The Handbook of Security

Also by Martin Gill

ASSESSING THE IMPACT OF CCTV, Home Office Research Study 292 (*co-author with A. Spriggs*)

MANAGING SECURITY, Crime at Work Series, Vol. III (*editor*)

CCTV, Crime at Work Series, Vol. IV (*editor*)

VIOLENCE AT WORK: Causes, Patterns and Prevention (*co-editor with B. Fisher and V. Bowie*)

COMMERCIAL ROBBERY: Offenders' Perspectives on Security and Crime Prevention

CRIME AT WORK: Increasing the Risk for Offenders, Crime at Work Series, Vol. II (*editor*)

ISSUES IN MARITIME CRIME: Mayhem at Sea, Crime and Security Shorter Studies Series (*editor*)

CRIME AT WORK: Studies in Security and Crime Prevention, Crime at Work Series, Vol. I (*editor*)

THE IMPACT OF PACE: Policing in a Northern Force (*co-author with A.K. Bottomley, C. Coleman, D. Dixon and D. Wall*)

A SPECIAL CONSTABLE (*co-author with R.I. Mawby*)

VOLUNTEERS IN THE CRIMINAL JUSTICE SYSTEM: A Comparative Study of Probation Police and Victim Support (*co-author with R.I. Mawby*)

CRIME VICTIMS: Needs Services and the Voluntary Sector (*co-author with R.I. Mawby*)

The Handbook of Security

Edited by
Martin Gill

© Palgrave Macmillan Ltd 2006

All rights reserved. No reproduction, copy or transmission of this publication may be made without written permission.

No portion of this publication may be reproduced, copied or transmitted save with written permission or in accordance with the provisions of the Copyright, Designs and Patents Act 1988, or under the terms of any licence permitting limited copying issued by the Copyright Licensing Agency, Saffron House, 6–10 Kirby Street, London EC1N 8TS.

Any person who does any unauthorized act in relation to this publication may be liable to criminal prosecution and civil claims for damages.

The authors have asserted their rights to be identified as the authors of this work in accordance with the Copyright, Designs and Patents Act 1988.

First published 2006 by
PALGRAVE MACMILLAN

Palgrave Macmillan in the UK is an imprint of Macmillan Publishers Limited, registered in England, company number 785998, of Houndmills, Basingstoke, Hampshire RG21 6XS.

Palgrave Macmillan in the US is a division of St Martin's Press LLC, 175 Fifth Avenue, New York, NY 10010.

Palgrave Macmillan is the global academic imprint of the above companies and has companies and representatives throughout the world.

Palgrave® and Macmillan® are registered trademarks in the United States, the United Kingdom, Europe and other countries.

ISBN-13: 978–0–230–00680–5   hardback
ISBN-10: 0–230–00680–9   hardback

This book is printed on paper suitable for recycling and made from fully managed and sustained forest sources. Logging, pulping and manufacturing processes are expected to conform to the environmental regulations of the country of origin.

A catalogue record for this book is available from the British Library.

Library of Congress Cataloging-in-Publication Data
The handbook of security / edited by Martin Gill.
        p. cm.
    Includes bibliographical references and index.
    ISBN 0–230–00680–9 (cloth)
    1. Private security services. 2. Security systems. 3. Corporations–Security measures. 4. Crime prevention. I. Gill, M. L.

HV8290.H346 2006
658.4'7–dc22

2005057769

Contents

List of Tables

List of Figures

List of Abbreviations

ACE	Access Control Entries
ACL	Access Control List
ACPO	Association of Chief Police Officers
AES	Advanced Exterior Sensor
AFSCME	American Federation of State County and Municipal Employees
AIVD	Algemene Inlichtingen- en Veiligheidsdienst
ALF	Animal Liberal Front
ALO	Architectural Liaison Officers
AM	Acousto-Magnetic
AMETHYST	AutoMatic Event autTHentication sYSTem
ANZUS	Australia-New Zealand-United States Security Treaty
ASIS	American Society for Industrial Security
ASTM	American Society for Testing and Materials
ATM	automated teller machine
BCC	British Chambers of Commerce
BCS	British Crime Survey
BID	Business Improvement District
BLS	Bureau of Labor Statistics
BSI	British Standards Institution
BSIA	British Security Industry Association
BCM	business continuity management
BCP	business continuity planning
BIA	business impact analysis
BIE	business impact evaluation
BSI	British Standards Institution
BUPA	British United Provident Association
CASPIAN	Consumers Against Supermarket Privacy Invasion and Numbering
CBCS	Cornwall Business Crime Survey
CBRN	Chemical, Biological, Radiological, and Nuclear
CC.OO.	Confederation of Workers' Commissions
CCD	charged couple device
CCTV	closed circuit television
CDRP	Crime and Disorder Reduction Partnership
CEO	Chief Executive Officer
CIA	Central Intelligence Agency
CIT	cash-in-transit
COESS	Confederation of European Security Services
COPS	community oriented policing
CPTED	Crime Prevention Through Environmental Design
CPU	Central Processing Unit

CRAVED	Concealable, Removable, Available, Valuable, Enjoyable and Disposable
CUPE	Canadian Union of Public Employees
CVS	crime victim survey / Commercial Victimization Survey
DARPA	Defense Advanced Research Projects Agency
DBT	design basis threat
DCI	Director of Central Intelligence
DDoS	Distribution Denial of Service
DI	Directorate of Intelligence
DIA	Defense Intelligence Agency
DiD	Defence in Depth
DIY	do-it-yourself
DOE	Department of Energy (United States)
DoS	denial of service
DNI	Director of National Intelligence
EAN	International Article Numbering Association
EAS	electronic article surveillance
EASHW	European Agency for Safety and Health at Work
EASI	Estimate of Adversary Sequence
ECOSOC	Economic and Social Council
EDRA	Environmental Design Research Association
EFTPOS	electronic funds transfer at point of sale
ENIAC	Electronic Numerical Integrator and Computer
EPC	Electronic Product Code
ETA	Euzkadi Ta Askatasuna (Basque Fatherland and Liberty)
EU	European Union
FAR	false alarm rate / false acceptance rate
FARC	Fuerzas Armadas Revolucionarias de Colombia (Revolutionary Armed Forces of Colombia)
FBI	Federal Bureau of Investigation
FEMA	Federal Emergency Management Agency
FMCG	Fast Moving Consumer Goods
FRR	false rejection rate
GCHQ	Government Communications Headquarters
GDP	gross domestic product
GIS	geographic information systems
GPS	global positioning system
HRM	human resource management
HSE	Health and Safety Executive
HTTP	Hypertext Transfer Protocol
HUMINT	human intelligence
ICBS	International Crimes against Businesses Survey
ICN	International Council of Nurses
ICVS	International Crime Victimization Survey
IDS	Intrusion Detection System

IEAS	Intelligent Electronic Article Surveillance
IETF	Internet Engineering Task Force
IGO	International Governmental Organization
ILO	International Labor Organization
IP	Internet Protocol
IPS	Intrusion Prevention System
IRA	Irish Republican Army
IT	information technology
JCATS	Joint Combat and Tactical Simulation
JTAC	Joint Terrorism Analysis Centre
KPI	key performance indicators
LAN	local area network
LP	loss prevention
MAC	message authentication code
MANPAD	Man-Portable Air Defense
MIS	management information system
NAR	nuisance alarm rate
NATO	North Atlantic Treaty Organization
NBFAA	National Burglar and Fire Alarm Association
NCAVC	National Center for the Analysis of Violent Crime
NCVS	National Crime Victimization Survey
NGO	non-governmental organization
NHMRC	National Health and Medical Research Council
NIRS	near infrared spectroscopy
NOHSC	National Occupational Health and Safety Commission
NSA	National Security Agency
NSC	National Security Council
NSI	National Security Inspectorate
NTOF	National Traumatic Occupational Fatalities
NVQ	National Vocational Qualification
ONE	Office of National Estimates
OSCE	Organization for Security and Co-Operation in Europe
OSHA	Occupational Safety and Health Administration
OSS	Office of Strategic Services
Pd	probability of detection
PESTEL	Political, Economic, Social, Technological, Environmental, Legal
PIN	personal identification number
PIR	passive infrared
PSI	Public Services International
PTL	pan, tilt and zoom
PTSD	Post Traumatic Stress Syndrome
R&A	research and analysis
RAM-W	Risk Assessment Methodology for Water System Protection
RDD	Radiological Dispersal Device
RF	Radio Frequency

RFC	Requests For Comments
RFID	Radio Frequency Identification
ROI	return on investment
RSPCA	Royal Society for the Prevention of Cruelty to Animals
SBD	Secure By Design
SEIA	Security Equipment Industry Association
SEIU	Service Employees International Union
SIA	Security Industry Authority
SID	security identifier
SMP	the Safer Merseyside Partnership
SNR	signal-to-noise ratio
SRDA	Small Retailers in Deprived Areas
SSBC	Scottish Survey of Business Crime
SSH	Secure Shell
SSL	Secure Socket Layer
SWOT	Strengths, Weaknesses, Opportunities and Threats
TCP/IP	Transport Control Protocol/Internet Protocol
TLS	Transport Layer Security
UCC	Uniform Code Council
UCLA	University of California, Los Angeles
UN	United Nations
UPC	Universal Product Code
VA	vulnerability assessment
VMD	video motion detection
VPN	Virtual Private Network
WHO	World Health Organization
WMD	weapons of mass destruction
WTO	World Trade Organization
WV	workplace violence
XML	eXtensible Markup Language

Acknowledgements

There are many groups who in different ways encouraged this book or facilitated it not least in helping me define its parameters. I benefited immensely from discussions I have had over the years with members of various organizations including the British Industry Security Association, The Security Industry Authority, The Risk and Security Management Forum, The Security Institute, The National Security Inspectorate and ASIS international. Various individuals have helped me and influenced my thinking including, Ron Clarke, Marcus Felson, David Gilmore, Colin Peacock, Carl Richards and Bob Rowe. Most importantly I would like to thank my colleagues here at Perpetuity Research and Consultancy International (PRCI) who have been a very positive influence.

I am grateful to all the contributors, they all seemed enthusiastic about the venture and clearly they have delivered (some of them on time!). I sent all the chapters for independent review and I am grateful to all those who offered their advice and made some excellent comments, they by necessity must remain anonymous. I would like to thank the staff at Palgrave Macmillan for their help in bringing this work to publication, especially Shirley Tan.

Putting this volume together has been a massive undertaking involving many others and I would like to thank all those who have helped bring it to fruition, not least my family. I hope that they and you the reader will find it a useful reference point and are inspired to think about improving the provision and study of security, there has never been a more important time for that.

Martin Gill
Perpetuity Research and Consultancy International
Spring 2006

List of Contributors

Joshua Bamfield is Director of the Centre for Retail Research, Nottingham, and is a Visiting Professor of Management at Nottingham Trent University. He has carried out research and consultancy into retail security issues for 20 years. He has been Head of a Business School and taught and led Management programmes from undergraduate to MBA. After leaving his University College post, he established and ran for six years the UK civil recovery programme with retailers and the police. Professor Bamfield's security publications concern inter-country crime comparisons, employee crime and anti-crime technology. He is a Chartered Member of the British Computer Society and a member of the Society of Security Professionals.

Adrian Beck is currently a Reader in Criminology at the University of Leicester, where he has worked since 1989. In 1991 he set up the first UK postgraduate degree in Security Management and has lectured widely on crime in the workplace and the use of technologies. His research interests are primarily focused on crime against the retail sector, including violence against staff, evaluating security equipment, the use of CCTV, the potential of RFID tagging technologies to tackle stock loss, staff dishonesty and shop theft. He has also co-developed a unique security management 'road map' to enable practitioners to adopt a more systematic approach to problem solving. He recently completed the second pan-European study on the extent of the problem of shrinkage throughout the European Fast Moving Consumer Goods Sector, and is currently working with ECR Europe on a project looking at identifying shrinkage hot spots in supply chains. He has published extensively on the subject of security management, including numerous books, articles in the academic and trade press and reports.

Mark Button is a Principal Lecturer and Associate Head (Curriculum) at the Institute of Criminal Justice Studies, University of Portsmouth. He has been based at Portsmouth for eight years, before which he was a Research Assistant for Bruce George MP specializing in policing and security. Mark has authored two books, *Private Policing* and *Private Security*, co-authored with Bruce George and written dozens of articles and chapters in books. These have covered regulation of private security, private policing, the policing of environmental protests and terrorism. He was between 1997–2005 completing research on the legal powers of security officers and about to embark upon a project reviewing counter-fraud strategies of UK Government departments.

James D. Calder is Professor of Political Science at the University of Texas at San Antonio. His academic career spans 28 years. He also served for 14 years in professional security positions in two aerospace firms and as a military intelligence officer. He has taught a variety of courses in security management, crime prevention, policing, national security intelligence, organized and transnational crime and justice policy history. Dr Calder has authored two books, one on presidential crime control policy and one on intelligence and espionage scholarship. His journal articles have addressed issues in organized crime, private security history, security management and security litigation. He has served as an expert witness in premises liability litigations in several jurisdictions. Dr Calder is a Certified Protection Profession (CPP), and he is a member of the Underwriters Laboratories Security Systems Council, the International Association for the Study of Organized Crime, and the Association of Former Intelligence Officers. Currently, he is writing a comprehensive history of the US Department of Justice Strike Force units and a history of auxiliary military police in World War II.

Caroline Cardone attended Skidmore College where in 1997 she graduated *summa cum laude* with a BA in English Literature. She then spent five years as manager and copy editor at Redspring Communications, a small custom publisher in upstate New York. In 2002, she began her graduate work in interior design at the Academy of Art in San Francisco, CA. After transferring to the Master of Interior Design programme at the University of Florida in 2003, she refined her academic focus to the study of retail design – specifically, its impact on loss prevention and store security. She is currently completing her Masters thesis on the effects of retail environments have on shoplifters' decisions to steal.

Dennis Challinger is a Fellow of the Criminology Department at the University of Melbourne and also a consultant criminologist in private practice. Over the last 15 years he has worked as a security executive for three of Australia's leading companies, (Telecom Australia, Coles Myer Ltd and the Mayne Group Ltd) focusing on reducing crime-related losses within those companies. Prior to that he worked for 16 years in the academic sphere, serving as Assistant Director of the Australian Institute of Criminology after leaving the University of Melbourne as Head of the Criminology Department. Dennis has a BSc (Hons) from Monash University, an MA in Criminology from the University of Melbourne and an MPhil in Criminology from the University of Cambridge.

Jason Crampton is a Lecturer in the Information Security Group at Royal Holloway, University of London, and an Associate Research Fellow at Birkbeck, University of London. Dr Crampton's main research interests are administrative models and constraint enforcement mechanisms for role-based access control and the use of partial order theory in modelling computer security systems. He is a member of the editorial board of the Information Security Technical Report.

Jason L. Davis is a visiting instructor at the University of South Florida, St Petersburg. He received his baccalaureate degree from Augusta State University and his Masters degree from the University of Florida. He is currently pursuing his doctorate from the University of Florida. His dissertation topic focuses on the corporate sanctioning under Federal Sentencing Guidelines for Organization. His research interests are related to the topic of corporate crime and retail theft. He previously worked as a graduate assistant for the National Retail Security Survey

(NRSS), an annual survey that measures retail financial loss and prevention strategies used to deter retail loss. He is currently a member of The American Society of Criminology, one of the leading criminology organizations.

Dominic Elliott (PhD) is currently Professor of Business Continuity and Strategic Management at the University of Liverpool Management School. He has published many articles and books in the fields of Strategic and Crisis Management and Business Continuity. Reflecting the practical focus of his work, he has worked with senior executives from a range of organizations including, IBM, Philips, Government of Lesotho, Football Association, Merrill Lynch, BNP-Paribas, Royal Mail, Transco and the Department of Trade and Industry. Professor Elliot has been editor of *Risk Management: An International Journal* since 2000.

Graham Farrell (PhD, Manchester 1993/94) is Professor of Criminology and Director of the Midlands Centre for Criminology and Criminal Justice at Loughborough University, where he is also programme director for the MSc in Criminology and Criminal Justice. He has worked and taught at a range of institutions in the UK and abroad, and is interested in hearing from potential PhD students who want to develop crime analysis and prevention research relating to the security industry.

Bonnie S. Fisher is a Professor in the Division of Criminal Justice at the University of Cincinnati. She received her PhD in political science from Northwestern University in 1988. Her current research interests include the extent and nature of, and proactive and reactive strategies to domestic violence in the workplace, repeat victimization among college women, and comparative victimology among university students. She has written several articles that examine workplace violence issues and is the co-editor of the *Security Journal* (with Professor Martin Gill). Professor Fisher recently co-edited with Vaughan Bowie and Professor Cary Cooper, her second workplace violence-related volume (the first volume, *Violence at Work: Causes, patterns and prevention*, was co-edited with Professor Martin Gill and Vaughan Bowie in 2002).

Mary Lynn Garcia is a Principal Staff Member at Sandia National Laboratories in Albuquerque, NM. She has 30 years experience in medical research, engineering application, project management and teaching. She has worked for the last 18 years designing hardware and software for physical security systems, specializing in systems engineering and analysis. More recently, she helped create new security education curricula at US universities that merge principles from the disciplines of business, criminal justice and engineering to make these programmes more science-based. She has been a Faculty Associate at Arizona State University, New Mexico State University, and the New Mexico Institute of Mining and Technology. She is the author of two textbooks entitled *The Design and Evaluation of Physical Protection Systems* (2001), and (2005) *Vulnerability Assessment of Physical Protection Systems*. She has also been published in *Security Management* magazine and the *Journal of the Institute of Nuclear Materials Management* and has contributed chapters to other works. She is a member of

ASIS, International and has been a Certified Protection Professional since December 1997.

Bruce George has been the Labour Member of Parliament for Walsall South since February 1974. Since 1977 he has campaigned for regulation of the British security industry introducing several bills to parliament. During this period he has written dozens of articles on private security including the book, *Private Security*, co-authored with Mark Button. Bruce is currently Chairman of the House of Commons Defence Committee and has been a major influence upon the Government's creation of the Security Industry Authority to regulate the British private security industry in the UK.

Martin Gill is Director of Perpetuity Research and Consultancy International (PRCI) a spin out company from the University of Leicester where he is a Professor of Criminology. The company specializes in the areas of security management, risk management, crime analysis, community safety and crime prevention. Professor Gill has been actively involved in a range of studies relating to different aspects of business crime including the causes of false burglar alarms, why fraudsters steal, dishonest staff, the effectiveness of CCTV, the effectiveness of security guards, whether property marking works, how companies protect their brand image, the generators of illicit markets and stolen goods, and counterfeiting to name a few. He has published widely with over 100 articles and 11 books. The latest two, *Managing Security* and *CCTV* were published in 2003. He is a Fellow of The Security Institute, a member of the Risk and Security Management Forum, the Fraud Advisory Panel and the Company of Security Professionals (and a Freeman of the City of London). He is also Chair of the ASIS Research Council and an overseas representative on the ASIS International Academic Programs Committee.

Suzette Grillot is an Associate Professor of Political Science and International and Area Studies at the University of Oklahoma in Norman. Her research and teaching focus generally on issues of international security and foreign policy. Currently she is completing a book on small arms in Central and Eastern Europe that includes intensive field work on arms control mechanisms and motivation in 13 countries. Her previous books include *Arms on the Market* (co-edited with Gary K. Bertsch, 1998) and *Arms and the Environment* (co-edited with Lakshman Guruswamy, 2002). Her research has also been published in various academic journals, such as *International Politics, British Journal of Political Science, Political Psychology, Journal of Southern Europe and the Balkans, The Nonproliferation Review* and *The Southeastern Political Review*.

Read Hayes, PhD, CPP is director of the Loss Prevention Research Council and co-ordinator of the Loss Prevention Research Team, DCP, of the University of Florida. Dr Hayes has more than 28 years' hands-on crime and loss control experience, providing expertise to numerous organizations worldwide including Target, Home Depot, Bloomingdales, Coles Meyer, Disney, Proctor and Gamble and Wal-Mart. Dr Hayes co-founded the University of Florida's National Retail

Security Survey in 1989, and his current research focus includes offender decision-making, total supply chain protection, asset and key product protection and premises violence, security and safeness.

Richard C. Hollinger is a Professor in the Department of Criminology, Law & Society at the University of Florida located in Gainesville. Dr Hollinger is also the Director of the 'Security Research Project' – an academic research institute that focuses exclusively on retail loss prevention and security issues. The Security Research Project annually conducts the *National Retail Security Survey* along with a number of other empirical research activities. In addition to numerous articles published in scholarly and professional journals, he is the author of three books, *Theft by Employees* (with John P. Clark, 1983), *Dishonesty in the Workplace: A Manager's Guide to Preventing Employee Theft*, 1989, and *Crime, Deviance and the Computer* (1997). He currently serves on the editorial advisory board of the *Security Journal* and is a regular columnist for *Loss Prevention Magazine*. He sits on the Loss Prevention Advisory Committee of the National Retail Federation.

Daniel B. Kennedy, PhD, is a forensic criminologist specializing in security and police issues. Before joining the sociology and criminal justice faculty at the University of Detroit Mercy in 1976, he was employed as an urban renewal worker, probation officer, and police academy director. Dr Kennedy has served as an expert witness throughout the US, Canada, Mexico and the Caribbean. He is Board Certified in Security Management and has published widely in various issues of *Security Journal, Journal of Security Administration, Journal of Criminal Justice, Crime and Delinquency, Criminal Justice and Behavior, Justice Quarterly, Professional Psychology, Victimology* and *Security Management*.

Michael Levi is a Professor of Criminology at Cardiff University. He has researched and published widely on corruption, international fraud (particularly payment card fraud), money laundering and organized crime, as well as on violent crime and policing. Recent and pending books include *Drugs and Money, White-Collar Crime and its Victims* and *The Media and Social Construction of White-Collar Crimes*. He has held a variety of international and national public roles including Scientific Expert on Organized Crime to the Council of Europe, Parliamentary Specialist Adviser on Policing and Anti-Social Behaviour, a review for the Royal Commission of Criminal Justice of the *Investigation, Prosecution and Trial of Serious Fraud*; and membership of the Criminological and Scientific Council of the Council of Europe; the Executive of the British Society of Criminology; a Reflections Committee on the 1990 Council of Europe Money-Laundering Convention; and the Steering Committee of the UK Cabinet Office PIU review of proceeds of crime and their enforcement. He has received an award from the American Society of Criminology for outstanding research scholarship.

Elena Licu is an advanced PhD student in the Division of Criminal Justice at the University of Cincinnati, specializing in crime prevention. She received her BS and MS degrees in criminal justice from the same university. Her research interests include victimology, transnational crimes, particularly trafficking of human beings for purposes of sexual exploitation and illicit labour, and workplace violence.

Giovanni Manunta, PhD FsyI is President of the Security and Risk Studies Institute, and External Examiner at the Scarman Centre, Leicester University. Formerly Director of the MA 'Intelligence and Security' at Link Campus University of Malta, Academic Leader and Senior Lecturer in the MSc in Corporate Security Management at Cranfield RMCS Shrivenham. He occasionally lectures at the Universities of Bologna, Barcelona (Universitat Central and Pompeu Fabra) and Southampton. He is also a Fellow of the Security Institute, UK, member of the Advisory Board of the Security Journal, of the Academic Board of the ERI (Espionage Research Institute, Washington DC), and AIPROS (Associazione Italiana Professionisti di Sicurezza).

Roberto Manunta, BSc, MSc is Vice President of the Security and Risk Studies Institute and Profesor Asociado at Barcelona Universidad Central. He holds a degree in Economics and Politics in Bath University, UK, and a MSc in Military Operational Research a Cranfield-RMCS, UK. He has lectured on 'Security Modelling Techniques' at Cranfield-RMCS, at Link Campus University of Rome. He is a member of ASIS International and AIPROS (Associazione Italiana Professionisti di Sicurezza).

Rob I. Mawby is Professor of Criminology and Criminal Justice and Director of the Community Justice Research Centre, University of Plymouth, England. He is the author of eight books and numerous articles in academic books and journals. His main research interests cover policing, victim issues, crime reduction and tourism and crime. His research has a particular cross-national emphasis, but he has also been closely involved in local research, most recently carrying out the first two Cornwall Crime Surveys and Cornwall Business Crime Surveys in 2001 and 2004. His most recent books include, *Policing across the world: issues for the twenty-first century* (1999) (editor) and *Burglary* (2001).

Robert D. McCrie is Professor of Security Management at John Jay College of Criminal Justice, the City University of New York. He was the founding editor-in-chief of *Security Journal* and has edited *Security Letter* since its founding in 1970. He has published widely in the security field, and he is also the author of *Security Operations Management* and *Readings in Security Management*.

Kenneth G. Paterson holds the title of Professor of Information Security at Royal Holloway, University of London. He obtained a BSc in 1990 from the University of Glasgow and a PhD from the University of London in 1993, both in Mathematics. He was a Royal Society Fellow at the Institute for Signal and Information Processing at the Swiss Federal Institute of Technology, Zurich from 1993 to 1994, then a Lloyd's of London Tercentenary Foundation Research Fellow at Royal Holloway, University of London from 1994 to 1996. He then joined the Mathematics Group at Hewlett-Packard Laboratories Bristol, becoming project manager of the Mathematics, Cryptography and Security Group in 1999. He re-joined the Information Security Group at Royal Holloway in 2001, becoming a Reader in

2002 and Professor in 2004. His current research interests are in the areas of Cryptography and Network Security. He is currently Associate Editor for *Sequences for the IEEE Transactions on Information Theory* and a member of the International Board of Referees for Computers & Security.

Ken Pease, now retired from full-time work, is Visiting Professor at the University of Loughborough and University College London. He retains his practising certificate as Chartered Forensic Psychologist and sits on the Home Office Science and Technology Reference Group. Recent published work includes studies of offender targeting and the uses of hard science in crime reduction. He is currently funded by the European Commission in collaborative work on the 'crime-proofing' of products, services and legislation.

Fred Piper has been Professor of Mathematics at the University of London since 1975 and has worked in security since 1979. He is currently Director of the Information Security Group (ISG) at Royal Holloway. The ISG at Royal Holloway offers an MSc in Information Security and Secure Electronic Commerce and has a PhD programme that has produced over 100 doctorates. Fred has published more than 100 research papers and is co-author of *Cipher Systems* (1982), one of the first books to be published on the subject of protection of communications, *Secure Speech Communications* (1985), *Cryptography: A Very Short Introduction* (2002), and an ISACA research monograph on *Digital Signatures* (1999). He has been a member of a number of DTI advisory committees and is a member of the Board of Trustees for Bletchley Park. In 2002 he was awarded an IMA Gold Medal for 'Services to Mathematics'. Also in 2002, he was awarded the first honorary CISSP for a European. This was for 'leadership in Information Security'. In 2003 Professor Piper received an honorary CISM for 'globally recognized leadership' and 'contribution to the Information Security Profession'.

Tim Prenzler lectures in the School of Criminology and Criminal Justice, Griffith University, Brisbane, Australia. His research interests include all aspects of security work, crime prevention, police integrity management, gender equality in policing and innovations in criminal justice. He is currently working on a study of the dimensions of the security industry in Australia and a prevention-oriented study of police deaths on duty.

Matthew J.B. Robshaw recently joined France Telecom Research and Development in Paris. Dr Robshaw was a Reader of Information Security within the Information Security Group at Royal Holloway, University of London. After completing his PhD Dr Robshaw joined RSA Laboratories, the research and consultation division of RSA Security, Inc., leaving as Principal Research Scientist after more than six years. During this time his research interests focused on the design, analysis and deployment of cryptographic algorithms and he was a co-designer of one of the five finalist algorithms for the AES. Dr Robshaw has published widely within academia and industry.

Bradley B. Rogers is an Professor of Mechanical Engineering Technology at Arizona State University. His academic background spans 20 years of research and teaching in engineering and applied mathematics, and includes security systems engineering and security technology. In partnership with Sandia National Laboratories, he developed the MSc programme in Security Engineering Technology at ASU. In addition to security engineering and security education, his journal publications and articles have addressed topics in applied mathematics, mechanics, fluid mechanics, heat transfer, magnetohydrodynamics, energy conversion and fuel cells. He has worked for private industry in the aerospace and energy research sectors, and as a private consultant for a wide variety of engineering topics. He holds BS and MS degrees in Mechanical Engineering from Montana State University, and a PhD in Mechanical Engineering from Arizona State University.

Richard H. Schneider is Professor of Urban and Regional Planning at the University of Florida's College of Design, Construction and Planning. He is a charter member of the American Planning Association and helped write the APA's national security planning policy. He serves on the Board of the Florida CPTED Network and has had a long teaching research interest in the field of place-based crime prevention security issues. Dr Schneider has served as consultant to police agencies relative to crime mapping and crime prevention planning issues and has been visiting scholar and research fellow at the University of Manchester Institute of Science and Technology and at the University of Arizona, where he lectured on conflict management, planning and security issues. He is co-author (with Professor Ted Kitchen at Sheffield Hallam University) of *Planning for Crime Prevention: A TransAtlantic Perspective* (2002) and has written numerous articles on planning and security design. He has served as editor for the *Journal of Architectural and Planning Research's* CPTED theme issue and his most recent book (with Ted Kitchen) is *Crime Prevention and the Built Environment*, scheduled to be released in 2006.

Stephen Sloan holds the title of University Professor and Fellow in the Office of Global Perspectives at the University of Central Florida. He was a Samuel Roberts Noble Professor of Political Science and is now Professor Emeritus at the University of Oklahoma. He has been involved in the study of terrorism, political violence and conflict for over 30 years. Professor Sloan pioneered the development of simulations of incidents of terrorism and has trained military, law enforcement personnel and corporate personnel in the US and overseas. He has also advised governments on counterterrorism doctrine, strategy and training. He is the author of nine books and numerous articles. His latest book co-authored with Sean K. Anderson is *Terrorism: Assassins to Zealots*.

Clifton Smith is Associate Professor, Security Science at Edith Cowan University, Perth, Western Australia, and is a Visiting Professor at Nottingham Trent University, UK. Professor Smith initiated and developed the Security Science programme at Edith Cowan University, with the Bachelor degree and Post Graduate research Masters and PhD degrees as international courses in security. He has been involved in lecturing the management of security technology, physical security, and security research methodology for about 15 years. His research interests include biometric imaging, forensic ballistics imaging, testing security systems, and security education. He has published extensively in *IEEE*, ballistics and security journals, and appropriate conference proceedings. Professor Smith is a member of the Australian Institute of Physics and a member of the Institute of Electrical and Electronic Engineers.

Craig Stapley recently completed his doctorate at the University of Oklahoma with an emphasis in international relations and comparative politics. His dissertation, entitled *NGOs is the Crosshairs: Non-Governmental Organizations and the Terrorist Threat* assesses the targeting priorities of terrorist groups and seeks to explain the threat to non-governmental groups which he is planning to develop into a book. He is a former NGO volunteer and prior to returning to graduate school, was an insurance loss professional who investigated and evaluated losses associated with both natural disasters and terrorist attacks. He has completed research on terrorism and public opinion, natural disasters and democracy, and Mad Cow disease and institutional change.

Alison Wakefield is a Lecturer in Criminology at City University, having previously taught security and risk management at the University of Leicester and undertaken doctoral research at the University of Cambridge. Her research interests have centred on private security, public policing and crime prevention, with a particular emphasis on human rights and civil liberties issues. She is currently carrying out research on foot patrol in public and private policing. Among her publications, Dr Wakefield has authored *Selling Security: The Private Policing of Public Space* (2003), and is editor of *Ethical and Social Perspectives on Situational Crime Prevention* with Andrew von Hirsch and David Garland (2000). She is Executive Secretary of the British Society of Criminology (BSC), Secretary of the BSC Southern Regional Group, and a board member of the International Institute of Security.

Paul Wilkinson is Professor of International Relations and Chairman of the Advisory Board of the Centre for the Study of Terrorism and Political Violence (CSTPV) at the University of St Andrews. Prior to his appointment at St Andrews in 1989 he was Professor of International Relations, University of Aberdeen 1979–89. He was Visiting Fellow at Trinity Hall, Cambridge in 1997–98 and is Honorary Fellow of University of Wales, Swansea. His publications include *Political Terrorism* (1974), *Terrorism and the Liberal State* (1977/1986), *The New Fascists* (1981/1983), *Contemporary Research on Terrorism* (as co-editor, 1987), *Aviation Terrorism and Security* (as co-editor, 1999) and *Terrorism versus Democracy: The Liberal State Response* (2001). He co-authored with Joseph S. Nye Jr and Yukio Satoh the report to the Trilateral Commission (May 2003) Addressing the New International Terrorism; Prevention, Intervention and Multilateral Co-operation. He is co-editor of the academic journal *Terrorism and Political Violence* and has recently (March 2005) co-edited with Dr Magnus Ranstorp, the *Special Issue on Terrorism and Human Rights*.

1
Introduction

Martin Gill

The nature of security threats is changing and so too are the types of responses. Worldwide there has generally been a move away from concern about nuclear bombs aimed at countries to terrorist attacks aimed at individuals, organizations and communities. The focus on a nation's ability to strike has largely been replaced by individual, community and organizational awareness to resist and react.

Yet in only some cases has security achieved a greater significance on the corporate agenda. In many ways security suffers from being a grudge purpose, important it may be, but it is not a welcome spend all too often associated with the unattractive features of a 'locks and bolts' approach, or what is its modern equivalent of 'cameras, tags and alarms'. Measures can be functional, but they are not always viewed as attractive and it is not always obvious to all parties what benefits they generate. Perhaps the real limitation of modern security management is that it has, in general, failed to talk the language of business not least in showing how it systematically impacts (positively or negatively) on the bottom line. There are of course many very effective security departments, some excellent security companies, and some extremely astute security personnel, but all too often security is seen as the poor relation both in the corporate hierarchy and as a member of the extended law enforcement family.

At least part of the reason for this is that the study of private/corporate security has to be regarded as an embryonic discipline, perhaps at the stage computer science was 30 years ago and environmental science 20 years ago. There are still major definitional problems that have never been satisfactorily resolved (see for e.g. Johnston, 2000; Johnston and Shearing, 2003). As many texts on security note, while in English 'security' and 'safety' are different words with different meanings, in other languages one word describes the two. And different disciplines use 'security' to refer to quite different things. For example, it can refer to security on the streets and in homes and then it becomes part of the discipline of policing or crime prevention, where it focuses on organizational assets it comes under the umbrella of security management and occasionally business or organizational studies. In a different way it can refer to the defence of a country where it becomes part of the discipline of war studies, or peace studies or defence

1

studies and so on. Indeed, the emergence of private military groups offers new forms of security and new areas of study.[1] Moreover, within these disciplines there is relatively little cross referencing (but see Chapter 3).

The problem of definition is not an abstract one deserving only the attention of academics, it has practical implications. On one level security regulators need to know what to include and what to exclude and definitions are crucial to guiding that choice. In a different way perceptions of what is a security context (see the final chapter of this book for a discussion) will influence what is an appropriate security response. As Johnston and Shearing (2003: 3) note:

> Our objective 'sense of security' (our feelings of safety) is just as important to most of us as any objective measure of our 'actual security' (i.e. the risks that we actually face). However, if the discrepancy between the two grows too wide, we are liable to be warned either that we have a 'false sense of security' or that we are 'paranoid'. Thus, to be effective security measures must address our subjective perceptions as well as more objectively identifiable threats to our safety.

The fact that security is still evolving as a distinct area of study in part explains the reason for preparing this book. Later the content and the rationale will be introduced but as a backdrop there are two issues that are in different ways core to assessing the current state of security. The first involves a short commentary on the extent of security which includes a consideration of the way it is provided, and second, a review of what we know about good security in terms of its effectiveness.

Security: here, there and everywhere

Security is omni-present; there are clearly limits to what the State can provide (see, Garland, 1996)[2] and this has enabled the private sector to flourish.[3] Private security has expanded (see George and Button, 2000),[4] and in many ways the services offered mirrors and then extends those of the State. As Johnston and Shearing (2003: 32–3) drawing on the work of a range of studies note:

> It is now virtually impossible to identify any function within the governance of security in democratic states that is not, somewhere and under some circumstances, performed by non-state authorities as well as by state ones. As a result, policy-makers are now ready to accept that the effective governance of security requires co-operation, collaboration and 'networking' between partners and that exact demarcation between the respective responsibilities of partners may be difficult, or even impossible to establish.

In practice partnerships can be problematic (although what partnerships aren't at least from time to time?), not least because the parties involved emerge from a set of conflicting principles (see, Prenzler and Sarre, 2002). In general, the private sector is accountable only to those who pay for it, and it is geared towards profit, somewhat in contrast to providers of state services. Each type of service generates different benefits and associated with some limitations leading Johnston and Shearing (2003) to advocate a 'nodal' approach with the nodes representing a set of 'shifting alliances' consisting of state sector, corporate or business sector, non governmental organizations, and the informal or voluntary sector. As they point out (p. 148):

> ... by linking up – or 'networking' – non state nodes of security with each other, and with state nodes, it is possible that some of the strengths of 'private' forms of provision may be maximised, and some of their dangers minimised.

There are a range of reasons why partnerships are problematic. Indeed, the study of the privatization of security has included fairly extensive discussion in the literature where a prime focus has been the relationship between private policing and alternatives forms of provision (especially the State) (e.g. Bayley and Shearing, 2001; Button, 2002, 2004; De Waard, 1999; Gill and Hart, 1997; Johnston, 2000; King, and Prenzler, 2003; Prenzler, 2004; Prenzler and Sarre, 2002; Sarre, 2005; Sarre and Prenzler, 1999, 2000; Shearing, 1992). The difficulties in a partnership approach extend beyond mere ideological differences (see, McLeod, 2002; Rigakos, 2002). For example, the method used by Governments to allocate budgets is generally prescriptive specifying how money should be spent. It would seem much more sensible to provide a budget to the local police chief and ask him or her to develop a policing plan responding to local circumstances that would then need to be approved by local representatives. It may be prudent to have fewer police and more support officers, or perhaps some of the money spent on police would be better spent providing administrative help or specialist private security expertise. Indeed, the way budgets are allocated has as much to do with the limited role of security as any ideological differences, and as security develops an expertise in a march to professionalization it could be the main factor that keeps it at arms length.[5] Certainly, it should not be assumed that the public are against the use of private security officers in public space (Noakes, 2000).

Already it can be seen that the term 'private security' used as an umbrella phase can refer to different activities. Table 1.1 is an attempt to highlight some of the ways in which security can be provided in what I have called 'The Mixed Economy of Security'. For each type or sector of provision some of the key ways that security is provided are listed with examples. Thus although it is not uncommon to discuss policing provision in terms of private, public, voluntary and informal (see Gill and Mawby, 1990a, b; Mawby, 2005) breaking these down further illustrates the very varied types of ways in which security can and is supplied and paid for. Private does not just mean a security company providing its services directly to clients, there might also be an internal market within an organization, even a public one. Or individuals working for an employer may spend some of their time working for someone else, including for the benefit of the

Table 1.1 'The mixed economy of security'

Type of provision	How security service is provided	Service provided to whom	Who pays	Example	Range of services
Private	Directly by company	To whoever will pay	The client	Personnel typically works for a security company and the company is contracted by a client to offer some types of service.	Potentially any type
	In-house/Proprietary	To the employer	The company/organization pays for its security personnel as employees alongside other staff	In-house officers are different from State officers because the employers are not state organizations, as such powers will most likely be restricted. Security officers work directly for the company/organization and are not normally clients.	Potentially any type
	In-house/Proprietary	To parts of the employer organization who will pay	Other parts of the company or Group of companies	Until a few years ago, the Security and Investigation Service sold their services to 21 business units within the British Royal Mail Group. Effectively services are provided under contract.	Potentially any type
	By employees	An organization or company chosen by the employer.*	The employer	Some train companies agreed to pay for staff to be employed by the British Transport Police. The train companies pay and the police deploy. This has required a cultural shift on the part of both companies.	Usually restricted
	By employees	To the public	The employer	Some retailers in London have agreed that their staff can serve as Special Constables (police volunteers) while on duty. In this role they are providing a service to the community.	Mostly routine tasks

Table 1.1 'The mixed economy of security' – *continued*

Type of provision	How security service is provided	Service provided to whom	Who pays	Example	Range of services
				In the UK the police may formally accredit some individuals to help support policing. They have limited powers and sometimes none at all, but are invested with a duty to assist the police. Some private security officers have been accredited and they may undertake this work during working hours.	
State	Directly by the State	To the public	The State	The State employs a wide range of security personnel, including private security personnel to protect public buildings. Of course, a range of law enforcement and military personnel are employed directly by the State.	Potentially any type
	Directly by the State – (mostly) external market	To whoever will pay who fall within ambit (usually regulated)	The State	'Police Security Services Branch (PSSB), which is a publicly-funded body employing public servants who are not sworn police officers, competing in the same market-place with private security firms in providing fee-for-service security advice, protective security risk reviews, alarm monitoring, patrol and personnel services.' (Sarre, 2005: 60)	Usually restricted by Statute

6

Table 1.1 'The mixed economy of security' – *continued*

Type of provision	How security service is provided	Service provided to whom	Who pays	Example	Range of services
	Directly by the State – (mostly) internal market	To other State (like) organizations prepared to pay for the service	State (like) organizations	'The Australian Protective Service (APS), which acts under the auspices of the Commonwealth Attorney-General's Department. Established in 1984, the APS is a government agency that provides specialist protective security to government departments on a contractual "fee-for-service" basis.' (Sarre, 2005: 60)	Usually restricted by Statute
Voluntary/ Charitable	By individuals	To the community usually locally	Effectively provided free, may sometimes include bursary	Lots of 'security-related' agencies use volunteers to enhance the work they do. The police, prison service and probation service all use volunteers.	Usually restricted
	By individuals (sometimes as part of a group)	To the immediate community	Effectively provided free of charge	'Watch' schemes, the most commonly referred to is Neighbourhood Watch	Usually restricted to routine duties
	By groups (sometimes individually)	By vigilantes to those defined as in need	By voluntary contributions	Guardian Angels	Restricted
Informal	By individuals	To family members	No payment as such, mostly a social and sometimes legal obligation to look after each other	Parents are obliged to look after their children to protect them from harm, and most importantly, to educate them on how to protect themselves from danger.	All encompassing

Table 1.1 'The mixed economy of security' – *continued*

Type of provision	How security service is provided	Service provided to whom	Who pays	Example	Range of services
	By individuals	To neighbours and friends	By individuals to neighbours and friends although the costs are usually in time spent	Security is often provided informally. Keeping an informal watch over neighbours' property while they are away is one example. Promoting security amongst family and friends is another example. Some positions have an informal role in promoting security, caretakers and janitors being examples.	Usually restricted

[*]All employees and not just those in a security function, may play a part in providing security within the company and beyond, by, for example, looking out for trespassers and 'strangers' on the premises, or by looking for and reporting suspicious behaviour on the way to and from work and while out and about. Sales assistants may have a role in assisting with fraud prevention. In some countries, the USA being a case in point, police officers may work in private security when off duty.

public. Public employees may become involved in different ways too, and the voluntary sector can include anything from benign vigilantes[6] to police volunteers. And the informal sector is a major provider of security, considerable protection is provided by the family and friends and neighbours.

The main purpose here is to illustrate the varied and very different ways in which security is provided and to note that there are different implications in terms of quality and type of service, and accountability issues in these diverse arrangements, and this is likely to have different implications for measures of effectiveness too. This is not intended to imply that there is a best way of providing security, they all might be best for particular circumstances, it is more a case of truly understanding the dimensions of each in order to understand what is appropriate or best in a given context. Clearly, the next important step (other than to refine and improve Table 1.1) is to assess which types of provision are suited to a particular set of circumstances and to try and highlight the strengths and weaknesses of each and to compare them. It says much about the state of research on security and private policing that these issues have yet to be put under the microscope. Doing so will entail a broader multi-disciplinary approach, and will certainly require researchers to move outside the boundaries of single disciplines (Johnston and Shearing, 2003).

How good is security?

There is a common-sense answer that it must be good. Few people, it seems, doubt the wisdom and certainly appear to accept detailed screening at airports, or the need for access controls to some premises. And evidence that security is valued can be derived from business practice which continues to purchase security, and in some cases invest more each year (Collins *et al.*, 2005). It is difficult to imagine bottom line focused organizations continuing with investments that they thought they could do without or did not believe were working. But of course this does not mean to say that they have carefully costed this, nor that what they have is the best. Indeed, many organizations do not have developed return on investment models for security operations, and few companies, and this includes security manufacturers and suppliers have collated credible independent evidence that their products specifically work to achieve clients' objectives. Too often a range of measures cause an effect and it is not always easy to identify which ones can claim credit for the success.

This does not mean to say that there is no good evidence of security working both effectively and cost-effectively (see Welsh and Farrington, 1999). But the problem is that there is relatively little research explaining what works and why, or for that matter what does not work and why which is arguably just as helpful. Within the criminology literature there has been a lot of work devoted to reducing opportunities for crime by applying a range of 'situational prevention' techniques. In a recent review of the approach (Clarke, 2005), its main proponent, Ron Clarke, has helpfully outlined a defence against some of the main criticisms of situational prevention although, from my point of view at least, it misses one important element, and that is that situational prevention over simplifies the solution. As an approach – and it provides an excellent framework for security – it has not so far located itself within a management framework, yet many security projects/measures fail to succeed because they are poorly conceived or because they are badly implemented (for example, see, Gill and Spriggs, 2005). It is all too easy to claim that a measure or measures have not worked without being clear why, was it a failure of the measure, or the way it was implemented, in short a failure of theory or practice?

Corporate security is a world desperate for more quality evaluations helping to explain what works, what does not and crucially, why this is the case. Certainly there is a greater need for evaluation approaches that are more practical for end users. And most importantly, there is a need to communicate the findings to those at the sharp end of practice. Indeed, the whole process of communicating findings effectively to audiences who have learned to be sceptical of 'academic' studies is a task in itself. Very little attention has been paid to identifying specific skill sets and thinking through how these can be communicated or translated into training programmes aimed at practitioners and policy makers. Indeed, much more information is needed on how practitioners absorb information and the forms they need it in in order to make the most use of it. Certainly the timescales of research and evaluation do not meet the more immediate requirements of those charged with taking actions that require more immediate solutions. And there has been a lack of investment in security theory looking at developing principles and testing theory application in different contexts.

There is one other thing that needs to be discussed in the context of the study of private or corporate security, and that is a body of writings which question its value or perhaps more its role in democratic societies. This is not necessarily a Marxist critique that calls for the overthrow of anything private, more a case of a critical approach to the role of (private) security that is potentially divisive in a democracy because it is accountable only to those who can pay. Loader (1997a) is concerned about the inequalities of private security provision, in that it is provided on the basis of an ability to pay and 'without reference to the common good'. It can be especially problematic, 'if those able to secure protection in the market place begin to resent paying – through general taxation – for public policing (on the grounds that they will then be paying twice)' (p. 385). Loader's point is not that all security should be provided by the State, more that there are issues about how private security is provided that should concern all democratic societies, or, specifically:

> What kinds of limits would a political community committed to equal citizenship and concerned to encourage social cohesion among its members place on the market exchange of security provision? (p. 385)

In a similar way Zedner (2003: 179) notes in the conclusion to her paper entitled 'Too Much Security?'; 'I have sought to show that the pursuit of security is by no means an unequivocal good,' and she does this by identifying six paradoxes of security, these are:

> ... that security pursues risk reduction but presumes the persistence of crime; that the expansion of security has enlarged not diminished the penal state; that security promises reassurance but in fact increases anxiety; that security is posited as a universal good but presumes social exclusion; that security promises freedom but erodes civil liberties; and finally that security is posited as a public good but its pursuit is inimical to the good society. (pp. 179–80)

There is not the space here to examine these arguments (see also Loader, 1997b), and others like them, but they do offer an important counter to the belief that security can only be a good thing (see also, Brodeur and Shearing, 2005), understandably perhaps a view held by those who work within it. These writings principally question the social role of security, but economically it has long been recognized that organizations, and especially those in business need to build an economic as well as social rationality into protecting themselves. Retailers could do a lot more to prevent shop theft, they could put more goods behind counters, employ more staff, search all customers entering and exiting the store and so on, but this is not economically rational.

These critiques are fundamental to developing a rigorous body of knowledge for the study of security. It is this last point that brings us back to the purpose of this book containing, as it does, a range of insights and critiques into the study of security. The next section introduces the main areas of focus and outlines a little more about the content of each chapter.

This book

At a security symposium held in the USA delegates discussed the various subject areas or disciplines that contribute to security, and, after some debate concluded that there were none that didn't. Moving on to consider areas of trade or activity where security was important, the delegates concluded there were none where it was not. Security then, to a lesser or greater degree, is a facet of every feature of our lives. The difficulty of prioritizing the areas of interest and focus will no doubt have troubled writers and editors of many a security text, and it certainly has this editor of this book. Therefore, the process by which topics and authors have been chosen is perhaps worthy of comment.

In each section of the book it will be easy to think of other relevant chapters that could, or even should have been included. In my judgment the chapters for this Handbook provide the foundation on which future editions may build. The authors were chosen because they are scholars with a recognized expertise in their area. It may be of some interest that of all the authors that were approached and asked to contribute only one was unable, because of illness. Precisely because they are all experts, they were invited to propose their own outline for the chapter taking into account the need to provide an authoritative review of research, current issues and thinking in their area of expertise. Their initial outlines were sometimes modified, often to avoid overlap,[7] but never to any great extent. Once the chapter outline was agreed authors were typically given about 12 months to think about and write their contribution. When it was received it was sent for independent review, and suggestions and ideas were sent back to authors who were asked to prepare a final draft taking account of any recommendations that had been made.

The content

The first section of this book considers security as a discipline. In Chapter 2 Bob McCrie traces the history of security showing how it facilitated the development of early civilization and has remained a core part of the functioning and development of individuals, enterprises, institutions, regions, and nations. His account marks the impact of industrialism and modernism on the creation of the modern military, public policing, and the private security industry.

In Chapter 3 Craig Stapley, Suzette Grillot, and Steve Sloan argue that the fields of corporate and traditional security studies have not readily adjusted to the changes in international affairs. They argue the need to bridge the gap between traditional and corporate security studies, not least because the modern world where the distinction between domestic and foreign threats has become blurred, and where 'non-state' actors are increasingly challenging the monopoly of force and the centrality of the State on the international stage.

In Chapter 4 Brad Rogers examines the contribution of engineering studies to security. He notes that most managers responsible for the engineering of solutions to security problems are not professional engineers, but may benefit from a greater understanding of the engineering design process. He examines a security system as a collection of interacting components, policies and procedures that are integrated and organized to react to a malevolent human attack in a manner that results in a protected asset and a defeated adversary. He outlines a methodology that is appropriate for examining all security systems.

In Chapter 5 Richard Schneider examines the link between environmental science and security. Schneider shows that while research and practice suggest there are broad place-based crime prevention theories that describe and predict criminal behaviour, the application of effective security design tends to be context dependent. For him environmental studies related to security demonstrate the importance of theory and practice influencing each other and spurring new developments in each.

Chapter 6 tackles the study of forensic security and the law. Daniel Kennedy shows how responsibility for security shortcomings which result in attack, can be attributed. He discusses 'crime foreseeability' and shows how it can be established by examining a property's criminal history and social ecology and how this can then be linked to determining what is or should have been an appropriate security response.

In Chapter 7 James D. Calder suggests that the lack of a scholarly approach in security studies could be corrected by learning from the study of national security intelligence, particularly in terms of the research and analysis functions that became core elements in most post-World War II national security decision processes. Similarly in Chapter 8 Graham Farrell and Ken Pease highlight the historical lack of interest by criminologists in security, albeit that the 'situational crime prevention' framework is a good one for studying security. The main contribution of criminology to the security industry is, the authors contend, to provide a range of approaches and tools for preventing crime and thereby an understanding of the mechanisms whereby they are likely to succeed or fail. They note the development of a discipline of Crime Science by the incorporation of contributions from a range of crime-relevant science disciplines.

The second section of this book assesses studies of offence types that are associated with organizations. Once again this does not cover all offences although in the space available the focus has been on those that are prominent. In Chapter 9 Richard Hollinger and Jason Davis discuss the study of dishonest staff. They note that employee theft is the single most costly form of larceny experienced by the business world, and that in some work settings, from a statistical standpoint, the 'deviant' employee is the worker who is *not* stealing. No wonder then that a major proportion of business failures are directly or indirectly related to employee theft or dishonesty. They trace various ways of explaining dishonest behaviour which is a basis for determining effective responses. Intriguingly they note that some companies tolerate some offending because it is significantly less expensive than paying employees a more equitable wage. They suggest a combination of strategies to guide the study and practice of security.

In Chapter 10 Elena Licu and Bonnie Fisher examine issues relating to workplace violence. They helpfully take a global perspective examining definitional issues, the scale of victimization and characteristics that are most likely to result in it, as well as documenting the negative physical, psychological and financial toll on employees and the organization. The authors suggest a focus for prevention efforts that is derived from evidence-based research.

In Chapter 11 Mike Levi tackles the issue of white collar crime. He looks at the features that render organizations more vulnerable to both fraud and money laundering and the connections between them. He moves on to assess responses and examines the management of reputational damage, the actual and appropriate roles of the criminal law and policing in the mitigation of business fraud and money laundering risks, and the role of collective business action against white-collar crimes.

In Chapter 12 Rob Mawby discusses research on commercial burglary across the world. He finds that while the extent of commercial burglary varies between countries, it is universally more common than household burglary. And the impact is considerable in financial and emotional terms. Despite this he finds that business people are sometimes ambivalent about the threat posed by burglars, and demonstrate a reluctance to invest in security. Conversely retailers have invested heavily in security to prevent shop theft, the focus of Chapter 13. Read Hayes and Caroline Cardone found the impact to be considerable, in addition to the obvious financial loss offences also disrupt processes, reduce product availability and introduce violence into shops. Their analysis of various patterns of offending leads them to assess the characteristics of an effective response.

In Chapter 14 Paul Wilkinson seeks to clarify our understanding of the concept of terrorism and other forms of violence, and the New Terrorism of the al-Qaeda Network and its implications for security are examined highlighting its capability for mass-casualty attack in western cities as well as its continuing intensive terrorist activity in the front line states in the Middle East. Wilkinson observes that terrorists have only rarely attained their strategic objectives by terrorism alone, although the events of 9/11 underline the enormous impact they can have. An outline is provided of the main elements of an effective strategy to dismantle the al-Qaeda Network including the management of the media.

In Chapter 15 Jason Crampton, Kenneth Paterson, Fred Piper and Matthew Robshaw discuss the latest developments in information security research. Their discussion focuses initially on cryptographic algorithms. They argue that while they often enjoy a highly visible public profile, in practice they are only a very small part of the security solution. They note that the security features offered by modern computer systems are improving all the time, but care must be taken when configuring these features to ensure that they implement the security required. They argue the case for an effective programme of information security management.

The third section of the book includes five chapters on key security services and products, three of these focus on people services and two on technology, although they overlap. In Chapter 16 Alison Wakefield assesses the role of security officers, which as she notes, are omnipresent. She argues that the development of the security industry has included the emergence of new and increasingly sophisticated opportunities for security personnel. Consequently the stereotypes of unskilled, uneducated security personnel may have become less relevant as the industry has moved into more demanding and prominent areas of work. Thus, in jurisdictions such as the UK and many US states, low pay and long hours belie the growing levels of responsibility for security officers, while reward levels in some European countries suggest that lessons may be learned through international comparisons. Her analysis includes a discussion of the role of private security in and with law enforcement. In Chapter 17 Read Hayes tackles another type of security delivered by people, the under-researched area of store detectives. He discusses their role and assesses the impact they have in stores concluding they have a vital role to play in the protection of assets.

In Chapter 18 Tim Prenzler assesses the role of private investigators which he sees as extremely diverse and often highly sophisticated, including covert surveillance, legal enquiries, fraud investigations, debt recovery, serving of legal notices, tracing missing persons, forensic accounting and security risk assessments. He assesses the potential inequalities and injustices that can result from the expansion of forms of 'private justice' based on a clients' capacity to pay. He welcomes licensing to protect clients and innocent third parties from poor quality service and from violations of civil liberties.

In Chapter 19 I discuss research on CCTV and in particular assess the evidence on its effectiveness taking a broader approach than just a consideration of the impact on crime rates. Although this is important, the extent of CCTV and the concerns about intrusions into people's civil liberties also matter. Discussion is also focused on the impact of CCTV on the public's feelings of safety and the pressing worry that CCTV merely displaces crime. In short, it is argued that while CCTV may well become, if it has not already, the essential security tool there is still a lot of learning to be done to use it to maximum advantage.

In Chapter 20 Adrian Beck evaluates research on RFID which, as he notes, is viewed by some as the next generation of barcode, enabling products, cases and pallets to be identified uniquely and without the need for direct human intervention. Beck believes it could revolutionize the way in which supply chains are managed and protected but is less convinced at its potential to seriously impact on theft by staff and customers. In any event he argues that there are still many technological hurdles standing in the way of the wider adoption of RFID and consumer concerns about privacy have yet to be fully addressed. For Beck RFID should not be seen as a panacea to the problems of shrinkage, as it clearly is not, but more as a potentially powerful tool to enable stock loss practitioners to manage the problem much more effectively.

The fourth section of the book focuses on management issues. In Chapter 21 Joshua Bamfield assesses the role of security as a part of management, dealing with planning, leading, organization, controlling, staffing, co-ordinating, and motivating. He examines the role of the security manager including their responsibility for configuring key variables including *tasks, structure, information and decision processes, security investment, reward systems,* and *people* to produce the greatest security results from a given security budget without imperilling the organization's future.

In Chapter 22 Mary Lynn Garcia discusses security risk management and specifically its focus on risk assessment, which attempts to establish what can go wrong, the likelihood that this will occur, and the consequences. The answers to these questions help identify and evaluate risks. She contends that risk management builds on risk assessment by considering available options, their associated tradeoffs in terms of costs, benefits, and risks, and the impacts of management decisions on future options. Her analysis incorporates a discussion of the business case for security and the options for a response including the use of avoidance, reduction, spreading, transfer, and acceptance alternatives.

In Chapter 23 Dominic Elliott discusses how some organizations possess crisis prone characteristics and how an organizational crisis can result from the actions and inactions of management regardless of the events that trigger them. He notes how crises possess both technical and human characteristics which both need to be effectively managed. Importantly, he discussed how managers may learn from the study of organizational failures elsewhere and how the process of Business Continuity Management provides an opportunity to identify potential weaknesses, the resources and competences required to meet customer needs and to develop crisis resilience alongside contingency plans.

The fifth and final section of the book is focused on a range of issues central to any discussion of modern security management. In Chapter 24 Mark Button and Bruce George discuss models of regulation including radical ones, and they draw upon world-wide experiences. They also refine and develop the model of private security regulation they initially presented in 1997. In Chapter 25 Dennis Challinger assesses the impact of security on the 'bottom line'. He argues that corporate security delivers value to a corporation through a range of activities the absence of which would likely lead to losses. For Challinger there is potential for a properly embedded security programme to contribute its expertise to all parts of the business.

In Chapter 26 Clifton Smith reviews trends in security technology. He argues that the application of security technology to protect assets needs – amongst other things – to be justified according to established criteria such as theories and principles, and uses the *defence in depth* and *crime prevention through environmental design* frameworks to guide his analysis. A hierarchy classification of intrusion detection systems is presented in an attempt to classify different types of security technology systems. He ends his analysis looking at the potential of security technology in the future.

In the final chapter Giovanni and Roberto Manunta theorize about what is a security context or situation and therefore what is not. They outline a methodology which invites readers to look at security as part of a much wider set of processes. They argue that to be effective a security system must be driven by a set of ethical, political and economic considerations proper to its specific context, level of analysis and situation. To be effective and useful as a system, security needs a clear definition of scope, relations and goals, of inputs, processes and outputs and they suggest how this might be achieved.

And so this is the first edition of the Handbook of Security. What it confirms, as if it needed confirming, is that security is a broad subject as a practice and as a discipline. It would be possible to envisage a book this size on each of the chapters presented. But it is a foundation on which to build. Indeed, I would be delighted to receive your thoughts on the content of this Handbook, and your suggestions on topics you believe should be covered next time around.[8] The development of the security body of knowledge is inevitably a long intellectual journey, this book can perhaps best be viewed as a small contribution along the way.

Notes

1 See interview with Clifford Shearing in the International Observer, produced by the International centre for the Prevention of Crime; http://www.crime-prevention-intl.org/io_view.php?io_id=125&io_page_id=559

2 Much police work is not crime-related (see, Bayley, 1996), indeed only a small proportion of the police strength is on the beat at any one time (Morgan and Newburn, 1997).

3 For a good discussion of the expansion of private security see, Jones and Newburn (1998).

4 It is worth noting the growing recognition that all staff in a company fulfil a security function. In a recent study of shop theft conducted by the author, shoplifters drew

attention to sales staff interest in them being a deterrent, good customer service is an effective crime prevention measure.

5 It needs to be emphasized that whatever plan emerged would need to be agreed with local representatives but it would mean that the full range of different forms of security provision could be incorporated into a single plan.

6 A malign form would be organized protection rackets which can inflict serious violence. They are of course another way of providing security illustrating still further the dimensions of the 'mixed economy of security'.

7 There has been no attempt to present a specific line of argument in this book, indeed that would be counter productive. Rather the objective has been to tap into the expertise of the authors in defining the salient themes and issues. Unsurprisingly then, as will become evident, contrary views emerge.

8 Please forward any suggestions or ideas to Martin Gill on, m.gill@perpetuitygroup.com.

References

Bayley, D.H. (1996) 'What Do the Police Do?'. In Saulsbury, W., Mott, J. and Newburn, T. (eds) *Themes in Contemporary Policing*. London: Independent Committee of Inquiry into the Roles and Responsibilities of the Police.

Bayley, D. and Shearing, C. (2001) *The New Structure of Policing: Description, Conceptualization and Research Agenda*, Research Report NCJ 187083. Washington DC: National Institute of Justice.

Brodeur, J.P. and Shearing, C. (2005) 'Configuring Security and Justice', *European Journal of Criminology*, 2(4): 379–406.

Button, M. (2002) *Private Policing*. Collumpton: Devon.

Button, M. (2004) '"Softly, Softly", Private Security and the Policing of Corporate Space'. In Hopkins Burke, R. (ed.) *Hard Cop, Soft Cop: Dilemmas and Debates in Contemporary Policing*. Collumpton: Devon.

Clarke, R.V.G. (2005) 'Seven Misconceptions of Situational Crime Prevention'. In Tilley, N. (ed.) *Handbook of Crime Prevention*. Collumpton: Devon.

Collins, P., Cordner, G. and Scarborough, K. (2005) *The ASIS Foundation Security Report: Scope and Emerging Trends*. Alexandria, US: ASIS International.

De Waard, J. (1999) 'The Private Security Industry in International Perspective', *European Journal on Criminal Policy and Research*, 7(2): 143–74.

Garland, D. (1996) 'The Limits of the Sovereign State: Strategies of Crime Control in Contemporary Society', *British Journal of Criminology*, 36(4): 445–71.

George, B. and Button, M. (2000) *Private Security*. Leicester: Perpetuity Press.

Gill, M. and Spriggs, A. (2005) *Assessing the Impact of CCTV*, Home Office Research Study number 292. London: Home Office. http://www.homeoffice.gov.uk/rds/pdfs05/hors292.pdf.

Gill, M. and Hart, J. (1997) 'Policing as a Business: the Organisation and Structure of Private Investigation', *Policing and Society*, 7: 117–41.

Gill, M.L. and Mawby, R.I. (1990a) *A Special Constable: A Study of the Police Reserve*. Aldershot: Avebury.

Gill, M.L. and Mawby, R.I. (1990b) *Volunteers in the Criminal Justice System: A Comparative Study of Probation, Police and Victim Support*. Milton Keynes: Open University Press.

Johnston, L. (2000) *Policing Britain: Risk, Security and Governance*. London: Routledge.

Johnston, L. and Shearing, C. (2003) *Governing Security*. London: Routledge.

Jones, T. and Newburn, T. (1998) *Private Security and Public Policing*. Oxford: Clarendon Press.

King, M. and Prenzler, T. (2003) 'Private Inquiry Agents: Ethical Challenges and Accountability', *Security Journal*, 16(3): 7–18.

Loader, I. (1997a) 'Thinking Normatively About Private Security', *Journal of Law and Society*, 24(3): 377–94.

Loader, I. (1997b) 'Private Security and the Demand for Protection in Contemporary Britain', *Policing and Society*, 7: 143–62.

Mawby, R. (2005) *From Police Science to the Science of Policing*. CEPOL police studies subgroup, Amsterdam, August.

McLeod, R. (2002) *Parapolice: A Revolution in the Business of Law Enforcement*. Toronto: Boheme Press.

Morgan, R. and Newburn, T. (1997) *The Future of Policing*. Oxford: Clarendon Press.

Noakes, L. (2000) 'Private Cops on the Block: A Review of the Role of Private Security in Residential Communities', *Policing and Society*, 10: 143–61.

Prenzler, T. (2004) 'The Privatization of Policing'. In Sarre, R. and Tomaino, J. (eds) *Key Issues in Criminal Justice*. Adelaide: Australian Humanities Press.

Prenzler, T. and Sarre, R. (2002) 'The Policing Complex'. In Graycar, A. and Grabosky, P. (eds) *The Cambridge Handbook of Australian Criminology*. Melbourne: Cambridge University Press, 52–72.

Rigakos, G. (2002) *The New Parapolice*. Toronto: University of Toronto Press.

Sarre, R. (2005) 'Researching Private Policing: Challenges and Agendas for Researchers', *Security Journal*, 18(4): 18–31.

Sarre, R. and Prenzler, T. (1999) 'The Regulation of Private Policing: Reviewing Mechanisms of Accountability', *Crime Prevention and Community Safety: An International Journal*, 1(3): 17–28.

Sarre, R. and Prenzler, T. (2000) 'The Relationship Between Police and Private Security: Models and Future Directions', *International Journal of Comparative and Applied Criminal Justice*, 24(1): 91–113.

Shearing, C. (1992) 'The Relation Between Public and Private Policing'. In Tonry, M. and Morris, N. (eds) *Modern Policing: An Annual Review of Research*. Chicago: University of Chicago Press, 15: 399–434.

Welsh, B. and Farrington, D. (1999) 'Value for Money? A Review of the Costs and Benefits of Situational Prevention', *British Journal of Criminology*, 39(3): 345–68.

Zedner, L. (2003) 'Too Much Security', *International Journal of the Sociology of Law*, 31(3): 155–84.

Part I
Security as a Discipline

2
A History of Security

Robert D. McCrie[1]

This chapter describes processes by which security has been, or has sought to be. achieved by and why it is requisite for human society. The term derives from the Latin *securus* and *securitas,* feeling no care or apprehension, the safeguarding of (the interests of) a state, organization, or persons; safe. Four interlinking factors have evolved to make individuals, enterprises, institutions, and society as a whole secure:

1. Physical security measures
2. Public protection forces and tactics
3. Private security personnel and technology
4. Individual efforts for protection and maintenance of order

This chapter will argue that society endeavors to achieve security through mutual connections between the public and private sectors, as well as from individual effort. Risks constantly change due to the development of new conditions, procedures and technology; security changes in response to this evolution.

Physical security measures

From earliest known evidence, security became necessary for human existence. This is due partially to the relationship between population and resources. As population increased in early societies, pressure for self-sustenance often led to exploration, domination of vulnerable populations, and exploitation. A study of prehistory suggests that warfare due to population pressures is related. Robert L. Carneiro (2003) theorizes that the rise of the first states in Egypt, Mesopotamia, and Peru were linked to increasing conflict between neighboring villages once it was no longer possible for villagers in one sector to cultivate land sufficiently to feed their hungry. Neighboring communities battled with each other as a consequence of limited resources. These conflicts added to the creation of hierarchical structures in early society. Farming societies gradually created chiefdoms, reinforced by kinship, partially to create order. The presence of stratification in early society produced numerous effects including establishing codes (laws) to assure peaceful coexistence, to stimulate commerce, to encourage development of specialized work, and to provide a structure for dealing with threats from external forces. The successful leader was likely to be one who could be most effective in rousing the clan, band, tribe, or community to fight ferociously and successfully against aggressors, or to lead people in attacks against others to increase their own resources.

As societies became larger, they developed stratification with kings, or their equivalents, serving as a leadership élite with subordinate categories of social, political, and economic distinctions. Often these positions became hereditary and self-reinforcing. This evolving creation of proto-government is explained by a complex existence with competition for limited resources which threatened the security and safety of the community.

The development of early communities, the accumulation of wealth, and the improvement of local agricultural lands made existence precarious from outside attack by those who coveted such assets and resources. The fear of attacks led to the evolution of defensive means to protect the community. A fundamental strategy was to use physical implementation wherever possible to protect from external incursions. Often geographic location could be significant for protection such as being situated on high locations or surrounded by or alongside bodies of water. While geography eased the vulnerability for some communities, others required additional means of protection. From Neolithic times on, excavated villages revealed fortified living areas for individual families (Saint-Blanquat, 1986). An encompassing wall or physical barriers for protection often surrounded

Table 2.1   Basic physical and animate security resources

Type	Main Advantages	Main Disadvantages
Protected location, e.g., on heights or water-protected	Harder to attack than low, flat areas	Possible inconvenience; construction difficulties
Walls	Strong deterrence; intimidating	Costly to construct, enlarge and maintain
Animals, especially dogs	Acute sight and hearing; trainable for various tasks	Fatigue; need for constant re-enforcement
Safes and vaults	Easy to lock and unlock	Can be defeated given sufficient time and skill
Locks	Inexpensive, easy to operate	May be picked or overcome by other means
Hiding places	Easy to create outside or inside	Eventually discoverable; locations may be forgotten
Traps	Inexpensive; of deterrent value	Accidental unintended injury or death

these in turn. Posts, thick enclosures, heavy doors with stout closures, animals, and traps all served to protect *fore*communities from attack from alien forces. Thus, a variety of physical and animate security resources emerged (Table 2.1). Yet nothing was comparable to the wall in terms of simplicity of concept, construction requirements, the extent of operating and construction costs, and the resultant shaping of the protected community into a distinctive political entity.

The wall as an organizing structure

Walls over the millennia protected entire nations, provinces, cities, villages, military fortifications, castles, and individual living units. The wall was by far the most costly defensive or public works expenditure a community might have to sustain. The wall was a critical aid to civility and security at least from the later part of the Stone Age until the 19ᵗʰ century, and continues in modern times on a more restricted basis. From the Roman tradition on, the medieval town or city wall contained three elements: the wall itself, towers, and gates. The wall could be one to three meters wide with heights sometimes over 20 meters. Towers would be situated at periodic distances along the extent of the wall in which soldiers or lookouts could be stationed. Gates controlled access to the interior. Beyond controlling entrance and egress, gates could be points where visitors sometimes may be charged a gate fee to enter, or visitors were obliged to provide evidence of their reliability. This physical structure significantly controlled internal and external features to life on both sides of the wall.

Construction sometimes was a matter of urgency involving the assistance of all able bodied people in its completion. Local materials normally were used for the structure if available, though substances for construction frequently had to be transported from great distances. Then when the wall had been completed, over time with an increase in population, enlargements and extensions became necessary. These again became extraordinary costs, which the community would accept only under compelling necessity. The physical construction of an enlargement of the wall additionally would require more guards or watchmen to staff the new gate and tower extension (Mumford, 1961; Pirenne, 1969; Turner, 1941).

Remnants of early walled communities exist today in hundreds of European and Asian cities. In Howard Saalman's *Medieval Cities*, figures depicting excavations of 50 medieval communities are presented: they all have walls. Walled cities raised the sense of significance of who could live and practice trades within the city. To live within a walled community was a privilege to be earned with alacrity and retained with diligence. Walls expressed the power and promise of urban life. The word *urban* itself derives from the Latin *urbs*, or city; this was the center of civility, borrowed from the Latin *civis*, or citizen. A walled community evoked psychological, economic, military, and political impediments for attackers. Aside from the construction, maintenance, and operations of the wall, the central reason for being was physical security of the population within its confines.

The demand to live within the walled city often was greater than the capacity to fulfill it. People settled – or attempted to – outside the walls if they could not live within. These new communities were called *faubourgs*. In effect, the wall became the organizing structure to orderly community life. When gates descended at sundown, no one could enter or leave. An early surveillance society imbued the walled city. Individuals who sought to stay within the walled compound overnight in some locations would have to have a current resident authorize their stay and take responsibility for their behavior while present. The ecosystem within the community was fragile. Disease could spread rapidly, decimating the population quickly. Additionally, risks of fire were constant threats as wood, straw, and other flammable materials were used within early habitations. Still, the walled castle, village, or city acted as a magnet for persons who wished to aspire to opportunities of urbanity as well as to achieve a higher degree of personal security.

Walls protected cities and towns from earliest recorded history in Mesopotamia and Phoenicia. Castles protected less populated regions located distant from population centers, though sometimes castle created sizeable adjacent communities capable of withstanding extensive sieges. With the development of modern siegecraft, however, the castle or walled community was placed at greater risk. Battering rams and catapults and the building of attack hills near the protected wall increased the chances of success by the forces laying siege. By the 15th century the development of artillery made the confidence in fixed fortifications less assured. Nonetheless, artillery attacks had limitations. In many examples, the greatest means of defeating the besieged structure or community was by cutting off needed supplies over extensive periods of time starving the inhabitants into surrendering. Castles could be large enough to protect not only royal or feudal personages and their entourages, but also to sustain soldiers, peasants, and others in safety over an extended siege. Protection was not limited to communal, residential, or military constructions. Even religious structures could serve as protective locations for the faithful. An extant example is the fortified cathedral of Sainte-Cécile in Albi, France.

While castles could exist within walled cities, usually they were located in a strategic position some distance from population centers. Castles were meant to dominate and were constructed to meet exigent military requirements. The Normans were able to enforce their feudal structure partly because of the capacity to build well and quickly. The crown owned castles and nobles pledged to support the crown with their own castles. Castles served both as centers of power to maintain the *status quo* domestically as well as to provide a defensive focus to repel invaders (Hogg, 1988).

Walls also served to protect entire populations. Fortifications in Central Asia date from the 4th century BC. The Great Wall of China began during the reign of Emperor Shih Huang-ti in 214 BC in which he linked earlier walled sections (Gaubatz, 1996; Luo, 1981). The object was to protect ethnic Chinese mainly against the northern Huns; the effect largely was successful. Over subsequent centuries the Great Wall was expanded, eventually to reach over 2400 kilometers from the Gulf of Chihli of the Yellow Sea to deep in Central Asia. Hadrian's Wall, 2nd century AD, was constructed to seal the Romans and Saxons from warring Celtic tribes to the north. When the southern part of Scotland was partially subdued, another wall was constructed beginning 138 AD farther north between the Clyde and the Forth of Firth. This was the Antonine Wall, named for Antoninus Pius, the Roman emperor (Hanson and Maxwell, 1986). While vast walls covering great distances were successful at deterring invaders for considerable time, some walls eventually failed due to the great cost of guarding and maintenance. A series of castles could accomplish the same objective at less cost in enforcing hegemony within a proximate area (Bradbury, 1992; Johnson, 2002; Singman, 1999).

Further, the advent of gunpowder changed the defensive capacity of castle walls. Gunpowder is an explosive mixture of saltpeter (potassium nitrate), sulfur, and charcoal. Believed to be originally used by the Chinese for fireworks as early as the 9th century, gunpowder was introduced by the 14th century in Asia and Europe for warfare. Other means of attacking walled communities and structures had been used for centuries earlier. Greek fire – the projecting of a flammable material that was catapulted over a wall – was a principal weapon used to attack those behind walls (Partington, 1999). The advent of gunpowder, however, meant that previously impenetrable walls were vulnerable from persistent, well-supported attackers. Furthermore, growth of urban populations forced periodic enlargements of many city or town walls, a costly expenditure and the defensive utility of the wall declined due to changing technology and military strategy. In the mid-19th century the invention of nitroglycerine produced an even more powerful agent against earthen and masonry construction. The nature of threats to communities had changed. Cities began removing their walls due to their needs for expansion and the limited use of historic walls in a modern era.

In contemporary experience the wall remains as an important protective structure: military outposts, utilities, factories, and research and development facilities are among the facilities where walls remain significant structures for protection. Gated communities protect millions of affluent and semi-affluent residents throughout the world. Walls were never ultimate barriers. They could be penetrated by a sustained direct attack, dug under, or surmounted. The wall remains important, nonetheless, for its symbolic as well as its actual significance in deterring access and providing physical security. Walls reference protection that is both ancient and contemporary. Physical and psychological effort are required to surpass them (Low, 2003).

Animals for protection

Animals probably preceded defensive structures to protect people. Dogs are particularly suitable for security purposes. Egyptian kings used sulukis to guard the kings' residences. The Egyptians also raised greyhounds and mastiffs to protect property. Dogs were valuable also as canine alarms, to attack intruders, for hunting, and for companionship. Egyptian families would grieve when a favorite dog died. The Romans employed rottweilers as sentries to guard storage depots against thieves.

From the Middle Ages through the advent of modern policing, guard dogs were important to protect homes, places of work and storage, and boats.

Watchmen patrolled the wharves with dogs to detect and deter thieves. In modern times canine patrols serve law enforcement around the world. They are used to detect illegal contraband, the smuggling of people, and the presence of prohibited foods, plants, narcotics, and explosives. Further millions of private citizens use dogs for companionship and as well as security aids (Bryson, 1996; Orbaan, 1968; Chapman, 1990).

Other animals besides dogs have played roles in protecting people and property. Livy described how geese in one of the Roman hills sounded an alarm to warn about Gaelic invaders seeking to attack an army encampment at night from a steep and unprotected side of a hill (Sélincourt, 1960). Other birds capable of making loud noise when disturbed have been put to use to protect prisons from escapees and military facilities from unauthorized presence of people. Similarly, the warhorse was important for military use since early civilizations (Hyland, 2003).

Protecting the interior of structures

Security is needed within as well as without a walled community or structure. To protect precious objects, including vital documents; hidden places within walls or furniture or under floors were frequently created. These were inexpensive to construct, but might be discovered eventually by others. Traps sometimes ensnared users who attempted to open a door but failed to know the secret of the combination. Similarly, traps and snares were employed frequently for protection in grounds and within structures. The disadvantage with traps is that persons setting them sometimes are injured, and others are inadvertently hurt. Safes and strong boxes have served as protected containers since ancient Egypt (Eras, 1974; Buehr, 1953). Locks are among the oldest mechanisms invented. The Lock Museum of America in Terryville, Connecticut, contains an Egyptian pin lock, perhaps 4000 years old. Through the centuries the need to protect precious metals and stones and important documents created a market that advanced safe and vault construction skills. Lockable chests, often protected with ingenuous, elaborate mechanisms, were common at the court during early medieval times. The oldest piece of furniture owned by the Bank of England is a multi-point locking secured chest dated from about 1700, visible today in the bank's museum.

Mechanical locks were developed earlier than combination mechanisms. Mechanical locks have three parts: the bolt, which must not be easily accessible, the obstacle, and the key. Locks with keys were widely available for purchase from artisans from the Middle Ages on. They were created as an inexpensive reliable means of deterring access. Metal locks made in Nüremberg were especially appreciated for their workmanship. By the 17th century, metal locks made in France developed their own caché for artistry as well as protection (Hopkins, 1928).

In the 19th century, vault door manufacturers in the United Kingdom and the United States sometimes employed the language 'burglar-proof' as part of their marketing efforts. This was an exaggeration as, in reality, no vault or safe is absolutely burglarproof and can be defeated by insider knowledge or brute attack; however, burglars have never defeated some mechanical locks to date in criminal attempts. Attacks on keyed and combination locks occur throughout the history of these security containers. Safes and vaults could be attacked forcefully by tools, torches, explosives, and acid; or skilled safe crackers hardly would leave a trace of their presence by opening the combination lock on the safe or vault door with finesse. Safe and vault makers steadily have sought to improve the resistance of their products to criminal intents. Combined with modern alarm systems, this target largely has been achieved, evidenced through the long-term decline in high-loss commercial burglary rates among Western nations.

In the first quarter of the 20th century, customers for anti-burglary products demanded assurances that devices could actually accomplish what they were supposed to. The standards movement resulted. In the United States, Underwriters Laboratories (UL) promulgated consensual standards for safe and vault door construction beginning in 1924. In subsequent years UL developed a gradation of the burglary resistance of certain products presented to it for possible approval.[2] In addition to safes and vault doors, UL added a variety of other security products for which security standards are set and tests are conducted. Some of these are: night depositories, vault ventilating ports and ventilators, timelocks, and combination locks, in addition to locking cylinders. These are mostly mechanical safeguards. With the advent of electric alarms, discussed later in this chapter, the requirement of protecting against brute strength or stealth attacks against such structures has declined.

UL in the United States and Canada represents only a partial reflection of standards-setting activities that have guided the evolution and development of physical security products. In the United States, other physical security standards have been developed by such organizations as ASTM International (formerly the American Society for Testing and Materials) and the Security Equipment Industry Association (SEIA). The National Institute of Justice issues standards for police equipment and supplies, which also may have relevance to private security equipment purchasers. Still, other organizations set standards for safety and fire-resistance of products and materials. In the United Kingdom, extensive standards involving electronic, mechanical, quality control, and procedural issues have been issued by the British Standards Institution (BSI). Many of the aspects of security alarm and system design recognized by BSI have been proposed under the authority of the Association of Chief Police Officers (ACPO). The British Security Industry Association (BSIA), the National Security Inspectorate (NSI), and other organizations have set standards for physical security products. On the Continent, standards for certain physical security products emanate from the European Fire and Security Group and Eurosafe. Conceptually, formal consensual standards took hold because they increased the minimum level of security and reliability provided by a product or material and simplified product-type options. They may be regarded as a historical stage in the evolvement of technology.

In the current era, mechanical locks remain an important part of security. Derived from principles over 4000 years old, locking systems in use today bear many similarities in concept and function to the earliest forms of locking protection. In the 21st century, electronic computer-operated safe and vault doors have become available providing systems-based advantages for formerly mechanical fixtures.

Public protection forces and tactics

Since the first duty of the community is to protect itself through government and personal initiative, hierarchical stratification in early society occurred partially to provide leadership for defensive purposes. According to the archeologist Robert Wenke (1999), human society evolved from bands, consisting of foragers with 50 or fewer members, to tribes, larger than bands and relying on kinship, then to chiefdoms, consisting of a leader who would direct the activities of those within his sphere of control. Beyond this, kingdoms, and occasionally queendoms, arose to advance mutual defense and economic vitality. In ultimate examples, empires emerged which combined multiple countries with various forms of governance.

Over the millennia, kingdoms, or their titular equivalents, turned to forces of men for defense and offense. For most of history, these forces were convened on an *ad hoc* basis. When the need for fighters in defensive or offensive actions had passed, the groups were disbanded. As the techniques of warfare evolved and the need for ready forces grew, the concept of having a dedicated stipendiary cadre of armed forces became initially tolerated and eventually regarded as imperative (Wright, 1965).

The concept of an organized military

In the Western experience early forms of military forces could be found among the Phoenicians and early Hebrews. The rise of the Greeks eventually challenged the Phoenicians' maritime power. The ensuing Hellenistic culture thrived until Rome absorbed it. Military forces in Roman times illustrate a high degree of organization and discipline (Watson, 1985). For the most part, soldiers or sailors had fixed commitments of service, respect for a hierarchy, the development of specialized skills, and a structure for compensation and rewards. This 'professional' army was important to extend the empire; it also was vital to maintain it. After conquest, Roman soldiers used their architectural and engineering skills to construct public works, ready or improve fortifications, and lay out the grid for the conquered or newly established communities. Beyond these tasks of community building, the military could play dominant or subordinate roles in the operations of the community, depending on local circumstances.

Control of the seas was also significant in assuring hegemony (David, 2003). Warships were first recorded by the Egyptians in 3000 BC. This is established by archeological evidence, which indicates that Egyptian ships were designed to support offensive or defensive maneuvers, and not merely fitted for conventional transportation.

While military forces were convened and disbanded as needed over the centuries, by contrast, rulers frequently had personal security forces on a permanent basis dedicated for their safety. Nonetheless, over time, the need for permanent military forces evolved. With foreign occupation, soldiers were vital for maintaining stability and assuring that the agenda set by the occupiers was respected. In times of national emergencies, such as attacks from foreign powers, military leaders required volunteers to augment the core forces. These *ad hoc* warriors might be amply available, or they might have to be called to service through coercion (conscription), suasion, or enticements.

While permitting the monarch his or her own personal protection forces and perhaps a dedicated military corps, contravening centers of power generally sought to limit the extent of standing armies. Standing armies with no engagements, represented, in the Middle Ages and Renaissance, a threat to freedom from royal subjugation, hard won over the centuries, as well as a source of recurring cost to be met. In times of extensive military action, nonetheless, the military became quasi-permanent. In modern times, with the period of continuous European conflict from approximately 1685 to 1714, the need to retain a skilled, well-supplied military became apparent for national interests. European states then created standing armies and navies with attendant bureaucracies to support them.[3] Insightful writers as diverse as Sun-Tzu (2002) and Julius Caesar (1998) centuries earlier had shared their thoughts on the conduct of war. The modern army, however, was characterized by a more faceted preparation than in the past. Theories and practices of military conduct emerged in the early 18th century, which drew upon rapidly expanding technical innovations. These developments helped solidify the position of permanent status for the nation's protective interests (Howard, 1966).

However, through all this period, the military had auxiliary, temporary duties when domestic conflicts or other emergencies occurred that surpassed the capacity of society to deal with them routinely. The military was always the nation's ultimate power to maintain order within cities when existing measures were overwhelmed. Military forces also might be needed within the countryside, which could be dangerous for farmers and travelers beset by itinerant criminal gangs. But soldiers and sailors were never ideal peacekeepers within a disorderly community. Trained and urged to kill in battle, they were inept at responding with a measured, minimally oppressive way to a disorderly citizenry. Public fear and loathing of loutish military behavior within cities when their presence was required increased pressure to find an option; the era of public police began. The separation of military and law enforcement as public security forces recognizes their different histories, goals, and methods. British general Sir John Hackett stated: 'To employ soldiers as police, or police as soldiers...is grossly inefficient and contains a serious threat to freedom' (Villiers, 1998). By the 21st century, military response to civilian domestic emergencies and disasters became controlled and nuanced relative to earlier times. In addition to the military, two other types of security forces emerged within the past two centuries (Table 2.2) Public policing is discussed next.

Table 2.2   Modern types of resources for security

Quality	Permanent Military	Police	Private Security
Origins	Early 18th century	1829, Metropolitan Police Act, UK	1850, founding Pinkerton's, US
Expectations	National safety and interests	Local order	Protection of assets from loss
Primary mandate	Defensive or offensive in the	To suppress crime and disorder public's interest	To safeguard people
Secondary mandate	Aid in times of emergencies or great disorders	To enforce laws	To deter and detect crime
Legal authority	National	Local and national	Local, usually
Compelling deadly force	Approved use of someone for charges	May arrest and hold resources as needed	Protects private feature
Growth pattern	Declining	Steady	Increasing

The emergence of law enforcement

Policing is inextricably linked to the emergence of the city. The word derives from the Greek *polis*, referring to the city-state, that is, organized government, the perfect community. While the word *polis* may still be used to define *civil administration*, since the 18th century the derivative term *police* has been associated internationally with a civil force entrusted with the maintenance of public order, enforcing regulations, punishing breaches of the law, and detecting crime.

The police historian Charles Reith describes in *The Blind Eye of History* (1975) early law enforcement in Greek, Roman, Byzantine, and Islamic empires and carries the discourse through policing in Britain and the United States until the mid-20th century. Reith notes an important distinction between totalitarian police, in which agents of control were appointed and had tacit or direct responsibility to the government or ruler, and police in democratic environments with responsibilities to the law.

The term law enforcement significantly reflects the supremacy of law, not the whims of an autocrat, local politician, or power broker. The term also implies that law enforcement involves more than police, incorporating specialized units generally possessing police powers but operating separately from the regular police of city and town. The law enforcement system today incorporates these general and specialized police units as well as probation, corrections, parole, and the criminal courts. However, this discussion, drawing relationships among the military and private security, concerns primarily urban policing services.

The era that developed modern policing in the British experience geographically is centered on Bow Street in London. Here the first police office and later the most important magistrates' court was found. Henry Fielding (1707–54), a magistrate and noted novelist, proposed the idea of permanent, paid, honest magistrates who would command a small force of permanent constables in district police offices (Battestin, 1989; Thomas, 1991). Fielding's prototype police force began in 1753 with seven men, six of whom previously had been parish constables. The newly organized constables quickly arrested a large gang of thieves. On the recommendations of the court, the constables might receive a reward that then could be divided between police officers and victims of the crime. Thus the Bow Street Patrols – later popularly called Bow Street Runners – earned bonuses on top of their regular income. Rewards were higher for solving particularly vexing crimes (Goddard, 1957).

Originally dressed in civilian clothing, the constables carried short crowned tipstaves as a symbol of their authority.[4] They worked with informants with whom they might share their bonuses following successful arrests. By the early 19th century, the uniformed Bow Street police squad began. A foot patrol was started at night, and a horse patrol was tried briefly.

Two generations after organized protective forces began on Bow Street, losses from crime imperiled the shipping industry centered in London. Merchant shippers turned in 1798 to a quasi-civilian group for protective services, called River Police or Maritime Police. Patrick Colquhoun (1745–1820) and John Harriott (1745–1817), both magistrates, conceived the idea of creating this dedicated force to protect ships at port and storage facilities associated with them. The West India Company agreed to pay 80 percent initially of the costs. The officers possessed civil authority. In July 1798, the Marine Police Office in Wapping High Street was opened and employed about 200 constables and guards. Colquhoun and Harriott seemed to espouse the concept of Cesare di Beccaria (1739–1794) that crime was best mitigated with the likelihood of swift detection and arrest rather than the severity of the punishment.

The first months provided a severe testing for the incipient law enforcement group. On October 16, just three months after formation, two river police officers arrested three men for stealing coal and fined each £2, a large sum at the time. That night a crowd of 100 of the men's supporters attacked the police office with sticks and cobblestones. Magistrate Colquhoun read them the Riot Act, ordering the mob to disperse immediately. They didn't. Pistols were distributed to the constables who fired to disperse the rioters. Some rioters also had weapons and fired back. Three constables were hit by gunfire and one died; five rioters were killed and several more, injured. Civilian militia responded to support the police, ending further chances of injury. The riot spanned less then three hours but established the point that police would not retreat from a mob.[5] In the first full year of operations the Maritime Police enormously cut crime from earlier levels, immediately justifying their cost. Felonies were eliminated, and over 2000 misdemeanor arrests were tallied in the first year of operations. The stalwart performance of the River Police helped create support for the creation of the Metropolitan Police three decades later.

Urban disorder reportedly grew in the early decades of the 18th century reflecting rapid urban growth from growing industrialization. Robert Peel (1788–1850), a pivotal figure in modern policing, served as chief secretary for Ireland from 1810–12. While there, he formed the Irish Peace Preservation Police chiefly to patrol rural areas where a variety of baronial police and rival oath-bound secret societies used terror as a weapon. This force grew to become the Royal Irish Constabulary. In London in 1822, as home secretary, Peel sought to respond to disorder by creating a Select Committee to evaluate possibly merging the regular constables, the parish constables, the Bow Street patrols, the River Police, and the night watch into a new coherent whole. Peel left office before the committee's influence was fully achieved but returned in 1828, and renewed the growing interest in establishing a dedicated quasi-military police force, but not one like the French in which espionage was part of the job description. This innovation culminated in passage of the Metropolitan Police Bill of 1829, which established a police force for London under a unified command (Ramsay, 1971; Evans, 1991). The act passed according to Reith 'in the face of intense and almost unanimous public opposition by what amounts to little more than a political party trick.' The act created a force of paid, round-the-clock constables, the new police. Charles Rowan (c.1782–1852) and Richard Mayne (1796–1868) teamed as joint commissioners from 1829 until Rowan died in 1852. The cabinet thought that co-commissioners made the strongest management team and Mayne, who continued in office, was joined by a co-commissioner for three years. Thereafter, Mayne continued as sole commissioner 1855–68 (Cobb, 1957). They created a force that was to inspire, within just a few years, the establishment of modern police departments in other parts of Britain and the world. The force was devoid of serious endemic corruption or the political tyranny that had fanned fears prior to passage of the act. The new police were unarmed except for a short wooden baton, a truncheon, concealed under their coats.[6] They would be uniformed. Rather than only learning by doing, a *General Instructions* book described command structure and provided practice guidelines. Constables were trained to respect civil rights of the public and to treat the public with courtesy and to use the least firmness necessary in the event of personal contact or arrest. The new police could be and were terminated for drunkenness on duty, absenteeism, talking with prostitutes, talking too long with women who were not prostitutes, unnecessarily rough behavior in making arrests, or associating with criminals. Emphasis on prevention of crime over detection of criminality became a characteristic.

The City of New York was among the cities which took notice of the new policing structure of London. The city had had a daytime constabulary system and a night watch since the Dutch era of the 17th century. The system had become ineffective as New York City exploded with growth supported by the surge of industrialization in the early 19th century (Costello, 1972). While Boston had created the first American major urban police department in 1838 (Lane,

1967), the reorganization in the City of New York seven years later was to have a great impact on the rest of the new nation. Using the Metropolitan Police as the principal model, New York revised its policing, adopting many of the same characteristics from London. The New York version of policing differed in some major aspects. For the earliest decades New York police officers first were reappointed on an annual basis then later for a biennial period. Support of a local politician was needed to secure a position. When a new mayor was elected, some police officers would be terminated immediately to be replaced by the winner's supporters. In the last quarter of the 19th century, political cronyism ceased to be the primary factor in selecting and retaining officers. Men were chosen for their abilities, and would have lifetime tenure if their records were clean for several years (Richardson, 1970).

The nexus between police and the military

If the military is primarily responsible for macro risks generally occurring outside of the nation, police are responsible for internal micro risks within the community. To manage the peace sworn police officers always have possessed a special power: to deprive people temporarily of their liberty for reasonable cause. What might be called the traditional, orthodox (Whig), or Reithian, view of policing is as follows: In the 19th century, an era of increased urbanization, industrialization, and economic change reshaped Western society. Advances in communications and transportation drew workers from the farms and other nations into cities for employment and opportunity. Along with these changes, violent and property crime increased markedly. Though police statistics were not accurate at that time, the consensus was that urban society was imperiled from waves of disorder, which had no adequate countervailing response from government.

The old system of policing was inefficient, inappropriate, political, and sometimes corrupt and tyrannical. The new policing system would concentrate on diminishing crime and enforcing laws. The clarity of purpose and the urgency of the need are why the new policing was invented and spread rapidly. But a few revisionist criminologists have argued that police fundamentally were class warriors fighting to enforce bourgeois values. The police were promoting codes of conduct, as 'blue-coated "domestic missionaries"', concomitant with a long period of political struggle between different economic and social forces (Philips and Storch, 1999). Sometimes crime-fighting seemed like an after-thought to those appointed to provide it. David Taylor (1997) mentions the 'Huddersfield Crusade' of the 19th century in which the chief constable imposed his own view on social issues in his district to an extreme degree. In one instant, police there arrested three men for watching a cricket match on Sunday, when they had been ordered to attend church.[7]

English-speaking nations follow the organizational structure of the new police in London. On the Continent cities also developed comparable modern police forces. But in smaller communities and the countryside, gendarmes, a military force historically linked to Revolutionary and Napoleonic armies, provide policing services (Emsley, 1999; Stead, 1983). In China, policing grew out of a system of civil surveillance and control from a feudal past (Dutton, 1992). For ancient to modern history of China, the state police controlled behavior through family intervention. In recent times state policing involves multiple forces: the armed police, administrative police, and criminal police. Also, the army may intervene in broader threats to the nation. At times when policing is inadequate for whatever reason, the private sector provides protection for itself. Eventually this will foster the rise of private security services and systems.

Private security personnel and technology

While the era of modern policing began in England, the security industry had its origins as a commercial enterprise in the United States. Development occurred in distinct ways.

Guarding and patrolling

No person contributed more to the origin of modern, profit-making security services than Allan Pinkerton did. The son of a Glasgow police sergeant, young Pinkerton immigrated to the United States in 1842. After an apprenticeship as a cooper, a barrel maker, Pinkerton settled in Dundee, 38 miles northwest of Chicago. His business prospered: three years later eight men were working for him. One day in 1846, Pinkerton was searching for trees to fell for barrels. He encountered the remnants of a recent campfire on a seldom-visited island. It was a suspicious location for such a fire as travelers would not have camped there and picnics were not family activities that time of the year. On several occasions he returned and found the location deserted as usual. Still curious he returned one evening at dark and his suspicions were confirmed. Pinkerton detected counterfeiters meeting around the campfire. Without being discovered, Pinkerton returned to town and described what he had observed to the sheriff. The sheriff, Pinkerton, and a posse returned one evening and arrested a band who were seized with bogus dimes and tools to make them. It was an event that would shape the cooper's life (Mackay, 1996; Morn, 1982; Horan, 1962).

Counterfeiting was a serious problem for commerce in mid-19th century America; it was the most serious type of fraud. Pinkerton soon learned about the presence of counterfeit ten-dollar banknotes being passed in his community. At the time numerous small banks issued their own notes. The only institution whose banknotes were trusted in Dundee were those issued by the Wisconsin Marine and Fire Insurance Company of Chicago. Pinkerton was tipped off that the suspected counterfeiter of the notes was at work in Dundee. Pinkerton angled to meet the man. Dressed in overalls and barefooted, he said that he was working at a cooperage but casually added that he was looking for 'a good scheme' that would bring him some fast cash.

After some effort Pinkerton was able to purchase a few counterfeit banknotes and quickly thereafter the counterfeiter was arrested. Allan Pinkerton became an instant local hero. The sheriff of much more populous Cook County which embraced fast-growing Chicago, faced the same problems of reducing the prevalence of counterfeiting. The sheriff offered Pinkerton a position as a deputy, the county's first and only investigator. Pinkerton accepted and moved to Chicago. Significant arrests soon followed. In 1850, Pinkerton resigned but was quickly hired by the United States Post Office, which appointed him as a special agent in charge of solving a series of mail thefts. Pinkerton's suspicion fell upon a mail sorter: but where was the evidence of his thefts? The suspect showed no indication that he was living above his means from the money supposedly stolen from the mails. An arrest was made and the suspect's boarding house simple room was searched without success. Finally, Pinkerton suggested examining the pictures on the wall. Concealed behind the pictures $3738 was found. Pinkerton's investigative sagesse had paid off.

Pinkerton, with a partner briefly, established an investigative office in Chicago. The incipient firm began working for a consortium of railroads which operated in Chicago. By 1854, he had received retainers from six railroads for investigative work. Their main problem was robbery: thieves could stop the train at a remote junction and steal cash and other valuables with impunity. Frequently, passengers on the trains also would be robbed. Local law enforcement was not equipped to trace the robbers when they left the jurisdiction of their crime. 'The Pinkertons' proved adept at tracking and apprehending train robbers, returning them to justice, and handing over the entire amount of the loot recovered, excepting what the criminals had spent during their short-lived celebrations. Another problem was internal crime within the railroads, which the firm also investigated. The firm, meanwhile, continued to provide investigative services for Cook County and for the United States Post Office.

Investigation was the original service offered by Pinkerton and his staff. (Pinkerton hired the first woman detective, Kate Warne, in 1856.) Eventually some railroad clients accepted Pinkerton's suggestion that his company provide armed guards to ride with the trains and to provide a deterrence when precious metal or other valuables were transferred. Guarding became a new source of revenue. With the start of the American Civil War, Pinkerton personally provided protective services briefly for the president, Abraham Lincoln, who was the target of a presumed early assassination attempt.[8] Later in the war, Pinkerton's organization created an intelligence gathering operation for the army. Pinkerton quickly devised means whereby he could collect intelligence from undercover agents. He placed or found operatives who were able to collect vital information on strategy and tactics of the seceding Southern states. With the end of the American Civil War, industrialization in the Northern states surged and Pinkerton's security business grew along with it. Allan Pinkerton was succeeded by sons, Robert and William, who advanced the business in their turn. The firm, which operated from numerous offices by the 20th century, came to provide security-consulting services to its clients in industrial America. Within the first generation of its founding, Pinkerton's firm had made seminal contributions to: commercial investigation, guarding, executive protection, intelligence collection, and consulting services. These services would develop separately in specialized areas over the decades to come.

Over the span of 20th century security services businesses grew resolutely. The Pinkertons were first and largest, but numerous other competitors emerged. By the 1950s, some security services businesses expanded from the United States to other nations. By the 21st century in the United States alone, over 8000 private security guard firms operated around the nation. Additionally, perhaps 11,000 investigators (detectives) operated. Further, security consultants – both generalists and specialists – plied their services. In the United States, Securitas, with headquarters in London and Stockholm, acquired Pinkerton, Burns International Security Services and others.

Elsewhere, the industry grew serving the security needs of an expanding industrial base. In England and Wales such firms as Group 4 Securitas and Securicor (now merged into Group 4 Securicor), Securitas (founded in Sweden in 1913), and Reliance Initial were the largest firms based on employment and revenues. But perhaps 2000 smaller local and regional watch, guard, and patrol companies operated as of 2005.

These security service workers are contract employees and are in addition to the thousands of proprietary (employed directly by the organization) employees working for organizations. The trend for the past half-century is for employers to contract-out routine security services, while maintaining in-house supervisory and management responsibilities for the security program.[9] This partially explains why guarding services have grown steadily in the past half century. Whereas contract security employees were in the minority for most of the brief history of the security services industry, they are now in the majority in many industrial countries. Private security personnel have also seized opportunities for privatization of public services. Today private security personnel offer their clients flexibility, specialized skills, insurance covering job-related liabilities, and cost-effective services making the choice attractive for clients. Private security firms sometimes operate for-profit correctional facilities and provide services in government offices, educational and research institutions, and within military compounds.

Security management

Security management emerged as a differentiative discipline in the second half of the 20th century (McCrie, 1997). Protection of assets from loss always mattered to profit-making organizations, and guards, regular patrols, and watchmen were tasked to protect private property from theft, fire, and vandalism based on early payroll records. But in the Cold War era of the 1950s conditions were right for development that produced first a few, then more, finally thousands of managers and executives directing ways to reduce losses in organizations and having the authority and resources to establish programs to meet those objectives. The Cold War was postulated on the belief that risks from the Soviet bloc threatened life in the West. The military-industrial complex would provide the products and technology to deter risks and to respond, should an attack actually occur. That meant that the industry must continue to develop advanced and better technology with military and civilian significance.

In the United States, the American Society for Industrial Security (now ASIS International) began in 1954 when five men, holding responsibilities for security at high-tech production facilities, met to discuss the need for a professional association (McCrie, 2005). Later that year over 200 persons would join the incipient trade and professional organization. By 2005, ASIS International had over 30,000 members throughout the world with an extensive program of chapter activities, publications, and certifications. The Security Industry Association began in 1967; the National Council of Investigation and Security Services started in 1975; and the International Security Management Association began in 1976. Elsewhere, interest in the field was also blooming. In Britain, the BSIA was founded in 1967; the International Institute of Security in 1968; and the Scottish Security Association was formed in 1996. Beyond these examples most other industrialized nations created their own professional and trade associations for enterprises that provide security services, products, and systems. These groups started to improve the tradecraft of security practitioners variously through education, training, legislation standards, and mutual assistance. Industry development has occurred because of the particular nature of security needs within organizations. While all organizations need security, not all organizations require security directors and personnel *per se*. Frequently, the duties can be devolved to others. Nonetheless, certain industries have security as a requirement. Others see improved protection as a cost-effective means of maintaining optimal operations.

Alarms

The earliest alarms to signal the approach of strangers were animate and communications depended upon smoke and light signals. In the modern era Information Technology (IT) traces its origins to the patent of the telegraph by William Cooke and Charles Wheatstone in 1836. Three decades later, a functioning transatlantic cable had been laid. Remote voice communication became possible by Alexander Graham Bell's patent of the telephone in 1876 (Greer, 1979; Grosvenor, 1997).

Mechanical alarms first were offered in the mid-19th century. An Englishman named Tildesley invented the first burglar alarm. This mechanical device was linked to a set of chimes connected to a door lock which would chime when opened at an unauthorized time. The only sale Tildesley made was to a bank in Massachusetts. In 1852, a Boston inventor, Augustus R. Pope, filed a patent for the first electronic alarm. Pope's invention could sound an alarm at the unauthorized opening of doors or windows; it could also signal for the fire department or to fetch a messenger. The burglar alarm feature operated, once the system was 'alarmed', when a magnetic contact between the door or window and its frame was broken by unauthorized entry. Without producing a commercial prototype, Pope sold the invention in 1857 to Edwin T. Holmes of Boston. Holmes improved the system's reliability, reducing the chances of error from electrical shorts. He then tried without success to market the alarm service in the Boston area. Failing that, he moved operations to a more attractive market for possible exploitation: the City of New York. The alarm industry grew in tandem with the telephone. Holmes was able to have cable for alarm connections laid at the same time cables for telephones were being installed (Holmes, 1990).

The principle remained the same from the earliest mechanical lock: an electrified magnetic contact between two points was established. When a door or window was opened without authorization, an alarm condition, monitored at a central station, would result. Personnel at the central station monitoring burglar alarms would respond by contacting police, or sending a guard or runner from the alarm monitoring office for verification, or both.

While Holmes originally had envisioned the alarm service to protect residences of wealthy individuals, the commercial and industrial markets had become quickly more important for the alarm industry. Alarms could be monitored from a central location operated by a contract service, or firms could monitor their own alarms, or both, could occur. For those unwilling to pay for an alarm monitoring service or who were too far away to benefit from one, local alarms could sound a loud noise in the immediate area with the hope burglars would leave quickly.

Wires historically transmitted alarm signals. These signals may travel on a proprietary connection or on a common carrier (telephone line) of various types. If a burglar cuts the common carrier, alarm monitoring for a large number of customers may be disrupted. For most of the 20th century a monitoring clerk at the central alarm station could not be sure if such alarms had been sounded due to electrical shorts, cut by a storm or by accident, or if burglars had knocked out the conduit to make identification of the crime difficult. At such times monitoring personnel might notify customers and the police that regular signals are not being received. Another alarm type, where customers face high risks of burglary, depends upon tiny microphones monitored by computers that signal an alarm if human voices are heard when facilities are supposed to be vacant. Some facilities use two or more alarm systems to assure backup in the event that one system is inadvertently inoperative or compromised. In recent decades wireless communications and computer-based systems have increased the reliability of such signals. An operator in a monitoring station no longer is bound to record routine opening and closing signals. Now the operator can be alert to any exceptions to the system and respond to them without distraction (Mahoney, 1995).

Armored transport (cash-in-transit)

Moving money is a security business; it is also a transportation enterprise. In 1859, Washington Perry Brink began a package and furniture delivery business in Chicago with one horse and wagon (Seng, 1959). Brink was committed to reliable service. He selected personnel carefully and slowly expanded his delivery service by assuring reliability. After over two decades of activity, Brink realized the many advantages of delivering small, valuable objects over heavy, inexpensive ones. It was gentler on the backs of workers, easier for horses, fast to complete, and more profitable. Money and monetary instruments became first a specialty, then the main activity. Most corporations believed it was their duty to transport funds to their banks or fetch funds for payrolls. Brink slowly convinced customers that his firm was able to perform these services at less cost and frustration.

By the turn of the 19th century, Brinks, the money movers, transmitted funds to and from banks and among business offices. Payrolls were made by Brink cash handlers for customers and the funds were distributed at the workplace, increasing workers' productive time on the job. In the era during which funds were transported by buggy and wagon, the driver or an assistant carried a rifle on the floor. After a robbery early in the 20th century, the money movers realized that their vehicles must conform to an era of greater risks and be better protected. In more recent times Brinks and its competitors have provided services to financial institutions for their automated teller machines (ATMs) by replacing canisters of money. Separate workers, usually, handle maintenance of the ATMs. Many banks find that contracting-out for cash-handling services is cost-effective and reliable. As a result, armored transit firms now often process cash for banks and other large cash-handling operations (Dunbar and Kingwell, 2003).

Related to this business are the transport, storage, and service of computer tapes for which originals need to be stored off-site as a precaution. While these tapes are not ordinarily the subject of burglars' interest, the tapes themselves are valuable and could represent serious loss to an organization should they be lost, destroyed, or fall into the hands of competitors.

Electronic systems

The physical security measures of earlier centuries have been enhanced first by electrification and later by computerization. A broad range of sensors has been developed for: CCTV, intrusion detection, access control, and communications systems, as well as for alarms previously discussed. Intrusion detection has been improved in utility by the use of biometric-based automatic identification systems. These assure with a higher degree of certainty that individuals who present themselves at a security checkpoint are who they say they are.

The first biometric systems – hand geometry and retinal identification – reached the marketplace in the 1960s.[10] Acceptance was slow due to the high cost, degree of reliability, and invasiveness (requiring physical contact) of early systems. Biometric systems rely on unique physical features possessed by an individual: fingerprints, iris, retina, physical appearance, signature dynamics, voice, gait, and other characteristics. Combined with an identification card and a personal identification number, a system using biometric features will have a higher likelihood of reliability than systems with fewer requirements.

Control, command, communications, computer resources and intelligence (C^{4}I) collection and analysis characterize modern large-scale systems. All of these functions may be integrated into a whole system that can be backed up and difficult for unauthorized to penetrate. Interoperability refers to the capacity of interconnected parts and subsystems to function without lapses. Managers desire to monitor security systems from anywhere they may be. In the past security operations were centered only in a security office. The trend is toward information disbursal, aided by internet power, so that the master system can be accessed at the security center, at personal workstations, from laptops or personal digital assistants, or from cell-phones. This systems approach has a brief history and continues to evolve quickly.

Cybercrime countermeasures

Computer (or IT) security became a concern barely a dozen years after the computer was invented. The Electronic Numerical Integrator and Computer (ENIAC) was constructed in 1946 at the University of Pennsylvania. Transistors were invented in 1958. About that time the first computer crimes occurred: mostly theft of output and misuse of computing time (theft of services). The first federal prosecution of a computer crime in the United States was in 1966. Since computing and particularly the internet were not developed with security as a foremost consideration, it was inevitable that serious abuses would emerge, leading eventually to what some people consider a current crisis (Schell, 2004; Parker, 1976, 1998).

A variety of types of computer crime now challenge management. Some of these are cyberstalking, extortion, fraud, hacking or cracking, identity theft, intellectual property theft, and theft of money or assets. Anarchists, common criminals, organized crime syndicates, and terrorists use IT resources for their own advantages.

The original hackers were computer students at Massachusetts Institute of Technology in the 1960s. They believed in freedom of communications and freedom of information, but they also espoused a moral code against criminal use of computing resources. Moral code alone would be insufficient to mitigate what was to occur in the next few years. Brute attacks on computing began in the 1970s. Particularly significant was the 1983 hacking of a Pentagon computer system by Kevin David Mitnick. Jim Hauser, a Californian, claims he wrote the first computer virus in 1982. (Other hackers have disputed the claim.) In 1988, Robert Tappan Morris, Jr., a graduate student at Cornell University, introduced a worm (like a virus, spreading itself among computers but without attaching itself to programs in the process). The Morris worm attacked 6000 computers using the Unix platform. He was sentenced to probation, community service, and a fine of $10,000. Today, virus-writing skills are detailed in books, traded on the internet, and taught in computer security courses.

The protection of computer communications, databases, and data integrity requires electronic measures to protect access. Anti-virus and anti-hacking software programs have become a major industry that shows no sign of diminishing. Cybercrime and other IT issues have expanded at an extraordinary rate. Their history is only a generation old.

Individual efforts for protection and order maintenance

From the earliest evidence of human experience, individuals have taken responsibility for their own security. This involved physical measures, described earlier in the chapter, as well as protective procedures taken both individually and collectively. While the military, civilian police, private security, and indeed numerous other organizations provided by the state offer protection, individual efforts are the oldest, most prevalent, and most difficult activity to assess quantitatively and qualitatively.

Programs provided by the state and not-for-profit organizations have been developed to mitigate risks in modern times. Recently, innovative ways have helped communities reduce crime and increase the perception of safety. These include public/private programs like community policing. A French scholar, Franck Vindevogel (2002), collected and analyzed data on how private efforts were related to the decline of crime in New York City during the 1990s. In addition to private security services, Vindevogel's study also includes volunteer programs such as the Guardian Angels. This organization is analogous to a vigilance committee in early America, prior to organized police. Business Improvement Districts (BIDs) represent another significant grassroots innovation. BIDs are organizations that provide services a specific geographic area desires but which are beyond the budget of government to provide. Greater protection was the primary goal of urban commercial enterprises. BIDs were approved by the New York State legislature in the early 1980s, but almost a decade was required for the first BID to begin operations. Today hundreds of BIDs, supported by additional taxes voluntarily agreed to, operate throughout North America.

In the past half century numerous non-police-oriented, private sector directed organizations have developed anti-crime programs to support security of individual homes, neighborhoods, and commercial enterprises. A directory of the National Crime Prevention Council (2005) in the United States lists over 75 of such resources. Other Western nations similarly seek to involve the private sector in working together to enhance protection.

Conclusion

Without security civilization could not have developed. Without the continuance of security future progress is imperiled because of the *un*certainty from danger of loss or harm. Security is not only a human need it also is a human right. The *Universal Declaration of Human Rights* of the United Nations in 1948 began: '*Whereas* recognition of the inherent dignity and the equal and inalienable rights of all members of the human family is the foundation of freedom, justice, and peace in the world'. Then *Article 3* states: 'Everyone has the right to life, liberty, and the security of person'. Much of this *Declaration* focuses on individual freedom from unreasonable encroachment by the state. But the same words may be read to include the concept that the state similarly has a general duty of protection to the public from untoward risks.

A safe society depends upon application of numerous resources described in this chapter: situational, individual, military, law enforcement, technical, and from the private sector. Such resources and procedures are likely to continue to evolve as society itself changes.

Notes

1 The author wishes to thank Fulvia Madia McCrie for considerable help with this chapter and the National Police Library, Bramshill, England, for its extensive resources.

2 For example, a safe that is tool-resistant would meet a number of criteria: constructed of one-inch thick steel meeting specified criteria and weighing at least 750 lbs. or, as is more usual, equipped with suitable anchors to a substrate. Safes that are presented for testing would be subjected to UL's best efforts to gain entry within a measured period of time. If the skilled crackers did not succeed within 30 minutes, for example, the manufacturer would be able to list UL's registered name or symbol in combination with the product name as meeting TL-30 (tool-resistant for 30 minutes), a control number, and the word *Listed*.

3 Mercenaries, professional soldiers hired by foreign countries, have long existed. The Persians used 4000 Greek mercenaries against Alexander the Great. The incessant war between the City States of Renaissance Italy was conducted by *condottieri* offering their services to the highest bidders. The English East India Company employed its own private army of 100,000 soldiers from several nations to gain control of the subcontinent. Contemporary mercenaries until recently called 'dogs of war', now are referred as 'private military contractors' (*The Week*, 4 September 2004, p. 13).

4 The tipstave had a crown at one end. If a constable struck someone with it, he was said to be 'crowned'.

5 This is the only time rioters have been killed by gunfire from a police force in the history of Britain.

6 Metropolitan police (bobbies) could carry revolvers from 1884 to 1936; thereafter, the force has been unarmed, except for a specialized squad (Fido, M. and Skinner, K. *The Official Encyclopedia of Scotland Yard*. London: Virgin, 1999).

7 In contemporary experience, police chiefs may concentrate crime-suppression efforts on matters that are unrelated to control of serious offences. Such officers may place an emphasis on traffic enforcement, while ignoring property or violent incidents. In the era of J. Edgar Hoover in the United States, who headed the Federal Bureau of Investigation 1924–72, considerable attention was paid to automobile thefts and property recoveries while the brass of the Bureau denied the existence of organized crime, which then flourished (Theoharis, A.G. *J. Edgar Hoover, Sex, and Crime: An Historical Antidote*. Chicago: Ivan R. Dee, 1995).

8 Lincoln was assassinated in April 1865, during a time when the office of the president had no personal security agents assigned for his protection.

9 Reasons for this development are discussed in: McCrie, R. *Security Operations Management*. Boston and Oxford: Butterworth-Heinemann, 2001, pp. 36–40.

10 Biometric features were used in ancient China where thumbprints were found on clay seals. They were also used to conclude business transactions in Babylon. By contrast, contemporary biometric systems analyze distinct physical features automatically for identification.

Key readings

The detailed references and the notes to this chapter constitute a full bibliography. However, some useful texts, not otherwise cited, may be mentioned to provide further context. A guide to military issues is provided by: Chris Bellamy, *The Evolution of Modern Warfare: Theory and Practice*. London and New York: Routledge, 1990; for early policing: Joan R. Kent, *The English Village Constable 1580–1642: A Social and Administrative Study*. Oxford: Clarendon Press, 1986; for later British policing: T.A. Critchley, *A History of the Police in England and Wales*. London: Constable, 1978; for the security industry in the United States: Milton Lipson, *On Guard: The Business of Private Security*. New York: Quadrangle/New York Times Book Company, 1975; for the security industry in Britain: Nigel South, *Policing for Profit*. London and Newbury Park: SAGE Publications, 1988; for the public/private police interface in Britain: Les Johnston, *The Rebirth of Private Policing*. London and New York: Routledge, 1992.

Bibliography

Battestin, M.C. (1989) *Henry Fielding: A Life*. New York: Routledge.

Bradbury, J. (1992)*The Medieval Siege*. Woodbridge, Suffolk and Rochester, NY: Boydell Press.

Bryson, S. (1996) *Police Dog Tactics*. New York: McGraw-Hill.

Buehr, W. (1953)*The Story of Locks*. New York: Scribner.

Caesar, J. (1998) *Seven Commentaries on the Gallic War*. Oxford and New York: Oxford University Press.

Carneiro, R.L. (2003) *Evolutionism in Cultural Anthropology: A Critical History*. Cambridge, MA: Westview Press.

Chapman, S.G. (1990) *Police Dogs in North America*. Springfield, IL: CC Thomas.

Cobb, B. (1957) *The First Detectives and the Early Career of Richard Mayne, Commissioner of Police*. London: Faber and Faber.

Costello, A.E. (1972) *Our Police Protector: History of the New York Police from the Earliest Period to the Present Time*. Montclair, NJ: Patterson Smith. (Reprint of the 1885 ed.)

David, A.R. (2003) *Handbook to Life in Ancient Egypt*. New York: Facts on File.

Dunbar, J.L. and Kingwell, R.G. (2003) *Bulletproof: A History of Armored Cars and the Colorful Characters Who Ran Them, Rode Them, and Sometimes Robbed Them*. Baltimore: MidAtlantic Book & Journals.

Dutton, M.R. (1992) *Policing and Punishment in China*. Cambridge: Cambridge University Press.

Emsley, C. (1999) *Gendarmes and the State in Nineteenth-Century Europe*. Oxford and New York: Oxford University Press.

Eras, V.J.M. (1974) *Locks and Keys Throughout the Ages*. Folkestone: Bailey and Swinfen.

Evans, E.J. (1991) *Sir Robert Peel*. London and New York: Routledge.

Fido, M. and Skinner, K. (1999) *The Official Encyclopedia of Scotland Yard*. London: Virgin.

Gaubatz, P.R. (1996) *Beyond the Great Wall: Urban Form and Transformation on the Chinese Frontiers*. Stanford, CA: Stanford University Press.

Goddard, H. (1957) *Memoires of a Bow Street Runner*. New York: Morrow.

Greer, W. (1979) *A History of Alarm Security*. Washington, DC: National Burglar & Fire Alarm Association. (The fire alarm industry history is covered in: Haywood, G.F. (1967) *General Alarm: A Dramatic Account of Fires and Firefighting in America*). New York: Dodd, Mead.

Grosvenor, E.S. (1997) *Alexander Graham Bell: The Life and Time of the Man Who Invented the Telephone*. New York: Harry Abrams.

Hanson, W.S. and Maxwell, G.S. (1986) *Rome's North West Frontier: The Antonine Wall*. Edinburgh: Edinburgh University Press.

Holmes, E. (1990) *A Wonderful Fifty Years*. New York: Holmes Protection. (Originally published 1917.)

Hogg, I. (1988) *The History of Forts and Castles*. London: Macdonald & Co.

Hopkins, A.A. (1928) *Lure of the Lock*. New York: General Society of Mechanics and Tradesmen, pp. 29–31.

Horan, J. (1962) *The Pinkertons*. New York: Bonanza Books.

Howard, M.E. (ed.) (1966) *The Theory and Practice of War*. New York: Praeger.

Hyland, A. (2003) *The Horse in the Ancient World*. Westport, CT: Praeger.

Johnson, M. (2002) *Behind the Castle Gate: From Medieval to Renaissance*. London and New York: Routledge.

Lane, R. (1967) *Policing the City: Boston*. Cambridge, MA: Harvard University Press.

Low, S. M. (2003) *Behind the Gates: Life, Security, and the Pursuit of Happiness in Fortress America*. New York: Routledge.

Luo, Z., Wilson, D. and Drege, J.-P. (1981) *The Great Wall*. New York: McGraw-Hill.

Mackay, J. (1996) *Allan Pinkerton: The Eye Who Never Slept*. Edinburgh and London: Mainstream Publishing.

Mahoney, R.W. (1995) *Diebold, Incorporated: From Safes to Software*. New York: Newcomen Society of the United States.

McCrie, R. (1997) 'A Brief History of the Security Industry in the United States'. In Felson, M. and Clarke, R. (eds) *Business and Crime Prevention*. Monsey, NY: Criminal Justice Press.

—— (2001) *Security Operations Management*. Boston and Oxford: Butterworth-Heinemann.

—— (2005) 'ASIS International'. In Sullivan, L. (ed.) *Encyclopedia of Law Enforcement*. Thousand Oaks, CA: SAGE Publications.

Morn, F. (1982) *The Eye That Never Sleeps*. Bloomington, IN: Indiana University Press.

Mumford, L. (1961) *The City in History*. New York: Harcourt, Brace & World.

National Crime Prevention Council (2005) *Catalyst*. Vol. 25, No. 1.

Nicholas, D. (1997) *The Growth of the Medieval City: From Late Antiquity to the Early Fourteenth Century*. New York: Longman.

Orbaan, A. (1968) *Dogs Against Crime*. New York: John Day.

Parker, D.D. (1976) *Crime by Computer*. New York: Scribners.

—— (1998) *Fighting Computer Crime: A New Framework for Protecting Information*. New York: John Wiley.

Partington, J.R. (1999) *A History of Greek Fire and Gunpowder*. Baltimore: Johns Hopkins University Press.

Philips, D. and Storch, R.D. (1999) *Policing Provincial England 1829–1856*. London and New York: Leicester University Press.

Pirenne, H. (1969) *Medieval Cities*. Princeton: Princeton University Press.

Ramsay, A.A.W. (1971) *Sir Robert Peel*. New York: Barnes & Noble.

Reith, C. (1975) *The Blind Eye of History*. Montclair, NJ: Patterson Smith (originally published 1952 by Faber & Faber, London.)

Richardson, J.F. (1970) *The New York Police: Colonial Times to 1901*. New York: Oxford University Press.

Saalam, H. (1968) *Medieval Cities*. New York: George Braziller.

Saint-Blanquat, H. (1986) *The First Settlements*. Trans. A. Ridett. Morristown, NJ: Silver Burdett.

Schell, B.H. (2004) *Cybercrime: A Reference Handbook*. Santa Barbara, CA: ABC-CLIO.

Sélincourt, A. de (trans.) (1960) *Livy: The Early History of Rome*. Baltimore, MD: Penguin Books, pp. 376–7.

Seng, R.A. (1959) *Brinks, the Money Movers: The Story of a Century of Service*. Chicago: Lakeside Press.

Singman, J.L. (1999) *Daily Life in Medieval Europe*. Westport, CT: Greenword Press.

Stead P.J. (1983) *The Police of France*. New York and London: Macmillan.

Sunzi. (2002) *The Art of War*. Boston: Shambhala.

Taylor, D. (1997) *The New Police in Nineteenth-Century England*. Manchester and New York: Manchester University Press.

Theoharis, A.G. (1995) *J. Edgar Hoover, Sex, and Crime: An Historical Antidote*. Chicago: Ivan R. Dee.

Thomas, D. (1991) *Henry Fielding*. New York: St. Martin's Press.

Turner, R.E. (1941) *The Great Cultural Traditions*, Vol. 1 *The Ancient Cities*. New York and London: McGraw-Hill.

Villiers, P. (1998) *The First 50 Years: The History of the Police Staff College*. Bramshill, Hants: Police Staff College, p. 44.

Vindevogel, F. (2002) *Sécurité Publique et Initiative Privée: Un Partenariat pour le Mantien de l'Ordre à New York*. PhD thesis, Université Paris VIII, Vincennes-St. Denis.

Watson, G.R. (1985) *The Roman Soldier*. Ithaca, NY: Cornell University Press.

Wenke, R. (1999) *Patterns in Prehistory: Humankind's First Three Million Years*. 4th edn. New York: Oxford University Press.

Wright, Q. (1965) *A Study of War*. 2nd edn. Chicago: University of Chicago Press.

3

The Study of National Security Versus the Study of Corporate Security: What Can They Learn From Each Other?

Craig Stapley, Suzette Grillot and Stephen Sloan

The profound shock waves that were generated by the events of 9/11 have increasingly forced those involved in the study and application of corporate and national security measures to adjust to a new threat environment. Certainly, the events of September 11 led to many changes within US national security agencies, as well as within US businesses. Defense and intelligence budgets have increased substantially to address the new and complex threats to US national security (Center for Defense Information, 2003). US businesses are also feeling the pinch. A recent US Business Roundtable survey of 100 American CEOs showed that 99 percent of the respondents had increased their company's physical security and 100 percent had increased their cyber security. The survey also recorded double digit increases in security spending (Cain, 2004).

Even before 9/11, however, the landscape of the international environment was being altered as a result of many factors. During the Cold War years, students and professionals in national and corporate security focused on fairly identifiable threats. Since the end of the Cold War era, however, the world system has produced a more complex security environment with multiple threat axes. While the Soviet Union is no longer the threat it was, the weapons it stockpiled may be. Additionally, threats from other states, such as North Korea, Iran, and others, have become more salient. Interstate warfare remains, of course, a potent national security threat. The primary immediate threat to national security, however, has shifted from state belligerents to terrorist groups. Moreover, corporate security efforts, which in the past were focused on protecting proprietary information and profits, have changed to include protecting agents and assets from terrorist threats and non-state actors as well. Organized crime has also emerged as a potent threat to both corporate and national security.

This study begins a much needed discussion about the study of national versus corporate security, and how and why national and corporate security studies can and should learn from each other. We first highlight the ways in which the international security environment has changed since the end of the Cold War as such changes have implications for the study of national and corporate security.

Second, we examine the resulting shifts in national and corporate security studies, as well as the important connections or disconnections between these two subjects of study. Third, we provide specific issue areas where traditional, state security studies and corporate security concerns diverge. Finally, we conclude with the argument that in today's security environment, the gaps between these two forms of security issues should be bridged in an effort to better manage contemporary problems and complexities. While this chapter does not focus primarily on terrorism, we do believe that terrorism has arguably become a primary threat to national security, as well as an increasingly important consideration for corporate security. The issue of national and corporate security studies cannot, therefore, be considered without some discussion of terrorism. Similarly, given that intelligence is crucial to security studies, some discussion of that topic is also presented.

A changing international environment

A number of factors have contributed to a changed and complex international security environment. The first factor relates to the end of the arbitrary equilibrium created by the Cold War, which placed a lid on ethnic, religious and other primordial demands that were often suppressed or hidden by the East-West standoff. With the breakdown of the Berlin Wall, deeply held beliefs came to the surface as the call for 'self-determination' created instability, conflict and violence, which replaced the outward order maintained by 'the balance of nuclear terror.' A wide variety of internal wars and regional conflicts marked the end of the bipolar super power competition (Davis, 1996; Snow, 1997; Richardson, 2003). Whether those internal wars and regional conflicts were a byproduct of the end of the Cold War or a result of globalization and its accompanying technological shifts, the result was the same. Additionally, weapons and information that were once controlled by the superpowers were then free to go to the highest bidder. Chemical and nuclear weapons scientists and materials are available worldwide. Thus, rogue nations and terrorist groups have greater access to weapons of mass destruction making the security environment much more dangerous. Moreover, these groups cannot be dissuaded by traditional deterrence (Thachuk, 2001).

The second factor altering the landscape of the international security environment relates to the erosion of the traditional nation-state. The domination of the classic 'state centric system,' originating from the Treaty of Westphalia in 1648 and being reinforced by the Congress of Vienna in 1815, is being increasingly challenged (Strange, 1996). The international activities of significant 'non-state actors' ranging from multinational corporations to transnational terrorists and criminal networks are eroding traditional state primacy (Tolentino, 2001; Gabel and Bruner, 2003; Sageman, 2004). Moreover, the explosive growth and influence of non-governmental organizations and regional entities such as the EU have challenged the primacy of the nation-state as the leading actor in the international arena (Keck and Sikkink, 1998; Boli and Thomas, 1999; Iriye, 2004). It may be argued that international law still considers states to be the primary actors in the international system. However, international law itself is but an amalgam of treaties, customs and traditions. As the world changes so does international law. As intergovernmental organizations and non-state actors gain acceptance as players on the world stage, so too will international law change (Slaughter, 2004).

It is the case that the primary actors in international bodies such as the UN and the WTO are nation-states. This too, however, is changing. Based on the work that NGOs are undertaking, they have increasingly demanded a place at the table of international policy creation and execution. The global community as well as sovereign governments have seemed willing to allow them that place (Spiro, 1995; Fitzduff and Church, 2004). Currently, NGOs have obtained consultative status on the Security Council of the United Nations through the Economic and Social Council (ECOSOC) based on article 71, which grants ECOSOC the right to 'make suitable arrangements for consultation with non-governmental organizations which are concerned with matters within its competence' (UN Charter, Article 71). In this capacity, qualifying NGOs are granted the right to propose ECOSOC agenda items as well as the right to supply information in conferences and committee hearings (Weiss and Gordenker, 1996). Moreover, the interaction between NGOs and the UN, as well as other organizations, plays a prominent role in international relations literature (White, 1951; Spiro, 1995; Willetts, 1982).

Nation-states are also voluntarily relinquishing powers that have been traditionally exercised solely by governments. Examples include policing and security responsibilities as well as economic regulation activities (Thompson, 1995). This aspect of state devolvement and NGO expansion of scope became widely publicized in UN Secretary General Boutros Boutros-Ghali's *An Agenda for Peace,* which suggested that the duty of the international community, including NGOs, is to become involved in what in the past were considered sovereign issues when matters of human rights or humanitarian interests were at stake (Ghali, 1992). In these and other cases, the principle most sacrosanct in the Westphalian order – sovereignty – is often ignored (Shotwell, 2001).

Why the increase in the scope, size and importance of NGOs? The answer may lie primarily in the accepted assumptions that as private, non-state entities that must compete for resources, NGOs are more efficient and effective than government. In addition, NGOs typically spotlight one specific sector of policy, allowing them to focus and, therefore, amass greater information and expertise than governments, which suffer from budget constraints and bureaucratic sclerosis. The reliance of governments and International Governmental Organizations (IGOs) on expertise available from NGOs creates other problems, as NGOs might be biased in their collection and advice on policy specifics (Edwards and Hume, 1996).

The erosion of state power may also be a result of globalization. Thomas Friedman defined globalization as a dynamic process which involves 'the inexorable integration of markets, nation-states and technologies to a degree never witnessed before' (Friedman, 1999: 9). This includes the economic collapse and restructuring that have occurred since 1989. At the end of the Cold War, Soviet client states were destabilized and Western client states received less money. At the same time, the number of failed states was on the rise and an overall increase in instability and social conflict occurred. There was also more space for civil society due to a trend toward democratization. The influence of the state also diminished because of a decrease in social spending and an increase in privatization. During this time, NGOs were able to fill the vacuum left by the diminished state due to an increase in giving to NGOs as well as incentives created by intergovernmental organizations (Lindenberg and Bryant, 2001).

State erosion may also be the result of enhancing representation. It is thought that IGOs obtain their legitimacy not only from the democratic governments that participate in their organizations, but also through the participation of NGOs, which represent another form of citizenship. 'In sum, the direct participation of private organizations lends a democratic quality to the management of intergovernmental organizations and is, therefore, an indispensable contribution to global politics' (Ronit and Schneider, 2000: 13; Weiss and Gordenker, 1996).

Regardless of the causes of state power erosion, the result is an environment in which security threats abound. Organized crime organizations have benefited from the reduced controls on trade and have taken advantage of the free movement of goods, services, and money to make inroads in fraud and money laundering (Thachuk, 2001). As national boundaries are loosened and travel access eased, organized criminals have been able to enhance their efforts. Similarly, in an environment of eased regulations on company formation and transnational ownership, investigation and prosecution have become much more difficult. As organized criminals mirror other transnational corporations, they become more difficult to distinguish from legal organizations (Thachuk, 2001). The success of organized crime may also speed the erosion of the nation state. The corruption of public officials erodes public confidence, which leads to an environment that fosters more corruption (Thachuk, 2001; Bruggeman, 2002).

This factor has also made terrorism a more dangerous phenomenon. During the Cold War era, many terrorist groups were financed and directed by state actors. Such groups often mirrored the ideology of the controlling states. In the post-Cold War era, proxy wars have ended and terrorist groups have few ties or allegiance to particular states. Thus, traditional means of diplomatic pressure are ineffective at reducing terrorism (Thachuk, 2001).

The third factor altering the landscape of the international environment relates to increases in technological breakthroughs. The world has become 'smaller' and society has become more global as a result of modern technology. Modern technology has been profoundly important for many reasons that relate directly to security issues. The introduction of jet aircraft in the late 1950s and early 1960s brought about the emergence of 'non-territorial terrorism – a form of terrorism that is not confined to a clearly delineated geographical area' (Sloan, 1978). The technological shifts in transportation allowed terrorists to commit acts of violence and literally disappear across states borders and travel half a world away in a few hours. This phenomenon is also evident in both state and private espionage as well as traditional state security situations where invading armies, missiles and aircraft can be anywhere in the world within a matter of hours. Organized crime also benefits from this phenomenon, as crime does not require a territorial base (Thachuk, 2001).

The emergence of television and satellite communication, and the accompanying global advances in information technologies, has created a new security environment for both state and private security entities. The advances in telecommunications have created a global audience for terrorists. Furthermore these individuals and groups have enhanced their global operations by utilizing the internet both as a target and as a means of logistical support. Traditionally, ideologically leftist groups such as Sendaro Luminoso have secured funds through the sales of t-shirts on the internet (Weimann, 2004). Terrorists and security threats can communicate in relative security in the anonymity of cyberspace. Viruses, worms and trojans are the means by which groups can acquire information and funding through internet fraud. The internet also provides a relatively risk free environment for intelligence gathering and technological transfers of attack methods (Weimann, 2004; Richardson, 2005).

The internet offers targets that can be harmed with real monetary losses without physical risk to the terrorists themselves. Given a choice of targets, terrorist groups will invariably attack those that afford the smallest risk (Briggs, 1991; Drake, 1998). These types of cyber attacks are effective. While it is true that some groups specialize in self-destructive suicide attacks, the vast majority of security threats are those that will attack the target that poses the least amount of risk of apprehension or damage to the attackers themselves. Terrorists now have the capability of attacking the 'soft underbelly' of data and the critical infrastructures that are essential for information driven post-industrial societies (Denning, 1998; Boni and Kovacich, 2000; Blane, 2001; Dunnigan, 2003).

The internet has also proved beneficial to terrorist groups who utilize it as a media and propaganda outlet. Gone are the days when terrorist groups were at the mercy of Western-allied media outlets for the dissemination of their message and actions (Crenlinsten, 1987; Schaffert, 1992; Weimann, 1994). Technologically savvy terrorist groups have bypassed the media and showed carefully edited video clips on their own home web pages. As a result, security challenges have moved from territorial to non-territorial based threats to the uncharted dimensions of cyber-space.

Organized crime has also benefited by technological advances. Criminal elements have used e-businesses and virtual identities to facilitate and then cover up criminal activities. Organized criminals also enjoy the illicit business opportunities provided by internet pornography and prostitution. The development of high-resolution printers and scanners has also increased the capacity of organized criminal groups to produce counterfeit documents. Web-based financial transactions make money transfers quick and easy, and detection difficult. The use of cellular and satellite phones has also made communication easier and monitoring more difficult (Bruggeman, 2002; Bailey, 2004).

The fourth factor contributing to the changing security environment is very much a product of the uneven and hard to predict processes resulting from globalization (Friedman, 2000; Held and McGrew, 2002). We now live in a world where an expanding technological universe has created more interdependence and accompanying vulnerabilities. The processes of globalization, with their emphasis on one dominant culture, often alienate ethnic or religious traditions (Flanagan, 2001; Johnson, 2001). This, then, may explain the reassertion of traditional values and the rejection of modernization by many ethnic and religious fundamentalist groups (Billet, 1993; Barber, 1996; Mousseau, 2002/03; Stern, 2003; Juegensmeyer, 2003). This is particularly important as those reasserting traditional ways may be more than willing to employ modern technology as a means of destroying post-industrial societies. The Neo-Luddites of today may be quite willing to use technology with potentially disastrous consequences (Gray, 2003; Clarke, 2004).

Malcontent individuals who in the past were isolated, now have the ability to communicate with like-minded others and create movements (Frost, 2001). Criminal or revolutionary organizations that in the past were hierarchical now operate in loose confederations or cells. This makes it difficult for security entities to infiltrate, monitor and apprehend or eliminate such groups (Bruggerman, 2002). Thus, those who have engaged in the 'new mode of conflict' (Jenkins, 1981) have declared and in many cases are executing their form of global war that ignores the boundaries of nation-states and the geographically based military fields of operations and police jurisdictions.

There has been, therefore, an inevitable shift in terrorist targeting patterns. As traditional, government targets are hardened and become more difficult to attack successfully, terrorists are changing their targeting priorities to include less hardened, corporate, targets. Furthermore, corporations are often seen as the vehicle for globalization. As such, the global environment and the accompanying pressures brought about by non-governmental influences, such as product marketing and cultural imperialism, make corporate targets more attractive (Stapley, 2004). In 1997, 85 percent of all American terrorist victims were non-governmental (Hoffman, 2001). In 2003 the numbers are more conclusive. 90.5 percent of all terrorist casualties were non-governmental personnel (State Department, 2003). Figure 3.1 illustrates the percentage of non-governmental targets since 1998 (State Department, 2003).

This shift may also be due to successes in the war on terror. As governments willing to support terrorist groups diminish, those terrorist groups are pressed to provide the assets required for their struggle. Terrorist groups may, therefore, target corporations and private businessmen as a means of securing financial and or logistical support through ransoms and extortion (see Wilson, 2004; and Whitlock, 2004).

Finally, and perhaps most alarming, we see a substantial increase in the destructive capability of both state and non-state actors who, in the pursuit of fundamentalist goals (often driven by religious conviction) are not concerned with public opinion. The ideologies that drive many terrorist groups have shifted

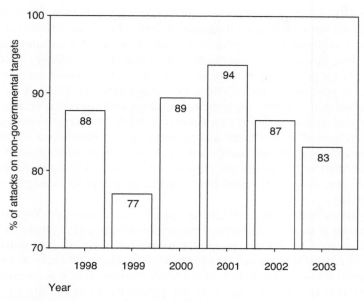

Figure 3.1 Non-governmental targets of terrorism 1998 to 2003

from political to ethnic and/or religious causes. Because these 'new' types of terrorists are not trying to gain political, mainstream power, and are not concerned with the goodwill of those not within their faction, they are more willing to use extreme methods (Schweitzer, 1998; Laqueur, 1999; Lifton, 1999). The September 11 attacks, with the devastating loss and destruction of civilian life, may be the ultimate example of this concept. Further, religious minorities may be more willing to utilize methods that bring about catastrophic loss by rationalizing that the victims were infidels or that it was God's will (Lifton, 1999; Juegensmeyer, 2003). These actors, therefore, do not face the same constraints regarding the use of weapons of mass destruction as do governments or terrorist groups of the past. Aum Shinrikyo embraced the use of WMD and actually used them in attacks in Japan in order to bring about their religious goals (Lifton, 1999). Moreover, given today's global reality, with Russia unable to properly police its nuclear stockpile, many actors may someday have the capability to develop, acquire and use such weapons (Stern, 2000; Allison, 2004).

National and corporate security studies

Given these very disturbing realities, one must address whether the field of security studies (in both state and corporate areas) is undergoing a shift to meet what may ultimately be a fundamental transformation in the international order. Although it is our contention that a shift in the international security environment has occurred, it is by no mean entirely clear if and when a transformation will take place in the intellectual arena where scholars, ideally working with policy makers and executives, can provide strategic assessments and guidance to meet future challenges in both the public and private sectors of national, regional and international arenas. The need for an integrated effort is, we believe, necessary to meet today's demands, but we recognize that those responsible for providing security are understandably focused on meeting the pressures of putting out today's fires. They, therefore, have little time 'to look over the horizon,' identify long-term problems and concerns, and prepare to take the initiative to respond to future challenges. In both governmental and non-governmental sectors 'crisis management' is no longer a process only to be used in exceptional circumstances, but has become institutionalized as a means of conducting the public's or the corporation's business in a threatening environment. This may be a logical consequence of trying to manage a complex environment.

What we see today, therefore, is an apparent disconnection between traditional, national security studies and corporate/private sector security concerns. There may well be numerous explanations for such discontinuity, but a number of critical reasons can be addressed. First, the divide may in part reflect the inherent conservative nature of academic inquiry. While academics, particularly in the social sciences, may be perceived to be politically liberal, they tend to be conservative regarding how they approach their respective disciplines. Instead of pursuing groundbreaking innovation in a particular discipline, which comes with an associated professional risk, emphasis is often placed on an incremental approach predicated on the refinement of previous studies. Instead of the occasional breakthrough of pioneering theory and method, more emphasis is placed on drawing on the research of authorities and accepting the existing 'conventional wisdom' (see Boyer, 1997). For example, one of the co-author's fields (terrorism studies) has been, for most of the 30 years over which he has engaged in research and application, largely intellectually quarantined as a 'problem area' of inquiry and not viewed to be in the 'mainstream' of political science in general and international relations and security studies in particular (Wieviorka, 1995).

Leading journals on international politics and security have not, over the years, focused on terrorism as a long-term threat that should be subject to an extensive and rigorous research agenda. Rather, articles, books and other publications on terrorism tended to be episodic in response to the latest incident. Certainly since 9/11 changes have been taking place, but in many instances such changes are essentially reactive and unsystematic in nature. In the academic journals that focus on national security studies, such as *Defense and Peace Economics, Contemporary Security Policy, Security Studies, Journal of Security Studies, Intelligence and National Security, Defense Studies, Defense and Security Analysis* and *Security and Defense Review*, analysis based on the interaction of states in global and regional arenas still takes precedence over the evolving significance of non-state actors and terrorist networks as central topics of international politics. The same assessment could be given to the most widely read journals in the policy arena – namely *Foreign Affairs. Foreign Policy* has widened the span of topics it covers, but the fact remains that it is primarily a policy journal dealing with the interaction of states.

Moreover, while there are specialized journals associated with terrorism and other less traditional forms of warfare, such as *Studies in Conflict and Terrorism, Terrorism and Political Violence, Conflict Quarterly* and *The Journal of Conflict and Law Enforcement,* articles published there are primarily written by individuals who have a sub-specialization in the field. The problem is further exacerbated by the fact that the journal primarily intended for national security specialists, *Security Studies,* is not typically read by the general population within the discipline of political science. There is a real gap, therefore, between the traditional field of national security studies and the growing issues of terrorism and non-state actors. In addition, the specialized journals focusing on corporate security, like *Security Journal* for example, are also not typically read by a larger audience – and certainly not by those focusing on national security concerns. In other words, those involved in the fields of terrorism, corporate security and crisis management are discreet groups of scholars conducting research in their own specialties – and the study of these specialties is considered to be out of the mainstream by general political scientists. As a result, interaction between these groups and the greater mainstream, along with the accompanying growth in the fields brought about by such intercourse, is lacking. Furthermore, there is a real disconnection between traditional national security and corporate security studies. The following explanations may help us further understand the differences in orientation.

For instance, mainstream national security studies place emphasis on the development of theories and concepts that can be employed to analyse the relations among nation-states. In contrast, studies associated with corporate security tend to be less theoretical and stress the need to address operational concerns. The gap between the academic and the practitioner is quite discernable. In their focus on the development of theory, national security scholars often look at such underlying issues as the causes of inter-state conflict and seek to engage in broader strategic assessment of future trends, especially in the light of international interactions (see Waltz, 1979; Morgenthau, 1985). In contrast, corporate security research tends to address current tactical problems and seeks to address the response to challenges instead of the reasons for their development (Hulnick, 2002; Halibozek and Kovacich, 2003; Bennett, 2003). In effect they tend to focus on the symptoms rather than an idealized cure.

Another important aspect of this disconnection can be understood when traditionally academic national security professionals are compared with practitioner corporate security professionals. Universities provide education that prepare future national security professionals through specific coursework aimed at understanding international affairs and the theoretical frameworks by which the world works. Further, these future professionals are also prepared through general cognitive training and intellectual winnowing that allow governments the ability to choose from those who have demonstrated their abilities academically.

Private firms are often limited in seeking security professionals with transferable skills. Corporate security professionals must be trained in-house to respond to the unique needs of the company. While professionals may move from one corporation to another, they may face a difficult task when transferring knowledge between clients. Many of the security assets must be tailored to fit the specific needs of the corporate client. Corporate security professionals note that a good corporate security shop would need to know as much about the research, marketing and distribution of their company's goods as they do about general security in order to be able to adequately secure the company's personnel and assets (Criscuoli, 1988; Rogalski, 2004). As a result, there is a considerable learning curve associated with new security employees. Independent security shops have less of a learning curve relating to basic security principles, but must work without some of the specialized knowledge that an in-house shop would provide. Another aspect of this difficulty is the fact that one of the major threats to operational security is someone on the inside. This may reduce the willingness of management to give proprietary information to specialized security firms (Semko, 2004). All of these factors combine to exacerbate the difficulty in finding competent security professionals.

Moreover, there are few academic programs providing the background needed for security professionals and many in the field are retired law enforcement and military personnel. While there may be some instances of shared expertise between corporate security and law enforcement and military experience, the requirements for each are markedly different, as is the preparation required for professionals in each field. Thus, it does not necessarily follow that law enforcement and military personnel will make good corporate security personnel. When such personnel are unable to meet the requirements for corporate security and fail to make the requisite transition, difficulties occur. This creates another basic problem within the corporate security field: the lack of credibility given to security professionals by the general public, company employees, corporate management and scholars studying corporate security phenomena. Many in these groups consider private security professionals to be nothing more than 'Barney Fife' rent-a-cops good for little more than window dressing. Certainly, that perception alone reduces the security professional's ability to adequately perform their function (Criscuoli, 1988). Much of corporate security rests on active co-operation between street level employees and corporate management. Thus, distrust of security professionals reduces overall security (Miller, 2004; Collins, 2004). There are further disconnects in terms of security professional licensing and standards that heighten the distrust for security professionals (Leonard, 2004).

Another factor is that traditional, national security emphasizes requirements associated with diplomatic methods as a means of resolving potential problems and conflicts in the international order (see Freeman, 1997; Berridge, 2002). Recent developments in intelligence sharing to combat the al-Qaeda threat are illustrative of this concept. The costs of intelligence gathering and counter-terrorism programs are spread across entire citizenries making the cost of such programs acceptable. In contrast, corporate security often emphasizes the need for the company to work alone in order to achieve a competitive edge and will usually only address cooperation with other corporations as part of tactical, short term objectives (see Sally, 1995; Allard, 2003). Traditionally, corporate security operations focused solely on protecting proprietary information or market advantage. The threat locus was small and the corporate security expertise was developed to address this locus only. This made information sharing less beneficial as any cooperative endeavors must then be adjusted for the specific application of each corporation. The current threats axes not only include the traditional market/informational threats, but have also expanded to include attacks on corporate personnel for ransom or attacks on company assets.

The contrast between national and private security is heightened when the cost of security programs are considered. Dean Carter, National Counterintelligence Officer for Economics, estimates the annual US cost of economic espionage alone to be $300 billion a year (Carver, 2004). The budgetary constraints forced on corporate security professionals by parent company incentives for profitability must be considered. Concrete programs to reduce threat exposure are costly and must be balanced against loss exposure. Further, the cost of corporate security programs are borne solely by the parent company and cost sharing with other companies is rare. The expense of training personnel must also be considered. True professionals with the training and experience to combat security threats are a limited commodity and expensive to retain (Radcliff, 2000; Rothkopf, 2002). The expense of such programs has led to dangerous gaps in America's security armor. Recent cooperation between US national government entities and private corporations in terms of the development of security hardware and software may help diffuse these costs. As such companies become more essential to national security, and government sources may help to defray security costs (Rothkopf, 2002). Because of the diffuse threat of national security, the state is more willing to expend resources on academic research. Thus, there are various state subsidized programs studying national security. Because of the focused threat of corporate security and the prohibitive cost of these security programs, corporations are less likely to fund research on security in this area.

Also a factor contributing to this divide is the fact that, given its theoretical and strategic concerns, national security scholars tend to focus on 'the big picture' or strategic issues despite the fact that they may be carried out at any level of government. However, corporations, with their operational concerns, emphasize concrete tactical or procedural measures to deal with security problems. There is a significant difference between the broad sweeps of a study on conflict prevention and resolution on a global, regional, national or local level and detailed descriptions of plans and methods associated with crisis management techniques that can be used by a company to handle an immediate challenge to its operations. The conflict prevention literature includes work on preventive diplomacy, demobilization, disarmament and intelligence led security. The crisis management literature dealing with corporate and private security, however, seems lacking in a preventative aspect and seems to be more oriented towards 'cleaning up the mess' after a crisis (Stapley interview with public security official, 2004).

Finally, and perhaps most importantly, national security specialists in addressing causes of war and peace, conflict and compromise, and associated issues deal with the very difficult task of analyzing the cost, effectiveness and requirements related to protecting a country's population, resources and basic values (see Snyder, 2000). In contrast, the corporation has a much more specific and easier to measure motive – the so-called 'bottom line' (see Bakan, 2004). Admittedly, an assessment of surrounding threats that can challenge company operations and indeed survival in a very competitive environment are quite complex, but the measures are often easier to calculate than such 'abstract' topics as national interest, will, or resolve, and the often disorderly process known as politics.

Comparing security studies: traditional versus corporate

Beyond these factors, however, there are even more specific differences that can be discerned between the focus on traditional academic security studies and corporate security issues. These include differences between governmental and private intelligence gathering, differences in private and traditional security measures, and the difference between corporate and national security proactive (offensive) and reactive (defensive) postures.

Intelligence gathering and analysis

Intelligence is defined in terms of providing external security, pursuing foreign policy objectives, or providing domestic security through police intelligence activities (see Deibert, 2003; Gorman, 2003; Chapman, 2004). Similar to corporate intelligence gathering, national security intelligence gathering was historically segmented into more discreet axes based on the type of threat, the type of intelligence, and the agency collecting the intelligence. The degree to which the agencies then shared collected intelligence depended on the nature of the threat as well as the degree of inter-agency conflict in an environment where agencies competed for budgetary largess. Certainly in the aftermath of the 9/11 Report, and the resulting intelligence overhaul, it is hoped that the level of interagency co-operation as well as international intelligence sharing will be increased.

In the aftermath of the Church Commission in the 1970s, and as a response to perceived misuses by the Presidential administration, intelligence-gathering agencies were put under a much finer microscope in terms of oversight (Goldstein, 2001). As a result, there was and still is a major focus on oversight especially in reference to a democratic political order. The methods by which intelligence agencies can operate were also examined and limited. The emphasis on human intelligence (HUMINT) sources was reduced and the use of electronic and satellite intelligence gathering was increased. This was certainly in keeping with the perception of the Cold War threat. In the post-Cold War world, the emphasis on electronic and satellite intelligence gathering was further expanded. The events of 9/11 switched the emphasis back toward HUMINT sources. This contributes to intelligence difficulties in that the creation and maintenance of a HUMINT network is a time consuming endeavor (Dreyfuss, 2001; Drogan, 2001).

Another difficulty endemic to national security intelligence gathering relates to analysis. For national security agencies, the difficulty is not necessarily a problem in intelligence gathering or a lack of intelligence. The problem is quite the opposite – too much intelligence. The various intelligence agencies gather an astounding amount of intelligence. The major difficulty lies in the intelligence analysis: determining what information is credible, important and actionable.

An additional distinction between national security intelligence gathering and corporate or private security intelligence gathering is the purpose for which the intelligence is intended. This distinction is important as it relates to the agencies using the intelligence. While an important part of the domestic intelligence gathering aegis, the FBI is a law enforcement agency that in the past was more concerned with law enforcement and suspect prosecution than threat avoidance. A suspect could not be arrested until a law had actually been broken, in contrast to taking action to ensure the law was never broken in the first place. In the US, there are many intelligence-gathering agencies tasked with specific missions. Expanding beyond that mission is sometimes difficult. For example, the Defense Intelligence Agency (DIA) is mainly concerned with gathering intelligence that will affect strategic and tactical military operations. Specifically, the DIA is concerned with how that intelligence will affect force protection or the success of an offensive or defensive operation. Intelligence that does not relate to that specific mission may be discarded as superfluous. Thus intelligence that could make a difference in reducing a future threat is wasted. The CIA is tasked with overall intelligence gathering for national security threats, but problems with interagency interfacing and legal authorization to act limit the effectiveness of national security agencies (Lowenthal, 2000; Berkowitz and Goodman, 2000).

Intelligence in the corporate security field is defined in terms of protecting proprietary information and actively engaging in competitive intelligence gathering to maximize one's market share. The threat axis traditionally has been very restricted. As the nature of the terrorist threat against corporate targets has changed and corporate security professionals have to deal with this increased threat, the need for broader security covering a wider number of subjects has also increased. Corporate security groups are hamstrung, however, by the lack of intelligence gathering assets available. Certainly deep cover HUMINT resources are precluded given the difficulty of insertion and cost of operation. As a result, corporate security professionals must rely on short-term human intelligence sources. This is problematic as the reliability of information provided by short-term, human intelligence sources is difficult to establish. Corporate security professionals also face difficulties from an electronic and photographic intelligence gathering perspective. The broad coverage often required for these kinds of intelligence gathering assets are prohibitively expensive for private companies and concerns over legality further reduce the ability of corporate security to effectively gather intelligence (Hulnick, 2002).

This question of legality shapes much of corporate intelligence-gathering capabilities. Concern about public oversight is limited to more narrow questions of legality and liability (see Kakalik and Wildhorn, 1971; Mendell, 1997; Hulnick, 2002). Private companies are legally unable to engage in covert intelligence-gathering, such as wire-tapping, even if sufficient cause could be shown. This limitation is ameliorated somewhat, however, in the case of in-house surveillance. In the case where security professionals wish to collect electronic or photographic intelligence within the company itself, the only limits are those that are self-imposed.

There does seem, however, to be some crossover between business and government security studies. Recent institutional creations, such as the Terrorist Threat Integration Center, seem to be breaking through the difficulties of integration with calls for greater co-operation in sharing intelligence between national and corporate security (Brennan, 2004). Intelligence-led security is becoming a new focus for law enforcement. There have also been some discussions and attempts at intelligence-led security among corporate security firms. Perhaps this new focus will help to bring national and private intelligence entities together.

National and corporate security measures

Traditionally, national security focuses on knowing adversaries, intentions and capabilities. There are also aspects of counter-intelligence and threat reduction. Of necessity, these measures should be both strategic and tactical to deal with specific threats, such as terrorist attacks, or more broad and diffuse concerns, such as general threats from potential adversaries. The strategic measures are perhaps most associated with national security measures. Strategic measures include efforts to control the spread of information that would threaten the security of the nation. Examples of this type of information include intelligence on troop movements and weapon systems, as well as delicate information relating to technologies such as nuclear and biological programs. Emphasis is also placed on protecting the homeland and interests abroad from foreign and domestic threats (see Snyder, 2000). Theoretically, such measures would allow national security professionals to manipulate policy and forecast action, countering threats (Waltz, 1979; Morgenthau, 1985; Allison, 1999).

These measures are necessarily broad and resource intensive. The laws permitting such measures, while subject to oversight, allow for threat elimination given sufficient parameters have been met. The tactical measures used by national security apparatus are meant to take advantage of actionable information for specific operations. Examples could include the use of addresses of terrorist cell leaders, their weapons and capabilities, and their travel plans in order to target and eliminate them. Such information has a limited usable lifespan before being rendered obsolete. Certainly national security agencies engage in both strategic and tactical measures. The emphasis, however, seems to be biased towards strategic measures.

Corporate security, on the other hand, has its own biases. In the case of corporate security, little effort is given to strategic security measures. Instead, efforts and resources are focused on tactics for protecting specific threats to employees, data, and assets. Emphasis is placed on physical security measures (see Salkever, 2001; Conlin *et al.*, 2001). The corporate security literature focuses almost exclusively on concrete tactical actions intended to reduce the profile or exposure of corporate targets. These types of tactical measures consist of how-to type instructions for reducing specific threats such as varying the route company personnel use when traveling. (Cunningham and Gross, 1978; Fuqua and Wilson, 1978).

The differences between traditional and corporate security measures have, however, diminished since 9/11 with both placing heavy emphasis on the requirements for physical security to protect 'critical infrastructure' in the public and corporate sectors. Corporate security actors do engage in some strategic security measures. Systemic measures to protect informational and computer leaks are engaged in an effort to eliminate or reduce the threat to the private organization. In these cases, these efforts are purely defensive in nature – meant to deter an attack from taking place or to reduce the exposure or damage from an attack. This, then, leads to the next difference between traditional national security and the newly emerging corporate security fields: offensive or proactive postures versus defensive or reactive postures.

Offensive (proactive) versus defensive (reactive) postures

Traditional national security studies address both offensive and defensive foreign policies and strategies to protect national security (see Grieco, 1990; Mearsheimer, 2001). Clearly the goal of national security agencies, especially in light of the horrendous possibilities of terrorist groups using weapons of mass destruction, is the pre-emptive elimination of threats before such attacks can take place. Such attacks cannot be allowed to happen and so security agencies focus resources on offensive, proactive postures. This offensive posturing is reinforced by various security and intelligence agencies whose entire capabilities are bent towards elimination of threats proactively. Such agencies include the Central Intelligence and National Security Agencies. These agencies have no domestic law enforcement authority. They are tasked, however, with protecting the national security of the United States. Certainly those agencies tasked with law enforcement also carry the onus of reacting once an attack has been committed. In those cases, national security agencies undertake defensive or reactive postures attempting to apprehend and eliminate perpetrators who have already committed violence against a national entity. (Richelson, 1999; Berkowittz and Goodman, 2000; Lowenthal, 2000; Smith and Deutch, 2002)

In the corporate arena, postures accepted by private corporations are primarily defensive and reactive (see Halibozek and Kovacich, 2003). This is partially a result of the differing nature of the threat posed to private entities or corporations. In most cases, catastrophic loss due to the use of weapons of mass destruction is a miniscule threat. Much more likely are threats posed to individuals as a result of kidnapping or hostage taking, or threats to the corporate infrastructure. Kidnapping seems to be a growing problem with an estimated 10,000 kidnappings each year worldwide (Briggs, 1991). As a result, corporate security can focus primarily on defensive or reactive posturing. This concept is reinforced by the literature dealing with private or corporate security threats. In these cases, it is almost exclusively reactive or defensive in nature (Bolz *et al.*, 1990). A good example of this is the series of books Richard Clutterbuck has written explaining the threats of hostage taking and what to do in the eventuality of such an attack. In every case, the actions are in response to an attack rather than actions to remove the threat pre-emptively. The titles are illustrative of this point: *Kidnap and Ransom: The Response*, and *Kidnap, Hijack and Extortion: The Response.* Notice both titles end in 'the Response.' There is no attempt at proactive or offensive actions meant to eliminate the threat (Clutterbuck, 1978, 1987). There have been calls for a more proactive and preventive approach, which might set a new tone for discussions about security issues in a multidimensional environment, but full implementation has yet to be realized (Briggs, 1991; Prime Minister's Strategy Unit, 2005).

These differences are, however, increasingly being blurred as corporations develop their own well-trained security forces and are more willing to take the initiative offensively when governments in areas in which they operate cannot provide security. Moreover, many corporations are now providing personnel and resources in support of military operations and in some cases are directly involved in addressing security issues in a conflict zone. Note, for example, the rapid growth of private counterterrorism firms in the wake of 9/11 (Olsen, 2002).

Conclusion

As stated earlier, one must address a very significant set of new players in the international arena. Both traditional security studies and those associated with the corporate sector will have to assess what the security requirements are for what can be called 'hybrid actors' in international politics in general and international security and corporate security studies in particular.

Finally, the fundamental shift in global interactions that blurs the lines between domestic and international security and, therefore, the lines between national and corporate security, must be subject to extensive research and refinement by both scholars and practitioners. If terrorists, organized criminal enterprises, and other illegal entities have achieved a unity of purpose to engage in international operations on a global scale, there is now the requirement for scholars and practitioners to also achieve an integration of effort. The arbitrary line between traditional security studies and corporate security concerns needs to be breeched.

Key readings

For an introduction to US foreign policy and the foundations of US global interactions, see Stephen E. Ambrose and Douglas G. Brinkley *Rise to Globalism: American Foreign Policy since 1938,* Eighth revised edition, New York: Penguin Publishing (1997). For an interesting discussion of the concept of globalization, please see Thomas L. Friedman's *The Lexus and the Olive Tree: Understanding Globalization.* New York: Knopf Publishing (2000). The topic of globalization's impact on world security is comprehensively addressed in *The Global Century: Globalization and National Security Volumes I & II.* Richard Kugler and Ellen Frost (eds) (2001) Washington DC: National Defense University Press. These edited volumes cover many of the threats facing the new global environment including religious fundamentalism, organized crime, and terrorism. For a discussion of corporate security in a global environment please see the following: Brian Bennet (2003) 'Terrorism' in *Professional Safety*. Vol. 48, pp. 31–9; and Michelle Conlin *et al.* (2001) When the Office is the War Zone. *Business Week*. Issue 3758, p. 38; Edward Halibozek and Gerald Kovacich (2003), 'Securing Corporate Assets' *Industrial Engineer*. Vol. 35, pp. 39–44; Arthur S. Hulnick (2002), 'Risky Business: Private Sector Intelligence in the United States' *Harvard International Review*. Vol. 24, pp. 68–72; Alex Salkever (2001), 'Coming to Grips with an Unsafe World' *Business Week Online*, 5 December 2001; and Dan Verton (2003), 'Corporate Security Still Lacks Focus Two Years After 9/11' *Computerworld*. Vol. 37, p. 13.

References

Allard, K. (2003) *Business as War: Battling for Competitive Advantage*, Brisbane: John Wiley and Sons, Inc.

Allison, G.T. and Zelikow, P. (1999) *Essence of Decision: Explaining the Cuban Missile Crisis* (2nd edn), NY: Longman.

Allison, G. (2004) *Nuclear Terrorism: The Ultimate Preventable Catastrophe*, NY: Henry Holt and Company, Inc.

Bailey, L.E. (2004) Computer Crime: Threats, Trends, and Solutions. Address to the National Security Institute's *Impact: National Security Forum and Exhibition*. Tuesday, April 27, 2004.

Bakan, J. (2004) *Corporation: The Pathological Pursuit of Profit and Power*, London: Simon and Schuster.

Barber, B. (1996) *Jihad vs. McWorld*, NY: Times Books.

Bennett, B.T. (2003) 'Terrorism: Assessing the Risk and Minimizing Exposure,' *Professional Safety*, Vol. 48, pp. 31–9.

Berridge, G.R. (2002) *Diplomacy: Theory and Practice*, NY: Palgrave Macmillan.

Berkowitz, B.D. and Goodman, A.E. (2000) *Best Truth: Intelligence in the Information Age*, New Haven: Yale University Press.

Billet, B. (1993) *Modernization Theory and Economic Theory: Discontent in the Developing World*, Westport, CT: Greenwood Publishing Group, Inc.

Blane, J.V. (2001) *Cyberwarfare: Terror at a Click*, Hauppauge: Nova Science Publishers, Inc.

Boli, J. and Thomas, G.M. (1999) *Constructing World Culture: International Nongovernmental Organizations Since 1875*, Palo Alto, CA: Stanford University Press.

Bolz, F. Jr., Dudonis, K.J. and Schulz, D.P. (1990) *The Counter-Terrorism Handbook: Tactics, Procedures and Techniques*, NY: Elsevier Science Publishing Company.

Boni, W.C. and Kovacich, G.L. (2000) *Netspionage: The Global Threats to Information*, Burlington, MA: Butterworth-Heinemann.

Boyer, E.L. (1997) *Scholarship Reconsidered: Priorities of the Professoriate*, San Francisco: Jossey-Bass, Inc.

Brennan, J.O. (2004) Global Terrorism: Confronting the New Security Realities. Address to the National Security Institute's *Impact: National Security Forum and Exhibition*. Tuesday, April 27, 2004.

Briggs, R. (1991) *The Kidnapping Business*, London: Foreign Policy Center.

Bruggeman, W. (2002) 'Security and Combating Organized Crime and Terrorism,' *European Community Studies Association* December 5, 2002. http://www.ecsanet.org/ecsaworld6/contributions/session1/Bruggeman.doc.

Cain, D. (2004) Companies Better Prepared for Terrorism than Prior to Attacks, Business Survey Says, BNA. Inc, Tuesday, March 2, 2004. http://subscript.bna.com/samples/hsd.nsf/0/4cccaab1b374545f85256e4b0002161e?OpenDocument.

Carver, D.W. (2004) Recognizing and Managing the Threat from Foreign Economic Espionage. Address to the National Security Institute's *Impact: National Security Forum and Exhibition*. Tuesday, April 27, 2004.

Center for Defense Information (2003) *Security After 9/11: Strategy Choices and Budget Tradeoffs*, Washington DC: Center for Defense Information.

Chapman, B.T. *Researching National Security and Intelligence Policy: A Research Guide*, Washington DC: CQ Press.

Clarke, D. (2004) *Technology and Terrorism*, Somerset, NJ: Transaction Publishers.

Clutterbuck, R. (1978) *Kidnap and Ransom: The Response*, Boston, MA: Faber and Faber.

Clutterbuck, R. (1987) *Kidnap, Hijack and Extortion: The Response*, London, UK: MacMillan Press.

Collins, D. (2004) Professional Development: How to 'Speak Security' to Upper Management. Address to the National Security Institute's *Impact: National Security Forum and Exhibition*. Tuesday, April 27, 2004.

Conlin, M., Thornton, E., Foust, D. and Welch, D. (2001) 'When the Office is the War Zone,' *Business Week*, Issue 3758, p. 38.

Crenlinsten, R.D. (1987) 'Terrorism as Political Communication: The Relationship Between the Controller and the Controlled,' *Contemporary Research on Terrorism*, Aberdeen: Aberdeen University Press.

Criscuoli, E. (1998) 'The Time Has Come to Acknowledge Security as a Profession,' *Annals of the American Academy of Political and Social Science*, Vol. 498, The Private Security Industry: Issues and Trends (July), pp. 98–107.

Cunningham, W. and Gross, P.J. (eds) (1978) *Prevention of Terrorism: Security Guidelines for Businesses and Other Organizations*, McLean, VA: Hallcrest Press.

Davis, M.J. (ed.) (1996) *Security Issues in the Post-Cold War World*, Cheltenham, UK: Edward Elgar Publishing, Inc.

Deibert, R.J. (2003) 'Deep Probe: The Evolution of Network Intelligence,' *Intelligence and National Security*, Vol. 18, pp. 175–93.

Denning, D.E. (1998) *Warfare and Security*, Boston: Addison-Wesley.

Drake, C.J.M. (1998) *Terrorist's Target Selection*, NY: St. Martin's Press.

Dreyfuss, R. (2001) 'Dim Intelligence,' *The American Prospect*, Vol. 12, Issue 18. October 22, 2001.

Drogan, B. 'New War Strains CIA Resources,' *Los Angeles Times*. December 10, 2001.

Dunnigan, J.F. (2003) *The Next War Zone: Confronting the Global Threat of Cyberterrorism*, NY: Kensington Publishing Corporation.

Edwards, M. and Hume, D. (1996) *Beyond the Magic Bullet: NGO Accountability in the Post-Cold War World*, West Hartford, Connecticut: Kumarian Press.

Fitzduff, M. and Church, C. (2004) *NGOs at the Table: Strategies for Influencing Policies in Areas of Conflict*, Maryland: Rowman & Littlefield Publishers, Inc.

Flanagan, S.J. (2001) 'Meeting the Challenges of the Global Century,' *The Global Century: Globalization and National Security Volume II*. Edited by Richard Kugler and Ellen Frost, Washington DC: National Defense University Press.

Freeman, C.W., Jr. (1997) *Arts of Power: Statecraft and Diplomacy*, Washington DC: USIP Press.

Friedman, T.L. (2000) *The Lexus and the Olive Tree: Understanding Globalization*, NY: Knopf Publishing.

Frost, E.L. (2001) 'Globalization and National Security: A Strategic Agenda,' *The Global Century: Globalization and National Security Volume II*. Edited by Richard Kugler and Ellen Frost. Washington DC: National Defense University Press.

Fuqua, P. and Wilson, J.V. (1978) *Terrorism: The Executive's Guide to Survival*, Houston, TX: Gulf Publishing Company.

Gabel, M. and Bruner, H. (2003) *Global, INC*, NY: The New Press.

Ghali, B.B. (1992) *An Agenda For Peace*, NY: United Nations.

Goldstein, D. (2001) 'Current CIA Policy Chills Information Gathering, Critics Say,' *Kansas City Star*, September 21, 2001.

Gorman, S. (2003) 'Homeland Security: Law Enforcement, Intelligence,' *National Journal*, Vol. 35, p. 3667.

Gray, J. (2003) *Al Qaeda and What It Means to Be Modern*, NY: The New Press.

Grieco, J. (1990) *Cooperation Among Nations*, Ithaca: Cornell University Press.

Halibozek, E. and Kovacich, G. (2003) 'Securing Corporate Assets,' *Industrial Engineer*, Vol. 35, pp. 39–44.

Held, D. and McGrew, A. (2002) *Globalization and Anti-Globalization*, Cambridge, UK: Polity Press.

Hoffman, B. (2001) Protecting American Interests Abroad: U.S. Citizens, Businesses and Non-Governmental Organizations. Testimony to the Subcommittee on National Security, Veterans Affairs, and International Relations, House Committee on Government Reform, April 3, 2001.

Hulnick, A.S. (2002) 'Risky Business: Private Sector Intelligence in the United States,' *Harvard International Review*, Vol. 24, pp. 68–72.

Iriye, A. (2004) *Global Community: The Role of International Organizations in the Making of the Contemporary World*, Berkeley: University of California Press.

Jenkins, B.M. (1981) *The Study of Terrorism: Definitional Problems*. P-6563, Santa Monica, CA: RAND Corporation.

Jeurgensmeyer, M. (2003) *Terror in the Mind of God: The Global Rise of Religious Violence*, 3rd edn, University of California Press.

Johnson, D.M. (2001) Religion and Culture: Human Dimensions of Globalization. *The Global Century: Globalization and National Security Volume II*. Edited by Richard Kugler and Ellen Frost. Washington DC: National Defense University Press.

Kakalik, J.S. and Wildhorn, S. (1971) *The Law and Private Police*, Santa Monica: Rand Corporation.

Keck, M. and Sikkink, K. (1998) *Activists Beyond Borders: Advocacy Networks in International Politics*, Ithaca: Cornell University Press.

Laqueur, W. (1999) *The New Terrorism, Fanaticism and the Arms of Mass Destruction*, Oxford: Oxford University Press.

Leonard, J.W. (2004) Solving the Problem in NISP: Issues and Answers. Address to the National Security Institute's *Impact: National Security Forum and Exhibition*. Tuesday, April 27, 2004.

Lifton, R.J. (1999) *Destroying the World to Save It: Aum Shinrikyo, Apocalyptic Violence, and the New Global Terrorism*, Metropolitan Books; 1st edition.

Lindenberg, M. and Bryant, C. (2001) *Going Global: Transforming Relief and Development NGOs*, Connecticut: Kumarian.

Lowenthal, M.M. (2000) *Intelligence: From Secrets to Policy*, Washington DC: CQ Press.

Mearsheimer, J. (2001) *The Tragedy of Great Power Politics*, NY: W.W. Norton.

Mendell, R. (1997) 'Using Intelligence Wisely,' *Security Management*, Vol. 41, pp. 115–23.

Miller, B.K. (2004) Building an Effective Security Awareness Program: Keys to Success. Address to the National Security Institute's *Impact: National Security Forum and Exhibition*. Tuesday, April 27, 2004.

Morgenthau, H. (1985) *Politics Among Nations*. 6th edn, NY: McGraw-Hill.

Mousseau, M. (2002/03) 'Market Civilization and Its Clash with Terror,' *International Security*, Vol. 27, pp. 5–29.

Olsen, P. (2002) 'Corporate Protection in a Violent World,' *New York Times*, 23 June 2002, p. 14.

Prime Minister's Strategy Unit, *Investing in Prevention: A Prime Minister's Strategy Unit Report to the Government: An International Strategy to Manage Risks of Instability and Improve Crisis Response*. February 2005. www.strategy.gov.uk. Accessed March 15, 2005.

Radcliff, D. (2000) 'Wanted: Security Supermen,' *Computerworld*, September 25, 2000. http://www.computerworld.com/securitytopics/security/story/0,10801,51025,00.html. Accessed March 3, 2005.

Richardson, L. (2003) 'Global Rebels: Terrorist Organizations as Trans-National Actors,' *Terrorism and Counterterrorism: Understanding the New Security Environment*. Guilford, CT: McGraw Hill.

Richardson, L. (2005) 'The Myth of Cyberterrorism: The Internet as a Tool or Target of the Terrorists' part of the Distinguished Lecture Series on Computation and Society, sponsored by the Center for Research on Computation and Society, Harvard University, February 24, 2005.

Richelson, J.T. (1999) *The U.S. Intelligence Community*, 4th edn, Boulder, CO: Westview Press.

Rogalski, R.W. (2004) Excellence in Security Management: Best Practices. Address to the National Security Institute's *Impact: National Security Forum and Exhibition*. Tuesday, April 27, 2004.

Ronit, K. and Schneider, V. (eds) (2000) *Private Organizations in Global Politics*, NY: Routledge.

Rothkopf, D.J. (2002) 'Business Versus Terror,' *Foreign Policy* May/June 2002. http://www.foreignpolicy.com/Ning/archive/archive/130/Rothkopf.pdf. Accessed March 2, 2005.

Sageman, M. (2004) *Understanding Terror Networks*, Philadelphia: University of Pennsylvania Press.

Salkever, A. (2001) 'Coming to Grips with an Unsafe World,' *Business Week Online*, 5 December 2001.

Sally, R. (1995) *States and Firms: Multinational Firms in Institutional Competition*, NY: Routledge.

Schaffert, R.W. (1992) *Media Coverage and Political Terrorists: A Quantitative Analysis*, NY: Praeger Publishers.

Schweitzer, G. (1998) *Superterrorism: Assassins, Mobsters and Weapons of Mass Destruction*, NY: Plenum Press.

Shotwell, C.B. (2001) 'International Law and Institutions: A Post-Westphalian Landscape,' *The Global Century: Globalization and National Security Volume II*. Edited by Richard Kugler and Ellen Frost, Washington DC: National Defense University Press.

Semko, R. (2004) D*I*C*E 2004: Countering Threats to Sensitive and Classified Information. Address to the National Security Institute's *Impact: National Security Forum and Exhibition*. Tuesday, April 27, 2004.

Slaughter, A.M. (2004) *New World Order*, Princeton, NJ: Princeton University Press.

Sloan, S. (1978) *The Anatomy of Non-Territorial Terrorism*, International Association of Chiefs of Police.

Smith, J.H. and Deutch, J. (2002) 'Smarter Intelligence' *Foreign Policy*, January/February 2002, http://www.foreignpolicy.com/story/files/story1889.php. Accessed April 2, 2005.

Snow, D.M. (1997) *Distant Thunder: Patterns of Conflict in the Developing World*, Armonk, NY: M.E. Sharpe.

Snyder, C.A. (2000) *Contemporary Security and Strategy*, NY: Routledge.

Spiro, P.J. (1995) 'New Global Communities: Nongovernmental Organizations in International Decision-making Institutions,' *Washington Quarterly*, Vol. 18, No. 1, Winter.

Stapley, C.S. (2004) *NGOs in the Crosshairs: Non-Governmental Agencies and the Terrorist Threat*, UMI Distributing.

Stern, J. (2000) *Ultimate Terrorists*, Cambridge: Harvard University Press.

Stern, J. (2003) *Terror in the Name of God: Why Religious Militants Kill*, Ecco/Harper Collins.

Strange, S. (1996) *The Retreat of the State: The Diffusion of Power in the World Economy*, Cambridge: Cambridge University Press.

Thachuk, K.L. (2001) 'The Sinister Underbelly: Organized Crime and Terrorism,' *The Global Century: Globalization and National Security Volume II*. Edited by Richard Kugler and Ellen Frost, Washington DC: National Defense University Press.

Thompson, J. (1995) 'State Sovereignty in International Relations: Bridging the Gap Between Theory and Empirical Research,' *International Studies Quarterly*, Vol. 39, No. 2 (June), pp. 213–33.

Tolentino, P.E. (2001) *Multinational Corporations: Emergence and Evolution*, New York: Routledge.

United States Department of State (2005) *Patterns of Global Terrorism 2003*. http://www.state.gov/s/ct/rls/pgtrpt/2003/c12108.htm. Accessed March 9, 2005.

Verton, D. (2003) 'Corporate Security Still Lacks Focus Two Years After 9/11,' *Computerworld*, Vol. 37, p. 13.

Waltz, K. (1979) *Theory of International Politics*, NY: McGraw-Hill.

Weimann, G. (1994) *The Theater of Terror: Mass Media and International Terrorism*, White Plaines, NY: Longman Publishing Group.

Weimann, G. (2004) *www.terror.net: How Modern Terrorism uses the Internet.* Special report. United States Institute of Peace. http://www.usip.org/pubs/specialreports/sr116.pdf. Accessed March 25, 2004.

Weiss, T.G. and Gordenker, L. (1996) *NGOs, the UN and Global Governance*, Boulder, CO: Lynne Rienner Publishers.

White, L.C. (1951) *International Non-Governmental Organizations*, New Brunswick: Rutgers University Press.

Whitlock, C. (2004) 'Al Qaeda Claims to Kidnap American,' *Washington Post*, June 13, p. A01, available at http://www.washingtonpost.com/wp-dyn/articles/A37583-2004Jun12.html.

Willetts, P. (ed.) (1982) *Pressure Groups in the Global System: The Transnational Relations of Issue-Oriented Non-Governmental Organizations*, London: Pinter.

Wilson, B. (2004) 'Iraq Contractors Weather Security Storm,' *BBC* September 21, available at http://newsbbc.co.uk/1/hi/business/3676856.stm.

Wieviorka, M. (1995) 'Terrorism in the Context of Academic Research,' Crenshaw, Martha (ed.) *Terrorism in Context*, University Park, PA: Pennsylvania State University Press.

4

Engineering Principles for Security Managers

Bradley B. Rogers

Introduction

Security managers are responsible for directing the solution of security problems in a cost and performance effective manner. Put more succinctly, the security manager is responsible for *engineering* the solution of security problems. In this context the noun 'engineer' does not necessarily refer to a person in possession of specific credentials, but rather to any professional who is responsible for engineering solutions in the security field. This chapter discusses application of engineering principles to security, so that security managers may become more effective engineers.

Engineering is a broad, well developed and mature discipline, and there are many specialties within engineering that are important to the field of security. For example, engineers are involved in security research at a fundamental level, they drive the development of security technology, and they are responsible for the use and development of a broad range of analyses, such as prediction of blast effects, and system performance predictions. At the interface between the disciplines of engineering and management is the field of systems engineering, in which fundamental engineering principles are applied to what are effectively management problems. In particular, systems engineering manages the integration of technologies, personnel, policies and procedures into complex systems. This chapter will outline the application of systems engineering principles and apply them to the field of security.

In this chapter, security is defined as the protection of an asset from a malevolent human attack. There are several methods available to a manager for dealing with security risks, including buying insurance, or simply accepting the risk (see Chapter 22; Grose, 1987). A security system functions to *reduce* the risk of loss of an asset, and the installation of a security system should be justified by the risk evaluation. Herein, it is assumed that the risk analyses has been completed, and the decision has already been made to protect assets either by installing a new security system, or by evaluating the performance of an existing system, and upgrading if necessary.

Systems and the systems approach to problem solving

The meaning of the word *system* has subtle variations for different disciplines and applications. For example, in thermodynamics a system is everything contained in a volume of space enclosed by an arbitrarily chosen boundary, while mathematicians refer to a system of equations. From an abstract viewpoint these (and other) definitions are analogous, but in practice they are based on different physical and mathematical concepts. Consequently, at the outset it is important to carefully define what we mean by the word system. In this chapter, a definition utilized in the field of systems engineering will be used: a system is a collection of interacting components, policies and procedures that are integrated and organized to react to an input and produce a predictable output (Blanchard and Fabrycky, 1998). Everything that is not a part of the system is called the surroundings. The basic input/output model of a system is illustrated below, in Figure 4.1.

In this model of a security system, the input is a malevolent human attack upon an asset, and the desired output is a defeated adversary and an intact asset. The security system, including all technological, procedural and human components, is in place to produce this output.

A *complex system* is defined as a diverse system of sub-systems working together toward a common goal. Each of the subsystems contributes a unique function that is utilized by the global system. The subsystems themselves may be complex, resulting in a multi-level hierarchy of functions. All of these functions must be integrated by the global system in a coherent and efficient manner, and the performance of the global system is a function based not only on the performance of the subsystems, but how well the integrated parts perform together (Kossiakoff and Sweet, 2003). A security system, utilizing a combination of technological, human and procedural components, fits the definition of a complex system.

Complex systems can be categorized in several ways. For example, they may be classified according to their output, such as service oriented or product oriented (Sage and Armstrong, 2000). A shopping mall is an example of a service oriented system, while a factory is an example of a product oriented system. Furthermore, systems may be *deterministic* or *probabilistic*. The goal of a deterministic system is to produce the same output every time given a specific input. An example of a deterministic system is an automobile,

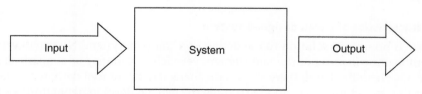

Figure 4.1   Input/output model of a system

which is designed to predictably function based on specific inputs from the driver. The performance of a deterministic system can be modeled and predicted by mathematical tools such as algebra and calculus. On the other hand, probabilistic systems do not always produce the same output, but rather a distributed output with a central tendency. An example of a probabilistic system is a public school system which is designed to produce educated graduates, given entering students with modest capabilities. The final outputs of this system, including the graduates as well as those that don't complete the curriculum, vary widely in capabilities. The measure of the success of a probabilistic system is quantified by use of the tools of probability and statistics. In some cases, complex systems may be assembled from deterministic and quasi-deterministic subsystems, but the complexity and nonlinearity of element interactions, human components, and input variability can result in a system that is effectively probabilistic. This is very often the case in the field of security.

Engineering and management of complex systems requires a *systems perspective*, in which difficult, multifaceted problems are viewed in total. In the systems perspective the system is viewed from outside, and performance is measured only by the effectiveness of the system in producing the desired output. While the failure of a subsystem may result in global system failure, *operating* subsystem components usually have only a secondary effect on the performance of the global system. The performance of the complete system depends primarily on how the subsystems interact with each other, and how well they are integrated together into the global system.

In the development of complex systems, specialists produce system components, and project managers must integrate them into the global system. With existing systems, subsystem components may need replacement, or decisions concerning upgrades may have to be made as new technologies become available. The systems viewpoint requires that the project manager maintain focus on the ultimate goal, which is an integrated system that reliably produces the desired input/output relation. For example, the replacement of existing technology that is well integrated into a system with new aggressively marketed technology may be detrimental to the overall system performance if the deployment of and transition to the new equipment is troublesome. The project manager must always be the advocate for the system – a decision to deploy new technology should be based on the effect it will have on the overall system performance (Kossiakoff and Sweet, 2003).

Characteristics of a well designed system

There is no unique solution to the design of a complex system. No two development teams will arrive at the same design, yet each design may be similarly effective. On the other hand, there are certain characteristics of well designed systems that the project manager can use to guide the general development efforts of the design team (Kossiakoff and Sweet, 2003; Sage and Armstrong, 2000; Eisner, 1997;

Adamsen, 2000; Grady, 1994). These characteristics relate equally to technologies, personnel, policies and procedures. A summary is given below:

1 The system is both **performance** and **cost effective**. In the development of a complex system, there will always be a tradeoff between cost and performance. A well designed system provides the **necessary** performance at the **minimum** cost.
2 The system is **reliable**, **maintainable**, and **upgradeable**. A well designed system utilizes technologies and procedures that minimize failures. When a failure does occur, it is easy to identify the cause and correct the problem. If the failures involve technological components, replacement parts are standard and easy to obtain and, if upgrades are necessary, new technologies are standard and backward compatible with existing systems. In terms of personnel, the system operation does not depend on the expertise of a single individual.
3 The system is **flexible** and **adaptable**. During the life cycle of a complex system, the original goals and constraints used to develop the system may change. A well designed system can evolve to meet new requirements.
4 The system is **verifiable** and **predictable**. In a well designed system, it is possible to test and ensure the system is working as required. The behavior of the system is well understood, and it is possible to accurately predict and test how the system will perform as scenarios change.

A systematic approach to problem solving

In addition to the concept of a system as a collection of interlaced parts, a system may also be a set of policies and procedures. All (competent) scientists and engineers follow such a systematic procedure, sometimes referred to as the scientific method, when confronting a problem. While simple explanations of the scientific method ignore important aspects of how science actually gets done, such as insight and interactions between scientists, it is certainly true that scientific and engineering progress is made by application of a rigorous, disciplined and systematic approach to problem solving (Gauch, 2003). This system is broadly outlined by the following three steps:

1 Define the Problem.
2 Solve the Problem.
3 Check the Solution.

If, in the third step, the proposed solution is found to be inadequate, the problem must be re-evaluated to determine if there is an error in the solution, or perhaps a flaw in the problem definition. At the leading edge of engineering, science and mathematics the details may be very complicated, but the procedure is easily recognized: a problem is put forward, a solution is proposed, and the solution is checked by recognized and knowledgeable experts. In practice, the procedure is often less formal, and a single individual may carry out the entire process. However, this system has been proven to provide effective and sustained progress on any problem.

In practice, the final step – checking the solution – is sometimes neglected. The result is that resources are wasted on systems and policies that have no effect, and may even be counterproductive. There are many instances of such practice in the security field. For example, as discussed in the chapter of this book dedicated to CCTV (see Chapter 19), research has shown that although the use of surveillance video cameras is not suitable in every situation, resources continue to be spent on these systems without regard to their effectiveness.

The sophistication of the analysis effort should depend on the consequence of loss of the asset, and can vary from qualitative evaluation through complex and expensive quantitative analyses. For the most part, solutions of deterministic problems can be checked against accepted scientific principles and observations with mathematical precision. On the other hand many probabilistic problems are lacking well defined and broadly accepted principles that have been formulated with mathematical clarity. Progress in these areas requires insight coupled with skillful statistical evaluation of data (Kumamoto and Henley, 1996). In general, it is easier to make rapid progress in understanding when problems are deterministic in nature, and more difficult as they become probabilistic. Therefore, in complex problems such as security that are quasi-probabilistic in nature, it is advantageous to develop and utilize analysis tools that are as deterministic as possible.

As problems become more complex, it becomes unlikely that a single individual will possess all of the knowledge and talent necessary to solve the problem, and an interdisciplinary team of specialists must be assembled. In this case, the systematic approach to problem solving must be *managed*, and it is the responsibility of the project manager to ensure that decisions are based on a sound methodology. In many cases specialists tend to work in isolation with little understanding of how their efforts contribute to those of the team. On the other hand, progress can be greatly accelerated when diverse specialists work toward a commonly understood goal, following a methodology based on accepted and sound principles, and with an appreciation of the capabilities, constraints and limitations of other specialists. Security is a field which draws from an extremely diverse talent pool. Consequently, a particular challenge for a security project manager is to communicate the objectives and methodology directly as well as to facilitate communications throughout the development team. Furthermore, the project manager must always base decisions on how they will affect the global system. (This requires a degree of technical sophistication because of the proliferation of new security technologies and the lack of general standards by which to evaluate these products.)

In summary, it is worth emphasizing again that a systematic approach to problem solving is not a defined set of procedures, but rather a philosophy of approaching problems. The approach is equally applicable to the solution of very simple problems, requiring only a few minutes, as it is to the development of a PhD dissertation. In some of the sections that follow, a systematic engineering approach to addressing security problems is described which includes rather detailed procedures. It is important to understand that these discussions involve the application of *one* systematic methodology to security. No claim is being made that every security problem justifies the level of detail that will be described in these sections, or that this is the only scientifically rigorous approach to the problem. The key is not the detailed procedures that are discussed, but rather the high level methodology. This can be summarized by the following axiom: 'It is impossible to solve a problem that hasn't been defined, and it is impossible to finish a problem if the validity of the proposed solution is not known.'

Principles of engineering design

The practice of engineering design is a creative process that involves tradeoffs and compromises to achieve a design that meets as many objectives as possible without violating certain constraints. There is no single correct answer to a design problem – many solutions are possible, and sometimes the possible solutions are surprisingly diverse. On the other hand, effective design practice in engineering requires a methodical scientific approach to the problem, as outlined in the previous section.

As has been discussed previously, the first step in attacking a design problem is to define and understand the problem. This will result in a list of constraints that must be met by the design. A constraint is a requirement that encapsulates the design. Constraints include externally imposed requirements, such as budgets, timelines and performance parameters, as well as those imposed by scientific principles and limits of technology. The first type of constraints, which are essentially design requirements, are identified and imposed during the problem definition phase of a design project. These constraints do not generally require specialized scientific knowledge to establish, but, for a number of reasons, they may change and evolve during the design process. The second type of constraints, those due to physical laws or the limits of technology, do not change, and they may require substantial expertise to understand and evaluate. (In some cases the design requirements may be physically impossible to meet, requiring a re-evaluation of the imposed constraints.) Proposed designs are evaluated and compared by their performance against all design constraints. Consequently, a design cannot logically proceed until constraints are established. In the following sections, the establishment of constraints for security systems based on technological capabilities and physical principles will be discussed.

After the constraints are established, the design proceeds through phases, from conception to embodiment to detail design (Haik, 2003). The conceptual design phase specifies the basic framework and essential functions of the design, and often several conceptual designs are proposed before one is selected for further development. For example, in a physical security application, a conceptual design would include determination of the areas to be protected, and the basic configuration of the detection, delay and response components of the system (Garcia, 2001). This leads into the embodiment of the design, in which preliminary layouts are established, and the performance of proposed designs are analysed and compared with respect to the constraints. The final phase is that of detail design, in which specific components and technologies are specified, and detailed descriptions of their placement and configurations are developed. The final phase of the design process is the most time consuming, and it is important that the analysis of the proposed designs in the embodiment phase be done as well as possible to avoid wasted effort.

In most cases, the entire design process involves continuous feedback and improvement, since the design of complex systems always involves some uncertainty. As more is learned about a problem, design improvements may become clear, or alternative approaches may come to light that merit evaluation. Thus the design process becomes one of iteration, which continues until a design is produced that meets or exceeds the imposed constraints.

A systematic approach to security systems engineering

The development of a new security system, or the evaluation of an existing system, involves the methodical solution of a complex systems engineering problem. The objectives must be specified (problem definition), a solution must be developed (problem solution) and the validity of the solution must be verified. Examples of systematic approaches to security include the Risk Assessment Methodology for Water System Protection, RAM-W, (Sandia National Labs, 2003) and the National Institute of Justice publication concerning vulnerability of chemical facilities (NIJ, 2002). These methodologies have been developed for specific security applications. On the other hand, it is advantageous to consider the problem as generally as possible, so that the principles common to the engineering of all security systems are first developed, with specific applications following. A particularly general articulation of security system engineering methodology has been developed at Sandia National Laboratories over the last 50 years, and was driven by the need to protect the nation's nuclear infrastructure (Garcia, 2001). This articulation, known as the Sandia Methodology, serves as a roadmap to guide the effective design, analysis and implementation of security systems, and is illustrated graphically in Figure 4.2.

This diagram includes the basic problem solving strategy discussed in the previous section in which a problem is defined, a solution is developed, and the solution is verified. By inference, this diagram also identifies specific tasks that are necessary for the development of any security system, and guides the engineering project.

While specific analytical tools, technological components and procedures necessary to accomplish the tasks identified in Figure 4.2 will vary according to the application, the basic methodology is applicable to all security problems. Details necessary for cyber security will be different than those required for physical security and other applications, and the relative sophistication and cost of the system analysis should vary according to the consequence of loss of the asset. For example, in the protection of low-value assets, the cost of a complete quantitative evaluation, such as will be described below, could never be justified. In these cases, a more qualitative approach is needed. On the other hand, in all cases it is

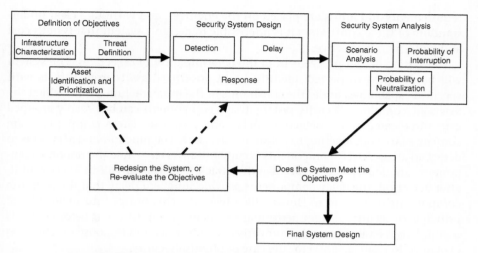

Figure 4.2 The Sandia security systems engineering methodology

impossible to solve a problem that hasn't been defined, or to analyse a design that hasn't been developed.

The methodology illustrated on Figure 4.2 involves continuous feedback and adjustment, and is a very nonlinear process. This feedback process is partially illustrated on the figure, but the need for a robust and flexible design is not clearly apparent. Security systems are unusual in the sense that they are designed to stop an adversary whose goal is to defeat the system. Consequently, as adversary capabilities change, and threat scenarios evolve, a security system must be able to rapidly evolve as well. Thus the need for continuous evaluation of security systems, and the ability to predict the performance of the system against changing scenarios.

The high-level tasks in the Sandia methodology shown on Figure 4.2 are determination of objectives, system design, and system analysis. Determination of objectives for a security system is the problem definition step – the engineer must determine the environment and constraints under which the security system must operate, identify what is to be protected, and from whom it must be protected. This step forms the 'boundary conditions' for the system design process. For example, a constraint on a cyber-security system installed within an information technology system at a university to protect student records, financial transactions, and other information is that it must not seriously degrade needed access from students, faculty and staff. Some requirements are easier to meet than others. In this example, the problem of preventing access to grades from student accounts is much simpler than that of stopping a corrupt employee of the university information technology department from gaining the same access. The consequence of loss of an asset is also a consideration – unauthorized access to financial records and accounts is much more serious than the defacing of a department's home page. In all security applications, similar requirements and limits are placed on the engineer, and without a clear understanding of these constraints it is impossible to design a system that is both cost and performance effective.

The system design proceeds from the determination of objectives. The system will be designed to protect identified and prioritized assets from threats with specified capabilities, under the constraints of the infrastructure within which the assets are contained. Security system design components can be broadly grouped into three categories – detection, delay and response. These components are configured to work together to defeat an adversary. The function of detection is to detect an attack. Delay components occupy the adversary while the response components are deployed to neutralize the attack. The system will be successful if, after detection, the delay components provide sufficient delay that the response components have time to thwart the adversary. This brings into focus a basic principle of security system performance – detection must occur before delay is useful. This is easily proven by comparison of adversary and response timelines, as explained in (Garcia, 2001) for the case of physical security.

The development of a complex system is an open-ended design problem. There is no single 'correct' solution, but rather a continuum of solutions, some of which will perform better than others (Haik, 2003). A practical reality of complex systems is that new technologies continuously appear, the system environment continuously evolves, and it is always possible to envision an 'improvement' to the system. However, the quest for the 'best possible' system can become prohibitively expensive. For example, in the security field the expenditure of limited resources on small improvements to an existing system can result in insufficient resources for the protection of other valuable assets. At the design phase it is important to be able to establish the cost and performance effectiveness of a proposed design or system upgrade so that time and resources are not wasted on marginal improvements, or the deployment of a flawed system which fails to meet objectives and may leave critical assets unprotected. This is accomplished through security system analysis.

The goals of security system analysis are to establish measurable performance outcomes, identify shortcomings and weaknesses, and ensure the system meets the original objectives. The analysis may include determining performance parameters of the system, verifying proposed designs and design changes, continuous improvement and tradeoff studies, and investigation of evolving threats and scenarios. Analysis techniques vary from basic qualitative evaluation to extremely sophisticated simulations of multiple adversary and response paths and neutralization techniques. The level of complexity of the analysis is driven by the consequence of loss of an asset and by the analytical tools and capabilities available to the security team. However, the importance of the analysis step should not be overlooked.

The general methodology shown on Figure 4.2 can be applied to virtually any security problem. Obviously, applications differ and, at some level of detail, the technologies and tasks required to engineer these systems must diverge. In the practice of systems engineering, however, it is advantageous to delay this divergence as long as possible so that as many common principles as possible can be developed. The questions, from a systems point of view, becomes: What is common to all security systems, and to what level of detail can we expand the procedures in Figure 4.2 without sacrificing generality? The following discussions, while using examples from particular branches of the security field, strive to present material that can be generally applied across the discipline.

Determination of objectives of a security system

The determination of objectives task has been further broken down into three general subtasks, referred to as infrastructure characterization, threat definition, and asset identification and prioritization on Figure 4.2. These tasks identify the constraints under which the security system must operate, what is to be protected, and from whom it is to be protected.

Infrastructure characterization

The importance of an asset to an organization does not simply depend on the monetary cost of the asset, but rather is based on the value of the asset to the organization. Before a consequence of loss of an asset can be reasonably evaluated, the organization itself must be thoroughly understood, which is the purpose of an infrastructure characterization. The infrastructure characterization seeks to gain an appreciation of this organizational environment and to establish design constraints under which the security system must operate. An infrastructure characterization consists of defining the critical missions and goals of the organization, the infrastructure that is necessary to accomplish this mission, the legal, regulatory, safety and corporate framework, and the vulnerabilities that the organization faces. As an example, eight essential tasks identified for physical security applications are discussed in (Garcia, 2001), and are listed below:

1 Operations
2 Condition and layout
3 Policies and procedures
4 Regulatory requirements
5 Safety considerations
6 Legal issues
7 Organization goals and objectives
8 Vulnerabilities

The goals and purposes of each of these tasks is explained in detail in Garcia, 2001. These tasks cannot be completely generalized to all security applications. For example, safety considerations are probably of indirect concern in cybersecurity. On the other hand, this list does provide a comprehensive framework for a thorough infrastructure characterization. In general, for all security applications the goal of the infrastructure characterization is to provide the information that is necessary to identify critical assets and establish some of the design constraints for the security system, as well as to understand and model the environment so that analysis of proposed designs and upgrades can be critically and continuously evaluated. For example, vulnerability analysis refers to identifying weaknesses that may be exploited by an adversary. As a security system is designed to mitigate particular vulnerabilities against specific threats, the most susceptible target will change. Furthermore, the capabilities and tactics of the threats continuously evolve as well. Consequently, the infrastructure characterization in general and vulnerability analysis in particular are not static tasks, but rather dynamic, ongoing processes integrated in to the security system management framework.

Asset identification and prioritization

From the systems engineering viewpoint, asset identification and prioritization is the process of identifying assets to be protected without consideration of the threat or the difficulty of providing protection (Garcia, 2001). Similar to the infrastructure characterization, this is a ongoing process. This is because both threats and organizations continuously evolve, and the value of an asset can only be established within the context of the organization and the threats to that organization. For example, recent intelligence has indicated that certain financial institutions have become terrorists targets. Previously, these institutions developed security to protect assets that were likely theft targets, but the most attractive targets for sabotage by a terrorist attack, such as the buildings and personnel, are essentially unprotected by these systems.

Details of the asset identification procedure depend on the complexity and importance of the infrastructures and assets that are being protected. In a small facility the assets may be relatively obvious, and can be identified by careful inspection. On the other hand, when considering sabotage threats at a major oil refinery or chemical facility, the complexity of the technology means that the disruption of seemingly innocuous support processes, or even procedures, can trigger sequences of events that result in catastrophic consequences, especially when initiated by a knowledgeable insider. In this case, use of special analytical tools including complex fault tree analyses, such as those used in safety and risk analysis, is justified (Garcia, 2001; Kumamoto and Henley, 1996).

The asset identification and prioritization effort can be enhanced by the use of the principles of risk analysis, since the security risk and the security risk equation theoretically provides a convenient means to establish the value of an asset. Risk is defined as the Probability of Occurrence of a loss, P_O, multiplied by the Consequence of the loss, C (see Chapter 22). In security applications, the probability of occurrence is given by:

$$P_O = P_A (1 - P_E), \tag{1}$$

where P_A is the Probability of Attack, and P_E is the Probability of Effectiveness of the security system. The Probability of Effectiveness is the Probability of Interruption of adversary action, P_I, multiplied by the Probability of Neutralization, given a successful interruption, P_N. Unfortunately, in many cases direct application of the risk equation is impossible because the uncertainty in the probability of an attack is very large. This is a consequence of the probabilistic nature of risk.

Consider, for example, the security risk equation for a single asset in its common form for security:

$$R = P_A (1 - P_I P_N)C. \tag{2}$$

This equation is often erroneously interpreted in absolute terms, with the terms treated as absolute rather than random variables. The equation is perfectly valid, as long as it is interpreted in terms of random variables. That is, R is the most probable Risk, P_A is the most probable probability of attack, P_I is the most probable probability of interruption of the attack, P_N is the most probable probability of neutralization of the attack given a successful interruption and C is the most probable consequence of loss. Because these are random variables, there is uncertainty associated with each variable. To establish the uncertainty in risk, the complete risk equation at a given uncertainty level is written:

$$R \pm u_R = [P_A \pm u_{P_A}][1 - (P_I \pm u_{P_I})(P_N \pm u_{P_N})][C \pm u_C] \tag{3}$$

where the u_i's refer to the uncertainty of the variables at a particular confidence level, such as 95 percent. Determination of the uncertainty in the dependent variable of risk, u_R, based on the uncertainties of the independent variables is a straightforward procedure, although the details do require a certain mathematical maturity (Figliola and Beasley, 1995; Coleman and Steele, 1989). However, for the purposes of this discussion it is sufficient to point out that the uncertainty in risk, u_R, will depend on a mathematical combination of the uncertainties of the independent variables, and will necessarily be greater than the largest of these uncertainties. Two particular mathematical problems arise in the analysis. First, if any of the uncertainties of the independent variables cannot be established, then it becomes impossible to directly quantify the risk. Second, if the uncertainty of any one of the independent variables is too large, the series used to establish the uncertainty in the risk, u_R, will 'diverge.' Put more plainly, there will be no solution to the equation.

In some security applications, such as retail crime, enough statistics exist to ascertain a probability of attack. This is the exception rather than the rule, however, and the probability of attack is usually the most troublesome variable to establish. This is especially true when considering very low probability very high consequence events, as discussed in Waller and Covello, 1984. When the probability of attack is unknown, but the need for security is established, it is still possible to prioritize assets using the principles of risk management by comparative analysis. To do this, consider the ratio of the most probable security risks for two assets for which the probabilities of attack are unknown, but assumed to be similar:

$$\frac{R_1}{R_2} = \frac{(P_{A_1})(1 - P_{I_1}P_{N_1})C_1}{(P_{A_2})(1 - P_{I_2}P_{N_2})C_2} = \frac{(1 - P_{I_1}P_{N_1})C_1}{(1 - P_{I_2}P_{N_2})C_2} \tag{4}$$

This equation establishes the ratio of risks for two assets, in terms of variables which are typically easier to determine then the probability of attack. The consequence of loss of an asset can almost always be established, and the probability of interruption and neutralization can be estimated using the design and analysis tools to be discussed in subsequent sections. At this point, certain design constraints can be established based on risk. One possible criterion is that the security system be designed with the goal that the risk for all assets is equal. That is, $R_1=R_2=\dots .=R_N$. The criteria for equal risks is then:

$$\frac{R_1}{R_2} = 1 = \frac{\left(1-P_{I_1}P_{N_1}\right)C_1}{\left(1-P_{I_2}P_{N_2}\right)C_2} \tag{5}$$

$$\therefore \left(1-P_{I_1}P_{N_1}\right)C_1 = \left(1-P_{I_2}P_{N_2}\right)C_2$$

If $C_1>C_2$, then the design goal is to increase the values of the P_{I1} and P_{N1}, so that the product shown in equation 5, $(1-P_{I1}P_{N1})C_1$, is reduced. In this case, the design constraints direct resources to improve the system performance variables, P_I and P_N. *The result of this criteria is that resources will be managed so that high consequence of loss assets will receive more protection than those of lower consequence.*

Another design criteria that is sometimes proposed is that all assets receive equal protection, so that the system design results in $P_{I1}P_{N1}=P_{I2}P_{N2}= \dots =P_{IN}P_{NN}$. If this criteria is used, however, the risk ratio becomes simply the ratio of the consequences of loss, $R_1/R_2=C_1/C_2$. The result is that high consequence items are left at high risk, while resources are wasted on low value assets. Clearly, this is a flawed requirement, since any performance criteria used as a design constraint should result in prioritized protection of higher value assets.

This discussion has demonstrated that asset prioritization in security problems in which the probability of attack is unknown or very uncertain can still be rigorously established from the principles of risk management through a comparative analysis of the consequences of loss of the assets. A logical design criteria in which resources are appropriately directed to higher value assets follows from the analysis. Therefore, from a systems engineering standpoint, the key task necessary for asset prioritization is establishing the consequence of loss of the asset.

It is worthwhile to point out that the preceding quantitative analysis can be costly and is most appropriate for high value assets – lower value assets may be analysed qualitatively. The analysis will follow the same principles, but more uncertainty can be tolerated in the analysis because the consequence of loss is lower.

The asset prioritization begins with a listing of undesirable consequences that may occur due to an attack by an adversary. Undesirable consequences can include loss of reputation, financial loss, injury or loss of life, and other measures. Unfortunately, there is no direct way to compare these consequences, since they are measured in different units. For example, it is not reasonable to try to place a monetary value on a human life, and in some applications, consequences may be so serious that financial measurement is meaningless. If problems in which all assets can be measured using the same units, such as a monetary value, the problem is straightforward. If this is not the case, the security manager must establish a criteria that can be used to compare consequences. For example, the most unacceptable consequence may be assigned a numerical value of 1, with other consequences following (Garcia, 2001).

Typically, assets that have a have a high monetary value are easily identified and prioritized. On the other hand, many assets of smaller direct economic value may be critically important for facility operation or, in some applications, human life or safety may depend on them. These assets are identified by recognition of all sequences that can lead to an undesired event. In simple situations, this may be a straightforward process. In complex problems analytical techniques such as event tree and fault tree analysis are helpful in identifying critical components since all assets that can lead to a failure sequence must be protected with equal diligence. Fault tree analysis is a highly developed field, and software packages have been developed to aid in the process. For an introduction to the techniques, readers are referred to Garcia, 2001, while a more complete treatment is given in Kumamoto and Henley, 1996. In complex problems, adding specialists in fault tree analysis to the security team to aid in this effort may be justified.

Threat definition

In addition to deciding what to protect, the security system engineer must determine from whom the asset is to be protected. This determination is the threat definition, and really forms the core about which the entire systems engineering process revolves. This is because a system is designed to deal with a threat that has certain capabilities and will employ specific tactics. No security system will be equally effective against all threats, and in some cases may become ineffective as threat scenarios change. As threat capabilities and tactics evolve, a well designed system may also evolve to meet the new threats to a certain extent. On the other hand, in some situations, a complete redesign may be necessary. For instance, in the example used earlier, the threat to large financial institutions has expanded beyond theft to include the possibility of terrorist attacks (DHS, 2004). As another example, a system designed to deal with outsiders may be nearly useless against an insider.

The threat assessment effort occurs in parallel with that of asset identification, since threats with different goals, motivations and tactics may choose different targets for attack. For high consequence assets, this can be a very large effort, in some cases requiring teams of specialists. In the context of security systems engineering, however, what is needed from these efforts is a threat description sufficient to engineer a system to mitigate the threat. This description is called the design basis threat (DBT). Therefore, in this section the gathering of threat information is not discussed in great detail, nor is the evaluation of the greatest credible threat. Instead, the use of threat information and the type of information needed so that an effective system can be designed is emphasized.

The DBT statement is a profile of the type, capabilities, intentions and tactics of internal and/or external adversaries who may seek to attack assets. This statement is a description of the threat against which assets must be protected, and upon which the security system engineering is based. Therefore, the DBT statement must carry sufficient information to make design decisions regarding system elements and configurations. These statements may vary substantially from one type of application to another. For example, typical DBT statements for cyber-security will bear minimal detailed resemblance to those for physical security. On the other hand, at least at an abstract level, the threat types, intentions, capabilities and tactics are similar.

Threat types include insiders, outsiders, and insiders colluding with outsiders. Outsider threats are those adversaries that do not have authorized access to assets, while insiders are adversaries that have such access. In general, security systems all involve integrated detection, delay and response functions and technologies. However, a system designed to detect an external intruder is very unlikely to be effective against an insider, while policies and procedures that are in place to detect insider action will do little against an outsider. In many cases, the security system may need to protect against both insider and outsider threats. If this is the case, then the system must be designed to deal with both threats.

Adversaries, both insiders and outsiders, may employ a variety of tactics, including speed, force, stealth and deceit, as well as diversionary tactics. In attacks relying on speed, adversaries simply try to accomplish their goals before a response arrives, such as a criminal that smashes a store window, removes items, and leaves before the police arrive. A force tactic is similar, but the adversaries in this case attempt to overpower any barriers or response effort. In stealth attacks, adversaries seek to accomplish their goals without being detected in a timely manner, while deceit involves gaining access to assets through apparent authorized admission. It is clear that different security measures will be appropriate for different tactics. For example, in physical security additional investment in detection technologies may be inappropriate if the DBT intends to employ force tactics, since additional detection will not improve the performance of a system that undergoes a speed/force attack.

Adversary capabilities may include the number of attackers, their weapons, equipment, technologies, skills and knowledge. Intentions of the adversary may include such goals as theft, sabotage, extortion, blackmail, and other crimes. The design of a security system will vary depending on these tactics. Some adversaries may be highly motivated and willing to use deadly force. The security system engineer must ensure that the system is designed to protect against adversary intentions and counter adversary capabilities. For example, it is much more difficult to protect an asset against sabotage than theft, since an adversary simply needs to reach the asset to complete the sabotage task.

The type of information that may be directly used in the engineering of a security system can be illuminated by example. The following is a portion of a DBT statement for a physical security application pertaining to a sabotage threat on a very high consequence target (NRC, 2004).

The threat consists of:

A determined violent external assault, attack by stealth, or deceptive actions, of several persons with the following attributes, assistance and equipment:

a Well-trained (including military training and skills) and dedicated individuals,
b Inside assistance which may include a knowledgeable individual who attempts to participate in a passive role (e.g. provide information), an active role (e.g. facilitate entrance and exit, disable alarms and communications, participate in violent attack), or both,
c Suitable weapons, up to and including hand-held automatic weapons, equipped with silencers and having effective long range accuracy,
d Hand-carried equipment, including incapacitating agents and explosives for use as tools of entry or for otherwise destroying reactor, facility, transporter, or container integrity or features of the safeguards system, and
e A four-wheel drive land vehicle used for transporting personnel and their hand-carried equipment to the proximity of vital areas, and

An internal threat of an insider, including an employee (in any position), and
A four-wheel drive land vehicle bomb.

The preceding threat definition is an illustration of specific threat information that the system engineer can use to design the system. For example, perimeter fences, barriers and gates must be capable of preventing penetration by a four wheel drive vehicle. The response force must be equipped and trained to intercept and neutralize adversaries carrying sophisticated weapons. Policies and procedures must be in place to deal with insider threats, and so on. The point is that from a systems engineering standpoint, the threat definition must contain information that the system engineer can act on. In this case, a sophisticated and dangerous adversary necessitates the development of a sophisticated (and expensive) security system. In other applications, less sophisticated threats will require less expensive systems to overcome. Therefore, effective use of limited resources for security requires identification of the characteristics of the DBT.

Security system design

Security systems consist of detection, delay and response elements and subsystems. These components are configured to protect an asset by preventing an adversary from accomplishing their goal. For the security system to function effectively the components must be configured and integrated into a complex global system based on the principles of systems engineering. This is the security system design effort – the proposed solution to the problem defined by the determination of objectives.

As with all complex systems, the performance of a security system depends only indirectly on the human and technological components and subsystems that make up the global system. The performance primarily depends on how these components are integrated together into a global system. Consequently, it is important to establish the 'transfer function' that produces the desired input/output relation for the system illustrated in Figure 4.1 so that the available components may be configured correctly. In this case, the input to the system is an attack by an adversary on an asset, and the desired output is an intact asset and a defeated adversary.

Any attack on an asset by an adversary requires a certain amount of time. This time consists of overcoming obstacles and completing tasks until the adversary completes their mission. This time sequence is referred to as the adversary timeline. After an attack is detected, a system response is initiated that seeks to prevent the adversary from completing their task. Similar to the adversary, the response requires time to intercept and neutralize the adversary. This time sequence is the response timeline. As the adversary approaches their goal, the adversary timeline decreases, and the available time for successful response likewise decreases. By this model, an attack on an asset may be described as a race between the adversary and the response effort, with the adversary winning the race if their task is accomplished before the response is complete.

In many applications, such as physical security, the response effort involves a human response force. On the other hand, in applications such as cyber security, the response may be semi-automated. However, in each case, the fundamental problem is similar – the response effort must intercept and neutralize the adversary before their task is complete. Obviously, for the response to be successful, the response timeline must be shorter than the adversary timeline. This brings up the fundamental principle of security system design – the response timeline cannot begin until an attack has been detected. Attempting to lengthen an adversary timeline by placing delay elements outside of detection elements does not improve the performance of the system since the only times that matter in the 'race' are the required response time in comparison to the remaining adversary time once detection occurs.

Based on this principle, the probability of a successful response to an attack is maximized if a security system is configured with detection components around the perimeter (physical or virtual), and delay increasing as the asset is approached. To effectively design the system, performance characteristics of these elements need to be quantified in the context of the DBT.

Detection element design characteristics

Detection is the discovery of an attack by a malevolent adversary. While simple human observation may serve as the sole detection element, in most cases this observation is enhanced through the application of subsystems and technologies designed to provide a warning, or alarm, to alert the security system of a possible attack. However, detection is not complete at the observation of an alarm. The warning must then be assessed to determine the validity of the alarm, and detection is complete when the validity of the alarm has been assessed and verified

(Garcia, 2001). Quantification of the system performance, which is necessary for evaluation of proposed designs, requires the performance of the detection system be likewise quantified.

In this section, intrusion detection differs from entry control in the sense that entry control is designed to prevent unauthorized access to assets along paths normally utilized by authorized personnel, while intrusion detection seeks to identify attempts at access to assets along paths that are not normally used. In this context, a perimeter detection system in a physical security system is an example of an intrusion detection system, while a username and password on a network is an example of entry control. Adversaries may seek access to assets by defeating either of these subsystems. However, since the functions of these systems differ, the necessary design parameters for each subsystem differ as well.

Intrusion detection elements are characterized by the Probability of Detection, P_D, the Nuisance Alarm Rate (NAR), and the Vulnerability to Defeat. The probability of detection at any layer is defined as the probability that an attack will be successfully detected and assessed. Therefore, P_D is the product of the probability of an alarm and the probability of successful assessment of that alarm. (It is important to understand this distinction, since data is published and systems are often marketed claiming a certain P_D, when in reality they are reporting the probability of an alarm.) The NAR is the frequency of alarms that are not due to attacks. From the standpoint of system design, the goal is to maximize the probability of detection, while minimizing the NAR. The vulnerability to defeat refers to weaknesses in the technology that may be exploited by a skilled adversary. Both the vulnerability to defeat and the probability of detection are highly dependent on the skill of an adversary and the attack scenario, while NAR depends primarily on the system technology and tuning, and on the installation environment. Technologies used in intrusion detection subsystems differ depending on the type of security. Details of intrusion detection technologies and subsystems for physical security and similar applications may be found in Garcia, 2001; DARPA, 1997 and Barnard, 1988. Intrusion detection in cyber-systems is discussed in Escamilla, 1998.

As mentioned, the probability of detection is a parameter that is dependent on the adversary skill and the attack scenario. While the level of skill necessary to defeat a detection technology varies, all technologies do have certain vulnerabilities to defeat that an adversary may seek to exploit. As an example of scenario dependence, in physical security the performance of some technologies may degrade during inclement weather. Consequently, the system must be engineered in the context of its performance against the DBT, as well as all attack scenarios that may be utilized. Vulnerabilities of particular technologies may be minimized by utilizing a design principle known as 'protection in depth.' Protection in depth means that to accomplish a goal, the adversary must defeat layers of detection and delay devices in series. This is especially effective if different technologies, requiring different skills and methods to defeat, are utilized at each layer (Garcia, 2001).

Entry control, designed to prevent unauthorized access to assets along paths normally utilized by authorized personnel, also may include delay. Properly designed and operated entry control systems are especially effective in dealing with many insider threats. In physical security applications, these systems also serve the function of contraband detection.

From an engineering design perspective, the relevant performance measures for an entry control system are throughput and error rate. The throughput is the time it takes for an authorized person to pass through the entry control system. Possible errors include false rejection (rejection of an authorized user) and false acceptance (admission of an unauthorized user.) These parameters can be used to design the system, based on the needed throughput, and to predict its performance, based on the error rates. Details of entry control technologies and subsystems for physical security and similar applications may be found in Garcia, 2001 and DARPA, 1997. Entry control in cyber-systems is discussed in Anderson, 2001.

Delay element design characteristics

The basic design parameter for the delay subsystem is that of delay time, while constraints that guide the design include the principles of balanced protection and protection in depth. These will be briefly clarified below. Detailed explanations of these principles can be found in Garcia, 2001.

Delay mechanisms can be passive or active. Examples of passive delay mechanisms in physical security include barriers, locks, and distance, while in cyber-security this may involve password protection, or other authentication that adversaries may try to overcome through tactics such as a dictionary attack (Anderson, 2001). Active delay elements are those that are activated by the attack, such as active barriers, and redirection. From the system engineering perspective, the measure of delay effectiveness is the time it takes the adversary to pass through a delay element. The delay time depends on the capabilities and tactics of the adversary, and must be estimated based on the DBT. The basic design criteria for delay components is that for a system to be successful, delay time after detection must be long enough to allow a successful response. Consequently, design of delay elements must proceed in parallel with that of the detection and response elements.

In general, the delay time between the adversary and the asset will not be the same along all possible paths. However, system effectiveness will not be improved if delay is concentrated along a few obvious routes, but a 'back door' is left open. Consequently, another design constraint for the delay elements, known as the principle of balanced protection, is that all paths to the target be equally difficult. In practice, this may be difficult to achieve to a high degree. On the other hand, applying this constraint as part of the design process ensures that no paths are left open, and guides decisions regarding expenditures on delay elements.

A final constraint that guides design decisions on delay components is the principle of protection in depth discussed earlier. This principle states that the tactics and skills necessary to overcome delay elements at each protection layer should differ, so that adversaries must increase their sophistication and arsenal to effectively overcome the delay element series.

Response element design characteristics

The response elements of the security system consist of actions taken to prevent the adversaries from accomplishing their goals. In general, response actions may be categorized as timely response, recovery response, or indirect response. Timely response refers to systems in which the response elements are designed to intercept and neutralize the attackers. Recovery response, logically utilized for theft of lower consequence of loss assets, are systems, such as video surveillance, which aid in the recovery of stolen items. Indirect response is that which occurs when adversaries accomplish all of their goals, but are ultimately captured and removed from society so that they can't repeat their actions. Clearly, not all assets require a timely response. However, in this chapter, the engineering requirements for security systems based on timely response are discussed as an illustrative example of the security system engineering process. If timely response is not justified, engineering requirements will change appropriately.

The basic design parameter for response systems is the response time, which is the time between notification of an attack, and the interception of the adversary. The necessary response time for system success is driven by the remaining adversary time, which decreases if the adversary evades detection at any protection layer. Improvements in system performance achieved if response time is decreased are similar to the improvements achieved by additional delay. This principle may be used as a constraint to guide expenditures during the design process. Specifically, is it more cost effective to increase delay times or reduce response times?

Response element characteristics differ substantially between physical and cyber security. In physical security applications, response usually involves a response force, which deploys and seeks to intercept and neutralize the adversary. The response force may be stationed on-site, or local law enforcement may be utilized. The type of response necessary to neutralize the adversary after a successful task interruption depends on the motivations and capabilities of the attacker, and in some cases, a simple command is all that is needed. In this case, if the adversary is interrupted, the probability of neutralization is $P_N=1$, and no special weapons or tactics are required. On the other hand, if the adversary is prepared to use force, the response team must be prepared to react appropriately. Therefore, a response design constraint is that the response force be capable of neutralizing the DBT. Expertise in neutralization analysis is a specialty, and, if the DBT capabilities are high and consequence of loss of the asset is significant, such an expert should be added to the security design team. (The cost of a military style on-site response team is rather staggering. This can only be justified for high value assets.)

In cyber-security applications attacks through networks can occur from almost anywhere in the world, and response to these attacks typically does not involve direct confrontation of the adversary (see Chapter 15). However, the basic principles of security system design continue to apply – after an attack is detected, the response time must be less than the remaining adversary time for system success. Response to attacks on information security systems is discussed in Escamilla (1998).

Security system analysis

The final component of a scientific problem solving methodology is that of evaluation and analysis. As discussed, a security system is a probabilistic system – it has a certain probability of success. As a consequence, measures of system performance are based on statistical and probabilistic variables. The probability of interruption, P_I, is defined as the probability that an adversary will be interrupted before completion of their task. Against certain threats, interruption is all that is required for success, while in some cases the response must not only interrupt the adversary, but neutralize them as well. In any such conflict, the response force will have a certain probability of success, quantified by the probability of neutralization, P_N. In this case, the system is only successful if the adversary is interrupted and neutralized by the response force, and the probability of success is given by the product $P_I P_N$. Therefore, analysis of security systems seeks to predict the performance of an existing or proposed system through the determination of P_I and, if necessary, P_N. This is accomplished by application of standard mathematical and statistical principles.

As was discussed earlier, it is easier to make rapid progress in understanding when problems are deterministic in nature, and more difficult as they become probabilistic. From the systems engineering viewpoint, it is advantageous to develop and utilize analysis tools that are as deterministic as possible. However, the cost of a sophisticated, rigorous quantitative analysis can only be justified for very high consequence targets, and qualitative analyses are used for lower value assets. When qualitative methods are utilized, it is important that the analyses incorporate a consistent enumeration of the subjective evaluations. For example, following Garcia (2001), when a verbal description of a probability is determined to be 'very low' it may be assigned a probability of 0.1, and so on. This is necessary so that meaningful comparisons of different systems and scenarios can be made. Quantitative and qualitative procedures utilized for security system analyses are discussed and contrasted in detail in Garcia (2001).

There are several specific types of analyses that may be used in the design and performance evaluation of security systems. These include path analysis, scenario analysis, neutralization analysis, and risk and vulnerability analysis. Risk and vulnerability analysis is discussed elsewhere (see Chapter 22). While in depth discussions of the other techniques are beyond the scope of this chapter, brief descriptions are given below.

Path analysis refers to the evaluation of possible adversary paths to an asset. A path is a sequence of actions that an adversary must take to complete their goals. This may be an actual path, in the case of physical security, or a virtual path in the case of cyber-security. The goal of the analysis is to identify the weak paths and vulnerabilities. The output of a path analysis is the probability of interruption, P_I. Readers are referred to Garcia (2001) for detailed information concerning path analysis, including access to the EASI (Estimate of Adversary Sequence

Interruption) computer code developed at Sandia National Laboratories (Chapman and Harlon, 1985).

In physical security, neutralization analysis is an analysis of force-on-force action between the response force and the attackers. Neutralization is successful if the response force is able to subdue the adversaries. In cyber-security, this concept is slightly more abstract in the sense that the adversary does not typically pose a physical threat. In this case, neutralization is successful if, after detection of an attack, the system operators, serving as the response force, are able to prevent the adversary from continuing the attack. The quantitative prediction of the outcome of force-on-force action has been a subject of intense study, and has led to the development of highly capable tools such as the Joint Combat and Tactical Simulation code (JCATS) developed at Lawrence Livermore laboratories. On the other hand, in less critical applications, a qualitative analysis is more appropriate, in which qualified experts identify the needed equipment and training necessary for successful neutralization based on the DBT description.

Scenario analysis is really the heart of the analysis procedures, and results in a comprehensive evaluation of a security system. In this analysis, different scenarios are proposed, and the performance of the security system is evaluated in light of these scenarios using path analysis and, if necessary, neutralization analysis. For example, in a physical security application, there is a possibility that the site may be attacked during inclement weather, in which the performance of the detection subsystems will be degraded. Another scenario might be an initial direct attack on the response force, followed by an attack on the asset. A large number of reasonable scenarios can be envisioned and analysed in a short time if analysis procedures (either qualitative or quantitative) are available for path and neutralization analyses. This is particularly useful in evaluating the effectiveness of an existing system against an evolving DBT.

Finally, it is worthwhile to emphasize once more that the principles of systems engineering require that the analysis step be integrated into the process. In many cases, the cost of some of the sophisticated quantitative analyses referred to in this section may not be justified. If this is the case, less expensive qualitative analyses techniques, such as described in Garcia (2001) can be utilized. However, from the engineering viewpoint, no system design is complete until analysis indicates that the objectives have been met.

Summary

The goal of this chapter was to explain the basic principles of systems engineering, and to illustrate how these principles may be applied to the problem of security system design. These principles are essentially a statement of the scientific method: 1) define the problem, 2) solve the problem, and 3) check the solution. In terms of security systems, these steps correspond to the determination of objectives, the security system design, and the analysis of the security system. While details differ for each application, these principles are equally valid for the engineering of all types of security systems. The discussion of these primary engineering tasks has been presented in a linear fashion, and there is a temptation to resort to a design 'checklist,' similar to that which a mechanical engineer might use to specify a machine component. In the engineering of complex systems, however, things are not this simple because the development and management of these systems is not a linear process, but rather one of continuous feedback, in which the processes are highly interdependent, with many of the processes occurring in parallel. A security problem is defined, a solution is proposed, the solution is analysed, and the process continues until analysis demonstrates that the objectives have been met. In the security field threats continually evolve, and new scenarios emerge. A well engineered system can be continuously evaluated against these scenarios, and redesigned and upgraded as necessary.

Key readings

An excellent source that provides details of the Security System Engineering Design Process is given by Garcia (2001) The Design and Evaluation of Physical Protection Systems, Butterworth/Heinemann. Systems Engineering is a highly developed and mature field, and there are many excellent references available. The text by Sage and Armstrong (2000), Introduction to Systems Engineering, Wiley, provides an excellent introduction to the field in the first chapter, while the text by Eisner (1997) Essentials of Project and Systems Engineering Management, Wiley, discusses management aspects of complex system development. A systematic approach to Risk Management which utilizes a 'risk totem pole' approach that can be adapted to security applications is given by Grose, V.L. (1987) Managing Risk: Systematic Loss Prevention for Executives, Prentice Hall. Readers interested in critical asset identification through analytical techniques, including fault tree analysis, are referred to Kumamoto and Henley (1996), Probabilistic Risk Assessment and Management for Engineers and Scientists, IEEE press. Techniques for quantification of uncertainty are developed and discussed in Coleman and Steele (1989) Experimentation and Uncertainty Analysis for Engineers, Wiley. Using intrusion detection technology as an example, a presentation of the type of data that is particularly useful for security systems engineering can be found in the Defense Advanced Research Projects Agency (DARPA) Perimeter Security Sensor Technologies Handbook (1997), www. nlectc.org/perimetr/full2.htm.

References

Adamsen, P. (2000) *A Framework for Complex System Development*, London: CRC Press.

Anderson, R. (2001) *Security Engineering: A Guide to Building Dependable Distributed Systems*, New York: Wiley.

Barnard, R. (1988) *Intrusion Detection Systems*, 2nd edn, Stoneham, MA: Butterworth Publishers.

Blanchard, B. and Fabrycky, W. (1998) *Systems Engineering and Analysis*, 3rd edn, Upper Saddle River, NJ: Prentice Hall.

Chapman, L.D. and Harlon, C.P. (1985) EASI, Estimate of Adversary Sequence Interruption on an IBM PC, SAND Report 851105.

Coleman, H. and Steele, W.G. (1989) *Experimentation and Uncertainty Analysis for Engineers*, New York: Wiley.

Defense Advanced Research Projects Agency (DARPA) (1997) Perimeter Security Sensor Technologies Handbook, www. nlectc.org/perimetr/full2.htm, last accessed November 2004.

Department of Homeland Security Advisory System, August 1, 2004, HS Advisory System Increased to ORANGE for Financial Institutions in Specific Geographical Areas, http://www.dhs.gov/interweb/assetlibrary/IAIP_AdvisoryOrangeFinancialInst_080104.pdf, last accessed February 2005.

Eisner, H. (1997) *Essentials of Project and Systems Engineering Management*, New York: Wiley.

Escamilla, T. (1998) *Intrusion Detection: Network Security Beyond the Firewall*, New York: Wiley.

Figliola, R. and Beasley, D. (1995) *Theory and Design for Mechanical Measurements*, 2nd edn, New York: Wiley.

Garcia, M.L. (2001) *The Design and Evaluation of Physical Security Systems*, Boston, MA: Butterworth/Heinemann.

Gauch, H. (2003) *Scientific Method in Practice*, Cambridge: Cambridge Press.

Grady, J. (1994) *System Integration*, London: CRC Press.

Grose, V. (1987) *Systematic Loss Prevention for Executives*, Upper Saddle River, NJ: Prentice Hall.

Haik, Y. (2003) *Engineering Design Process*, Pacific Grove, CA: Thomson-Engineering.

Kossiakoff, A. and Sweet, W. (2003) *Systems Engineering: Principles and Practice*, Hoboken, NJ: Wiley.

Kumamoto, H. and Henley, E. (1996) *Probabilistic Risk Assessment and Management for Engineers and Scientists*, 2nd edn, Piscataway, NJ: IEEE Press.

National Institute of Justice Report NCJ 195171 (2002) A Method to Assess the Vulnerability of U.S. Chemical Facilities. Can be accessed at: www.ncjrs.org/pdffiles1/ nij/195171.pdf, last accessed November 2004.

NRC Regulations Title 10, part 73, Physical protection of plants and materials, www.nrc.gov/reading-rm/doc-collections/cfr/part073/part073-0001.html, last accessed November 2004.

Sage, A. and Armstrong, J. (2000) *Introduction to Systems Engineering*, New York: Wiley.

Sandia National Labs (2003) Water Infrastructure and Risk Assessment, can be accessed at: www.sandia.gov/water/FactSheets/WIFS_RAnew.pdf, last accessed November 2004.

Waller, R. and Covello, V. (eds) (1984) *Low-Probability High-Consequence Risk Analysis: Issues, Methods, and Case Studies*, New York: Plenum Press.

5

Contributions of Environmental Studies to Security

Richard H. Schneider

Introduction

Chapter overview

This chapter identifies significant contributions that *environmental studies* have made and continue to make to security scholarship and practice. To do so, we define the terms *environment* and *security* and briefly review the history of connections between them using evidence from early human settlement planning and design as well as modern examples. We examine the linkage of industrialization, urbanization and the evolution of security concerns and practices, including early theories linking social and physical environmental influences to criminal behavior. Place-based theories of criminal behavior are discussed as outgrowths of these foundations, including defensible space, crime prevention through environmental design, situational criminology and environmental criminology. Other concepts with security implications such as space syntax, new urbanism, rational choice, routine activity and pattern theory are also reviewed. We conclude the chapter by looking at future challenges to security-environment study and practice that are related to technologies used to combat crime and terrorism such as geographic information systems (GIS), global position radio-navigation systems (GPS) and closed circuit television (CCTV).

We make no claim that this is an exhaustive discussion of the contributions of environmental studies to security, which entail large, diverse and rapidly growing fields of knowledge and practice. The aim of this chapter is to point to some of the notable research contributions that have been made over the years. That some work is not mentioned does not mean it is not significant, but rather a function of limits to time and space. The reader is directed to other chapters in this Handbook to fill in those gaps.

Definitions and distinctions

Anthropologist/architect Amos Rapoport (1977) reviewed competing definitions of the term environment and concluded they had two common concepts: all identified multiple elements – social, cultural and physical – and all suggested a linkage among alterations in physical elements and changes in the other elements. He concluded that, 'The environment is a series of relation-ships among elements and people and these relationships are orderly – they have pattern.' (p. 9). In seeking to describe a subset of those patterns, this chapter focuses on studies that primarily speak to the impacts that social and physical environmental issues have had on human behavior relative to secu-rity. We do not use the term environment in the ecological sense, or relative to social movements that target environmental decline, hazards or to relation-ships between environmental issues and social justice although we acknow-ledge that these are important subjects. They are outside the range of present concentration.

Rather, the focus centers on the influence that environmental factors such as land form and topography, industrialization, place and space design, community layout and plans, building and store configuration, and climatic variation (to name but a few) have had on the evolution of modern security planning and practice. A growing number of disciplines – anthropology, architecture, business and marketing, criminology, geography, psychology and social psychology, soci-ology and urban planning – have produced research and practice strategies that connect these topics either directly or indirectly with security.

Security is also a term with a vast and growing array of modifiers, especially in recent years where terrorist threats around the world have greatly expanded its use in everyday life. It has been linked to everything from agriculture to zoonotic diseases (those that can be transmitted from animal to humans). We define *security* here to mean 'the condition of being protected from or not exposed to danger; safety.' (Oxford English Dictionary, 1982: 2705) In this context we refer to physical security as distinct from economic or psycholo-gical security, although they are ultimately interrelated. We further distinguish security from *life safety* issues, which are the subject of planning and building codes, regulations and standards that protect against unintentional acts and natural calamities such as flood, fire, storms, and earthquakes. Even though such codes relate to the *effects* of terrorist acts, such as the possibility of pro-gressive collapse or fires resulting from bomb blasts in high rise buildings (DiMaggio, 2004), we are primarily concerned with environment and security relationships that are associated with the *causes of* criminal acts – intentional human behavior including terrorism.

As suggested above, an array of disciplines has contributed studies and research conclusions to the linkage of environment and security issues. In many cases, contributions span disciplines such that it is unproductive to apportion them to distinctive fields of study. Typical of this heterogeneity is the Environmental Design Research Association (EDRA), whose membership spans many fields and which has contributed many modern security-related studies through its journal, *Environment and Behavior*, published since the 1960s. History that is unwritten but nevertheless etched in the landscape of human evolution also tells of the long connection between the shape and composition of the natural and man-built environment and security, and we turn to that as the context in which to set our discussion.

Historical roots of the connection between environment and security

Throughout history, human beings have consciously altered their physical environment in order to protect themselves, their belongings, and their civilizations. As McCrie suggests in this volume relative to the history of security, the development of security measures parallels the history of humankind's competition for scarce resources. Security decisions were fundamental *survival* strategies (Maslow, 1968) that are just as relevant today as they were in ancient times and there is much to be learned from both their substance and durability. Many environmental security strategies – such as those related to site design and selection, hardening targets, layering defenses, access control, protection of territorial integrity and surveillance – are intuitive and have been 'rediscovered' by successive generations. Indeed, these strategies are part and parcel of modern anti-terrorism security planning, a topic we shall return to at the conclusion of this chapter. It is only relatively recently, however, that scientific study has organized them into relatively discrete crime prevention and security theories and has provided empirical data to argue (or refute) their cases.

Site selection and layered defenses

One of our species' earliest and most intuitive defensive strategies was to live in areas that provided protective cover as well as easy surveillance and defense. Archeological records of European and Asian cave dwellings indicate that early inhabitants chose sites with protective, border-defined topography, such as at mountain bases or rivers' edges. Defensibility was not the only reason for such choices; other explanations included access to resources including fertile soils and potable water, transportation access, linkage to other settlements, as well as religious and spiritual reasons (Mumford, 1961). Nevertheless, security was a primary concern since once established, places needed to be defensible if their inhabitants were to survive. As these sites developed into communities they often evolved layered security strategies consisting of rings of defensive design elements that might incorporate the backs of houses, rammed-earth walls and natural land features. Masonry castles, citadels and spiritual centers developed over long time periods and were the most protected locations. Medieval castles sheltered the king and his court in the castle keep, the last and best defended refuge for the most valuable community assets (Kenyon, 1990).

Layered defense planning remain fundamental principles of security at community, neighborhood, site and building levels. A recent publication by the Federal Emergency Management Agency (FEMA), now part of the US Department of Homeland Security, predicates its anti-terrorist building site and layout design guidance on medieval castle design models, depicted complete with outer and inner gates, wards, and landscape features. The guide notes that '... the objective of layers of defense is to create succeeding more difficult layers of security to penetrate, provide additional warning and response time, and allow building occupants to move into defensive positions or designated Safe Haven Protection.' (Kennett, 2004: 37) This basic military strategy is exemplified in a wide range of civilian applications, evident in the growing gated community enclaves presently being built in the United States (Blakely and Snyder, 1999). It is also found in advice given by retail security and loss prevention researchers to store owners/managers as a means to protect stock against shoplifters (Moussatche *et al.*, 2004). For example, modern 'store-within-a-store' layouts offer not only merchandising benefits, but also the opportunity to layer design and guardianship strategies around especially desirable or 'hot' items.

Renaissance wall systems and access control

During the Renaissance, many European cities developed elaborate perimeter edges that far surpassed the curtain walls of the medieval castle and city. These expensive wall systems – designed largely to resist the onslaught of new gunpowder-based technologies – also served a variety of important social, political, economic and general security functions (Kostof, 1991, 1992). They were, as McRie points out in this volume, fundamental organizing elements for emerging cities. Walls controlled access to markets and to city life (civilization) by virtue of their intimidating physical bulk which thrust bastions outwards like thorns into the surrounding landscape and used gates as valves augmented by watchful guards. Together, these elements comprised a system of natural (design-based), mechanical and organized (human) access control principles that are directly analogous to those embodied in modern crime prevention strategies such as defensible space and crime prevention through environmental design, or CPTED. We shall return to defensible space and CPTED in the discussion of modern security theory, below.

In some cases the walls of Renaissance cities deterred assault by marauding or invading armies: however, in the face of protracted siege they were almost always defeated, despite their elaborate design. One well-documented lesson was that while access control devices can *deter* and *delay* attack, they generally cannot deny it altogether. Determined, motivated offenders will ultimately evade even the best access control. In the same way, modern criminals and terrorists, like bandits of old, are highly adaptive and learn ways to circumvent even the best environmental security devices and systems. Because of this, security specialists are increasingly cautioned to be one step ahead – to 'think thief' or, in the modern case, to 'think terrorist' wherever feasible (Ekblom, 1997; Design Council, 2003). Experience and research argue that confidence in security design and technology must be tempered by continuous observation and systems evaluation, bearing in mind that criminals throughout history have continuously adapted to security defenses.

Environmental cues and messages in security design

Access control devices such as walls can serve symbolic as well as practical purposes. In so doing they convey 'environmental cues' – messages derived from the design and management of the physical environment – that are interpreted variably by people. For example, picket fences mark boundaries and present psychological barriers but do not otherwise control access (the police call them 'recreational height' fences). While some studies have suggested that most burglars' decisions are primarily motivated by beliefs about the availability of valuable household goods and the need for cash, environmental factors and cues in terms of escape routes and surveillance opportunities were nevertheless factors that others strongly considered (Hearnden and Magill, 2002). Even mere images can send environmental cues such as where burglars and police interpret the defensibility of types of housing designs based on photographs. (Cozens *et al.*, 2001). Theory and supporting evidence argues that criminals notice these messages and the ways in which they are read can impact a variety of goals, including security (Wilson and Kelling, 1982; Pascoe, 1993; Clarke, 1997; Wright and Decker, 1997; Poyner, 1998). Some designers and researchers have paid particular attention to social, psychological and political messages that access control devices such as gates, barricades and walls present. (Marcuse, 1997; Blakely and Snyder, 1999; Zelinka and Brennan, 2001). The public's *perceptions* of safety and risk in places occasioned by overt security strategies may negatively impact overall community goals relative to the notion of *civitas*, defined as a communal commitment to civic and public life. Blakely and Snyder make the case that that the growth of gated communities in the United States, predicated at least in part on security goals, is emblematic of deeper societal divisions and which tend to splinter the communal fabric – the civitas – of cities and towns. This includes heightening fears that do not necessarily correspond to actual security risks or vulnerabilities (Wilson-Doenges, 2000).

Changing technology and industrialization

Throughout history, changing technology has been a potent force related to both environmental and security concerns. The industrialization of Western Europe and the United States on the heels of Watt's steam engines in the 1780s illustrates the linkage between technological advance, environmental change and security. Following Watt and other inventors, advances in agricultural technology made farms more efficient, transformed cottage industries into large-scale factory production, and hastened the growth of low cost rail and steamboat transportation (Levy, 2002).

The result combined to both force and attract large numbers of rural people to cities in Britain and the United States, although industrial innovation also affected Germany and France, especially Berlin and Paris. Housing supply, sanitary facilities and social service could not match needs and consequently cities in 19th century Britain and America became crowded with poor, low-skilled workers. (Booth, 1888) Hall has characterized London, Paris, Berlin and New York collectively as 'The City of Dreadful Night' after a poem of the same name. (Hall, 1988) By the 1890's conditions in New York and London were so odious that state and national commissions had been convened to assess the problems and recommend solutions. One of them, the New York State Tenement House Commission concluded:

> The tenement districts of New York are places in which thousands of people are living in the smallest place in which it is possible for human beings to exist – crowded together in dark, ill-ventilated rooms, in many of which the sunlight never enters and in most of which fresh air is unknown. They are centers of disease, poverty, vice, and crime, where it is a marvel, not that some children grow up to be thieves, drunkards and prostitutes, but that so many should ever grow up to be decent and self-respecting. (DeForest and Veiller, 1903: 10)

There are fewer more stark linkages between environmental conditions and criminal behavior then those that flow from this era. The populist idea that large cities were dangerous and insecure places, which was part of American folklore at least since Jefferson declared them to be 'penitential to the morals, the health, and the liberties of man', (Clapp, 1984: 129) was reinforced a hundredfold by the reality and myths emanating from the urban places of the era. Response from the budding security community varied and ranged from the development of organized police forces in Britain and the United States (see McCrie's discussion of the evolution of policing in this volume), to development of theories designed to account for the origins of criminal behavior.

Some of these echoed earlier 'classical' school theorists such as Beccaria (1764) who argued that crime was the result of individuals' rational choice and maximized self-interest and could best be deterred by swift and certain punishment. Security policy approaches, especially those advocated by conservatives, can be linked to Beccaria's theory. These concepts resonate with modern routine activity and rational choice theory (Cohen and Felson, 1979; Cornish and Clarke, 1985, 2003), discussed below. Others searched for biological explanations of crime and insecurity. Lombroso (1911) suggested that genetic and evolutionary differences between people accounted for criminal behavior and that physical traits could be used to distinguish 'born criminals' from law-abiding citizens. While discredited, his approaches nevertheless helped establish the 'positivist' school of criminology, which attempted to establish the causes of crime through observation and testing.

Connecting criminal behavior with social and economic environments

By the turn of the 19th century, urban changes occasioned largely by the forces let loose by the industrial revolution led researchers to search for explanations of how external forces – environmental factors outside individuals – led people to become criminals. Chicago proved to be a natural laboratory for such work by virtue of its dramatic growth and industrialization. Sociologists influenced by the University of Chicago hypothesized relationships between city locations and delinquency rates, suggesting ultimately that a variety of social and economic conditions (transient and heterogeneous populations, poverty, rapid population growth and fractured families) caused social disorganization, the predicate of higher crime and delinquency rates.

Building on Burgess's urban zone development concepts (1925), Shaw and MacKay (1942) argued that the disorganized social environment in neighborhoods contributed to development of delinquency and its persistence across generations. Others elaborated on this foundation relative to social learning theory (Sutherland, 1939; Akers, 1985) and control and containment concepts (Reckless, 1961; Hirschi, 1969). A glue binding all the above together is the assumption that offenders' *sociological* and *economic* environments were at fault and required treatment, insomuch as the 'root causes' of crime were seen to stem from inadequacies there. These emphases on social factors as the genesis of criminal and delinquent behavior formed the bases of public security policy in the United States for decades. The resulting public policies dictated crime prevention aimed primarily at the amelioration of the basic social and economic problems that gave rise to criminal behavior. As Schneider and Kitchen (2002) note, 'Although its adherents used such spatial and ecological terms as city "sectors, rings and zones" it is clear that this school of thought was concerned with the social and economic fabric of crime rather than its physical environment'(p. 12).

Connecting behavior with physical environments

Theories supporting connections between human behavior and the physical environment began to emerge in the 1940s and 50s based on earlier stimulus/response studies in psychology, on ongoing sociological research on the nature of deviancy and delinquent behavior as described above and on growing concerns relative to what Sommer (1983) has termed 'social design,' a philosophy seeking to 'humanize the process by which buildings, neighborhoods and cities were planned.' (p. 6) By the 1960s and early 1970s a few social and behavioral scientists, designers and criminologists expressed interest in the relationships between social conditions and community characteristics with a special focus on connections between crime and the physical environment. Some, such as Jeffrey (1971) went so far as to argue that criminal behavior could be understood as a function of environmental learning, relatively independent from social conditions.

This view, which was radical in its time, contended that elements of the physical environment were conducive to some types of criminal behavior. The basic premise was that the environment could be more significant to the *immediate* decision to commit a crime than underlying social or economic factors that nevertheless represented fundamental *causes* of crime and delinquency. Prior to this, criminal behavior was considered to be almost entirely captive to the external social and economic environments, to genetic dysfunction, moral imperfection or to psychological impulses driving the human psyche. Subsequent behavioral science research and theory supported the notion that aspects of the physical environment could indeed be 'criminogenic', or crime-causing. Elizabeth Wood's study of public housing projects in Chicago in the 1950s, Edward Hall's work (1966) on personal space, and Jane Jacobs' writings (1961) on the importance of vibrant street life and 'eyes on the street' as a deterrent to crime, came to influence some urban designers, environmental psychologists and criminologists who saw increasingly direct relationships between the physical environment and criminal behavior. Emerging from this heterogeneous background was a family of place-based crime prevention theories and associated security strategies that are in common use today.

Modern theory and practice

Virtually all modern place-based crime prevention theory and applications – defensible space, CPTED, situational crime prevention, and environmental criminology – are related to the historical antecedents discussed above. Moreover, although each evolved from different sources and influences, they are interconnected in their application in 'real-life' security applications.

Defensible space

The theory of defensible space originates from architect Oscar Newman's critical observations of public housing projects in St. Louis and New York City (1973) and the behaviors he associated with residents and visitors based on specific design elements. Newman wondered why housing projects that were adjacent to each other and possessed similar population characteristics had such varying degrees of criminality associated with them. He suspected that the discrepancy was caused by design differences and identified several design elements as the main culprits. Among these were:

– *Territoriality*: The organization, definition, and design of spaces and places such that residents feel responsibility, defensiveness, and control toward the space, whether they own it or not.
– *Natural surveillance*: The '...capacity of the physical environment to provide surveillance opportunities for residents and their agents' (1973: 78). For example, this means the design and placement of windows and building entrances to maximize the abilities of residents and other 'legitimate' users to see interior and exterior spaces. In practice, natural surveillance can be augmented by electronic devices and facilitated by appropriate lighting, discussed below.
– *Boundary definition:* Closely related to territoriality, this is the dividing and marking of spaces to clearly identify the gradations between public and private places. It may involve implementation of real and symbolic barriers as *access control* between places, aimed especially at blocking offenders.

Territoriality

Territoriality, one of the primary concepts of defensible space, applies not only to places and spaces that people own, but also to places that they may only rent or occupy temporarily. Even in transient environmental settings such as the beach, people may become temporarily territorial about their small patch of sand, protecting and defending that space against intruders. Though first applied to residential settings, territoriality has been useful in security planning for institutional and retail environments such as schools and stores. In its most controversial adaptation, defensible space strategies have been extended to community street layouts to restrict access and thereby reduce neighborhood 'permeability'. It is asserted that design elements – including the use of real and symbolic space markers and boundaries – as well as the design process itself (especially when it involves users as participants) can help make legitimate users feel and act protectively about space or items within it and help deter misbehavior and crime. (Newman, 1973, 1981, 1995)

One example of using territoriality as a crime and disorder reduction strategy comes from modern school security design practice in the United States where studies have identified parking lots as significant crime venues, especially prone to fighting and assaults (FDOE, 2003). A solution has been for some school administrators to assign numbered spaces and to allow students to personalize them through artwork. Although empirical studies of the effects are not completed, the strategy anticipates reduced confrontations over otherwise ambiguous areas in locales that traditionally have low levels of guardianship. Obviously, management practices can reinforce territorial feelings and behavior and some of these can help extend the effects of good defensive design and planning beyond the immediate target environment into the community itself. This is especially evident when there is a 'diffusion of benefits' – whereby positive effects (e.g. less crime) extend beyond the initial implementation site to other, possibly adjacent areas (Clarke and Weisburd, 1994).

Natural surveillance

Natural surveillance is facilitated by building and site planning, design and maintenance that permits space users, including owners, renters, passersby, and employees (who are not normally tasked with guardianship responsibilities) to easily see what is transpiring within their physical domain. As such, it incorporates the notion of site transparency and is augmented by appropriate site, street and interior lighting, building layout and orientation relative to adjacent structures, and landscape maintenance. As with all security design and planning, management is a vital component and bad practices can defeat good design, such as when policies permit users to cover windows with posters and advertisements, a common practice in convenience stores (Hunter and Jeffrey, 1992) and at schools (FDOE). Beside natural surveillance, Crowe (2000) has divided surveillance into two additional categories – organized and mechanical.

Organized surveillance is exemplified by employees in commercial establishments such as clerks or counter staff who are trained to watch for shoplifters, by the normal duties of police, private security forces and some military personnel, and by motivated citizens who form street crime fighting groups. In this context, organized surveillance is also described as *formal* surveillance. Clarke (1997) reports a range of empirical studies supporting the use of organized surveillance to reduce crime and misbehavior. These include bike patrols in Vancouver, tram and train security officers in the Netherlands, and daily inventory counting of high risk items by security staff in retail stores as effective techniques to reduce crime and vandalism in specific circumstances. (Of course, informal, unorganized surveillance, such as that provided by customers in stores or passersby on streets also is widely relied upon to prevent crime.) Appropriate security design facilitates the use of organized as well as natural surveillance and incorporates context based technology, such as lighting and CCTV, components of mechanical surveillance as described below.

Mechanical surveillance is defined by devices that extend the ability to detect and understand events that transpire at targeted locations. Examples include the use of improved lighting and mirrors in stores to amplify employee observation of valuable inventory, CCTV in banks, department stores and at sporting events, and electronic audio surveillance of schools and other vulnerable facilities, especially after hours. The sophistication of mechanical surveillance devices has burgeoned with the development of computers, wireless technology and the miniaturization of components, and the ubiquity of mechanical surveillance will undoubtedly continue to grow.

Surveillance facilitators: lighting and CCTV

Lighting

A fundamental surveillance facilitator, improved lighting can enhance the defensibility of spaces by increasing public use through optimized sightlines and increased pedestrianism. Both can contribute to the sense of community control (Samuels, 2005). From the standpoint of situational crime prevention (discussed below), better lighting increases perceived risk to offenders in terms of visibility and the concern that witnesses' testimony might be more reliable (Clarke, 1997).

The development of lighting standards were first spurred by security needs during World War I and II at key production industries and received further impetus by virtue of heightened domestic crime concerns in the US and Britain in the 1960s. It was not until the early 1980s however that scientific study began to produce the first reliable evidence that improved street lighting reduced the level of street crime *as well as* the fear of crime (IESNA, 2003). A flurry of subsequent studies in the United Kingdom produced variable results relative to crime occurrence and lighting, although most confirmed that the *fear* of crime was reduced by better lighting. Among the most extensive and convincing studies have been those conducted by Painter whose long-term focus led to a seminal publication (Painter and Farrington, 1997) providing clear evidence that improving lighting led to sweeping crime reductions in a British community. Farrington and Welsh's (2002) multi-national, meta analysis of the impact of street lighting on crime support these conclusions on a broader scale.

Lighting improvements are fundamental elements of community regeneration. Environmental design and behavior research at the community level has shown that it is not only the *quantity* of light that is important in deterring crime and reducing the fear of crime but the *quality* and blending of light as well at the street level (Stollard, 1991; OPDM, 2004; Samuels, 2005). As one researcher notes,

> The night-light relationship is the best understood element of the afterdark paradigm, but even here a subtle mix of illumination levels is required to accommodate the ambience or mood of different places. Appropriate lighting in the public domain is not accomplished through flooding places with light, nor should it cast deep shadows, or be filtered through foliage. Furthermore, paths and the edges of open spaces must be adequately lit and nowhere should users be isolated in a pool of light within a dark context (Samuels, 2005: 6).

The determination of appropriate security lighting is both a science and an art. In this respect, a clear message from much of the lighting research is that lighting applications must be tailored to the individual contexts and circumstances including relevant physical, social and cultural environments.

Closed Circuit Television (CCTV)

Besides lighting, CCTV is probably the most ubiquitous surveillance facilitator in modern use. First employed by British police to identify troublemakers at mass sporting events, such as football matches, its use has spread rapidly throughout the United Kingdom (Norris and Armstrong, 1999; McCahill and Norris, 2003). Though initially resisted in the United States due to privacy concerns, it has become a more acceptable security tradeoff among Americans following the September 11, 2001 terrorist attacks. There is a large and growing body of work commenting on CCTV's impacts and variable effectiveness in a variety of settings (Mayhew *et al.*, 1979; Poyner, 1991; Gill and Mathews, 1994; Brown, 1995; Wright and Decker, 1997; Welsh and Farrington, 2002). The reader is directed to the extensive discussion of CCTV provided in this volume.

Boundary definition

Relative to defensible space, boundary definition incorporates both symbolic and real methods of access controls that impede the movements of offenders and help alert residents of their presence. Boundary marking may also facilitate territorial impulses and behavior. A wide range of design elements can constitute boundary markers at the macro – neighborhood and community – level including appropriate signage, paving, fences (real and symbolic) and lighting. At a micro level – say the interior of a retail store, boundary markers might include color-coded tiles, ceiling and wall treatments, lighting, and wall displays. As suggested by the theory, these need not necessarily be actual barriers but may be simple differences in material or color, symbolizing a change in space control or ownership. Such design elements can also highlight high-risk areas of a site, building or retail store, indicating places where potential offenders are likely to be, or where the crime targets are located.

One security strategy derived from Newman's research relates to activity genera-tion and space use. Depending on the context, it may be good advice to locate high-risk areas next to low-risk areas because the latter helps protect the former. A number of retailers, including Wal*mart (Mexico), Exito (Colombia), Salcobrand (Chile), Power Oral Care and Home Depot have employed this strategy, often in combination with 'store-within-a-store' strategies, and have generally been suc-cessful in reducing theft and related losses (Moussatche, 2004). Do-it-yourself (DIY) home improvement retailers have experienced considerable losses in their tools department, particularly theft of electric drills and drill kits. As noted previ-ously, 'store-within-a-store' tactics have reduced the opportunity for theft of these items by marking boundaries, limiting access points, and increasing formal guardianship by employees.

Newman's theory of defensive design remains highly influential. His conclu-sions related to the linkage of large scale, anonymous high-rise public housing with crime and disorder, helped convince housing authorities across the devel-oped world that 'certain types of housing types were having disastrous effects on their occupants.' (1973: xiii) although many scholars believe that the connection is far too simplistic and that a broad combination of factors are responsible (Taylor, 2002). It also has been the foundation for much of the 'Secure By Design' (SBD) advice given by police Architectural Liaison Officers (ALOs) to British developers and to the public for more than a decade (Kitchen, 2005).

Despite its influence, defensible space remains controversial. Some scholars and practitioners question the research methodologies on which it rests and the security design strategies that are derived from the research (Bottoms, 1974; Mayhew, 1979). Both 'Space Syntax' theory, pioneered by Hillier (1996, 2002), and 'new urbanism' design theory challenge Newman's fundamental concepts in urban settings and specifically those that flow from the linkage of territoriality into controlled access neighborhoods. Hillier is especially critical of defensible spaces' 'strangers equal danger mentality and its reliance on curtain twitching residents in cul de sacs [as] the best protection against crime.' (p. 36)

As distinct from Newman's approach, space syntax is concerned primarily with the morphology and configuration of space insomuch as these affect accessibility and the movement choices that people make, primarily in urban settings. According to the theory, these choices tend to be influenced by sight-lines, such that people move in the directions of what they see. Within this context, some space syntax-based empirical studies find that the relationships between urban space layouts and crime are much more complicated than defensible space theory suggests and that connected and open street networks are generally safer places from some crimes, such as burglary than closed cul de sacs. On the other hand, there remain significant evidence that restricting street access works in many circumstances. For example, Taylor points to a range of scientific study over three decades that 'operates consistently in the same direction across studies: more permeability, more crime.' (2002: 419)

While starting from different premises new urbanist design theorists reach a similar conclusion as Space Syntax advocates relative to street layout and urban design. Like defensible space, new urbanism traces its lineage back to Jane Jacobs (1961) and the belief that bustling, pedestrian oriented street life is a good defense against street crime. But new urbanists expand this and related premises into a holistic theory of urban design that, among other notions, explicitly values the permeability of the interconnected street grid above the sheltered street favored by defensible space.

In this context, the Charter of the Congress for New Urbanism states as its third principle relative to blocks, streets and buildings that, 'The revitalization of urban places depends on safety and security. The design of streets and buildings should reinforce safe environments, but not at the expense of accessibility and openness' (CNU, 2004). As of this writing, there is more rhetoric than evidence to support new urbanist views about crime and design. Moreover, recent controversial research presents evidence that new urbanist design tends to increase both crime rates as well as the costs of policing in some British communities (Town, 2003). Despite that, new urbanist design has many positive aesthetic, design and sustainability features that have made it and related 'smart growth' development policies dominant paradigms of urban planning and design in much of the English-speaking world.

A future prospect is the development of better comparative evaluations of the applications of defensible space, space syntax and new urbanist crime reduction theories in real life settings, something that is admittedly difficult to do since the laboratory is ever-changing. Nevertheless, attempts to reconcile these theories are likely to produce much fuller understanding of the security implications of site and urban design decisions.

Crime Prevention Through Environmental Design (CPTED)

CPTED is more widely known (especially as the acronym) than defensible space though it emerged as a place-based crime prevention theory at about the same time in the United States (1970s). It developed out of criminologist C. Ray Jeffrey's frustration with the ineffectiveness of the criminal justice system in preventing crime. His search for a new approach to crime prevention based on the relationship between people and their environments (1971, 1977) gave way to an approach that was grounded in a blend of psychological, behavioral and learning theory.

While the focus of CPTED was much broader than Newman's research on public housing projects, the fundamental principles it embraces are similar to Newman's: surveillance, boundary definition, access control, and the interconnectivity between land use, location and activity. Human territoriality is less emphasized since it is a challenging concept to define and measure, even though it is almost universally acknowledged to be a real phenomenon. Crowe (1997) suggests nine fundamental CPTED strategies that build on the basic principles above. These include:

1. Providing clear border definitions of controlled space
2. Providing clearly marked transitional zones

3. Relocating of gathering areas
4. Placing safe activities in unsafe locations
5. Placing unsafe activities in safe locations
6. Re-designating the use of space to provide natural barriers
7. Improving space scheduling
8. Redesigning space to increase the perception of natural surveillance
9. Overcome distance and isolation

One implied CPTED principle is *maintenance*. This principle gained importance following the publication and subsequent elaboration of the 'broken windows' theory (Wilson and Kelling, 1982; Kelling and Coles, 1996) and was further emphasized by Alice Coleman's extensive work on British council housing estates (1990), in which she stressed the importance of signs of incivility (i.e. graffiti, trashed entranceways, vandalism) as factors conducive to criminal acts, although her conclusions on design disadvantagment and enclosure have been largely discredited (ODPM, 2004; DOE, 1997). At its base, the broken windows theory suggests that unchallenged 'small' acts of incivility (such as swearing, public urination, intoxication) as well as disregard for physical decline of the local environment (litter, graffiti, broken windows) lead to larger, sometimes criminal acts insomuch as they tell people that 'no one cares' about this place and hence, no one will defend it. While this has been a very popular theory, recent scholarly work suggests that its impacts have been overstated and that other factors may be more important to the generation of crime at places (Taylor, 2000; Miller, 2001).

Some CPTED practitioners and consultants categorize surveillance and access control according to their methods of implementation: *natural, organized, and mechanical*. It is important to note, however, that in practice, these subcategories are not mutually exclusive and are often used in conjunction with one another. For example, if we were to apply them to the principle of access control we might examine how entrances to retail stores are protected by the placement of windows that look out onto to entry paths and doorways (natural surveillance), the deployment of security guards (organized surveillance), or the use of CCTV (mechanical/electronic surveillance). Again, it is not uncommon to find all three elements operating at once, especially in upscale residential areas or in retail establishments in high crime neighborhoods.

CPTED applications and awareness – embodying defensible space concepts at their core – are widely used in police agencies in the United States and Britain and now are considered 'mainstream' crime prevention techniques. CPTED is also used as a public relations vehicle for several high profile crime prevention campaigns such as those conducted by the US National Crime Prevention Council and by large police departments. The British government has formally adopted both defensible space and CPTED concepts in the context of its SBD program, which applies to land use developments of all types and to building fittings (especially door and window hardware). (OPDM, 2004)

While common sense supports the application of CPTED-based security strategies, definitive scientific validation as to whether they *really* do prevent or deter crime – remains elusive. Taylor (2002) suggests the dimensions of the issue. He contends that CPTED is variably effective depending on many factors that make every situation unique, suggesting that the crime-environment connection is so complicated by site features and surrounding elements (man-built and natural) that the evaluation of CPTED effectiveness depends upon 'how you define key terms, how rigorous is the proof you demand, and how complete an answer you seek.' (p. 423) Others, including Samuels (2005) point out that CPTED 'is a misnomer' since design cannot 'cause or prevent crime' by itself but is a facilitating agent among many other potentially more cogent factors. Additional research provides tangential support by emphasizing that workable applications are highly context-sensitive, such that solutions must be customized and geared to specific circumstances (ODPM, 2004; Schneider and Kitchen, 2002; Ekblom, 2002).

Nevertheless, evidence is accumulating that place-based crime prevention strategies, including CPTED, do work or are promising in specific circumstances (Sherman *et al.*, 1997; Loukaitou-Sideris, 1999; Taylor, 2002). The evidence, though not conclusive still is persuasive enough that it ought to be seriously considered as one of the many strategies that security professionals can choose from in making places safer. Thus, it is arguable that while the role of physical design is often difficult to assess in making crime more or less likely to occur, it plays a role nonetheless.

Situational crime prevention

Like defensible space and CPTED as described above, situational crime prevention is an approach that de-emphasizes offender dispositions and motivations in favor of concentrating on the criminal event itself. It focuses on crime *opportunities* and the specific circumstances – the *situation* surrounding the crime event. Originating independently of defensible space and CPTED in the British Home Office Research Unit's work on correctional treatments done in the 1960s and 70s, it was first detailed by Ronald V. Clarke, a criminologist (1992, 1997). Since then, situational crime prevention has gained widespread popularity with the crime prevention community, including police and security agencies around the globe. A later development, the 'problem oriented policing' approach uses a similar research framework, but is much narrower in scope insomuch as it focuses largely on police administration and practice (Goldstein, 1979, 1990). Like many of the earlier sociological and human ecology theories of crime as well as Jeffrey's CPTED concept, initial situational crime prevention theory and applications arose out of work with youthful offenders but has since been extended to all types of offenders and offenses.

Situational crime prevention encompasses both spatial and non-spatial variables by incorporating management advice and data from the use and users of spaces and services. Thus, while its adherents acknowledge the importance that physical design and physical environments have (and the contributions of defensible space and CPTED theory) on criminal behavior, they cast a wider net and extend the zone of influence to include a variety of non-physical factors as well.

As such situational crime prevention has been identified as an underlying theoretical basis for the British SBD approach noted above (Town *et al.*, 2003) It also frames the American 'community oriented policing' (COPS) strategy.

While the Criminology chapter in this volume provides an in-depth discussion of situational crime prevention and related theories, we point out that it is intimately connected to routine activity theory as described by Cohen and Felson (1979) and rational choice theory (Clarke and Cornish, 1985; Cornish and Clarke, 2003). Routine activity theory focuses on understanding the patterns of offender and offending activity, concentrating primarily on the criminal event instead of the criminal's state of mind or background. Clarke and Felson (1993) note that there are '... three minimal elements for direct-contact predatory crime: a likely offender, a suitable target, and the absence of a capable guardian against crime.' (p. 2)

Routine activity theory also lends itself to the geographic and quantitative analysis of crime patterns and trends and is associated with theories of behavioral geography and environmental criminology. Changes in routine activities (whether associated with the perpetrator or the targets) can be associated with changes in crime rates. Cohen and Felson suggested, for example, that the rise in burglary rates beginning in 1960 was associated with increases in empty homes occasioned by more working women and the increased availability of portable, valuable electronic items such as radios and stereo systems (1979). Likely targets may therefore be associated with the ease of opportunity (as noted above) and, in the case of retail theft, resale value. Thus, items that fit the CRAVED definition – Concealable, Removable, Available, Valuable, Enjoyable, and Disposable – are predictably 'hot items' (Clarke, 1999) and vulnerable to offenders' routine activities.

Rational choice theory is related to routine activity theory and undergirds situational crime prevention. It assumes that physical or other environmental factors influence offenders' choices and that they commit crimes within the context of a 'bounded' rationality (Cornish and Clarke, 1986). Rational choice takes into account the notion that while individuals' perceptions of situations vary they generally are the result of a calculation that acknowledges the costs (which include effort expended), benefits (potential reward) and risks associated with those acts. The theory also incorporates fundamental defensible space and CPTED principles to the extent that offenders are swayed by environmental elements within the context of the immediate decision to commit crimes. It is, however, distinguishable from other place-related or based theory insomuch as it accounts for criminal disposition and is derived largely from psychology and economics although it has some foundations in sociology and criminology as well.

Situational crime prevention is not without its critics. Some contend that because it emphasizes increasing effort and risk to offenders its crime prevention interventions too often wind up hardening targets. This is expensive and may result in fortress effects (like grilled windows and community gating), that have unacceptable social costs (Forrest and Kennett, 1977). A response is that this is but one aspect of an approach that extends crime prevention into the realm of place and space management (Taylor, 2002) and further, seeks to account for user (target) behavior or location as it influences offender decisions. Together situational crime prevention, rational choice and routine activity theories help explain and predict crime based on opportunity and the resulting choices that offenders make. The patterns that are discernable from the aggregation of these choices are largely the foci of environmental criminology, the last modern place-based crime prevention theory that we shall consider here.

Environmental criminology

Environmental criminology shares a number of fundamental tenets with situational criminology, among them the belief that crime is not a random event, but rather the result of a rational search and decision process guided by the perception of opportunity characteristics in the environment. These are presented as environmental cues such as may be interpreted by burglars (Bennett, 1989; Pascoe, 1993; Cozens *et al.*, 2001), armed robbers (Wright and Decker, 1997) and shoplifters (Carroll and Weaver, 1986). It diverges significantly from situational criminology however in its focus on spatial, movement, location and geographical elements in the analysis of criminal events. In this context it owes a debt to urban design and planning, and especially to Lynch who described cities in terms of pathways, nodes, edges, landmarks, and districts (1960). These elements constrain, contain and mold the substantive components of criminal events insomuch as they connect '… victims or criminal targets in specific settings at particular times and places.' (Brantingham and Brantingham, 1991: 2). To environmental criminologists the spatial-temporal dimension is considered as the focal component of the criminal event, which also is defined by laws that are broken, offenders, and crime targets.

Academic and theoretical influences on environmental criminology include the Chicago School social and spatial ecologists (who were, in turn influenced by the social problems spawned by industrial cities of the 19th century), Jeffrey's concept of crime prevention through environmental design, Newman's defensible space, and rational choice and routine activity theories. At its core environmental criminology suggests that:

> …criminal events can be understood in the context of people's normal movement through normal settings in the course of everyday life. Offenders commit their offenses near the places where they spend most of their time – home, work, school, shopping, entertainment – and along the major pathways between them. Similarly, victims are victimized near places where they spend most of their time and along the major pathways in between. This line of theory implies that criminal events can be understood and predicted through analysis of offenders' residences; targets such as unattended residences or parked automobiles; the daily activity patterns of teenagers and housewives, postal workers, bank clerks, physicians, timber brokers, auto workers and school teachers; and common recreational patterns such as a trip

to the movies, an evening at a favorite pub, or a dinner with friends. It also implies that crime can be understood and predicted through the analysis of a city's land use patterns, its street network, and its transportation system. (Brantingham and Brantingham, 1991: 2)

It seeks to explain the behavioral geography of offender and offence occurrences at activity nodes (places that attract people such as bars, schools, shopping centers) along pathways (which connect nodes) and edges (for example, boundary zones between neighborhoods which are often ambiguous, hence dangerous places) (Brantingham and Brantingham, 1993). These elements help environmental criminologists describe and delineate the 'activity spaces' of offenders (all locations frequented) and their 'awareness spaces' (all locations which they know about) relative to the determination of 'search areas' (potential offending areas). The theory predicates that these areas are not uniform but vary with offender age, race and socioeconomic status as well as by the availability of low risk (hence attractive) targets across the urban landscape (which is also variable). It suggests too that offenders talk to each other and thereby exchange information that modify their awareness spaces. The Brantinghams modeled a series of hypothetical cases based on these assumptions and produced predictions of offence occurrence linked to city form (1991). For example, they suggested that 'areas with grid networks, in general, have higher potential crime rates then areas with organic street patterns' and that 'the shifting of work areas out of core areas into fringe areas of a city will tend to increase crime in suburban areas.' (pp. 51–2).

Environmental criminology involves the depiction and analysis of crime patterns across large swaths of territory, often using statistical methods. Modern technology, and especially computer-based mapping using GIS allow users to see connections among map elements, such as the relationship between land values and property crimes. These programs, inspired by the analytic geometry of environmental criminology, also permit users to 'drill down' to mid-range or smaller crime patterns and look at connections among offenders and environmental features, such as roadways (paths) and commercial land uses (nodes) such as nightclubs suspected to be associated with specific crimes like armed robberies. Recent research based upon interviews supports the long-observed phenomenon that burglars – often driven by the immediate need for cash or drugs – tend to stay close to home areas in target selection and crime commission (Hearnden and Magill, 2002).

Pattern theory and micro-level applications have proven useful in explaining and predicting crime probabilities at vulnerable points and has helped designers, planners, police and the security industry formulate strategies based on their analysis (Rossmo, 1999; Bromley and Nelson, 2002). Crime patterns analyses are regularly conducted by British ALOs and by American police crime analysts for local constituents and consist of crime series identification as well as trend, hot spot and general profile analyses. (OPDM, 2004) Even though it has been sometimes difficult to translate its theoretical components into some fields of practice (Zahm, 2005; Rondeau, Brantingham and Brantingham, 2005), environmental criminology nevertheless has been extraordinarily important to the evolution of modern place-based crime prevention theory and has helped inspire modern technological security applications.

Future directions

While the future directions of environmental studies with security-related implications and applications are as varied as the many academic fields that have produced them to date, two major forces – technology and world terrorism – are likely to be powerful influences. The effects of these forces converge as they tend to drive each other. One salient example of this is the increasing use of the Internet by terrorist organizations who, ironically, are taking full advantage of this most democratic of all technologies to spread anti-democratic messages. Other technical advances, in electronic access control, intrusion detection and monitoring devices, CCTV and lighting technology are likely to stimulate new environmental research and study related to security issues. The reality and threat of terrorism will no doubt continue to influence technology, but will also impact environment-based research and thought about the nature of city building and design, and ultimately, we suspect, the actual shape and structure of cities themselves.

Computer-related technology

Aside from the dissemination of information, advances in computer technology have empowered our abilities to collect, process and analyze vast quantities of data in the past four decades. These advances have facilitated the development of a range of environmental studies that are linked, directly or indirectly, to security applications. For instance, computer technology has helped reinvigorate flagging research on relationships among climate, weather and crime (Rotton and Cohn, 2002) as well as the development of building technologies to protect against crime, including terrorist attacks (Grassie, 2004).

Technology has made 'hot-spot' crime maps available to police through GIS applications, as noted above, and has made urban street and crime scenes come to life through the magic of computer simulation and advanced visualization programs (Brantingham and Brantingham, 2004). These same programs have been used to enhance public participation techniques through computer-based collaborative mapping and design approaches (Al-Kodmany, 2000), and they promise to make community-based security design easier as new visualization programs become more user friendly. The growing linkage of GPS technology to GIS crime data will markedly enhance the accuracy of crime and incident mapping, allowing law enforcement and security personnel to pinpoint locations through 'X and Y' coordinates on the surface of the earth, as distinct from using street addresses (Sorensen, 1997). This undoubtedly will be amplified by the evolution of inexpensive hand-held GPS devices and their subsequent dissemination to local police and security personnel for use in the field.

Such technological advances have often proceeded hand in hand with environmental theory and in many cases it is impossible to unravel their interconnected evolution since new tools tend to drive new theory and vice versa. For example, while the ability to quickly aggregate and query vast crime data sets is a function of the available technology, theories such as situational criminology, environmental criminology and space syntax have provided roadmaps to organize the data into intelligible patterns and explainable events, transforming it from raw numbers into knowledge. This in turn has spurred the development of new data inquiry tools, such as those produced by the growing number of consulting firms that specialize in police records management and mapping applications.

As Block (1997) notes, theory and technology must support each other and connect realistically to the community of users, whether they are in public or private security practice. This is particularly true since technology has the ability to produce a surfeit of data that can overwhelm, not inform users. A challenge to security researchers and professionals is to develop strategies to organize and manage the easy wealth of data made possible by computer technology so as to provide better analysis and decision-making tools.

Terrorism and environment/security studies

This challenge is made more imperative by the vast array of new security technology developed or refined in response, at least in part, to recent terrorist attacks. These range from refined electronic intrusion and access control devices such as exterior and interior sensors (fiber-optic, ported coaxial cable, microwave, ultrasonic, pulsed infrared beam, and basic electric door contacts, etc.) to electronic control devices that read identification cards, code numbers, or biometric information, such as hand shape or eye characteristics (Grassie, 2004). McCrie's chapter in this handbook provides a fascinating account of the evolution of some of these security devices. With some exceptions, this technology has not been studied in detail by behavioral and social scientists or criminologists. Rather, environmental studies have tended to concentrate on two older technologies, CCTV and lighting because of their relative longevity, because of their connection to surveillance strategies, and as noted previously, because of public policy concerns relative to privacy issues. But renewed emphasis on combating terrorism has begun to direct the interests of many academics and security professionals to revisit other technical and strategic issues that link environmental studies with security.

The literature in this area is rapidly growing. It can be divided into two broad, but non-exclusive types: the first deals with *counter*-terrorism and the second group concentrating on *anti*-terrorism. Counter-terrorism primarily refers to *offensive* measures taken by military intelligence and national law enforcement agencies to combat terrorist activity at its sources. Anti-terrorism is defined as *defensive* strategies including a wide array of activities undertaken by public and private groups and that include prevention and mitigation efforts. (FEMA, 2002) While environmentally-related research no doubt informs both sides of this equation, much of the contribution have been to terrorism mitigation and prevention efforts.

Mitigation is concerned with minimizing damage to targets or displacing it to other targets that are less vulnerable but that also are less desirable (from the perpetrator's point of view) and may involve both prevention and response efforts. A small sampling of the mitigation literature includes technical architectural and engineering studies seeking to explain the effects of bomb blasts on structures and devise new approaches to harden targets (Conrath, 1999; Schmidt, 2003; Nadel, 2004), recommendations on fire, security and evacuation route optimization (Institution of Structural Engineers, 2002), and recommendations relative to improving the performance of materials affected by blasts and fire (Maréchaux, 2001). Mitigation also focuses on public policies aimed at the regeneration of communities after attacks. (Kitchen, 2001; FEMA, 2002)

Terrorism *prevention* entails, among many other threads, the modern place based crime prevention strategies discussed previously but with increased emphasis on risk and vulnerability *assessments*, concepts particularly associated with situational crime prevention and CPTED. Challenges to environmental design academics and security professionals include developing new anti-terrorist planning and design theory and approaches that connect with constantly changing risk and vulnerability.

This is made much more problematic for terrorism prevention because the number of terrorist incidents are so small (in comparison to crime incidents) which renders them statistically unpredictable (FEMA, 2002). Moreover, the number of potential terrorist targets is so huge that it obviates much of what we know about repeat victimization (Sherman, 1995; Sherman *et al.*, 1997) largely inapplicable relative to terrorist target selection, the several attempts on the World Trade Center notwithstanding. Challenges thus remain relative to sorting out conflicting crime prevention evidence that may or may not be germane to anti-terrorism planning (such as that dealing with street permeability), applying context-specific solutions as distinct from cook-book formulations (applicable to both crime and terrorism prevention) and reconciling conflicting advice and philosophies relative to such areas as community design.

For instance, large stand-off distance recommendations to separate vehicular traffic (and bomb blasts) from some infrastructure and building facades are generally at odds with urban design philosophies, such as new urbanism, that seek close connections between buildings and the street. Other fundamental challenges for environmental research with security practice implications involves investigating the use of GIS, GPS and CCTV so that they serve the purposes for which they are intended yet respect the values of free and open societies. Moreover, a developing area for research is on the emerging synergistic combinations of technology with community-based anti-crime and terrorism efforts, such as local police and citizen partnerships in Britain and community-based policing in the United States. Realized in part by crime maps that are uploaded onto public Internet sites maintained by police agencies, this is a nexus of technology, public participation and security unique in human history.

In the final analysis, while ordinary street crime and terrorism are different in many respects, they share many prevention and mitigation principles and strategies derived from overlapping environmental, and especially place-based crime prevention, research ancestries. Throughout history, environmental studies have made a vast contribution to security applications. Given advances in theory development, the growth of new technologies, and the increased drumbeat of international terrorism, there is every reason to believe that this co-evolutionary process will continue in the future.

Summary

This chapter has sampled the vast contributions of environmental studies to security beginning with unwritten but nevertheless recorded evidence left by our ancestors carved into the landscape, through early theories of the causes of criminal behavior translated into social, economic and psychological research. Technology, industrialization, and urbanization also were seen as forces driving the development of later theories of criminal behavior that were linked to the environment in terms of the physical design, management and use of places. Place-based theory – including defensible space, crime prevention through environmental design, situational crime prevention and environmental criminology – were described as producing a wealth of studies, including those related to security facilitators such as improved lighting and CCTV. Studies have also produced contradictory results that remain to be reconciled, such as those related to urban layout and street patterns. Nevertheless the literature tends to point to common directions relative to verification based on empirical evidence and to the notion that security strategies are very much context dependent, such that solutions applied in one place may not always fit another. The chapter concluded with a discussion of the importance of technology and terrorism as compelling influences on emerging security theory and practice, with these elements co-evolving, having driven each other in the past and being likely to do so in the future.

Key points
- Security is intimately connected to human survival and to the natural and man-built environment such that civilization, security design and environmental design have co-evolved.
- Many, often widely disparate, disciplines and fields of study contribute to security and environmental design and planning.
- Research and practice suggest that although there are broad place-based crime prevention theories that describe and predict criminal behavior, the application of effective security design tends to be context dependent.
- Throughout history the introduction and diffusion of new technology have driven the development and obsolescence of much security design and planning. In the modern world, technology *and* the fear and reality of terrorism are becoming the primary forces behind the development of new security theory and applications.

- A fundamental challenge to the use of computer aided technology in security analyses is to be able to organize and make intelligible the vast amounts of data that can be generated.
- Environmental studies related to security demonstrate the importance of theory and practice influencing each other and spurring new developments in each.

Key readings

The fundamental work on defensible space remains Oscar Newman's (1973) *Defensible Space: Crime Prevention Through Urban Design*, New York: Macmillan. It is out of print but nevertheless available. It is updated and re-defended by his 1995 article for the American Planning Association. Jeffrey's (1977) *Crime Prevention Through Environmental Design.* 2nd edn, Beverly Hills, Ca.: Sage, provides the most complete theoretical discussion of the original conception of CPTED, but should be read in conjunction with Taylor's article, (2002) *Crime Prevention through Environmental Design (CPTED): Yes, No, Maybe, Unknowable, and All of the Above*. In Bechtel, R.B. and Churchman, A. (ed.) *Handbook of Environmental Psychology*. New York: John Wiley, pp. 413–26, which puts CPTED and other place-based crime prevention theories into context relative to their effectiveness as security strategies. See Clarke, R.V.'s (1997) *Situational Crime Prevention: Successful Case Studies*. 2nd edn, Albany, NY: Harrow and Heston, for a broad variety of situational crime prevention applications, ranging from those with environmental connections to those that are strictly based on management practice. Likewise, the Brantinghams' edited text (1991) *Environmental Criminology*. Prospect Height, Ill.: Waveland Press, presents a range of studies that discuss the use of crime patterning techniques and the Sherman *et al.* study (1997) *Preventing Crime: What Works, What Doesn't, What's Promising*? National Institute of Justice Research, Washington DC: US Department of Justice, provides an assessment of many environmentally-based crime prevention and security strategies (among others), based upon empirical standards and review.

References

Akers, R.L. (1985) *Deviant Behavior: A Social Learning Approach*. Belmont, California: Wadsworth.

Al-Kodmany, K. (2000) 'Extending Geographic Information Systems to Meet Neighborhood Needs: Recent work of the University of Illinois at Chicago.' *The Journal of Urban and Regional Information Systems Association* 12, 3 (Summer): 19–37.

Beccaria, C. (1764) *Essay on Crimes and Punishments*. Reprinted 1983. Brookline Village, MA: Branden Press.

Bechtel, R, and Churchman, A. (2002) *Handbook of Environmental Psychology*. New York: Wiley and Sons.

Bennett, T. (1989) 'Burglars Choice of Targets.' In Evans, D.J. and Herbert, D.T. (eds) *The Geography of Crime*. London: Routledge.

Blakely, E.J. and Snyder, M.G. (1999) *Fortress America: Gated Communities in the United States*. Washington DC: Brookings Institution Press.

Block, C.R. (1997) 'The Geoarchive: An Information Foundation for Community Policing.' In Weisburd, D. and McEwen, T. (1997) *Crime Mapping and Crime Prevention*. Monsey, NY: Criminal Justice Press, pp. 27–81.

Booth, C. (1888) 'Conditions and Occupations of the People of East London and Hackney,' *Journal of the Royal Statistical Society*, Vol. 51, pp. 326–91.

Bottoms, A.E. (1974) 'Review of Defensible Space by Oscar Newman,' *British Journal of Criminology*, 14: 203–6.

Brantingham, P.L. and Brantingham, P.J. (1991) (eds) *Environmental Criminology*. Prospect Height, Ill.: Waveland Press.

Brantingham, P.L. and Brantingham, P.J. (1993) 'Paths, Nodes, Edges: Considerations on the Complexity of Crime and the Physical Environment,' *Journal of Environmental Psychology*, Vol. 13, pp. 3–28.

Brantingham, P. and Brantingham, P. (2004) 'Computer Simulation as a Tool for Environmental Criminologists,' *Security Journal*, Vol. 17, No. 1, pp. 21–30.

Bromley, R.D.F. and Nelson, A.L. (2002) 'Alcohol-related Crime and Disorder Across Urban Space and Time: Evidence from a British City,' *Geoforum*, 22: 239–54.

Brown, B. (1995) 'CCTV in town centres: Three Case Studies,' *Police Research Group Crime Detection and Prevention Series Paper*, #68. London, UK: Home Office.

Burgess, E.W. (1925) 'The Growth of the City: An Introduction to a Research Project.' In Park, R.E., Burgess, E.W. and McKenzie, M. (eds), *The City*, pp. 47–62. Chicago: University of Chicago Press.

Carroll, J. and Weaver, F. (1986) 'Shoplifter's Perceptions of Crime Opportunities: A Process Tracing Study.' In Cornish, D. and Clarke, R.V. (eds) *The Reasoning Criminal*. New York: Springer Verlag, pp. 19–38.

Clapp, J.A. (1984) Thomas Jefferson quote from a letter to Benjamin Rush *The City, A Dictionary of Quotable Thought on Cities and Urban Life*. New Brunswick: Center for Urban Policy Research.

Clarke, R.V. (1992) *Situational Crime Prevention: Successful Case Studies*. Albany, NY: Harrrow and Heston.

Clarke, R.V. (1997) *Situational Crime Prevention: Successful Case Studies*. 2nd edn. Albany, NY: Harrrow and Heston.

Clarke, R.V. (1999) 'Hot Products: Understanding, Anticipating and Reducing Demand for Stolen Goods,' *Police Research Series Paper 112*. London: Home Office, Policing and Reducing Crime Unit. See also See http://crimeprevention.rutgers.edu/case_studies/effort/hot_products/cravedlist.htm. Last accessed September 2004.

Clarke, R.V. and Cornish, D.B. (1985) 'Modeling Offenders' Decisions: A Framework for Policy and Research.' In Tonry, M. and Morris, N. (eds), *Crime and Justice: An Annual Review of Research*, Vol. 6. Chicago: University of Chicago Press, pp. 147– 85.

Clarke, R.V. and Felson, W. (1993) (eds) *Routine Activity and Rational Choice. Advances in Criminological Theory*, Vol. 5. New Brunswick and London: Transaction Publishers.

Clarke, R.V. and Weisburd, D. (1994) 'Diffusion of Crime Control Benefits: Observations on the Reverse of Displacement.' In Clarke, R.V. (ed) *Crime Prevention Studies*, Vol. 2. Monsey, NY: Criminal Justice Press.

Cohen, L.E. and Felson, M. (1979) 'Social Change and Crime Rate Trends: A Routine Activities Approach.' *American Sociological Review*, Vol. 44., pp. 588–608.

Coleman, A. (1990) *Utopia on Trial*, revised edition. London: Hilary Shipman.

Congress for the New Urbanism (2004) Last accessed November 2004 at http://www.cnu.org/index.cfm.

Cornish, D.B. and Clarke, R.V. (eds) (1986) *The Reasoning Criminal*. New York: Springer-Verlag.

Cornish, D.B. and Clarke, R.V. (2003) 'Crime As a Rational Choice.' In *Criminological Theory – Past to Present*, 2nd edn. Cullen, F. and Agnew, R. Los Angeles: Roxbury Publishing Company.

Conrath, E.J. (1999) *Structural Design for Physical Security: State of the Practice*, American Society of Civil Engineers. Reston: ASCE Press.

Cozens, P., Hillier, D. and Prescott, G. (2001) 'Defensible Space: Burglars and Police Evaluate Urban Residential Design,' *Security Journal*, Vol. 14, No. 4, pp. 43–62.

Crowe, T. (1997) 'Crime Prevention Through Environmental Design Strategies and Applications.' In Fennelly L.J., Effective Physical Security, 2nd edn. Boston, MA: Butterworth-Heinemann, pp. 35–88.

Crowe, T. (2000) *Crime Prevention Through Environmental Design*, 2nd edn. Boston: Butterworth-Heinemann.

Design Council (2003). *Think Thief – A Designers Guide to Designing Out Crime*, London. http://www.crimereduction.gov.uk/business32.pdf.

DeForest, R.W. and Veiller, L. (eds) (1903) *The Tenement House Problem: Including the Report of the New York State Tenement House Commission of 1900*, 2 vols. New York: Macmillan.

DiMaggio, P. (2004) 'Building Hardening.' In *Security Planning and Design: A Guide for Architects and Building Design Professionals*, Demkin, J. (ed.) Hoboken, NJ: John Wiley & Sons, pp. 83–106.

Department of the Environment (1997) 'An Evaluation of DICE Schemes,' *Regeneration Research Summary No. 11*, London: DOE (now ODPM).

Ekblom, P. (1997) 'Gearing Up Against Crime: A Dynamic Framework to Help Designers Keep Up with the Adaptive Criminal in a Changing World,' *International Journal of Risk, Security and Crime Prevention*, Vol. 2, No. 4, pp. 249–65.

Ekblom, P. (2002) 'From the Source to the Mainstream is Uphill: The Challenge of Transferring Knowledge of Crime Prevention through Replication, Innovation and Anticipation.' In Tilley (ed.) *Analysis for Crime Prevention, Crime Prevention Studies 13*: 131–203. Monsey, NY: Criminal Justice Press.

Farrington, D. and Welsh, B. (2002) 'Effects of Improved Street Lighting on Crime: A Systematic Review,' *Home Office Research Study 251*.

Federal Emergency Management Agency/FEMA (2002) *Integrating Human-Caused Hazards Into Mitigation Planning*. Publication #386-7 Washington, DC: Government Printing Office.

Florida Department of Education (2003) Florida Safe School Design Guidelines: Strategies to Enhance Security and Reduce Vandalism. Last accessed October 2004 at http://www.firn.edu/doe/edfacil/safe_schools.htm.

Forrest, R. and Kennett, P. (1977) 'Risk, Residence and the Post-Fordist City,' *American Behavioral Scientist*, 41: 342–59.

Gill, M. and Mathews, R. (1994) 'Robbers on Robbery.' In Gill, M. (ed.) *Crime at Work*. Leicester: Perpetuity Press.

Goldstein, H. (1979) 'Improving Policing: A Problem Oriented Approach,' *Crime and Delinquency*, 25: 236–58.

Goldstein, H. (1990) *Problem Oriented Policing*. New York: McGraw Hill.

Grassie, R.P. (2004) 'Building Security Technologies.' In *Security Planning and Design: A Guide for Architects and Building Design Professionals*, Demkin, J. (ed.). Hoboken, NJ: John Wiley & Sons, pp. 107–36.

Hall, E.T. (1966) *The Hidden Dimension*. Garden City, NY: Doubleday.

Hall, P. (1988) *Cities of Tomorrow*. Oxford: Basil Blackwell.

Hearnden, I. and Magill, C. (2002) 'Decision Making by House Burglars: Offenders Perspectives,' *Home Office Research* Study 249. London: Home Office.

Hillier, B. (1996) *Space is the Machine*. Cambridge: Cambridge University Press.

Hillier, B. (2002) *Can Streets be Made Safe?* London: Space Syntax.

Hillier, B. and Shu, S. (1999) 'Designing for Secure Spaces,' *Planning in London*. Vol. 29 (April) pp. 36–8.

Hirschi, T. (1969) *Causes of Delinquency*. Berkeley, California: University of California Press.

Hunter, R.D. and Jeffrey, C.R. (1992) 'Preventing Convenience Store Robbery Through Environmental Design.' In Clarke, R.V. (1997) *Situational Crime Prevention: Successful Case Studies*, 2nd edn. Albany: Harrow and Heston, pp. 191–9.

Illuminating Engineering Society of North America (2003) *Guideline for Security Lighting for People, Property and Public Space*. G-1-103. New York: IESNA.

Institution of Structural Engineers (2002) *Safety in Tall Buildings and Other Buildings of Large Occupancy*. Reference Number 344. London: ISE.

Jacobs, J. (1961) *The Death and Life of Great American Cities*. New York: Vintage Books.

Jeffrey, C.R. (1971) *Crime Prevention Through Environmental Design*. Beverly Hills, CA: Sage.

Jeffrey, C.R. (1977) *Crime Prevention Through Environmental Design*, 2nd edn. Beverly Hills, CA: Sage.

Maréchaux, T.G. (2001) 'Better Materials Can Reduce the Threat from Terrorism,' *Journal of the Mineral, Metals and Materials Society*, 53: 12, pp. 12–13.

Kelling, G.L. and Coles, C.M. (1996) *Fixing Broken Windows: Restoring Order in American Cities*, with Coles, C.M. New York: The Free Press.

Kenyon, J.R. (1990) *Medieval Fortifications*. Leicester: Leicester University Press.

Kennett, M. (2004) *Symposium Abstracts: The Risk Management Series and FEMA 430, Building Site and Layout Design Guidance to Mitigate Potential Terrorist Attacks*. Presentation at the American Society of Landscape Architects Security Design Symposium, July 2004, Chicago Ill.

Kitchen, T. (2001) 'Planning in Response to Terrorism: The Case of Manchester, England,' *Journal of Architectural and Planning Research*. Vol. 18, No. 4 Winter, pp. 325–40.

Kitchen, T. (2005) 'New Urbansim and Secure by Design in the British Planning System: Some Critical Reflections,' *Journal of Architectural and Planning Research*. Vol. 22, No. 4, Winter, pp. 342–57.

Kostof, S. (1991) *The City Shaped*. Boston: Little, Brown & Company.

Kostof, S. (1992) *The City Assembled*. Boston: Little, Brown & Company.

Levy, J.M. (2002) *Contemporary Urban Planning*, 6th edn. Upper Saddle River, New Jersey: Prentice Hall.

Lombroso, C. (1911) *The Criminal Man in Criminological Theory – Past to Present* (2nd edn, 2003) Cullen, F. and Agnew, R. Los Angeles: Roxbury Publishing Company.

Loukaitou-Sideris, A. (1999) 'Hot Spots of Bus Stop Crime: The Importance of Environmental Attributes,' *Journal of the American Planning Association*, 65, 4: 395–411.

Lynch, K. (1960) *Image of the City*. Cambridge, MA: MIT Press.

Marcuse, P. (1997) 'Walls of Fear and Walls of Support.' In Ellin N. *Architecture of Fear*. Princeton, New Jersey: Princeton Architectural Press, pp. 101–14.

Maslow, A.H. (1968) *Toward a Psychology of Being*, Princeton: Van Nostrand Company.

Mayhew, P. (1979) 'Defensible Space: The Current Status of a Crime Prevention Theory,' *The Howard Journal of Penology and Crime Prevention*, 18: 150–9.

Mayhew, P., Clarke, R.V., Burrows, J.N., Hough, J.M. and Winchester, S.W.C. (1979) *Crime in Public View*. Home Office Research Study No. 49. London: HM Stationary Office.

McCahill, M. and Norris, C. (2003) 'Estimating the Extent, Sophistication and Legality of CCTV in London.' In M. Gill (ed.) *CCTV*. Leicester: Perpetuity Press.

Miller, D.W. (2001) 'Poking Holes in the Theory of Broken Windows,' *Chronicle of Higher Education*, February 9, 2001.

Moussatche, H., Hayes, R., Schneider, R., McLeod, R., Abbott, P. and Kohen, M. (2004) *Reducing Loss Through Retail Store Design and Layout*. Unpublished Report for the Gillette Corporation. Loss Prevention Research Team. Gainesville, Florida: Loss Prevention Research Center.

Mumford, L. (1961) *The City in History*. Orlando, Florida: Harcourt.

Nadel, B. (2004) *Building Security: A Handbook for Architectural Planning Design*. New York: McGraw-Hill.

Newman, O. (1973) *Defensible Space: Crime Prevention Through Urban Design*. New York: Macmillan.

Newman, O. (1981) *Community of Interest*. Garden City, NY: Anchor Press/Doubleday.

Newman, O. (1995) 'Defensible Space: A New Physical Planning Tool for Urban Revitalization,' *Journal of the American Planning Association*, Vol. 61, No. 2, pp. 149–55.

Norris, C. and Armstrong, G. (1999) *The Maximum Surveillance Society. The Rise of CCTV*. Oxford/New York: Berg.

ODPM and Home Office (2004) *Safer Places: The Planning System and Crime Prevention*. London: HMSO.

Oxford English Dictionary (1982) Oxford: Oxford University Press.

Pascoe, T. (1993) 'Domestic Burglaries: The Burglar's View,' *BRE Information Paper 19/93*. Garston, Watford: Building Research Establishment.

Painter, K. and Farrington, D.P. (1997) 'The Crime Reducing Effect of Improved Street Lighting: The Dudley Project.' In Clarke, R.V. (ed.), *Situational Crime Prevention: Successful Case Studies*, 2nd edn. Albany, New York: Harrow and Heston, pp. 209–26.

Poyner, B. (1991) 'Situational Crime Prevention in Two Car Parks,' *Security Journal*, Vol. 2, pp. 96–101.

Poyner, B. (1998) 'The Case for Design.' In Felson, M. and Peiser, R. *Reducing Crime Through Real Estate Development and Management*. Washington, DC: Urban Land Institute.

Rapoport, A. (1977) *Human Aspects of Urban Form: Toward a Man-Environment Approach to Urban Form and Design*. Oxford: Pergamon Press.

Reckless, W.C. (1961) *The Crime Problem*, 3rd edn. New York: Appleton-Century Crofts.

Rondeau, M.B., Brantingham, P.L. and Brantingham, P.J. (2005) 'The Value of Environmental Criminology for the Design Professions of Architecture, Urban Design, Landscape Architecture and Planning,' *Journal of Architectural and Planning Research*. Vol. 22, No. 4, Winter, pp. 294–304.

Rossmo, D.K. (1999) *Geographic Profiling*. New York: CRC Press.

Rotton, J. and Cohn, E. (2002) 'Climate, Weather and Crime.' In Bechtel, R. and Churchman, A. *Handbook of Environmental Psychology*. New York: Wiley and Sons, pp. 481–98.

Samuels, R. (2005) 'After-Dark Design, Night Animation and Interpersonal Interaction: Towards a Community-security Paradigm,' *Journal of Architectural and Planning Research*. Vol. 22, No. 4, Winter, pp. 305–18.

Schmidt, J.A. (2003) Structural Design for External Terrorist Bomb Attacks. At http://www.structuremag.org/archives/2003/march/Blast.pdf. Last accessed November 2004.

Schneider, R.H. and Kitchen, T. (2002) *Planning for Crime Prevention: A Trans Atlantic Perspective*. London and New York: Routledge.

Shaw, C.R. and MacKay, H.D. (1942) *Juvenile Delinquency and Urban Areas*. Chicago: University of Chicago Press.

Sherman, L.W. (1995) 'Hot Spots of Crime and Criminal Careers of Places.' In Eck, J.E. and Wisburd, D. (eds), *Crime and Place*. Monsey, NY: Criminal Justice Press, pp. 36–7.

Sherman, L.W., Gottfredson, D.C., Mackenzie, D.C., Eck, J., Reuter, P. and Bushway, S.D. (1997) *Preventing Crime: What Works, What Doesn't, What's Promising?* National Institute of Justice Research, Washington DC: US Department of Justice.

Sommer, R. (1983) *Social Design: Creating Buildings with People in Mind*. Englewood-Cliffs, NJ: Prentice Hall.

Sorensen, S.L. (1997) 'Smart Mapping for Law Enforcement Settings: Integrating GIS and GPS for Dynamic, Near Real Time Applications and Analyses.' In Weisburd, D. and McEwen, T. (1997) *Crime Mapping and Crime Prevention*. Monsey, NY: Criminal Justice Press.

Stollard, P. (1991) (ed.) *Crime Prevention Through Housing Design*. London: E & FN Spon.

Sutherland, E.H. (1939) *Principles of Criminology*. Chicago: J B Lippincott Co.

Taylor, R.B. (2000) *Breaking Away from Broken Windows: Baltimore Neighborhoods and the Nationwide Fight Against Crime, Grime, Fear and Decline*. Boulder, Colorado: Westview Press.

Taylor, R.B. (2002) *Crime Prevention Through Environmental Design (CPTED): Yes, No, Maybe, Unknowable, and All of the Above*. In Bechtel, R.B. and Churchman, A. (ed.) *Handbook of Environmental Psychology*. New York: John Wiley, pp. 413–26.

Town, S. (2003) Permeability, Access Control and Crime. Unpublished Paper West Yorkshire Police.

Town, S., Davey, C.L. and Wooton, A.B. (2003) Design Against Crime: Secure Urban Environments by Design. Salford: University of Salford.

Weisburd, D. and McEwen, T. (1997) *Crime Mapping and Crime Prevention*. Monsey, NY: Criminal Justice Press.

Welsh, B. and Farrington, D.P. (2002) Crime Prevention Effects of Closed Circuit Television: A Systematic Review. London: *Home Office Research Study 252*. Home Office.

Wilson-Doenges, G. (2000) 'An Exploration of Sense of Community and Fear of Crime in Gated Communities,' *Environment and Behavior*, 32: 597–612.

Wilson, J.Q. and Kelling, G.L. (1982) 'Broken windows,' *The Atlantic Monthly*, No. 211, March, pp. 29–38.

Wright, R.T. and Decker, S.H. (1997) *Armed Robbers in Action: Stickups and Street Culture.* Boston: Northeastern University Press.

Wood, E. (1961) *Housing Design: A Social Theory.* New York: New York Citizens' Housing and Planning Council.

Zahm, D. (2005) 'Learning, Translating and Implementing CPTED,' *Journal of Architectural and Planning Research*, Vol. 22, No. 4, Winter, pp. 284–93.

Zelinka, A. and Brennan, D. (2001) *SafeScape: Creating Safer, More Liveable Communities through Planning and Design.* Chicago: Planners Press.

6
Forensic Security and the Law

Daniel B. Kennedy

Introduction to forensic security

Historical overview of forensic sciences

In ancient Rome, a forum was a public place where important governmental debates were held. Sometimes it was a town square or even a marketplace. Gradually, the forum also became a sort of public 'courthouse,' where various trials of importance to the citizenry were held. Etymologically, the word forensic may be traced to the Latin *forensis*, for 'public,' and to *forensus*, meaning 'of the forum.' In some centers of higher learning, forensic studies came to mean the art or study of argumentative discourse, while in others the legal and judicial aspects of forensics were emphasized. In modern times, the term forensic has been applied to a body of knowledge useful to the courts in the resolution of conflicts within a legal context.

The word 'science' also comes to us from the Latin word *scire*, meaning 'to know.' Forensic science in its broadest definition, then, is the application of science to law. Essentially, a forensic scientist is one who relies on a systematically collected body of knowledge in order to provide relevant information to courts of law tasked with resolving legal issues. Although one might speak of science in service to the law, certain conflicts are inevitable in that the classic goal of science is the production of truth, while the goal of the law is to achieve justice.[1] Forensic scientists must recognize that they are but guests of the court, invited for the court's purposes. It is not unexpected that, from time to time, 'scientific truth' will be subordinated to 'legal truth.' Such is the reality of the adversary system, and one which every forensic scientist must be prepared to accept if he or she is to engage in the modern forum.[2]

Because of the wide breadth of knowledge potentially useful to the courts, numerous classification schemes have been proposed for the forensic sciences. Some authors have claimed that forensic science is simply a more generic term for criminalistics, the application of natural science to the detection of crime (Gilbert, 1986). Saferstein (2001) argues that, for all intents and purposes, the two terms are taken to be one and the same. Other scholars believe this approach is too narrow and exclusionary. For example, Moenssens, Starrs, Henderson and

Inbau (1995) consider scientific evidence in civil and criminal cases to be comprised of evidence based on the biological and life sciences, evidence based on the physical sciences, and behavioral science evidence. Thus, biological and life science evidence would consist of forensic pathology, serology and toxicology, drug analysis, DNA testing, and forensic odontology. Forensic anthropology and osteology (see Bass and Jefferson, 2003) would also be included within this rubric.

Forensic evidence based on the physical sciences would include questioned documents, ballistics, firearms identification and micrography, trace evidence, arson and explosives, spectographic voice recognition, and fingerprint identification.[3] In such a scheme, behavioral science evidence would be derived primarily from psychiatry, psychology and, to a limited extent, the detection of deception through polygraphy, hypnosis, narcoanalysis, and voice stress analysis.

In this chapter, however, we shall follow the lead of James and Nordby (2003), who argue that forensic science is much more comprehensive than criminalistics and related laboratory subjects. In addition to the conventional areas of study mentioned above, the field of forensic science 'constantly expands to include many additional areas of expertise' (James and Nordby, 2003: xvi). Thus, these scholars also include analyses of bloodstain pattern interpretation, forensic engineering, forensic cybertechnology, and criminal personality profiling in their recently edited textbook. Other subjects which may be routinely included one day are forensic economics, forensic photography, forensic radiology, and forensic accounting.

While the modern security manager would instantly understand the relevance of forensic accounting to his or her loss prevention responsibilities, certain social sciences are also becoming more forensically relevant to security concerns (Faigman, Kaye, Saks, Sanders, 2002b; Monahan and Walker, 1998). Certainly, there is a developing forensic sociology (Colquitt, 1988; Jenkins and Kroll-Smith, 1996; Moore and Friedman, 1993; Roesch, Golding, Hans and Reppucci, 1991) as well as a forensic criminology (Anderson and Winfree, 1987; Kennedy and Homant, 1996; Thornton and Voigt, 1988; Wolfgang, 1974). As will be seen below, there is also an emerging specialty known as forensic security with which today's loss prevention manager must become quite familiar if he or she is to successfully respond to the growing challenge of premises liability for negligent security litigation facing today's businesses, corporations, and commercial/residential landlords.

Because security litigation can be a rather complex matter, it is best understood from the perspective of the security expert witness so often called up by the courts or by attorneys for either plaintiffs or defendants.[4] The consulting or testifying expert must understand completely the event in question as well as the parts played in it by all parties. The expert witness must also be aware of a property's history, all security-related policies and procedures, relevant industry standards, and the legal process as well. It is from this comprehensive perspective, then, that much of the ensuing material will be presented.

Forensic security and premises liability litigation

Among the myriad duties of the modern security manager is the responsibility to limit an organization's exposure to premises liability for negligent security. As a result of the evolution of case law in the US and Commonwealth countries over the past three decades, landowners and landlords of all stripes may be legally liable should a passenger, customer, client, tenant, guest, or other category of visitor to the premises be assaulted while on property under their control. For example, merchants may be sued by a customer attacked in a store's restroom or car park. A hotel guest sexually assaulted in her room by a nighttime intruder may have a cause of action against hotel management. Students at a university, visitors to a corporate headquarters, and passengers of common carriers are increasingly looking to the courts to order compensation from the owners and managers of the property whereupon their injuries were sustained (Michael and Ellis, 2003). The actual perpetrators of these acts are unlikely targets of such lawsuits since their identities often remain unknown or they themselves are simply uncollectible. This leaves, of course, the third-party corporate entity which is often looked upon as a 'deep pockets' defendant.

Not only might a commercial enterprise be sued for a criminal act occurring on its property, a lawsuit might arise out of the actions of its own employees. Should a salesperson assault a customer, or a contract security officer wrongfully detain a suspected shoplifter, liability may attach. In addition to crimes by employees, modern organizations must be concerned about crimes *against* employees. Traditionally, business entities had been relatively immune from lawsuits instituted against them by their own employees for injuries sustained while at work because in many jurisdictions workers' compensation was their exclusive remedy. Even this barrier, however, is beginning to erode as more and more courts are carving out exceptions to workers' compensation laws and allowing increasing numbers of employees or their heirs to successfully sue employers for crime-related injuries sustained while on the job (Sakis and Kennedy, 2002). As one member of the defense bar has observed, 'Today, premises security lawsuits are among the fastest growing segment of personal injury lawsuits' (Kaminsky, 2001). This same source goes on to suggest that claims alleging inadequate security soon will be second only to general negligence/slip-and-fall cases as the most common lawsuit brought against landowners and landlords. Based on a recent survey of businesses, the Institute of Management and Administration reported that one out of every five organizations faced a security-related lawsuit in 2003, and nearly one in two large companies (30,000 employees or more) suffered the same fate ('A New Look at How to Prevent Security-Related Lawsuits,' 2004). Accordingly, security and loss prevention professionals must be increasingly prepared to deal with forensic issues as they help guide their organizations into the 21st century. Indeed, the forensic security specialist should be prepared not only to assist his or her employer in avoiding litigation in the first place but also to help manage the defense of a lawsuit should one be filed notwithstanding preventive efforts.

The forensic security expert can seek to prevent litigation by developing a familiarity with a property's crime problems and implementing security measures appropriate to the threat, a form of 'negligence proofing,' if you will (deTreville, 2004; Bottom, 1985). In the event litigation proceeds nonetheless, the forensic expert can assist counsel in pointing out faulty opposing arguments, preparing witnesses, and marshaling affirmative defenses. The importance of these efforts cannot be denied, particularly given the millions of dollars in punitive and compensatory damages frequently awarded to plaintiffs by sympathetic juries (Anderson, 2002). For example, juries in the United States have recently awarded damages totaling over $20 million dollars to a bank employee rendered paraplegic during an armed robbery, $18 million to the guest of a motel who suffered a particularly violent group rape, and $12 million to a mother who lost her son to murder at another motel. Other juries awarded over $2 million to the child survivors of a woman killed by her former lover while both were working in an automobile plant, and $1 million to the victim of a sexual assault in the parking lot of a major retailer. A bar was held liable for $18 million in compensatory and punitive damages awarded to a family for the loss of a son killed while fleeing his drunken attackers. These reported cases are only the tip of the iceberg, however. Far more cases go unreported because they are resolved by settlement between the parties before trial, and these settlements can often involve amounts exceeding a million dollars.[5] A perusal of such monthly publications as *Crime Liability Monthly* (The National Center for Victims of Crime) or *Private Security Case Law Reporter* (Strafford Publications) will reveal the pervasive nature of premises liability litigation in the US. These trends are becoming evident in other common-law countries as well.

History and nature of premises security litigation

The growth of security-related litigation in common-law countries around the world is closely related to the worldwide victims' rights movement, which was significantly influenced by the efforts of English magistrate Margery Fry to secure financial compensation for crime victims. Partially in response to her efforts, New Zealand set up a fund in 1963, followed by Great Britain in 1964, and by several Australian states and Canadian provinces during the next few years. In the US, California established the first government-funded victim compensation program in 1965 (Karmen, 2004; Tobolowsky, 2001; Wallace, 1998).

While the concept of making a victim whole is not new (e.g. Code of Hammurabi), the renewed emphasis on victims' rights, including the right to sue criminal perpetrators and third parties whose negligence is causally related to the criminal attack, must be viewed in the context of a broader 'due process' revolution which began to sweep over much of Western society in the 1960s. The civil rights, anti-war, consumerist, and women's movements all emphasized the rights of individuals to seek redress from the broader social institutions which had been viewed as insensitive to their just needs (Pointing and Maguire, 1988). Also, as more and more innocent citizens suffered the ravages of crime, the stage was set for a sea change concerning the duty of property owners and managers to provide proper security for all those people rightfully on the premises (see, generally, Kennedy, 1998).

In the US, two cases are widely regarded as the forerunners of third-party litigation against landlords, businesses, and corporate entities. In the 1970 case of *Kline v. 1500 Massachusetts Avenue Apartment Corporation*, a tenant sued her landlord for allowing the apartment building's security to deteriorate after she had moved in.[6] Ms Kline was subsequently assaulted and robbed. Ultimately, the appeals court ruled the landlord had a duty to take steps to protect Ms. Kline since only the landlord had sufficient control of the premises to do so. The court ruled the landlord-tenant contract required the landlord to provide those protective measures which are within his reasonable capacity. It also noted that the relationship of the modern apartment house dweller to a landlord is akin to that of innkeeper and guest, and, therefore, a duty similar to that imposed on innkeepers would apply (Carrington and Rapp, 1991).

The Garzilli case, also known as the 'Connie Francis' case, has given great impetus to victims' rights litigation. In *Garzilli v. Howard Johnson's Motor Lodges, Inc.*, the internationally known recording artist was assaulted in 1974 while in her motel suite. The unit's sliding glass doors gave the appearance of being locked, but the faulty latches were easily defeated by an intruder.[7] The property manager had known the locks were defective but had not yet provided for secondary-locking devices. The notoriety of the Connie Francis case came because of her star status and because the jury initially awarded her over two million dollars in compensatory damages (Carrington and Rapp, 1991).[8] Thereafter, crime victims were more inclined to pursue redress through the civil courts and soon found their pleas resonating with plaintiffs' attorneys, juries, and the judiciary as well.

Although the specialist in forensic security is not expected to be a lawyer, he or she must possess a comprehensive understanding of the legal context in which he or she will be operating. Generally speaking, negligent security constitutes a tort at English common law. A tort is a civil wrong for which the plaintiff hopes to receive compensation. In order to prove his or her case, the plaintiff must establish by a preponderance of the evidence that the defendant (1) owed the plaintiff a *duty* to act in a certain way, that (2) the defendant *breached* his or her duty by failing to act as the duty required, and that this (3) *caused* some (4) *harm* to the plaintiff. This chapter will explore in some detail the concepts of foreseeability, breach of duty, and causation as they relate to premises liability for negligent security.[9] As will be shown, underlying all arguments advanced by plaintiff and defense is the understanding that, generally speaking, the defendant had a duty to act as a reasonable person would act under similar circumstances (Best and Barnes, 2003).

For the purposes of this discussion, no duty exists without both a special relationship and crime foreseeability. As a general proposition, no duty is owed to another unless there is a special relationship between the two parties such as that of merchant-invitee, landlord-tenant, innkeeper-guest, public carrier-passenger or the like. The existence of a special relationship is generally a matter decided by the law of the particular jurisdiction as applied by the judge, and forensic security experts have little or no input into this determination. On the other hand, assessing the foreseeability of a crime is a vital task to be performed by the forensic security specialist.

Without foreseeability, there is no duty to provide security, and conventional premises liability for negligent security cases will fail in the absence of foreseeability. To establish that a crime was foreseeable to a defendant, the plaintiff must show that the defendant knew or should have known that a crime was reasonably likely to occur (Kaminsky, 2001). Many lawyers believe foreseeability is the most important element of a negligent tort since it is seen to put a defendant on notice that an injury will occur; it is a form of notice to the defendant not generally available to the plaintiff. The question of foreseeability may be approached in a number of different ways, depending upon the jurisdiction in which the case is to be heard.

Foreseeability of criminal attack

Definitions and tests

There is no simple universal definition for the legal concept of foreseeability. Each jurisdiction which addresses the issue will generally do so through its own case law and will often provide more than one definitional approach to the concept. In its abridged fifth edition, Black's Law Dictionary defines foreseeability as 'the reasonable anticipation that harm or injury is a likely result of acts or omissions.' This definition can be misleading to some interpreters, however, because the word 'likely' could be taken to mean 'more likely than not.' In no jurisdiction does foreseeability require such a degree of probability, 51 percent or higher, since even in the worst part of the worst neighborhood, crime does not occur in 51 of 100 instances wherein it is possible to occur. Most jurisdictions instead use such language as 'reasonably likely to occur,' 'reasonable cause to anticipate,' or 'appreciable chance.' Other jurisdictions define foreseeability by citing the anticipated behavior of reasonable citizens. For example, in *Samson v. Saginaw*, 'foreseeability depends upon whether or not a reasonable man could anticipate that a given event might occur under certain conditions.'[10] In the California case of *Onciano v. Golden Palace Restaurant*, an event is foreseeable 'if it is likely enough in the setting of modern life that a reasonably thoughtful person would take account of it in guiding practical conduct.'[11] As is the case with many legal definitions, however, the practical meaning of foreseeability remains elusive. In order to provide guidelines on how to apply foreseeability to the fact pattern of a case at bar, many jurisdictions provide for certain 'tests' of foreseeability. While a definition of foreseeability is useful in orienting the security manager to the concept, a test of foreseeability tells him or her which analytical steps a court is likely to follow in order to determine whether or not a certain crime was foreseeable, and thus whether a duty to protect can be said to have existed. For analytic purposes, foreseeability should be considered a continuous rather than a discrete variable. In other words, foreseeability should be assessed on a continuum from not foreseeable to highly foreseeable.

Currently, there are four tests of foreseeability which are routinely applied in common law jurisdictions. While some jurisdictions have used the same test of foreseeability for many years, others have adopted one or another of the tests as they have begun to examine more and more premises liability cases. The four most popular approaches are: the imminent or specific harm test, the prior similar acts test, the totality of the circumstances test, and the balancing test (Donohue, 2002).

Imminent harm test

Also known as the specific harm test, this approach to foreseeability is one of the older and more conservative tests and has lost favor in many jurisdictions because it constitutes such a formidable barrier for most plaintiffs to penetrate. Essentially, this test requires the plaintiff to show that a landlord was aware that a specific individual was acting in such a manner as to pose a clear threat to the safety of an identifiable target. Given the large size of much commercial property open for business to the public, it is unlikely that landlords or their agents will be physically present at many emergent situations, thus effectively absolving them of liability. As a matter of public policy, for example, the Michigan Supreme Court recently ruled that a merchant's duty is limited to responding reasonably to 'situations occurring on the premises that pose a risk of imminent and foreseeable harm to identifiable invitees.'[12] The court reasoned that to rule otherwise would have a pernicious and devastating effect on the many commercial businesses located in Michigan's urban and high-crime areas (e.g. Detroit). For the good of urban merchants, businesses, and metropolitan-area economies, then, at least one higher court has curtailed a great deal of third-party litigation concerning criminal attack. Most courts, however, are unwilling to hold that a criminal act is foreseeable only in such specific and limited situations. Accordingly, several jurisdictions have adopted one of the remaining three tests of foreseeability.

Prior similar acts test

It is almost axiomatic in forensic criminology and psychology that the best predictor of future behavior is past behavior. Empirical research involving the course of crime at 'hot spots' has shown, for example, that in one major city, each location had initially only an 8 percent chance of suffering a predatory offense. Once such an offense occurred, however, the chance of a second increased to 26 percent. After a third offense, the risk of a fourth within the year exceeded 50 percent (Sherman, Gartin, and Buerger, 1989). Should a burglary take place at a residential location, the likelihood it will be reburglarized may increase up to fourfold (Weisel, 2002). Similar patterns may be applied to individuals. Criminal recidivism rates often reach 60 to 70 percent (Austin and Irwin, 2001). The more crimes an individual has committed in the past, the more crimes he is likely to commit in the future. This is particularly true of early-onset delinquents and psychopaths (Lykken, 1995; Piquero and Mazerolle, 2001). Given the importance of past history in attempting to forecast future events, the forensic security expert should immediately acquaint himself with the history of a property either to be protected or which has already become the subject of litigation. Jurisdictions will vary as to whether prior crime must be substantially similar to the litigated crime or whether, for example, as in Georgia, crimes against property may also make crimes against persons foreseeable (Gorby, 1998).

A related question refers to the appropriate time period for which prior similar acts should be evaluated. While plaintiff security experts would wish to extend the number of years back in time upon which to focus their attention, defense experts would probably prefer that a much shorter period of time be considered. Although the International Association of Professional Security Consultants suggests three to five years prior to the date of the incident as a relevant time frame, as does the General Security Risk Assessment published by the American Society for Industrial Security, many courts seem to consider a two- to three-year prior history not to be so remote in time as to be irrelevant. Time limitations on prior similar acts are most likely to be decided during *in limine* motions preceding trial.

An excellent framework for considering the most pertinent aspects of prior acts was provided in the Texas case of *Timberwalk Apartments, Partners, Inc. et al. v. Cain.*[13] The court in that case decided that five factors must be considered together to determine whether criminal conduct was foreseeable: proximity, recency, frequency, similarity, and publicity. Thus, courts would consider whether any criminal conduct previously occurred on or near the property in question.[14] However, many courts require that prior similar incidents be somewhat numerous. One or two prior incidents have been found insufficient to put certain properties on notice. Ten armed robberies in a three-year period were enough to put a fast-food restaurant on notice. The issue of numerosity seems to be determined more by the nature of each case rather than by any pat formula.[15]

Also important in determining foreseeability is how recently crime occurred, how often it occurred, how similar[16] the conduct was to conduct on the property and, finally, what publicity was there to indicate the landlord knew or should have known about the crime on or near the property. Any forensic security expert charged with planning for security protection or tasked with helping to defend a landlord being sued should be familiar with these five factors.

The data which will provide the basis for this historical evaluation will come from an organization's own incident reports, proprietary guard service incident reports, and public police records. Because 'calls for police service' records can both overestimate and underestimate actual crime (Klinger and Bridges, 1997), the forensic security expert is expected to consult records of crime *known* to the police and the actual narrative reports composed by responding officers. A close reading of these narratives can provide the security specialist with a deeper, qualitative appreciation of the nature of crime at a property. For example, an initial report classified as domestic assault and battery may reveal, upon closer reading, that the battery arose out of a dispute over the proceeds of drug sales in an apartment complex. Such a revelation would, of course, present more profound implications for any security manager to consider.

In order to develop an appreciation of the broader neighborhood context, forensic specialists will sometimes compare the number of crimes committed in a property's police district with crimes in other districts. Since disparities may be explained by differential population size rather than by actual risk, the analyst should develop comparative crime rates per 100,000, where possible. Some police agencies keep records of crimes within census tract boundaries (e.g. Milwaukee, Columbus), thus facilitating this task. Most police agencies, however, do not match population data with crime data except, of course, at the city level. Given the need for analytical information of this kind, the forensic security specialist may wish to develop skills and techniques approaching those possessed by public police crime analysts (Clarke and Eck, 2003; D'Addario, 1989; Gottlieb, Arenberg and Singh, 1994; Osborne and Warnicke, 2003; Peterson, 1998).

Totality of the circumstances test

There are many jurisdictions which do not require the existence of prior similar acts in order to conclude that a given crime was foreseeable. Known as 'totality of the circumstances' jurisdictions, foreseeability is determined therein by the existence of various social and environmental factors known to be associated with crime, which may or may not include prior crimes. For example, in one case a physician was shot in a poorly lit section of a hospital emergency room parking lot located in a 'high crime' area. The emergency room area was the site of many incidents of harassment yet was insufficiently secured. The court ruled that a landowner should not get 'one free assault' before he can be held liable for criminal acts which occur on his property.[17] The court further commented that parking lots, by their very nature, create an especial temptation and opportunity for criminal misconduct.[18] The Nevada Supreme Court, commenting further on parking lots, observed that the place and character of a hotel/casino's business, where 'cash and liquor are constantly flowing,' may provide a fertile environment for criminal conduct such as robbery and assault.[19]

Of primary importance to the forensic security analyst is the specific location of a property whereupon a criminal attack has taken place. The census tract in which this property is located can readily be determined so that the socioeconomic characteristics of the immediate population can be reviewed and compared with the rest of the city. For example, median family income, unemployment rate, proportion of population beneath the poverty level, population mobility, population density, percentage of female heads of household with children, and percentage of married-couple households have been correlated with criminal behavior in an urban setting (Figlio, Hakim and Rengert, 1986; Roncek, 1981; Stark, 1987). Canadian criminologists Paul and Patricia Brantingham (1981/1991, 1984) have documented the travel patterns and thought processes of criminals as they navigate the urban landscape. The implications of their environmental criminology are obvious for the security manager responsible for customer and employee safety. A proximity hypothesis suggests that people within a one to two mile radius of a potentially criminal population are at risk for criminal victimization (Meadows, 1998).[20]

In addition to considering the proximity of criminal populations, the security manager must also note the differential land use of surrounding properties. For example, certain high schools, housing projects, fast-food restaurants, and even shopping centers have been found by various researchers to be linked with crime in a neighborhood (Roncek, Bell and Francik, 1981; Roncek and Lobosco, 1983; Roncek and Maier, 1991). Australian researcher Ross Homel and colleagues (1997) have documented the incidence of crime attendant to selected entertainment areas, much as Roncek and Maier (1991) have done for bars and taverns in the US.

Further related to land use, an interesting distinction can be made between properties described as crime 'attractors' and those described as crime 'generators' (Brantingham and Brantingham, 1995). The former tend to experience more crime than other locations simply because there are more potential victims from which criminals may choose although the level of risk per individual may not be heightened. Crime generators, on the other hand, foretell more crime because of the illicit nature of activities on the premises, such as illegal gambling, prostitution, and drug trafficking. Since the association between drug use, drug trafficking, and crime is so well established (Goldstein, 1985), security managers must take action to both prevent and aggressively respond to any such activities occurring on the properties for which they are responsible.

Certainly, all the variables which might be considered in a 'totality of the circumstances' test of foreseeability have not been discussed. Additional criminological concepts such as crime displacement, vehicle and pedestrian travel patterns, critical intensity, criminal mental mapping, and Crime Prevention Through Environmental Design issues may impact on crime foreseeability (Kennedy, 1993). The forensic analyst must learn to recognize potentially violent situations which might arise out of a myriad mix of variables. For example, might violence be foreseen by a Manager On Duty at a hotel where a teenager has rented a room on a Saturday night and where dozens of underage and unchaperoned juveniles, many unknown to each other, are making a great deal of noise and acting belligerently while appearing to be under the influence of alcohol? Some acts of violence would be reasonably foreseeable here. Is violence in the parking lot of a gay bar foreseeable in a lower-income urban area where there have been taunts and threats of a 'hate crime' nature, but no known attacks? It would seem so. If one were to add a history of prior attacks under similar circumstances at these properties, it would seem a foregone conclusion that these crimes were foreseeable. On the other hand, if a woman was suddenly struck and robbed during daylight hours at a small strip mall parking lot which had no criminal history, was located in an upper-middle class suburb, and where there were several bystander witnesses in the area, would a court consider this attack to have been foreseeable? It is doubtful that a court would find that such an act should have been foreseen. Ultimately, the forensic analyst must familiarize himself with relevant cultural and social factors of the vicinity in which a security incident occurred. Local judges and juries will evaluate any given case in the context of informal history and community attitudes as well as the formal legal record. The effective expert will be aware of these variables as well.

To summarize, a crime is foreseeable under the 'totality of the circumstances' test if a reasonable person would be able to identify the presence of one or more social facts commonly associated with crime. Courts would consider all of the circumstances surrounding an event, including the nature, condition, and location of the land, the nature of human behavior regularly occurring on the property, as well as prior similar incidents, if any. Because this approach may render the foreseeability question too broad and too easily answered in the affirmative, a number of courts are turning to a fourth test of foreseeability, the balancing test.

Balancing test

As we have seen so far, some courts believe the specific harm test is too limited. Others find that the prior similar incidents test can unfairly relieve landowners of liability, at least insofar as the first victim is concerned. The totality of circumstances test is seen by other courts as rendering foreseeability simply too easy to establish. The balancing test offers a fourth alternative as jurisdictions around the world seek the appropriate approach to the question of foreseeability.

Essentially, the balancing test seeks to balance the level of harm to be anticipated against the burden of the duty to be imposed. As the gravity of the possible harm increases, the likelihood of its occurrence needs to be correspondingly less in order to trigger the implementation of appropriate security measures. Correspondingly, a merchant should not be expected to take burdensome security precautions unless their need is convincingly established, often through the occurrence of prior similar acts.

Early versions of the balancing test could be quite complex, as in Judge Learned Hand's algebraic formula for ascertaining negligent conduct: If the burden (i.e. cost) of providing the security is less than the probability of criminal attack multiplied by the seriousness of the potential injury, the landlord will be liable. If, on the other hand, the burden outweighs the probability times the harm, then there is no negligence (Tarantino and Dombroff, 1990).

A recent Tennessee Supreme Court case lists a number of factors to be reviewed under the balancing test as courts seek to balance the burden of the duty with the rights to be protected. These include the foreseeability and magnitude of the harm, the importance or social value of the defendant's activity, the feasibility of alternative, safer conduct, and the relative costs and burdens associated with that conduct.[21] Because the forensic security specialist is rarely a trained lawyer, he or she might find the balancing tests somewhat difficult to apply in any immediately practical fashion. For those responsible for designing security in a balancing-test jurisdiction, a 'three-way' test of security adequacy is recommended as a threshold assessment. The three prongs of this test are: (1) the level of crime foreseeability, (2) the likelihood a given combination of security measures will prevent future harm, and (3) the burden of taking such precautions (McGoey, 1990). These three issues constitute the core of current balancing tests and are quite manageable for the purposes of case analysis.[22]

Breach of duty

Reasonableness and standards of care

Once a special relationship and foreseeability have come together to impose upon a landlord a duty to protect someone on his property, the question becomes whether the duty was breached or whether it was discharged reasonably. The concept of reasonableness is a mainstay of common law, no less so in premises liability for negligent security cases. At the heart of all such cases is whether a landlord or property manager took appropriate steps to prevent a foreseeable harm from occurring. Although no landlord is expected to be a guarantor of invitee, licensee or trespasser safety, reasonable steps must be taken to avoid injury.[23] Because a landlord is in control of a property and in a better position to know the condition of a property, the law may place upon him a duty to act reasonably on behalf of people who come upon the property.

The issue, of course, is what constitutes reasonable behavior? Reasonable behavior is nothing more than that which a landlord or security manager of ordinary prudence would do under similar circumstances (Bilek, Klotter and Federal, 1981). While some courts are content to let judge or jury decide what is reasonable based upon a combination of the evidence and their own background experiences, other courts welcome discussion of relevant benchmarks or other information which would help guide them in their assessment of what is reasonable.

To that end, litigants will often introduce evidence purporting to establish certain standards of care against which a defendant's conduct is to be compared. Theoretically, a jury's job would be much easier if it could simply assess a defendant's behavior and then compare it to a known, descriptive standard specifying what the behavior should have been. The problem, of course, is identifying just what the standard of care is for a given set of circumstances. Not only will knowledgeable people disagree as to the nature of the appropriate standard, debates over the meaning of related concepts such as 'guidelines' or 'best practices' are likely to ensue.[24] In order for the forensic security specialist to navigate in the legal arena, it is important for him or her to understand the sources of various standards of care pertaining to security.

Most industries sponsor or support professional or trade associations whose purpose is to advance members' interests. For example, the American Hotel and Lodging Association serves the hospitality industry. The International Council of Shopping Centers serves retailers and developers of varying sizes. The National Association of Convenience Stores serves small stores while the Food Marketing Institute serves larger ones. The National Apartment Association and the Institute of Real Estate Management represent the interests of property managers of varying sizes. The forensic specialist's first inquiry into appropriate standards (or guidelines) should be with the appropriate professional or trade organization.

Forensic security specialists would certainly approach their own professional associations to determine the nature of relevant security standards. The American Society for Industrial Security International (ASIS) has a worldwide membership of approximately 33,000 professionals representing all industries and publishes a monthly magazine as well as technical monographs. Security equipment manufacturers and service providers are also represented by such trade groups as the British Security Industry Association and, in the US, by the Security Industry Association. There are also smaller, specialty associations which are concerned with security in specific institutional settings. The International Association for Healthcare Security and Safety and the International Association of Campus Law Enforcement Administrators are but two such examples.

There are other sources of standards as well. Cross-cutting associations which provide specialized products and services through their members in a wide range of settings may also offer standards or guidelines. For example, the National Association of Security Companies represents the interests of contract and proprietary security officer providers in all settings. The Illuminating Engineering Society of North America publishes very comprehensive lighting standards. The National Parking Association and the Institutional and Municipal Parking Congress are two trade organizations whose members are very knowledgeable of appropriate parking practices. Organizations such as the American Society for Testing and Materials (ASTM), the American National Standards Institute (ANSI), and Underwriter's Laboratories (UL) are active in setting standards for security equipment.

Of course, the various associations just mentioned are but a tiny sample of the numerous trade groups and learned societies to which a forensic specialist might turn for guidance.[25] In any event, it is important first to develop an understanding of the very nature of standards themselves so that the credibility to be reposed in said standards might be better assessed.

Types of standards

Having sampled possible sources of security standards, it is also important to note the different types of standards routinely presented to civil courts in common law countries. Although there is no universally applicable standards typology, forensic security specialists often identify five categories: national consensus standards, community standards, self-imposed standards, mandatory standards and learned treatises.

National consensus standards are generated by neutral, consensus-setting organizations such as ASTM, ANSI, and Underwriters' Laboratories of Canada or by specialized professional societies such as ASIS and the National Fire Protection Association (NFPA). These organizations follow a formal procedure wherein standards are formulated, published, revised by consensus and eventually finalized. The idea, of course, is that consensus standards represent the best thinking of relevant stakeholders who have had multiple opportunities to contribute to the formulation of these standards. Both ASIS International and NFPA are in the process of developing numerous consensus standards through this process, and the forensic security specialist is well advised to keep informed of their efforts in this regard.[26]

Community standards refer to those practices commonly found in a given geographic area or those practices generally preferred by an entire specialized industry (Bates, 1997). For example, courts are routinely asked to assess the reasonableness of a company's security practices by comparing these practices to those of other companies in the same geographical area. The idea, of course, is that a security practice would appear to be all the more reasonable to the extent that numerous companies follow that practice. Unfortunately, of course, this has not always been the case. Community standards, in a broader sense, also relate to the security measures taken by a given industry throughout an entire region or nation. For example, how do most hotels in Australia handle guestroom key control? To what extent do enclosed malls throughout the United States patrol exterior parking lots? Do most British hospital maternity wards follow similar practices to ensure infant safety and security? Are criminal background checks done for people who are hired for security positions in all Commonwealth countries?

Self-imposed standards are those which organizations have set for themselves by inclusion in their own policies and procedures manuals. The first interrogatory questions or demands for production of documents in security litigation generally involve a defendant corporation's internal policy and training manuals. The idea, of course, is that a company will implement only those security measures which it deems reasonable. Thus, should a company violate its own reasonable practices, it is acting negligently. However, this is not necessarily the only proper conclusion to be drawn from a seeming contradiction between policies and actions.

Mandatory standards are taken to mean those nonelective measures formally mandated by state or provincial statute, municipal ordinance, administrative code, and the like. In some jurisdictions, negligence *per se* may apply where legally required security measures have not been implemented. Examples of mandatory standards include lighting levels for municipal car parks, security officer staffing at shopping malls, the number of clerks on duty at convenience stores by time of day, ventilation window locks for rental property windows, alcohol server training in certain states, pub doorman licensing, pre-assignment security officer training, and the installation of secondary door and window-locking devices.

Finally, the recommendations of learned treatises and expert opinion are to be considered. It is not unusual for judges to cite academic literature in their opinions. The scholarly works of natural and social scientists as well as legal philosophers routinely impact judicial thinking (Erickson and Simon, 1998; Faigman, 2000; Homant and Kennedy, 1995). Where an established expert has provided substantial evidence in a security-related case, his or her thoughts on reasonable security measures can play a significant role in a judge's formulation of case law and, in effect, become somewhat of a standard, at least in that particular jurisdiction.[27] Because most cases do not reach trial stage, the importance of a written expert report cannot be overemphasized. In the United Kingdom, expert reports must comply with Civil Procedure Rules, Part 35, while in the US, Rule 26 of the Federal Rules of Civil Procedure controls the structure and goals of expert reports. Forensic experts must be skilled in the written explication of their opinions and also must be prepared to defend these opinions in open court under often rigorous cross-examination. For these and other reasons, forensic knowledge alone is insufficient to qualify one as an effective forensic expert.[28]

Presumptive standards of care

On the one hand, industry leaders and security professionals are expected to formalize a set of broadly applicable standards in order to optimize protective efforts on behalf of all citizens. On the other hand, enlightened observes realize that most properties are somewhat unique in their configurations and in the threats they face. A shopping mall with a specific tenant mix located in a certain kind of neighborhood may have different security requirements than another mall with a different tenant mix located in a much poorer or richer part of town. One size does *not* fit all and, to a certain extent, security efforts must be tailored to fit each particular property or land usage. It is largely because of these conflicting themes that security standards have not been universally adopted and their impact on premises liability only partly understood.[29] A possible solution to this problem may lie in the notion of 'presumptive standards,' a concept borrowed from the field of corrections and its use of presumptive sentencing.

In presumptive sentencing, a somewhat narrow range of months of incarceration is established for a given crime (a standard sentence). This presumptive sentence, however, may be increased by aggravating factors or decreased by mitigating factors. Such a sentencing format, it is believed, will reduce inappropriate sentencing disparity (Clear and Cole, 1997; Schmalleger and Smykla, 2005). A similar approach to security standards may increase the uniformity of protective services both within and between nations and still take into account the unique requirements of each individual property. Consider the common question of appropriate security officer-to-patron ratios. How many security officers per 100 concertgoers is appropriate?

Although most security experts are reluctant to identify any ratios at all, some have ventured conditional recommendations. For example, Poulin (1992) has suggested assigning one security officer for every 100 concert patrons. Under a presumptive standards approach, venue managers might then assign one officer per every 50 patrons of a heavy metal or gangster rap concert (aggravating factors) and one officer per every 150 patrons of a Johnny Mathis or Yanni concert (mitigating factors). The parking lot of a hospital in an urban area might require security fencing for access control while a rural hospital might require no such measure. In both scenarios, however, a presumptive security standard would have required security managers to consider the issue of parking lot access control.

It seems, then, that the finder of fact in a premises liability lawsuit will face two major tasks concerning breach of duty. The first will be to determine what behavior should reasonably have been expected on the part of the defendant. What was the appropriate standard of care given the defendant's circumstances? The second task, of course, is to determine whether the defendant failed to live up to these expectations. In numerous instances, both plaintiff and defendant will concur on the appropriate standard of care to be applied. They may disagree on whether the standard of care was actually breached. As will be seen, however, a defendant will not become liable for negligence unless it can be shown by a preponderance of evidence that the failure to act reasonably was causally related to the injuries sustained. In other words, had the defendant properly discharged his duty, it is more likely than not the crime would not have occurred.

Causation

Proximate cause and cause in fact

Even if crime at a property was foreseeable and there was breach of a standard of care, plaintiffs in civil litigation must still prove by a preponderance of evidence that the breach caused harm to the plaintiffs. Causation in the legal sense is not so rigorously defined as in the social sciences[30] and can generally be broken down into two parts: proximate cause and cause-in-fact.

Proximate cause is often defined as 'that, which in a natural and continuous sequence, unbroken by any efficient intervening cause, produces injury, and without which the result would not have occurred' (Nolan and Connolly, 1983: 641). Legal practitioners often take this definition to once again encompass the notion of foreseeability. In other words, not only must a crime be foreseeable for duty to attach, it must also be foreseeable that a given breach would lead to injury.

Cause in fact refers to the actual cause of an injury. One test of actual cause is the 'but for' test. But for the failure to implement a reasonable security program, would the plaintiff have been injured? Another very common test is the 'substantial factor' test. Was the failure to implement a reasonable security program a substantial factor in the plaintiff's injury or loss? Causation issues are generally left to the decider of fact.

Forensic security practitioners must be aware of the concept of 'abstract negligence' if called upon to defend a corporate security program.[31] Plaintiff security experts will often criticize multiple aspects of a defendant's security program even if these aspects of the program were totally unrelated to the criminal attack. For example, an expert might criticize a landlord's key control or access control program even though an attacker entered upon the property legally as an invited guest. A security officer's training history may be criticized even though his actions at the scene of an incident were completely appropriate. A defendant landlord's failure to repair a garage security gate cannot be the legal cause of an assault if there is no evidence a perpetrator actually entered through the open gate. Without proving the critical element of causation, of course, the plaintiff cannot make his or her case.[32]

Evidence-based security measures

Evidence-Based Medicine and Evidence-Based Policing should serve as models for security specialists intent on developing and implementing effective security measures (Sherman, 1998; 2003). By adhering as closely as possible to scientific methodologies in evaluating the efficacy of security programming, researchers and practitioners can more effectively inform juries about appropriate standards of care for the security industry. For example, lighting is not the automatic crime deterrent it is thought to be by so many laymen (Farrington and Welsh, 2002; Marchant, 2004) nor does CCTV function universally to deter crimes against the person (Gill and Loveday, 2003; Painter and Tilley, 1999; Welsh and Farrington, 2003; Welsh and Farrington, 2004). Just as random police patrol is losing ground to directed patrol, security managers may need to rethink standard security officer deployment practices based on the best empirical evidence available (e.g. Sherman, Gottfredson, MacKenzie, Eck, Reuter and Bushway, 1997).

The forensic implications of these critical evaluations are obvious: improved lighting may not have prevented an attack in a parking lot so there may be no obvious causal relationship between a defendant's lighting levels and the crime. If CCTV does not prevent violent crimes in convenience stores, how can failure to install CCTV at a given location be the cause of a clerk's attack? On the other hand, lighting and CCTV may manifest preventive benefits in certain circumstances involving certain perpetrators. Lighting, for example, seems to be the catalyst which provides for the synergy of several security measures working together to more effectively harden a target. Hence, the liability implications of conventional security measures still need to be sorted out on a case-by-case basis. Lighting, CCTV, and preventive patrol are mentioned only as examples of popular security practices which need to be evaluated for the purposes of each particular property. Other security measures should also be realistically assessed before implementation so that a false sense of security is not generated.

Individual deterrence

Rather than focusing exclusively on the efficacy of security hardware, many forensic behavioral scientists also consider the criminal's susceptibility to deterrence.[33] Can all criminals be deterred? Is the deterrence threshold higher for criminals with certain cognitive characteristics than for others? Once again, each criminal must be evaluated on an individual basis.

Homant (1999) believes offenders can be placed in one of four categories based on their desire to avoid capture interacting with their motivation to commit a particular crime. Thus, the opportunistic offender who is not highly motivated to commit a particular crime and is highly motivated to avoid capture may be readily deterred (e.g. a professional criminal with many available targets). On the other hand, it is extremely difficult to deter an individual who is highly motivated to commit a particular crime yet not very motivated to avoid capture (e.g. a suicide bomber). Another approach to the question of individual deterrence involves a relatively new investigative technique known as 'criminal profiling.' Former law enforcement profilers sometimes have been retained in civil litigation to assess the behavioral characteristics of unknown offenders and to opine on the likelihood that certain security measures would have deterred them. While such crime scene profiling may occasionally prove helpful in an investigative sense, caution must be employed lest such profiling be applied with unfounded confidence to inappropriate cases (Kennedy and Homant, 1997).

More recently, Jacobs (2004) has offered eight variables which serve to make an offender more or less risk-sensitive. The implication is that less risk-sensitive offenders will be less deterrable and vice-versa. Thus, impulsive offenders are less deterrable (see, also, Webster and Jackson, 1997) as are those who believe their appearances, altered by disguises, render them anonymous. The presence of bystanders can deter some criminals, while crime sprees generally reflect risk insensitivity. Other considerations include presence of a prior record, intoxication, whether an offender is 'dared' to do a crime, and whether there are perceived injustices to be corrected (Kennedy, Homant and Homant, 2004).

There are additional considerations when assessing the deterrability of a given offender. Psychopaths, for example, do not experience fear as others do (Hare, 1993) and might be less deterrable. Offenders can be intensely motivated by paraphilias (Abel and Osborn, 1992) and some rapists (Salter, 2003) and pedophiles (van Dam, 2001) actually find the risk of getting caught to be a big part of the thrill of the crime (Katz, 1988). Some gang members may be relatively impervious to conventional perceptual security measures since their prestige is often derived from 'La Locura,' or acting out in an outrageous fashion regardless of the obvious consequences (Moore, 1991; Yablonsky, 1997). As a practical matter, criminologists have generally found the criminal who acts instrumentally to be more deterrable (or displaceable) than one whose crimes tend to be expressive in nature (cf. Nettler, 1989). Thus, a professional criminal who tends to choose a lucrative target carefully might be more sensitive to security measures than a morbidly jealous man who charges into his girlfriend's place of work and shoots her in front of many witnesses because he had recently heard rumors of her infidelity.

Lifestyle and causation

The forensic security specialist will find study of the criminological subdiscipline of victimology quite useful in understanding alternative theories of causation. A major concern of early victimologists was the role played by the victim himself in helping to cause his own victimization. It is known that young males are several times more likely to be homicide victims than are older females. This disparity is largely due to lifestyle differences (Fattah, 1991; Karmen, 2004). For example, young males are more likely to go out to public unsupervised places late at night and consume alcohol while in the proximity of other young males in groups who are strangers to them. Ego contests and disputes over females often lead to violence. Additionally, to the extent young males engage in criminal behavior with other young criminals, they themselves are more likely to be victimized as well. As Wolfgang (1957) explained many years ago, it is often a matter of chance alone that determines which individual becomes the perpetrator and which becomes the victim of violence.

The implications of these youthful lifestyle choices for landlords of mass private property (cf. Shearing and Stenning, 1983) are obvious. A young man injured at a shopping center or apartment complex while engaging in drug selling or 'gangbanging' will sometimes elect to sue property management for failing to protect him from the degradations of his peers. For example, a recent Texas case involved a young man who was shot at 4:30 a.m. while in the parking lot of his apartment building. Earlier in the day, he had beaten another young man in the same parking lot, and that youngster had vowed to return and take his revenge. The 'victim' was shot while selling drugs during the early morning hours, although he told the court he was in the lot at that hour only because his uncle was coming to pick him up early for day labor. Another case in California was brought by a gang member who was attacked in the parking lot of a large shopping mall. This 'victim' was attacked in retaliation for his own attack on the perpetrator earlier in the week. Clearly, both attacks were more related to pre-existing animosities than to any given condition of the property. Thus, in these instances the landlords can argue that there was no causal relationship between a property's security measures and the violent outbursts. Furthermore, it is particularly difficult to foresee the appearance of two antagonists at the same time and place.

To the extent security personnel understand relevant victimological theories, they can better explain to a jury that the real 'cause' of an injury might be an individual's own behavior rather than a landlord's negligence. Judges and juries must decide to what extent a landlord should compensate an individual for the negative consequences of his own lifestyle choices.

Conclusions

Forensic studies run the gamut from applied physics, entomology, and engineering to psychology, psychiatry, and criminology. Forensic security involves efforts to prevent litigation and to defend against it should lawsuits ensue. As we have seen in this chapter, premises liability for negligent security has become a billion dollar problem worldwide which no forward thinking business organization can afford to ignore. Accordingly, modern security managers must become familiar with tort law and master operational meanings of foreseeability, standards of care, and legal causation. Although forensic security specialists are not expected to become lawyers, their understanding of criminal behavior, security systems, and legal principles should make them indispensable assets to corporate leadership in this litigious business environment.

There are several areas of security litigation not yet touched upon in these limited pages. Security litigation is usually more complex than simply determining the quality of lighting in a distant car park. Subrogation often pits one insurance company against another, as when an insurance company pays off on a large claim and then sues for recovery. Many English cases involve contract disputes over delivery of services or system failures, as well as large financial losses due to theft or damage.

While a corporate or business entity may be vicariously liable under *respondeat superior* for the negligent acts of its employees committed within the scope of their employment, there is also the notion of direct liability to consider. Here the organization may be deemed culpable if it negligently hired, retained, entrusted, supervised, assigned, directed, or trained an employee (Maxwell, 1993). Legal commentators expect new tort actions to evolve. For example, various companies sometimes issue false letters of recommendation to rid themselves of troublesome employees. From time to time other companies may arbitrarily and capriciously fire employees who then extract workplace revenge on other workers. While negligent referral and negligent firing are not as yet fully established causes of action, several such lawsuits have already been filed.

Other topics of concern for the forensic security expert, particularly in the retail sector, involve false arrest, false imprisonment, defamation of character, and excessive force. Banks have been sued for faulty alarm systems, construction engineers have been sued for failing to secure construction sites, and hotels have been sued for allowing unsupervised access to swimming pools. Lawyers have even been sued for failing to properly prosecute negligent security claims. The point here, of course, is that modern commerce requires attention to security issues; and where there is a security issue, there is the possibility of security litigation.

Notes

1 Of course, it would be naive to presume that all forensic scientists place the concern for truth above partisan and ideological considerations. Examples of 'junk science' abound in public health (Milloy, 1995), psychiatric (Kirk and Kutchins, 1992), psychological (Hagen, 1997) and public policy literature (Gilbert, 1997; Hunt, 1999). Even worse, Turvey (2003) has documented an alarming number of cases in which forensic scientists in criminal cases have deliberately offered fraudulent evidence to the courts. Ever since the US Supreme Court case of *Daubert v. Merrell Dow Pharmaceuticals, Inc.*, 509 US 579 (1993), federal trial judges have served as 'gatekeepers' to try and ensure that the claimed basis for scientific and other expert testimony is valid. Daubert and other related cases, however, have raised as many questions as they have answered (Faigman, 2000).

2 This snapshot of the evolution of forensic science is derived from discussions found in Faigman, Kaye, Saks, and Sanders (2002a), Osterburg and Ward (1997), and Saferstein (2001).

3 To be sure, most of these forensic specialities would be of more direct concern to public law enforcement agencies and public prosecutors than to the private security community. It is important, however, that private sector security professionals understand the role of physical evidence in the investigative process so that private property crime scenes can be protected, and relevant leads can be provided to the public authorities.

4 Expert witnesses are utilized in Australia, New Zealand, Canada, the United States and the United Kingdom, albeit with some minor differences. Due to their expertise, they are allowed to render opinions to the jury rather than simply relay facts. Ward (1999, 2004) points out some interesting distinctions among the common law countries and discusses the evolution of both civil and criminal expert evidence as well.

5 Historically, corporate executives and business owners would occasionally dismiss the need to implement security measures in order to prevent incidents by quipping, 'That's what we have insurance for.' In many instances, however, organizations are self-insured up to, for example $250,000. In other words, there is a large deductible which the company will have to pay itself. It is also important to consider the nonrecoverable

personnel costs involved in locating, duplicating, and producing documents, sitting for
lengthy depositions, hosting site inspections and tolerating disruption of executive
schedules. Bad publicity, loss of good will, divulgence of embarrassing information,
negative career consequences, and personal stress are also part and parcel of the litigation process. Effective security proactively seeks to avoid litigation by preventing
adverse incidents from occurring in the first place.

6   439 F.2d 477 (D.C. Cir. 1970).

7   419 F. Supp. 1210 (E.D.N.Y. 1976).

8   Until his untimely death in 1992, Frank Carrington was clearly the leading legal advocate for litigation on behalf of crime victims in the US (see also, Carrington, 1978,
1983 and 1988). Much of his work is carried on through the National Crime Victim Bar
Association, an affiliate of the National Center for Victims of Crime in Washington,
DC. Its quarterly magazine, *Victim Advocate*, carries scholarly articles written by legal
professionals and forensic security experts addressing premises liability and other types
of third-party litigation on behalf of victims of crime and terrorism. Readers interested
in additional treatises addressing premises security should consult Bakken and Abele
(1995), Homant and Kennedy (1995), Kuhlman (1989),Talley (1994), and Tarantino
and Dombroff (1990). Consult Blake and Bradley (1999) and McGoey (1990) for legal
and professional texts and Kennedy (1993) for an academic treatise authored by a
forensic security specialist. Those interested in far greater legal detail should consult
the legal series *Proof of Facts* and *Causes of Action*.

9   The concept of harm translates to financial damages to be awarded a plaintiff. Damage
experts are generally physicians, psychotherapists, rehabilitation specialists, and forensic economists. Forensic security experts are rarely involved in damages issues so these
matters will not be discussed herein.

10   *Samson v. Saginaw Professional Building, Inc.*, 393 Mich. 393 (1975).

11   269 California Reporter 96 (Cal. App. 2 Dist. 1990).

12   464 Mich. 322, 628 N.W.2d 33 (2001).

13   972 S.W.2d 749 (Tex. 1998).

14   As will be seen in subsequent discussions, the occurrence of crime in nearby areas is
generally associated with the foreseeability of crime on a particular property.
Environmental criminology and journey-to-crime research (Kennedy, 1990) also attest
to the importance of location and neighboring land use for assessing a property's
susceptibility to criminal attack.

15   *Boren v. Worthen National Bank of Arkansas, 324 Ark. 416, 921 S.W.2d 934 (1996).*

16   According to the Timberwalk court, supra, note 11, assaults and robberies in an apartment complex make the risk of other violent crimes like murder and rape foreseeable.
However, a spate of domestic violence in the complex would not portend predatory
sexual assaults or robberies. Crimes between acquaintances or lovers generally emanate
from prior disagreements, are expressive rather than instrumental in nature, and are
not related to the condition of the property.

17   *Mervyn Issaacs, et al. v. Huntington Memorial Hospital*, 685 P.2d 653 (Cal. 1985).

18   Subsequent research by British and American scholars has established that certain
parking lots can, indeed, be problematic (Clark and Mayhew, 1998; Smith, 1996).
Parking structures can be particularly threatening because their environment contains
multiple impediments which block victims' sightlines. Garages also offer multiple locations for offender concealment and often limit avenues of escape (Nasar and Fisher,
1993).

19   *Doud v. Las Vegas Hilton Corp.*, 864 P.2d 796 (Nev. 1993).

20   The security director interested in advanced environmental criminology is referred to
Goldsmith, McGuire, Mollenkopf, and Ross (2000) and Paulsen and Robinson (2004),
particularly Chapter 5, 'Behavioral Geography and Criminal Behavior.' English scholar
David Canter (2003) and Canadian criminologist Kim Rossmo (2000) are well known
for their work in geographic profiling, a topic also of interest to security analysts. These

and other specialties can make substantial contributions to an evolving field of study and practice known as forensic criminology.

21 *McClung v. Delta Square Limited Partnership*, 937 S.W. 2d 901 (Tenn, 1995).

22 The four tests of foreseeability discussed herein do not exhaust all approaches to the question, although they do constitute the dominant approaches. Two additional approaches to foreseeability are worthy of mention, however. One jurisdiction specifically declines to articulate a test for foreseeability, deciding on a case-by-case basis whether a reasonably prudent person would have anticipated danger and provided against it. See *L.A.C. v. Ward Parkway Shopping Center Company*, L.P. 75 S.W. 3d 247 (Missouri, 2002). In *Mary Ann Workman v. United Methodist Committee on Relief*, 320 F. 3d 259 (D.C. Cir. 2003), there is a relational component to the question of foreseeability. If the relationship between the parties strongly suggests a duty of protection, specific evidence of foreseeability is less important. If the relationship is not clearly of a type that entails a higher duty of protection, then the evidentiary hurdle is higher.

23 In many jurisdictions a greater or lesser duty owed to visitors to a property depending upon the nature of their invitation and the likely beneficiary of their visit. Invitees are owed the highest duty. The landowner/occupier should attempt to discover any unreasonably dangerous conditions on the premises and either make them safe or warn the invitee of the danger. The licensee takes the premises as he finds them, although a landlord may be liable to a licensee if the danger of the premises is concealed or cannot reasonably be anticipated and no warnings were given, or there were no attempts to make the conditions safe. Finally, a trespasser is owed no duty, although the landowner must refrain from willful or wanton misconduct toward him (Page, 1988; Tarantino and Dombroff, 1990).

24 For example, security professionals often prefer to use the term 'guideline,' believing this term will convey to a jury the need for professional discretion in the development of security policies and procedures. Many forensic security experts fear the term 'standard' would be taken to mean that a given security practice or device must be applied uniformly across all properties regardless of the unique nature of a given property. This, of course, would not be appropriate practice.

25 Effective litigation is generally characterized by a multidisciplinary approach. Security experts may also be called upon to work with lighting engineers, human factors experts, architects and behavior scientists, to name but a few examples. Artificial disciplinary boundaries should not impede a barrister's ability to present an intelligible yet succinct case to a jury.

26 The American Society for Industrial Security International is currently creating formal 'guidelines' pertaining to business continuity, investigations, risk assessment, security officer selection and training, information protection, security countermeasures, museum security, threat advisory response, workplace violence, and the Chief Security Officer. See www.asisonline.org/guidelines/guidelines.htm.

The National Fire Protection Association is preparing an extensive 'Guide for Premises Security' (NFPA 730), which consists of 22 chapters. Topics include vulnerability assessment, security devices and systems, security personnel, educational and healthcare facilities, apartment buildings, lodging facilities, shopping centers, retail establishments, office buildings, parking facilities, restaurants, and special events. See www.nfpa.org/codes/index.asp.

27 Expert testimony in premises liability cases is subject to differing admissibility tests depending upon the jurisdiction. In the US, for example, several states apply what is known as the federal *Daubert* test, first articulated in *Daubert v. Merrell Dow Pharmaceuticals, Inc.*, 509 U.S. 579, 113 S. Ct. 2786 (1993). In essence, *Daubert* requires judges to be the gatekeepers of expert testimony and to ensure that such testimony is relevant and reliable. The March 1999 issue of *Psychology, Public Policy, and Law* is devoted to an analysis of *Daubert's* impact on social science evidence. See also, Britt (2001) for a plaintiff attorney's perspective and Patterson (2003) for a defense attorney's

perspective. Overall judicial and attorney responses to *Daubert* are addressed by Krafka, Dunn, Johnson, Cecil and Miletich (2002) and Groscup (2004).

28   Lawyers and experts in all common law countries would benefit from articles by Black (2003) and Wivell (2003), both of whom write from the perspective of a litigator who wishes to introduce expert evidence to the court.

29   At least one publication written from the forensic security practitioner's viewpoint does a good job of applying various industry standards to litigation and liability issues. Mattman, Kaufer and Chaney (1997) discuss foreseeability, forensic consulting, and security case law pertinent to eight settings.

30   For example, Hagan (2003) points out that causality in science involves demonstrating a covariance between variables, establishing the time sequence of this relationship (for A to cause B, it must precede B) and ruling out rival explanations for the purported causal relationship between the variables.

31   *See Nola M. v. University of Southern California*, 16 Cal. App. 4th 421 (1993) and Leslie G. v. Perry and Associates, 43 Cal. App. 4th 472 (1996).

32   In addition to the question of 'abstract negligence,' corporate defendants must also beware of an expert who argues for or against a particular standard of care without being able to cite a foundation for his opinion other than his own personal predilections. Such 'personal standards' evidence does not automatically constitute generally accepted standards and should be closely scrutinized (Jackson, 2004).

33   Criminologists are beginning to explore the intermediate notion of displacement rather than limiting themselves to deterrence alone (Repetto, 1976; Clark, 1997). In other words, might someone who is hard to deter be easier to displace? Are these distinctions without a difference? Most landlords would be satisfied with simply displacing the criminal, at least from a liability point of view. Society as a whole, however, would be better served by absolute deterrence.

Key readings

There are several excellent texts available to the attorney or security manager interested in further information concerning forensic security and the law. For a pioneering and very comprehensive treatment, see Carrington, F. and Rapp, J. (1991) *Victims' Rights: Law and Litigation*. New York: Matthew Bender. A plaintiff attorney's perspective is presented by Kuhlman, R. (1989) *Safe Places? Security Planning and Litigation*. Charlottesville, Virginia: The Michie Company. The defense perspective is offered by Kaminsky, A. (2001) *A Complete Guide to Premises Security Litigation*, 2nd ed., Chicago: American Bar Association. A recent text on the subject is Perline, I. and Goldschmidt, J. (2004) *The Psychology and Law of Workplace Violence*. Springfield: Charles C. Thomas.

References

Abel, G. and Osborn, C. (1992) 'The Paraphilias: The Extent and Nature of Sexually Deviant and Criminal Behavior,' *Psychiatric Clinics of North America*, Vol. 15, No. 3, pp. 675–87.

Anderson, P. and Winfree, L. (eds) (1987) *Expert Witnesses: Criminologists in the Courtroom*, Albany: State University of New York Press.

Anderson, T. (2002) 'Laying Down the Law: A Review of Trends in Liability Lawsuits,' *Security Management*, Vol. 46, No. 10, pp. 42–51.

Austin, J. and Irwin, J. (2001) *It's About Time*, 3rd edn, Belmont, CA: Wadsworth.

Bakken, G. and Abele, J. (1995) *Innkeeper's Liability Management*, Tucson: Lawyers and Judges Publishing Company.

Bass, B. and Jefferson, J. (2003) *Death's Acre*, New York: G.P. Putnam.

Bates, N. (1997) 'Foreseeability of Crime and Adequacy of Security.' In Lack, R. (ed.) *Accident Prevention Manual for Business and Industry: Security Management*, Itasca, IL: National Safety Council.

Best, A. and Barnes, D. (2003) *Basic Tort Law: Cases, Statutes, and Problems*, New York: Aspen Publishers.

Bilek, A., Klotter, J. and Federal, K. (1981) *Legal Aspects of Private Security*, Cincinnati: Anderson.

Black, B. (2003) 'Focus on Science, Not Checklists,' *Trial*, Vol. 39, No. 13, pp. 24–32.

Blake, W. and Bradley, W. (1999) *Premises Security: A Guide for Security Professionals and Attorneys*, Boston: Butterworth-Heineman.

Bottom, N. (1985) *Security/Loss Control Negligence*, Columbia, MD: Hanrow Press.

Brantingham, P. and Brantingham, P. (eds) (1981/1991) *Environmental Criminology*, Prospect Heights, IL: Waveland Press.

Brantingham, P. and Brantingham, P. (1984) *Patterns in Crime*, New York: Macmillan.

Brantingham, P. and Brantingham, P. (1995) 'Criminality of Place: Crime Generators and Crime Attractors,' *European Journal on Criminal Policy and Research*, Vol. 3, No. 1, pp. 5–26.

Britt, C. (2001) 'Getting Your Security Expert Over the *Daubert* Hurdle,' *Trial*, Vol. 37, No. 12, pp. 31–7.

Canter, D. (2003) *Mapping Murder: The Secrets of Geographical Profiling*, London: Virgin Press.

Carrington, F. (1978) 'Victims' Rights: A New Tort?,' *Trial*, Vol. 14, No. 6, pp. 39–41, 58.

Carrington, F. (1983) 'A New Tort? Five Years Later,' *Trial*, Vol. 19, No. 12, pp. 51–3, 95.

Carrington, F. (1988) 'Crime Victims' Rights: Courts Are More Willing to Grant Remedies,' *Trial*, Vol. 24, No. 1, pp. 79–83.

Carrington, F. and Rapp, J. (1991) *Victims' Rights: Law and Litigation*, New York: Matthew Bender.

Clark, R. (ed.) (1997) *Situational Crime Prevention* 2nd edn, Guilderland, NY: Harrow and Heston.

Clarke, R. and Eck, J. (2003) *Become a Problem-Solving Crime Analyst*, London: Jill Dando Institute of Crime Science.

Clarke, R. and Mayhew, P. (1998) 'Preventing Crime in Parking Lots: What We Know and What We Need to Know.' In Felson, M. and Peiser, R. (eds) *Reducing Crime Through Real Estate Development and Management*, Washington, DC: Urban Land Institute.

Clear, T. and Cole, G. (1997) *American Corrections* 4th edn, Belmont, CA: Wadsworth Publishing.

Colquitt, J. (1988) 'Judicial Use of Social Science Evidence at Trial,' *Arizona Law Review*, Vol. 30, No. 4, pp. 51–84.

D'Addario, F. (1989) *Loss Prevention Through Crime Analysis*, Boston: Butterworths.

deTreville, R. (2004) 'Time to Check Out Liability Trends,' *Security Management*, Vol. 48, No. 2, pp. 61–5.

Donohue, K. (2002) 'MacDonald v. PKT, Inc.: Who is Responsible for Your Protection?: The Michigan Supreme Court Limits a Merchant's Duty,' *University of Detroit Mercy Law Review*, Vol. 80, No. 1, pp. 127–47.

Erickson, R. and Simon, R. (1998) *The Use of Social Science Data in Supreme Court Decisions*, Urbana: University of Illinois Press.

Faigman, D. (2000) *Legal Alchemy: The Use and Misuse of Science in the Law*, New York: W. H. Freeman.

Faigman, D., Kaye, D., Saks, M. and Sanders, J. (eds) (2002a) *Science in the Law: Forensic Science Issues*, St. Paul, MN: West Group.

Faigman, D., Kaye, D., Saks, M. and Sanders, J. (eds) (2002b) *Science in the Law: Social and Behavioral Science Issues*, St. Paul, MN: West Group.

Farrington, D. and Welsh, B. (2002) 'Improved Street Lighting and Crime Prevention,' *Justice Quarterly*, Vol. 19, No. 2, pp. 313–42.

Fattah, E. (1991) *Understanding Criminal Victimization*, Scarborough, Ontario: Prentice-Hall Canada.

Figlio, R., Hakim, S. and Rengert, G. (eds) (1986) *Metropolitan Crime Patterns*, Monsey, NY: Criminal Justice Press.

Gilbert, J. (1986) *Criminal Investigation* 2nd edn, Columbus, OH: Charles E. Merrill Publishing Company.

Gilbert, N. (1997) 'Advocacy Research and Social Policy.' In Tonry, M. (ed.) *Crime and Justice: A Review of Research*, Chicago: University of Chicago Press.

Gill, M. and Loveday, K. (2003) 'What Do Offenders Think About CCTV?' *Crime Prevention and Community Safety*, Vol. 5, No. 3, pp. 17–25.

Goldsmith, V., McGuire, P., Mollenkopf, J. and Ross, T. (eds) (2000) *Analyzing Crime Patterns*, Thousand Oaks, CA: Sage Publications.

Goldstein, P. (1985) 'The Drugs/Violence Nexus: A Tripartite Conceptual Approach,' *Journal of Drug Issues*, Vol. 15, No. 1, pp. 493–506.

Gorby, M. (1998) *Premises Liability in Georgia*, Norcross, GA: The Harrison Company.

Gottlieb, S., Arenberg, S. and Singh, R. (1994) *Crime Analysis: From First Report to Final Arrest*, Montclair, CA: Alpha Publishing.

Groscup, J. (2004) 'Judicial Decision Making About Expert Testimony in the Aftermath of Daubert and Kumho,' *Journal of Forensic Psychology Practice*, Vol. 4, No. 2, pp. 57–66.

Hagan, F. (2003) *Research Methods in Criminal Justice and Criminology* 6th edn, Boston: Allyn and Bacon.

Hagen, M. (1997) *Whores of the Court: The Fraud of Psychiatric Testimony and the Rape of American Justice*, New York: Regan Books.

Hare, R. (1993) *Without Conscience: The Disturbing World of the Psychopaths Among Us*, New York: The Guilford Press.

Homant, R. (1999) 'Crime Scene Profiling in Premises Security Litigation,' *Security Journal*, Vol. 12, No. 4, pp. 7–15.

Homant, R. and Kennedy, D. (1995) 'Landholder Responsibility for Third Party Crimes in Michigan: An Analysis of Underlying Legal Values,' *University of Toledo Law Review*, Vol. 27, No. 1, pp. 115–47.

Homel, R. (ed.) (1997) *Policing for Prevention: Reducing Crime, Public Intoxication and Injury*, Vol. 7, Monsey, NY: Criminal Justice Press.

Hunt, M. (1999) *The New Know-Nothings: The Political Foes of the Scientific Study of Human Nature*, New Brunswick, NJ: Transaction Publishers.

Jackson, J. (2004) 'Impeachment With "Personal Standards" Evidence,' *For the Defense*, Vol. 46, No. 7, pp. 49–54.

Jacobs, B. (2004) 'The Undeterrable Offender,' *For the Defense*, Vol. 46, No. 4, pp. 16–19.

James, S. and Nordby, J. (eds) (2003) *Forensic Science: An Introduction to Scientific and Investigative Techniques*, Boca Raton, FL: CRC Press.

Jenkins, P. and Kroll-Smith, S. (eds) (1996) *Witnessing for Sociology: Sociologists in Court*, Westport, CT: Praeger.

Kaminsky, A. (2001) *A Complete Guide to Premises Security Litigation* 2nd edn, Chicago: American Bar Association.

Karmen, A. (2004) *Crime Victims: An Introduction to Victimology* 5th edn, Belmont, CA: Wadsworth.

Katz, J. (1988) *Seductions of Crime*, New York: Basic Books.

Kennedy, D. (1990) 'Facility Site Selection and Analysis Through Environmental Criminology', *Journal of Criminal Justice*, Vol. 18, No. 3, pp. 239–52.

Kennedy, D. (1993) 'Architectural Concerns Regarding Security and Premises Liability,' *Journal of Architectural Planning and Research*, Vol. 10, No. 2, pp. 105–29.

Kennedy, D. (1998) 'Apartment Security and Litigation: Key Issues,' *Security Journal*, Vol. 11, No. 1, pp. 21–8.

Kennedy, D. and Homant, R. (1996) 'The Role of the Criminologist in Negligent Security Cases.' In Wiley Law Editorial Staff (eds) *1996 Wiley Expert Witness Update: New Developments in Personal Injury Litigation*, New York: John Wiley & Sons.

Kennedy, D. and Homant, R. (1997) 'Problems With the Use of Criminal Profiling in Premises Security Litigation,' *Trial Diplomacy Journal*, Vol. 20, No. 4, pp. 223–9.

Kennedy, D., Homant, R. and Homant M. (2004) 'Perception of Injustice as a Determinant of Support for Workplace Aggression,' *Journal of Business and Psychology*, Vol. 18, No. 3, pp. 323–36.

Kirk, S. and Kutchins, H. (1992) *The Selling of DSM: The Rhetoric of Science in Psychiatry*, New York: Aldine de Gruyter.

Klinger, D. and Bridges, G. (1997) 'Measurement Error in Calls-For-Service as an Indicator of Crime,' *Criminology*, Vol. 33, No. 4, pp. 705–26.

Krafka, C., Dunn, M., Johnson, M., Cecil, J. and Miletich, D. (2002) 'Judge and Attorney Experiences, Practices, and Concerns Regarding Expert Testimony in Federal Civil Trials,' *Psychology, Public Policy, and the Law*, Vol. 8, No. 3, pp. 309–32.

Kuhlman, R. (1989) *Safe Places? Security Planning and Litigation*, Charlottesville, VA: The Michie Company.

Lykken, D. (1995) *The Antisocial Personalities*, Hillsdale, NJ: Lawrence Erlbaum.

Marchant, P. (2004) 'A Demonstration that the Claim that Brighter Lighting Reduces Crime is Unfounded,' *British Journal of Criminology*, Vol. 44, No. 3, pp. 441–7.

Mattman, J., Kaufer, S. and Chaney, J. (1997) *Premises Security and Liability: A Comprehensive Guide from the Experts*, Laguna Beach, CA: Workplace Violence Research Institute.

Maxwell, D. (1993) *Private Security Law*, Boston: Butterworth-Heinemann.

McGoey, C. (1990) *Security: Adequate or Not?* Oakland, CA: Aegis.

Meadows, R. (1998) *Understanding Violence and Victimization*, Upper Saddle River, NJ: Prentice-Hall, Inc.

Michael, K. and Ellis, Z. (2003) *Avoiding Liability in Premises Security*, 5th edn, Atlanta: Strafford Publications.

Milloy, S. (1995) *Science Without Sense: The Risky Business of Public Health Research*, Washington, DC: Cato Institute.

Monahan, J. and Walker, L. (1998) *Social Science in Law*, Westbury, NY: The Foundation Press.

Moenssens, A., Starrs, J., Henderson, C. and Inbau, F. (eds) (1995) *Scientific Evidence in Civil and Criminal Cases*, Westbury, NY: The Foundation Press.

Moore, H. and Friedman, J. (1993) 'Courtroom Observation and Applied Litigation Research: A Case History of Jury Decision-Making,' *Clinical Sociology Review*, Vol. 11, pp. 123–41.

Moore, J. (1991) *Going Down to the Barrio: Homeboys and Homegirls in Change*, Philadelphia: Temple University.

Nasar, J. and Fisher, B. (1993) 'Hot Spots of Fear and Crime: A Multi-Method Investigation,' *Journal of Environmental Psychology*, Vol. 13, No. 3, pp. 187–206.

Nettler, G. (1989) *Criminology Lessons*, Cincinnati: Anderson.

A New Look at How to Prevent Security-Related Lawsuits. (2004, May) *IOMA's Security Director's Report*, No. 4–5, pp. 6–7.

Nolan, J. and Connolly, M. (1983) *Black's Law Dictionary*. Abridged Fifth Edition, St Paul, MN: West.

Osborne, D. and Wernicke, S. (2003) *Introduction to Crime Analysis*, New York: The Haworth Press.

Osterburg, J. and Ward, R. (1997) *Criminal Investigation: A Method for Reconstructing the Past* 2nd edn, Cincinnati: Anderson Publishing Company.

Page, J. (1988) *The Law of Premises Liability* 2nd edn, Cincinnati: Anderson Publishing Company.

Painter, K. and Tilley, N. (eds) (1999) *Surveillance of Public Space: CCTV, Street Lighting and Crime Prevention*, Monsey, NY: Criminal Justice Press.

Patterson, D. (2003) 'Challenging the Opposing Expert at Deposition,' *For the Defense*, Vol. 45, No. 8, pp. 12–19.

Paulsen, D. and Robinson, M. (2004) *Spatial Aspects of Crime: Theory and Practice*, Boston: Allyn and Bacon.

Peterson, M. (1998) *Applications In Criminal Analysis*, Westport, CT: Praeger Publishers.

Piquero, A. and Mazerolle, P. (eds) (2001) *Life-Course Criminology: Contemporary and Classic Readings*, Belmont, CA: Wadsworth.

Pointing, J. and Maguire, M. (1988) 'Introduction: The Rediscovery of the Crime Victim.' In Maguire, M. and Pointing, J. (eds) *Victims of Crime: A New Deal?* Milton Keynes: Open University Press.

Poulin, K. (1992) *Special Events: Avoiding the Disaster*, Okotoks, Alberta: International Foundation for Protection Officers.

Reppetto, T. (1976) 'Crime Prevention and the Displacement Phenomenon,' *Crime and Delinquency*, Vol. 22, No. 2, pp. 166–77.

Roesch, R., Golding, S., Hans, V. and Reppucci, N. (1991) 'Social Science and the Courts: The Role of Amicus Curiae Briefs,' *Law and Human Behavior*, Vol. 15, No. 1, pp. 1–11.

Roncek, D. (1981) 'Dangerous Places: Crime and Residential Environment,' *Social Forces*, Vol. 60, No. 1, pp. 74–96.

Roncek, D., Bell, R. and Francik, J. (1981) 'Housing Projects and Crime,' *Social Problems*, Vol. 29, No. 2, pp. 151–66.

Roncek, D. and Lobosco, A. (1983) 'The Effect of High Schools on Crime in Their Neighborhoods,' *Social Science Quarterly*, Vol. 64, No. 3, pp. 598–613.

Roncek, D. and Maier, P. (1991) 'Bars, Blocks and Crimes Revisited: Linking the Theory of Routine Activities to the Empiricism of "Hot Spots."' *Criminology*, Vol. 29, No. 4, pp. 725–53.

Rossmo, K. (2000) *Geographic Profiling*, Boca Raton, FL: CRC Press.

Saferstein, R. (2001) *Criminalistics: An Introduction to Forensic Science* 7th edn, Upper Saddle River, NJ: Prentice-Hall.

Sakis, J. and Kennedy, D. (2002) 'Violence at Work,' *Trial*, Vol. 38, No. 12, pp. 32–6.

Salter, A. (2003) *Predators: Paedophiles, Rapists, and Other Sex Offenders*, New York: Basic Books.

Schmalleger, F. and Smykla, J. (2005) *Corrections in the 21st Century*, New York: McGraw-Hill.

Shearing, C. and Stenning, P. (1983) *Private Security and Private Justice: The Challenge of the 80s*, Montreal: The Institute for Research on Public Policy.

Sherman, L. (1998) *Evidence-Based Policing*, Washington, DC: Police Foundation.

Sherman, L. (2003) 'Misleading Evidence and Evidence-Led Policy: Making Social Science More Experimental,' *Annals of the American Academy of Political and Social Science*, Vol. 589, September, pp. 6–19.

Sherman, L., Gartin, P. and Buerger, M. (1989) 'Hot Spots of Predatory Crime: Routine Activities and the Criminology of Place,' *Criminology*, Vol. 27, No. 1, pp. 27–55.

Sherman, L., Gottfredson, D., MacKenzie, D., Eck, J., Reuter, P. and Bushway, S. (1997) *Preventing Crime: What Works, What Doesn't and What's Promising*, Washington, DC: US Department of Justice.

Smith, M. (1996) *Crime Prevention Through Environmental Design in Parking Facilities*, Washington, DC: US Department of Justice.

Stark, R. (1987) 'Deviant Places: A Theory of the Ecology of Crime,' *Criminology*, Vol. 25, No. 4, pp. 893–909.

Talley, L. (1994) *Are You Really Safe: Protecting Yourself in America Today*, Marietta, GA: Longstreet Press.

Tarantino, J. and Dombroff, M. (1990) *Premises Security: Law and Practice*, New York: John Wiley and Sons.

Thornton, W. and Voigt, L. (1988) 'Roles and Ethics of the Practicing Sociologist,' *Clinical Sociology Review*, Vol. 6, pp. 113–33.

Tobolowsky, P. (2001) *Crime Victim Rights and Remedies*, Durham, NC: Carolina Academic Press.

Turvey, B. (2003) 'Forensic Frauds: A Study of 42 Cases,' *Journal of Behavioral Profiling*, Vol. 4, No. 1. Retrieved July 25, 2004, from http://www.profiling.org/journal/subscribers/vol4_no1/jbp_4-1_ff.html

van Dam, C. (2001) *Identifying Child Molesters*, New York: The Haworth Maltreatment and Trauma Press.

Wallace, H. (1998) *Victimology: Legal, Psychological, and Social Perspectives*, Boston: Allyn and Bacon.

Ward, T. (1999) 'Liars, Damned Liars and Expert Witnesses: Video Identification and the Law of Expert Evidence,' *Security Journal*, Vol. 12, No. 1, pp. 29–39.

Ward, T. (2004) 'Expert Testimony Issues in the UK,' *Security Journal*, Vol. 17, No. 3, pp. 41–9.

Webster, C. and Jackson, M. (eds) (1997) *Impulsivity: Theory, Assessment and Treatment*, New York: The Guilford Press.

Weisel, D. (2002) *Burglary of Single Family Houses*, Washington, DC: US Department of Justice.

Welsh, B. and Farrington, D. (2003) 'Effects of Closed-Circuit Television on Crime,' *Annals of the American Academy of Political and Social Science*, Vol. 587, May, pp. 110–35.

Welsh, B. and Farrington, D. (2004) 'Surveillance for Crime Prevention in Public Space: Results and Policy Choices in Britain and America,' *Criminology and Public Policy*, Vol. 3, No. 3, pp. 497–525.

Wivell, M. (2003) 'Deliver a Daubert-Proof Expert Report,' *Trial*, Vol. 39, No. 13, pp. 38–40.

Wolfgang, M. (1957) 'Victim-Precipitated Criminal Homicide,' *Journal of Criminal Law and Criminology*, Vol. 48, No. 1, pp. 1–11.

Wolfgang, M. (1974) 'The Social Scientist in Court,' *Journal of Criminal Law and Criminology*, Vol. 65, No. 2, pp. 239–47.

Yablonsky, L. (1997) *Gangsters*, New York: New York University Press.

7
The Study of Intelligence and Its Contributions to Security

James D. Calder

Introduction

In 2001 the United States and the world were reminded that major acts of terrorism cause severe emotional and physical devastation in ways that are somewhat similar to the effects of all-out military invasion. In the United States at the time, comparisons between the Twin Towers attack and the 1941 Pearl Harbor attack were not overlooked. In each case enemies achieved strategic surprise by bold violations of national (or external) and domestic (or internal) security. Authorities were criticized for actions or inactions associated with implementing defensive measures, for the adequacy of oversight of intelligence systems, and for proper outfitting of all elements of domestic or homeland security. In the United States and the United Kingdom, especially, intelligence and security services encountered blistering probes by legislative bodies. Most questions concerned what was known, when it was known, and what decisions were taken. The US Congress altered dramatically the organizational structure of the US intelligence community, and the US Department of Homeland security consolidated domestic security functions and rose to a new cabinet-rank position in the Executive Branch. Policy-makers set forth priorities to tighten fragmented intelligence reporting practices and to modernize out-dated and largely inefficient internal security capabilities. Multiple congressional inquiries exposed terrorist methods, particularly those aimed at positioning mole-like cells, conspiratorial associations and how to discover them, and breaches of security procedures and systems. Intelligence and investigative services were challenged on their competence in collecting, evaluating, and reporting circumstances of terrorist planning. Indeed, withering cross-examination of witnesses revealed disturbing weaknesses all across the security front, giving rise to plans for reorganizing intelligence analysis, internal security, undercover operations, and counter-terrorism measures (Best, 2005; National Commission, 2004).

In current times it is safe to assume that domestic security functions will draw closer in partnership with the intelligence services in the larger framework of national security protection. Each element will be asked to give new thought to important new questions, and to reflect more deeply on how they sift and correlate evidence, and how they report findings to key public and private decision-makers. If it is not already obvious, the national security intelligence element will have an advantage in these activities because of its history of research and analysis (R & A) and its well-rooted experience in informing the highest levels of the policy process. There can be no claim that intelligence R & A has always performed up to expectations, however, or that it has been error-free, but they have evolved to indispensability and to an overall standing of reliability in national security decision-making. The domestic security realm, on the other hand, has neither a comparable history nor an institutional focus on R & A to inform decision-making. Consequently, domestic security management is painfully hindered and marked by marginal credibility in circles of high-level decision-making in the public and private sectors. The expectation, and the focus of this chapter, is the possibilities for improving domestic security in a manner that is comparable to the evolution since World War II in the intelligence field. A first order of business will be domestic security's commitment to an institutionalized orientation to independent R & A conducted within organizations similar in design and function to the current intelligence community's R & A units. A giant step of this kind will require, of course, a change in mind-set, large investments of human and monetary resources, and an argument for doing so (George, 2004). This chapter is largely about the latter issue. The intellectual capital for taking the leap is available but it remains to be organized, focused, and underwritten.

Discussion about this change should begin by examining the evolution of some of the key features of national security intelligence services, most notably the analytical functions (Anonymous, 1986; Davis, 1995; Ford, 1995; Johnston, 2005). In this regard space limitations limit discussion to the American experience, but there is no implication that this is the only setting in which useful lessons can be learned. Sixty years ago the US Congress and the American national security leadership formally recognized the need for a major investment in analytical resources (Jeffreys-Jones, 1989; Johnson, 1989a; Overton, 1992). The concept of a centralized R & A branch was ultimately located in the Central Intelligence Agency's Directorate of Intelligence (DI) (Ransom, 1958; Shulsky, 1991; Taubman, 2003; Thomas, 1995).[1] Positioned as a resource to investigate and interpret conditions of the world and national security threats, the DI evolved rapidly as the most reliable authority for informing major decisions made by the President and the National Security Council. The analytical function was, and continues to be, the most important of four major organizational activities of the CIA (Berkowitz and Goodman, 2000). Brevity compels that we defer discussion of the administrative, operational, scientific and technological elements of CIA,[2] suggesting that the reader refer to bibliographies of the massive scholarly literature for additional readings (Calder, 1999). Essentially, the DI serves as a loose comparative organizational model for a R & A function. It can serve as a preliminary model for innovating a similar function in the domestic security community. Its historical evolution is unique in many respects (Berkowitz and Goodman, 1989). Profoundly, it reached center stage in the US intelligence community from a position of relative obscurity in less than a decade. Its rapid rise to prominence and respect was largely due to the ideas and leadership of a small band of brilliant analysts and academics (Thomas, 1995). The critical mass of creativity produced a sea change in the demand for and supply of grounded decision-making, thus causing the intelligence community to dramatically shift priorities away from wartime operational specializations to research and analytical expertise suitable for a post-war national security system (Ransom, 1958; Darling, 1990; Westfield, 1995).

Close study of the intelligence community reveals a history sharply contrasted with developments in domestic security. In the latter case, regular and nearly exclusive investments were made, first, in labor-intensive human resources, and second, in technologies to replace the high costs and errors of human interventions. Security leaders responded to the demands of private and public clients who favored immediate operational performance regardless of evidence of effectiveness or value. The horizons of response were generally limited to low-level domestic roles in what was termed 'crime prevention' and to a few roles in internal security where human and other threats were regarded as part of the overall national security picture (i.e., defence plants, nuclear facilities, transportation, waterfronts, airports, etc.). While growing and diversifying at a rate substantially faster than police organizations, the domestic security field ignored the growing need for an institutional framework for R & A. In simple terms, the field showed little interest in evaluating its perceived accomplishments and its productivity. Rarely did it search library resources for vetted research to inform decision-making processes. From time to time, major security problems arose, such as rising crime rates, aircraft hijackings, executive hostage takings, and embassy bombings. The focus, however, was always on quick, post-event solutions and to physical security measures for preventing mainly property crime. Occasionally, security experts were invited to propose incremental and profit-generating responses to white-collar crime schemes, to respond to public fears about violent crime, and to advise the political community on human and technological security resources. Security service companies, both in the US and abroad, grew ever larger to meet the operational expectations of the marketplace, all fixed on business priorities of profitability and competitive positions. The business of security, in fact, controlled the direction of security advancement (George and Button, 2000; Institute, 1974; Johnston, 1992; Jones and Newburn, 1998; Kakalik and Wildhorn, 1977; Shearing and Stenning, 1987).

Grounding domestic security's decision-making in an evidence-based approach and methodology was not often considered, thus not accomplished. The fault lay mainly in ignoring what had been so central to post-war national security thinking: significant investment in R & A. The vast majority of funding was put into operations and technological devices for sale in the marketplace. Only in recent years has the field shown interest in research, as evidenced by a small but growing base of vetted literature appearing in scholarly journals. The larger failure to muster broad support for research and its translation into decision processes has not slowed security's self-proclaimed march toward professional standing, however. This cart-before-the-horse result is not unique to domestic security. Policing and corrections, two related criminal justice functions, have also claimed professional standing despite the fact that more than three decades of significant intellectual investment followed the proclamation. Domestic security's failures stemmed from ignoring an evidence-based approach to linking R & A to operational productivity. Most assuredly it failed to lead in the use of scientific findings in the assessment and reduction of security risks, choosing instead to follow events and market trends.

Rudiments of a new research commitment are straining for recognition. Substantial work remains, however, to design of an intensive research-analysis organization similar to units in the intelligence community, to create a centralized library of vetted scientific knowledge, and to underwrite a cadre of research scholars to carry out a focused research agenda.[3] In the end, the most important objective is for the domestic security community to have an identified and respected seat at all executive and policy-making tables where grounded R & A contributes significantly to domestic security decisions. True professional development, a status clearly evident in the intelligence community by the 1950s, will come when the domestic security profession recognizes that its central redeeming value is the credibility of its critical decisions. Such recognition is widely evident in other areas of human service delivery, such as education, policing, public health, nursing, and social work. At present the domestic security community, including some of its main branches in crime prevention, economic crime investigations and systems, private security services, information collection, and technological innovations and applications, cannot claim to have centers of centralized R & A to which decision makers can turn. To move toward a new level of credibility in critical decision circles, it must give thought to transforming its long record of operational achievements into research questions, discard associations with widely accepted myths about what does or does not work in reducing risks, bring together scattered ideas about its place in community and national protection, focus and expand its currently unorganized body of research, assemble its currently scattered group of researchers and thinkers, and aim to strengthen its weak standing in the academic community.

In the following discussion, the two sectors of security, one domestic and the other international, will be compared. The objective is to stimulate new thinking about what domestic security management may wish to consider in terms of R & A priorities. Research and analysis, as generally practiced by CIA's DI, is a concerted, intensive, and never-ending process (Dulles, 1963; Lowenthal, 2003a). This is also true in the US Defense Intelligence Agency, and to lesser degrees of intensity and scope in many other branches of national security advisement. Each of these activities depends upon recruiting talented analysts from the best research institutions in the nation (Blash, 1993; Bodnar, 2003). Each employs the latest information technologies for mining data collected from human (e.g. case officers, diplomats, attaches, and spies) and technological devices (e.g. satellites, aircraft, ground equipment, signaling devices, etc.), and each employs a full range of methodologies (e.g. network analysis, opportunity analysis, linchpin analysis, etc.) for organizing data for decision purposes (Krizan, 1999; McCue, 2005). CIA's DI is mainly focused on preparing and submitting analytical reports through many horizontal and vertical vetting processes. Ultimately, reports find their way to key policy-makers. These are the end products of widely studied, collated, and critiqued interpretations of intelligence information relevant to national security decisions. There is no illusion, however, that data or the interpretations upon which they are based do not suffer a rate of error. Moreover, there are no guarantees about the applications policy-makers will make with the information they receive. Analysis concerns what happened five minutes or five months ago, and there are different types of analytical expertise called for in short-term and long-term analysis. It is part art, part science, and part estimation, all influenced by, and clearly dependent upon, the best available information. Whatever criticism it attracts, the DI remains one of most respected functions in the entire national security process, and its place in the intelligence community is guaranteed even though its credibility is sometimes challenged (Prillaman and Dempsey, 2004; Nolte, 2004; Shukman, 2000). Lessons from the intelligence community's development of core R & A functions, therefore, help to frame a conceptual direction for a comparable institution in the domestic security community. Formal configuration of a similar organization, loosely conceived as a center for domestic security R & A, must remain for another venue. Conceivably, however, such a center is an essential element in advancing government and private security sectors. Its philosophical support and its ultimate implementation, therefore, must come from public and commercial funds since its benefits will cut across all types of organizations and settings.

Historical setting of intelligence: overview of the American experience

Intelligence services in democratic states have always attracted skepticism and a certain amount of concern for excesses, fears of intrusiveness, analytical and operational failures, and misdirection. The secret world rarely acknowledges its successes, and it is disallowed from openly debating sources and methods. Despite periodic criticism, justified or not, the intelligence community has earned prominence as a credible and generally reliable element in national security decision-making. This achievement is relatively recent in origin, but it has occurred with approximately equal force in all developed democracies. Some part of this status, particularly in the American experience, may have resulted from post-World War II realities that have included nuclear weapons and mobile terrorist organizations. On the one hand there was no alternative to on-going, current, and detailed analyses of circumstances and events facing national security decision-makers. And on the other hand, analysis of critical world conditions was, and continues to be, conducted by human analysts who, from time to time, make mistakes. For purposes of this chapter, we must step around a comprehensive historical perspective on the US intelligence community, leaving that to others (e.g. Andrew, 1995; Corson, 1977; Jeffreys-Jones, 1989). A more limited use of the history is in order, thus allowing us to highlight what can be learned from the American intelligence community's R & A activities since World War II.[4]

The modern American intelligence community originated with the National Security Act of 1947, a statutory innovation that encountered great struggle on the path to implementation (Zegart, 1999).[5] The community's organizational framework was intentionally designed to address problems of intelligence co-ordination and integration across agency and departmental lines. The superior co-ordinative function, including advice to the President, was assigned to the National Security Council (NSC) comprised of four permanent members (i.e. the President of the United States, the Vice President, the Secretary of Defense, and the Secretary of State). Among other provisions of the Act, a director of central intelligence was created to serve as the President's intelligence advisor and as head of the Central Intelligence Agency.[6] CIA was placed at the center of a federated relationship with the other intelligence organizations (i.e. State Department, FBI, military services, etc.), responsible for co-ordination and guidance of all foreign intelligence work. CIA's charge was to advise the NSC on foreign intelligence matters, co-ordination of intelligence, correlation analysis, and dissemination of intelligence among government agencies.[7]

In the first decade of operations, Congress and the Executive branch continued efforts to craft additional elements of the intelligence community. The wartime intelligence unit named the Office of Strategic Services (OSS) had been disbanded in 1945 and a large number of its personnel resources moved to an interim Central Intelligence Group and then to CIA's ranks in 1947. Early and sustained commitment was given to forming a small army of analysts who possessed transferable intelligence experience, language skills, and extensive familiarity with areas of regional conflict. OSS personnel, especially those who had served in field operations in war zones or in the military, filled those needs (Katz, 1989; O'Donnell, 2004). Many had strong academic records and some held professorial positions in prestigious Ivy League colleges. Many had extensive overseas experience serving in R & A functions (Doob, 1947; Jeffreys-Jones, 2000; MacPherson, 2002; Winks, 1987). The code-making and code-breaking dimensions of intelligence, which had been highly developed by the British in their long history of the Government Communications Headquarters (GCHQ), was formalized in 1952 at the National Security Agency (NSA) (Aid, 2001; Aldrich, 2001; Andrew, 1986; Bamford, 1982, 2001; Budiansky, 2000). This organization became the nation's eyes and ears in worldwide communications. Military specialists in signals intelligence operated listening posts and electronic technologies at stations around the world while mathematicians and scientists invented and advanced code systems.[8] In the aftermath of the Bay of Pigs scandal in 1961, President John F. Kennedy pressed the Congress to create the Defense Intelligence Agency (DIA) to provide the military services with strategic and tactical intelligence most relevant to their missions and to serve as an alternate pool of Executive information analysis (Andrew, 1995; Richelson, 1999). The Federal Bureau of Investigation (FBI) continued its domestic law enforcement and intelligence roles mainly targeted at enforcing federal criminal statutes but also keeping up its massive information gathering and forensics capabilities (Kessler, 1993; Powers, 2004). In recent decades, modern intelligence communities in the US and the UK have been under extreme pressure to reinvent themselves and to remodel seemingly failed elements of the past, all the while retaining principal focus on providing high level, vetted, and credible analysis to inform the policy process (Andrew, 2004; Lander, 2002; National Commission, 2004; Taylor and Goldman, 2004; West, 2005; Wolfberg, 2004).

The US intelligence community is a relative newcomer to the world of national intelligence services (Corson, 1977; Keegan, 2003; O'Toole, 1991). Spies and analysts have worked for rulers of all stripes, and their positions of access, influence, and power have varied greatly. British, French, and other European nations have long histories of employing spy services dating to the 16th century (Andrew, 1986; Champion, 1998; Faligot and Krop, 1985; Keegan, 2003; Kennedy, 2003; Porch, 1995; Powers, 2002; Richelson, 1988; Stieber, 1979; West, 1981). Long ago these services encountered the whims of their leaders, administrative or political. They were tested on their capacities to discover intrigues and enemy invasion plans, to guard against theft of secrets associated with weapons production and military assets, and to uncover conspiracies of internal subversion (Haswell, 1977).[9] General (later President) George Washington ran a primitive but successful intelligence service during the American Revolution. Significant developments in tradecraft and the use of intelligence in military plans evolved during the Civil War (1861–1865) and thereafter (Andrew, 1995; Axelrod, 1992; Feis, 2002; Fishel, 1996; Jensen, 1991; Tidwell, 1995; Tidwell, Hall and Gaddy, 1988). Formalization of intelligence did not take shape until 1885 when the Army organized the Military Information (later Intelligence) Division and the Navy opened the Office of Naval Intelligence in 1887 (Dorwart, 1979; Dorwart, 1983; Hamm, 1987; Powe, 1975). But these beginnings failed to institutionalize a comprehensive intelligence function. Operational responsibilities remained in the hands of lower ranking officers far removed from the top echelons of a small military structure in a small federal government. There was no command leadership to give priority to intelligence. In the aftermath of wars from 1898 to 1941 most intelligence work faded into departmental shadows. Most notably, the American habit of demobilizing military and intelligence functions after every major internal and international conflict frustrated career commitments by officers and civilians who had served in intelligence-related units from the 1880s to the 1930s. Neither the Executive branch nor the Congress displayed any interest in having a stream of codified intelligence information. Fortunately, a few dedicated Army and Navy officers, FBI's J. Edgar Hoover, and code experts in the State Department continued their work, often in secret and on non-budgeted resources (Jensen, 1991; Kahn, 1991; Knightley, 1986; Powers, 2004). They built and maintained card files on foreign and domestic circumstances. By contrast, European intelligence services were regularly deployed in war service and their staff functions were formally sustained in peacetime. The British improved on their analytical skills based on intelligence collection activities in several regions of the world, and they greatly reinforced counter-espionage defenses beginning in 1909 (Andrew, 1986; Knightley, 1986).

Fragmented American intelligence remained buried in military bureaucracies and weakly planned preparedness before World War II, woefully deficient in several areas but particularly in information analysis. Signals intelligence had advanced during World War I but significant progress was stifled in 1929 when Secretary of State Henry L. Stimson closed the State Department's code and cipher operations (Alvarez, 2000; Bamford, 1982; Yardley, 1931). Records and reports remained dispersed at operational levels in the Army and Navy. There was little initiative to collate information across agency lines and to put informational tidbits in a suitable condition for handy reference. Maps and mapping functions also remained reclusive and unacknowledged for possible contributions in warfare.[10] In essence, before 1941 intelligence expertise was scattered. Its aggregate capacity for contributing anything of value to senior policy-makers was unknown (Corson, 1977; Wohlstetter, 1962). The pioneers in a new order of priorities and information specialties remained unrecognized before the outbreak of war. Despite small achievements, they remained unable to give a unified voice to crises looming in Asia and Europe (Aldrich, 2000). When war finally came it was vital to overcome the burdens of the new emergency and an outmoded military mindset. With few exceptions, there was inadequate administrative and political interest in looking closely at European intelligence services, although it is fair to conclude that the onset of any war leaves only small windows of opportunity for creativity and deep consideration of advanced ideas. In general, American intelligence services failed to study other intelligence functions and to mine the knowledge that, arguably, may have changed rapidly the advancing crises on two fronts.[11]

The tragedy of the 1941 Pearl Harbor attack has been laid at several doorsteps and attributed to many causes, not the least of which was the inability of the Executive branch, civilian diplomats, and military leaders to make coherent assessments of enemy capabilities and intentions (Wohlstetter, 1962). Fragmentation of focus, organizational incoherence, and lack of resources perpetuated separate and jealously guarded intelligence operations in the Army, Navy, and Federal Bureau of Investigation (Corson, 1977). Not until summer 1941 did President Roosevelt create the position of Coordinator of Information, the predecessor of the wartime OSS begun in 1942 under the command of William 'Wild Bill' Donovan (Brown, 1982; McIntosh, 1998; Smith, 1983; Smith, 1972).[12] Immediately after Pearl Harbor the United States and its allies marked the end of an era and the beginning of an entirely new way of looking at external and internal security. The concept of a centrally directed intelligence community evolved, despite the fact that it would require wartime experiences to test and refine. Some intelligence hands, in fact, argued that it was miraculous that the US found the wherewithal to organize an effective intelligence system since it had lacked earlier preparedness (Cline, 1981: 21). After a slow start and numerous failures, a pattern of successes followed, such as the compromise of Japanese codes and ciphers that produced victory in the 1942 Battle of Midway and the grand allied deceptions that enabled the Normandy landings in 1944 (Kahn, 1967; West, 1988). The combination of OSS and military successes gave indications that future modes of national security decision-making would allow for greatly expanded collection and analysis, channeled dissent and rebuttal, and career commitments for analysts and tacticians. Ultimately, the wartime challenges caused policy-makers to break with the previous tradition of demobilization of the intelligence tool. At war's end, however, the organizational design to link the participating elements in an intelligence network was not immediately forthcoming. Realities of a post-war nuclear world and the memories of Pearl Harbor raised the importance of intelligence analysis. The basic facts were clear: information had frequently been incomplete, it had been poorly evaluated and compiled, it had been incompletely transmitted, and it had been ineffectively considered in the policy process.

The CIA opened in the summer of 1947 amid a barrage of negative and positive background conditions. Resentment arose over a congressionally crafted design of intelligence organization, from insecure military commanders, and from a suspicious and jealous FBI director, J. Edgar Hoover. President Harry Truman's polite but sudden firing of William Donovan in 1945 introduced new confusion since it had been the former OSS chief's vision to create a civilian-operated and centrally directed intelligence function (Ranelagh, 1986: 110). Donovan was summoned to the White House in September, awarded a congratulatory medal for wartime service, and dismissed. On a positive note, however, CIA was born in an atmosphere charged with an abiding sense of balance between the operational side of intelligence work (spying, counterintelligence, military and international liaisons, and covert actions) and the bread and butter work of analysis. That said, the analytical component did not find its niche in the Truman administration until the Korean War surprises occurred in June and October of 1950 (Laqueur, 1985).

Interagency squabbling during the first five years of CIA's life made the road to credibility in the early 1950s more than a little difficult. The agency's first director, Roscoe H. Hillenkoetter, was not spared from the wrath of bureaucratic resentments (Darling, 1990: 193), but he was able to hold his position by remaining loyal to the legislative mandates and by strengthening the base of analytical skill. He understood that the CIA provided the President and the Council with the best available intelligence, fully collated, integrated, and worthy of citation credibility. Hillenkoetter's success, in part, was his ability to balance the pulls of the covert action enthusiasts, especially the needed holdovers from the OSS, with the new demands of analytical strength and a consistent flow of credible, well-grounded intelligence reports. Over the next few years the CIA's initial jitters were survived largely due to an institutional durability to stay the course and to rise above agency narrowness (Ambrose, 1981). Its prestige grew with a remarkable pace, quickly gaining the respect of presidents and key committees of Congress. Budget allocations for analysis and operations expanded rapidly. The analytical agenda was filled. Dozens of active projects addressed international security crises tied to Korea, India, the Middle East, Soviet Union and other spots on the globe (Andrew, 1995). CIA's Research and Analysis Branch produced an extensive collection of threat assessments concerning Chinese and Soviet intrigues designed to attract allies. Priority was given to measuring the progress of arms buildups and sponsorship of revolutionary actions in Third World nations. The sheer workload and demands for intellectual talent convinced CIA leaders of the need to hire the top talent that American universities could produce. The agency invested heavily in recruiting diversified analytical skills across traditional and non-traditional disciplines.

One of the most prominent features of the CIA's early years was the Agency's direct associations with the academic community. The Agency created an internal work climate that was akin to academe, and through its recruitment of social scientists, engineers, linguists, and other disciplines it expanded and refined methods of scientific analysis. Unquestionably, the Agency recruited the best analysts and field case officers from the OSS, but hundreds of new analysts were also drawn from top academic institutions. Set against the swashbuckling operational focus of William Donovan and OSS's wartime field successes, the new CIA attracted young scholars from Harvard, Princeton, Yale, and respected publicly funded schools. The objective was to transform agency focus to analysis and research. Many bright new analysts were assigned tasks of summarizing conditions surrounding the world's hot spots and threats to regional security. Almost instantaneously their findings were presented to the highest levels of the diplomatic, military, and policy communities. Their work products resulted in the first National Intelligence Estimates of post-war threats. Reports reflected their abilities to read and understand foreign languages and cultures, to interpret experiences from foreign travel, to lend perspectives on scientific and technological advancements, and to incorporate into their reports knowledge from their broad liberal arts education in cultural traditions, economics, history, and psychology. The total effort constituted a profound leap forward and a rather amazing transformation of a vital national security function. It was achieved through insightful commitment to R & A, and to delivering the findings from that work to top government leaders. In time, the credibility of their assessments was tested and new analytical strategies were introduced. As such, R & A advanced to high standing in the intelligence community and in the Executive Branch (Andrew, 1995; Garthoff, 1984). It would be intellectually dishonest, however, to ignore the fact that successes in analysis were not matched by some mistakes, overestimates, under-estimates, and missed opportunities (Betts, 1978), particularly with respect to some aspects of Soviet capabilities and intentions. The saving factor, although unappreciated at the time, was that Soviet intelligence analysts made many of the same errors in estimating US capabilities and intentions (Andrew and Mitrokhin, 1999: 180).

The key to achieving a durable position at the table of national security policy making was CIA's leadership in recruiting strong intellectual capital to lead its critical departments. The Agency, as Robin Winks has pointed out, demanded '...the ability to learn at speed, a good mind with, preferably but not indispensably, a broad education, a sense of personal balance, and awareness of nuance that would lead to discretion, specialized knowledge and, ideally, one or two foreign languages at a level of competence above the textbook' (1987: 58). Two of the most prominent names in American intelligence history include William Langer and Sherman Kent. Langer was chosen for the CIA's Research and Analysis Branch, a continuation of the same function in OSS, known then as "the campus." Historian by training and Harvard professor on leave for nine years in service at CIA, Langer organized and led the Office of National Estimates (ONE) to its premier position in the Agency's hierarchy. Still clinging to his academic roots, Langer promoted the idea that universities were important assets in supplying the intelligence agencies with brilliant young talent, and that federal funds should be invested in programs to train the next generation of analysts (Winks, 1987: 81).

Langer's successor was one of the biggest names in American intelligence history, Sherman Kent. As a young professor of history at Yale, Kent was recruited into OSS under Langer, later working his way to the top echelons of CIA. Kent held on to his academic orientation by developing a theory of intelligence. *Strategic Intelligence for American World Policy* observed that intelligence is knowledge of the world's conditions and nations; it is organization of foreign surveillance, organization of central intelligence, and organization of the departmental functions; and it is the activity involving a methodology to frame the problem, to collect and evaluate the data, to build a working hypothesis, and to make a presentation of findings (Davis, 1992; Kent, 1949). His academic leanings, like Langer's, led to the creation of the inhouse journal, *Studies in Intelligence*, which began in 1955 as a classified outlet for exchanging ideas and methodologies, both essential to the development of a true profession. A major contributor to the intellectual development of intelligence, Kent insisted that the body of literature must address theory construction and missions and methods for investigating the world of human actions and intrigues. It must also have clear definitions of terms and it must elevate the discussion by debate and examination of foundations (Kent, 1955).

There were dozens of other key contributors to the analytical side of the intelligence community's rise in national security decision-making. The wartime experiences of OSS and post-war years of CIA benefited equally from full deployment of academic scholarship organized around and directed at the problems of their respective eras. Kent's notions of a body of literature for intelligence analysis and theory construction were operationalized by men like Donald Downes, Joseph Curtiss, Thomas Mendenhall, Walter Pforzheimer, and Bernard Knollenberg who created the Yale Library Project. A giant undertaking, the Project gathered and catalogued massive collections of documents, artifacts, and studies from around the world (Nolte, 2001; Winks, 1987). Ready availability of these resources was an important key to the success of wartime OSS intelligence analysts.[13] OSS, and later CIA, built a significant part of the analytical foundation around a cohort of professors, among them Norman Pearson, another Yale scholar who found favor with British intelligence services. James Angleton, later one of the most reclusive individuals in CIA history, moved from analysis to operations of the Agency's counterintelligence function. He was known for his perspective that analysts were '...theoreticians of human nature, with the human condition fragmented into that easy and admittedly at times misleading set of receptacles for collecting and analyzing data, the nation state' (Winks, 1987: 323). From 1947 to the present, the themes of close and continuing associations in academe, research scholarship, intensive library development, use of the latest in methodological approaches, honing of interagency co-operation and communications, and a persistent record of technological sophistication sustained the Agency's viability in the national security arena. There was never a claim of perfection or invincibility; there were only the human resources and the policy commitments to building a R & A function from the best available talent.

Intelligence community mainstay: the analytical function

The importance of the analytical function at the Central Intelligence Agency is demonstrated by the position it holds in the hierarchy of the intelligence community. The Directorate of Intelligence (DI) is located on the fourth tier of the community's organization chart, directly below the President and National Security Council (top tier), the new Director of National Intelligence (DNI, as of May 2005) (second tier), and the Director of Central Intelligence (DCI) (third tier). The new Director of National Intelligence and his principal deputy have broad power over 15 intelligence agencies, and they are responsible for White House briefings of the president and the NSC, receiving additional support from the deputy director for intelligence (analysis) and the DCI. Daily and long term assignments consistently focus on such critical questions as 'what do we know,' 'how long have we known it,' and 'what are our options.' The heartbeat of the DI's function never stops, and the analysis directorate is a highly respected player in the minute-by-minute assessment of world conditions. It should not go unrecognized that the importance of accuracy and reliability of the DI's work was given yet another check in the recent creation of the DNI.

The DI functions as a concentration of analysts who, in theory at least, are prepared to gather, evaluate, and compile information derived or acquired from the community's collection functions (human and technical). The work is one of close study, digestion of vast quantities of information, team input, report writing, individual and group editing, internal and external vetting for competitive views, and estimations (not predictions) about threats to instability affecting national security interests. These normal capacities are followed by a most critical step in the process – informing policy makers about the results. That end process, of course, draws responses ranging from congratulations to harsh ridicule. The DI is responsible for warnings about potential attacks on the United States and its allies, a task that keeps it well connected to military preparations and to plans for strategic and tactical responses. This function has never been, and will never be, immune to failures (Bozeman, 1992; Burris, 1993; Helms and Hood, 2003; Hughes, 1976; Lowenthal, 2003a; Mahle, 2004). It recognizes that safety from embarrassment or from estimative failure may mean that the analysis was too guarded or too shallow. A few years ago, one CIA director suggested that one way to measure how comprehensive an analytical product had been was the amount of criticism it attracted from consumers (Gates, 1997). Analysis of failure teaches valuable lessons; but failure to analyse teaches nothing. In practical terms, there has been no retreat at CIA from a persistent commitment to improve the quality of analytical methodologies and products, even though analyst managers clearly recognize that a failure rate is an inherent feature of the job (Dupont, 2003; Gates, 1992 & 1997; Grabo, 2002; Heuer, 2003; Lowenthal, 2003b; MacEachin, 1994).

Intelligence analysis is fundamentally an activity involving intensive research, writing, verification, and re-writing. Written products are subjected to an extensive vetting process involving an array of internal and external critiques (Lefebvre, 2004; Lowenthal, 2003a). Normally, work is performed in teams, a process factor that requires shared goals, interdependence, accountability, and close supervision (Johnston, 2005: 68–70). Community and agency management assign projects in response to the information needs of the President, the National Security Council or other community agencies. Intelligence analysts work in offices at CIA headquarters in Langley, Virginia. They read, download, organize, and summarize massive quantities of information on topics directed by questions from consumers or policy-makers. Analysts, also, are asked to give informed estimates on issues and circumstances that policy-makers may not have considered or may not have requested. The DI's internal atmosphere, according to one recent characterization, is analogous to academia on steroids, driven by events and a sense of urgency (Mahle, 2004: 94). Raw and digested intelligence appear in paper documents, microfiche, film, satellite images, ground-based photographs, and even physical objects. New analysts quickly become topical and/or regional experts since the information they work with is at the cutting edge of actual occurrence or is rapidly accessible by comparison with what outsiders can learn in real time and space. They provide orderliness to a volume of seemingly disparate pieces of evidence. The analyst's objectives are thorough research and timely reporting in ways that are meaningful to information consumers. They draw factual and insightful information from a massive body of open sources and classified reports stored throughout the intelligence community. Reports attempt to inform while reconciling as best they can the competing views of the same information. Since analysis drives collection activities, senior analysts participate in the hierarchical and lateral communications processes that identify the types of information that must be collected. The environment of analysis is premised on competition, that is, analysts may find that the subject of their analysis is also under consideration by other analysts in other analytical functions in the community, e.g. DIA or the State Department. Multiple layers of analysis and review offer decision-makers an opportunity to consider both coherence and conflict of viewpoints, thereby calling for further analysis if views are too divergent. The objective is to produce reports for decision-makers reflecting collated and correlated findings, including clarifications and qualifying notes where the evidence is weak or in significant conflict with other inputs. Final products delivered up to national security officials should not reflect mere consensus drawn together to please or to find favor, but rather to stand on the evidence while acknowledging any weaknesses in the data employed or the limitations of the methodology (Clark, 2004; Clark, 1975; Lahneman, 2004–2005; Shultz, Godson and Quester, 1997).

Intelligence analysis results in both short-term, or 'current,' intelligence reporting and long-term intelligence products in various documentary forms. Each type of analysis calls for special expertise. There is never a sense that the results, especially with regard to long-term analysis, guarantee that every aspect of the problem has been fully understood or that revisions will not be needed. The objectives are always to be accurate, timely, and relevant (Lowenthal, 2003a; Mahle, 2004). Analysts may be uncomfortable admitting that their business is mainly about outcome predictions, but they all participate in processes that measure their work in terms of predictive mediocrity or competence (Mahle, 2004: 90). Clearly, at one time or another they are all engaged in estimating outcome probabilities (Rieber, 2004). Some of the analytical products of the DI include the President's Daily Briefing (delivered each morning to the White House), the Senior Executive Intelligence Briefing (or National Intelligence Daily delivered daily to senior government officials in the Executive branch and Congress), National Intelligence Estimates (prepared for the director of central intelligence and reflecting the community views for DCI approval and delivery to the President), and other more narrowly focused special reports (Smith, 1999). Each president has a different practice for reading, digesting, and asking further questions about the daily intelligence reports, and each one relies on different members of the national security community to conduct his briefings and to call attention to matters that are more compelling or critical (Mahle, 2004: 91).

Essentially, current intelligence concerns the events occurring in the minutes and hours before the President and other key government officials are briefed. Sharply contrasted, long-range intelligence concerns the unfolding events and developments that have been studied over a longer period of time, generally within a year's time. Current intelligence analysis is a discrete specialization demanding high-level analytical skill and extensive experience working in an environment of high pressure and quick comprehension of developing events. It most certainly requires careful interpretation, rapid reporting, and consistent accuracy. Current intelligence analysts live in a tension-filled corridor between their offices in Virginia, the White House Oval Office, the Defense Department executive offices, the State Department, and in the company of congressional oversight committee leaders on Capitol Hill. It is work that is perpetually tuned to the breaking events that may be transformed into mere historical artifacts within hours. As they say in the current intelligence field, when the page is turned there is little further concern for its contents. Current intelligence analysts are normally fixed on horizons outside the nation and their scope of interest is world events sliced into minutes and hours, including the data elements from satellites and aircraft platforms.

Analysts who work in areas of long-range research and reporting encounter an entirely different environment. Project tasking takes a more deliberative course through meetings, back-and-forth discussions, and measured research initiatives. Horizons of time to reach completion are usually months or a year in the future. Typically reports are lengthy and more detailed accounts containing detailed citations to original or documentary sources. In theory, most analysis should be based on carefully crafted and more strategically considered perspectives. One cold reality analysts always face is that targeted consumers, mainly high level policy makers, have limited time to read detailed reports, frequently relying instead on a diet of current intelligence. In recent years, in fact, CIA's analytical component has been chastised for spending so much time answering policy-maker questions at the expense of independent contemplation of significant world events (Mahle, 2004). Indeed, current and long-range intelligence analysis are miles apart in their horizons of time and perspectives on the immediacy of relevant circumstances, but clearly their respective products hold independent value at the highest and most critical levels of national security decision-making.

Analysis proceeds from methodologies associated with mining massive quantities of information, a challenge to, yet an expectation of, all researchers and scholars. Information storage and retrieval technologies in the intelligence community are, perhaps, the best available systems in the world. They are so good, in fact, that decisions about what information to select and how much to include in finished products are persistent challenges to analysts who are driven by a desire to be comprehensive in their assessments. Daily survival and career development depend, in part, on efficiency in information mining and succinctness in subject matter summation. Policy-makers are always impatient to receive brief and highly focused and timely material. Over time, analysts develop in-depth expertise in one or more subject areas, thus adding to an analytical function's critical mass of diverse library resources. Intensity of analytical operations cause managers concern for burnout and learned biases. These potential results are subtle and potentially dangerous byproducts of repetitive responses under time pressures, organizational socialization, and topical turf defensiveness. It is presumed that the group context in which analysis occurs alleviates and checks some, and hopefully most of the negative effects of intense research on subjects of vital importance to national security (Godson, May and Schmitt, 1995; Johnston, 2005; Lowenthal, 2003b; Marrin, 2003–2004; Medina, 2002, Swenson, 2003).

The modern analyst is a dedicated student of topics under investigation. Typically, analysts are expected to hold graduate degrees in international affairs, politics, regional studies, languages, history, and culture from strong academic institutions. As they invest in their career path, analysts become national security assets. Daily, each analyst adds to the total body of knowledge. Hundreds of individual and team products combine to cause exponential growth of information resources. Simultaneously, analysts are hunters and gatherers, adding interpretations of meaning to raw data, a process, some argue, often focused on passive rather than active modes of collection resources

(Cogan, 2004). Reasonably, analysts expect to be recognized for contributions to major national security decisions, but they all recognize, too, that they must remain intensely dedicated and reclusive researchers of world conditions. They are all susceptible to bureaucratic politics and information manipulation, and they are all subject to sharp criticism, mirror imaging, confirmation bias, default to standard peer perspectives, the need to please bosses, and co-optation by the organizational culture (Betts, 1978; Hughes, 1976; Johnston, 2005; Lowenthal, 2003a). Groupthink, or susceptibility to it, is always an element in the daily organizational reality.

There are two critical characteristics of the analytical process. First, success in intelligence analysis means that a requisite amount of information has crossed organizational lines and that no elements of critical information have been ignored or withheld. The original design of the intelligence community stressed the importance of interagency discussions and information sharing, now fulfilled in practice through interagency committees, document exchanges, individual and small group meetings, visitations to target sites, and horizontal and vertical vetting of draft reports. Unquestionably, bureaucratic barriers are raised to control the amount of interagency sharing. Individual analysts find ways to acquire information, however, to exchange insights and valuable perspectives with counterparts in other agencies, and to work across lines of separation that usually carry more meaning to managers than to people on operational levels. Second, intelligence analysis is grounded in human interpretation, thus the analytical function remains, in theory anyway, open to dissent and to entirely different conclusions (Nolte, 2004; O'Connell, 2004). Analysis means criticism, challenges, competition, and the full range of human tendencies to mediate strongly held views. In a manner similar to processes associated with academic publishing, and perhaps with a vetting intensity carrying greater consequences for inaccurate assessment, successful analysts recognize and adapt to internal dissent. In theory, institutionalization of dissent induces deeper, more careful research, arguably improving the accuracy of the final product (Lowenthal, 2003a; MacEachin, 1994). It is never assumed to be a perfect process. But, it is a process that is unlikely to be replaced, only improved.

One final and critical element in the bag of intelligence research resources is the library. As the founders of the Yale Library Project knew intuitively, analysis requires a library of information, arranged according to a rational taxonomy of topics. The library represents the body of knowledge from which the analyst assembles perspectives and answers to questions posed by policy-makers. The vast majority of the body of knowledge is found in open sources, the remainder derived from sensitive human and technological sources. Unquestionably, then, the intelligence community library must command top-level sophistication in terms of its internal development. The library's goal is superiority over every other depository in the world of knowledge. To support storage and information retrieval objectives, the community, principally CIA, NSA, the State Department, and FBI, invest heavily in the most advanced computer systems that technology can build. The body of knowledge, small in the days of Sherman Kent and the founders of CIA's analytical branch, itself is a national treasure for analyst consultation and further expansion. Its resources are mined for tidbits of new information and unique perspectives. Known facts are placed alongside contemporary ways of thinking on the path to assembling perspectives associated with critical and direction-changing decisions. It is a heady business. Significant prestige accrues to the analytical function in a position to conduct vital activities at the heart of the national security system, and most importantly, to add new knowledge to the library collection. The days of the 'old boy'[14] networks (Hersh, 1992) based on informal communications and trusted insider opinions have faded to near extinction, replaced by systematic analytical activities grounded in scientific method (Johnson, 1989b; Herman, 2001; Heuer, 2003; Grabo, 2002). There is no comparable organization in the domestic sector anywhere in the world. It is a model worthy of partial replication in the realm of domestic security. The demands for intelligence in the international business community, and on privately contracted security services, are having their effects on how corporate executives and domestic security companies use information (Cooper, 1996).

Domestic security in America: a contrasting overview

The evolution of the domestic security community stands in sharp contrast to the American intelligence community. No formal domestic security organization existed in America before the late 1860s. Evolution in the late 19th century was mainly in response to private self-help actions in response to rising opportunities for crime. Self-help remained a byproduct of national expansion for several decades. Protective responses to predators eventually spawned a cottage industry in security enterprises, all operating in parallel to emergent but primitive police departments. Scottish immigrant Allan Pinkerton, a man who gained significant reputation in the first years of the Civil War, established the first American company (Horan, 1962; McCrie, 1988; Morn, 1982; Pinkerton, 1883; Tidwell, Hall and Gaddy, 1988).[15] The detective business spread across developed and undeveloped territories as banks, merchants, railroads, and town governments required investigative assistance. After the Civil War, industrial organizations were transformed into the manufacturing of commercial products, workforces grew in size and companies often moved to locations distant from town centers where law enforcement hardly existed. By 1900, Pinkerton's detective agency dominated the provision of security services. Small armies of industrial guards were contracted to work directly for industrialists and plant directors to control labor organizing, crime, and general order maintenance.

Arguably, the value of security organizations to the quality of life was in chasing fugitives, protecting property, and investigating crimes. The early security industry never contemplated any sort of self-evaluation of its performance, seeking only to meet consumer demand for services and to pursue profits. Lack of analysis and foresight led ultimately to excessive conduct in the last decades of the 19th century. The Pinkerton agency, for example, learned hard lessons from embarrassments suffered in labor conflicts in the 1890s (Calder, 1985; McCrie,

1988). Unlike other companies in industrial protection, however, the Pinkerton agency turned attention to expanding intelligence files and to initiatives aimed at broadening crime analysis at the federal level. By distinguishing itself in this area, and by carefully analyzing new markets for security services, the Pinkerton agency endeared itself to the Bureau of Investigation (later the FBI) and other intelligence services both civilian and military (Minahan, 1994). The Burns International Detective Agency was also intimately connected with a resource-strapped Bureau of Investigation in the years after 1908 (Theoharis, 2000: 170). The close ties between public and private sectors were confirmed in the appointments of William Flynn and William Burns, both master detectives, to head the Bureau from 1917 to 1924 (Powers, 2004: 123). These were entrepreneurs and leaders of domestic security operations, but they had no visions of a broader context of security in American society or the world.

Only insignificant differences in approach, conduct, and results were manifested in the operations of private security companies between 1865 and 1935 (Calder, 1985). During these 'mean years,' industrialists and plant foremen continued the practice of hiring guard companies and labor spies to protect property, to undermine labor-organizing initiatives, and to control unruly workers (Shalloo, 1933).[16] One can argue that most manufacturers had admirable and legitimate economic interests at heart. Some, however, affiliated with criminal elements and corrupt politicians, thus carrying on the image of rank abuse of workers in service of corporate greed (Calder, 1985; McCrie, 1988; Sward, 1968). In some cases the loss of perspective, a consequence of high profitability, demonstrated the belligerence of private interests gone mad. Government intervention remained inept, also, until the National Labor Relations Act of 1935 granted workers collective bargaining rights and a qualified right to strike. Industrial guards, too, achieved standing in law as they were permitted to join collective bargaining units like other workers. Industrial riots in 1936 and 1937 were evidence that the law could not manufacture industrial peace. Security companies still lacked internal discipline and self-reflection. Congressional investigations and demands for severe disciplinary actions threatened to force company owners to control the brutal, largely uneducated, and frequently corrupt domestic guard forces (Maney, 1978; Shearing and Stenning, 1987). In essence, by the late 1930s the domestic security function had not escaped its negative image and it showed no signs of contemplation about how to move to higher ground of public respect.[17] In general, the industry had no interest in a coherent and focused strategy to earn public respect or approval by police organizations. Moreover, private security seemed uninterested in creating an image for its role in the national efforts against crime. Simply put, it looked for no such role, it planned for no role, and it lived only in the operational moment. Most noteworthy, there was no voice of dissent among industry leaders about the need to change directions and priorities.

In ways quite similar to the intelligence function, Pearl Harbor forever changed the domestic security function. On the American home front internal security was entirely unprepared for emergencies occurring outside company property.

The security industry was frozen in 19th century thinking, modernized only by a few technological innovations that were largely irrelevant to national security assistance. When this reality set in, corporate leaders, mainly in coastal regions, panicked. They all feared second-wave attacks upon mainland industries in places like Los Angeles, Santa Barbara, and San Francisco. General Joseph Stilwell, then West Coast Deputy Army commander, was bombarded with requests to supply armed soldiers to protect company properties (Tuchman, 1970: 298). Quickly it was clear that the entire complement of domestic protection was disorganized, a ragtag collection of corporate guards who owed allegiance to company owners. It seemed that domestic security was little more than a scattered force of contract personnel with no concept of a larger purpose in the national emergency, no loyalty except to a paycheck, and no sense of the public welfare. Few had any advanced police or military training. Company managements continued deployment of company guards in essentially the same manner as they had done since the late 19th century. The security posture was focused on the internal details of company order maintenance, monitoring of potential labor-management conflict, and ordinary day-to-day routines of gates, locks, patrols, and report writing. Security functions, with few exceptions, were far removed from the upper echelons of decision-making, remaining for years to follow in the lowest ranks of the administrative position and priority. At the top levels of American corporations no appreciable analysis of security needs was associated with wartime contingencies.

Militarization of the industrial guard forces was a government-directed emergency response. As a story saved for another venue, this action allowed regular Army troops to leave defensive guard positions for war-fighting duties. Army or Navy officers were assigned to war production plants to organize guard force training and to introduce wartime security procedures. Military methods were employed to impose physical and operational security on war factories.[18] By war's end, however, the obvious lessons for emergency response planning were not preserved, relegated to mere artifacts of wartime crisis and response, not of advanced thinking or decisions based on studied analysis.

Another decade passed before a national organization was formed to represent industrial security. The American Society for Industrial Security (ASIS) was formed in 1955, mainly an organization of corporate security leaders in national defense and allied industries and in natural resources and manufacturing. In the post-war period of economic boom, the business community was largely uninterested in domestic security preparedness. Some attention was given to relatively low-level civil defense initiatives in response to the Soviet nuclear threat, but there was no clarion call for significant improvements in private or government security preparedness. In civilian society juvenile crime and property theft increased sharply during the 1950s. Private contract security expanded but it developed no special identity in connection with crime prevention initiatives. It was impossible for ASIS (currently ASIS, International) to speak for all elements in the domestic security realm because there was no coherent understanding of its role, contributions to crime prevention, and professional standing. In essence, what little imagery there was of domestic security emanated from large corporate in-house security operations and from security guard and private investigative companies. Guard and investigations companies were mainly interested in market share expansion, acquisitions and mergers, and profits. Unquestionably, ASIS represented a step in the direction toward a distinctive role definition for domestic security. It distinguished the professional leadership of the security industry from the operational levels of security in the guard industry, private detectives, money courier firms, etc. It limited membership to a select few managers and directors of security operations, and to associate members drawn from the new class of corporate security professionals. Research interests of ASIS languished for nearly four more decades, but the industry in general failed to take up any significant interest in grounding decisions in research evidence. Essentially, there was no triggering mechanism in society, the political community, or economics to cause the industry or its budding associations to invest in a costly and labor-intensive research enterprise.

In the two decades between 1955 and 1975, domestic security organizations grew in proportion to perceptions and realities associated with the American crime wave. As police organizations retreated from property protection, the private security sector recognized that it stood alone in times of emergency, generally during riots and major natural disasters. A combination of fear of inaction and action merely for the sake of action stimulated a kind of 'boots-on-the-ground' approach to security, thus intensifying an already labor-intensive industry. The same basic phenomenon of rapid unplanned expansion also occurred in the UK in this period (Jones and Newburn, 1998). Beginning anew in 1961 and rising steadily for two decades, aircraft hijackings caused substantial increases in airport and air carrier security. College and university campuses were forced to introduce major investments in campus policing and security when anti-war riots destroyed property and the general serenity of campus life. The Bank Protection Act of 1968 shifted responsibility to federally insured banks to institute security programs to deter armed robberies, an initiative long favored by the FBI. In fact, crime and rising expectations about property protection greatly expanded all aspects of domestic security. Responses by private and public sectors to sharply rising crime rates were all fundamentally defensive in nature, stimulated by federal attention, initiated well after problems had festered, and with few exceptions, guided by outmoded physical security measures.

In the decades after World War II the domestic security realm has been engaged mainly in tasks associated with corporate asset protection ranging from low-tech human systems to high-tech gadgetry. Persistent innovation by criminals has produced corresponding innovations in security devices, but individual manufacturers have been reluctant to engage in analysis of how systems could be more strategically integrated. The threat of losing intellectual property has always been in the foreground of reasons for avoiding objective vetting of security devices. The coherence of security responses, challenges, and risks associated with the crime problem has remained an illusive objective. Emphasis instead was placed on internal expansion of corporate security operations, especially in the manufacturing sector, and rabbit-like reproduction of the security service industry. All of this economic investment stimulated significant growth and diversification of products and services, representing a sincere interest in addressing the crime problem without reflection on objectives, research grounding, and applications across sub-fields or specializations.

Security organizations evolved from relative obscurity in wartime to fixtures on the crime prevention landscape throughout the developed and developing world. Security presence became an obtrusive element in all well traveled urban commercial places (e.g. airports, banks, entertainment and sports venues, malls, theatres, etc.). The industry employed hundreds of thousands of people in jobs primarily oriented to standing watch or in gate-keeping functions. Other elements of human security, although less obvious in daily life, included investigative, managerial, and technical personnel paid higher salaries to perform higher order protection tasks. The technological departments of domestic security invented, manufactured, and sold technical equipment intended mainly to replace or to supplement human security. In the past sixty years, the vast majority of security work has been in private crime prevention (e.g. alarm response, guard, and investigative services). Various forms of domestic security have been linked to national defence (e.g. government agency protection, background investigations, and technical assignments) (Parfomak, 2004; White, 2004). The private sector, by contrast, has remained free to invent itself in a fragmented way, driven by the profit motive under conditions of minimal regulatory oversight (Button and George, 2001; George and Button, 2000; Farnell and Shearing, 1977; Gill and Hart, 1996; Jones and Newburn, 1998; Kennedy, 1995).

The domestic security community has made a few attempts at self-diagnosis, but analysis has tended to remain at the descriptive level. Individual researchers and government-sponsored projects have characterized demands for security services, components of private security, major security business interests, and estimates of industry growth in technologies and services. It is clear that state governments were reluctant to impose regulatory standards as a vehicle for introducing self-analysis and industry improvement (Hemmens, Maahs, Scarborough and Collins, 2001). In the years between primitive studies by the 1930 Wickersham Crime Commission (Calder, 1993), the 1933 study of private police in Pennsylvania by Professor John P. Shalloo, and federally sponsored studies in the 1970s, concerns that domestic security had not moved beyond descriptive analysis remained unnoticed. No political or policy interests stirred critical attention to the massive growth, diversification, and role expansion of domestic security.[19] Private security remained a patchwork of private companies largely unchanged since World War II, and an internally incoherent enterprise that claimed professional standing while manifesting few characteristics of a real profession. These were revelations of the 1971 Rand Report on private security, the product of a US Justice Department grant to the Rand Research Corporation (Kakalik and Wildhorn, 1977).[20] An obvious irony, not lost on the few analysts at the time, was that federal funds for research were used to inform a large, wealthy, predominantly private industry of its failings and its needs.

Expectations of closer co-operation with police caused the Justice Department to fund another batch of initiatives that resulted in an investigation by the National Advisory Committee on Criminal Justice Standards and Goals (1976). The Committee's report on private security observed that, 'the absence of reliable research has made planning and decision-making difficult in the field,' proposing in response to form an institute to 'further the development of a body of knowledge for use in educational institutions, and to provide a foundation for the development of new and improved strategies to optimize private security capacity in crime prevention and reduction' (National Advisory Committee, 1976: 259). In the following year (1977), the authors of the original Rand Report revisited their findings, concluding that few significant improvements had occurred (Kakalik and Wildhorn, 1977). The Centre of Criminology at the University of Toronto published a series of descriptive studies on private security in 1977 but the focus of attention was narrowly limited to Canadian legal issues, in-house or proprietary security operations, and statistics representing the Canadian security industry (Farnell and Shearing, 1977). Similar studies were conducted in the UK in the late 1970s. In the US, one final attempt at critical evaluation was reported out as the 'Hallcrest Report.' In editions appearing in 1985 and 1990, additional government-funded research described the conditions of domestic private security. Recommendations were projected to the year 2000. The Hallcrest investigators recommended an 'Economic Crime Research Center' (or Institute) to bring uniformity to definitions and terms, to measure economic crime's impact, to co-ordinate economic crime data across trade and industry associations, to fund research, and to promote awareness of countermeasures (Cunningham, Strauchs and Van Meter, 1990: 313). At no time in the 1990s were formal studies initiated to closely examine the operations, performance, and prospective futures of government security. Moreover, at no time in the history of private security has R & A taken center stage, remaining instead a vague peripheral concept without significant advocacy. Perhaps the most disheartening result of government-funded research initiatives on domestic security is confirmation that the field of security management has failed to declare a priority interest in R & A. Admittedly, it shows that a small group of dedicated researchers were willing to undertake sizeable investigations that served to enlighten public knowledge of domestic security's scope and operations. This result stands in contrast to the tremendous growth, financial success, and increasing technical capacity of the security field in many parts of the world.

Domestic security: can it learn from the intelligence community?

This chapter has contrasted the manner in which two related security communities have attributed value to the role of R & A in the development of their respective areas of responsibility. Arguably, the domestic security community stands in sharp contrast to the intelligence community. Its interests in grounding decision-making processes in independent research findings have been limited, scattered, and peripheral at best. The experience of the intelligence community has shown quite the opposite result: extensive, focused, and central to major decision-making concerns. That said, we advance to key questions associated with domestic security management's ability to learn from this contrast. First, will the domestic security community continue to grow its operational capabilities in the absence of investment in independent R & A? Second, will the domestic security community commit to a significant change in its thinking about its decision-making processes, in part, by critical self-evaluation of the extent to which decisions are grounded in theory development and testing, in evidence-based and vetted crime prevention and risk reduction strategies, and in critical assessments by independent researchers of all applications of technology used in protective/preventive capacities? Third, will the domestic security community undertake critical self-analysis to learn what measurable contributions it makes to solutions to real social or technical problems associated with crime, terrorism, and other forms of risks to human safety and property protection? Finally, and perhaps most importantly, can the domestic security community expect to reach a level of credibility and sustained consultation with high-level policymakers in private and public life without a long-term investment in R & A? These and related questions may well guide part of the future agenda of domestic security. The answers are not possible at this time, and they will not serve any significant purpose if they do not find a responsive audience in the nation's highest levels of security management leadership.

One outcome is certain, however. The major elements of the intelligence community, both civilian and military in all the developed and developing nations, will advance rapidly toward greater emphasis on analysis (Henderson, 2003; Johnston, 2005). Evidence of rapid advancement is found in the American experience with the Joint Military Intelligence College (founded in 1962), the CIA's new internal organization known as the Sherman Kent School for Intelligence Analysis (founded in 2000), and the FBI's recent work to develop an internal College of Analytical Studies (under construction in 2004) to train analysts for its new Office of Intelligence (Hitz and Weiss, 2004; Swenson, 2003). Presently, there are no comparable institutions serving the domestic security community, specifically organizations focused on a domestic R & A agenda. For the sake of clarity, the reference here is not to the creation of private intelligence organizations similar to government security agencies, but rather to organization(s) designed specifically to conduct R & A in the same intensive manner as intelligence organizations but with the intent of improving the quality of decision-making applicable to domestic security (private and public).

For the moment, and to serve the limited objectives of this chapter, we now point directly to the lessons learned from close study of the field of intelligence and its R & A foci. The lessons listed below will not find favor with all readers. They should, however, provoke critique and discussion by professionals and scholars who are interested in advancing the credibility and place of domestic security in decision-making circles.

Transferable lessons from the study of intelligence and intelligence analysis:

- The Pearl Harbor disaster compelled political leaders to construct a centralized intelligence analysis function. That function selected top intellectual talent, built a library of knowledge, and evolved to a status of high reputation by the end of World War II.
- The Central Intelligence Agency, the core agency in the national security intelligence community, developed a calling among national security leaders at the highest levels of government; thereby influencing continued support for the R & A functions in all major organizations of the community.
- The primary analysis organization in the intelligence community has been the CIA's Directorate of Intelligence, a center of analytical excellence that draws on its own resources for R & A and upon other analytical centers throughout the national security community. Analytical functions in other intelligence organizations reinforce competitiveness as an essential element in decision-making objectivity.
- Decisions on all significant national security policies have been grounded in the correlated and integrated intelligence assessments provided by the CIA, including relevant input from other community analytical functions.
- The internal strength of CIA's analytical function evolved from the investments in the best and brightest analysts drawn from top colleges and universities.
- Intelligence analysis was founded on the principle of diversity of research interests across all academic disciplines and realms of knowledge.
- A theory of intelligence analysis was constructed as a vehicle for advancing the art and science of interpretation of world conditions and the methodologies employed to build the base of data and the continuity of intellectual discovery. Theory development continues, and must continue to be, uninterrupted (Andrew, 2004; Kahn, 2001).
- A body of knowledge in intelligence-relevant areas was gathered, organized, and placed in a library retrieval system.
- Intelligence analysis and research activities evolved into specializations using diverse methodologies to inform the national security structure on current and long-term concerns.
- Intelligence analysis and research have become discrete specializations in the intelligence community meriting special training carried out by colleges and universities and by the community's internal schools of advanced development.
- No one has ever claimed that intelligence analysis, based on the very best human resources, data, methodologies, and techniques of evaluation, is a perfect or error-free process. By the same token, no one in any responsible position in the national security system has claimed (or is likely to claim) that decisions of the President and the National Security Council can ignore the input of analysis and research from the intelligence community, regardless of mistakes the analysis process has made and may make in the future.

Final thoughts

National and domestic security organizations have been asked to reevaluate their respective contributions to the overall security posture of the nation. In the foreseeable future, these organizations will be asked to measure operational integrity, human resource competencies, and procedures aimed at protecting the nation's most vulnerable locations. New benchmarks can be expected to measure how well the domestic security community in the Western nations succeeds in developing an institutional framework for internal advancement and for contributions it makes to security preparedness (Marrin, 2004). One purpose of benchmarks, of course, is to measure the progress of domestic security in its quest to achieve standing and credibility comparable to what was achieved by the national security intelligence community. Several decades ago the US intelligence community recognized that similar weaknesses affected its own intellectual and professional standing. It made a concerted and successful effort to improve its position in the national security policy arena. Lessons from this history are directly insightful to speeding up the transformation of the domestic security community. If they are learned well and institutionalized, the domestic security community will be afforded with a critical tool for elevating a currently disaggregated collection of private interests fixed only on profit-making to a position of high professional respect comparable to the intelligence community (Garcia, 2000). Clearly, the 21st century security professional is challenged to apply the latest analytical tools and vetted research in decision-making, risk assessment, and countermeasures planning. To reach the objective of universal acceptance of the role of R & A in all of these areas of decision-making, the domestic security community has much work to do. It must develop a theory of domestic security to include conceptualization of how the community contributes to the quality of life in democratic societies. It must institutionalize a research agenda to inform private and public decisions. It must sustain a tradition of internal criticism across its research agenda. It must recruit and underwrite the work of a cohort of intellectual talent across disciplinary lines. And it must create a center of research excellence, including a library for an expanding body of vetted knowledge. The work ahead will be challenging, and at times frustrating. The intelligence community has supplied a highly useful model for setting a course of action, imperfect by design and experience, but nonetheless, a model tested by long-term measures of credibility and experience. Intelligence analysis has risen to a level of indispensability in national security decision-making. It has reached a developmental stage in which the frustrations and calls for change are about qualitative improvements in collection resources and analytical methodologies, not about the need or value of vetted analysis. The domestic security community has created no comparable institutional setting, and for the most part it cannot claim that its critical decision-making is based on any significant level of R & A. Frankly, in 2006 and beyond it would be better to have debates among security professionals over the quality and methodological rigor of its research output than to argue for a research priority in the first place. The field has the capacity to create an institutional setting for formal R & A but so far it has lacked the will to do so. That result needs to change.

Notes

1 It should not be misunderstood that many other organizations in the US intelligence community also conduct R & A. The CIA, however, conducts its own R & A and it is charged with the central co-ordinative function for the community.

2 As currently designed, for example, the CIA has three other major units: Directorate of Administration, Directorate of Operations, and Directorate of Science and Technology.

3 The authors reflected in this collection of chapters may well serve as pioneers in this effort.

4 A very large historical literature on intelligence is available to inform the learning process but it is too voluminous to list here. The bibliography below provides some beginning literature.

5 Considerations of space and relevance prevent discussion of the total context in which the American intelligence and national security system was instituted in 1947.

6 In early 2005, President George W. Bush appointed a new director of national intelligence to serve in the capacity of the president's primary adviser on intelligence matters and co-ordinator of intelligence policy across the many agencies in the national security community, as distinguished from the Director of the Central Intelligence Agency.

7 Two other provisions were added to the charter of responsibilities that allowed for flexibility in the duties that the NSC might assign with respect to how information would be gathered or services performed in later years. In this connection, the statutory provision has been the source for planning and conducting covert and paramilitary operations. The looseness of the language of these provisions was considered negative at the time of the Reagan administration's scandal involving arms for hostages, but it may now be viewed more positively in light of global terrorism.

8 Excellent histories of these developments are included in the bibliography, particularly works by James Bamford, David Kahn, and Nigel West.

9 It is even more accurate to date the British intelligence service to 1587 and the role of Sir Francis Walsingham in introducing the first analytical report of foreign threats, the *Plot for Intelligence Out of Spain*, a document summarizing the development of a Spanish fleet of fighting ships. Great Britain emerged as a leader in the intelligence field in the early 20th century with the development of the War Office Intelligence Branch and the better-funded Naval Intelligence department. The French history of intelligence is also richly relevant to American developments. The literature on German secret services is entirely too voluminous to cite here, and most of it dates from Adolph Hitler's era. The vast majority of literature on Russian and Soviet intelligence services dates from the origins of the KGB, once again a massive collection.

10 This author's father, William D. Calder, began his 33-year career in the US Army Map Service (later Defense Mapping Agency and now part of the National Geospatial-Intelligence Agency) in Washington, DC in 1941. In an interview in the mid-1980s, he acknowledged the assistance given by British intelligence services and mapping functions. The US military services desperately needed this assistance since they could not plan invasions in unfamiliar areas nor make reliable maps available to commanders without new mapmaking techniques. The British had long before made detailed maps of many parts of the world and they had perfected a variety of mapping techniques.

11 The litany of intelligence blunders and missed opportunities in this era are exceptionally well documented in the book and journal scholarship. Unrelenting efforts of Herbert Yardley and William Friedman, however, carried on the work of code breakers during the inter-war years.

12 There are many excellent memoirs of OSS service. The close reader of this service should consider that there are many myths about the effectiveness of OSS analytical capabilities.

13 Downes claimed to have begun the project in secret at Yale. He had been a Yale student, then worked in the OSS. Curtiss was a Yale professor of English. Mendenhall, a Yale history professor, served as a collector of funds from donors and laundered the money to keep the project secret. Pforzheimer, a Wall Street broker, supervised the

funds and the laundering efforts. Knollenberg, a well-known tax lawyer, was Yale's librarian, responsible for rounding up a diverse collection of materials to make Yale one of the largest libraries in the world.

14   'Old boys' is a term referring mainly to ranking members of the British security services who, usually by retirement, become employed by other government agencies or the private security industry. It is rumored that the British security services have encouraged and aided such transitions in order to sustain the influence of security services by maintaining informal communications and whereabouts, by preserving consultative resources in experienced personnel, and generally by enhancing continuity of roles between the work of government analysts and operators and the private sector. The 'old boy' phenomenon has also been influential in sustaining the links between the US intelligence community and domestic industrial security. No assessment has yet been made of the influence and roles of American 'old boys' who retire from CIA, FBI, and other national level intelligence and security organizations to key positions in domestic security organizations. It is difficult to measure the impact of the 'old boy' members of security associations and societies of former government agents (e.g. ASIS, International (formerly the American Society for Industrial Security), Association of Former Intelligence Officers, Federal Law Enforcement Agents Association, and the Society of Former Agents of the FBI) on the policy community. Corporate executives may assume that such persons carry into the private realm the competencies needed to perform security functions with distinction, but we have no confirmation of that assumption.

15   Pinkerton has several books attributed to his name. Many suspicions have arisen as to authenticity and accuracy. Nonetheless, they are interesting period pieces.

16   The first formal study of private security in America was conducted by a young assistant professor of sociology at the University of Pennsylvania, John P. Shalloo.

17   There were, without a doubt, tales of heroic couriers who defended money and property in their work for armored transport companies. Others served as night watchmen who prevented a fire or who saved a life, and as private detectives who helped police find stolen goods.

18   During the war many industrial guard units served with distinction, despite significant tensions between military commanders and company managements. Militarization affected approximately 200,000 service personnel.

19   The police community, by sharp comparison, encountered a different experience in these years, spurred on by the intellectual leadership of August Vollmer, Bruce Smith, O.W. Wilson, Raymond Fosdick, V.A. Leonard, and others. By the early 1970s, despite poor responses to major changes in crime statistics and to obvious abuse and ineptitude in handling civil rights, policing made remarkable advances.

20   The five-volume report represented the first modern investigation into the private protection industry in the US. Constructively, this research energized closer study of private security, introduced improvements in co-operation between police and security organizations, and stimulated interest in new government policies and regulations.

Key readings

See an important, if somewhat incomplete and narrowly framed study that magnifies the point of this chapter and the need for extensive, focused analysis of security protection in Parfomak, P.W. (2004) *Guarding America: Security Guards and U.S. Critical Infrastructure Protection*. Washington, DC: Congressional Research Service. A broader perspective on the role of analysis in homeland protection is found in Marrin, S. (2003) Homeland Security and the Analysis of Foreign Intelligence. *The Intelligencer: Journal of U.S. Intelligence Studies*. Vol. 13, No. 2, pp. 25–36. For a hefty reference volume to more than 10,000 scholarly articles on intelligence and espionage, including discussions of analysis and security services, see Calder, J.D. (1999) *Intelligence, Espionage and Related Topics: An Annotated Bibliography of Serial Journal and Magazine Scholarship, 1844–1998*. Westport, CT: Greenwood Group.

Dozens of excellent articles on intelligence analysis can be found in the scholarly journals, such as Herman, M. (2003) Intelligence's Future: Learning from the Past. *The Journal of Intelligence History*. Vol. 3, No. 2, pp. 1–19; Johnston, R. (2003) Reducing Analytic Error: Integrating Methodologists into Teams of Substantive Experts. *Studies in Intelligence*. Vol. 47, No. 1, pp. 57–65 and Dupont, A. (2003) Intelligence for the Twenty-First Century. *Intelligence and National Security*. Vol. 18, No. 4, pp. 15–39.

Bibliography

Aid, M.M. (2001) 'The National Security Agency and the Cold War,' *Intelligence and National Security*. Vol. 16, No. 1, pp. 27–66.

Aldrich, R.J. (2001) 'GCHQ and Sigint in the Early Cold War 1945–70,' *Intelligence and National Security*. Vol. 16, No. 1, pp. 67–96.

Aldrich, R.J. (2000) *Intelligence and the War Against Japan: Britain, America and the Politics of Secret Service*. Cambridge, UK: Cambridge University.

Alvarez, D. (2000) *Secret Messages: Codebreaking and American Diplomacy, 1930–1945*. Manhattan, KS: University Press of Kansas.

Ambrose, S.E. (1981) *Ike's Spies: Eisenhower and the Espionage Establishment*. Garden City, NY: Doubleday.

Andrew, C. (2004) 'Intelligence, International Relations, and "Under-theorisation",' *Intelligence and National Security*, Vol. 19, No. 2, pp. 170–84.

Andrew, C. (1995) *For the President's Eyes Only: Secret Intelligence and the American Presidency from Washington to Bush*. New York: Harper Collins.

Andrew, C. (1986) *Her Majesty's Secret Service: The Making of the British Intelligence Community*. New York: Viking Penguin.

Andrew, C. and Mitrokhin, V.I. (1999) *The Sword and the Shield: The Mitrokhin Archive and the Secret History of the KGB*. New York: Basic Books.

Anonymous (1986) 'The Art of Intelligence Analysis,' *Studies in Intelligence*. Vol. 30, No. 3, pp. 1–11.

Axelrod, A. (1992) *The War Between the Spies: A History of Espionage During the Civil War*. New York: Atlantic Monthly.

Bamford, J. (1982) *The Puzzle Palace: A Report on NSA, America's Most Secret Agency*. Boston: Houghton Mifflin.

Bamford, J. (2001) *Body of Secrets: Anatomy of the Ultra-Secret National Security Agency from the Cold War Through the Dawn of a New Century*. New York: Doubleday.

Berkowitz, B.D. and Goodman, A.E. (1989) *Strategic Intelligence for American National Security*. Princeton, NJ: Princeton University.

Berkowitz, B.D. and Goodman, A.E. (2000) *Best Truth: Intelligence in the Information Age*. New Haven, CT: Yale University.

Best, R.A., Jr. (2005) 'Intelligence Issues for Congress,' *CRS Issue Brief for Congress*. Washington, DC: Congressional Research Service.

Betts, R.K. (1978) 'Analysis, War, and Decision: Why Intelligence Allures Are Inevitable,' *World Politics*. Vol. 31, No. 1, pp. 61–89.

Blash, E.C., II (1993) 'Strategic Intelligence Analysis and National Decisionmaking: A Systems Management Approach,' *International Journal of Intelligence and Counterintelligence*. Vol. 6, No. 1, pp. 55–68.

Bodnar, J.W. (2003) *Warning Analysis for the Information Age: Rethinking the Intelligence Process*. Washington, DC: Center for Strategic Intelligence Research, Joint Military Intelligence College.

Bozeman, A.B. (1992) *Strategic Intelligence & Statecraft: Selected Essays*. Washington, DC: Brassey's.

Brown, A.C. (1982) *Wild Bill Donovan: The Last Hero*. New York: Times Books.

Budiansky, S. (2000) *Battle of Wits: The Complete Story of Codebreaking in World War II*. New York: Free Press.

Button, M. and George, B. (2001) 'Government Regulation in the United Kingdom Private Security Industry: The Myth of Non-Regulation,' *Security Journal*. Vol. 14, No. 1, pp. 55–66.

Burris, W.C. (1993) 'The Uses of History of Intelligence Analysis,' *International Journal of Intelligence and Counterintelligence*. Vol. 6, No. 3, pp. 297–302.

Calder, J.D. (1999) *Intelligence, Espionage and Related Topics: An Annotated Bibliography of Serial Journal and Magazine Scholarship, 1844–1998*. Westport, CT: Greenwood Group.

Calder, J.D. (1993) *The Origins and Development of Federal Crime Control Policy: Herbert Hoover's Initiatives*. Westport, CT: Praeger.

Calder, J.D. (1985) 'Industrial Guards in the Nineteenth and Twentieth Centuries: The Mean Years,' *Journal of Security Administration*. Vol. 8, No. 2, pp. 11–21.

Champion, B. (1998) A Review of Selected Cases of Industrial Espionage and Economic Spying, 1568–1945. *Intelligence and National Security*. Vol. 13, No. 2, pp. 123–43.

Clark, R.M. (2004) *Intelligence Analysis: A Target-Centric Approach*. Washington, DC: CQ Press.

Clark, R.M. (1975) Scientific and Technical Intelligence Analysis. *Studies in Intelligence*. Vol. 19, No. 1, pp. 39–48.

Cline, R.S. (1981) *The CIA under Reagan, Bush & Casey: The Evolution of the Agency from Roosevelt to Reagan*. Washington, DC: Acropolis.

Cogan, C. (2004) Hunters Not Gatherers: Intelligence in the Twenty-First Century. *Intelligence and National Security*. Vol. 19, No. 2, pp. 304–21.

Cooper, H.H.A. (1996) *Business Intelligence: A Primer*. Berryville, VA: Executive Protection Institute.

Corson, W.R. (1977) *Armies of Ignorance: The Rise of the American Intelligence Empire*. New York: Dial Press.

Cunningham, W.C., Strauchs, J.J. and Van Meter, C.W. (1990) *Private Security Trends 1970–2000: The Hallcrest Report II*. McLean, VA: Hallcrest Systems.

Darling, A.B. (1990) *The Central Intelligence Agency: An Instrument of Government, to 1950*. University Park, PA: Pennsylvania State University.

Davis, J. (1995) 'A Policymaker's Perspective On Intelligence Analysis,' *Studies in Intelligence*. Vol. 38, No. 5, pp. 7–15.

Davis, J. (1992) 'The Kent-Kendall Debate of 1949,' *Studies in Intelligence*. Vol. 36, No. 5, pp. 91–103.

Doob, L.W. (1947) 'The Utilization of Social Scientists in the Overseas Branch of the Office of War Information,' *American Political Science Review*. Vol. 41, No. 4, pp. 649–67.

Dorwart, J.M. (1979) *The Office of Naval Intelligence: The Birth of America's First Intelligence Agency, 1865–1918*. Annapolis, MD: Naval Institute Press.

Dorwart, J.M. (1983) *Conflict of Duty: The U.S. Navy's Intelligence Dilemma, 1919–1945*. Annapolis, MD: Naval Institute Press.

Dupont, A. (2003) 'Intelligence for the Twenty-First Century,' *Intelligence and National Security*. Vol. 18, No. 4, pp. 15–39.

Dulles, A.W. (1963) *The Craft of Intelligence*. New York: Harper & Row.

Faligot, R. and Krop, P. (1985) *La Piscine: The French Secret Service since 1944*. Oxford, UK: Basil Blackwell.

Farnell, M.B. and Shearing, C.D. (1977) *Private Security: An Examination of Canadian Statistics, 1961–1971*. Toronto, Canada: University of Toronto.

Feis, W.B. (2002) *Grant's Secret Service: The Intelligence War from Belmont to Appomattox*. Lincoln, NB: University of Nebraska.

Fishel, E.C. (1996) *The Secret War for the Union: The Untold Story of Military Intelligence in the Civil War*. Boston, MA: Houghton Mifflin.

Ford, H.P. (1995) 'The US Government's Experience with Intelligence Analysis: Pluses and Minuses,' *Intelligence and National Security*. Vol. 10, No. 4, pp. 34–53.

Garcia, M.L. (2000) 'Raising the Bar for Security Professionals,' *Security Journal*. Vol. 13, No. 4, pp. 79–81.

Garthoff, R.L. (1984) *Intelligence Assessment and Policymaking: A Decision Point in the Kennedy Administration.* Washington, DC: Brookings Institution.

Gates, R.M. (1997) *From the Shadows: The Ultimate Insider's Story of Five Presidents and How They Won the Cold War.* New York: Simon and Schuster.

Gates, R.M. (1992) 'Guarding Against Politicization: A Message to Analysts,' *Studies in Intelligence.* Vol. 22, No. 2, pp. 5–13.

George, B. and Button, M. (2000) *Private Security, Volume 1.* Leicester, UK: Perpetuity Press.

George, R.Z. (2004) 'Fixing the Problem of Analytical Mind-Sets: Alternative Analysis,' *International Journal of Intelligence and Counterintelligence.* Vol. 17, No. 3, pp. 385–404.

Gill, M. and Hart, J. (1996) 'Historical Perspectives on Private Investigation in Britain and the US,' *Security Journal.* Vol. 7, No. 4, pp. 273–80.

Godson, R., May, E.R. and Schmitt, G.J. (1995) *U.S. Intelligence at the Crossroads: Agendas for Reform.* Washington, DC: Brassey's.

Grabo, C.M. (2002) *Anticipating Surprise: Analysis for Strategic Warning.* Washington, DC: Joint Military Intelligence College.

Hamm, D.L. (ed.) (1987) *Military Intelligence: Its Heroes and Legends.* Washington, DC: Government Printing Office.

Haswell, J. (1977) *Spies & Spymasters: A Concise History of Intelligence.* London: Thames and Hudson.

Helms, R. and Hood, W. (2003) *A Look Over My Shoulder: A Life in the Central Intelligence Agency.* New York: Random House.

Hemmens, C., Maahs, J., Scarborough, K.E. and Collins, P.A. (2001) 'Watching the Watchmen: State Regulation of Private Security 1982–1998,' *Security Journal.* Vol. 14, No. 4, pp. 17–28.

Henderson, R.D.A. (2003) *Brassey's International Intelligence Yearbook, 2003 Edition.* Washington, DC: Brassey's.

Herman, M. (2001) *Intelligence Services in the Information Age.* London: Frank Cass.

Hersh, B. (1992) *The Old Boys: The American Elite and the Origins of the CIA.* St. Petersburg, FL: Tree Farm.

Heuer, R.J. (2003) *Psychology of Intelligence Analysis.* Washington, DC: Center for the Study of Intelligence, Central Intelligence Agency.

Hitz, F.P. and Weiss, B.J. (2004) 'Helping the CIA and FBI Connect the Dots in the War on Terror,' *International Journal of Intelligence and Counterintelligence.* Vol. 17, No. 1, pp. 1–41.

Horan, F. (1962) *The Pinkertons: The Detective Dynasty that Made History.* New York: Crown.

Hughes, T.L. (1976) *The Fate of Facts in a World of Men: Foreign Policy and Intelligence-Making.* New York: Foreign Policy Association.

Institute for Local Self Government (1974) *Private Security and the Public Interest.* Sacramento, CA: Institute.

Jeffreys-Jones, R. (2000) 'The Role of British Intelligence in the Mythologies Underpinning the OSS and the Early CIA,' *Intelligence and National Security.* Vol. 15, No. 2, pp. 5–19.

Jeffreys-Jones, R. (1989) *The CIA & American Democracy.* New Haven, CT: Yale University Press.

Jensen, J.M. (1991) *Army Surveillance in America, 1775–1980.* New Haven, CT: Yale University.

Johnson, L.K. (1989a) *America's Secret Power: The CIA in Democratic Society.* New York: Oxford University Press.

Johnson, L.K. (1989b) 'Strategic Intelligence; An American Perspective,' *International Journal of Intelligence and Counterintelligence.* Vol. 3, No. 3, pp. 299–332.

Johnston, L. (1992) *The Rebirth of Private Policing.* London: Routledge.

Johnston, R. (2005) *Analytic Culture in the U.S. Intelligence Community: An Ethnographic Study.* Washington, DC: Central Intelligence Agency.

Jones, T. and Newburn, T. (1998) *Private Security and Public Policing.* Oxford, UK: Clarendon Press.

Kahn, D. (2001) 'An Historical Theory of Intelligence,' *Intelligence and National Security*. Vol. 16, No. 3, pp. 79–92.

Kahn, D. (1991) *Seizing the Enigma: The Race to Break the German U-Boat Codes, 1939–1943*. New York: Houghton Mifflin.

Kahn, D. (1967) *The Code-Breakers: The Story of Secret Writing*. New York: Macmillan.

Kakalik, J.S. and Wildhorn, S. (1977) *The Private Police: Security and Danger*. New York: Crane, Russak.

Katz, B.M. (1989) *Foreign Intelligence: Research and Analysis in the Office of Strategic Services 1942–1945*. Cambridge, MA: Harvard University.

Keegan, J. (2003) *Intelligence in War: Knowledge of the Enemy from Napolean to Al-Qaeda*. New York: Alfred A. Knopf.

Kennedy, D.B. (1995) 'A Synopsis of Private Security in the United States,' *Security Journal*. Vol. 6, No. 2, pp. 101–5.

Kennedy, P.C. (2003) 'The Secret Service Department: A British Intelligence Bureau in Mid-Victorian London, September 1867 to April 1868,' *Intelligence and National Security*. Vol. 18, No. 3, pp. 100–27.

Kent, S. (1955) 'The Need for an Intelligence Literature,' *Studies in Intelligence*. Vol. 1, No. 1, pp. 1–11 (reprinted in special edition volume, 2000).

Kent, S. (1949) *Strategic Intelligence for American World Policy*. Princeton, NJ: Princeton University.

Kessler, R. (1993) *The FBI: Inside the World's Most Powerful Law Enforcement Agency*. New York: Pocket Books.

Knightley, P. (1986) *The Second Oldest Profession: Spies and Spying in the Twentieth Century*. New York: W.W. Norton.

Krizan, L. (1999) *Intelligence Essentials for Everyone*. Washington, DC: Joint Military Intelligence College.

Lahneman, W.J. (2004–2005) 'Knowledge-Sharing in the Intelligence Community After 9/11,' *International Journal of Intelligence and Counterintelligence*. Vol. 17, No. 4, pp. 614–33.

Lander, S. (2002) 'British Intelligence in the Twentieth Century,' *Intelligence and National Security*. Vol. 17, No. 1, pp. 7–20.

Laqueur, W. (1985) *A World of Secrets: The Uses and Limits of Intelligence*. New York: Basic Books.

Lefebvre, S. (2004) 'A Look at Intelligence Analysis', *International Journal of Intelligence and Counterintelligence*. Vol. 17, No. 2, pp. 231–64.

Lowenthal, M.M. (2003a) *Intelligence: From Secrets to Policy* (2nd ed.). Washington, DC: CQ Press.

Lowenthal, M.M. (2003b) *Bringing Intelligence About: Practitioners Reflect on Best Practices*. Washington, DC: Joint Military Intelligence College.

MacEachin, D.J. (1994) *The Tradecraft of Analysis: Challenge and Change in the CIA*. Washington, DC: Consortium for the Study of Intelligence.

MacPherson, N. (2002) *Reducio Ad Absurdum*: The R&A Branch of OSS/London. *International Journal of Intelligence and Counterintelligence*. Vol. 15, No. 3, pp. 390–414.

Mahle, M.B. (2004) *Denial and Deception: An Insider's View of the CIA from Iran-Contra to 9/11*. New York: Nation Books.

Maney, P.J. (1978) *'Young Bob' La Follette: A Biography of Robert M. La Follette, Jr., 1895–1953*. Columbia, MO: University of Missouri.

Marrin, S. (2003–2004) 'CIA's Kent School: Improving Training for New Analysts,' *International Journal of Intelligence and Counterintelligence*. Vol. 16, No. 4, pp. 609–37.

Marrin, S. (2004) 'Homeland Security Intelligence: Just the Beginning,' *Intelligencer: Journal of U.S. Intelligence Studies*. Vol. 14, No. 1, pp. 43–52.

McCrie, R.D. (1988) 'The Development of the U.S. Security Industry,' *Annals of the American Academy of Political and Social Science*. Vol. 498, pp. 23–33.

McCue, C. (2005) 'Data Mining and Predictive Analytics: Battlespace Awareness for the War on Terrorism,' *Defense Intelligence Journal*. Vol. 13, Nos 1 & 2, pp. 47–63.

McIntosh, E.P. (1998) *Sisterhood of Spies: The Women of the OSS.* Annapolis, MD: Naval Institute Press.

Medina, C.A. (2002) 'What to Do When Traditional Models Fail: The Coming Revolution in Intelligence Analysis,' *Studies in Intelligence.* Vol. 46, No. 3, pp. 23–8.

Minahan, J. (1994) *The Quiet American: A Biography of George R. Wackenhut.* Westport, CT: International Publishing Group.

Morn, F. (1982) *The Eye That Never Sleeps.* Bloomington, IN: Indiana University.

National Advisory Committee on Criminal Justice Standards and Goals (1976) *Private Security: Report of the Task Force on Private Security.* Washington, DC: Government Printing Office.

National Commission on Terrorist Attacks Upon the United States (2004) *The 9/11 Report.* New York: St. Martin's.

Nolte, W. (2004) 'Preserving Central Intelligence: Assessment and Evaluation in Support of the DCI,' *Studies in Intelligence.* Vol. 48, No. 3, pp. 21–5.

Nolte, W. (2001) 'Interviewing an Intelligence Icon: Walter Pforzheimer Reminisces,' *Studies in Intelligence.* Vol. 45, No. 10, pp. 39–48.

O'Connell, K. (2004) 'Thinking About Intelligence Comparatively,' *Brown Journal of World Affairs.* Vol. 11, No. 1, pp. 189–99.

O'Donnell, P.K. (2004) *Operatives, Spies, and Saboteurs: The Unknown Story of the Men and Women of WWII's OSS.* New York: Free Press.

O'Toole, G.J.A. (1991) *Honorable Treachery: A History of U.S. Intelligence, Espionage, and Covert Action from the American Revolution to the CIA.* New York: Atlantic Monthly.

Overton, D.W. (1992) 'The DI Ten Years After Reorganisation: Stresses, Successes, and the Future,' *Studies in Intelligence.* Vol. 36, No. 5, pp. 45–54.

Parfomak, P.W. (2004) *Guarding America: Security Guards and U.S. Critical Infrastructure Protection.* Washington, DC: Congressional Research Service.

Pinkerton, A. (1883) *The Spy of the Rebellion.* Hartford, CT: M.A. Winter & Hatch.

Porch, D. (1995) *The French Secret Services: From the Dreyfus Affair to the Gulf War.* New York: Farrar, Straus and Giroux.

Powe, M.B. (1975) *The Emergence of the War Department Intelligence Agency, 1885–1918.* Manhattan, KS: Military Affairs/Aerospace Historian Publishing.

Powers, R.G. (2004) *Broken: The Troubled Past and Uncertain Future of the FBI.* New York: Free Press.

Powers, T. (2002) *Intelligence Wars: American Secret History from Hitler to al-Qaeda.* New York: New York Review of Books.

Prillaman, W.C. and Dempsey, M.P. (2004) 'Mything the Point: What's Wrong with the Conventional Wisdom about the CIA,' *Intelligence and National Security.* Vol. 19, No. 1, pp. 1–28.

Ranelagh, J. (1986) *The Agency: The Rise and Decline of the CIA.* New York: Simon & Schuster.

Ransom, H.H. (1958) *Central Intelligence and National Security.* Cambridge, MA: Harvard University.

Richelson, J.T. (1999) *The U.S. Intelligence Community.* 4th ed. Boulder, CO: Westview Press.

Richelson, J.T. (1988) *Foreign Intelligence Organisations.* Cambridge, MA: Ballinger.

Rieber, S. (2004) 'Intelligence Analysis and Judgmental Calibration,' *International Journal of Intelligence and Counterintelligence.* Vol. 17, No. 1, pp. 97–112.

Shalloo, J.P. (1933) 'The Private Police of Pennsylvania,' *Annals of the American Academy of Political and Social Science.* Vol. 146, pp. 55–62.

Shearing, C.D. and Stenning, P.C. (eds) (1987) *Private Policing.* Newbury Park, CA: Sage.

Shukman, H. (ed.) (2000) *Agents for Change: Intelligence Services in the 21st Century.* London: St. Ermin's Press.

Shulsky, A.N. (1991) *Silent Warfare: Understanding the World of Intelligence.* Washington, DC: Brassey's.

Shultz, R.H. Jr., Godson, R. and Quester, G.H. (eds) (1997) *Security Studies for the 21st Century.* Washington, DC: Brassey's.

Smith, B.F. (1983)*The Shadow Warriors: O.S.S. and the Origins of the C.I.A.* New York: Basic Books.

Smith, M.D. (1999) 'CIA Publications: Serving the President with Daily Intelligence,' *International Journal of Intelligence and Counterintelligence.* Vol. 12, No. 2, pp. 201–6.

Smith, R.H. (1972) *OSS: The Secret History of America's First Central Intelligence Agency.* Berkeley, CA: University of California.

Stieber, W.J.C.E. (1979) *The Chancellor's Spy: The Revelations of the Chief of Bismarck's Secret Service.* New York: Grove.

Sward, K. (1968) *The Legend of Henry Ford.* New York: Russell & Russell.

Swenson, R.G. (2003) 'Intelligence Education in the Americas,' *International Journal of Intelligence and Counterintelligence.* Vol. 16, No. 1, pp. 108–30.

Taubman, P. (2003) *Secret Empire: Eisenhower, the CIA, and the Hidden Story of America's Space Espionage.* New York: Simon & Schuster.

Taylor, S.A. and Goldman, D. (2004) Intelligence Reform: Will More Agencies, Money, and Personnel Help? *Intelligence and National Security.* Vol. 19, No. 3, pp. 416–35.

Theoharis, A.G. (ed.) (2000) *The FBI: A Comprehensive Reference Guide.* New York: Checkmark.

Thomas, E. (1995) *The Very Best Men: Four Who Dared: The Early Years of the CIA.* New York: Simon & Schuster.

Tidwell, W.A. (1995) *April '65: Confederate Covert Action in the American Civil War.* Kent, OH: Kent State University.

Tidwell, W.A., Hall, J.O. and Gaddy, D.W. (1988) *Come Retribution: The Confederate Secret Service and the Assassination of Lincoln.* Jackson, MS: University Press of Mississippi.

Tuchman, B.W. (1970) *Stilwell and the American Experience in China 1911–45.* New York: Macmillan.

West, N. (2005) 'The UK's Not Quite So Secret Services,' *International Journal of Intelligence and Counterintelligence.* Vol. 18, No. 1, pp. 23–30.

West, N. (1988) *The SIGINT Secrets: The Signals Intelligence War, 1900 to Today.* New York: William Morrow.

West, N. (1981) *MI5: British Security Service Operations 1909–1945.* New York: Stein and Day.

Westfield, H.B. (ed.) (1995) *Inside CIA's Private World: Declassified Articles from the Agency's Internal Journal 1955–1992.* New Haven, CT: Yale University.

White, J.R. (2004) *Defending the Homeland: Domestic Intelligence, Law Enforcement, and Security.* Belmont, CA: Wadsworth.

Winks, R.W. (1987) *Cloak & Gown: Scholars in the Secret War, 1939–1961.* New York: William Morrow.

Wohlstetter, R. (1962) *Pearl Harbor: Warning and Decision.* Stanford, CA: Stanford University.

Wolfberg, A. (2004) 'The Challenges of Creating and New Analytical Culture,' *American Intelligence Journal.* Spring–Summer, pp. 11–20.

Yardley, H.O. (1931) *The American Black Chamber.* Indianapolis, IN: Bobbs-Merrill.

Zegart, A.B. (1999) *Flawed by Design: The Evolution of the CIA, JCS, and NSC.* Stanford, CA: Stanford University.

8

Criminology and Security

Graham Farrell and Ken Pease

The attempt to reduce the number of crime events and/or the loss and harm resulting from crime events is the core work of both the security industry and the police, with their local authority partners. The difference is that the former does its work for its employers (where the security is in-house) or for paying clients. The police act as the National Health Service to the security industry's BUPA, with many of the same tensions that arise at the points of connection.

This chapter seeks to outline key aspects of criminology that, in the view of the authors, make a significant and continuing contribution to the security industry. Its main aim therefore, is to present an introduction to crime prevention and crime science for a readership working in the security industry. Enough case studies of successful crime reduction efforts have now been published to provide a source of information and possible emulation for anyone in the public or private sector seriously interested in crime and loss reduction.

There is a lot of scepticism about the contribution of the academic discipline criminology to the security industry. Much of the scepticism is justified. Criminology had its roots in attempts to understand the offending person, or 'the causes and treatment of delinquency' as the early publication series of the UK's Home Office research in crime was titled. The title was understandable in that the government was also responsible for the processing and punishment of offenders in the criminal justice system – not that such attempts at 'treating' delinquency have been markedly successful. Some parts of criminology were reinvented as the sociology of deviance, whereby study of the individual characteristics of offenders was eschewed in favour of study of the 'social facts' of power relations and demography which were held responsible for crime. These were not (and were not intended to be) helpful to policing, still less to the security industry.

However, the last quarter century has seen the gradual emergence of some serious scholarship directed towards reduction of the extent of crime and the loss and suffering it causes. One strand in this has come to be known as situational crime prevention, wherein techniques to reduce the supply of opportunities for crime are examined. These have grown into more recent efforts to develop criminology into a distinct discipline of 'crime science' which draws on contributions from all branches of science in the service of crime reduction.

The chapter does not purport to cover every intricacy of the subject – impossible in the space available – but will have succeeded if it whets the appetite. It will provide extensive directions to further reading. If even a few of those reading the chapter feel moved to add their work to the published literature, that would be an immense bonus.

A roadmap to this chapter

Such theory as the chapter addresses (routine activity, crime-as-pollution, and rational choice), is straightforward and short on jargon. The chapter reviews domino effects (displacement, diffusion) and risk-focused crime prevention in the hope of making them conceptual tools that security experts can plunder and apply. The chapter only gives a glimpse at the evidence relating to the effectiveness of crime prevention, but a table of recommended further sources, many of them online, is given in the section on the evidence base.

The sections that follow are:

1. Routine activity theory
2. Crime pollution theory
3. Rational choice theory
4. The 25 techniques of situational crime prevention
5. Designing-out crime
6. Domino effects
   - Displacement and deflection
   - Diffused and anticipatory benefits
7. The benefits of security
8. Getting security where it is needed: Risk focused crime prevention
   - Repeat offenders
   - Repeat victimization
   - Risky facilities
   - Hot products
   - Hotspots and prospective mapping
9. The evidence base
10. Concluding comments

Routine activity theory

Routine activity theory is magnificent. While easy to grasp, it can be almost universally applied to provide insight for crime prevention. It is arguably the simplest theory of crime, but astonishing in its flexibility: it is deceptively powerful and insightful and, to be blunt, a downright useful way of thinking about both crime and its prevention.

Cohen and Felson originally proposed the theory in a famous 1979 article. Marcus Felson has gone on to develop it more clearly and extensively in a book now in its third edition (Felson, 1994, 1998, 2002). The theory can be summarized as:

- A crime occurs when a *suitable target* and a *potential offender* meet at a *suitable time and place* lacking *capable guardianship*.

These are the minimal elements and conditions for a crime to occur. They must all come together. A missing element means that no crime will occur there and then. Consequently, routine activity theory reminds us that a crime requires more than just a potential offender – it requires a suitable target and a conducive environment. Once it is acknowledged that crime requires suitable targets and environments, then these elements can be shaped in ways that reduce or prevent crime. A crime will not occur if either a potential target or situation is not 'suitable' for a particular crime to take place.

The shaping of elements can be done with a subtlety limited only by one's imagination. When silver mining opened up in California, silver was cast in ingots for transport to the East. This was stolen *en route*, despite protection by guards. The thefts ceased when the metal was cast in the largest available cannon ball mould. This was transported East on unprotected wagons without further problem (Lingenfelter, 1986). The target ceased to be suitable.

The term 'suitable target' can refer to a person, a business or other premises, a vehicle, or a particular consumer product *perceived in a particular way*. If the crime is a burglary of a business, then a 'suitable target' may be premises which are believed to contain cash, or products with a high re-sale value. If the crime is street robbery then a 'suitable target' may be a person who is perceived to carry things of value, be unarmed and be unlikely to fight back. Note the importance of the terms 'perceived' and 'suitable'. The same target may be perceived as suitable by one offender but not another. Crime risk is reduced if perceived target suitability is decreased or, conversely, its security increased. Many of the techniques of situational crime prevention (detailed below) seek to reduce perceived suitability or increased security of potential targets.

A *potential offender* can be anyone although a relatively small number of career criminals account for a disproportionate amount of serious crime (see p. 193), and there are many personality and demographic traits associated with serious criminality (see Walsh and Ellis, 2003). Nonetheless it can be any of us – including you – depending on the circumstances, and if you the reader engages in attack testing in some rigorous form it is likely that many of the crime-prone features of situations and victims can be designed out. Most of us have an inner criminal as well as an inner child, well capable of 'thinking thief'. If late for a meeting, most people speed in their cars if they can get away with it. One study found that people are less likely to post a 'lost' stamped-addressed letter if it contained money because 'opportunity makes the thief' (Farrington and Knight, 1980 in Felson and Clarke, 1998) . Under the influence of alcohol and excitement, far more of us are disorderly or prone to tinder-box anger and argument. Sufficiently provoked, even the most amiable person retaliates. If there is something around that is grabbed as a weapon, even the pacifist may become a serious offender. People who already have some criminal experience will be more likely to perceive and exploit easy criminal opportunities that arise (the unlocked car, the solitary bag, the unguarded mobile phone or credit card), but this further illustrates the flexibility of the terms *potential*, *likely* or *motivated* offender. The term is not restricted to hardened criminal specialists and planners, and the line between 'them' and 'us' is often blurred – but there is a seriously committed 'them' out there, fortunately sufficiently like us to enable most of their moves to be anticipated!

The *capable guardianship* that may prevent a crime is similarly flexible, and again is a question of perception as much as fact. A guardian can be anyone depending on the circumstances. The term does not just refer to the police or a CCTV camera. A guardian may be an office worker whose window overlooks a street and who might be thought to be looking out. In an early study, Pat Mayhew and her colleagues (1979) showed that the degree of vandalism to phone kiosks was predictable from the number of overlooking windows. Guardians are 'capable' if they are perceived likely to call the police or intervene directly. In office buildings, receptionists provide guardianship if their desk position allows surveillance of people coming and going. Bus drivers, train drivers and staff at restaurants, shops and entertainment centres all provide a form of guardianship. Marcus Felson writes of how trimming garden bushes can increase the guardianship capacity of neighbours by allowing them to see if anyone is snooping around property. The *capability* of a guardian depends upon the circumstances. Friends and colleagues implicitly co-operate as guardians when they walk or travel together, as do parents who accompany their children. In severe circumstances, neither may in fact be *capable* as guardians. However, the capability of guardianship is enhanced by carrying a mobile phone which can mobilize an intervention (or threatens photographic evidence). There is a direct link between guardianship and the various surveillance types discussed as techniques of situational crime prevention. The notion of capable guardianship becomes very important and complex when we think about cybercrime. CISCO Systems advertise their products as protecting 'against human nature' which is a nice way of encapsulating routine activity thinking. How one presents portals (just as how one marks roads in cul-de-sacs) has relevance in terms of perceived guardianship, as are the automated checks on identity which are becoming ubiquitous.

Finally, the fact that the suitable target and potential offender must interact *in time and space* is important. Even where they both exist, keep them separate and no crime occurs (as in the management of soccer crowds). Alternatively, when it is inevitable they will meet, make sure there is capable guardianship when they coincide and no crime occurs (as in the weigh-ins before highly-charged boxing matches).

The *environment* in which crime-prone interactions occur is influential and so some aspects of crime-reductive criminology concentrating on the design of places is called environmental criminology (Brantingham and Brantingham, 1981). In whole or in part, particular places, buildings and other facilities generate or attract far more crime than others – for example the accident and emergency facilities in hospitals. The environment includes streets and transportation systems, building designs and the urban (or rural) landscape more generally. The design of the environment significantly influences people's perceptions, their routine movements, their surveillance and other capabilities, and therefore directly influences the likelihood of criminal opportunities arising. Felson's study of the re-design of New York City's Port Authority Bus Station shows how the overt shaping of the environment and thereby the movement and perceptions of passengers and others, had a major crime reduction effect (Felson *et al.*, 1996).

While it is less intuitively obvious that routine activity theory can be applied to 'victimless' crimes such as drug taking and prostitution, they do fit into the theory. For such crimes, it is easiest to think of the state (that is the country, the government, the legal system) as the suitable victim. This means that such crimes take place whenever a motivated offender finds him or herself in the absence of capable guardianship. In the case of prostitution or drug dealing, for instance, the crime occurs when motivated offenders interact (that is, both parties in the transaction) in the absence of capable guardianship.

It is through the flexibility of its seemingly innocuous terms that routine activity theory derives its power. Since each of the simple terms really applies to an almost endless list of possibilities, then routine activity theory has an infinite number of permutations.

Another virtue of routine activities, implicit in the examples above and which it shares with the notion of problem-oriented policing (see Goldstein, 1990) is that it invites one to think in terms of crimes in clusters rather than one at a time. If some things about a victim, perpetrator or place make crime likely, understanding what those things are make it clear what aspects of the environment or victim or offender one needs to attend to. Until Dr John Snow recognized that the common factor in cholera cases was the pump from which people took their drinking water, the disease could not be prevented.[1] Likewise, understanding the common features of the three elements which make a crime possible is important for prevention.

Crime pollution theory

Air, water and noise pollution are well known. They occur when the producer imposes an unwanted cost on others. In essence, the polluter profits while others incur the expense – whether toxic hazard or lost sleep. Some types of crime can be viewed as pollutants in a similar fashion (Farrell, 2000; Farrell and Roman, 2005; Clarke and Newman, forthcoming). A bar or club which promotes cheap and rapid consumption of alcohol during happy hours can produce an environment and intoxicated individuals that generate assaults and disorder. Similarly, the manufacture of attractive insecure targets imposes a crime pollution cost on society that the manufacturer does not bear. High value hot-products include mobile phones and portable MP3 players, which make easy targets for theft and robbery. Cars which are manufactured without due attention to anti-theft security produce a significant crime cost that manufacturers do not cover. In each case, producers or manufacturers make fortunes in sales but bear none of the risk-cost that customers unwittingly bear when making the purchase. These costs include the harm and damage to individuals and property including health service costs, the expense of policing, resulting lost productivity of individuals, plus any knock-on costs of the criminal justice system (see e.g. Brand and Price, 2000; Miller *et al.*, 1996 and Mayhew, 2003 for, respectively, UK, US and Australian national cost-of-crime estimates).

So what? In the field of vehicle accidents, it is known that, irrespective of the role or culpability of the driver, a certain percentage of cars will be involved in accidents. Consequently, car manufacturers are legally obliged to produce products that meet specified safety standards (called an *Enhanced Injury Doctrine* in US legal terms). Perhaps the manufacturers of cars and other consumer products, or the owners of bars and other crime-prone premises, should be subject to an *Enhanced Crime Doctrine*. Since it is known that a certain percentage of many types of product will be stolen, irrespective of any role played by the victim, it should behoove manufacturers to produce products that minimize crime risk and resultant harms. The theory can apply to many crime and disorder problems across the range. The seemingly trivial problem of chewing-gum grime littering city streets might be tackled if manufacturers were held accountable. If they were obliged to pay a clean-up tax, the long-term result might be that this incentive caused them to develop alternative approaches to the problem.

To some extent, the theory of crime pollution relates to shifting responsibilities, which has previously been suggested in relation to policing (Goldstein, 1990; Clarke and Eck, 2003). There are also parallels with the UK's Crime and Disorder Act 1998 which legislates for local authorities, working with the police as Crime and Disorder Reduction Partnerships, to take responsibility for crime related to their work and activities. S17 of the Act imposes a statutory duty to consider the crime implications of all decisions taken by local authorities.

Many forms of pollution are tackled via regulation and fines. Recently, such traditional punitive measures have been complemented by measures that seek to harness market forces to reduce pollution. Hence tax breaks and incentives for those who emit little pollution, and patents for those who introduce innovative technologies and processes, have been introduced. Systems of tradeable permits have been introduced whereby heavy polluters can purchase further pollution 'allowance' from those who produce little pollution (the Kyoto protocol is the most famous example relating to climate-change and carbon emissions trading). The effect is to reward low-emitters and punish heavy emitters. Such market-based incentives may have the potential to be transferred to crime pollution. Supplementing traditional punitive approaches they could generate an 'incentivized' crime prevention philosophy.

Although this is an emerging area of theory and research, and undoubtedly potentially controversial, it is presented here as illustrative of the contribution to security studies made by crime prevention theory and its relation to policy and practice. While it may appear that a 'crime as pollution' perspective appears to promote primarily a legislative approach, this is not really the case. Any such legislation is really a means of implementing crime prevention by stemming them at source. The security industry could benefit greatly from identifying and advising upon potential areas of crime pollution, as well as in devising innovative preventive responses.

A useful categorization of approaches is Goldstein's hierarchy (see Scott, 2000). This is presented here as Figure 8.1. Reading from the bottom, it indicates increasingly severe means of addressing 'polluters'. Of course, private security has a particular role in this perspective, in that bringing in a private security company may be one legitimate means by which crime polluters are pressured to address the problem. In-house security facilities provide the most obvious means whereby crime pollution can be addressed by means such as re-design, product registration or activation procedures, or any comparable low cost approaches to product security.

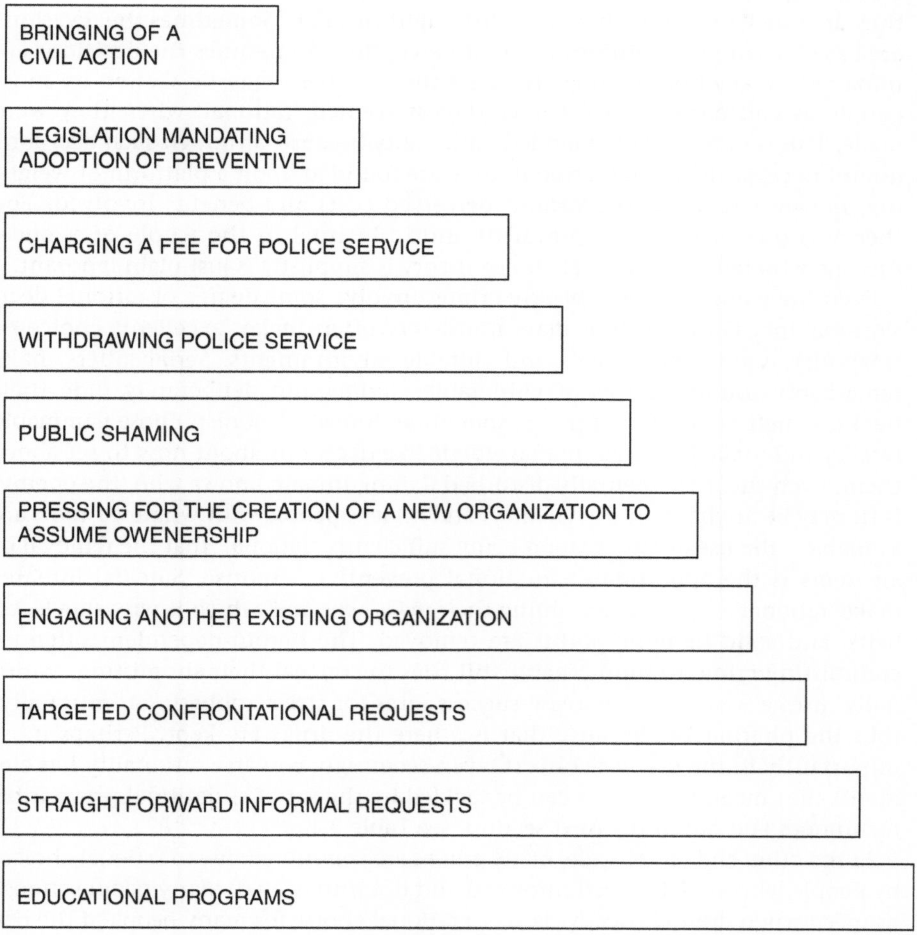

BRINGING OF A
CIVIL ACTION

LEGISLATION MANDATING
ADOPTION OF PREVENTIVE

CHARGING A FEE FOR POLICE SERVICE

WITHDRAWING POLICE SERVICE

PUBLIC SHAMING

PRESSING FOR THE CREATION OF A NEW ORGANIZATION TO
ASSUME OWENERSHIP

ENGAGING ANOTHER EXISTING ORGANIZATION

TARGETED CONFRONTATIONAL REQUESTS

STRAIGHTFORWARD INFORMAL REQUESTS

EDUCATIONAL PROGRAMS

Figure 8.1 Hierarchy of means utilized in the shifting of ownership for crime prevention strategies emerging from the current wave of reforms in policing

Rational choice theory

Rational choice theory is an all-encompassing theory of offending. Like routine activity theory, its basic elements are simple yet strong and flexible. It can be caricatured as simplistic, which it is not: There is a world of difference between a simple foundation and a simplistic foundation. A simple foundation is a general perspective which follows understanding. A simplistic foundation is a general perspective which precedes understanding.

People make choices between alternatives. Active offenders make choices among criminal and non-criminal alternatives.[2] Most active offenders are 'adolescent limited', that is, they cease substantial offending as maturity kicks in (Moffitt, 1993). Some have changes of perspective which lead them to desist. Others don't (Maruna, 2001). The point is that the criminal career (like others) is a seething mass of moment to moment and day to day decisions.[3] Sometimes they are quick decisions that are not thought through. Sometimes the decisions are based on imperfect information or perception. Sometimes the decisions are impaired by alcohol or drugs. Hence although these may be viewed by most people as bad decisions they nevertheless seemed 'rational' when they were made. This is often called 'bounded' rationality because, although such decisions do not necessarily appear rational, they are founded upon a platform of weighing, however roughly, the various perceived costs and benefits involved. The theory is one of the most prevalent and influential in the whole of science. Anyone who tells you rational choice theory is simplistic is just plain ignorant.

Even the wildest or most bizarre crimes involve some degree of rational decision-making. Gun-wielding mass murderers often make 'excellent' choice of weaponry, vulnerable targets and suitable environments. Serial killers make remarkably sound choices of vulnerable victims and deliberately hide their tracks, sometimes for long periods, sometimes forever. Arsonists chose flammable targets and make informed management-like decisions about how to set about them. Even the most mentally disturbed flailing inmate knows who 'the enemy' is (it may be anybody in the vicinity) and attacks people with whatever tools are available – the use of any weapon being sufficiently 'rational' that the removal of all items is the appropriate situational preventive response. Suicidal inmates make 'rational' choices determining their *modus operandi* which is why shoelaces, belts, and solid hanging points are removed. The heroin-dependent offender committing crime to fund a habit still tries to conceal their shoplifting, 'rationally' uses a weapon to increase success rates for street robbery, or 'rationally' robs the pharmacists because that is where the drugs are kept. Perhaps most importantly in the present context, even seemingly perverse rationality has elements that mean the crimes can be tackled by the set of situational prevention techniques laid out in the next section, see Table 8.1.

At the other end of the scale, many crimes are committed due to rational choices by people who are fairly well informed and not intoxicated. Many people choose to speed when driving. Tax evasion is a rational choice for many people if the risk of detection appears low, and can occur if income is 'accidentally' not declared.

Table 8.1   Bad decisions are still bounded 'rational' choices

Type of Decision	Example / Caricature
Quick decision (not thought through)	It seemed like a good idea at the time. I wasn't really thinking – I just did it. Now I regret it.
Decisions based on imperfect information	I didn't know they had a dog. I didn't know he would hit me back. I didn't know they had a silent alarm. I didn't know I was on CCTV. At the time, I didn't think of the consequences.
Impaired decision (including emotional decision)	I wasn't thinking straight. It was the alcohol acting, not me.

Decisions involve weighing the various perceived costs and benefits involved, and choosing what appears to be the decision option that maximizes the benefit (even though, as mentioned, the offender may be mistaken in his or her reasoning). The most obvious benefits of crime are financial – cash or goods that are the proceeds of crime. Yet benefits are often psychological, including the perceived 'benefit' of being able to control another individual through violence or threats. Likewise, the thrill of committing a crime or impressing potential sexual partners or on-looking peers, are forms of reward or benefit that can influence a decision. This means that perceived benefits from committing a crime can often be subjective.

Rational choice theory can be interpreted as 'all encompassing' as far as other theories of offending are concerned. There are many so-called theories of offending which examine the influences of peers and peer-pressure, the role of the family and parenting, the role of education, the role of deprivation (or relative deprivation), the role of learning about crime, and the role of individual biology, genetics and psychology. There is no doubt that a range of factors influence decision-making – but that is what they are – influences. A potential offender who is less well-off makes a decision in different circumstances than one who is well-off, just as someone experiencing the goading of peers makes a decision under different constraints to someone on their own in a similar situation. Each decision depends upon the individuals concerned as well as upon the situation. From a crime prevention perspective, the factors that can be most immediately influenced are the immediate circumstances and context. This does not mean that other social problems should not be tackled – they should – but they are primarily tackled for reasons other than crime prevention. In contrast, influencing the immediate circumstances and context in which the crime takes (or does not take) place is the avenue with the greatest chance of preventive success (see Sherman *et al.*, 1997). Put in a more homely way, in the foreseeable future more blind people will be saved from death by others guiding them away from danger (and designing-out dangerous places) than by medical research into blindness. Blindness is a 'root cause' of the problem, and the medical research is to be applauded. But the guiding hand and environmental facilitators are not to be derided.

The obvious question is: How does rational choice theory relate to security and crime prevention? It is directly linked because of the elements of costs and benefits involved in offender decision-making. Security and crime prevention seek to increase the costs or reduce the benefits, thus nudging decisions away from offending. The various means by which decisions can be influenced are described in the section below on the 25 techniques. It also allows one to second-guess offender choices, since they are made with roughly the same mental apparatus as the security practitioner or academic. The practitioner can hypothesis-test about offender choices, and match patterns of deployment accordingly. One approach that could be said to flow from this approach is that of prospective crime mapping, where emerging patterns of offender choice dictate where patrolling should occur (see Bowers *et al.*, 2004).

The 25 techniques of situational crime prevention

The 25 techniques comprise an extremely useful typology that applies directly to many areas of security. It is thought-provoking in the ways it identifies many mechanisms by which crime can be prevented. Security and crime prevention are too often stereotyped as 'target hardening', yet here this becomes just one of 25 techniques. Likewise, security and crime prevention are too often stereotyped as intrusive, abusive of civil liberties, or creating the atmosphere of a fortress society. Such instances are the unfortunate exceptions rather than the rule. It illustrates how security can bring not only freedom and enhanced civil liberties, but can do so in unobtrusive ways and, perhaps surprisingly, often bring additional unanticipated social benefits. In short, the 25 techniques open up a range of ways of thinking about promoting security and crime prevention.

There is a friendly colourful presentation of the techniques at http://www.pop-center.org/25techniques.htm which gives excellent summaries, description and evidence. The reader is encouraged to take a brief look because it gives good pop-up examples of the application of the techniques in a manner that cannot be attempted here.

Ron Clarke developed the set of techniques and has been improving and revising them for nearly three decades (since Clarke, 1980 with major revisions in Clarke, 1992 and Clarke and Homel, 1997). Their latest version is to be found as Cornish and Clarke (2003) but watch out for further revisions. One area that is arguably not wholly developed in the typology is the distinction between actual and perceived risks and costs/benefits. Measures that trick, fool or mislead offenders by increasing perceived risk or effort, or by reducing perceived rewards, is an emerging area of crime prevention and security. Just as many security experts have long known that fake alarm boxes and fake lights to enhance effectiveness, recent evaluation work suggests that publicity can play an important role (Bowers and Johnson, 2003). The reader is reminded of the emphasis on perception earlier in this chapter. It is what people believe to be true that matters in crime reduction (as in war and politics).

Designing-out crime

Designing-out crime is an important and growing contribution that splits roughly into the design of the built environment and the design of consumer products. The design of the built environment including streets, street layout and furniture, building design and accoutrements, can all play a role in crime, and the area has evolved via Crime Prevention Through Environmental Design (CPTED, Jeffrey, 1971) and environmental criminology (Brantingham and Brantingham, 1981). Of particular recent note has been the evaluation of Secured by Design (SBD) housing.[4] SBD offers crime prevention standards for buildings. Recent research suggests that levels of crime in SBD housing are some 30 percent lower than in equivalent housing not built to SBD standards (Armitage, 2000). Armitage (2005) shows the scope for further design-driven reductions in burglary in particular. Such issues are tackled more fully in the excellent Chapter 5 by Schneider.

The design profession has recently become involved in crime reduction. The Royal Society of Arts has recently introduced crime reduction to its student competitions.[5] These have included projects to make mobile phones less crime prone, student accommodation less liable to burglary, design of house entry points to facilitate secure delivery of goods ordered on-line, and bicycles less vulnerable to theft. The Design Council is engaged with a consortium of design schools to incorporate crime-reductive considerations in industries in which such considerations have not hitherto been common.[6] Central Saint Martins Design School in London has exhibited designs of chairs for pubs and cafes. These chairs have ingenious means of attaching bags, making them difficult to steal. The same School has exhibited handbags resistant to common methods of theft.[7] Crime Reduction Through Product Design (Lester, 2001) is a developing area that is becoming increasingly important (see also Ekblom, 2005).

In many ways, the security industry has to deal with the criminogenic environment as it exists. However, a special case could be made for the involvement of in-house security personnel in the design of systems which are less crime-prone, a point which was touched upon in the earlier discussion of crime as pollution. Just as the crime reduction officer role in the police has developed into the Architectural Liaison Officer, advising on structures before they are built, one should encourage in-house security to try to get upstream of crime problems by addressing the work systems and practices which give rise to them. Of course, there is the particular problem that a degree of minor illegality by employees is often tolerated in the interests of smooth running and staff morale, so security personnel will be aware of the trade-off between crime reduction and such 'easing' practices.

Table 8.2   Domino effects

	Displacement/deflection effects	Bonus (diffused and anticipatory benefit) effects
Individual effects		
Spatial	Offender commits the crime at different location	Offender reduces offending elsewhere
Temporal	Offender commits the crime at a different time	Offender reduces offending at other times as well
Tactical	Offender commits crime using different tactic	Offender reduces offending using other tactics as well
Crime-type	Offender switches to committing other types of crime	Offender reduces rates of offending across other crime types as well
Aggregate effects		
Offenders	Different offender moves in to take the criminal opportunity	Other offenders also reduce offending in the face of reduced opportunity
Market effects	Reduced supply increases prices and profit, causing new offenders to commit crime	Reduced supply shrinks crime market causing others to also stop this type of offending
Agency and victim effects	Individuals or agencies perceive prevention as ineffective and reduce effort in despair (a vicious spiral)	Individuals and agencies recognize effectiveness of crime prevention and are prompted to take action (a positive spiral)

Domino effects

Crime prevention induces a range of important secondary knock-on or domino effects. Theory and evidence suggest that these are likely to be, for the most part, positive effects. However, it is still certainly the case that popular opinion alights upon the exceptional case of 'net-loss displacement' to develop an improper knee-jerk reaction against crime prevention, see Table 8.2.

Displacement and deflection

Crime prevention efforts have sometimes been criticized as merely shuffling crime around, deflecting crime to different places and targets. Do offenders just deflect or displace to other targets, other crimes, or use other tactics to try to get around security measures? It is now recognized that crime does move around but that the recognition of this in no way reduces the proper role for crime reduction. For deflection to occur it must mean that crime prevention can work – because a crime has to be prevented in one place if it is to move to another. The second reason is that any secondary target (or change in *modus operandi*) to which an offender shifts must, by definition, be at best their second choice. This means it was initially less desirable, being more difficult, risky, requiring more time and effort, or being less rewarding.

In the early days of crime prevention work, this phenomenon was more often referred to as 'displacement'. It is now recognized that this term has negative connotations reflecting an incorrect understanding of the nature of crime and its prevention. Barr and Pease (1990) noted that 'deflection' is a more accurate representation of commensurately greater heuristic value. The term better captures the fact that crime can be deliberately shaped, for the betterment of society, by prevention efforts. Even if displacement was 100 percent in terms of the number of crimes occurring (unlikely), society can still be better off if the crimes occur where there is less overall harm to society. They cite the illustrative case of the politician who inquired if crime could be displaced as far as the border. They also propose that an offender who displaces from murder to criminal damage is a benign form of displacement, like the movement of prostitution away from population centres to locations out of town.

Perhaps most importantly, the evidence suggests that displacement does occur but at a rate less than 100 percent (Eck, 1993; Hesseling, 1994). This is of critical importance because it means that, even when displacement occurs, there is a net benefit from prevention efforts. The probability of malign displacement (a switch to more serious or more frequent crime) is low and can usually be anticipated, managed and avoided. In general therefore, the deflection or displacement of crime is generally a good thing – it shows crime can be prevented and is usually far less harmful than the previous crime patterns. In the private sector, of course, there is a particular issue – namely that it may advantage one company if the crime it suffers moves to victimize a competitor.

Diffused and anticipatory benefits

Security experts will benefit from understanding the beneficial domino effects of crime prevention. While an emerging area that remains to be fully charted, it is a substantive contribution of criminology to security studies. In short, it means that crime prevention practice often has a knock-on beneficial effect beyond the parameters of its original intention. The general form of 'diffusion of benefits' and the more specific form of anticipatory benefits warrant further explanation.

Crime prevention can produce unanticipated beneficial effects. If many business premises are secure and alarmed, the remainder may benefit if offenders are uncertain which are the more and which the less secure and hence cease to burgle any of them. Clarke and Weisburd (1994) termed this unanticipated crime reduction a *diffusion of benefits*. They argue that it is the opposite of displacement insofar as it is the *prevention* rather than the *crime* which is displaced.

When offenders know that a crime prevention measure is due to be introduced, they will change behaviour in anticipation (Smith *et al.*, 2003). This is only rational. It makes sense to adapt to reduce risk of apprehension or wasted effort. This phenomenon links to the role of publicity mentioned earlier, where publicity in advance of a crime prevention effort can trigger an anticipatory reduction in crime. Smith *et al.* termed the phenomenon *anticipatory diffusion of benefits*. The interesting question which it opens up concerns whether one can get crime reduction by saying one is about to mount a crime reduction initiative without actually doing it. The answer, from the Smith *et al.* work, is probably yes. Attempts made by the second author to interest various police forces in testing this idea have met with no success, and some ethical queasiness.[8] This may be a case where the private sector is better placed to evaluate the idea.

Other types of positive domino effect have been identified but are less commonly recognized. Farrell *et al.* (1993) hypothesized that agency effect would exist whereby agents were stimulated into action upon perceiving the beneficial effects of crime prevention, are prompted or inspired to inject new momentum into their own anti-crime efforts. *Market effects* have been identified to refer to instances where crime is driven by market forces to produce effects that appear similar to displacement. For example, if law enforcement reduces drug supply, this causes drug prices to rise which, in turn, encourages new traffickers and dealers to enter the more lucrative market even though they may be supplying from a different geographical location (Farrell and Thorne, 2005). The market effect may explain why crimes which are more directly driven by market mechanisms, often those which are more organized crimes as a result, may have greater rates of displacement and be more robust in the face of crime prevention (although remaining far from immune).

The benefits of security

The security industry is comprised of businesses. Firms encounter scepticism when potential customers do not perceive or comprehend the likely benefits of improved security and prevented crime. It is easier to save money by avoiding investment in security if the benefits are unclear or uncertain or are enjoyed by others than the immediate client. Criminology has made relevant and rapid progress in recent years in the estimation of the costs of crime. Perhaps the most significant relevant development has been the inclusion of the intangible (psychological, emotional) costs of crime in addition to the more tangible financial costs of crime.

The most recent estimates of the costs of crime are far higher than previously thought. These more realistic estimates are potentially beneficial to the security industry insofar as they provide clear and independent evidence of greater likely benefit per pound invested in security. The large qualifier is that the costs are those incurred by all the players combined, not just the immediate commercial or individual victim.

Mark Cohen is one of the leading scholars in the field of cost estimation. His most recent estimates of the cost of crime are based upon the established methodology termed 'Willingness-to-pay' or WTP (Cohen *et al.*, 2004). In essence, interviewees are asked how much they would be willing to pay to reduce the crime risk by a particular amount. The findings – the most recent available to our knowledge at the time of writing – are summarized in Table 8.3. The estimates are presented in their original US dollar currency to avoid any problems due to changing exchange rates. While these estimates are higher than many

Table 8.3 The benefits of security per crime prevented (average US$ per crime)

Crime	Benefit per crime prevented
Burglary	$25,500
Armed robbery	$244,000
Serious assaults	$71,500
Rape and sexual assaults	$249,000
Murder	$9,750,000

Note: Based on Cohen *et al.* (2004, table on p. 103).

previous estimates, they clearly illustrate the potentially significant benefits that such studies suggest can derive from the work of the security industry.

Getting security where it is needed: risk focused crime prevention

It is all well and good having theories to understand how crime and offending occur, and frameworks to aid the development of prevention and to understand the subsequent knock-on effects. However, critical to the security and crime prevention enterprise is getting the grease to the squeak (Hough and Tilley, 1998). The delineation of appropriate nodes or focal points around which crime clusters can be tackled has arguably been one of criminology's main contributions in recent years. Five such nodes are outlined briefly here. In each instance, crime clusters so that a small proportion of the group in focus (offenders, targets/victims, areas, product-types) experience a grossly disproportionate amount of the crime. Each of the main categories is outlined briefly here as they constitute what we perceive to be significant contributions of criminological analysis that are, or deserve to be, drawn upon by the security industry. A conceptual representation of the manner in which most of these concepts overlap is presented as Figure 8.2 (prospective mapping is not shown).

It has long been known that a large proportion of offending is committed by a relatively small proportion of offenders. This has been used to focus various anticrime responses, from incapacitative sentencing, intensive probation, and police detection efforts. Offender detection is (depending upon the context) a key performance indicator for the security industry. Recent developments in electronic surveillance and biometric testing may assist these efforts. In particular, recent detection efforts using DNA processing (Webb *et al.*, 2005; Townsley *et al.*, 2005) may prove fruitful, a means whereby which the security industry prospers in the future.

Repeat victimization, is far more likely to occur than first victimization, that is, the proportion of those victimized who are victimized again is much higher than the proportion of people, homes or businesses suffering for the first time. In fact, one victimization often triggers another, and the repeats are likely to be committed by the same offender(s). This is most evident in crimes such as domestic violence but is true of all crimes (except murder, for obvious reasons) studied

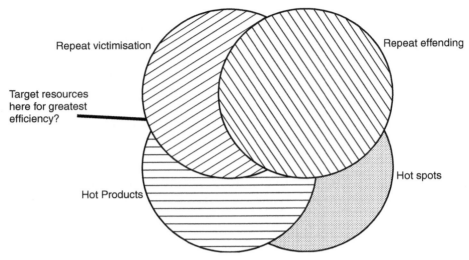

Figure 8.2   Overlap between repeat victimization, hot spots, repeat offending and hot products
Source: Adapted from Farrell, G. and Sousa, W. (2001)
Note: Diagram not to scale

to date, from commercial burglary and bank robbery to computer network hacking (see Farrell, 2005 for a recent review). Repeats, when they happen, tend to happen soon after the last victimization. Consequently, crime prevention or security resources that are quickly focused upon existing victims or targets, are more likely to be in the right place at the right time to prevent further crime. It has also been shown that repeat victimization or 'hot dots' (as they appear on crime maps) contribute disproportionately to the make-up of crime hot-spots. Further, since repeat offenders commit repeat victimization, placing detection efforts at the location of targets likely to be repeatedly victimized has been suggested to be a possibly fruitful form of detecting offenders.

Hot-products are those frequently stolen (Clarke, 1999). Valuable and highly portable electronic goods make extremely attractive targets of theft. Warehouses, shops or vehicles containing such products make similarly attractive targets. Likewise, certain types of cars, due to their particular characteristics (whether easy to steal, or particularly desirable or ideally both depending upon the motivation of the offender), make attractive targets. Designing consumer products in ways that make them either less attractive or less vulnerable to theft, or less rewarding if stolen, has become an increasingly important area of research in recent years.

Hotspots are spatial crime clusters. However, the term hotspot is applied in many different ways and there is arguably little common understanding of the size, scope, duration or level of crime required to constitute a hotspot (Townsley and Pease, 2003). The term 'hot-spot' was popularized by a 1989 study by Sherman, Gartin and Buerger which found that around 3 percent of street corners accounted for around 50 percent of calls to police. The term has gained popular usage in parallel with computerized crime mapping efforts and prevention and policing resources are often focused upon perceived hotspots.

Prospective mapping is the more recent and powerful combination of hotspots and repeat victimization work (Johnson *et al.*, 2005). Almost all previous hotspot analysis was static in assuming that crime will occur in the same places. Rather than assuming that crime will occur in the same places or against the same targets, prospective mapping approaches crime as dynamic and shifting over time and place. At the time of writing it is gaining currency and is likely to be highly influential in the future of crime mapping.

The clusters or foci outlined here all exhibit unusual concentrations of crime. In essence, they predict where crime will occur in some fashion. Their key contribution to the work of the security industry is that they provide natural points upon which effort should be focused.

The evidence base

There are now many case studies demonstrating the effectiveness of efforts to prevent crime. There is no single tactic or strategy that guarantees effectiveness. What appears to work best is the application of a methodology involving action research, crime analysis and problem solving, whereby a crime problem is assessed and appropriate prevention efforts are then identified. Highly replicable strategies and tactics are very welcome but may lead to complacency due to the highly adaptable nature of crime and offending. No crime remedy is forever. The process is one of co-evolution or an arms race between offender and preventer (Ekblom, 2005). The security industry will need to be continually evolving its responses to crime, but the existing evidence base will certainly provide examples, pointers and lessons that will assist this process. Many of the best sources of information on crime prevention are relatively concentrated, and many are summarized in Table 8.4.

Table 8.4 Key readings and information sources

Title	Publishers and Availability
Crime Prevention Studies (chapter-length peer-reviewed studies)	Publishers: www.criminaljusticepress.com. Many chapters free in PDF from http://www.popcenter.org/library-crime_prevention.htm
Crime Prevention Unit papers, which later became the *Policing and Reducing* Crime series: 155 studies of preventing crime	Publishers: UK government's Home Office. Free in PDF from: http://www.homeoffice.gov.uk/rds/policerspubs1.html (series unfortunately after Home Office restructuring)
Crime Reduction Research Series: 13 studies mainly relating to crime prevention	Publishers: UK government's Home Office Free in PDF from: http://www.homeoffice.gov.uk/rds/crimreducpubs1.html (series unfortunately after Home Office restructuring)

Table 8.4   Key readings and information sources – *continued*

Title	Publishers and Availability
The Centre for Problem-Oriented Policing	Fabulous online information source and library at www.popcentre.org (although it says 'policing' there is much for a general security audience)
The *Problem-Oriented Guide* series	Publishers: US Department of Justice (COPS Office). Series of crime-specific guides reviewing evidence and known prevention methods. Free in PDF from: www.popcentre.org
Development and Practice Reports, Research Studies, Online Reports	Since 2003, the UK government's Home Office has foolishly chosen to mix its crime prevention publications into its criminal justice and other crime-related series. So, while it involves some sifting it is still often worth it. Free in PDF from http://www.homeoffice.gov.uk/rds/pubsintro1.html
Crime Prevention and Community Safety: An International Journal	Publishers: Palgrave, www.palgrave-journals.com[1]
Security Journal	Publishers: Palgrave, www.palgrave-journals.com
The Handbook of Crime Prevention and Community Safety. Excellent book edited by Nick Tilley (2006).	Publishers: Willan Press, www.willanpublishing.co.uk

Note: Other criminology-related journals tend to include occasional studies on crime prevention but this list covers many of the main dedicated sources.

Concluding comments

The contribution of criminology, and its emergent successor crime science, to the security industry is not always apparent. It is clearest in those works which seek to tackle crime, but such a perspective unfortunately cannot be taken for granted. That criminological work which has developed under the rubric of situational crime prevention, environmental criminology, and problem-oriented policing, more recently grouped into Crime Science, is that which most obviously complements the work of the security industry. This body of work takes the prevention of crime as its primary goal:

> Crime science values detection of criminals and the prevention of crime harms, just as medicine values the curing of illness and the prevention of sickness and its consequences. (Laycock and Tilley, forthcoming).

With respect to the future, it is to be hoped that the concerns of the security industry will become increasingly central to the criminological enterprise. The theory, frameworks and evidence presented here are, it is hoped, among those which will help promote that process.

Notes

1 http://www.makingthemodernworld.org.uk/learning_modules/geography/05.TU.01/?section=2
2 This phrasing reflects the fact that even the most active offenders choose non-criminal options.
3 A strong case could be made for the inclusion of a section on criminal careers and how they unfold in this chapter. Space and internal coherence precludes such inclusion.
4 http://www.securedbydesign.com/
5 http://www.rsa-sda.net/
6 http://www.design-council.org.uk/design/
7 http://www.research.linst.ac.uk/dac
8 Rather odd in that there are plenty of cases when police initiatives launched with fanfares enjoy only token implementation.
9 Palgrave acquired the journals from Perpetuity Press in October 2005.

Key readings

Marcus Felson's 'Crime and Everyday Life', now its third edition (Sage publications, 2002), is a provocative introductory text. Felson is an original thinker, and the book's accessible style belies its biting critique of many ways of thinking about crime that have been too-long accepted. Nick Tilley's 'Handbook of Crime Prevention and Community Safety' (Willan Press, 2005) would be a useful complement to the present volume for anyone wanting a greater criminological emphasis. Ron Clarke's 'Situational Crime Prevention: Successful Case Studies' (Harrow and Heston, 1992) remains a useful text, with an excellent introductory overview introducing a set of insightful preventive efforts. At the time of writing there are 19 volumes in the set of 'Crime Prevention Studies' (Criminal Justice Press), each of which present case studies and crime analysis, typically with a thematic focus for each volume. Anthony Braga's 'Problem-Oriented Policing and Crime Prevention' (Criminal Justice Press, 2002) gives a clearly written introduction to many key issues. The *Problem-Oriented Guide* series (Office of Community Policing Services, US Department of Justice) are useful practical guides focused on specific crime topics and available free from www.popcenter.org. http://www.crimereduction.gov.uk/ is the closest UK equivalent.

References

Armitage, R. (2000) *An Evolution of Secured by Design Housing Within West Yorkshire*. Home Office Briefing Note 7/00. London: Home Office.
Armitage, R. (2005) *Designing out Crime in Residential Housing*. Unpublished, PhD, University of Huddersfield.
Barr, R. and Pease, K. (1990) 'Crime Placement, Displacement, and Deflection', *Crime and Justice 12*. Chicago: University of Chicago Press.
Bowers, K.J. and Johnson, S.D. (2003a) *The Role of Publicity in Crime Reduction: Findings from the Reducing Burglary Initiative*. Home Office Research Study 272. London: Home Office.
Bowers, K.J. and Johnson, S.D. (2003b) 'Measuring the Geographical Displacement of Crime', *Journal of Quantitative Criminology*, 19(3): 275–301.
Bowers, K.J., Johnson, S.D. and Pease, K. (2004) 'Prospective Hot-spotting: The Future of Crime Mapping?' *British Journal of Criminology*, 44: 641–58.
Brand, S. and Price, R. (2000) 'The Economic and Social Costs of Crime', *Home Office Research Study 217*, London: Home Office. At http://www.homeoffice.gov.uk/rds/pdfs/hors217.pdf
Brantingham, P.J. and Brantingham, P.L. (1981) *Environmental Criminology*. Beverly Hills, CA: Sage.

Clarke, R.V. and Eck, J. (2003) *Become a Problem-Solving Crime Analyst*. London: Jill Dando Institute.

Clarke, R.V. (1992) Situational Crime Prevention: Successful Case Studies. New York: Harrow and Heston.

Clarke, R.V. (1980) '"Situational" Crime Prevention: Theory and Practice', *British Journal of Criminology*, 20: 136–47.

Clarke, R.V. and Homel, R. (1997) 'A Revised Classification of Situational Crime Prevention Techniques'. In S.P. Lab (ed.), *Crime Prevention at a Crossroads*. Cincinnati, OH: Anderson.

Clarke, R.V. and Newman, G. (forthcoming) 'Security Coding of Electronic Products', *Crime Prevention Studies*.

Clarke, R.V. and Weisburd, D. (1994) 'Diffusion of Crime Control Benefits: Observations on the Reverse of Displacement', *Crime Prevention Studies*, 2: 165–84.

Clarke, R.V. (1999) *Hot Products: Understanding, Anticipating and Reducing Demand for Stolen Goods*. Police Research Series Paper 112. London, UK: Home Office.

Cohen, L.E. and Felson, M. (1979) 'Social Change and Crime Rate Trends: A Routine Activity Approach', *American Sociological Review*, 44: 588–608.

Cohen, M., Rust, R.T., Steen, S. and Tidd, S.T. (2004) 'Willingness-to-pay for Crime Control Programs', *Criminology*, 42: 89–109.

Cornish, D.B. and Clarke, R.V (2003) 'Opportunities, Precipitators and Criminal Decisions: A Reply to Wortley's Critique of Situational Crime Prevention', *Crime Prevention Studies*, 16: 41–96.

Eck, J. (1993) 'The Threat of Crime Displacement', *Criminal Justice Abstracts*, 25: 527–46.

Ekblom, P. (2005) 'Designing Products Against Crime'. In N. Tilley (ed.) *Handbook of Crime Prevention and Community Safety*. Cullompton, Devon: Willan Publishing.

Farrell, G. (2005) 'Progress and Prospects in the Prevention of Repeat Victimisation'. In N. Tilley (ed.) *The Handbook of Crime Prevention and Community Safety*. Cullompton, Devon: Willan Publishing.

Farrell, G., Buck, W. and Pease, K. (1993) 'The Merseyside Domestic Violence Prevention Project: Some Costs and Benefits', *Studies on Crime and Crime Prevention*, Vol. 2, pp. 21–33.

Farrell, G. (2000) 'Crime prevention'. In D. Levinson (ed.) *Encyclopedia of Criminology and Deviant Behavior*. London: Taylor and Francis.

Farrell, G. and Roman, J. (2005) 'Crime as Pollution: Proposal for Market-Based Incentives to Reduce Crime Externalities'. In K. Moss and M. Stephens (eds) *Crime Reduction and the Law*. London: Routledge.

Farrell, G. and Sousa, W. (2001) 'Repeat Victimization and "Hot Spots": The Overlap and its Implications for Crime Prevention and Problem-oriented Policing', *Crime Prevention Studies*, 12: 221–40.

Farrell, G. and Thorne, J. (2005) 'Where Have All the Flowers Gone?: Evaluation of the Taliban Crackdown on Opium Poppy Cultivation in Afghanistan', *International Journal of Drug Policy*, 16(2): 81–91.

Farrington, D.P. and Knight, B.J. (1980) 'Stealing From a "Lost" Letter', *Criminal Justice and Behaviour*, 7: 423–36.

Felson, M. (1994) *Crime and Everyday Life*. Thousand Oaks, California: Pine Forge Press.

Felson, M. (1998) *Crime and Everyday Life, 2nd Edition*. Thousand Oaks, California: Pine Forge Press.

Felson, M. (2002) *Crime and Everyday Life, 3rd Edition*. Thousand Oaks, California: Sage.

Felson, M. and Clarke, R.V. (1998) *Opportunity Makes the Thief: Practical Theory for Crime Prevention*, Police Research Series paper 98. London: Home Office.

Felson, M. *et al.* (1996) 'Redesigning Hell: Preventing Crime and Disorder at the Port Authority Bus Terminal'. In Clarke R.V. (ed.) *Preventing Mass Transit Crime*. Monsey, NY: Criminal Justice Press.

Goldstein, H. (1990) *Problem-Oriented Policing*. Philadelphia: Temple University Press.

Hesseling, R. (1994) 'Displacement: A Review of the Empirical Literature', *Crime Prevention Studies 3*, (ed.) Clarke R.V. Monsey, NY: Criminal Justice Press.

Hough, M. and Tilley, N. (1998) Getting the Grease to the Squeak: Research Lessons for Crime Prevention. Home Office Crime Prevention and Detection series paper 85. London: Home Office. At: http://www.homeoffice.gov.uk/rds/pdfs05/cdps85.pdf

Laycock, G. and Tilley, N. (forthcoming) 'From Crime Prevention to Crime Science'. In G. Farrell, K. Bowers, S.D. Johnson and M. Townsley (eds) *Imagination for Crime Prevention: Essays in Honor of Ken Pease*, volume of *Crime Prevention Studies*. Criminal Justice Press.

Lester, D. (2001) *Crime Reduction Through Product Design*. Australian Institute of Criminology Trends and Issues in Crime and Criminal Justice paper 206. Canberra: Australian Institute of Criminology.

Jeffrey, C.R. (1971). *Crime Prevention Through Environmental Design*. London: Sage.

Johnson, S.D., Bowers, K.J., Birks, D. and McLaughlin, L. (2005) Burglary Prediction, Theory, Flow and Friction. Paper presented at the *British Society of Criminology Conference*, July, Leeds, UK.

Johnson, S.D., Bowers, K.J. and Pease, K. (2004) 'Predicting the Future or Summarising the Past? Crime Mapping as Anticipation'. In Melissa Smith and Nick Tilley (eds) *Launching Crime Science*. London: Willan, pp. 145–63.

Lingenfelter R.E. (1986) *Death Valley and the Amargosa: A Land of Illusion*. Berkeley: University of California Press.

Maruna, S. (2001) *Making Good*. Washington, DC: American Psychological Association.

Mayhew, P.M., Clarke, R.V.G, Burrows, J.N., Hough, J.M. and Winchester, S.W.C. (1979) *Crime in Public View*. Home Office Research Study No. 49. London: HMSO.

Mayhew, P. (2003) Counting the Cost of Crime in Australia. Crime Trends and Issues in Crime and Criminal Justice. Canberra: Australian Institute of Criminology. At: http://www.aic.gov.au/publications/tandi/ti247.pdf

Miller, T., Cohen, M.A. and Wiersema, B. (1996) Victim Costs and Consequences: A New Look. National Institute of Justice Research Report. Washington, DC: NIJ. Also at: http://www.ncjrs.org/pdffiles/victcost.pdf

Moffitt, T.E. (1993) 'Life Course Persistent and Adolescent Limited Antisocial Behaviour: A Developmental Taxonomy.' *Psychological Review*, 100: 674–701.

Schneider, R.H. (this volume) 'Contributions of environmental studies to security'. In M. Gill (ed.) Handbook of Security. Basingstoke: Palgrave Macmillan.

Scott, M.S. (2000) *Problem-Oriented Policing: Reflections on the First 20 Years*. Washington DC: US Department of Justice Office of Community Oriented Policing Services.

Sherman L.W., Gottfredson, D., MacKenzie, D., *et al.* (1997) *Preventing Crime: What Works, What Doesn't, What's Promising*. Washington, DC: US Office of Justice Programs.

Sherman, L.W., Gartin, P.R. and Buerger, M.E. (1989) 'Hot Spots of Predatory Crime: Routine Activities and the Criminology of Place', *Criminology*, 27: 27–55.

Smith, M., Clarke, R.V. and Pease, K. (2002) 'Anticipatory Benefits in Crime Prevention'. In Tilley, N. *Analysis for Crime Prevention*. Monsey, NY: Criminal Justice Press.

Tilley, N. (2006, ed.) *Handbook of Crime Prevention and Community Safety*. Collumpton: Willan.

Townsley, M. and Pease, K. (2003) 'Hot Spots and Cold Comfort: The Importance of Having a Working Thermometer'. In N. Tilley (ed.) *Analysis for Crime Prevention*, *Crime Prevention Studies*, 13: 59–70.

Townsley, M., Smith, C. and Pease, K. (2005) *Using DNA to Catch Offenders Quicker: Serious Detections Arising from Criminal Justice Samples*. London: Jill Dando Institute of Crime Science, University College London.

Walsh, A. and Ellis, L. (2003) (eds) *Biosocial Criminology*. New York: Nova.

Webb, B., Smith, C., Brock, A. and Townsley, M. (2005) 'DNA Fast-Tracking'. In M. Smith and N. Tilley (eds) *Crime Science: New Approaches to Preventing and Detecting Crime*. Cullompton, Devon: Willan Publishing.

Part II

Crimes and Organizations

9

Employee Theft and Staff Dishonesty

Richard C. Hollinger and Jason L. Davis

Introduction

The concept of 'white collar crime' was formally introduced during Edwin Sutherland's presidential address to the American Sociological Society in Philadelphia in 1939. Sutherland (1949) used the term to help establish his new crime theory, differential association, by challenging the discipline of criminology to pay more attention to crimes 'committed by persons of respectability and high social status in the course of his/her [legitimate] occupation.' Today, 'white collar crime' has become an umbrella concept often used to describe a host of criminal behaviors, including but not limited to, illegal financial acts, deceitful or dishonest business practices, or abuses of state power. Scholars generally include employee theft, embezzlement, corporate crime, computer crimes and even political or governmental crimes as primary examples. While white collar crime continues to be used as a crime category, most scholars have developed more precise definitions that focus on specific types of either occupational or corporate crime. An early landmark work in this area was the classic study by Donald Cressey (1953) who interviewed numerous incarcerated embezzlers. Perhaps the most widely recognized differentiation of the major sub-types of white collar crime is represented in Clinard and Quinney's (1973) effort which dichotomized the concept of white collar crime into two subcategories, namely, occupational and corporate crime. They asserted that white collar crime was too broad a topic and could not be classified as a single group of acts. Separating the concept into two sub-categories, Clinard and Quinney, were the first to distinguish clearly occupational crime from corporate crime. These offenses include violations of criminal law committed by an individual or group of individuals during the course of activity within a legitimate occupation for personal gain. The importance of this division is that occupational crime focuses exclusively on criminal acts that benefit the individual, and specifically excludes Sutherland's emphasis on 'high social status' offenders. Thus, a criminal act committed by any employee within an organization is considered occupational white collar crime. For Clinard and Quinney, Sutherland's use of 'respectable' or 'high status' restricted the breadth of white collar crime, since employees other than executives or managers could commit equally harmful or injurious acts. The alternative form of white collar crime specified by Clinard and Quinney (1973) was 'corporate crime.' Corporate crimes were offenses committed by executive officers and high ranking officials in the name of the organization that ultimately benefited, not victimized, the corporation.

Today, most scholars regard employee theft and staff dishonesty as a form of occupational crime. These definitions have virtually all specified that such crimes (1) take place during the course of a legitimate occupation; (2) involve a violation of trust; and (3) are committed primarily for the benefit of the individual either financially or in terms of social status. For example, the Association of Certified Fraud Examiners uses the term 'occupational fraud' to describe 'the use of one's occupation for personal enrichment through the deliberate misuse or misapplication of the employing organization's resources or assets.' They assert that any form of occupational fraud involves four critical elements including the notion that such activity (1) is clandestine; (2) violates the offender's fiduciary duties to the victim organization; (3) is committed for the purpose of direct or indirect financial benefit to the offender; and (4) costs the victim organization assets, revenue, or reserves (ACFE, 2004: 1).

Over the last several decades, a plethora of different studies have suggested that employee theft is one of the most widespread, pervasive, and costly form of crime (e.g. Astor, 1972; Bacas, 1987; Baker and Westin, 1988; Clark and Hollinger, 1979, 1980; Delaney, 1993; Franklin, 1975; Greenberg and Barling, 1996; Friedrichs, 2004; Hayes, 1993; Hollinger, 1989; Hollinger and Clark, 1983; Hollinger and Dabney, 1994; Jaspan, 1974; Jones, 1972; Lary, 1988; Lipman, 1973, 1988; Mars, 1982; Merriam, 1977; Murphy, 1993; Mustaine and Tewksbury, 2002; Niehoff and Paul, 2000; Robin, 1969, 1970, 1974; Shepard and Dustin, 1988; Slora, 1989; Terris, 1985; Thomas *et al.*, 2001; Wimbush, 1997). Estimates of the annual losses that US retail businesses suffer as a result of employee dishonesty typically range between five and ten billion dollars, but can reach upwards of hundreds of billions of dollars if all industry categories are included (Friedrichs, 2004; Lary, 1988). Obviously, the monetary costs of employee theft have substantial adverse effects on society and the economy. For example, employee theft results in an inflation of the price of consumer items by anywhere from 10 to 15 percent (Friedrichs, 2004; Hollinger and Clark, 1983) and costs the average American family approximately $400 dollars per year (*Consumer Reports*, 2002: 20). Additionally, losses from employee theft play a major part in the bankruptcies of between 30 to 50 percent of all insolvent organizations annually (Greenberg, 1997; Greenberg and Barling, 1996; Hollinger, 1989; Neihoff and Paul, 2000; Thomas *et al.*, 2001; US Chamber of Commerce, 1976).

Defining employee theft and staff dishonesty

One of the most widely accepted definitions of 'employee theft' (or 'staff dishonesty') is the one offered by Hollinger and Clark in 1983 who defined such theft as 'the unauthorized taking, control, or transfer of money and/or property of the formal work organization perpetrated by an employee during the course of occu-pational activity which is related to his or her employment' (1983: 1). They also distinguished between the two major forms of employee theft, namely, property deviance and production deviance. The former refers to situations in which employees illegally acquire or damage tangible property or organizational assets, whereas the latter concerns counterproductive behavior that violates the for-mally proscribed expectations of daily work production. Property deviance includes such acts as financial embezzlement, pilferage, theft of goods, or sabo-tage (Taylor and Walton, 1971). Alternatively, production deviance involves the 'stealing of time' in which workers get paid for hours not worked, absenteeism or tardiness, leave abuse, or failing to accomplish tasks in a timely manner (Hollinger and Clark, 1983). Although this chapter is primarily focused on prop-erty theft and dishonesty, there is extensive evidence that counterproductive workplace deviant behavior is closely related to property deviance. This body of literature is found not in criminology, but primarily in the sociology of work and occupation literature (e.g. Dalton (1959); Gouldner (1954); Kamp and Brooks (1991); Kemper (1966); Roethlisberger and Dickson (1939); Roy (1952, 1953, 1954, 1959); Ruggiero and Steinberg (1982)).

Prevalence of employee theft and staff dishonesty

Most early employee theft researchers were primarily interested in determining the incidence or prevalence of such crimes according to Hollinger (1989). The incidence of employee theft refers to the absolute number of times theft has occurred, while prevalence indicates the proportion of employees involved in theft. Answers to both questions have remained elusive and provide a constant challenge for researchers, primarily because there is a lack of official data that measures employee theft. Moreover, the majority of employee theft cases are not handled directly by law enforcement agencies, but rather, are dealt with inter-nally by security, loss prevention, asset protection, or human resource depart-ments. Instead of filing formal charges or calling police authorities, most business organizations that discover employee theft use alternative, non-criminal sanctions such as immediate dismissal, demotion, or civil tort remedies. The rationale for using non-criminal sanctions allows the company to avoid other potentially negative outcomes such as adverse publicity, retaliation or retribution from employees, or publicly advertising internal weaknesses that may cause the organization to be considered an easy target. As a result, there is no precise measure concerning the incident or prevalence of employee theft.

Since there is no official data available to examine, researchers have instead relied on case studies or self-report surveys to study the incidence and prevalence of employee theft and workplace dishonesty (Hollinger and Clark, 1983). In some cases, organizations also use indirect measures to estimate the extent of employee theft.

Retailers have been the industry to most aggressively study the problem. The method most commonly used in the retail industry for estimating levels of employee theft has been to track the percentage of unsold and unaccounted for merchandise when sales are subtracted from the actual remaining inventory. According to some scholars, the use of 'inventory shrinkage,' 'shortage,' or other terms such as 'loss' to describe employee theft tends to reflect an attitude of denial and ultimately decriminalizes the incident of employee theft as something other than criminal behavior (Oliphant and Oliphant, 2001). In any case, retail loss prevention and security researchers have continued to rely on organization's measurement of shrinkage in order to gauge the incident and prevalence of employee theft.

The oldest and most reliable source of data on the levels of employee theft in US retailing has been the University of Florida's *National Retail Security Survey (NRSS)*. Beginning in 1991, the University of Florida has conducted annual evaluations of retail industry crime and prevention strategies employed by companies to help prevent such crimes. In particular, the *NRSS* focuses on inventory shrinkage and asks retailers to estimate what percentage of loss can be attributed to four primary sources including (1) employee theft; (2) shoplifting; (3) bookkeeping errors; or (4) vendor fraud. One of the most consistent findings of the *NRSS* is that employee theft is believed to be the primary source of inventory shrinkage. In each year the *NRSS* conducted its survey, employee theft was believed to account for 40 or more percent of inventory loss. In 2003, employees were believed to account for nearly 47 percent of all inventory shrinkage losses in US retail stores (Hollinger and Langton, 2004).

Another source of employee theft information comes from the Association of Certified Fraud Examiners (ACFE). Beginning in 1996, the ACFE examined occupational fraud cases reported to the Certified Fraud Examiners (CFEs) and issued its first Report to the Nation on Occupational Fraud and Abuse with the intent of (1) summarizing the amount of lost revenue that could be attributed to occupational fraud, (2) examining the characteristics of the employees who committed occupational frauds, (3) determining which organizations were most likely to be victimized by occupational fraud, and (4) categorizing the ways in which fraud occurred. The latest 2004 *Report to the Nation* contains information from 508 occupational fraud cases. In all, these cases resulted in over $761 million in losses with an average loss of $100,000 per case.

Regardless of the source, most accounts of employee theft estimate that such crimes cost businesses billions of dollars each year. The 2004 *Report to the Nation* estimates that a typical organization loses 6 percent of its annual revenue to occupational fraud which translate into $660 billion in annual fraud losses (p. 8).

In this respect, employee theft can be considered the single largest form of larceny-theft in the United States (Hollinger and Langton, 2004). Indeed, in any given year employee theft generally costs more than all Type 1 UCR 'index property crimes' combined. The alarming rate of employee theft has at least two negative consequences (Parilla, Hollinger and Clark, 1988). First, employee theft results in stolen property that must be replaced. This causes a loss of money and time which undermines organizational productivity and goals such as profit accumulation. Secondly, employee theft creates uncertainty and disruptions that can lead to business failure. For instance, approximately 30 percent of all small business failures can be attributed to employee theft (Kuratko, Naffziger and Hodgetts, 2000). Others suggest the general public also suffers because of employee theft. More specifically, the general public pays a 'crime tax' whenever corporations are victimized because they must pay higher merchandise costs as well as increased insurance premiums (Bamfield and Hollinger, 1996).

Beyond the financial implications, employee theft can also have impacts on workplace morale and personal relationships at work (Hollinger, 1989). Pervasive employee dishonesty can strain workplace interactions and ultimately create a lack of trust between dishonest and honest employees. Subsequently, employee theft can decrease positive productivity and increase employee dissatisfaction levels. Understanding why employees commit theft is an important step in helping to reduce the significant financial and social impact of these crimes.

Why do employees steal and engage in dishonesty?

Explaining why employees steal from their employers is an extremely difficult task. What makes identifying the root causes of employee dishonesty so difficult is that there is no single factor or theory that can explain each and every occurrence. Instead, social scientists have concluded that a variety of factors may contribute to the occurrence of theft or dishonest behavior.

Most people employed in business organizations are conventionally socialized individuals. Generally speaking, the vast majority of employees are law-abiding citizens who know the difference between right and wrong. After all, to be hired they have survived a pretty extensive interview and screening process. For a theft to occur, then, it is necessary for these persons to believe their law-breaking activity as completely justified under the circumstances. These motivating circumstances either can be the result of economic problems external to the work setting or can originate from factors within the work organization itself.

Paradoxically we continue to observe increases in employee dishonesty while our country's official and self-reported larceny rates are both in decline. NRSS over the past ten years indicate that the increasing problem of employee dishonesty is not the result of a sudden breakdown in hiring practices. In fact, the NRSS has shown in each of the past ten years that increasingly more numerous and sophisticated screening tools are being routinely used by employers. This enhanced level of applicant screening often involves multiple interviews, drug testing, criminal background checks, credit evaluations, and honesty testing. These countermeasures have successfully eliminated many risky and marginal persons from the applicant pool. Nevertheless, despite our best efforts to screen-out known or potentially dishonest job candidates, employee theft not only persists but also seems to be increasing in prevalence. The critical question is 'why?' The most popular theories of employee theft tend to fall into three general categories including: (1) rational choice theories, (2) job satisfaction or workplace equity theories, and (3) organizational theories that concentrate on the effects of the informal workplace, that is, a 'culture of dishonesty.'

I   Rational choice theories

Rational choice theories combine elements of classical theory and economic theory to explain criminal behavior. From a classical perspective, humans are considered inherently rational and hedonistic beings who logically calculate the potential costs and benefits of a given act (Beccaria, 1764). Being hedonistic, humans will naturally make decisions that will avoid pain and provide the greatest amount of pleasure, even if it means violating the law (Bentham, 1789). Employees who steal from their employers are viewed as taking advantage of opportunities that have a low risk of detection or apprehension and at the same time provide the greatest potential for personal benefit. Building upon these classical theory principles, traditional rational choice theories utilized an economic model to assert that employees were self-interested offenders primarily motivated by the pursuit of financial gain.

External economic pressures

There is extensive debate among both scholars and security experts alike regarding the extent to which external (or non-work) economic pressures provide the principal motivation for employee dishonesty. Despite numerous anecdotal accounts, Hollinger and Clark concluded in their 1983 book, *Theft By Employees*, that most incidents of employee pilferage were unrelated to an employee's particular wage or level of compensation. In other words, highly paid employees reported taking property from the company just as often as did poorly paid employees. The data from nearly 9500 employees suggested that the adequacy of one's compensation is extremely relative. Employee satisfaction with pay seemed to be independent of the absolute amount of money received. Moreover, employees who reported having personal economic problems were no more theft-prone than those who did not. This research study, conducted over two decades ago, concluded that most employees do not steal from the company as a way of resolving their personal debts and other external economic pressures. This may not be the case today. In fact, as personal debt piles up, contemporary employees may be feeling much stronger economic pressures than their peers did 20 years ago. Many individuals today are seriously in debt. Personal bankruptcies are at record levels. Credit card debt among Americans currently averages nearly $9000. These substantial credit card debts and other economic difficulties result in what criminologist Donald Cressey called 'non-sharable problems.' Some people steal from their employers to meet their financial needs. In fact, some persons in a financial bind will elect to steal large amounts of money from their employers. In his now classic study of convicted embezzlers published in 1953, Cressey found that most became involved in 'trust violations' as a result of some personal financial problem that they could not share with anyone else. Perhaps they had incurred a sizable gambling debt, were involved in an expensive love affair, were secretly addicted to drugs, or made a bad financial mistake with the company's assets. All of the above are examples of 'non-sharable problems' which precipitated the 'borrowing' of a large amount of their employer's money to solve these personal problems.

For the classical theorist, the presence of formal mechanisms such as criminal law or severe punishments is needed to deter potential criminal behavior by making the costs of crime outweigh the expected benefits. In fact, Hollinger and Clark (1983) found evidence that formal constraints reduced rates of theft among retail, hospital, and manufacturing employees. In particular, the threat of apprehension appeared to have the strongest impact in terms of deterring criminality.

Some scholars have questioned the importance of economic needs. While large-scale embezzlements do occur – often crippling the business victimized – we must remember that these large thefts are quite rare. The typical employee thief is not a cash embezzler, but rather a person who pilfers much smaller amounts of company property and money on a more regular basis. It is this more prevalent 'nickel and dime' theft activity that over time costs companies far more in lost assets than all the embezzlers combined. It is for this reason that we need to look beyond purely economic motivations for an explanation of employee theft.

Most notably Cornish and Clarke (1986) suggested that offenders are not motivated solely by economic needs but instead engage in purposeful criminal behavior in order to meet immediate day-to-day financial needs such as food, housing, status, or entertainment. For example, Stone (1990) discovered that Michael Milken, the junk bond king of the savings and loans scandal of the 1980s, was driven largely by the fun, excitement, and adrenaline rush associated with stealing large sums of money. Furthermore, Cornish and Clarke (1986) maintained that an offender's decisions and choices are likely to be guided by external factors such as time, ability, and the availability of relevant information needed to commit an offense. An employee may consider the skills needed to commit certain types of offenses, what type of knowledge or understanding is needed to commit certain types of criminal behavior, and other considerations unrelated to pure economic needs. In perhaps the most inclusive rational choice model yet developed, Paternoster and Simpson (1993) maintain that offenders consider at least nine different factors before committing a crime. These factors include the perceived certainty and severity of formal sanctions such as criminal or civil outcomes; the perceived certainty and severity of informal sanctions including reactions by family and friends or the loss of career mobility; moral inhibitions which refers to the extent that an offender considers a specific criminal behavior to be wrong or offensive; the potential loss of self-respect as the offender ponders how criminal behavior will impact their self-image; the perceived costs of rule compliance in which the offender considers whether or not compliance will interfere with more important goals such as profitability or competitiveness; the benefits of noncompliance occurs when an offender assesses whether or not criminal behavior will result in more favorable personal benefits such as a promotion or enhanced financial status; the perceived legitimacy of the laws as offenders evaluate whether or not the existing rules and regulations are fair and consistent; and the characteristics of the criminal event in which the offenders considers the availability of criminal opportunities or how acceptable criminal behavior is within the organization. Paternoster and Simpson (1993) basically assert that the best predictor of criminal behavior is past offending in which case the offender has likely developed favorable attitudes to criminal activity.

Routine activities theory

Another similar theory that accounts for the factors that potential offenders consider includes Cohen and Felson's (1979) 'routine activities theory.' Specifically, this theory asserts that the occurrence of crime is a product of opportunity related to three factors: (1) motivated offenders, (2) suitable targets, and (3) the absence of capable guardians. These are the three logically required conditions which must be present before a theft can occur. This is sometimes called the 'theft triangle.' First, the deviant act must be motivated by one or more precipitating factors. Second, there must be ample opportunity present for the theft to occur. Third, there must be a perceived absence of deterrence or lack of a capable guardian.

First, Cohen and Felson maintain that everyone is a motivated offender because of their hedonistic or pleasure seeking nature. Given the opportunity, most people will engage in crime unless they are prevented or deterred from doing so. The second factor, a suitable target, refers to the attractiveness of potential targets including money, jewelry, or any other valuable asset. Finally, guardianship refers to the extent to which valuable property is monitored or regulated. When these three factors converge in time and space, the chances of criminal occurrences significantly increase. In other words, the spatial and temporal sequence of a crime must involve the offender and the victim in the same location at the same time without the presence of guardianship. Thus, from a routine activities perspective employees will take advantage of opportunities favorable or conducive to criminal behavior. Unlocked inventory doors, areas without alarms or surveillance, relatively easy access to valuable information or assets are conditions that lack effective guardianship. Under these conditions, rational or calculating employees will exploit these opportunities for individual benefit.

Opportunity

The amount, the frequency, and the prevalence of theft are also determined by the possible range of theft opportunities. Some jobs permit more opportunities for stealing as compared to other occupations, professions, or positions. If the product is without much value or no cash handling occurs, we would expect correspondingly less theft. Alternatively, if there are many things of value that can be taken from the workplace, we should not be surprised to discover higher prevalence levels of theft.

Unfortunately, almost everywhere one looks in the workplace, especially in retailing, we can find desirable merchandise of significant value, as well as plentiful amounts of cash. Given the high levels of opportunity for theft, it not surprising that employee dishonesty abounds in retailing. In fact, perhaps we should ask the question in the opposite direction, namely, 'why isn't there even more theft given the numerous opportunities for taking things in the retail store?' Reduce the levels of opportunity and theft rates should decline. The solution to the problem seems so obvious. Lowering levels of dishonesty should be the direct result of strictly limiting an employee's access both to money and merchandise. However, as we eventually discovered with shoplifting, simply constraining access can backfire, since physical controls can seriously interfere with the ability of the retail employee to do their job. Just as the shopper must be able to touch the merchandise to facilitate sales, the sales associate must also have unrestricted access to both merchandise and cash to serve the customer and to complete their purchase transactions. In other words, locking things up, putting items under the counter, or physically chaining things down may not be the ideal answer to this problem.

Thirty years ago, it seemed that most security experts believed that unlimited opportunity was the predominant or sole cause of dishonesty in the workplace. Virtually all argued that if items are not properly secured, eventually your merchandise will be taken. At the time it was very common to believe that all employees are vulnerable to temptation. While most experts feel that this is an overly pessimistic image of the typical employee, it is undeniable that opportunity can facilitate theft and dishonesty in the workplace. Given its obvious importance, we find it interesting that here has been so little systematic research on the role that opportunity plays in the employee theft equation.

In *Theft by Employees* (1983), Hollinger and Clark compared theft levels among the various occupations in three different industries, namely, retailing, healthcare, and manufacturing. Generally speaking, employees working in those jobs possessing the greatest uncontrolled access to money and property did report slightly higher levels of theft. It is also important to note, however, that the majority of employees with high opportunity to steal were not involved in dishonest activity. In other words, from my own research and other scholarly studies, it has become clear that just having access to things of value does not necessarily produce theft. Opportunity also has important subjective dimensions. Three factors that can most greatly affect the subjective value of merchandise include social desirability, concealability, and proximity.

Social desirability

Obviously, money has objective (or extrinsic) value. However, the same always can not always be said for merchandise, which has both objective (extrinsic) and subjective (intrinsic) value. Some merchandise in our stores is highly priced, but could not be given away. Other less expensive merchandise can not even be kept on the shelves. Most internal theft (and shoplifting) is focused on those items that are at present highly desirable. This is especially true for younger employees with minimal tenure with the firm. Opportunity then is not just access to merchandise, it is also directly dependent on how 'hot' the merchandise is. In other words is the item currently in vogue? Or, as my generation said, 'Is it cool?' We should not just ask ourselves whether stolen items can be fenced or sold to strangers? Of greater importance might include, does the merchandise in our stores have subjective value to the person who takes it, either for their personal use or to give to a close friend or family member? In other words, we need to continually re-evaluate the social desirability of the merchandise in the store.

Concealability

Can the item easily be hidden on one's person to be taken? Most people are afraid to violate another's private social space. This is why we have such objection to current airport security screening policies. Most things that are socially desirable are getting physically smaller and as a result, easier to conceal on our persons. Just think of how much easier it is to conceal a CD when compared to a vinyl record of an earlier generation, or a DVD when compared to a VHS tape in its box.

Proximity

The old saying goes, 'familiarity breeds contempt.' Perhaps in the retail store the saying should be re-stated 'proximity breeds devaluation.' Merchandise that is handled continuously every day can allow the employee to eventually view these items as just 'things' without great value to the company. POS terminals automatically price items that allows associates to lose appreciation for the real value and price of store merchandise. Eventually it just all becomes 'stuff' with little or unknown value, making much easier to steal and not worth protecting.

In summary, understanding the subjective dimensions of opportunity can help understand the cause of both internal and external theft. If an item of merchandise is socially desirable (i.e. envied and approved by one's closest peers), can be easily concealed because of its small size, and is in continuous, unsupervised proximity to the sales associate during the work day, we should not be surprised if it is stolen with regularity. In fact, alternatively, perhaps we should be examining those circumstances where we find high levels of opportunity but with very little theft! Quite possibly the sales associates in those low theft environments have internalized the real value of the merchandise, understand the harm that theft causes for the profitability of the firm, and have not yet rationalized away the wrongful nature of their dishonesty.

II   Job dissatisfaction and workplace equity theories

While rational choice theories suggest that employees engage in a personal cost-benefit analysis prior to committing crime, other theories maintain that employees are likely to steal because of the way they are treated by the organization and its managers. In recent years more and more scholars have found significant empirical support for the relationship between job dissatisfaction and employee dishonesty. One of the most commonly observed dishonesty explanations is based upon the assumption that disgruntled employees will steal from their employers in order to resolve feelings of perceived inequity in the way in which they have been treated. Generally speaking, if the prevailing worker attitudes toward the organization, management and supervisors are positive, one finds lower levels of all types of deviant behavior in the workplace, including theft and dishonesty. However, if the employees: 1) feel exploited by the work organization, 2) believe that supervisors are not interested in them as persons, and 3) are generally disgruntled with their work situation – we find higher than average levels of theft and deviance. High levels of turnover in the retail industry can be viewed as a barometer of this pervasive worker dissatisfaction problem. Theft is viewed as the employee's way of 'getting back' at an employer who does not provide a satisfactory work experience. In other words, employees 'rip off' the company when their employer is perceived as 'ripping' them off (Altheide *et al.*, 1978).

The relationship between job dissatisfaction and workplace deviance was first tested by Mangione and Quinn (1975), who found only mild support among males 30 and older. Later Hollinger and Clark (1982) examined job dissatisfaction hypothesis with a much larger data set, discovering a more consistent pattern of support. Among employees in three different industries studied, those dissatisfied with their present jobs and looking for another job were more involved in employee theft. Retail employee thieves were most unhappy with the inadequate 'task challenges' of their work and the fact that their employers seemed not to care about them. In the hospital, employees who take property were most unhappy about their employer's lack of caring, in addition to poor treatment by immediate supervisors and limited job responsibility. Although slightly less influential in the manufacturing plant, deviant employees were again more likely to express dissatisfaction both with their employers and with limited span of authority. In all three industries studied employees who felt that their employers were dishonest, unfair and uncaring about their workers were significantly more involved in theft and other forms of workplace deviance. Immediate supervisors were often viewed as the source of the workplace inequity, since employees usually view their supervisors as the personification of their employers.

A similar group of theories used to account for employee theft focus on employees' perceptions of equity within the organization and how these conditions can provide motivation for criminal behavior. In general, equity, retributive and distributive justice theories assert that in situations where employees feel they are treated unfairly, employee theft is more likely to occur. In a classic study, Ditton (1977) discovered that workers commit petty crimes such as pilfering or chiseling to compensate for low wages. These 'wages-in-kind' were considered legitimate forms of compensation by most workers. Similarly, Greenberg (1990) found that employees view theft as a form of debt collection for perceived salary inequalities. In other instances, employees may steal because of dissatisfaction with work conditions. As Greenberg (1997) points out in his STEAL motive theory, employees will engage in theft in order to 'even the score' and redress perceived inequity with their employers. That is, workers who perceive unequal outcomes in an exchange relation will resort to theft to reestablish a more equitable relationship.

There is a rich literature in this area of inquiry. According to Mars (1974), dockworkers considered pilfering an entitlement for exploitative work conditions. In a study of nursing home theft, Harris and Benson (1998) found that dissatisfied employees were more likely to steal than satisfied workers. Likewise, Greenberg and Scott (1996) discovered that employees justified theft as retributive justice for dissatisfaction over an employer's actions. In other words, employees rebelled against their treatment within the company.

Tucker (1989) describes similar behavior as a form of self help. In particular, this concept asserts lower status employees will commit offenses against their superiors in order to pursue justice. Since lower classes have less access to formal remedies when they seek to settle grievances against their superiors, they must take the law into their own hands and engage in alternative behaviors to help ensure a more equitable relationship. In most instances, these alternative behaviors are defined as criminal. Thus, when employees develop alternative behaviors to overcome a perceived injustice they are engaging in 'self-help' to pursue justice against a powerful organization. Indeed, Tucker (1989) found that the most marginalized workers including those that received the lowest wages, few or no benefits, and exerted little autonomy over their work conditions were those most likely to engage in theft. Similarly, Hollinger and Clark (1983) examined nearly 9500 employees representing the retail, medical, manufacturing industries and found that workers who felt exploited by the company were more likely to engage in acts detrimental to the organization. Finally, Baumgartner (1984) suggests that the origins of embezzlement can be found in grievances employees have against their companies. In order to settle these grievances, employees will engage in 'covert retaliation' such as theft or sabotage. Overall, studies related to equity theories indicate that employee theft is not necessarily an act of greed or opportunity. Instead, employee theft is a consequence of organizational characteristics that produce inequitable relationships. Employees steal to react against, counter, or control injustices in their work environment.

A recently published study entitled, 'Career Jobs, Survival Jobs, and Employee Deviance: A Social Investment Model of Workplace Misconduct,' concludes that while most of the research on employee theft conclusively shows a strong relationship to poor job satisfaction, there is yet another pathway to dishonesty (Huiras, Uggen and McMorris, 2000). After surveying a large sample of young high school students over a period of years, the authors conclude that the relationship between one's future career plans and current job can also be a strong predictor of employee deviance. In other words, for this mid-twenty age group the entry into a career marks the beginning of adulthood. When respondents were employed in meaningful jobs that were not just providing economic 'survival,' but were directly linked to their long term career plans, deviance levels on the job were significantly reduced. In short, people whose current jobs match their long term career goals have made a social investment that directly inhibits deviance in the job. Even among young people, who are most prone to higher levels of employee theft and workplace deviance, can be deterred from these activities when they see that their future might be adversely affected by their deviant actions.

III Culture of dishonesty

Other scholars have focused on the normative characteristics of the workplace in order to better understand how employees learn and justify their criminal behavior. For the most part, these theories have focused on the organizational culture and its informal structure to understand employee theft. This final group of theories used to explain employee theft focuses on organizational culture which refers to a set of shared meanings or understandings that influence organizational behavior by shaping employees' cognition and perceptions of reality (Ott, 1989). An important part of the informal organizational culture is the various peer subcultures of dishonesty that exist within a given workplace (Cherington and Cherington, 1985). In many instances, these subcultures often take precedence over the established formal guidelines and become the guiding force of employee behavior (Parilla, Hollinger and Clark, 1988). That is, employees become more influenced by the expectations of their workplace peers than by the formal rules established by executives and managers. According to Hollinger and Clark (1982), employee perceptions of informal co-worker sanctions had the strongest effect on deterring theft. In particular, employees appeared to be more constrained by the anticipated reaction from co-workers than by formal reactions from the organizational management. As such, the informal structure is considered the most important factor determining the incident and prevalence of employee theft. Through peer interaction and socialization, employees learn the techniques, motivations and rationalizations for criminal behavior (Shover and Hochstetler, 2002). The pioneer of white collar research, Edwin Sutherland, was the first scholar to discuss the importance of peer association and its influence on criminal behavior. His theory of 'differential association' was developed as general theory to help explain the occurrence of both conventional and white collar crime. Specifically, Sutherland's theory included nine propositions which asserted among other things that criminal behavior is learned through close interaction with others who hold favorable definitions to crime. Also within these interactions, offenders learn the techniques needed to commit specific types of crime and rationalizations used to justify criminal behavior. Sutherland argued that the longer and more frequent these criminal associations, the more likely a person would develop favorable attitudes toward crime and eventually engage in crime themselves. One of the more salient aspects of Sutherland's theory that scholars have continued to explore is the importance of rationalizations to help justify criminal behavior.

The vocabulary and language shared among organizational members is generally considered a salient feature of the informal structure. In terms of employee theft, the use of linguistic exchanges provides justifications that minimize the guilt and shame associated with crime (Shover and Hochstetler,

2002). In part, this helps explain why otherwise moral and decent people can 'drift' into criminal behavior (Matza, 1964). One of the most complicated behaviors that social scientists attempt to explain is the person who takes the property of another without feeling any guilt or remorse. Most security professionals continue to be amazed by how many dishonest employees fail to appreciate the wrongfulness of what they have just been caught doing. Apparently, many people believe that stealing is perfectly acceptable, especially if you do not get caught. This belief is most commonly observed when the victim of the theft is a large, faceless bureaucracy, such as the government or a business corporation. Indeed, Smigel (1970) found that respondents were less concerned about the consequences of stealing from large organizations because they were considered impersonal, ruthless, wealthy and powerful and thus deserving of victimization.

According to Sykes and Matza's (1957) techniques of neutralization theory and subsequent writings by other scholars, there are a handful of potential justifications offenders use prior to engaging in criminal behavior to reduce the anxiety caused by such acts.

Perhaps the primary reason for the continuing growth in the prevalence of dishonest employees is attributable to the fact that many conventionally socialized workers have discovered a way to overcome guilt for doing something that they know is wrong. In other words, normally honest and ethical employees are stealing without feeling remorse for their behavior. This process is not based on simple rationalizations in which one excuses or justifies unethical behavior 'after the fact.' No doubt many of us have engaged in these ex post facto rationalizations for our dishonesty after we have been caught doing something wrong or illegal. For example, the driver who receives a speeding ticket blames the police officer. The person who underreports their income blames the overly zealous tax auditor. The student who cheats on a test blames the instructor for preparing an extremely difficult exam.

These examples of 'after the fact' rationalizations are *not* causal explanations of behavior because they do not occur prior to the deviant act. To prove causation the factors which contribute to the origin of the behavior must be present before, not after, the offending behavior.

One of the most useful theories to explain why associates who have passed the rigorous interview and screening process will eventually steal is what criminologists, Gresham Sykes and David Matza (1957), call 'techniques of neutralization.' In other words, we need to understand how conventionally socialized persons negate the guilt or remorse that one should be expected to feel for their deviant behaviors. These techniques allow for the traditional ethical bonds of society to be temporarily broken or suspended. Prior to the introduction of this theory, crime was presumed to be a product of lower class life. Alternatively, this theory helped to explain why middle and upper class adolescents, after growing up in a morally and financially sound social background also engaged in delinquent behavior.

We have listed the major types below, along with a definition for each in words that a retail store employee might use to express the concept:

1. <u>Denial of Responsibility</u>
   'My store doesn't make any sincere attempt to protect its merchandise. We have no working cameras or EAS tag alarms like other retailers do, so it's not my fault when merchandise is missing. It's obvious the company doesn't care.'

2. <u>Denial of Injury</u>
   'My employer sells so much merchandise that nobody will miss the few items I take. They can afford it.'

3. <u>Denial of the Victim</u>
   'This company makes so much profit that they have no right to claim that they are hurt by a few petty thefts. I consider pilferage my "fringe benefit package."'

4. <u>Condemnation of the Condemner</u>
   'The store has no right to condemn me for stealing small amounts of money and merchandise. My manager shouldn't be surprised when we take things. In fact, if there is any victim around here it is me, given the pitifully low wages that we are paid. The company should not be surprised when their hard working employees steal. The more appropriate question they should be asking is, "why is everybody not stealing?"'

5. <u>Defense of Necessity</u>
   'I really need the money to buy food and pay my rent.' 'Or, If the company expects me to dress well at work then I am going to have to take money or merchandise to look presentable.'

6. <u>Appeal to Higher Loyalties</u>
   'My friends and family are far more important to me than this company that I have been working at for just a few short weeks. So, I let friends have free or reduced price items when I ring them up at the cash register.' Or, 'I need money to pay for my child's doctor bills, since my kids and family comes before my temporary allegiance to this company.'

7. <u>Metaphor of the Ledger</u>
   'We all work really hard around here, especially during the holiday season I keep track of what the company owes me in my head. If I steal it is only fair compensation for unpaid extra hard work.'

There is substantial empirical research support for this theory. Richard Hollinger (1991) found that many of the above-listed guilt neutralizing techniques were statistically more likely to be utilized by employees to excuse their dishonest behavior. Moreover, he discovered that techniques of neutralization were slightly more likely to be used by older, than the very youngest employees. Apparently, older associates, who understand better right from wrong, are more likely to need sophisticated guilt neutralizing vocabularies to excuse their own crimes.

In summary, employees' perceptions of how they are treated by management have a great deal to do with creating and perpetuating a 'climate of dishonesty' in the workplace. Research shows that the most productive explanations are based on variables directly related to perceived workplace conditions or the attitudes held by workers. Managers must be more attentive to the extent to which these neutralizing techniques are present within the culture of their organizations. If neutralizing language and expressions are commonly expressed by workers, managers should not be surprised to discover that rates of employee dishonesty are above an acceptable level.

Another important aspect of the workplace vocabulary occurs when peer subgroups define employee behavior that is acceptable and unacceptable. In a study of blue-collar workers at a Midwestern electronics assembly plant, Horning (1970) discovered that employees developed guidelines for the theft of property. More specifically, employees identified three types of property including company property; personal property; and uncertain property. In terms of company property, the subculture consensus held that expensive tools or items for which there was an established accounting procedure such as a checkout policy were off limits in terms of theft. Conversely, small, less expensive or plentiful company property including nails, screws, and bolts was considered acceptable for theft. Also, uncertain property in which there was no clear ownership such as tools replaced by newer equipment, scrap or waste materials, and broken or defective parts were viewed as acceptable for theft. In terms of personal property, there was a strong normative consensus that such property should not be stolen under any circumstance. According to Horning, the theft of personal property was considered more serious than the stealing of expensive company property. Indeed, employee's feelings were so strong and adamant that the stealing of personal property was unthinkable and considered taboo.

In other instances, the informal structure of an organization may define potentially criminal behavior as normal or commonplace. In this respect, the subculture language redefines criminal behavior as acceptable. For instance, Vaughan (1998) suggests that engineers at NASA continuously redefined problems associated with the solid rocket boosters (the cause of 1983 space shuttle Challenger explosion) as 'acceptable risk.' According to Vaughan, the work group's definition of the boosters as 'acceptable risk' became an institutionalized cultural belief that was not questioned by those within the organization. Ultimately, the vocabulary of the informal structure provided employees with the means to negate the moral dilemmas caused by apparent signs of danger and weakness associated with the boosters. Whichever theoretical perspective scholars adhere to, it is important to understand the different dynamics that influence employee behavior in order to develop effective control mechanisms to limit its occurrence.

Understanding deterrence

Perhaps the single most important factor influencing employees' decisions to steal involves whether they believe that they will get caught or not. This is known in criminology as the question of deterrence. Assuming that an employee wants to steal and has the prerequisite opportunity, he or she will be affected by the two primary dimensions of deterrence. The first dimension of deterrence is the offender's perceived certainty of detection. In other words, in the offender's own mind, what is the chance of getting caught? The second dimension of deterrence is known as the perceived severity of punishment. In other words, if the offender does get caught, what bad things do they believe will happen to him or her as a result? Notice that we have phrased this in terms of perceived deterrence. The actual (or objective) certainty of detection and severity of punishment are not really important. All that really matters is the perception reality on the part of the offender.

Both the perceived certainty of detection and the perceived severity of punishment work together in combination to provide the optimal deterrent effect. Put in the context of highway speeding, the perceived certainty of detection consists of 'what are the odds that I might get pulled over by the police if I exceed the speed limit?' In addition, the severity of punishment amounts to 'how many dollars will I be fined if given a ticket?' For deterrence to work effectively, the law violator must believe two things. First, that there is a high probability of getting caught, and second, if caught, that the punishment will be severe or costly.

Research has shown that most new employees believe (albeit inaccurately) that they will be caught if they attempt to steal from their employers. Fortunately for most businesses, the vast majority of these easily deterred employees will never attempt to steal. Most troubling, however, is that further research suggests that there is a small but significant number of employees who believe that there is little or no chance that they will ever be caught. Unfortunately, as we all secretly know, these employees are factually correct in their assessment that the risks of detection are quite low.

Moreover, even if detected, many employees correctly assume that they will not be punished very severely. In fact, the more times that they successfully steal without detection increases their assessment that they are invincible to the efforts of loss prevention. This is especially true for young males. In fact, many long-time thieves actually believe that they will never get caught and are quite surprised when they eventually do (Hollinger and Clark, 1983b).

Given the virtually impossible task of detecting employee theft, the unspoken truth remains – most dishonest workers will never be caught. And, even if they are detected, they know that realistically the worst consequence which can happen to them is that they will be fired. Most employees who are actively engaged in theft believe that they will not be criminally prosecuted. Unless the offense is particularly costly or notable, these offenders are, more often than not, correct.

If your company is not known to aggressively prosecute employee dishonesty cases in criminal court, this situation provides very little deterrence, especially to those younger employees who report the very highest levels of theft even when the chances of detection are significant. So, if the employees at the bottom of the bureaucratic hierarchy believe that they won't be prosecuted, and know that they can get another job the very next day, how can the employer ever hope to prevent theft? The answer is that in most companies there is very little perceived certainty of detection and even lower perceived severity of punishment. It would appear that for the very experienced and confident employee thief, whatever loss prevention is doing to deter theft simply does not work very well.

Responses to employee theft and dishonesty

The primary function of any organization is goal attainment. In a business organization one of the more important goals is profitability. Crimes committed against the company by its staff and employees negatively affect the attainment of this goal. In order to protect its interests, companies devote considerable resources to combat employee theft and other potential sources of financial loss. Indeed, most corporations have loss prevention departments dedicated to focusing on crime prevention strategies. Preventing workplace crime requires a multistage prevention and detection strategy that includes keeping potential thieves out of the company, increasing awareness of crime-related problems, preventing and detecting the crime of both employees and customers, and finally handling offenders when apprehended (Traub, 1996; Hayes, 1993; Gross-Schaefer *et al.*, 2000). Accordingly, most companies use a combination of four general prevention to limit sources of financial loss including: (a) pre-employment screening measures, (b) employee awareness programs, (c) employee or asset control policies, and (d) loss prevention and asset protection systems. In essence, such programs are based on deterrence principles which assert criminal behavior is the result of rational decision-making and opportunity. By limiting the opportunity to commit crime and/or increasing the certainty of apprehension, offenders will be less likely to commit a crime. As such, companies become more concerned with reducing the opportunity for crime rather than focusing on characteristics and motivations of offenders (Traub, 1996). In many ways, the prevention measures used by most corporations are closely related to Ronald Clarke's (1997) concept of situational crime prevention. This concept suggests retailers can prevent crime by manipulating the environment to make criminal opportunities less attractive. The following discussion will examine each strategy in more detail.

Pre-employment screening measures are designed to identify employees susceptible to criminal behavior. Such measures include multiple interviews, honesty tests, drug screening criminal, background checks, reference checks, and verification of past employment to name but a few. The use of multiple interviews provides employers with a sense of an applicant's demeanor and personality. Hayes (1993) points out that conducting at least two interviews allows employers to determine if an applicant is consistent and truthful in their responses or if they are being deceptive. Honesty tests are another method of determining the credibility of a potential employee. Since the enactment of the Polygraph Protection Act of 1988, US companies can no longer use lie detector tests during the screening process (Shepard and Dustin, 1988). Instead, many companies have turned to honesty tests which typically gauge an applicant's tolerance of deviant behaviors. Drug screening has proven to be an effective pre-vention measure since it immediately eliminates candidates that test positive. Likewise, criminal background, reference, and employment history checks imme-diately alert employers about applicants with less than exemplary criminal or work histories. According to Traub (1996), pre-employment screening strategies set the foundation for an effective crime prevention program. By preventing potentially deviant employees from entering the company, retailers can create an environment in which criminal practices are less likely to be developed or undertaken.

A second area in which companies attempt to prevent crime is through employee awareness programs. In general, these programs stress the importance of protecting company assets, the impact and costs associated with crime, and strategies to reduce criminal activity. Some examples of awareness measures are anonymous telephone hotlines so that employees can report wrongdoings, honesty or monetary incentives, training videos or programs, newsletters, and bulletin board notices and announcements. Since sales employees are the main defense against sources of financial loss, it is important for companies to develop programs that increase staff awareness or 'consciousness' concerning retail crime (Bamfield and Hollinger, 1996). In fact, employee commitment to the company has been shown to substantially reduce rates of inventory shrinkage (Hollinger and Dabney, 1994). A formal and consistent policy on issues related to theft alerts employees of the company's stance on crime and informs them of the con-sequences for violating such policies. Indeed, Traub (1996) notes the major purpose of employee awareness programs is to indicate that the company is serious about reducing crime. Not surprisingly, the use of certain awareness strategies have proven effective in reducing levels of inventory shrinkage. In par-ticular, companies that use honesty or monetary incentives, telephone hotlines, and periodic training lectures or programs have noticed declines in shrinkage rates (Traub, 1996).

A third type of prevention category companies rely on to control retail crimes include the use of employee or asset control policies. These include the use of cash register controls, inventory bar coding and scanning techniques, controlled cash handling procedures, and employee package checks. The use of point-of-sale (POS) exception-based reporting systems are employed to detect or track extraor-dinary register activity including voided sales, excessive refunds or discounts, and under-or-overcharges (Traub, 1996). In addition, companies use bar coding and scanning measures to prevent price switching and under-ringing of mer-chandise. The goal of these register controls is to quickly isolate employees involved in high-risk or questionable transactions (Hayes, 1993).

Increasingly, retailers have utilized electronic access controls to monitor and discourage employees from entering sensitive or restricted areas such as mer-chandise warehouses or cash handling areas. One of the more effective employee theft measures has been the use of periodic or daily merchandise audits. For instance, Masuda (1997) found that the use of a preventive audit survey (PAS) which consisted of daily cycle counts of camcorders and VCRs on display. These informal audits instantly lowered theft rates of these frequently stolen items. He asserted the drastic reduction was primarily due to the perceived risk and certainty of detection. In addition, Masuda discovered the PAS system also lowered theft rates of non-targeted products such as televisions, radar detectives and portable CD players. According to Clarke (1997), the implementation of prevention measures often creates a halo effect (called 'diffusion of benefits') whereby non-target crime items also experience a marked reduction in theft because opportunities for crime become uncertain and offenders perceive an increased risk of apprehension.

While the three previous categories focused primarily on internal threats (e.g. employees) to profits, the last prevention category centers on strategies to reduce external threats such as shoplifting. Most of these customer or loss prevention system techniques rely on surveillance and target hardening measures including closed-circuit televisions (CCTV), cameras, merchandise ink or electronic tags, the use of locks, alarms, and safes, and the use of store detectives or security personnel. Surveillance strategies significantly increase the risk of detection and apprehension, while target hardening devices attempt to physically obstruct offenders from valued merchandise by increasing the effort associated with committing crime.

Concerning surveillance measures, the presence of CCTV often serves as a psychological deterrence. Offenders know they are being closely monitored and thus will be more reluctant to commit an offense. In a study of supermarket thefts, the presence of CCTV dramatically lowered levels of shrinkage after being implemented (Brown, 1997). Similarly, security guards and store detectives also provide surveillance particularly over merchandise and items that can be concealed easily. Another monitoring strategy includes placing small and/or frequently stolen merchandise near employee work areas or stations.

Beyond surveillance or monitoring devices, retailers rely on several target hardening devices. For instance, electronic article surveillance (EAS) systems such as merchandise tags and electronic equipment source tags are specialized devices that can only be deactivated by cashiers using detachable machines. If illegally removed, audible alarms are sounded. In this way, EAS systems dramatically increase the risks of committing criminal offenses. Studies have shown that the use of EAS tags on clothing items significantly reduced levels of shoplifting (DiLonardo, 1997). Similar to EAS tags, retailers also rely on benefit denial devices (BDDs) such as fluid, ink, or mechanical tags that damage or destroy merchandise when tampered with (Hayes, 1993). Such devices remove the potential gain of stealing since offenders will be unable to use or re-sell these stolen goods.

Another loss prevention strategy company's use to limit customer theft is the use of refund controls. Challinger (1997) found that an authorization program introduced by Target stores reduced the number of customer-related frauds since 'proof of purchase' sales receipts were needed to obtain a refund. In essence, the refund system prevented offenders from stealing items and returning them for cash or store credits. The use of check approval screening systems also limits the ability of individual to fraudulently forge stolen checks.

In sum, the four major prevention categories including pre-employment screening measures, employee awareness programs, employee or asset control policies, and customer or loss prevention strategies are indicative of Ronald Clarke's (1997) concept of situational crime prevention. This concept refers to measures that manipulate the environment in order to reduce criminal opportunities. In effect, the situational crime prevention measures can make a company less vulnerable to victimization since these countermeasures can (1) increase the perceived effort of criminal behavior, (2) increase the perceived risks associated with crime, (3) reduce the anticipated rewards of crime, and (4) increase the shame or stigma related to criminal behavior. According to Clarke, these situational measures create physical and/or psychological deterrence barriers that make offending more difficult. While the use of these prevention strategies have proven to be effective, Shapland (1995) argues that many crime-prevention measures used by organizations have been implemented without regard to the actual crime problem and without consideration of location or geographic factors. In a study of manufacturing and wholesale organizations in England, Shapland (1995) found that the organizational design and layout as well as location were significantly related to the crime rate of the organization. Thus in order to develop effective crime prevention programs, organizations must implement policies that account for the potential impact of location factors.

Conclusion

It should be quite apparent by now to the reader that employee theft and staff dishonesty is not an easily understood phenomenon. It is hard to measure, difficult to theoretically explain, and almost impossible to prevent. Nevertheless, it has been well researched over the years, yielding a literature with many consistent findings and conclusions. First, while the typical worker is not dishonest, many employees do steal at work. In a typical year approximately one-third steal property and two-thirds engage in counter-productivity (i.e. production deviance) (Hollinger and Clark, 1983). Most do not think that what they are doing is very wrong, and some even justify their behavior. The majority of these employees feel disgruntled about their employers, supervisors, and workload. It should not be surprising then that one of the best predictors of employee deviance is the percentage of 'turnover' of staff in the workplace. People who are unhappy don't work productively, may steal, and eventually leave for 'greener pastures.' This should clearly suggest to employers that the way that employees are treated will affect every aspect of the work experience. Moreover, unhappy, marginalized and disgruntled staff will definitely be a detriment to the profitability and growth of the business in which they are employed. They will seek higher levels of remuneration, often in an illegal and unauthorized manner. Perhaps the old adage, 'pay me now or pay me later,' is an appropriate summary to the material covered in this chapter.

Key readings

The topic of employee theft and dishonesty has developed a long and distinguished literature. The most important works are listed below in alphabetical order by authors. An
excellent assessment of the subjective nature of theft is: Altheide, D.L., Adler, P.A.,
Adler, P. and Altheide, D.A. (1978). 'The social meanings of employee theft.' In
J.M. Johnson and J.D. Douglas (eds), *Crime at the Top*. Philadelphia: J.B. Lippincott. Even
after fifty years the classic study of convicted embezzlers is: Cressey, D.R. (1953). *Other
people's money*. Glencoe, IL: Free Press. One of the most important evaluations of the occupational subcultures of theft is: Ditton, J. (1977b). *'Part-time crime: An ethnography of fiddling
and pilferage.'* London: Macmillan. A concise statement using the 'distributive justice' explanations of employee dishonesty is: Greenberg, J. (1997a). 'A Social Influence Model of
Employee Theft: Beyond the Fraud Triangle.' In R.J. Lewicki, B.H. Sheppard and R.J. Bies
(eds), *Research on Negotiation in Organizations* (Vol. 5, pp. 29–51) Greenwich, CT: JAI Press. A
comprehensive explanatory model of theft from the point of view of the industrial/
organizational psychologist is: Greenberg, J. (1997b). 'The STEAL Motive: Managing the
Social Determinants of Employee Theft.' In R. Giacalone and J. Greenberg (eds), *Antisocial
Behavior in Organizations* (pp. 85–108) Thousand Oaks, CA: Sage. The largest and most comprehensive empirical study of employee theft ever conducted was by done by Hollinger,
Richard C. and Clark, John P. (1983a). *Theft by Employees*. Lexington, MA: Lexington Books.
Using their multi-industry, multi-city data set, Hollinger and Clark specifically examined
the effects of deterrence on theft in: Hollinger, R.C. and Clark, J.P. (1983b). 'Deterrence in
the workplace: Perceived certainty, Perceived severity and employee theft.' *Social Forces 62*:
398–418. A short but concise overview of employee dishonesty written with a specific focus
on training managers about the problem is: Hollinger, R.C. (1989). *Dishonesty in the workplace: A manager's guide to preventing employee theft*. Park Ridge, IL: London House Press.
Finally, Gerald Mars developed a comprehensive explanatory model of stealing in the
workplace from the perspective of the cultural anthropologist in: Mars, G. (1982). *Cheats at
work: An anthropology of workplace crime*. London: George Allen & Unwin.

References

Adams, J.S. (1965) 'Inequity in Social Exchange.' In L. Berkowitz (ed.) *Advances in
Experimental Social Psychology*. Vol. 2. (pp. 267–99). New York: Academic Press.
Adams, V. (1981) 'How to Keep 'em Honest: Honesty as an Organizational Policy Can Help
Prevent Employee Theft.' *Psychology Today*, 15 (11): 50, 53.
Albrecht, W.S. and Wernz, G.W. (1993) 'The Three Factors of Fraud.' *Security Management*
(July): 95–7.
Altheide, D.L., Adler, P.A., Adler, P. and Altheide, D.A. (1978) 'The Social Meanings of
Employee Theft.' In J.M. Johnson and J.D. Douglas (eds), *Crime at the Top*. Philadelphia:
J.B. Lippincott.
Association of Certified Fraud Examiners (2004) *Report to the Nation on Occupational Fraud
and Abuse*. http://www.cfenet.com/pdfs/2004RttN.pdf
Astor, S.D. (1972) 'Who's Doing the Stealing?' *Management Review, 61* (May): 34–5.
Bacas, H. (1987) 'To Stop a Thief.' *Nation's Business* (June): 16–23.
Baker, M.A. and Westin, A.F. (1988) *Employer Perceptions of Workplace Crime*. Washington,
DC: Bureau of Justice Statistics, US Department of Justice.
Bamfield, J. and Hollinger, R.C. (1996) 'Managing Losses in the Retail Store: A Comparison of
Loss Prevention Activity in the United States and Great Britain.' *Security Journal*, 7: 61–70.
Baumer, T.L. and Rosenbaum, D.P. (1984) *Combating Retail Theft: Programs and Strategies*.
Boston: Butterworth.
Baumgartner, M.P. (1984) 'Social Control from Below' pp. 303–45 in *Toward a General
Theory of Social Control Vol. I* by D. Black. Orlando, FL: Academic Press.
Beccaria, C. (1764) *On Crimes and Punishments*. Philadelphia: Philip H. Nicklin.
Bensman, J. and Gerver, I. (1963) 'Crime and Punishment in the Factory: The Function of
Deviancy in Maintaining the Social System.' *American Sociological Review, 28* : 588–98.

Bentham, J. (1789) *An Introduction to the Principles of Morals and Legislation*. New York: Macmillan.

Brown, B. (1997) 'CCTV in Three Town Centers in England.' In Ronald V. Clarke (ed.) *Situational Crime Prevention: Successful Case Studies*, 2nd edition. New York: Harrow and Heston.

Challinger, D. (1997) 'Refund Fraud in Retail Stores' pp. 250–62 in *Situational crime prevention*, 2nd edn edited by R.V. Clarke. Guilderland, NY: Harrow and Heston.

Cherrington, D.J. and Cherrington, J.O. (1985) 'The Climate of Honesty in Retail Stores.' In Terris W. (ed.) *Employee Theft: Research, Theory, and Applications*. Park Ridge, Illinois: London House Press.

Clark, J.P. and Hollinger, R.C. (1979) 'Workplace Theft.' *Assets Protection, 4* (December): 33–5.

Clark, J.P. and Hollinger, R.C. (1980) 'Theft by Employees.' *Security Management, 24* (September): 106–10.

Clarke, R.V. (1997) *Situational Crime Prevention*, 2nd edition. Guiderland, NY: Harrow and Heston.

Clinard, M.B. and Quinney, R. (1973) *Criminal Behavior Systems*. 2nd edn. New York: Holt, Rinehart and Winston.

Cohen, L.E. and Felson, M. (1979) 'Social Change and Crime Rate Trends: A Routine Activities Approach.' *American Sociological Review*, 44: 588–608.

Consumer Reports (2002) Vol. 67 (10: 10). 'Retail Theft: The Crime Tax.'

Cornish, D. and Clarke, R.V. (1986) *The Reasoning Criminal*. New York: Springer-Verlag.

Cressey, D.R. (1953) *Other People's Money*. Glencoe, IL: Free Press.

Dalton, M. (1959) *Men who manage*. New York: John Wiley.

Delaney, J. (1993) 'Handcuffing Employee Theft.' *Small Business Report, 18*(7): 29–38.

DiLonardo, R.L. (1997) 'The Economic Benefit of Electronic Article Surveillance,' pp. 122–31 in *Situational Crime Prevention*, 2nd edition edited by R.V. Clarke. Guilderland, NY: Harrow and Heston.

Ditton, J. (1977a) 'Perks, Pilferage, and the Fiddle: The Historical Structure of Invisible Wages.' *Theory and Society, 4:* 39–71.

Ditton, J. (1977b) *Part-time Crime: An Ethnography of Fiddling and Pilferage*. London: Macmillan.

Franklin, A.P. (1975) *Internal Theft in a Retail Organization: A Case Study*. Ph.D. dissertation, The Ohio State University. Ann Arbor, Michigan: University Microfilms.

Friedrichs, D. (2004) 'Enron et al.: Paradigmatic White Collar Crime Cases for the New Century.' *Critical Criminology, 12*: 113–32.

Giacalone, R.A. and Rosenfeld, P. (1987) 'Reasons for Employee Sabotage in the Workplace.' *Journal of Business and Psychology, 1*: 367–78.

Giacalone, R.A. and Greenberg, J. (1997) *Antisocial Behavior in Organizations*. Thousand Oaks, CA: Sage.

Gouldner, A.W. (1954) *Wildcat Strike: A Study in Worker-management Relationships*. New York: Harper and Row.

Greenberg, J. (1990) 'Employee Theft as a Reaction to Underpayment Inequity: The Hidden Costs of Pay Cuts.' *Journal of Applied Psychology, 75*: 561–8.

Greenberg, J. (1993) 'Stealing in the Name of Justice: Informational and Interpersonal Moderators of Theft Reactions to Underpayment Inequity.' *Organizational Behavior and Human Decision Processes, 54:* 81–103.

Greenberg, J. and Scott, K.S. (1996) 'Why Do Workers Bite the Hands That Feed Them? Employee Theft as a Social Exchange Process.' In B.M. Staw and L.L. Cummings (eds), *Research in Organizational Behavior, 18*: 111–56. Greenwich, CT: JAI Press.

Greenberg, J. (1997) 'The STEAL Motive: Managing the Social Determinants of Employee Theft. In R. Giacalone and J. Greenberg (eds), *Antisocial Behavior in Organizations*, 85–108. Thousand Oaks, CA: Sage.

Greenberg, L. and Barling, J. (1996) 'Employee Theft.' In C.L. Cooper and D.M. Rousseau (eds), *Trends in Organizational Behavior, 3*: 49–64. New York: Wiley.

Gross-Schaefer, A., Trigilio, J., Negus, J. and Ro, C-S. (2000) 'Ethics Education in the workplace: An Effective Tool to Combat Employee Theft.' *Journal of Business Ethics, 26*: 89–100.

Harris, D.K. and Benson, M.L. (1998) 'Nursing Home Theft: The Hidden Problem.' *Journal of Aging Studies, 12*: 57–67.

Hayes, R. (1993) *Employee theft control.* Orlando, FL: Prevention Press.

Hollinger, R.C. and Clark, J.P. (1982a) 'Employee Deviance: A Response to the Perceived Quality of the Work Experience.' *Work and Occupations, 9*: 97–114.

Hollinger, R.C. and Clark, J.P. (1982b) 'Formal and Informal Social Controls of Employee Deviance.' *The Sociological Quarterly, 23*: 333–43.

Hollinger, R.C. and Clark, J.P. (1983a) *Theft by Employees.* Lexington, MA: Lexington Books.

Hollinger, R.C. and Clark, J.P. (1983b) 'Deterrence in the Workplace: Perceived Certainty, Perceived Severity and Employee Theft.' *Social Forces 62*: 398–418.

Hollinger, R.C. (1986) 'Acts Against the Workplace: Social Bonding and Employee Deviance.' *Deviant Behavior: An Interdisciplinary Journal, 7*: 53–75.

Hollinger, R.C. (1989) *Dishonesty in the workplace: A Manager's Guide to Preventing Employee Theft.* Park Ridge, IL: London House Press.

Hollinger, R.C. (1991) 'Neutralizing in the Workplace: An Empirical Analysis of Property Theft and Production Deviance.' *Deviant Behavior: An Interdisciplinary Journal, 12*: 169–202.

Hollinger, R.C., Slora, K.B. and Terris, W. (1992) 'Deviance in the Fast-food Restaurant: Correlates of Employee Theft, Altruism, and Counter Productivity.' *Deviant Behavior. An Interdisciplinary Journal, 13*: 255–84.

Hollinger, R.C. and Langton, L. (2004) *2003 National Retail Security Survey: Final Report.* Gainesville, FL: Security Research Project, University of Florida.

Hollinger, R.C. and Dabney, D. (1994) 'Reducing Shrinkage in the Retail Store: It's Not Just a Job for the Loss Prevention Department.' *Security Journal, 5*: 2–10.

Horning, D.N.M. (1970) 'Blue Collar Theft: Conceptions of Property, Attitudes toward Pilfering, and Work Group Norms in a Modern Industrial Plant.' In E.O. Smigel and H.L. Ross (eds), *Crimes Against the Bureaucracy.* New York: Van Nostrand Reinhold.

Huiras, J., Uggen, C. and McMorris, B. (2000) 'Career Jobs, Survival Jobs, and Employee Deviance: A Social Investment Model of Workplace Misconduct.' *The Sociological Quarterly, 41*: 245–63.

Jaspan, N. (1974) *Mind Your Own Business.* Englewood Cliffs, NJ: Prentice Hall.

Jones, D.C. (1972) 'Employee Theft in Organizations.' *Society for the Advancement of Management, 37*: 59–63.

Kamp, J. and Brooks, P. (1991) 'Perceived Organizational Climate and Employee Counter-productivity.' *Journal of Business and Psychology, 5*(4): 447–58.

Kemper, T.D. (1966) 'Representative Roles and the Legitimization of Deviance.' *Social Problems, 13*: 288–98.

Kraut, R.E. (1976) 'Deterrent and Definitional Influences on Shoplifting.' *Social Problems 23*: 358–68.

Kuratko, D.F., Hornsby, J.S., Naffziger, D.W. and Hodgetts, R.M. (2000) 'Crime and Small Business: An Exploratory Study of Cost and Prevention Issues in US Firms.' *Journal of Small Business Management, 38.*

Kurks, M.L. (1991) 'Dishonesty, Corruption, and White-Collar Crime: Predicting Honesty and Integrity in the Workplace.' *Forensic Reports, 4*: 149–62.

Lary, B.K. (1988, May) 'Thievery on the Inside.' *Security Management, 32*: 79–84.

Lipman, M. (1973) 'Stealing: How America's Employees are Stealing their Companies Blind.' New York: Harper's Magazine Press.

Lipman, M. (1988) 'Employee Theft: A $40 Billion Industry.' *The Annals of the American Academy of Political and Social Sciences, 498*: 51–9.

Mangione, T.W. and Quinn, R.P. (1975) 'Job Satisfaction, Counter-productive Behavior, and Drug Use at Work.' *Journal of Applied Psychology, 11*: 114–16.

Mars, G. (1973) 'Chance, Punters, and the Fiddle: Institutionalized Pilferage in a Hotel Dining Room. In M. Warner (ed.), *The Sociology of the Workplace*. New York: Halsted Press.

Mars, G. (1974) 'Dock pilferage: A Case Study in Occupational Theft.' In P. Rock and M. McIntosh (eds), *Deviance and Social Control*, pp. 209–28. London: Tavistock.

Mars, G. (1982) *Cheats at Work: An Anthropology of Workplace Crime*. London: George Allen & Unwin.

Masuda, B. (1997) 'Reduction in Employee Theft in a Retail Environment: Displacement vs. diffusion of benefits,' pp. 183–90 in *Situational Crime Prevention*, 2nd edition edited by R.V. Clarke. Guilderland, NY: Harrow and Heston.

Matza, D. (1964) *Delinquency and Drift*. New York: Wiley.

Merriam, D. (1977) 'Employee theft.' *Criminal Justice Abstracts, 9*: 380–6.

Murphy, K.R. (1993) *Honesty in the Workplace*. Belmont, CA: Brooks Cole.

Mustaine, E. and Tewksbury, R. (2002) 'Workplace Theft: An Analysis of Student-employee Offenders and Job Attributes.' *American Journal of Criminal Justice, 27*(1): 111–27.

Neihoff, B.P. and Paul, R.J. (2000) 'Causes of Employee Theft and Strategies that HR Managers Can Use for Prevention.' *Human Resource Management, 39*(1): 51–64.

Oliphant, B.J. and Oliphant, G.C. (2001) 'Using a Behavior-based Method to Identify and Reduce Employee Theft.' *International Journal of Retail & Distribution Management, 10*: 442–51.

Ott, S.J. (1989) The *Organizational Culture Perspective*. Pacific Grove, CA: Brooks/Cole.

Parilla, P.F., Hollinger, R.C. and Clark, J.P. (1988) 'Organizational Control of Deviant Behavior: The Case of Employee Theft.' *Social Science Quarterly, 69*: 261–80.

Paternoster, R. and Simpson, S. (1993) 'A Rational Choice Theory of Corporate Crime,' pp. 37–58 in *Routine Activity and Rational Choice: Advances in Criminological Theory*, edited by R.V. Clarke and M. Felson. New Brunswick, NJ: Transaction Books.

Robin, G. (1969) 'Employees as Offenders.' *Journal of Research on Crime and Delinquency, 6*: 17–33.

Robin, G. (1970) 'The Corporate and Judicial Disposition of Employee Thieves.' In E.O. Smigel and H.L. Ross (eds), *Crimes against bureaucracy*. New York: Van Nostrand Reinhold.

Robin, G. (1974) 'White Collar Crime and Employee Theft.' *Crime and Delinquency, 20*: 251–62.

Robinson, S.L. and Greenberg, J. (1998) 'What's So Deviant About Organizational Deviance?' In D.M. Rousseau and C.L. Cooper (eds), *Trends in Organizational Behavior, 5*. New York: Wiley.

Robinson, S.L. (1998) 'Monkey See, Monkey Do.' *Academy of Management Journal 41*: 658–72.

Roethlisberger, F. and Dickson, W.J. (1939) *Management and the Worker*. Cambridge, Massachusetts: Harvard University Press.

Roy, D.F. (1952) 'Quota Restrictions and Goldbricking in a Machine Shop.' *American Journal of Sociology, 57*: 427–42.

Roy, D.F. (1953) 'Work Satisfaction and Social Reward in Quota Achievement: An Analysis of Piecework Incentive.' *American Sociological Review, 18*: 507–14.

Roy, D.F. (1954) 'Efficiency and the "Fix": Informal Intergroup Relations in a Piecework Machine Shop.' *American Journal of Sociology, 60*: 255–66.

Roy, D.F. (1959) 'Banana Time: Job Satisfaction and Informal Interaction.' *Human Organization, 18*: 158–68.

Ruggiero, W.G.E. and Steinberg, L.D. (1982) 'Occupational Deviance Among Adolescent Workers.' *Youth & Society, 13*(4): 423–48.

Shapland, J. (1995) 'Preventing Retail-sector Crimes,' pp. 263–342 in *Building a Safer Society Volume 19* edited by M. Tonry and D.P. Farrington. Chicago: The University of Chicago Press.

Shepard, I.M. and Duston, R. (1988) *Thieves at Work: An Employer's Guide to Combating Workplace Dishonesty*. Washington, DC: The Bureau of National Affairs.

Shover, N. and Hochstetler, A. (2002) 'Cultural Explanation and Organizational Crime.' *Crime, Law, & Social Change, 37:* 1–18.

Sieh, E.W. (1987) 'Garment Workers: Perceptions of Inequity and Employee Theft.' *British Journal of Criminology, 27:* 174–90.

Slora, K.B. (1989) 'An Empirical Approach to Determining Employee Deviance Base Rates.' *Journal of Business and Psychology,* 4(2): 199–219.

Smigel, E.O. (1956) 'Public Attitudes Toward Stealing as Related to the Size of the Victim Organization.' *American Sociological Review, 21:* 320–7.

Stone, D.G. (1990) *April Fools: An Insider's Account of the Rise and Collapse of Drexel Burnham.* New York: Donald Fine Company.

Sutherland, E.H. (1949) *White Collar Crime.* New York: Dryden Press.

Sykes, G. and Matza, D. (1957) 'Techniques of Neutralization: A Theory of Delinquency.' *American Sociological Review, 22:* 664–70.

Tatham, R.L. (1974) 'Employees' Views on Theft in Retailing.' *Journal of Retailing,* Fall: 49–55.

Taylor, L. and Walton, P. (1971) 'Industrial Sabotage: Motives and Meanings.' In S. Cohen (ed.), *Images of Deviance.* London: Penguin.

Terris, W. and Jones, J. (1982) 'Psychological Factors Related to Employees' Theft in the Convenience Store Industry.' *Psychological Reports, 51:* 1219–38.

Terris, W. (1985) *Employee Theft: Research, Theory, and Applications.* Park Ridge, Illinois: London House Press.

Thomas, P., Wolper, R., Scott, K. and Jones, D. (2001) 'The Relationship Between Immediate Turnover and Employee Theft in the Restaurant Industry.' *Journal of Business and Psychology,* 15(4): 561–77.

Trevino, L.X. and Youngblood, S.A. (1990) 'Bad Apples in Bad Barrels: A Causal Analysis of Ethical Decision-making Behavior.' *Journal of Applied Psychology, 75:* 378–81.

Traub, S.H. (1996) 'Battling Employee crime: A review of corporate strategies and programs.' *Crime and Delinquency, 42:* 244–56.

Tucker, J. (1989) 'Employee Theft as Social Control.' *Deviant Behavior, 10:* 319–34.

US Department of Commerce (1976a) *The Cost of Crimes Against Business.* Bureau of Domestic Commerce, Domestic and International Business Administration. Washington, DC: Superintendent of Documents.

US Department of Commerce (1976b) *Crimes Against Business: A Management Perspective.* Proceedings of a seminar held September 14, 1976 in New York, N.Y. Office of Business Research and Analysis, Bureau of Domestic Commerce, Domestic and International Business Administration. Washington, DC: Superintendent of Documents.

Vaughan, D. (1998) 'Rational Choice, Situated Action, and Social Control of Organizations.' *Law & Society Review, 32:* 23–61.

Wimbash, J.C. and Dalton, D.R. (1997) 'Base Rate for Employee Theft: Convergence of Multiple Methods.' *Journal of Applied Psychology, 82:* 756–63.

Zeitlin, L. (1971) 'A Little Larceny Can Do a Lot for Employee Morale.' *Psychology Today 5* (June): 22, 24, 26, and 64.

10
The Extent, Nature and Responses to Workplace Violence Globally: Issues and Findings

Elena Licu and Bonnie S. Fisher

Introduction

Workplace violence (WV) transcends national and international borders; it happens to employees in all types of job settings and occupation categories (Chappell and Di Martino, 1998a). Current workplace practices, cultural and organizational norms, and social structures continue to place workers' lives at risk of victimization. A lack of clear definitions of WV, the absence of formal legislation and, in some cases, organization-specific policies to adequately regulate and penalize violent behavior in the workplace, and the existence of cultural values that tolerate violent behavior are some of the contributing factors for WV (see Verdugo and Vere, 2003; Chappell and Di Martino, 2000). WV is a concern for all parties who have a vested interest in creating and maintaining a safe work environment. As the International Covenant of Economic, Social and Cultural Rights highlighted, WV is a human rights violation, as everyone is guaranteed the fundamental right to 'safe and healthy working conditions.' (1966, art. 7(b))

The global economic costs of WV are staggering. Annual estimates for the United States alone, suggest that there are between three million (using National Crime Victimization Survey data) and seven million (using National Violence Against Women data) lost work days per year, with a lower bound estimate of losses of $192 million shared by the victims and their employers (Farmer and Tiefenthaler, 2004). Further, research has established that experiencing violence at work takes a severe toll on the physical and mental health of the employee-victim and co-workers alike (see Fisher and Peek-Asa, 2005). The financial costs coupled with negative health effects are reasons why interested parties across the globe are steadfastly working to educate employers and employees as to the effects of WV and developing prevention and reaction policies and programs to reduce the incidence of such violence (International Labor Organization, 2003).

Routine international media coverage of sensational violent incidents in the workplace has brought much attention to this distinct category of crime. It is important to recognize, however, that such accounts mask the day-to-day risks that employees experience while on the job. The real image of WV moves beyond the media's breaking news: Disgruntled employees stalking, attacking or killing former or current superiors or co-workers due to stresses related to massive layoffs or an overall increasingly harsh working environment (Chappell and Di Martino, 2000).

These sensationalistic accounts of WV need to be tempered by a close examination of how WV has been defined and measured, by its extent and nature. This chapter examines these issues and discusses the impact and costs of WV, contributing risk factors, and current WV responses and prevention efforts. As shown throughout the chapter, researchers have made progress to advance our understanding of WV and related issues.

The chapter is organized into seven main sections. Section one defines WV and discusses four types of violence that have been the focus of research studies across a variety of disciplines. Section two acknowledges limitations related to WV measurement, data, and information availability. Section three examines the extent and nature of WV at global, regional, and national levels. Section four documents the impact and costs of WV on individuals, organizations, and society at large. The fifth section reviews the factors contributing to WV, including individual, organizational, situational, and structural characteristics. Section six outlines several responses to WV that have been offered by vested stakeholders, such as local and national governments, regional and international governing bodies and agencies, trade unions, organizations, and collaborations among law-enforcement and other community partners. Finally, section seven examines WV prevention, discussing evaluation and implementation challenges, as well as outlining appropriate recommendations.

What is violence in the workplace?

Defining what the concept 'violence in the workplace' entails is a challenging task in part because there is no internationally agreed definition of WV (Chappell and Di Martino, 2000). A commonly used definition, however, has been recently agreed to by the European Commission: 'Incidents where persons are abused, threatened or assaulted in circumstances related to their work, involving an explicit or implicit challenge to their safety, well-being, or health.' (cited in Leather *et al.*, 1999) The International Labor Organization (ILO) has defined violence to cover both physical and psychological behaviors. That is 'any attack, assault or threat that results in physical injury or in the psychological stress of an individual or group.' (Verdugo and Vere, 2003) Such actions, incidents or behaviors may take place between employees, including managers and supervisors (internal WV) or between employees and other persons present at the workplace such as, customers, clients or the general public (external WV), and occur during or as a result of one's work (ILO, 2003). In Australia, a widely used definition of occupational violence has been put forth by the National Occupational Health and Safety Commission (NOHSC): '[T]he attempted or actual exercise by a person of any force so as to cause injury to a worker, including any threatening statement or behavior which gives a worker a reasonable cause to believe he or she is at risk.' (1999: 1) In Britain, the Health and Safety Executive (HSE), in charge of regulating health and safety related risks in the workplace, defines work-related violence as: 'Any incident in which a person is abused, threatened or assaulted in circumstances related to their work.' (http://www.hse.gov.uk/violence/index.htm) This includes verbal abuse, threats, and physical attacks.

A generally accepted classification of WV by many disciplines is the 'three-types' classification developed by California Occupational Safety and Health Administration (Cal/OSHA) (Cal/OSHA, 1995). As can be seen in Table 10.1, the three types, external/intrusive violence, consumer/client-related violence, and relationship violence are based on the perpetrator's relationship to the workplace. Bowie (2005) has expanded the original Cal/OSHA typology to include a fourth category, organizational violence.

These four types of WV have been the focus of several published studies across a variety of disciplines, including criminology, psychology, law, economics, business, public health, and nursing (see Farmer and Tiefenthaler, 2004; Gill, Fisher,

Table 10.1   Expanded workplace violence typology

Type 1: External/Intrusive violence – Perpetrator has no legitimate relationship with the workplace or its employees
Criminal intent by strangers Terrorist acts Protest violence Mental illness or drug related aggression Random violence
Type 2: Consumer related violence – Perpetrator has a legitimate relationship with the workplace and commits violent acts during a work-related interaction
Consumer/clients/patients (and family) violence against staff Vicarious trauma to staff Staff violence to clients/consumers
Type 3: Relationship violence – Perpetrator may or may not have a legitimate relationship with the workplace but has a personal relationship with an employee
Staff on staff violence & bullying Domestic violence and sexual harassment at work Third party violence
Type 4: Organizational violence – Organizations are structured and managed in ways that may contribute to violence against workers and clients. Perpetrator has a legitimate relationship with the workplace.
Organizational violence against staff Organizational violence against consumers / clients / patients Organizational violence against other organizations or communities

Source: Bowie, 2005.

232 The Handbook of Security

Table 10.2   Types of violence and violent behaviors in the workplace

Type of Violence	Behavior
Physical	Assault/Attack (e.g. kicking, punching, scratching, squeezing, pinching and biting) Robbery Rape Homicide
Psychological	Bullying or Mobbing Threats or intimidation (e.g. swearing, shouting and interfering with work tools and equipment) Harassment (e.g. sexual, racial, and ethnic slurs, remarks and behavior) Stalking Deliberate silence Ostracism (e.g. exclusion or isolation)

and Bowie, 2002; Spector and Fox, 2005; Wilkinson and Peek-Asa, 2003). Within these types of WV, employee-initiated violence has captured much scholarly attention (and media, too) (for a discussion of the research within each type, see LeBlanc and Barling, 2005).

Domestic violence, including intimate partner violence, and stalking are rarely acknowledged in the WV research. However, this may be changing as researchers document the incidence of each spilling over in the workplace (both victimization and perpetration) and reveal the physical and psychological toll domestic violence and stalking have on abused employee, the perpetrator-employee, co-workers, and the costs to businesses (see Fisher and Peek-Asa, 2005; Rugala and Issacs, 2004).

As shown in Table 10.2, WV covers a wide range of types of violence that include physical and psychological behaviors, which are often interrelated and overlapping. To illustrate, psychological violence, in the form of threats or intimidation, often precludes physical violence such as attacks or assaults. Some of these actions are perceived differently across various contexts and cultures (Chappell and DiMartino, 1998a). Perception and understanding of sexual offenses, for example, and the attitudes and concerns about these crimes in the workplace, vary greatly from one country to another. Cultural differences play an important role. In a number of European countries, sexual harassment at work is associated with deeply rooted stereotypes about the social roles of males and females (Paoli and Merllié, 2001; Di Martino et al., 2003).

Measurement: data limitations and information availability

How much WV is there is a question that no one government agency, private firm, or research study can answer with certainty for two primary reasons. First, there are data limitations in that very few valid and reliable WV statistics are currently available. Second, and highly correlated with the first reason, there is a lack of responsibility in many countries, at least until recently, to systematically and routinely collect such information using either official law enforcement data systems or victimization survey data. Some exceptions, however, are the United States, England and Wales, Australia, and the European Union (EU) (Chappell and Di Martino, 2000). Individually many countries do not collect WV statistics. They depend on international organizations, such as the ILO or the UN, to periodically collect such data and disseminate it publicly. Both issues are more fully discussed below.

Data limitations

There are a handful of data sources in which WV estimates can be calculated. Among the international sources of WV is the International Crime Victimization Survey (ICVS). The survey has been conducted four times over a period of 12 years and provides self-reported victimization data from respondents in 25 industrialized countries and 46 cities across the globe (see Nieuwbeerta, 2002). Regional data sources, such as the European Survey on Working Conditions carried out every five years since 1990, provide significant insight about the risks of WV within the European Union countries (Paoli and Merllié, 2001). An ongoing national-level data source since 1982, conducted annually since 2001–2002, among the most frequently cited ones with respect to WV, is the British Crime Survey (BCS) (Budd, 2001; Upson, 2004). In the United States, the National Traumatic Occupational Fatalities (NTOF) and the Bureau of Labor Statistics (BLS) National Census for Fatal Occupational Injuries (for a more detailed description, see Bulatao and VandenBos, 1996: 4–8) are two national surveillance systems of workplace homicide. The National Crime Victimization Survey (NCVS), another on-going annual survey since the 1970s, provides estimates of non-fatal WV (Bachman, 1994; Warchol, 1998; Duhart, 2001). Each of these sources provides WV information, yet, note that none of these sources was specifically designed to identify the intersection between violence and the workplace or while at work.

Analysing WV data for comparative purposes is a difficult task. In addition to the limitations inherent in any crime or victimization data nationally, regionally and internationally WV research is fraught with unique measurement issues including: (1) the lack of agreement about how to define violence, work, and workplace; (2) the various approaches to measuring and operationalizing key violence constructs (e.g. the two distinct ways used to measure psychological violence render significantly different prevalence rates); and (3) different reporting practices due to different sensitivity to WV in different contexts and/or cultures (Licu *et al.*, 2005; Salin, 2001 cited in Di Martino *et al.*, 2003). For example, workplace victimization of women, in countries where obtaining employment outside the home is difficult, may go unreported as many women fear losing their jobs.

The definitions of the concepts 'violence,' and 'at or during work' or 'the workplace' vary across nations (Chappell and Di Martino, 2000). Sometime WV is broadly defined to incorporate perpetrators who are employed within the organization and those who do have a legitimate reason to be at the workplace, such as customer or patient, and those who do not have such reason, like someone who wanders off the street (Di Martino *et al.*, 2003). Some definitions exclude violence directed at property or psychological violence (Chappell and Di Martino, 2000).

Even across jurisdictions within a given country, such as in Australia, the legal elements necessary to define various crimes of violence can differ (Mukherjee, 1981). Finally, the definition of work or the workplace varies among official crime statistics, as some data reflect only violent offenses committed in traditional workplaces such as, offices, banks, schools, excluding mobile or geographically diverse occupational settings (Chappell and Di Martino, 2000). Estimating the extent of WV thus varies widely across individual countries, as no international set of standards in defining this crime has been developed to date (see Chappell and Di Martino, 2000; Alvazzi del Frate *et al.*, 2000). As a result, any comparisons must be mindful of these issues and their effects on the estimates of the extent of WV.

Information availability

Throughout this chapter an international perspective is presented. Due to the availability of cross-national WV data and published research in the English language, however, the discussion is bounded to those nations, regions, and international agencies (e.g. England and Wales, the United States, Canada, Australia, the European Union, and the UN's ILO) that publish WV estimates and relevant information in English and make publicly available printed or web-based reports, articles, or books.

Extent and nature of WV

Global trends

There are four primary sources of the extent and nature of WV globally. Each source is collected by different sponsors and hence the measurement issues discussed in the last section apply accordingly. Below each source is described.

International Crime Victimization Survey

The survey data collected by the ICVS in its third sweep (1996) measured, for the first time, workplace victimization (note that no definition of workplace was provided to respondents, see Chappell and Di Martino, 2000). This multinational comparative survey-based data are one of the most important sources of international information about violence at work. Approximately 130,000 employees aged 16 and over were randomly selected from 32 countries across the world (between 1000 and 2000 respondents per area surveyed). The respondents were interviewed about their experiences of sexual victimization (women only) and assaults and/or threats (of non-sexual nature) in several contexts, including at work (see 1996 questionnaires in ICVS, 1999). The main findings are summarized in Table 10.3.

Table 10.3 Prevalence rates of workplace victimization by type of incident, gender, region and country, ICVS 1996 (percentages)

Region/Country	Assaults*		Sexual Incidents#
	Male	Female	Female Only
Western Europe^	**3.6**	**3.6**	**7.0**
Austria	0.0	0.8	0.8
England & Wales	3.2	6.3	8.6
Northern Ireland	2.3	3.7	6.0
Scotland	3.1	2.6	6.2
France	11.2	8.9	19.8
Finland	3.1	4.3	6.6
Netherlands	3.6	3.8	7.6
Sweden	1.7	1.7	3.5
Switzerland	4.3	1.6	4.8
Countries in transition	**2.0**	**1.4**	**3.0**
Albania	0.4	0.4	0.8
Czech Republic	1.9	0.8	2.3
Georgia	1.7	0.9	2.1
Hungary	0.6	0.0	0.5
Kyrgyzstan	2.5	3.4	5.3
Latvia	1.0	0.8	1.5
Macedonia (former Yugoslavia)	0.8	0.5	1.4
Mongolia	1.4	1.6	2.8
Poland	0.9	1.3	1.9
Romania	8.7	4.1	10.8
Russian Federation	0.4	0.5	0.9
Yugoslavia (Federal Republic)	3.2	2.4	5.8
North America	**2.5**	**4.6**	**7.5**
Canada	3.9	5.0	9.7
United States	1.0	4.2	5.3
Latin America	**1.9**	**3.6**	**5.2**
Argentina	6.1	11.8	16.6
Bolivia	0.4	0.9	1.3
Brazil	0.2	0.4	0.8
Costa Rica	0.8	1.4	2.2
Asia	**0.4**	**1.0**	**1.3**
Indonesia	0.3	1.1	1.5
Philippines	0.5	0.8	1.0
Africa	**2.3**	**1.9**	**3.7**
South Africa	0.7	0.7	1.3
Uganda	3.2	4.3	7.2
Zimbabwe	3.0	0.7	2.6

Source: ILO, 1998 (http://www.ilo.org/public/english/bureau/inf/pr/1998/30.htm#N_2_)
* Defined as threat or physical attack of a non-sexual nature;
# Defined as rape, attempted rape, indecent assault, and offensive behavior, including harassment;
^ A discrepancy in the workplace victimization prevalence rates for the Western European region has been noted between rates reported in this table and those reported by ILO (2000) elsewhere, (see http://www.ilo.org/public/english/protection/safework/violence/intro/htm)

As Table 10.3 shows, the highest percentages of workplace victimization were observed for sexual incidents including rape, attempted rape, indecent assault and offensive behavior (including harassment). Victimization of both men and women were highest in industrial countries (Western Europe and North America). Rates of assault and sexual incidents of females were highest in North America, followed by Western Europe and Latin America.

In general, victimization risk in the workplace was higher for females than for males. On average, 10 percent of all the acts involving women victims, particularly sexual harassment and non-sexual assaults, happened at work (ICVS cited in Chappell and Di Martino, 2000).

Thirteen percent of all the incidents involving male victims occurred in the workplace. Workplace victimization affected victims aged 25 to 49. Female victims were, on average, younger than their male counterparts. Between 10 and 15 percent of females who have been assaulted reported being threatened with a weapon, while less than 5 percent of victims of attempted rape and indecent assault reported such experience. Finally, females and males alike were more likely to report victimization in the workplace (i.e. non-sexual assaults) to police and other authorities, compared to victimization that happened elsewhere (ICVS cited in Chappell and Di Martino, 2000).

International Commercial Crime Survey

Another source of information about violence at work at the international level is the International Commercial Crime Survey (ICCS) (Chappell and Di Martino, 2000). The ICCS is a survey of crime against businesses. It was conducted in 1994, when eight countries participated in the project. The results showed a high rate of crime victimization among retail businesses that resulted in significant financial costs. More than 25 percent of businesses in the retail sector reported to have been burgled during the previous year. Although personal or violent crimes such as robbery and assaults were reported less frequently, they too resulted in high financial costs, but also caused fear, anxiety and physical trauma they caused to workers and/or to organizations (Chappell and Di Martino, 2000).

Multi-agency sponsors

The third source of international information about WV is represented by specific country case studies or reports about a specific type of violence (e.g. sexual harassment) commissioned by and developed under the auspices of international organizations such as the ILO, the World Health Organization (WHO), the International Council of Nurses (ICN), and Public Services International (PSI). One example is a one-time multinational case study of WV in the health sector (Di Martino, 2002). Health sector personnel and other stakeholders, such as unions, employers' organizations, private owners of health services, and health authorities in seven countries (Brazil, Bulgaria, Lebanon, Portugal, South Africa, Thailand and Australia) participated in the study. Among the findings that were reported, 50 percent of the health care workers surveyed experienced at least one incident of physical or psychological violence during the 12 months before the survey was conducted. Variation across countries was reported. For example 75.8 percent of the health care workers in Bulgaria annually experienced at least one incident of either types of violence, followed by 67.2 percent in Australia, 61 percent in South Africa, 60 percent in Portugal, 54 percent in Thailand, and 46.7 percent in Brazil (Di Martino, 2002: 16). Verbal abuse was found to be widespread in all countries, too. Almost 40 percent of respondents in Brazil had experienced verbal abuse in the last year, around 33 percent in Bulgaria, 52 percent in South Africa, and 67 percent in Australia (Di Martino, 2002: 17). Bullying and mobbing, followed by racial and sexual harassment, have also emerged as two main areas of concern in all countries (see Einarsen *et al.*, 2002). Such studies provide an important and reliable account of the extent, patterns and impact of WV within specific industries.

Another report commissioned and developed by the ILO's advisory team in East Asia together with the Bangkok office, targeted sexual harassment at work in Asia and the Pacific (ILO, 2001). The report outlines various topics related to sexual harassment, including the incidence of this type of WV in the region. Among the most notable findings that are cited is a Japanese survey conducted under the auspices of the Ministry of Labor in this country, which found that two thirds of the women respondents had been sexually harassed at least once. Of these women, 11 percent said they had experienced a *quid pro quo* type of harassment, and 45 percent reported to have been subjected to a hostile working environment (Yamakawa, 2001 cited in ILO, 2001: 35). Similar trends were found in other countries in the region, such as Korea and the Philippines (ILO, 2001). In the Republic of Korea, a study of 567 public officers (of which, 345 men and 222 women), conducted in October 2000 in Seoul, found that almost 70 percent of women respondents had experienced sexual harassment in the workplace (ILO, 2001: 35). In the Philippines, a survey conducted by an organization of women workers in 1999, reported that 17 percent of both unionized (43) and non-unionized (291) establishments that had been surveyed, had records of sexual harassment cases (Ursua, 2001 cited in ILO, 2001: 35). Another survey conducted by the government in two Northern states in Malaysia, Penang and Perlis, found that 83 and respectively 88 percent of the female respondents experienced some form of sexual harassment (Zaitun, 2001 cited in ILO, 2001: 36).

Regional and national trends: Europe, United States and Australia

WV incidents are documented in Europe, United States (Chappell and Di Martino, 2000) and Australia (Perrone, 1999). The results from each area are respectively highlighted below.

Europe

Among the most notable regional and national data sources of WV are the European Survey on Working Conditions. The third European Survey on Working Conditions, in which 21,500 workers throughout the EU were interviewed, indicates that 2 percent (or approximately three million) workers are physically victimized in their workplace. Four percent (or about six million) employees in the EU experience this type of victimization from people outside the workplace. The highest exposure to physical violence is found in public administration (6 percent), trade and retail industries (5 percent). Two percent of workers in the EU report sexual harassment and 9 percent report being subject to bullying and intimidation in the workplace in 2000. Gender discrimination is reported to be as high as 3 percent in countries such as the Netherlands and the UK, while ethnic discrimination is reported by 2 percent of workers in countries like France and Luxembourg (Paoli and Merllié, 2001).

The extent and nature of violence in England and Wales is measured by the BCS. Results from 2002–3 BCS estimated that 1.7 percent of working adults were the victim of one or more violent incidents at work during 2001. An estimated 431,000 assaults and 418,000 threats occurred at work throughout England and Wales in 2001. Among the respondents that were most at risk of violence in the workplace were police officers, nurses and health professionals such as medical and dental practitioners. Science and technology professionals, such as mechanical engineers, were least at risk (Upson, 2004).

United States

The NCVS is a housing unit-based national representative sample conducted by the federal government. The NCVS collects information about criminal victimization incidents from all individuals age 12 and older who live in the selected housing units. During a seven-year period (1993 to 1999) an average of 1.7 million violent victimizations per year were committed against US persons age 12 or older who were at work or on duty. WV represented 18 percent of all violent crime during this period. In addition to the nonfatal violence measured by the NCVS (rape and sexual assault, robbery, aggravated assault and simple assault), data from the US BLS suggests that 900 work-related homicides occurred annually during the period 1993–99. Rape, sexual assault, robbery and homicide accounted for only 6 percent of all WV between 1993–99. Most violent incidents (19 out of 20) were aggravated or simple assaults. Males workers were victimized more compare to female workers during 1993–99 (15 versus 10 per 1000). The occupations most at risk were in the fields of law enforcement (police officers accounted for 11 percent of all workplace victimization), followed by mental health. Retail sales workers were victimized in the workplace at higher rates (20 per 1000 in the workforce) compared to teachers, bus and taxi cab drivers, and physicians, nurses and medical technicians (Duhart, 2001).

The most comprehensive information available internationally on work-related homicides comes from the National Traumatic Occupational Fatalities database in the US, maintained by the National Institute for Occupational Safety and Health (NIOSH, 2004) and also from the Census of Fatal Occupational Injuries, maintained by the US BLS (BLS, 2004). Work-related homicide data from the US reveals that between 1980 and 1990, this form of violence was the third most significant cause of workplace death in the United States, claiming approximately 7600 lives or almost 13 percent of the nation's total traumatic work-

related fatalities (Bell and Jenkins, 1992; OSHA, 1998). In the mid-1990s homicide accounted for 17 percent of all occupational fatalities, making it the second
leading cause of death in US workplaces (Jenkins, 1996). On average, 20 workers
are murdered each week in the United States (NIOSH, 1997). While 80 percent of
workplace homicide is perpetrated against males, homicide has become the
leading cause of occupationally related death for women (Jenkins, 1996). Of the
homicides against female workers, over 50 percent are reported in the retail
industry (BLS, 1994). National data for the 1993–96 period shows that sales
workers experienced the highest number of workplace homicides in the US (an
average of 327 annually), followed by executives and managers (average of
150 murders per year), taxi drivers and chauffeurs (averaging 74 per year), and
law enforcement officers killed while on duty (an average of 70 per year) (BLS,
1993–96 as cited in Warchol, 1998).

Australia

The Australian Work-Related Fatalities Studies is based on coroner records of
traumatic fatality (Driscoll, 1998 cited in Mayhew and Quinlan, 1999). The
second Australian Work-related Fatalities Studies (which covered the period
1989–92) reported that occupational homicides represented approximately
2 percent of all traumatic workplace deaths in Australia during this period. While
62 percent of the victims were employees, 36 percent were self-employed and
business-owners. The workers that were most commonly killed were those in
the community service sector, including police officers and medical staff
(24 percent); the whole sale and trade sector (22 percent); and the recreation,
personal and other services sector, which includes brothels (20 percent). Forty
nine percent of workplace homicides involved the use of a gun. In most
instances the assailant was a customer, client or patient (31 percent), a stranger
(29 percent), or either unknown or 'other' party (33 percent) (see, Driscoll, 1998
as cited in Mayhew and Quinlan, 1999).

The impact and costs of WV

Regardless of where globally WV happened, researchers have documented that it
takes a negative physical, psychological and financial toll on employees – abused
employee and perpetrator-employee, and co-workers – and the organization. In
the US it has been estimated to cost about 1.8 million lost working days every
year (NCVS, 1987–92 cited in Chappell and Di Martino, 2000). In Finland, a
study of bullying at two hospitals estimated the annual costs of absenteeism
from bullying to be approximately €200,000 (Kivimaki *et al.*, 2000). Three
percent of respondents to the British Chambers of Commerce Business Crime
Survey in 2001 reported that crime has cost them the equivalent of €156 in the
previous year (Di Martino *et al.*, 2003). In Australia, victimized small retail businesses such as restaurants, general and liquor stores, gas stations and pharmacies,
reported, on average, direct and indirect dollar losses between AUS$800 and
AUS$6950 during 1998–99 (Taylor and Mayhew, 2002).

Quantifying the costs associated with occupational stress and violence is a relatively recent endeavor (Chappell and Di Martino, 2000; Cooper, Liukkonen and Cartwright, 1996; Levi and Lunde-Jensen, 1995). As such, most analyses of work-related violence costs consider both tangible (i.e. loss of income and medical costs) and intangible costs (i.e. fear, pain, reduction in quality of life, and grief to friends and family) at individual, organizational, and societal level. Caution must be exercised with respect to actual figures, however, as too many uncertain variables and intangible factors make any estimation difficult (McCarthy, 2004; Hoel *et al.*, 2001).

The cost of WV to victim-employees include loss of income due to psychological conditions and physical injuries (bruises, concussions, broken bones and teeth) that bring about medical-related costs, poor work performance, absenteeism, and, in some cases, termination from the organization (see, Fisher and Peek-Asa, 2005; Hoel *et al.*, 2001; LeBlanc and Barling, 2005). To illustrate, work-related violence leads to physical and mental health impairment, sometimes with long-term traumatic effects, such as Post Traumatic Stress Syndrome (PTSD) (Flannery, 1996), experienced by victims of workplace bullying and sexual harassment (Einarsen *et al.*, 1994 cited in Hoel *et al.*, 2001; Koss, 1990). Exposure to workplace bullying and sexual harassment has been found to be associated with anxiety, depression and aggression (Quine, 1999). Other social and economic individual costs have been reported, such as divorce and loss of one's home, car or health insurance (Dorman, 2000).

The costs to organizations are related to abused employee sickness absence or premature retirement, reduced performance and productivity, replacement costs in relation to high turnover rates, increased insurance premiums and litigation and compensation costs, to name a few. Another more intangible cost to organizations is the loss of public 'goodwill' or reputation (Hoel *et al.*, 2001). Anecdotal evidence suggests that negative media coverage of WV at a specific business location may be costly as patrons shy away from doing business there (see LeBlanc and Barling, 2005). Finally, societal costs are related to health care and medical treatment, early retirement, long-term unemployment and welfare dependency, and potential loss of productive workforce (Di Martino *et al.*, 2003). Using data from a number of countries, Hoel *et al.* (2001) estimated that workplace stress and violence account for 1 to 3.5 percent of the GDP.

Furthermore, the impact of WV extends beyond the person(s) directly involved in the incident. Research findings suggest that witnessing violence has similar negative effects as being assaulted or attacked. This may result in fear of future violent incidents (Rogers and Kelloway, 1997; Leather *et al.*, 1998). Several studies have revealed that a significant number of third parties who witnessed workplace bullying (one in five respondents) report having left the organization as a result of their indirect experience of this form of violence (UNISON, 1997 and 2000 cited in Di Martino *et al.*, 2003). Co-workers of employees who experience domestic violence in the workplace experience negative effects similar to the victims (see Fisher and Peek-Asa, 2005).

Stress resulting from exposure to WV also impacts one's behavior and attitudes. Some examples of typical effects of stress are reduction in job satisfaction and/or commitment to the employer, unsafe behavior and an increased ability for accidents, and poor life style habits, such as increased smoking and alcohol consumption (Cooper *et al.*, 1996). Victims of WV experience concentration problems (Barling *et al.*, 1996), they are less self-confident and more withdrawn, thus becoming socially isolated (Brady, 1999), and their relationships with co-workers and others deteriorate (Stockdale, 1996).

At the organizational level, WV leads to an increase in sickness absenteeism, higher turnover rates and reduced productivity (Hoel *et al.*, 2001). Exposure to violent assaults or physical attacks is likely to cause one to miss work due to sickness (Warshaw and Messite, 1996). Health-related absence may extend long-term and sometime lead to early retirement. Not every violent episode, however, automatically results in the victim taking time off. In the health service, while physical violence and threats are very common, the majority of incidents do not lead to victim absenteeism (Boyd, 1995). Severe workplace bullying may also affect absenteeism and turnover rates. And exposure to sexual harassment is related to an increase in absences, transfers within the agency and a higher likelihood to leave the organization (Hoel *et al.*, 2001).

Society also incurs substantial costs associated to WV. Assault, bullying or sexual harassment victims suffer both physical and psychological injuries. For some workers, the onset of PTSD resulting from work-related violence may lead to long-term medical treatment and absenteeism, which in many countries will be supported in part or in full by society (Hoel *et al.*, 2001). WV also affects national productivity levels, due to the loss of productive workers and skills (Hoel *et al.*, 2001).

Despite the high costs associated with WV, the state of knowledge about this phenomenon, especially about non-fatal violence is rather limited (Castillo, 1995 cited in Hoel *et al.*, 2001). Therefore, caution must be exercised when attempting to assign monetary value to the costs of workplace victimization and violence.

Factors contributing to violence in the workplace

Researchers have determined which factors significantly contribute to the occurrence of WV. Bear in mind that most of the WV research is methodologically weak on several key scientific criteria. First, most of the research is atheoretical and cross-sectional. As a result, causal relationships between individual, situational, organizational or socio-economic risk factors and workplace violence have been difficult to establish (Di Martino *et al.*, 2003). Second, rigorous research on risk factors and their interaction and cumulative effects is limited at best. Third, most existent reports are case studies or 'accounts of personal experiences in workplace violence prevention.' (Bulatao and VandenBos, 1996: 16)

Despite much concern over WV, empirical studies that identify correlates of WV are scant. These studies have generally focused on the characteristics of two units of analysis: (1) the individual, and (2) the workplace (Peek-Asa and Jenkins, 2003).

Who are the perpetrators?

Available evidence suggests, that individuals displaying the following characteristics are more likely to commit WV: (1) young adult males; (2) with a history of violent behavior; (3) who have experienced difficulties during childhood, such inadequate parenting and low achievement in school; (4) have problems of psychotropic substance abuse, especially alcohol; (5) suffer from severe mental illness that is unidentified and uncontrolled through therapy; and (6) who find themselves in situations that are conducive to self-directed or interpersonal violence, such as having access to weapons (McDonald and Brown, 1997 cited in Chappell and Di Martino, 2000). As noted in Table 10.2, the violent perpetrator is likely to fall into three major categories: (1) a client of the particular organization or enterprise; (2) a colleague or fellow employee; or (3) a stranger (Chappell and Di Martino, 2000).

Who are the victims?

The attributes of workplace violence victims – usually employees, but who may also be customers – which are significant predictors of risk, include gender, appearance, health, age and experience, personality and temperament, attitudes and expectations (Chappell and Di Martino, 1998b: 65). Women are generally more vulnerable to certain types of attacks as they are more likely to be perceived as easy targets by perpetrators, especially if they are working alone (Davis *et al.*, 1987 cited in Perrone, 1999). Appearance is important in any job, as it can define interactions and shape the role characteristics for a given encounter (Chappell and Di Martino, 2000). The way in which employees interact with others in the workplace, whether co-workers or clients, is also likely to be affected by their personality – passive or aggressive, patient or intolerant – by their expectations about behavior, the workers' attitudes and health. It has been suggested that individuals who are highly stressed, lack the experience to deal with difficult situations in the workplace and face job instability, have, in general, aggressive personalities (Perrone, 1999). Victims of bullying, however, have been identified to have low self-esteem, high anxiety levels, to be introverted, conscientious, neurotic and submissive (Einarsen and Raknes cited in Di Martino *et al.*, 2003, 1991; Vartia, 1996).

An employee's age and level of experience or training are also important variables to consider. Older, more experienced workers can deal with difficult scenarios better, having more skills that allow them to cope and appropriately respond to threatening situations (Chappell, 1998 and Kposowa, 1999 cited in Perrone, 1999). Victims of sexual harassment in EU countries (European Commission, 1998) are more likely to be young (20–40 years of age), female, single or divorced, having completed a lower level of education, and with long-or short-term tenure (cited in Di Martino *et al.*, 2003).

Organizational characteristics

Research has reported several organizational characteristics contribute to opportunity for WV violence. First, poor work organization and inequitable workloads create potentially violent responses from clients. They may also undermine the employees' perception of fairness in the workplace, which affects the attitudes they form on the job as well as their behaviors, and may trigger deviance or aggression in the workplace (Snyder *et al.*, 2005). Excessive and sometimes unjustified delays or long line-ups are likely to instigate aggressive behavior. Insufficient staff or inadequate staff training may elicit similar effects (Di Martino *et al.*, 2003). Research findings attest to the positive relationship between workload and experienced frustration (Spector, 1997) and workload and hostility and complaining (Chen and Spector, 1992).

Second, organizational restructuring, such as down sizing, outsourcing, and privatization, especially during times of economic uncertainty, is also related to higher levels of WV and aggression (Elliot and Jarrett, 1994). Examining the relationship between workplace aggression and four types of organizational change (e.g. downsizing and layoffs, restructuring, increased diversity, and increased use of part time help), Baron and Newman (1998) found that such changes are associated with verbal aggression, obstructionism and physical attacks and theft in the workplace. These processes could result in tension among employees and also lead to more confrontational management styles (Babiak, 1995; McCarthy et al., 1995 cited in Perrone, 1999).

Third, leadership styles that rely on coercion and harsh discipline to achieve employee conformity may curtail employee autonomy and severely restrict communication and dialogue between employer and employees (Cappozzoli and McVey, 1996). Two management styles that have been found to be associated with harassment and bullying are the authoritarian style, described above, and the *laissez-faire* style (Di Martino *et al.*, 2003). Lack of leadership, is also associated to WV. As management ignores or fails to recognize and intervene when violence occurs, this conveys the message that such behavior is tolerated, acceptable.

Fourth, the culture or the structure, policies, and procedures of an organization are also related to aggressive behavior (Snyder *et al.*, 2005). Increased conflict and alienation (Hall, 1996 cited in Snyder *et al.*, 2005), or routinization (Tobin, 2001) have been found to mediate the relationship between organizational culture and frustration among employees. A growing body of research also identifies the passive or active roles organizations themselves play in creating a violent, oppressive culture (see McCarthy and Mayhew, 2004; Hearn and Parkin, 2001; White, 1997). The organizational culture may permit or even reward WV and other negative behaviors. To illustrate, in a study of fire brigades, Archer (1999) reported that the desire to perpetuate the continuation of a white male culture in the service led to the bullying of those individuals belonging to a minority group in terms of gender and race (cited in Einarsen *et al.*, 2005).

And fifth, the design of a workplace may either diffuse or make matters worse in regards to a potentially violent situation. Workspaces that cannot accommodate increased activity, such as restaurants, may result in overcrowding, which in turn will affect staff and patrons alike, generating hostility and friction (Perrone, 1999). Overcrowding, inadequate ventilation, excessive noise, as well as other poor architectural design features have been found to be associated with the incidence of destructive behaviors in and around bars, clubs and pubs and other such licensed premises (Homel and Clark, 1994; Beale *et al.*, 1998).

Situational characteristics

Research suggests that situational risk factors are associated with an individual's routine activities. To illustrate, studies have consistently shown that WV is clustered in certain occupational fields, such as the medical, mental health, teaching, law enforcement, retail sales, and transportation fields. During 1993–99, Americans working in these occupations have experienced violent victimization in the workplace (Duhart, 2001). In Canada and the UK, bank workers, retail sales staff, bar staff, milk delivery persons, and transport and taxi drivers are also at increased risk for victimization (Willis *et al.*, 1999). In Sweden, workplace violence concentrates in occupational fields, such as health care, social services, retail trade, post, banking, transport, security, police, education and child care (Chappell and Di Martino, 1998a).

Situations that place workers at risk include those associated with (1) working alone and/or in mobile workplaces; (2) working in contact with the public; (3) working late at night or early in the morning; (4) handling cash or valuables; (5) working in community-based settings; and (6) working with unstable or distressed people (Collins and Cox, 1987; Castillo and Jenkins, 1994; Budd, 1999 cited in Perrone, 1999; Di Martino *et al.*, 2003; NIOSH, 2004). Individuals whose occupation involves all of these features run the greatest risk of victimization. When one's employment involves direct contact with large number of clients on a routine basis, the handling of money, and routine travel or more than one work sites, that individual's risk of victimization is greater compared to someone who does not routinely perform these activities (Lynch, 1987).

Structural factors

Finally, the workplace violence research recognizes a third group of risk factors that is rooted in broader socio-economic explanations. At macro level, structural forces, such as (1) social inequality (Mayhew and Quinlan, 1999); (2) economic recession (Leck, 2002; Midiris, 2002 cited in Verdugo and Vere, 2003; Di Martino *et al.*, 2003); (3) an increase in drug dependency and gambling addiction across societies and the individuals' inability to finance these habits; (4) the break down of marriage, extended family and community support groups (Perrone, 1999); and (5) the introduction of immigrant- and foreign-born labor (Leck, 2002 cited in Verdugo and Vere, 2003) contribute to WV. Although their effect on WV is distal rather than proximate, socio-economic factors generate and exacerbate violence-producing behavior and environments (Blair, 1991; Flannery, 1992 cited in Perrone, 1999; Mayhew and Quinlan, 1999).

Responding to WV

Whether nationally, regionally or globally, several vested stakeholders have offered various solutions or responses to WV. First, local and national governments and regional and international governing bodies and agencies, such as the UN's ILO and the European Parliament use legislative and regulatory approaches to control and prevent WV. They also formulate and enforce guidelines to assist employers and workers in their efforts to prevent WV (see Di Martino *et al.*, 2003; Howard and Barish, 2003; OSHA, 2004) and fund and support WV research as well as data collection efforts (see Annest *et al.*, 1996; NIOSH, 2004a; NOHSC, 2004). Second, labor or trade unions across the world initiated various projects to combat WV (see *An End to Sexual Harassment at Work*, 2004). In countries such as Canada, and the US, unions play a key role in lobbying for the implementation of occupational safety guidelines in the affected industries, supporting the promulgation of mandatory workplace safety standards, and convincing employers to develop and use WV prevention strategies (Fisher and Peek-Asa, 2005; Rosen, 2001; Pizzino, 2002). Third, organizations have also invested in protecting workers from WV by implementing environmental and administrative controls, such as measures related to the architectural design and physical layout of the workplace, as well as various practices and policies (Marshall *et al.*, 2003). Finally, collaborative efforts among law-enforcement, private security firms, universities and organizations, rendered successful community partnerships aimed at reducing the incidence of WV (see Rugala and Isaacs, 2004; Rugala and Fitzgerald, 2003; Casteel *et al.*, 2003).

Legislative and regulatory approaches to WV prevention

Various governing bodies from international to local levels and their agencies have been actively involved in protecting employees against WV. In the US, the earliest governmental action intended to prevent WV took place in the 1990s, when state and local authorities adopted and passed legislation focusing on reducing injuries among workers in high-risk occupations, such as convenience store workers, taxi drivers and healthcare workers (Howard and Barish, 2003). In 1990, the Washington Industrial Safety and Health Services Agency (cited in Howard and Barish, 2003) adopted administrative regulations to protect convenience store workers against assault and other forms of WV. Florida followed suit, by passing similar legislation in 1990 and 1992. In Virginia, due to the risk of late night retail robbery expressed by franchisees, the state adopted legislation prohibiting gasoline retail franchisers to require franchisees to stay open over 16 hours per day or more than six days per week (see Howard and Barish, 2003).

Florida was the first state to adopt extensive retail crime prevention legislation. The law covers retail establishments who sell groceries and gasoline, which are open for business from 11 p.m. to 5 a.m. It addresses both employee training and environmental controls against robbery, as well as injury prevention in general. Among the measures imposed by the law are 'security cameras, drop safes for cash management, height markers at the entrance to stores, and silent alarm systems.' (Howard and Barish, 2003: 724) The Florida Attorney General is responsible for enforcing the statute (Howard and Barish, 2003).

At a local level in the US, municipalities have adopted city ordinances to protect taxi drivers. The following municipalities in the US have such ordinances: Los Angeles; Chicago; New York; Baltimore, Maryland; Boston; Albany, New York and Oakland, California (Rathbone, 1999, cited in Howard and Barish, 2003). These types of laws have been evaluated for their effectiveness in reducing worker injuries. Stone and Stevens (1999, cited in Howard and Barish, 2003) reported the following findings in regards to the implementation of the Baltimore, Maryland ordinance. Comparing the 12-month periods before and after the ordinance took effect the authors found a 56 percent reduction in assaults on taxi drivers. The same study also found that prior to the implementation of the ordinance a cab driver who worked without a barrier had a higher likelihood (five times greater) to be assaulted compared to a driver protected by a barrier.

The Canadian federal and provincial governments have also been actively addressing WV through legislation (see http://www.workplaceviolence.ca/legal/legal-intro.html). Most Canadian jurisdictions have a 'general duty provision' in their occupational health and safety legislation, which requires employers to take all reasonable precautions to protect employees from a known risk of WV. There is variation in WV coverage across the Canadian provinces. For example, British Columbia and Saskatchewan have specific WV prevention regulations. Nova Scotia has also drafted WV regulations. Manitoba has the 'Workers Working Alone Regulation' which addresses criminal violence victimization (see http://www.workplaceviolence.ca/legal/legal-intro.html).

In the UK, although no specific WV legislation exists, several general as well as occupational health and safety acts address violence in the workplace (Di Martino et al., 2003). *The Protection from Harassment Act 1997* (1997) has recently made harassment a criminal offence (whether occurring at the workplace or in other locations). Health and safety legislation, such as the *Health and Safety at Work Act 1974* (1974), emphasizes the employers' legal duties to protect workers health, safety, and welfare. Under this act, the employer's responsibilities can be extended to include protection from violence (Chappell and Di Martino, 2000). Similarly, *the Management of Health and Safety at Work Regulations 1992* (1992) requires employers to assess the risks to which workers are exposed to while at work.

In Australia, each state and territory are responsible for enacting legislation for the prevention of work-related injury and illness (Mayhew, 2004). Several state and territory health and safety acts, such as the *Workplace Health and Safety Act 1995* in Queensland (2004) and Tasmania (1995), although not expressly addressing WV, require employers to foster a work environment that is free from risks, hazards, and potential dangers (Perrone, 1999). According to this legislation, employers are obligated to address the potential for all forms of violence if this is an inherent feature of the working environment. The law is framed in such a way that prosecutions may ensue independent of whether or not actual harms occur (Russell, 1999 cited in Perrone, 1999).

Legislation has been adopted that addresses high-risk industries. Health care workers are also at increased risk for WV (Chappell and Di Martino, 1998a; Duhart, 2001). In the US, California and Washington have adopted legislation that mandates and structures health care employee training prevention (Howard and Barish, 2003). Other countries, such as New Zealand, have also passed legislation to address WV related issues in health care occupational settings. In 1992, the *Health and Safety Employment Act* took effect. This New Zealand statute has been used by employers and employees to develop and implement safety practices in the workplace, such as identifying and reducing the likelihood of hazards or other potential sources for injury in the workplace (cited in Chappell and Di Martino, 2000).

Similar WV prevention measures have been taken by governing bodies at regional level (e.g. the EU), as well as by international agencies (e.g. the UN). The European Commission's Treaty, article 13, addresses issues related to discrimination based on sex, race or ethnicity, religion or belief, disability, age or sexual orientation (see Di Martino *et al.*, 2003: 47). The provisions outlined in this article cover various workplace-related issues, from equal access to employment for men and women, to vocational training, promotion and working conditions.

Internationally, organizations such as the UN's ILO and the WHO have adopted landmark resolutions. The *International Covenant on Economic, Social and Cultural Rights* (1966) adopted by the UN, requires the nations governed by the act to recognize all individuals the right to a safe and healthy working environment. Another act adopted by the UN General Assembly, the *Convention on the Elimination of All Forms of Discrimination against Women (CEDAW)* (1979), demanded that ratifying states take measures to combat discrimination against women in the field of employment. The resolution adopted by the 49th World Health Assembly, titled *Prevention of Violence: Public Health Priority* (1996), acknowledged WV as a public health problem and recognized the grave health and psychological consequences associated with WV, as well as formulated ways to deal with the problem. Finally, the *ILO Declaration on Fundamental Principles and Rights at Work* (1998) has addressed broader workplace-related issues, such as discrimination in regards to employment and occupation, freedom of association, the right to collective bargaining, and the elimination of compulsory and child labor.

Guidelines for employers and employees

In the US, the Department of Labor's Occupational Safety and Health Administration (Fed-OSHA) and its state counterparts have been addressing WV issues since the 1990s. The primary role of federal and state occupational health and safety agencies is to find ways and to encourage organizations to safeguard workers not only from traditional dangers, such as toxic fumes, heavy machinery and other hazards, but also from the newly established threat – WV (Speer,

2003). In order to meet the challenge of WV, these agencies have adopted and enforced a general duty clause, which requires employers to provide a workplace that is 'free from recognizable hazards that are causing or likely to cause death or serious harm to employees.' (US Occupational Health and Safety Act, 1970) In 1992, Fed-OSHA issued a memorandum in which interpreted the clause to include WV as a recognized hazard (Speer, 2003).

Federal and state health and safety agencies in the US have also developed and implemented specific guidelines targeting those industries that have been disproportionately affected by WV (see the//www.osha.gov/SLTC/workplaceviolence/solutions.html). In 1998, OSHA issued such guidelines for night-retail establishments, social service and healthcare industries (Speer, 2003). The regulations require employers to implement WV prevention programs to include (1) risk analysis conducted by specialized threat-assessment teams; (2) administrative controls, such as employee training in regards to safety and security against violence; (3) and also environmental controls, such as improving lighting and cash-handling practices (see Speer, 2003).

In the UK, a similar approach to that of the US has been adopted. Several ministries, such as the Departments of Employment, Health, Transport, and Labor Research, have formulated violence and harassment guidelines for occupations at special risk. The guidelines complement existing legislation in these areas, and aim to protect bus drivers, health and social workers, and retail and education staff, against various forms of WV (see Di Martino *et al.*, 2003, p. 55). The Health and Safety Executive (HSE) has developed and published numerous WV reports, leaflets and guidance publications, including guides for employers (see http://www.hse.gov.uk/pubns/indg69.pdf), guidelines for solitary workers (see http://www.hse.gov.uk/pubns/indg73.pdf), as well as bank employees, educators, retail and health care staff (see http://www.hse.gov.uk/violence/information.htm).

In Australia, the federal government, as well as several states and territories have published various guidelines for the prevention of occupational violence (see http://www.aic.gov.au/research/cvp/occupational/initiatives.html#aust). The Australian National Health and Medical Research Council (NHMRC) has recently released a manual designed to assist healthcare workers in remote and rural areas prepare and respond to violence (see http://www.nhmrc.gov.au/publications/pdf/hp16.pdf). In New South Wales, Work Cover NSW, a statutory authority within the Ministry of Commerce, has produced several WV prevention guidelines and fact sheets, including (1) managing the risk of robbery and violence in the retail and wholesale industries (see http://www.workcover.nsw.gov.au/Publications/Industry/RetailandWholesale/default.htm); (2) prevention and management of workplace aggression in health and community service (http://www.workcover.nsw.gov.au/NR/rdonlyres/30A073EA-E492-45EA-8DDB-0E61CFDEE9E6/0/guide_wpaggression_4358.pdf); and (3) WV prevention in the finance sector (see http://www.workcover.nsw.gov.au/NR/rdonlyres/12175B50-FEEA-4AE2-9C77-7A3C77AC8566/0/guide_violencefin_4348.pdf).

WV research and data collection efforts

National governments and international agencies are also responsible for funding and supporting WV research and/or data collection efforts. In the US, the main objectives of the National Institute for Occupational Safety and Health (NIOSH) is to 'conduct research to reduce work-related illnesses and injuries.' (NIOSH, 2004) The National Center for Injury Prevention and Control (NCIPC), whose mission includes the improvement of injury data systems, conducted in 1996 an inventory of existing federal or federally-funded data systems that collect injury events or injury-related information (i.e. mortality, morbidity, and risk factors) (see Annest *et al.*, 1996). In Australia, the National Occupational Health and Safety Commission (NOHSC) collects work-related violence data, including accident notification and workers' compensation information (see NOHSC, 2004). The Australian commission works in partnership with the European Agency for Safety and Health at Work (EASHW), which also conducts research and collects occupational health and safety statistics regionally (see http://europe.osha.eu.int/), by sharing existing health and safety information (see http://www.nohsc-eu.gov.au/default.asp). In Britain, the HSE has commissioned research to prevent WV, focussing in particular on high-risk industries and work settings, such as the retail sector and solitary workers (see http://www.hse.gov.uk/violence/plans.htm), as well as on the prevention of post-traumatic stress disorder (PTSD) resulting from assaults in the workplace (see http://www.hse.gov.uk/research/crr_pdf/1998/crr98195.pdf). The same organization publishes its own health and safety statistics (see http://www.hse.gov.uk/statistics/index.htm) as well as the current findings from the BCS (see Budd 2001; Upson, 2004). Finally, the UN's ILO reviews and updates periodically current WV guidelines, policies and strategies (see Chappell and Di Martino, 2000).

Trade union efforts to reduce WV

Labor or trade unions across the world are also involved in WV prevention. To illustrate, the Spanish Trade Union Confederation of Workers' Commissions (CC.OO.), together with partner trade unions in Sweden and Ireland, undertook a research project whose goal was to understand and to reduce sexual harassment in the workplace (*see An End to Sexual Harassment at Work*, 2004). The Pandora Project was funded by the Daphne Program – an EU initiative to prevent violence against women, young adults and children – in 1998 and it examined trends, patterns and risk factors of sexual harassment in the workplace (see *Daphne II EU Programme*, 2004).

To reduce WV, labor unions in the US, such as the United Federation of Teachers, the Service Employees International Union (SEIU) and the American Federation of State County and Municipal Employees (AFSCME), conduct inspections, file complaints with enforcement agencies, negotiate contract language, and support the passage of mandatory workplace safety standards (Rosen, 2001). In Canada, the Canadian Union of Public Employees (CUPE) conducts WV research aimed at identifying at-risk occupations and work settings. The union continues to propose hazard and WV regulation as well as lobbies provincial, territorial and federal authorities to pass legislative protection from WV (Pizzino, 2002).

Organizational responses to WV

Organizations have also invested in protecting workers from WV. Two types of prevention measures have been recommended and implemented. These are environmental controls, which relate to the design of the workplace, and administrative controls, related to work practices and policies (Marshall *et al.*, 2003). Environmental modifications to reduce WV are based on the Crime Prevention through Environmental Design (CPTED) model (Jeffery, 1971). This model focuses on redesigning the environment to reduce both fear and incidence of crime (see http://www.cpted.net). Environmental controls include the following features: (1) bright exterior and interior lightning at the workplace; (2) surveillance equipment, such as alarms, cameras and CCTV; (3) design strategies that increase visibility of employees; (4) physical separators, such as bars, grills, and bullet-resistant barriers, aimed at reducing access; and (5) cash storage devices, such as time-release or drop safes. A comprehensive review of environmental controls applied and evaluated in retail settings suggested that programs that implemented such measures showed significant reductions in robbery and related injuries (Casteel and Peek-Asa, 2000).

Administrative measures refer to work practices and policies. They include (1) worker and management training programs aimed at improving social skills, conflict management, communication, leadership and administrative skills; (2) staffing procedures, such as number of staff on duty and additional staffing in high-risk locations and/or at high-risk times; (3) cash-handling procedures, such as performing frequent bank deposits; and (4) personnel selection or screening, including pre-employment testing (Marshall *et al.*, 2003; Runyan *et al.*, 2003; NIOSH, 2004; Snyder *et al.*, 2005).

Collaborative efforts to reduce WV

Partnerships formed by national or local police agencies, private security firms, universities, businesses and organizations, are yet another example of successful responses to prevent WV (see Casteel *et al.*, 2003; Rugala and Fitzgerald, 2003; Rugala and Isaacs, 2004). One such collaboration was formed in 2001 in California. The Oxnard Police Department, together with private security and the University of California, Los Angeles (UCLA), and with the assistance of business organizations, including the Korean American Grocers Association, undertook a WV prevention project that was modeled after the CPTED approach (briefly described above). The project was funded by NIOSH and focused on prevention of robbery and robbery-related injuries among high-risk retail and service establishments in the city of Los Angeles (Casteel *et al.*, 2003). Another example of such a partnership against WV is the ongoing relationship between the FBI's National Center for the Analysis of Violent Crime (NCAVC) and local police agencies, employers and other state or federal entities. Acting in consulting capacity, the NCAVC develops proactive approaches to WV prevention and is also called to assess the potential for WV in various locales (Rugala and Isaacs, 2004; Rugala and Fitzgerald, 2003).

Efforts to prevent WV

Methodological, evaluation, and implementation challenges

During the last decade, such WV prevention efforts have been outlined in scientific reviews (e.g. Cabral, 1996; Leymann, 1996; D'Addario, 1996; Neuman and Barron, 1997, 1998; Collins and Griffin, 1998; *Hoel et al.*, 1999; McClure, 1999; Pearson *et al.*, 2000 cited in Snyder *et al.*, 2005) and task force reports (e.g. United States Postal Service; Anfuso, 1994 cited in Snyder et al., 2005). The WV prevention literature, however, relies, by and large, on correlational studies and field experience (Hoel *et al.*, 1999 cited in Snyder *et al.*, 2005). In the US, several researchers have noted the need for more 'sophisticated analytical studies' in the field of WV (Casteel and Peek-Asa, 2000; Runyan *et al.*, 2000; Merchant and Lundell, 2000 and Runyan, 2001 cited in Marshall *et al.*, 2003: 759). Future WV prevention research should employ more advanced methodology, designs, such as case-control studies or randomized control intervention trials (Marshall *et al.*, 2003). Currently, most studies use simple evaluation designs and lack comparison groups or randomization. Furthermore, they include almost no process evaluation, a serious limitation to successful WV prevention (Marshall *et al.*, 2003).

There is a general lack for empirical evidence about the effectiveness of WV prevention strategies (in Snyder *et al.*, 2005). Evaluation of intervention strategies is a key component in the development of successful and cost-effective WV prevention, yet few interventions have been evaluated to date (see Casteel and Peek-Asa, 2000; Runyan *et al.*, 2000; Marshall *et al.*, 2003). In the US, most studies have focused their attention on robbery and robbery-related injury prevention in retail settings. Comparatively, evaluation research addressing disputes and injury outcomes in the workplace is rather scant (Runayan *et al.*, 2000). Surveys about WV programs in other occupational sectors than the retail industry, are scarce (Peek-Asa and Jenkins, 2003). This clearly suggests that WV prevention efforts, though possibly successful, are not evidence-based (Peek-Asa and Jenkins, 2003).

Finally, problems related to the implementation of existing WV prevention programs have also been attested. In the US, there seems to be a gap between what research findings suggest is effective in WV prevention and what organizations voluntarily implement (Peek-Asa and Jenkins, 2003). Upon reviewing 11 studies that identified risk factors and prevention strategies for robbery and violence prevention in the retail sector, Peek-Asa and Jenkins (2003) found an inverse relationship between WV prevention approaches that have been found to be successful and what organizations have implemented. To illustrate, almost 88 percent of these studies considered that cash-control policies are important in reducing the risk for robbery, yet only 10 percent of businesses had implemented appropriate cash-control policies. Security cameras, on the other hand, was found to be an important prevention strategy in only 33 percent of the studies, yet more than 70 percent of businesses had installed security cameras (Peek-Asa and Jenkins, 2003).

Implementation problems in other occupational sectors have also been attested. A US national survey about existing programs in city and county governmental offices found that only around 40 percent had WV policies or implemented full WV programs. Less than 42 percent of offices had a post-incident response plan. And zero-tolerance policies were the most common policy implemented (around 84 percent), despite the little evidence suggesting that these policies are effective (Nigro and Waugh, 1988 cited in Peek-Asa and Jenkins, 2003).

Recommendations

In October of 2003, experts nominated by governments of 12 countries (i.e. Algeria, Canada, Denmark, Germany, Japan, Malaysia, Mauritius, Peru, Philippines, South Africa, UK, and US), together with specialists selected by the ILO's Employers' and Workers' groups, met in Geneva to develop a WV prevention code for the service industry, including commerce, education, financial and professional services, healthcare, hotels, catering and tourism, media and entertainment industries, postal and telecommunications, as well transportation and public services (ILO, 2003).

Following are the recommendations that have been outlined. First, employers and workers should identify and assess the nature and magnitude of WV in a given setting. In doing so, the following indicators could be used: (1) national and local surveys on the extent of violence in the pertaining occupational field and similar workplaces or types of services; (2) absenteeism; (3) sick leaves; (4) accident rates; (5) personnel turnover; and (6) feedback from management, workers, safety and occupational health and social services personnel (ILO, 2003).

Second, employers and employees should support and participate in WV risk assessment. In conducting risk assessments, the following possible signs of WV should be considered: (1) physical injuries that lead to actual harm; (2) intense continual abuse, including (a) verbal abuse (e.g. swearing, insults, and condescending language); (b) aggressive body language meant to intimidate or express contempt; and (c) harassment (e.g. mobbing, bullying, and racial and sexual harassment); and (3) expressed intent to cause harm, including verbal and written threats and threatening behavior (ILO, 2003).

Third, incidents of WV should be recorded at organizational, sectoral, national, and international levels. Identifying the sources and forms of WV, its severity and incidence in particular area or task categories, and its possible contributing factors and situational contexts is important for the development of effective control measures. Fourth, governments, employers, employees and their representatives should also raise awareness about WV issues, by disseminating information about WV, and co-operate regionally and internationally in an effort to reduce WV (ILO, 2003).

The report also suggests that the following considerations are important when WV policies and strategies are to be developed: (1) analyzing the full range of factors that contribute to WV; (2) using evidence-based preventive measures, strategies that have been evaluated and proved to be effective; and (3) identifying short-and long-term objectives and planing intervention action while considering realistically achievable goals (ILO, 2003).

Organizational preventive measures are also outlined. The importance of communication among employers, employees, and clients is emphasized, as this could reduce the risk of WV. Preventive measures regarding work practices are also discussed. These pertain to (1) adequate staffing; (2) service capacity and resources; (3) workload; (4) scheduling practices; (5) security and the handling of valuables; and (6) proximity or the possibility of communication for isolated employees.

Prevention strategies related to the physical environment of the workplace are also mentioned. The report suggests that the physical features of a work setting could potentially defuse violent events in the workplace. To reduce the risk of WV (1) at-risk areas and their level of risk should be identified; (2) special attention should be paid to access to and from the workplace, such as parking areas and transportation facilities and to the security services that are in place; (3) barriers and other obstacles that impede a clear view at the workplace should be eliminated; (4) security systems, such as alarms should be installed in dangerous areas; (5) weapons should be banned from the premises, except when these are an inherent part of the occupation; (6) alcohol and drugs should be restricted; and (9) appropriate access control systems for both employees and visitors should be implemented (ILO, 2003).

Incident preparedness and response plans should be developed and maintained in all organizations. Management should be prepared to provide support to workers affected by WV. They should make available appropriate medical treatment and/or referral to all victims. Organizations should help those affected by WV by offering debriefing, explaining what has happened, offering reassurance and support, and informing them about available resources (ILO, 2003).

Last, but not least, current WV prevention practices and policies should be reviewed periodically by competent individuals. The results of the reviews should be communicated to all stakeholders. Evaluation of the effectiveness of WV prevention strategies should include (1) regular monitoring of strategies that were implemented and their results; (2) developing evaluation criteria, evaluating current policies and measures, and making modifications when necessary; (3) informing staff about the specific measures put in place and; (4) reviewing the management plan periodically (ILO, 2003).

Conclusions

Whether from either a domestic or international perspective, WV victimization or perpetration and their effects are realities of the global labor market. Researchers, practitioners and policy makers have made strides to address basic issues surrounding the conceptualization and measurement of WV, and unravel the complexities of the nature and effects of WV. Some organizations have designed and implemented prevention programs and response policies to reduce the incidence of WV in their workplaces, and sometimes in collaboration with other interested parties. Currently, however, WV prevention programs and response policies are far from being universally adopted by all organizations. And what comprises 'best' practices or 'what works,' is far from settled in the WV field as this type of evaluation is in its infancy stages of development.

The WV field is relatively young and hence, there are still several unanswered questions and gaps about the extent and nature of WV and the effectiveness of prevention programs and policies. First, defining what are the concepts of 'violence' and 'workplace' so comparable valid and reliable measures can be developed is much needed. Even if these definitions vary across countries (possibly due to statutory requirements), providing a definition of WV and the types of behaviors that comprise WV are important steps to understanding what phenomena are being measured. Second, developing data collection strategies, especially ones for which comparative WV research can be undertaken, is much needed. The ICVS is one source; other data sources need to be developed that take into account overlooked WV types, such as domestic and intimate partner violence and stalking. Related, the results from the data collected could aid our understanding of the individual, economic, social, and organizational and cultural predictors of WV and its effects on individuals and organizations. Only by understanding the complexities of the predictors of WV can comprehensive strategies be developed and then be effective prevention and security components of each workplace's policies. Fourth, the exchange of information about WV prevention program development, content, implementation and effectiveness worldwide is a critical gap that needs to be filled. Making available what types of WV programs and policies are currently implemented would be a great starting point. The evaluation of these programs and policies is also much needed. Both program content and evaluation information may provide models and incentives for employers to effectively address the incidence and effects of violence in their workplace.

Even with the noted gaps, the current WV body of knowledge has built a framework for future WV research and the development and evaluations of innovative WV policies and programs. This framework is only the beginning of a long-term WV agenda for employees, businesses, and governments. With growing concern by these parties about WV domestically and internationally, the safety and security of workers and organizations must be at the forefront of all research and program and policy development and evaluation.

Key readings

Spector and Fox's edited collection (2005), *Counterproductive Work Behavior: Investigations of Actors and Targets*, Washington, DC, APA, offers an integrative perspective to counterproductive behavior at work. The volume brings together various approaches to understanding how individual level and organizational characteristics create opportunities to experience and perpetrate counterproductive behaviors. Einarsen, Hoel, Zapf and Cooper's edited text (2002), *Bullying and Emotional Abuse in the Workplace: International Perspectives in Research and Practice*, Florida, CRC Press LLC, provides a comprehensive review of the theoretical developments and empirical findings, and practical interventions in the field of workplace bullying. As a companion to these two volumes, *Violence at Work: Causes, Patterns and Prevention*, Cullompton, UK, Willan, edited by Gill, Fisher and Bowie (2002) brings together researchers and practitioners from around the world who offer innovative perspectives and experiences. The chapters address a broad variety of WV issues. The International Labor Organization's *Violence and Stress at Work in Services Sectors* web site, http://www.ilo.org/public/english/dialogue/sector/themes/violence.htm, provides industry-specific information on WV, linking to additional sources on violence and stress around the world. The Health and Safety Executive's *Work Related Violence* web page, http://www.hse.gov.uk/violence/index.htm, presents current WV findings from the BCS, and also posts WV case studies, leaflets, and guidance publications for workers and employers in various industries, offering practical examples on how to reduce the risk of violence using simple and cost-effective measures. Another useful WV web resource is National Institute for Occupational Safety and Health's *Traumatic Occupational Injuries: Occupational Violence* web site, http://www.cdc.gov/niosh/injury/traumaviolence.html. This provides research projects and various publications on occupational violence and homicide in the United States, a searchable bibliographic database of occupational safety and health documents, grant reports, and journal articles, as well as other useful occupational violence links, such as the Bureau of Labor Statistics's occupation, demographic and homicide data.

References

Alvazzi del Frate, A., Hatalak, O. and Zvekic, U. (eds) (2000) *Surveying Crime: A Global Perspective*. Roma: Istituto Nazionale di Statistica (ISTAT).

Annest, J.L., Conn, J.M. and James, S. (1996) *Inventory of Federal Data Systems in the United States for Injury Surveillance, Research and Prevention Activities*. Atlanta, GE: National Center of Injury Prevention and Control, Center for Disease Control and Prevention http://www.cdc.gov/ncipc/pub-res/federal.pdf 24 January 2006.

Babiak, P. (1995) 'When Psychopaths Go to Work: A Case Study of an Industrial Psychopath,' *Applied Psychology*. Vol. 44, No. 2, pp. 171–88.

Bachman, R. (1994) *Violence and Theft in the Workplace*. NCJ study 148199. Washington, DC: US Department of Justice.

Barling, J., Dekker, I., Loughlin, C.A., Kelloway, E.K., Fullagar, C. and Johonson, D. (1996) 'Prediction and Replication of the Organizational and Personal Consequences of Workplace Sexual Harassment,' *Journal of Managerial Psychology*. Vol. 11, pp. 4–25.

Baron, R.A. and Neuman, J.H. (1998) 'Workplace Aggression – The Iceberg Beneath the Tip of Workplace Violence: Evidence on its Forms, Frequency, and Targets,' *Public Administration Quarterly*. Vol. 21, pp. 446–64.

Beale, D., Cox, T., Clarke, D., Lawrence, C. and Leather, P. (1998) 'Temporal Architecture of Violent Incidents,' *Journal of Occupational Health Psychology*. Vol. 3, No. 1, pp. 65–82.

Bell, C.A. and Jenkins, E.L. (1992) *Homicide in US Workplaces: A Strategy for Prevention and Research*. Morgantown: US Department of Health and Human Services, Public Health Center for Disease Control, NIOSH Division of Research.

Bowie, V. (2005) 'Terrorism and Workplace Violence.' In Bowie, V., Fisher, B.S. and Cooper, C.L. (eds) *Workplace Violence: Issues, Trends, Strategies*. Cullompton, UK: Willan.

Boyd, N. (1995) 'Violence in the Workplace in British Columbia: A Preliminary Investigation,' *Canadian Journal of Criminology*. October 1995, pp. 491–519.

Brady, C. (1999) 'Surviving the Incident.' In Leather, P., Brady, C., Lawrence, C., Beale, D. and Cox, T. (eds) *Work-related Violence: Assessment and Intervention*. London: Routledge.

Budd, T. (2001) *Violence at Work: New Findings from the 2000 British Crime Survey*. Home Office RDS Publication. London: Home Office. http://www.hse.gov.uk/violence/britishcrimesurvey.pdf 24 January 2006.

Bulatao, E. and VandenBos, G.R. (1996) 'Workplace Violence: Its Scope and the Issues.' In VandenBos, G.R. and Bulato, E. (eds) *Violence on the Job: Identifying Risks and Developing Solutions.* Washington, DC: APA.

Bureau of Labor Statistics (BLS) (2004) *Official Web Site.* http://www.bls.gov/ 24 January 2006.

BLS (1994) *Violence in the Workplace Comes under Closer Scrutiny.* Washington, DC: US Department of Labor. http://www.bls.gov/iif/oshwc/ossm0006.pdf 24 January 2006.

California Occupational Safety and Health Administration (Cal/OSHA) (1995) *Cal/OSHA Guidelines for Workplace Security.* San Francisco, CA: State of California Department of Industrial Relations, Californian Division of Occupational Safety and Health http://www.dir.ca.gov/dosh/dosh_publications/worksecurity.html 24 January 2006.

Cappozzoli, T.K. and McVey, R.S. (1996) *Managing Violence in the Workplace.* Florida: St. Lucie Press.

Casteel, C. and Peek-Asa, C. (2000) 'Effectiveness of Crime Prevention through Environmental Design (CPTED) in Reducing Robberies,' *American Journal of Preventive Medicine.* Vol. 18, No. 4, pp. 99–115.

Casteel, C., Chronister, T., Grayson, J.L. and Kraus, J.F. (2003) 'Partnerships and Collaborations to Prevent Robbery-Related Workplace Violence.' In Wilkinson, C. and Peek-Asa, C. (eds) *Clinics in Occupational and Environmental Medicine.* Vol. 3, No. 4, pp. 763–74. Philadelphia: W.B. Saunders.

Chappell, D. and Di Martino, V. (1998a) *Violence at Work.* Geneva: SAFEWORK, ILO. http://www.ilo.org/public/english/protection/safework/violence/violwk/violwk.pdf 24 January 2006.

Chappell, D. and Di Martino, V. (1998b) *Violence at Work.* Geneva: ILO.

Chappell, D. and Di Martino, V. (2000) *Violence at Work.* (2nd ed.). Geneva: ILO.

Chen, P.Y. and Spector, P.E. (1992) 'Relationship of Work Stressors with Aggression, Withdrawal, Theft and Substance Use: An Exploratory Study,' *Journal of Occupational and Organizational Psychology.* Vol. 65, pp. 177–84.

The *Convention on the Elimination of All Forms of Discrimination against Women (CEDAW)* (1979) http://www.un.org/womenwatch/daw/cedaw/ 24 January 2006.

Cooper, C.L., Liukkonen, P. and Cartwright, S. (1996) *Stress Prevention in the Workplace: Assessing the Costs and Benefits for Organizations.* Dublin: European Foundation for the Improvement of Living and Working Conditions.

Daphne II EU Programme (2004) http://europa.eu.int/comm/justice_home/funding/daphne/funding_daphne_en.htm 24 January 2006.

Di Martino, V., Hoel, H. and Cooper, C.L. (2003) *Preventing Violence and Harassment in the Workplace.* European Foundation for the Improvement of Living and Working Conditions. Luxembourg: Office for Official Publications of the European Communities. http://www.fr.eurofound.eu.int/publications/files/EF02109EN.pdf 24 January 2006.

Di Martino, V. (2002) *Workplace Violence in the Health Sector: Country Case Studies, Brazil, Bulgaria, Lebanon, Portugal, South Africa, Thailand and an Additional Australian Study.* Geneva: ICN. http://www.icn.ch/SynthesisReportWorkplaceViolenceHealthSector.pdf 24 January 2006.

Dorman, P. (2000) *The Economics of Safety, Health and Well-being at Work: An Overview.* Geneva: ILO. http://www.ilo.org/public/english/protection/safework/papers/ecoanal/ecoview.pdf 24 January 2006.

Duhart, E. (2001) *Bureau of Justice Statistics Special Report: Violence in the Workplace, 1993–99.* NCJ Study 190076. Washington, DC: US Department of Justice. http://www.ojp.usdoj.gov/bjs/pub/pdf/vw99.pdf 24 January 2006.

Einarsen, S., Hoel, H., Zapf, D. and Cooper, C.L. (eds) (2002) *Bullying and Emotional Abuse in the Workplace: International Perspectives in Research and Practice.* Boca Raton, Florida: CRC Press LLC.

Einarsen, S., Hoel, H., Zapf, D. and Cooper, C.L. (2005) 'Workplace bullying: Individual pathology or organizational culture?' In Bowie, V., Fisher, B.S. and Cooper, C.L. (eds) *Workplace Violence: Issues, Trends, Strategies.* Cullompton, UK: Willan.

Elliott, R.H. and Jarrett, J.T. (1994) 'Violence in the Workplace: The Role of Human Resource Management,' *Public Personnel Management*. Vol. 23, No. 2, pp. 287–300.

An End to Sexual Harassment at Work (2004) Daphne: An EU Response to Combat Violence Toward Children, Young People and Women, Illustrative Case # 6 http://europa.eu.int/comm/justice_home/funding/daphne/documents/illustrative_cases/illustrative_cases_en/06_pandora_en.pdf 18 December 2004.

Farmer, A. and Tiefenthaler, J. (2004) 'The Employment Effects of Domestic Violence,' *Research in Labor Economics*. Vol. 23, pp. 301–34.

Fisher, B.S. and Peek-Asa, C. (2005) 'Domestic Violence and the Workplace: Do We Know Too Much of Nothing?' In Bowie, V., Fisher, B.S. and Cooper, C. (eds) *Workplace Violence: Issues, Trends, Strategies*. Cullompton, UK: Willan.

Flannery, R.B. (1996) 'Violence in the Workplace, 1970–1995: A Review of the Literature,' *Aggression and Violent Behavior*. Vol. 1, pp. 57–68.

Gill, M., Fisher, B.S. and Bowie, V. (eds) (2002) *Violence at Work: Causes, Patterns and Prevention*. Cullompton, UK: Willan.

Health and Safety Executive (HSE): Work Related Violence (2005) *Official Web Site*. http://www.hse.gov.uk/violence/index.htm 24 January 2006.

The Health and Safety at Work Act 1974 (1974) Elizabeth II 1974, Chapter 37. Healthy and Safety Homepages. London: Professional Health and Safety Consultants Ltd. http://www.healthandsafety.co.uk/haswa.htm 24 January 2006.

Hearn J. and Parkin, W. (2001) *Gender, Sexuality and Violence in Organizations: The Unspoken Forces of Organization Violations*. London: Sage.

Hoel, H., Sparks, K. and Cooper, C.L. (2001) *The Cost of Violence/Stress at Work and The Benefits of a Violence/Stress-Free Working Environment*. Report Commissioned by the ILO Geneva http://www.ilo.org/public/english/protection/safework/whpwb/econo/costs.pdf 24 January 2006.

Homel, R. and Clark, J. (1994) 'The Prediction of Violence in Pubs and Clubs,' *Prevention Studies*. Vol. 3, pp. 1–46.

Howard, J. and Barish, R.C. (2003) 'Government Approaches to Reducing Workplace Violence.' In Wilkinson, C. and Peek-Asa, C. *Clinics in Occupational and Environmental Medicine*. Vol. 3, No. 4, pp. 721–32. Philadelphia: W.B. Saunders.

International Crime Victimization Survey (ICVS) (1999) Steinmetz Archive Documentation Set: Version 1.0. Amsterdam: Netherlands Institute for Scientific Information Services (NIWI) http://www.unicri.it/icvs/data/questionnaires/Questionnaires%201989_1996.pdf 18 December 2004.

International Labor Organization (ILO) (2004) *Official Web Site* http://www.ilo.org/ 24 January 2006.

ILO (2003) *Code of Practice on Workplace Violence in Services Sectors and Measures to Combat this Phenomenon*. ILO study MEVSWS/2003/11. Geneva: ILO http://www.ilo.org/public/english/dialogue/sector/techmeet/mevsws03/mevsws-cp.pdf 24 January 2006.

ILO (2001) *Action Against Sexual Harassment at Work in Asia and the Pacific: Technical Report for Discussion at the ILO/Japan Regional Tripartite Seminar on Action Against Sexual Harassment at Work in Asia and the Pacific, Penang, Malaysia, 2–4 October 2001*. ILO East Asia Multidisciplinary Advisory Team and Bangkok Area Office http://www.ilo.org/public/english/protection/condtrav/pdf/hvs-sh-tr-01.pdf. 18 December 2004.

The *ILO Declaration on Fundamental Principles and Rights at Work* (1998) http://www.ilo.org/dyn/declaris/DECLARATIONWEB.ABOUTDECLARATIONHOME?var_language=EN 24 January 2006.

The *International Covenant of Economic, Social and Cultural Rights* (1966) The United Nations: Office of the High Commissioner for Human Rights http://www.unhchr.ch/html/menu3/b/a_cescr.htm 24 January 2006.

Jeffery, C.R. (1971) Crime Prevention through Environmental Design. Beverly Hills, CA: Sage.

Jenkins, L.E. (1996) 'Workplace Homicide: Industries and Occupations at High Risk,' *Occupational Medicine*. Vol. 11, No. 2, pp. 219–25.

Kivimaki, K., Elovainio, M. and Vahtera, J. (2000) 'Workplace Bullying and Sickness Absence in Hospital Staff,' *Occupational and Environmental Medicine.* Vol. 57, pp. 656–60.

Koss, M.P. (1990) 'Changed Lives: The Psychological Impact of Sexual Harassment.' In Paludi, M. (ed.) *Ivory Power: Sexual Harassment on Campus.* Albany, NY: SUNY Press.

Leather, P., Brady, C., Lawrence, C., Beale, D. and Cox, T. (eds) (1999) Work-related Violence: Assessment and Intervention. London: Routledge.

Leather, P., Lawrence, C., Beale, D., Cox, T. and Dixon, R. (1998) *Exposure to Occupational Violence and the Buffering Effects of Intra-organizational Support. Work and Stress.* Vol. 12, pp. 161–78.

LeBlanc, M. and Barling, J. (2005) 'Understanding the many faces of workplace violence.' In Spector, P. and Fox, S. (eds) *Counterproductive behavior at work: Investigations of actors and targets.* Washington, DC: American Psychological Association.

Levi, L. and Lunde-Jensen, P. (1995) *A Model for Assessing the Costs of Stressors at National Level: Socio-Economic Costs of Stress in Two EU Member States.* Dublin: European Foundation for the Improvement of Living and Working Conditions.

Licu, E., Barberet, R. and Fisher, B.S. (2005) 'International Crime Statistics: Data Sources and Problems of Interpretation.' In Wright, R.A. and Miller, J.M. (eds). *Encyclopedia of Criminology.* New York: Routledge.

Lynch, J. (1987) 'Routine Activity and Victimization at Work,' *Journal of Quantitative Criminology,* Vol. 3, No. 4, pp. 282–300.

The Management of Health and Safety at Work Regulations 1992 (1992) Statutory Instrument 1992 No. 2051. Her Majesty's Stationery Office (HMSO). The Stationery Office Limited http://www.hmso.gov.uk/si/si1992/Uksi_19922051_en_1.htm#end 24 January 2006.

Marshall, S.W., Loomis, D.P. and Gurka, K.K. (2003) 'Preventing Workplace Violence through Environmental and Administrative Controls.' In Wilkinson, C. and Peek-Asa, C. *Clinics in Occupational and Environmental Medicine.* Vol. 3, No. 4, pp. 751–62. Philadelphia: W.B. Saunders.

Mayhew, C. and Quinlan, M. (1999) *The Relationships between Precarious Employment and Patterns of Occupational Violence: Survey Evidence from Thirteen Occupations.* In Isaksson, C., Hogstedt, C., Eriksson, C. and Theorell, T. (eds) Health Effects of the New Labor Market. New York: Kluwer Academic.

Mayhew, C. (2004) *Crime and Violence Prevention: Occupational Violence in Australia: An Annotated Bibliography of Prevention Policies, Strategies, and Guidance Materials.* http://www.aic.gov.au/research/cvp/occupational/ 18 December 2004.

McCarthy, P. (2004) 'Costs of Occupational Violence and Bullying.' In McCarthy, P. and Mayhew, C. (eds) *Safeguarding the Organization against Violence and Bullying: An International Perspective.* London: Palgrave Macmillan.

McCarthy, P. and Mayhew, C. (eds) (2004) *Safeguarding the Organization against Violence and Bullying: An International Perspective.* London: Palgrave Macmillan.

Mukherjee, S. (1981) *Crime Trends in Twentieth Century Australia.* Sydney: Allen and Unwin.

NIOSH (2004) *Violence in the Workplace: Risk Factors and Prevention Strategies* http://www.cdc.gov/niosh/violrisk.html 24 January 2006.

The National Institute for Occupational Safety and Health (NIOSH) (2004a) *About NIOSH.* Center for Disease Control (CDC) http://www.cdc.gov/niosh/about.html 24 January 2006.

NIOSH (1997) *NIOSH Facts: Violence in the Workplace.* Document 705002. NIOSH and CDC http://www.cdc.gov/niosh/violfs.html 24 January 2006.

Nieuwbeerta, P. (ed.) (2002) *Crime Victimization in Comparative Perspective: Results from the International Crime Victims Survey, 1989–2000.* The Hague: Boom Juridische uitgevers.

National Occupational Health and Safety Commission (NOHSC) (2004) Official Web Site. Australian Government http://www.nohsc.gov.au/ 24 January 2006.

NOHSC (1999) *Program One Report: Occupational Violence.* Paper discussed at the 51st Meeting of the Australian National Occupational Health and Safety Commission held 10 March 1999. Hobart, unpublished NOHSC papers.

Occupational Safety and Health Administration (OSHA) (1998) *Recommendations for Workplace Violence Prevention Programs in Late-Night Retail Establishments.* US Department of Labor, OSHA 3153 http://www.osha.gov/Publications/osha3153.pdf 24 January 2006.
OSHA (2004) *Laws, Regulations and Interpretations.* US Department of Labor http://www.osha.gov/comp-links.html 24 January 2006.
Paoli, P. and Merllié, D. (2001) *Third European on Working Conditions 2000.* European Foundation for the Improvement of Living and Working Conditions. Luxembourg: Office for Official Publications of the European Communities. http://www.eurofound.eu.int/publications/files/EF0121EN.pdf 24 January 2006.
Peek-Asa, C. and Jenkins, L. (2003) 'Workplace Violence: How Do We Improve Approaches to Prevention?' In Wilkinson, C. and Peek-Asa, C. (eds) *Clinics in Occupational and Environmental Medicine.* Vol. 3, No. 4, pp. 659–72. Philadelphia: W.B. Saunders.
Perrone, S. (1999) *Violence in the Workplace.* Australian Institute of Criminology (AIC) Research and Public Policy Series, 22. Canberra: AIC http://www.aic.gov.au/publications/rpp/22/ 24 January 2006.
Pizzino, A. (2002) 'Dealing with Violence in the Workplace: The Experience of Canadian Unions.' In Gill, M., Fisher, B. and Bowie, V. (eds) *Violence at Work: Causes, Patterns and Prevention.* Cullompton, UK: Willan.
The Protection from Harassment Act 1997 (1997) Chapter 40. Her Majesty's Stationery Office (HMSO). The Stationery Office Limited http://www.hmso.gov.uk/acts/acts1997/1997040.htm 24 January 2006.
Quine, L. (1999) 'Workplace Bullying in NHS Community Trust: Staff Questionnaire Survey,' *British Medical Journal.* Vol. 318, pp. 228–32.
Rogers, K. and Kelloway, E.K. (1997) 'Violence at Work: Personal and Organizational Outcomes,' *Journal of Occupational Health Psychology.* Vol. 2, pp. 63–71.
Rosen, J. (2001) 'A Labor Perspective of Workplace Violence Prevention: Identifying Research Needs,' *American Journal of Preventive Medicine.* Vol. 20, No. 2, pp. 161–8.
Rugala, E.A. and Fitzgerald, J.R. (2003) 'Workplace Violence: From Threat to Intervention.' In Wilkinson, C. and Peek-Asa, C. (eds) *Clinics in Occupational and Environmental Medicine.* Vol. 3, No. 4, pp. 775–81. Philadelphia: W.B. Saunders.
Rugala, EA.. and Isaacs, A.R. (eds) (2004) *Workplace Violence: Issues in Response.* US Department of Justice, FBI. Quanitco, Virginia: NCAVC, FBI Academy http://www.fbi.gov/publications/violence.pdf 24 January 2006.
Runyan, C.W., Schulman, M. and Hoffman, C.D. (2003) 'Understanding and Preventing Violence against Adolescent Workers: What Is Known and What Is Missing?' In Wilkinson, C. and Peek-Asa, C. (eds) *Clinics in Occupational and Environmental Medicine.* Vol. 3, No. 4, pp. 711–20. Philadelphia: W.B. Saunders.
Runyan, C.W., Zackocs, R.C. and Zwerling, C. (2000) 'Administrative and Behavioral Interventions for Workplace Violence Prevention,' *American Journal of Preventive Medicine.* Vol. 18, No. 4, pp. 116–27.
Spector, P.E. (1997) 'The Role of Frustration in Antisocial Behavior at Work.' In Giacalone, R.A. and Greenberg J. (eds) *Anti-Social Behaviors and Organizations.* Thousand Oaks, CA: Sage.
Spector, P. and Fox, S. (eds) (2005) *Counterproductive behavior at work: Investigations of actors and targets.* Washington, DC: American Psychological Association.
Speer, R.A. (2003) 'Workplace Violence: A Legal Perspective.' In Wilkinson, C. and Peek-Asa, C. (eds) *Clinics in Occupational and Environmental Medicine.* Vol. 3, No. 4, pp. 733–49. Philadelphia: W.B. Saunders.
Snyder, L.A., Chen, P., Grubb, P., Roberts, R., Sauter, S. and Swanson, N. (2005) 'Workplace Aggression and Violence against Individuals and Organizations: Causes, Consequences, and Interventions.' In Perrewe, P.L. and Ganster, D.C. (eds) *Research in Occupational Stress and Well Being: Exploring Interpersonal Dynamics.* Vol. 4, pp. 1–65. San Diego: Elsevier JAI.
Stockdale, M. (1996) 'What We Know and What We Need to Know about Sexual Harassment.' In Stockdale, M. (ed.) *Sexual Harassment in the Workplace: Perspectives, Frontiers and Response Strategies.* Thousand Oaks, CA: Sage.

Taylor, N. and Mayhew, P. (2002) *Financial and Psychological Costs of Crime for Small Retail Businesses*. Australian Institute of Criminology (AIC) Trends and Issues in Crime and Criminal Justice 229. Canberra: AIC http://www.aic.gov.au/publications/tandi/ti229.pdf 24 January 2006.

Tobin, T.J. (2001) 'Organizational Determinants of Violence in the Workplace,' *Aggression and Violent Behavior*. Vol. 6, pp. 91–102.

Upson, A. (2004) *Violence at Work: Findings from the 2002/2003 British Crime Survey*. Home Office Online Report. London: Home Office, RDS. http://www.hse.gov.uk/violence/bcsviolence0203.pdf 24 January 2006.

US Occupational Health and Safety Act (1970) http://www.osha-slc.gov/pls/oshaweb/owadisp.show_document?p_table=OSHACT&p_id=2743 24 January 2006.

Vartia, M. (1996) 'The Sources of Bullying: Psychological Work Environment and Organizational Climate,' *European Journal of Work and Organizational Psychology*. Vol. 52, pp. 203–14.

Verdugo, R. and Vere, A. (2003) *Workplace Violence in Service Sectors with Implications for the Education Sector: Issues, Solutions and Resources*. ILO Sectoral Activities Working Paper, 208. Geneva: ILO. http://www.ilo.org/public/english/dialogue/sector/papers/education/wp208.pdf 24 January 2006.

Warchol, G. (1998) *Workplace Violence, 1992–1996*. NCJ Study 169634. Washington, DC: US Department of Justice.

Warshaw, L.J. and Messite, J. (1996) 'Workplace Violence: Preventive and Interventive Strategies,' *Journal of Occupational and Environmental Medicine*. Vol. 38, pp. 993–1006.

White, W.L. (1997) *The Incestuous Workplace: Stress and Distress in the Organizational Family*. Center City, Minnesota: Hazelden.

Wilkinson, C. and Peek-Asa, C. (eds) (2003) 'Violence in the Workplace,' *Clinics in Occupational and Environmental Medicine*. Vol. 3, No. 4. Philadelphia: W.B. Saunders.

Willis, A., Beck, A. and Gill, M. (1999) 'Violent Victimization of Staff in the Retail Sector,' *Journal of Security Administration*. Vol. 22, No. 2, pp. 23–30.

Workplace Health and Safety Act 1995 (1995) Tasmanian Legislation: Tasmania's Legislation Consolidated Online http://www.thelaw.tas.gov.au/tocview/index.w3p;cond=;doc_id=13%2B%2B1995%2BAT%40EN%2B20041219000000;histon=;prompt=;rec=-1;term=18 December 2004.

Workplace Health and Safety Act 1995 (2004) Office of the Queensland Parliamentary Counsel http://www.legislation.qld.gov.au/LEGISLTN/CURRENT/W/WorkplHSaA95.pdf 18 December 2004.

World Health Assembly (1996) *Prevention of Violence: Public Health Priority*. Forty-Ninety World Health Assembly, Geneva http://www.who.int/violence_injury_prevention/resources/publications/en/WHA4925_eng.pdf 24 January 2006.

11

Combating White-Collar and Organized Economic Crimes: Some Reflections on the Role of Security

Michael Levi

Introduction

Business leaders commonly assert that brand reputation is one of the most important components of a business's assets. One might imagine that crime risks, and in particular crimes committed with the active or reckless participation of the business (including its agents), would constitute a significant component of reputational risk, at least if and when exposed or deemed plausibly likely to be exposed at some future date. Yet it is not obvious (1) who – within corporations or outside them – has ownership of the prevention of frauds by and against business, and (2) what the role of security and crime risk managers is in preventing before the fact or in dealing after the fact with financial crimes such as mis-selling of financial services products and of bribery committed with the apparent aim of helping the business (and the individuals' careers). Let us examine the first question. In the flourishing sense of crisis in 'law and order' in most Western countries, most focus has been on populist crimes against individuals, even including terrorism risks. In the particular case of fraud – white-collar or blue-collar – from the amount of governmental, academic and, to a lesser extent, private sector effort devoted to serious analysis of fraud issues in most Western countries, one would have to conclude 'no-one very much has ownership'. Negligible research funding has been allocated to this area by governmental criminological research agencies. Furthermore, the subject of financial crime also remained off the research agenda of UK business promotion and development agencies such as the UK Department of Trade and Industry until the creation of the (now disbanded) Crime Foresight Panel (2000) and before some technology and crime reduction initiatives in the early 21st century.[1] True, post-Enron and Parmalat, there has been a strong focus on corporate governance (Green, 2004), and compliance jobs have blossomed to deal with that (especially with the US Sarbanes-Oxley Act 2002) and (in financial services) with money-laundering: but the issues remain outside the crime control mainstream.

At the international level, the neglect of financial crime may be because the International Monetary Fund and similar bodies are concerned only with 'macro-economically relevant' phenomena and, with the exception of some offshore finance transparency issues highlighted in major frauds such as the Bank of Credit and Commerce International, Enron and Parmalat, very few frauds (and no other sorts of business crimes except, arguably, those that have a major effect on the financing of terrorism) qualify as macro-economically relevant, though some systemic corruption and related financial crimes by senior government personnel might do so. Capital flight and money-laundering have certainly become significant components of international banking and G7 deliberations (Gilmore, 2004; Levi and Gilmore, 2002), even before '9/11', but the admixture in the Anti-Money Laundering movement between crime and financial stability continues to be an uneasy one. At the national level, the neglect of financial crimes may also have something to do with the focus of government on the 'old' business sectors of manufacturing, wholesale and retail rather than the late modern service industry (including financial services) sectors, symbolized by the absence of those service sectors from the Home Office-funded Commercial Victimisation Surveys (Mirrlees-Black and Ross, 1995; Taylor, 2004). Although 'risk management' has entered Home Office and police thinking – for example over the management of sex offenders in the community and over serious crime investigations – neither bodies are well equipped to comprehend risk management in the contemporary business sense, despite the formation in 2004 of a small 'business and crime' section of the Home Office. Readers might give some thought to the question of why frauds attract such modest sympathy in the media, except for 'identity frauds' and 'widows and orphans frauds' that fall squarely within that populist agenda, though mostly for their effects upon individuals rather than upon businesses great and small (see Levi and Pithouse, forthcoming).

Although this chapter (and book) is written primarily for business security and compliance personnel and for scholars interested in those areas, it is important to place the fraud and other financial crime issues in a broader perspective of corporate social responsibility and legal liabilities. (The latter vary in different parts of the globe, corporate criminal liability being generated by actions much lower down the corporate ladder in the US than in the UK, and being jurisprudentially alien to the Germanic countries.) One might seek to differentiate between 'frauds for gain' and 'corporate crimes that deliberately or inadvertently hurt workers, customers or the environment'. However, though the harms caused by the latter may not be directly intended, it is normally more profitable for such crimes to occur than not to occur, so financial/career motives are often implicated in 'decisions' not to prevent them. Wider economic trends – such as the outsourcing of back office, call centres and physical production to legally separate businesses, often in the Third World, to reduce labour and compliance costs – under the vague banner of 'globalization' have affected many crime and business continuity risks and have often reduced direct corporate control over them, and these are security issues to be managed as well as employment issues that have aroused Western governments, more troubled by domestic job losses than about improving standards of living in the developing world. One of the risks not just from outsourcing but from transnational expansion generally is that corruption, family and group loyalties, and/or threats may more readily lead to subversion of employees (and possibly senior management too) in some Third World countries than in the UK; this may affect not just direct fraud and theft but also data security (for example payment card and customer/staff identification details held on corporate data systems). Nevertheless, for reasons of space, I have decided to focus here on the control of financial crimes involving the manipulation of trust. Some such crimes affect business directly as victims of fraud; others affect customers directly via mis-selling and may generate reputational risk and regulator/ investor reactions that can also be costly. A third category – money laundering – may not generate direct losses to anyone but may lead to regulatory sanctions and even criminal prosecutions for intermediaries.

Analytical perspectives on financial crime risks

Traditionally, white-collar crime scholars focused upon the inadequacies of conventional criminological theories (poverty, genetic defects, family pathology) to explain crimes by business, political and professional elites (see Croall, 2001; Nelken, 2002 – though see also Simpson and Piquero, 2002). Rather, they argued, one had to understand such crimes as the product of cultural and organizational learning processes, combined with the development of rationalizations that enabled white-collar offenders to see their conduct as being socially acceptable and not 'real crimes', a view reinforced by the rarity with which they are prosecuted and openly stigmatized (Benson, 1985; Willott *et al.*, 2001). However, considerable effort was expended in discussing what counted as sufficiently high socio-economic status to merit the label of white-collar criminal: did one have to be a minister or was being an MP enough? Were a bank manager or an accountant sufficiently high up? What about those high-class con artists whose professions were fraud – were they excluded? What kind of criteria other than a criminal conviction – e.g. administrative sanctions, media allegations of misconduct – were sufficient to qualify a business or an individual to be labelled a 'white-collar criminal'? In an attempt to focus on the characteristics of the crime rather than the socio-economic status of offenders, Shapiro (1990) suggests that we begin sampling from *settings* of trust and examine how fiduciaries define and enforce trust norms, the structural opportunities for abuse, the patterns of misconduct that ensue, and the social control processes – commercial, family and criminal justice – that respond. However, any 'trust violation' sample drawn from criminal court processes leaves us with what one might term 'blue-white collar crime' (see Hollinger and Davis, this volume), in the sense that the proportion of convicted offenders drawn from elite social and business networks is very small, even in countries such as the US that are more vigorous in pursuit of crimes by elite businesspeople and politicians than is the UK.[2]

As the definitional discussion above highlights, there is a need for clarity in the objectives regarding what *forms* of financial crime one wants to reduce and by how much. This is true even when we conduct a risk analysis of frauds against business. Since reliable and testable data are available most readily for volume crime, mostly by outsiders against companies, this might lead us to neglect frauds by senior management against companies or against the public (whether as consumers or taxpayers). Although this might include some areas of reputational risk such as identity fraud, it would exclude others such as mis-selling of financial services products, money laundering and self-dealing (insider dealing or corrupt purchasing arrangements) by senior corporate personnel, where evidence of incidence and prevalence is less certain. But even in the case of volume fraud, data on common frauds against insurance companies remain poor compared with payment card fraud data. Developing the revisionist situational crime prevention line of Clarke and Homel (1997), we can express the objectives and some possible ways of achieving them in the following formulation:

- Increase perceived effort of fraud and corruption
  - Targeted risk-based prevention efforts, with better regulation of contract bidding process and vetting, and measures to make fraudsters work harder for the same level of income
- Increase perceived risks from fraud and corruption
  - Faster reaction time in detecting fraudulent attempts; efficient and independent investigations and criminal justice process to balance consciousness-raising
  - Proactive integrity testing and independent complaints mechanisms
- Reduce the anticipated rewards from fraud and corruption
  - Catch the corrupt quicker at supplier and purchaser countries and better asset recovery[3]
- Reduce the excuses for fraud and corruption
  - Strengthen independence of media and civil society, with clear condemnation of behaviour,[4] and elite role models who are not themselves fraudulent or corrupt.

However, even excluding those forms of behaviour such as insider trading where there are no identifiable victims or, arguably, no victims at all, there are so many different types of fraud and of victim/offender relationships that it would be a mistake to take all these as a homogeneous issue. 'Fraud' includes, for example:

- *crimes by élites against consumers, clients or other, lower status businesspeople* e.g. the looting of a bank or building society in a country that does not have a full compensation scheme; misrepresentation of the quality of goods beyond mere inflation of the quality of what one is selling (for if the latter were included, most salespeople would be committing fraud).
- *crimes by businesspeople against consumers and employees*, e.g. knowingly or recklessly selling counterfeit goods as genuine ones, and pocketing the National Insurance and/or occupational pension contributions paid by staff in order to benefit personally and/or to keep the business running.[5]

- *crimes by professional criminals against élites/large corporations* e.g. bankruptcy 'long firm' fraud; major counterfeiting rings; mortgage frauds; 'advance fee' frauds.
- *crimes by blue-collar persistent offenders/opportunists against financial institutions* e.g. using lost and stolen payment card and cheque frauds.
- *crimes by individuals of various status against government* e.g. fraud against the financial interests of the European Union, social security frauds by landlords and claimants and tax evasion (including paying workers in cash without additional contributions).

Opportunities for crime: forms of social and technical organization as criminogenic factors

Shapiro (1990) notes that agents (in the legal sense) end up with a great deal of power because they hold information that cannot readily be assessed or verified by their principals: information about profitability and risks, for example; and information about how they have disbursed funds (including, in some cases, to themselves or to their covert nominees) – the asymmetric information is a principal cause of market failure.[6] Bank agents can make non-arms length loans to their friends, using collateral which is fictitious, forged (especially easy with new technologies), stolen, or grossly overvalued by supposedly independent professionals such as real estate valuers: principals who perceive that there is a serious risk of such fraud seek out as their agents people of 'good reputation' (about whom they and others may be mistaken or whose economic circumstances may have changed, leaving them vulnerable to deception). Principals can seldom physically see what their agents are doing but rely instead upon contracts that may require (in law) prior permission for particular sorts of transactions (e.g. futures contracts) beyond a particular sum of money, and upon the face validity of paperwork such as share certificates, bills of lading, contract notes, bank deposit certification or even a genuine-looking payment card and/or signature. They can also be deceived by new technologies such as the re-routing facilities generated by call-forwarding and outright telephone diversion, so that while they think they are checking something out with the British Embassy in Nigeria, they are in fact speaking to some conspirators of the Nigerians in an advance fee scam; or when they think they are phoning a number in one of the more respectable Offshore Finance Centres, they are speaking to a con artist in some completely different country. Often, only mobile phone numbers are left with the victim-to-be, and it is not easy for people to tell whether a foreign number is a landline or mobile phone.[7] In Internet fraud, imposing web-sites do not imply respectability (especially if the websites have been hi-jacked or phished). Indeed one may characterize the contemporary world as one in which *interpersonal* trust has largely been replaced by impersonal mechanisms such as international credit bureaux (for traders assessing their customers) or government/regulator sites warning of particular scams and listing firms who are authorized to trade in financial services (in the country concerned only, since their jurisdiction is based on territoriality): by inference, anyone not authorized has to be taken at the trader or investor's own risk, though the trader/investor may not appreciate this. (In 'advanced' societies, authorization for deposit and investment purposes[8] carries with it a variable State-backed guarantee of compensation should the financial institution collapse or the transactions prove fraudulent: this creates an incentive for regulators to detect and act against fraud and reckless trading.)

Although some organizations are merely instruments of fraud, for the most part, it appears that financial services malpractice often grows out of dependence on individual commission payments rather than salaries, which incentivizes lying as well as selling. In principle, this can be checked and controlled by 'mystery shopping' in which the employer checks whether or not its sales force actually conducted business in the way that they were supposed to: but whether from greed or from optimistic faith in their staff, this was very seldom done. (Indeed, unless offending was very common and widely distributed, it might not be considered cost-effective to adopt such strategies: without being very lucky and getting an early 'hit', it would be expensive to keep surveillance on over a lengthy period.) Following mis-selling of pensions scandals and large compensation payments and fines, major British life assurance companies have changed the salary balance for staff, reducing the proportion paid on commission, and have stopped door-to-door selling, whatever the effect on level of sales and corporate profitability. Second, an unintended consequence of bonus payments for senior executives, combined with high job mobility, is to make it less likely that there will be heavy upfront investment by business in long-term fraud prevention, since those making investment decisions do not expect to be around long enough to receive the benefits. Third, the status of regulatory roles such as compliance officer is normally much lower than those of sales or of Chief Financial Officers, on which corporate survival and growth depends. The exception to this is after a major scandal (such as the Bank of New York experienced following widespread allegations of Russian money-laundering at some of its branches), when compliance roles are mandated under severe pressure and intense regulatory monitoring.

Money laundering

The other major area of financial crime discussed here is money laundering. Financial services businesses should be interested in money laundering because if compliance officers – a type of security function – get things wrong, the institution may go out of business or at best be hit with a large fine, bad publicity and expensive rehabilitation. However, all businesses are affected because of the need to indicate who their beneficial owners are and by enhanced monitoring of business accounts to ensure that the business is operating as the bankers were told it would do. Some perspective is necessary. When merchants negotiated payments over long distances in ancient times, when usury was a crime as well as a sin, they would inflate exchange rates to cover interest. They would claim that interest charges were a special premium to compensate for risk and would make interest costs appear a penalty for late payment – while lender and borrower agreed in advance on a delay. They would 'lend' money to the equivalent of a shell company, then take payment, supposedly in profits, even though no profit had been made.

Three things brought about a transformation in the money laundering issue. First (stimulated by the need to finance world wars), governments shifted the fiscal base from taxing commodities to taxing income, putting a premium on evasion. Second, governments began to criminalize personal vice, requiring people earning illegal incomes from supplying wanted but forbidden desires to disguise the take. Third, came massive capital flight, and the growth of offshore financial centres: although most customers were (and still are) transnational corporations and wealthy rentiers aiming to reduce their tax liabilities, the facilities also attracted 'real criminals' (Naylor, 2004).

Properly defined in conceptual terms, money laundering is a three-stage process. It requires: first, moving the funds from direct association with the crime; second, disguising the trail to foil pursuit; and, third, making the funds again available to the instigator with their occupational origins hidden from view.[9] Thus money laundering is not burying cash in a large box in the middle of a garden in Liverpool, negotiating a bearer bond in a Swiss bank, or buying a BMW with a gold bar. Money is not truly laundered unless it is given sufficient appearance of legitimacy to permit it to be used openly, without fear of asset confiscation.

Nor is money laundering restricted to major cocaine or heroin traffickers. The techniques can be employed by small-town used-car dealers or company directors who want to evade payments to ex-wives or business creditors. If underground entrepreneurs – from stock market manipulators to cigarette smugglers – must launder money, so too must otherwise legitimate corporations to disguise a bribe to a customer or to a politician for a necessary permit: this is an issue that the firm's audit department and – where they have one – compliance officer may need to deal with proactively, but may not be within the remit of the security department unless large amounts of cash need to be collected or transported.

Legislators have drafted ever-more comprehensively in response to both national and international pressures, so that legal prohibitions include any storage or conversion of (a) proceeds of crime and (b) funds intended to finance terrorism, irrespective of whether anyone intended to go through the full concealment process. Hence corporate vehicles (including franchises), accountants, lawyers and bankers can fall foul of laundering legislation, if they are used as fronts or fail to make reports of conduct they found or ought have found to be suspicious.

The criminal can purchase a piece of property. The publicly recorded price, set well below market value, is paid with legitimately earned money by formal funds transfer. The rest is paid in cash under-the-table. The property is resold for full market value and the money recouped, with the illegal component appearing as a capital gain. Going one step further, a run-down building can be acquired using partly legal and partly illegal money, and builders – legal or illegal migrants

– hired and paid in cash (further dissipating the illicit funds). Since they are earning tax-free, they will not be inclined to talk. The building can be sold for a double capital gain, part due to the original undervaluation and part due to the renovations. Alternatively the building could be a rental property. Not only can illicit money partially fund its purchase, but more can be laundered by reporting the illicit funds as rent payments. (Whoever checks whether high rents were really paid by tenants?[10]) Inflated rental returns enhance the capital gain realizable on final sale. Or they can be the basis for a higher assessment to justify a bank lending more money which the entrepreneur can use to buy yet more buildings (Beare and Schneider, 1990; Middleton and Levi, 2005; Schneider, 2004). Such techniques can be employed only episodically and, usually, for relatively small sums (though large enough to be a material fraud upon the lender). To cover continuing flows, the best candidates are still in the retail service industries. They can credibly seem to generate large amounts of cash on an on-going basis. Services have a major advantage over physical goods. In the manufacturing industry, anyone who investigates seriously can expect to examine the flow of input that corresponds to the declared flow of output. But in services, there is only a fuzzy relationship between cost of physical input and value of output. Just as services are the best sector through which to evade taxes (by under-reporting income), so too they are also the best sector through which to launder money (by over-reporting income, though to launder properly, criminals have to be disciplined enough to pay the extra taxes, which may be beyond their temperament to do). The process has been rendered easier by recent structural changes in industrial economies, stimulating small service industry firms in the 'post-industrial society' such as car washes, video rentals and better still, night-time economy establishments where total receipts are easy to fake – particularly since the authorities are more likely to try to find out how much tax the owners evade, rather than to worry about how much they inflate their taxable earnings to cover for a money-washing operation.

All three stages of a laundering cycle can be integrated in one place by using a domestic cash-based retail service business. By physically running cash through the business, criminal money is separated from the act that generated it. By reporting it as earnings of that business, the trail is hidden. Then, once the firm's tax returns have been approved, the money can be used openly by the persons who initiated the operation or their nominees. This can be done both using cash and other financial instruments.

When the sums become larger and law enforcement more motivated, this stimulates international laundering. First, funds must be moved out of the country from which they originate. These can simply be flown out or placed in containers and shipped out, before being deposited. Once the money is in the bank – a task that probably has become harder due to money laundering controls – the depositor can convert it into cashiers' cheques, money orders or wire transfers and move it abroad. Alternatively, the monetary equivalent can be moved in high-value, low volume products such as diamonds or other precious metals. The underground banking mechanism uses standard banking techniques – the lateral transfer and the compensating balance – common in legal transactions, particularly with countries where there are exchange controls and/or legally inconvertible currencies.[11] Legitimate brokers as well as underground 'bankers' – often gold and jewellery shopkeepers – specialize in the arrangements.

There are many different forms bank secrecy might take, all of which are under attack from the Financial Action Task Force and other bodies. For example there are:

- Accounts where the client must reveal his/her identity but officials of the bank are bound by law never to reveal it without court authorization.
- Accounts coded so only the top management can know who the beneficial owner is, which secrecy laws prevent the management from revealing.
- Accounts protected by bank secrecy law and by nominee ownership in which the nominee and the beneficial owner are connected by civil contract and/or simply a bond of trust (or fear).
- Accounts in which a lawyer interposes him/herself between bank and client, thereby protecting the client's identity, first, by bank secrecy law, and, second, by a layer of lawyer–client privilege.
- Accounts where the client (perhaps under pressure from law enforcement) can request the bank to lift the protection of bank secrecy law.
- Accounts where bank-secrecy law forbids the bank to reveal information even if the client so requests.
- Accounts that are totally anonymous where no one in the bank can possibly know, unless the clients themselves reveal it, who the beneficial owners are.

Secrecy can be further facilitated by avoiding use of signatures. However, except in the case of totally anonymous accounts, which have almost been eliminated through Financial Action Task Force sanctions, bank secrecy can be waived by any financial haven in the event of a criminal investigation. It can also be broken by bribery or espionage. So the most rigorous launderers hold illicit money in corporate accounts. Therefore, prior to sending money to the haven of choice, the launderer will probably call on one of the many jurisdictions which sell 'offshore' corporations – licensed to conduct business only outside the country of incorporation, free of tax or regulation and protected by corporate secrecy laws. There are many options, though the traditional favourites have been Caribbean islands and especially Panama. Again, such activities have been under attack by the international community, but surveillance of corporate accounts is still more difficult than that of individuals.

In addition, some laundering schemes use yet a third layer of cover, that of the offshore trust. There are some legal reasons for the establishment of offshore trusts (mainly estate planning), some dubious ones (like dodging decisions of bankruptcy or divorce courts) and a few clearly criminal. When the owner of assets conveys ownership to a trust, it prevents those assets from being seized by creditors. The obvious disadvantage is the nominal loss of control by the owner – in theory, a deed of trust is irrevocable; and the former owner can influence, but not control the actions of the trustee. Many of the issues in this section lie outside the intervention needs of most security departments, but the focus of correspondent banking controls on Knowing the Correspondent Bankers' Customers may require due diligence involving understanding these techniques.

The control of white-collar crime

Recipes for 'effective' regulation can seldom have the same ingredients even within the first world, let alone throughout the whole world. Even allowing for the spreading of risks associated with globalization, 'what works' will depend on the particular histories and cultures of different countries or even regions within countries, but what is *actually* practised is subjected to fluctuations depending upon political and media pressures. At the level of policy instrument *adoption*, even before the push against terrorist finance, political pressure and the War on Drugs rhetoric have 'worked' in universalizing anti-laundering measures, while pressure for fairness in business contracts (and leftists crusades against widespread theft of public resources) have 'worked' in enactment of the 1997 OECD Convention prohibiting the bribery of foreign politicians and office-holders overseas, whose implementation has given many governments including the UK such difficulties, with the UK Department of Trade and Industry being forced after judicial review to reopen in early 2005 its relaxed rules covering Export Credit Guarantees on overseas sales, especially of armaments and aircraft.[12]

What constitutes effective fraud prevention *practice* at the operational level is, however, more obscure (see further, Comer, 2003; Doig, forthcoming; Wells, 2004). The routes through which white-collar crimes may sensibly be tackled are (a) rational choice theory, operating both on increasing the risks of detection and salient sanctions, and on reducing situational opportunities; (b) altering perceptions of harmfulness, reducing the cultural availability of 'techniques of neutralization' that make potential offenders comfortable about committing crimes; and (c) working creatively on ways in which people and corporations can prosper without breaking the law. But giving these hypotheses operational effect and evaluating these results is another issue.

Responses to financial crime

Criminal justice policies are both a reflection and a cause of perceptions of harm, and they generally are determined by what the political market will bear (and has become habituated to). This reflects populist pressures (including the media) and political lobbying. Unlike 'normal' crimes, most corporate crime control is conducted by *forward-looking* 'compliance' orientation: arrest, prosecution and imprisonment are viewed as a subordinate method of behavioural regulation, even where corporations are victims. Blue-collar frauds, lacking the drama of violence and with victims who usually have some contributory negligent role which makes them 'impure' victims, likewise are not treated severely: this enhances the trend towards self-reliance on the part of the commercial sector.

Compared with street crimes, it is hard to predict in advance 'hot spots' where *sophisticated* fraud takes place (or even to conceptualize what this might mean spatially), and – with the exception of some payment card counterfeiting and ATM-tampering gangs – there are fewer high-rate offenders against whom to mount surveillance operations (which, anyway, might have to take place for a long time before they detected any criminal plots, making them relatively expensive compared with street crime). Consequently, there are two strategic directions in which policing major fraud might go. First, both reactively and proactively, there is the development of long-term expertise and motivation among investigators and prosecutors, enhanced by the prospects of post-retirement jobs in the compliance and investigation parts of the business sector, including consultancy. Second, more controversially, there is the development of more proactive policing strategies, such as placing fake get-rich-quick scheme advertisements in the newspapers and then sending warning letters to those who reply, to be on their guard against such schemes; or undercover work to expose corruption, money laundering, and other financial crimes (Levi, 1995; Marx, 1977, 1988). At the more routine level, trading standards officers may test whether cooked or raw meats in supermarkets contain water in excess of the levels permitted, or whether 'fresh produce' has been illegally treated to preserve it for longer; or may send in under-age children to test purchase cigarettes or alcohol. Such mystery shopping may be conducted by security/compliance officers concerned about whether their controls are working properly. At the more dynamic end of the spectrum, however, one danger is not only the up-front cost but also the risk to civil liberties in all proactive policing: how are targets determined, and how does one ensure that their selection is 'reasonable' and is not politically motivated?[13] Adding this to the intra-corporate selection process in determining cases that will be reported to the authorities, problems of fairness are magnified.

Criminal prosecution has a considerable symbolic significance, and the redrawing of boundaries of behavioural acceptability by public degradation ceremonies such as prosecution can have a considerable impact, to the extent that for many white-collar defendants, the process is the punishment, irrespective of conviction outcomes (Levi, 1993, 2002). The American criminal justice system appears to have fewer difficulties in convicting white-collar accused than do its common law counterparts in England and Australia, or even in Canada, perhaps because lengthy sentences combined with plea bargaining generates defendant co-operation. Early Serious Fraud Office cases in the UK and the US insider dealing cases involving Boesky and Milken (however satirised by Tom Wolfe in *Bonfire of the Vanities*) did redraw the symbolic boundaries of law: but the serious investment deceptions within major financial institutions exposed in 2003–5 by the Attorney-General of New York Eliot Spitzer suggests that reappraisals of morality and/or risk in the financial services 'community' were very far from universal. Unlike for example the unauthorized use of computers to download pornographic images, such scams may be below the radar and even the formal remit of security departments within corporations, but their detection and prevention are the task of corporate audit and compliance officers: in all cases, the higher up the organization they are, the harder they are to deal with.

Fraud prevention and reduction

This brings me to consider the final element in this chapter: the prevention and reduction of fraud. Here, there is at least some evidence of 'what works' in highly defined fields. This can be taken at several levels: situational opportunity reduction, rationalization-stripping and motivation reduction (though rationalizations and motivation are connected). There are financial crimes where organizations themselves can be left to regulate in their own interests, and others where the state can (and/or should) play a role in ensuring protection for those 'incapable' of looking after themselves. (For example, in consumer fraud where no outsider can readily tell if impurities or if food content differs from that described on the label.) With regard to external regulation, at a *normative* level, one possibility is to aim for a system of regulation based on trust, with regular inspections and graduated punitive sanctions for those who show themselves to be unwilling to 'play the game'. Illustrating their theme with data from their study of nursing home compliance, Braithwaite and Makkai (1994) observe that nursing home misconduct can be picked out by inspectors, using subtle contextual knowledge as well as quantitative predictors, but when managers perceive that they are not trusted, their behaviour deteriorates. They recommend enhancing civic responsibility by creating dialogue between corporate managers and their staff and community groups. This trust approach contrasts with the 'amoral calculator' perspective implicit in the work of Shapiro and by some of the (particularly US-headquartered) corporations interviewed (Levi and Pithouse, forthcoming), which stresses sanction risks and levels as the only relevant influences. There is no obviously right answer as to which is the 'right approach': but without a thoughtful analysis of one's own corporate culture at all levels, one is unlikely to choose sensibly.

The choice of 'appropriate' regulatory strategy depends also on where the sources of harm are – from within the corporation or from outside it – and on whether or not violators see that they are 'doing wrong' or even are breaking the law at all. For example, if embezzlers truly believe that they are 'just borrowing', this may require a different control strategy from that if they are 'just stealing but reckon they won't be detected or prosecuted'. Given the flexibility of capital and the financial services industry in a globalized economy, the 'what works best' strategy may depend also on whether a tough policy will bring closure of the business: if a business is to go bust anyway, graduated sanctions are irrelevant to its managers and/or owners, and it remains open whether penal sanctions or the threat of disqualification from being company directors will have a significant effect at that stage. There is some 'shadow boxing' in business threats of movement away from 'over-regulated' economies – they may be just seeking the minimum expenditure possible on, in this context, consumer and investor protection – but even those who critique conventional economists' disregard of social values in utility maximization models would accept the relevance of such issues to corporate behaviour (Lehtola and Paksula, 1997; Korsell, 2005).

It is important to clarify one's target population for crime prevention measures. *Anyone* who has money or is able to borrow it is capable of being victimized by fraud: 'popular capitalism' has spread securities ownership to the middle and even working classes (particularly following privatization in Western Europe[14]) and if we add, to these, people who have an interest in investments via life assurance, personal pension schemes, and mortgages, the majority of the population are susceptible to being defrauded directly or indirectly. Only *some* of these victims are in a position to take evasive action to some kinds of fraud, though if they checked the regulators' websites on which regulated firms are listed, they could avoid investing with unregulated firms (except those who were simply impersonating legitimate businesses). Savers and investors can put pressure on the people they entrust with their money to take greater care of it (and upon compensation schemes which underwrite the conduct of the fraudulent and the reckless): but except for large institutional investors who have often proved reluctant to intervene, they cannot *dictate* the fraud prevention strategies of their management. This is one reason why the role of compliance and security personnel, as well as corporate investigators, is so crucial to defend the assets of the corporation against both outsiders and insiders. In some cases, for example mail-order and telemarketing frauds, it may be rational to impose third party liability on media advertising the activity, to ensure that they check that the firms exist and are properly set up for the kind of business that they advertise. Again, however, there is no evaluated evidence demonstrating the effectiveness of such advertising.

In the case of frauds *against* companies, prevention ideas must reach individuals at *all* levels of organizations. The credit manager or the head of security in a large company may be concerned about fraud, but the managing director may be more concerned about corporate image and sales, so if organizational policy is to be changed, it is the *senior* managerial personnel who have to be convinced about the desirability of or necessity for this. Fraud, in other words, should be part of the strategic plan of loss control within any organization (Levi *et al.*, 2003). The criminological and 'grey' policing literature contains very few examples of evaluated efforts to reduce any sophisticated forms of crime for serious economic gain. The modest literature indeed illustrates how difficult it is to get the authorities to act in a cross-cutting, inter-agency way against such sources of crime for gain. Though there have been a number of national and international surveys by major accounting firms (e.g. Ernst & Young, KPMG, PwC, RSM Robson Rhodes), there have been no major research studies in any key economic crime areas – whether fraud against business, fraud against the public, or fraud against the financial interests of the European Union – that conform to the normal canons of the Home Office crime reduction programme.

Preventing fraud on business

The aim of crime prevention is to keep the criminal out. Normally, this is conceived of in terms of steering columns, locks, and bolts: better physical protection. However, in the case of fraud, a different set of preventative methods must be employed. There are *some* physical measures that are relevant – access controls to reduce the risk of illicit entry to computers or computer areas, and random checks to ensure password change and difficult password availability – but the major threat comes from people with whom the defrauded party has a contractual relationship of some kind. In this sense, fraud prevention is closer to family violence prevention than to burglary prevention: the danger is already within but what businesspeople need to do is to take avoiding action and change the nature of the relationship.

(1) Entry control

The first line of defence against fraud is entry control, which may be applied both to employees and outside contractors. For *internal* frauds, entry controls may take the form of vetting employees or members of professional associations to ensure that they are 'fit and proper persons'. However, the absence of criminal convictions is by no means a guarantee of probity (nor is the presence of distant convictions an indicator of lack of probity). In the past (and, for the most part, the present too), the low rate of reporting and prosecution of fraud meant that fraudsters were unlikely to be convicted: many people suspected of dishonesty are allowed simply to resign rather than be prosecuted. But the absence of any real references on employees is commonplace in fraud cases, and temporary staff are often allowed access to sensitive locations where they may access computers, intellectual property or take/copy personal details that can be used later in identity frauds. Out-sourcing is a particular risk, as family/ethnic pressures (social and physical threats) may be exerted.

(2) Post-entry controls

Many of the largest frauds have been committed by people whose personal backgrounds are such that they would have satisfied the *prima facie* integrity and competence checks implicit in the Gottfredson and Hirschi (1990) model of generic anti-sociality and poor self-discipline (for examples, see Comer, 2003; Wells, 2004). Disciplined fraudsters (whether they began intending to defraud or not) will therefore readily pass this Maginot line. The focus then shifts to internal management systems and compliance monitoring (for internal frauds), and creditworthiness checking (for some external ones, though the quality of individual credit information is much poorer outside the UK and North America). Here, organizational tone is important. There is insufficient evidence to demonstrate any 'displacement effect' whereby intending fraudsters choose to work for organizations that have a lax reputation, but 'sucker lists' are passed around by *external* fraudsters, and this may be true of internal ones too. Though there will always be people whose ability to rationalize verges on the magical, clear policies which set out the acceptability and unacceptability of particular practices will diminish the scope for self-deception, particularly if they are applied consistently and fairly.

More generally, fraud prevention measures might involve educating colleagues and internal security to watch out for and enquire into the circumstances of employees who are living in a style far in excess of their salaries. Several defrauded firms had allowed employees on modest salaries to go on driving new Porsches and taking expensive holidays without conducting any enquiry or more than a superficial one into how they could afford this. Where the 'high liver' is a member of senior management, however, as many post-scandal reports have noted, there are serious difficulties in knowing to whom one should or can safely report. Here, non-executive directors can play a vital role as impartial insiders, but since they tend to be selected by the existing senior executives, measures to enhance the independence in reality might include 'public interest' directors, as well as 'whistleblowing' legislation (e.g. The Public Interest Disclosure Act 1998) which protects employees from dismissal and/or provides rewards. This is not a panacea, because the social stigma for 'betrayal' needs to be tackled. The underlying theory is that employees and 'the public' are all stakeholders directly and indirectly, and that they (along with minority shareholders) should be able to influence fraud prevention as well as other areas of potential misconduct by the corporation or its senior personnel.

Clear rules on own-account dealing by employees of financial institutions are vital. The mere existence of clear rules tells us nothing about whether they are followed. Although the Financial Action Task Force and OECD have been effective in reducing the number of jurisdictions offering nominee and bearer accounts, suspense accounts, from which one can load profitable deals into one's own account and unprofitable ones into the trust's accounts, are examples of activities which are difficult to monitor successfully unless the individual is very greedy or unless there is some reason why Stock Exchanges or other regulators mount special investigations, e.g. insider dealing suspicions arising from sudden market price movements prior to company announcements.

The role of 'ethical statements' is a controversial one in business schools and practice. Some multi-national companies have codes of ethics which are expressed strongly and are applied vigorously. Companies send letters annually to suppliers drawing their attention to the code of business ethics and in particular to the requirements not to make gifts or take other actions towards employees which would contravene this. All senior employees have to sign an annual representation to say that they are not aware of and have not during the year contravened the code of business ethics. There is a limit as to how much private sector monitoring can occur, but the important thing is to have lines of accountability which can lead subsequently to individually attributable blame.

Much more difficult to prevent are frauds that involve collusion, and they can occur in any area of business. The people in the cashier's department (perhaps in league with computer assistants) who pay phoney invoices against goods that have not been received. The people in the purchasing department (or, perhaps, more senior than that) who get a rake-off from the supplier. The manager who extends loans or credit terms to doubtful enterprises in which he or she has a covert interest. The main prevention method is to require standard devices like double signing of cheques, counter-signing of *records* of cheques, and careful controls over purchasing and contracting in public and private sectors, with *prompt* checks to verify claims about how the money was spent. However, where there is collusion, (and/or hostility to management and poor internal communications, often as a result of authoritarian management styles), the checks do not operate, and this increases the length of time that the fraud can continue undetected.

Crime prevention in the business world has to be seen in its economic, political, and social contexts (Burrows, 1997; Levi *et al.*, 2003). Theoretically, private sector judgments should differ from public sector concerns, because it may not – in narrow terms – be rational for private sector organizations to take into account the 'externalities' (i.e. the costs and benefits accruing to 'society at large') of their crime prevention decisions in the way that it would be rational for public sector organizations to do. (Thus, if opportunities to use stolen credit cards lead to street robberies and burglaries, this is not part of the private sector cost-benefit analysis.) In practice, of course, many public sector organizations behave as if they were private ones: they have their own organizational agendas, unless benefits to other public sector units can somehow be built into their own performance indicators. Even then, *personal* 'glory factors' often intervene to frustrate bureaucratic harmonization. However, the classical theory of the corporation as profit-maximizer would suggest that in the private sector, the *organizational* financial 'bottom line' reigns supreme, though the social and political advantages of being seen as a 'good corporate citizen' means that it is not easy to predict precisely what a rational corporation would do. Sometimes, as in the case of the Dedicated Cheque and Plastic Crime Unit (now wholly funded by the Association for Payment Clearing Services) and the fraud section of the Metropolitan Police Vehicle Crime Unit (currently funded by the Finance and Leasing Association), this can lead to hybrid private-public policing and to new accountability models that remain to be fully worked out (Levi and Pithouse, forthcoming).

Conclusions

Without being a detailed 'how to control fraud' exercise, this chapter has tried to indicate the inter-connectedness between the causes and control of white-collar crimes, in the sense that a cultural/organizational climate can be created (or inhibited) in which financial crimes of various kinds become commonplace. Conventional candidates for deterrence – imprisonment, director disqualification, and even social stigma – have not been seriously evaluated in the economic crime arena, and one may expect them to have different effects depending partly on how much fraudsters care about their local 'communities' and what they know or expect the reactions of friends and neighbours to be (Levi, 2002; Levi and Pithouse, forthcoming). 'Rationality' of both individuals and organizations, let alone of 'society as a whole', is a more difficult concept to operationalize than is commonly assumed, for it depends partly on value choices and risk orientations which can properly vary. With the devaluation of 'civic responsibility' in the rush for personal advancement as the engine of the enterprise culture, in the enhanced climate of job insecurity with which even the middle classes in the 'culture of contentment' have been plagued in the 1990s, the motivation to be honest has been submerged in the politics of envy. The tension between *laissez-faire* ideology and the control of fraud is clear, and particularly given the asymmetric information necessitated by the growth of agency and organizational complexity, not everyone is a good judge of their own interests, especially when they are being actively deceived.

To some extent, the anti-money laundering requirements of financial institutions to 'know their customer' and the customer's business may (or should) act as some sort of brake on fraud; and terrorist finance concerns with underground banking and false invoicing may also enhance the risk factor. Internally, this has certainly enhanced compliance systems including electronic 'unusual transaction monitoring'. However in the struggle against fraud, what is required is not just some modicum of initial vetting of the competence and integrity of those who hold funds in trust, but also a more continuous flow of monitoring which ensures that even if – as is inevitable – people are able to defraud, their gains will not be allowed to continue for long without detection, so the total losses will be diminished. (Similar issues of transparency arise in corruption.) For external credit fraud, private sector data sharing via CIFAS in the UK has proven effective, while within the public sector, large scale inter-agency data matching has had a significant impact on fraud losses.

In the aftermath of the collapses of the Bank of Credit and Commerce International and of the huge offshore derivatives firm Long-Term Capital Management, banking regulators moved towards a more integrated approach to global regulation, with clearer lines of responsibility for institutions operating in more than one market: how far the revised Bank of International Settlements guidelines of 2001 (generally known as Basel II) will improve this remains to be seen. Furthermore, in many first world countries – though not in the former Communist countries that remain vulnerable to fraudulent dream-sellers – national regulators such as the US Securities and Exchange Commission impose informational requirements upon those who wish to do business in their country, at least above a certain level of trading and share value. Nevertheless, unless businesspeople learn to share information to reduce their exposure to multiple victimization and unless we have the self-confidence to build up a more communitarian trust culture of regulation backed by sanctions, the nightmare of a de-centred universe of unregulatable institutions remains just around the corner, as countries vie with each other to underbid regulation in order to attract providers of employment. In order to be clearer about 'what works' in the prevention of economic crime, we have to be clearer about what we want to achieve, and at what costs in terms of interference with personal and commercial liberties. Until then, security and compliance managers in multinationals can expect to encounter different regulations and levels of enforcement in the environments in which they operate, so it is possible for fraud-minded staff to 'slip in under the wire' in some countries, while generating reputational risks for worldwide brands.

Notes

1 Interestingly, this is not true of the Scandinavian countries, where economic crime prevention and policing – especially but not exclusively tax and environmental offences – were central parts of the crime agenda (see Korsell, 2004 and Alvesalo and Tombs, 2001).
2 The question of what constitutes criminal justice effectiveness is too large a one for this chapter.
3 This is a particularly complex issue, as companies may feel driven to corruption either by having uncompetitive prices/quality or by having their superior prices/quality undermined by the known/anticipated corruption of public and private sector officials by their competitors.
4 How or indeed whether one can attain this outreach is a matter of some concern, especially where prosecutions are so few, and the media are normally dependent on some court or regulatory process on which to base their publicity: see Levi (forthcoming).
5 This category of offences is normally committed by small or medium-sized businesses. However, the creation of companies to purchase failing companies and offload their company pension liabilities is a social issue of growing importance, and is not restricted to SMEs.
6 Asymmetric information can lead to unforeseen moral hazard and adverse selection. Moral hazard means that people with insurance may take greater risks than they would do without it because they know they are protected, so the insurer may get more claims than it bargained for. When there is adverse selection, people who know they have a higher risk of claiming than the average of the group will buy the insurance, whereas those who have a below-average risk may decide it is too expensive to be worth buying. In this case, premiums set according to the average risk will not be sufficient to cover the claims that eventually arise, because among the people who have bought the policy more will have above-average risk than below-average risk. This happens whether or not there is fraud, but fraud obviously increases risks.
7 In developing countries such as China, where there are few legacy landline systems, mobiles have become the norm anyway.
8 This can be an arena of dispute but for the purposes of this business, policing and professional audience, corporates are only seldom major beneficiaries of such protection, since the upper limit is set below £40,000. The exception is fraud insurance and reinsurance, including the Export Credit Guarantee Department in the case of the UK.
9 This is slightly different from the definition of the Financial Action Task Force which divided money laundering into placement (the fusion of cash into the legal economy or smuggling it out of the country); layering (separation from source by creating complex covering structures) and integration (placing laundered funds back into the economy). The problem with this approach is that instead of three distinct stages it refers to an action, an intention and a perception, all of which may be true but do not give a really accurate picture of a *process*.
10 Such information asymmetry can also be used by landlords false claiming housing benefit for their tenants.
11 I am grateful to Tom Naylor for this and many other observations.
12 'Exports victory for anti-corruption group' *The Guardian*, 13 January 2005.
13 This causes controversy in police corruption investigations as well as in anti-laundering and other business crime stings.
14 Privatization in Central and Eastern Europe did not have this effect: from poverty and pressure, many sold their shares to business and crime entrepreneurs – almost indistinguishable categories – and the system replaced state oligarchy with private oligarchy.

Key readings

This is a wide topic, and a variety of academic and professional authors have contributed from a range of disciplines. For general reviews of findings on types of fraud and how they might be dealt with, see Comer, M. (2003) *Investigating Corporate Fraud*, Aldershot: Gower; Doig, A. (forthcoming, 2006) *Fraud*, Cullompton: Willan; and Wells, J. (2004) *Corporate Fraud Handbook: Prevention and Detection*, New York: John Wiley. There are also websites that are for business as well as for the private individual or investor, such as http://www.met.police.uk/fraudalert/index.htm; also, http://www.identity-theft.org.uk/. Also useful is a Swedish review by Korsell, L. (2005) *Methods to Prevent Economic Crime: Rapport 2005: 5*, Stockholm, Swedish National Council for Crime Prevention (from the website). For a helpful review of the thorny issue of whether directors are living up to their responsibilities to deal with business crime, see Levi, M., Morgan, J. and Burrows, J. (2003) Enhancing Business Crime Reduction: UK Directors' Responsibilities to Review the Impact of Crime on Business, *Security Journal*, 16(4), pp. 7–28.

More academic works that deal with motivation and rationalization include Benson, M. (1985) 'Denying the guilty mind: accounting for involvement in white-collar crime', *Criminology*, 23: 583–607; Shover N. and Hochstetler A (2002) Cultural explanation and organizational crime, *Crime Law Social Change*, 37(1): 1–18; Simpson, S. and Piquero, N. (2002) Low self-control, organizational theory, and corporate crime, *Law and Society Review*, Vol. 36, No. 3, pp. 509–47; and Willott S., Griffin, C. and Torrance, M. (2001) Snakes and ladders: Upper-middle class male offenders talk about economic crime, *Criminology*, 39(2): 441–66. An early study of planned bankruptcy fraud with an introduction discussing changes since the 1970s may be found in Levi, M. (2005) *The Phantom Capitalists*, Andover: Ashgate.

For comprehensible analyses of some money-laundering issues, accounts may be found in Blum, J., Levi, M., Naylor, R. and Williams, P. (1998) *Financial Havens, Banking Secrecy and Money-Laundering*, Issue 8, UNDCP Technical Series, New York: United Nations (1998) UN document V.98-55024 – http://www.cf.ac.uk/socsi/whoswho/levi-laundering.pdf; Howell, J. (2005) *ICC Guide to the Prevention of Money Laundering and Terrorist Financing*, London: International Chamber of Commerce; Clark, A. and Burrell, P. (eds) (2001) *A Practitioner's Guide to International Money-Laundering Law and Regulation*, London: City and Financial Planning (though as in all texts that deal with regulation and law, parts are outdated). A good study on how anti-money laundering measures are seen by practitioners is Gill, M. and Taylor, G. (2004) Preventing Money Laundering or Obstructing Business? Financial Companies' Perspectives on 'Know Your Customer' Procedures, *British Journal of Criminology*. 44, 4, July, pp. 582–94; and for wider discussion of impact, see Levi, M. (2002) Money laundering and its regulation, *Annals of the American Academy of Political and Social Science*, 582: July, pp. 181–94.

References

Alvesalo, A. and Tombs, S. (2001) 'The Emergence of a "War" on Economic Crime: The Case of Finland', *Business and Politics*, Vol. 3(3).

Beare, M. and Schneider, S. (1990) *Tracing Of Illicit Funds: Money Laundering in Canada*, Ottawa: Office of the Solicitor General.

Braithwaite, J. and Makkai, T. (1994) 'Trust and Compliance', *Policing and Society*, Vol. 4, pp. 1–12.

Burrows, J. (1997) 'Criminology and Business Crime: Building the Bridge'. In M. Felson and R. Clarke (eds) *Business and Crime Prevention*, New York: Harrow and Heston.

Clarke, R. and Homel, R. (1997) 'A Revised Classification of Situational Crime Prevention Techniques'. In S. Lab (ed.) *Crime Prevention at a Cross-roads*, Cincinnati: Anderson.

Comer, M. (2003) *Investigating Corporate Fraud*, Aldershot: Gower.

Croall, H. (2001) *White-Collar Crime*, 2nd edn, Milton Keynes: Open University Press.

Doig, A. (forthcoming) *Fraud*, Cullompton: Willan.

Foresight Crime Panel (2000) *Turning the Corner*, London: Department of Trade and Industry.

Gilmore, W. (2004) *Dirty Money*, Strasbourg: Council of Europe Press.

Gottfredson, M. and Hirschi, T. (1990) *A General Theory of Crime*, Stanford, CA: Stanford University Press.

Green, S. (2004) *Manager's Guide to the Sarbanes-Oxley Act: Improving Internal Controls to Prevent Fraud*, New York: John Wiley.

Korsell, L. (2005) *Methods to Prevent Economic Crime: Rapport 2005: 5*, Stockholm: Swedish National Council for Crime Prevention.

Lehtola, M. and Paksula, K. (1997) *Talousrikosten tillannetorjunta [Situational crime prevention and economic crime]*. Helsinki: Oikeuspoliittisen tutkimuslaitoksen julkaisuja 142.

Levi, M. (1993) *The Investigation, Prosecution, and Trial of Serious Fraud*, Royal Commission on Criminal Justice Research Study No. 14, London: HMSO.

Levi, M. (1995) 'Covert Operations and White-collar Crime'. In G. Marx and C. Fijnaut (eds) *Undercover: Police Surveillance in Comparative Perspective*, Daventer: Kluwer.

Levi, M. (2002) 'Suite Justice or Sweet Charity? Some Explorations of Shaming and Incapacitating Business Fraudsters', *Punishment and Society*, Vol. 4(2) pp. 147–63.

Levi, M. and Gilmore, W. (2002) 'Terrorist Finance, Money Laundering and the Rise and Rise of Mutual Evaluation: A New Paradigm for Crime Control?', *European Journal of Law Reform*, Vol. 4(2), pp. 337–64.

Levi, M., Morgan, J. and Burrows, J. (2003) 'Enhancing Business Crime Reduction: UK Directors' Responsibilities to Review the Impact of Crime on Business', *Security Journal*, Vol. 16(4), pp. 7–28.

Levi, M. and Pithouse, A. (forthcoming) *White-Collar Crime and its Victims*, Oxford: Clarendon Press.

Levi, M. (forthcoming) White-Collar Crimes in the Media, Oxford: Clarendon Press.

Marx, G. (1988) *Undercover*, Berkeley: University of California Press.

Middleton, D. and Levi, M. (2005) 'The Role of Solicitors in Facilitating 'Organized Crime': Situational Crime Opportunities and Their Regulation', *Crime, Law & Social Change*, Vol. 42 (2–3): 123–61.

Mirrlees-Black, C. and Ross, A. (1995) *Crime Against Retail and Manufacturing Premises: Findings from the 1994 Commercial Victimisation Survey*, London: HMSO.

Naylor, R. (2004) *Hot Money and the Politics of Debt*, Montreal: McGill University Press.

Nelken, D. (2002) 'White-Collar Crime'. In M. Maguire, R. Morgan, and R. Reiner (eds), *The Oxford Handbook of Criminology*. 3rd edn, Oxford: Oxford University Press.

Schneider, S. (2004) *Money Laundering in Canada: An Analysis of RCMP Cases*, Toronto: Nathanson Center.

Shapiro, S. (1990) 'Collaring the crime, Not the Criminal: Liberating the Concept of White-collar Crime', *American Sociological Review*, Vol. 55, pp. 346–64.

Simpson, S. and Piquero, N. (2002) 'Low Self-control, Organizational Theory, and Corporate Crime', *Law and Society Review*, Vol. 36, No. 3, pp. 509–47.

Taylor, J. (2004) *Crime Against Retail and Manufacturing Premises: Findings from the 2002 Commercial Victimisation Survey*, London: TSO.

Willott, S., Griffin, C. and Torrance, M. (2001) 'Snakes and Ladders: Upper-middle Class Male Offenders Talk about Economic Crime', *Criminology*, 39(2): 441–66.

Wells, J. (2004) *Corporate Fraud Handbook: Prevention and Detection*, New York: John Wiley.

12
Commercial Burglary

Rob I. Mawby

Introduction

Burglars may target residential or corporate property, of which some of the latter will be commercial premises but others not. While this chapter focuses on commercial burglary, the distinctions between this and both other corporate and residential burglary are sometimes more apparent than real. Thus, a school operated by local government would be excluded from a review of commercial burglary but a private school would qualify. Equally, the burglary of a small business might include the residential premises of the owner who lives on site. And a break-in to an office might involve theft of employees' personal possessions.

The legal definition of burglary varies between countries. However, the international crime victim survey (ICVS) defines burglary as where someone enters property without permission in order to steal something. That is, there is no need for forced entry, but rather it is the 'entry without permission' that distinguishes burglary from theft. Accordingly, a number of burglary scenarios can be distinguished:

- Forcible entry through a door, window or roof.
- Use other method (e.g. credit card) to enter through locked door or window without causing damage.
- Enter through an open door or window.
- Enter with permission, where the offender used trickery to gain access.

Forcible entry through a door or window is perhaps the most common type of commercial burglary, with ram raiding an extreme – and comparatively uncommon (Donald and Wilson, 2000; Jacques, 1994) – example of this. Access through subterfuge is a contemporary issue, generally associated with domestic burglary, where distraction burglary targeting older people has been the subject of recent government initiatives in Britain (Distraction Burglary Task Force, 2002; Home Office, 2002; Thornton *et al.*, 2003). However it is also manifest in the commercial sector: hotels rooms may be burgled, for example, by professional burglars gaining employment as service staff, or by offenders who con reception staff into passing over room keys.

That said, there is surprisingly little written about commercial burglary (Clarke, 2003). This is partly a reflection of the traditional emphasis placed upon residential or household crime. For example, although local, national and international household victim surveys have become common in the last 30 years, surveys of the business community are more recent. It also stems from difficulties with using police statistics. In English[1] criminal statistics, for example, the only distinction made is between residential burglaries and 'other' burglaries, which will include a variety of different incidents, including garage or outhouse break-ins as well as burglary of commercial and other corporate property (Redshaw and Mawby, 1996).

What has been written tends to fall under one or other of three headings. First, there are studies of burglary in general that include some comparison of household and corporate offences (Mawby, 2001). Second, surveys of business victimization allow for a comparison of burglary with other offences experienced by the business community. The 1994 International Crimes against Businesses Survey (ICBS) was conducted in eight European countries,[2] and paralleled surveys in Australia and South Africa (van Dijk and Terlouw, 1996). It was the first major survey of its kind, but was largely restricted to the retail sector. The Home Office in England helped run the ICBS, of which its Commercial Victimisation Survey (CVS) (Mirrlees-Black and Ross, 1995) was a part, and followed this with a second national survey in 2002 (Taylor, 2004).[3] National surveys have also been carried out elsewhere: for example in Scotland (Burrows *et al.*, 1999; Hopkins and Ingram, 2001)[4] and Australia (Perrone, 2000; Walker, 1996). Data from a number of local surveys in England and Wales (Johnston *et al.*, 1994; Mawby, 2003; Tilley, 1993; Wood, Wheelwright and Burrows, 1997) are also readily available. Finally, but less commonly, some studies have concentrated exclusively on commercial burglary: for example in England and Wales (Redshaw and Mawby, 1996; Taylor, 1999), the USA (Bichler-Robertson and Potchak, 2002; Hakim and Gaffney, 1994) and the Netherlands (Kruissink, 1995; Kruissink, 1996; Wiersma, 1996). Some such studies have specified particular targets: Laycock (1985) identified the particular problems of chemists shops, Beck and Willis (1991) reviewed burglary records kept by 22 out-of-town superstores, and Jones and Mawby (2005) researched hotel burglary. In a review of research from across the world, Clarke (2003) has recently discussed burglary of retail establishments.

The remainder of this chapter covers the available findings under six headings. First, in the light of emphasis upon 'fear' of burglary in the victimological literature, business people's perceptions of and concern about crime in general and burglary in particular is discussed. This is then contrasted with the extent and costs of commercial burglary. The following section then covers policy and practice, first in terms of police and policing and then crime reduction. Next, an attempt is made to explore the distribution of commercial burglary. Finally, research on those who commit commercial burglary is summarized. The findings are then drawn together in an attempt to explain the extent and distribution of commercial burglary. Where relevant, each section incorporates a brief review of the author's recent research on hotel burglary.[5]

Concern over burglary within the business sector

The concept of fear of or anxiety about crime has featured prominently in victimology. Anxiety or concern over crime has been measured by questions about safety, by questions that tap anxiety or worry, or by questions asking people to estimate risk (Ditton and Farrell, 2000; Hale, 1996; Hough, 1995). More recently the British Crime Survey (BCS) and other studies have incorporated questions about the crime situation and other 'public incivilities', locally or nationally (Ellis and Fletcher, 2003). Research has identified levels of concern or anxiety, variations between different subgroups of the population and the relationship between 'fear' and risk. Specifically, in demonstrating that 'fear' exceeds risk, researchers have attempted to explain this in terms of the extent to which citizens' concerns are well founded or irrational (Hough, 1995).

In contrast, surveys of the business sector have concentrated on behaviour rather than perceptions. However, where studies have assessed concern, the findings have been somewhat ambiguous. The Scottish Survey of Business Crime (SSBC), for example, found that only 11 percent of respondents felt that crime in the area immediately around their premises affected their ability to operate profitably; with regard to burglary 7 percent felt that residential burglary was a problem in the area, with 10 percent identifying burglary of businesses as a problem. This led the authors to conclude that crime was viewed with greater concern by the general Scottish population than by business people.

In England and Wales, the 2002 CVS (Taylor, 2004) did not ask specifically about perceptions of burglary. However about a third considered crime to be a problem for their business and the surrounding area and half felt that crime against businesses in the area was increasing. Teenagers hanging around and street drug misuse were considered the main local issues, with retailers generally more concerned than manufacturers.

More detailed questions were asked in the 2001 Cornwall Business Crime Survey (CBCS) (Mawby, 2004). In this predominantly rural and small-town county, respondents were given a list of possible issues and asked two questions:

> Thinking about the area in which your business is based, how much of a problem would you say the following were?

And

> How concerned are you about the effect the following are having on your business?

'Burglary/breaking into business premises' was considered an area problem by 36 percent of business people, with rather more (67 percent) thinking it had a detrimental affect on their business. However, noncrime issues, such as traffic congestion, and antisocial behaviour, such as 'children/teenagers hanging around on the street/public places' and public drug misuse, were rated as more immediate problems than burglary.

There were, moreover, marked variations in the perceptions of different subgroups of business people. For example, those based in the towns expressed more concern than those sited in villages. In particular though:

- Those who had been victims within the previous 13 months were significantly more likely to: consider crime a problem in the area where their business was located; feel that their business was affected by crimes such as burglary; and cite crime as a disadvantage of their business' location.
- The relationship was generally strongest where the offence cluster was closest to the object of concern – specifically, concern about burglary was greatest among those who had been burgled within the past year.

Despite the recent high profile accorded to business crime by the British government, there is thus some ambiguity about how far business people consider crime in general and burglary in particular to be a problem. The Scottish Executive research found that business people expressed less concern than the general public, but research in England and Wales suggests otherwise. Certainly, though, burglary is considered less of a priority for businesses than many other noncrime and public disorder issues. Our interviews with hoteliers in two tourist areas provide some explanation for this. Hoteliers saw burglary as a problem. But they felt that other issues, such as the difficulty of vehicular access to the resort and public disorder problems that might impact upon the popularity of the area with holidaymakers, had a greater impact on their businesses. These views are of direct relevance to the success of crime reduction initiatives. Most immediately, though, they raise questions about the extent and impact of burglary.

The extent of commercial burglary

In considering the extent of commercial burglary, two questions are pre-eminent. First, do commercial premises experience more burglary than residential property? Second, how does burglary compare with other crimes against businesses?

Overwhelmingly research has found that businesses experience more crime than do individuals, and the evidence for burglary parallels this. Van Dijk and Terlouw's (1996) discussion of the ICBS illustrates this. For those in the retail trade, a third had suffered a burglary (including attempts), and this was the second most common offence cited, after 'theft by persons'. The risk of burglary in the retail business was about ten times that among households. However, the proportion of the retail sector that had been burgled in the preceding year varied, ranging from 44 percent in South Africa and 31 percent in the Czech Republic to 16 percent in Switzerland and 9 percent in Italy.

In Australia, Walker (1996) found that reported rates for burglary were 38.34 per 1000 residential dwellings but 98.29 per 1000 business premises. According to the Australian component of the ICBS, around 4 percent of households were burgled each year in the early 1990s, but the first Australian business victimization survey revealed a rate of 27 percent, with burglary 'the most common form of crime occurring to businesses in 1992' (Walker, 1996: 283). Perrone's (2000) more recent survey of small businesses reiterates this, with shoplifting and burglary the most common offences experienced.

The Scottish business survey, while registering lower levels of victimization overall, also identified businesses as particularly susceptible to burglary. Vandalism was the most common offence cited, but 18 percent had experienced a (successful or attempted) break-in, and the incidence rate was over ten times that found in the Scottish Crime Survey.

In England and Wales, the first CVS also discovered high rates of burglary against retail and manufacturing premises (Mirrlees-Black and Ross, 1995). Among retail premises, 24 percent experienced a burglary in 1993, this being the second most common crime after theft by customers (cited by 47 percent). In comparison, 25 percent of manufacturing premises suffered a vehicle theft and 24 percent a burglary. In each case, burglary of commercial premises was more common than household burglary, suffered by 4 percent of households in the same year. The second CVS reported a fall in crimes against businesses since 1993 (Taylor, 2004). Nevertheless, risk from burglary was broadly similar, affecting 25 percent of retailers and 22 percent of manufacturers. Other English studies reiterate this pattern. In one study of crime on five industrial estates, for example, Johnston *et al.* (1994) identified burglary as one of the most common – and serious – crimes experienced by business units. The predominance of burglary was also confirmed in a subsequent analysis of 600 estates. Tilley's (1993) survey of crimes against small businesses similarly identified burglary as one of the most common crimes experienced. More recently, our own research identified burglary as the most common crime against hotels recorded by the police (43 percent–50 percent of crimes at hotels in the two areas studied), while a survey of hoteliers confirmed the extent of burglary (Jones and Mawby, 2005).

Repeat victimization has also been identified as an issue, and one that is particularly evident within the commercial sector. Although repeat burglary is less common than more interpersonal crimes, or offences where there is an ongoing relationship between offender and victim, it is scarcely the exception. Thus the ICBS identified it as an issue (van Dijk and Terlouw, 1996) and this is confirmed by national studies. In Australia, Walker (1996) noted that almost 60 percent of commercial burglary victims said they had been victimized more than once during the year, and Perrone (2000) found that 47 percent of burglary victims experienced another burglary within the year. The Scottish survey found that 8.4 percent of businesses had been burgled on one occasion, with 6.9 percent burgled 2–3 times and 2.2 percent four times or more, and that 40 percent of burglaries were suffered by the most victimized 10 percent of premises. The concentration of burglaries over a two year period was even more striking. In

England and Wales, the extent of repeat victimization has been highlighted by Taylor (1999), Taylor (2004), Johnston *et al.* (1994) and Tilley (1993). Redshaw and Mawby (1996) reported that 'only' 8 percent of their domestic burglary sample said they had been burgled before in the last 12 months, whereas exactly half their commercial burglary sample said they had. Our survey of hotels also found that no less than 37 percent of all hotel burglaries in one district that were reported to the police occurred at 17 hotels, out of some 450 establishments (Jones and Mawby, 2005).

The cost of commercial burglary

The ICBS emphasized the financial costs of burglaries against retail and manufacturing premises (van Dijk and Terlouw, 1996). Mirrlees-Black and Ross (1995) estimated that burglaries cost industries in England and Wales over £300 million in 1993. The average cost of a burglary was £2420 among manufacturers and £1660 among retailers, compared with £1370 for household burglary. In the most recent CVS, Taylor (2004) identified burglary as one of the most costly individual crimes. Moreover, given that burglary was more common than vehicle theft (the most costly crime), the overall cost of burglary to industry was particularly pronounced. This is well illustrated in the SBC. The average cost of a burglary was £3075, lower than that from vehicle theft (£5325) or fraud (£5142). However, the average cost of burglaries per business, at £539, was higher than for any other offence type, and accounted for 23.6 percent of the total cost of crime. Additional costs not included here involve the cost of crime prevention and insurance premiums (Taylor, 2004). Although much of the cost of burglary may be covered by insurance, insurance companies may react by increasing premiums (or even withdrawing cover in high risk areas) and requiring expensive security improvements. Crime prevention was estimated to be £10,092 per business in Scotland in 1998, while total spending on crime prevention among retailers amounted to £608m in Britain in 2001 (Keynote, 2002).

The costs of crime to businesses are, however, much broader than this. They include disruption to trading, loss of custom, lower staff morale and enforced moving of premises (British Chambers of Commerce, 2002). In the inner city areas of Britain attacks on Asian shops may impact on both the shopkeepers and the area, where much-needed local services may close (Eckblom and Simon, 1988). Among small businesses, crime may be the difference between survival and closure (Perrone, 2000). In the case of hotel burglary in tourist resorts the cost to the individual hotel and the area may be considerable where the victim is deterred from returning in future years (Mawby and Jones, 2004).

Moreover, it is not just the businesses concerned that are affected by burglary. Burglary may impact on both staff and customers. In the case of staff, for example, Redshaw and Mawby (1996) cited the case of an office burglary that resulted in cleaning staff being reluctant to work alone in the evenings. Customers also often bear the cost of burglaries: hotel break-ins, for example, generally involve theft of residents' rather than hotel property. However, while the emotional effect of burglary on victims of domestic burglary is well documented (Mawby, 2001), there is little information on the extent of any emotional effect on victims of commercial burglary. Indeed, the assumption seems to be made that victims are unaffected, with the result that Victim Support contact with victims of commercial burglary is extremely low. For example, a survey of Victim Support in one English city (Simmonds and Mawby, 2002) found that out of 102 cases of corporate crime, Victim Support did not attempt to contact any victims in person, and only communicated by letter on one occasion.

Crime reduction and commercial burglary

The ICBS found that burglaries were among the most common crimes reported to the police, noting that this largely reflected the commonality of insurance coverage and the greater willingness of businesses to report crimes committed by 'outsiders' rather than staff (van Dijk and Terlouw, 1996). The recent CVS in England concurred with this, with Taylor (2004) observing that reporting levels were higher than among burgled households interviewed as part of the BCS.

However, alongside this studies have revealed extensive criticism of police services from commercial victims. For example, Johnston *et al.* (1994) noted dissatisfaction among their sample, with victims criticizing the police for minimal effort, poor feedback and a low clear up rate. Respondents in general also complained at the lack of a visible police presence. Only 8 percent felt their estate was well policed. Tilley (1993) also reported that the need for a greater police presence was the most common recommendation made by small business operators. The BCC survey noted that the most common reason for not reporting crime was a lack of confidence in the police response (British Chambers of Commerce, 2002), a finding echoed in the second CVS (Taylor, 2004).[6] The latter also found that two fifths of business people thought that 'the police are becoming less responsive to crime against businesses in this area'. Victims in Redshaw and Mawby's (1996) survey were also asked about the service they received and expressed considerably more criticism than did individual victims.

Respondents to this survey were generally positive about *initial* police response, but they were more critical of follow-up services, as provided, for example, by scenes of crime officers. They were also less likely than victims of domestic burglaries to have been contacted again, either by the officers who first attended or by anyone else. As a result, they expressed more criticism of the police than did victims of household burglary *vis-à-vis* the failure of the police to keep them informed of progress or tell them the results of their investigation, and were also more likely to describe themselves as dissatisfied with some aspect of the service they had received. Most frequently cited reasons for dissatisfaction were a belief that the police should have made more effort in detecting crime, that victims were not given any kind of progress report and a perception that the police were not interested in pursuing the matter.

The commercial sector faces a particular set of problems in attempting to prevent burglary. On the one hand, premises are often relatively large, empty at night and at weekends, and located in non-residential areas where the possibility of natural surveillance is limited. On the other hand, restricted public access to retail premises and commercial premises like shopping malls inhibits routine surveillance.

One common response across the world, encouraged by dissatisfaction with the public police and the spread of 'mass private property' (Bayley and Shearing, 1996; Johnson, 1992; Jones and Newburn, 1995), has been a shift towards private policing alternatives. In 2001 in Britain, retailers spent some £171m on contract security staff and £134m on in-house security staff (Keynote, 2002). Nevertheless, only a minority of businesses invest in security personnel.[7] Our recent (unpublished) research in one rural county in England indicates that in 2004 10.7 percent of businesses paid an outside security company to patrol their premises while 14.9 percent employed in-house security. However, internal security staff – or at least the presence of a resident caretaker – regularly feature in industrialized societies such as France, Canada, the US and the Netherlands (Mayhew and van Dijk, 1997).

Alternatively, there has been an increased emphasis on physical aspects of security, with – as we have seen – considerable financial implications. In 2001 in Britain, retailers spent some £15m on alarm systems and an additional £9m on 'anti-burglary equipment' (Keynote, 2002). Recent findings from the second CVS in England and Wales indicate that target hardening measures among businesses have become near-universal. Thus in 2002:

> The vast majority reported having protective door and/or window measures. Burglar alarms and measures to protect the outside of the premises such as CCTV or fencing were also commonplace (Taylor, 2004: 5).

Similar findings have been reported from abroad. Van Dijk and Terlouw (1996: 165) concluded that, 'The anti-burglary measures taken most in all countries are the installation of burglar alarms with or without follow-up by security companies, lighting and window security.'[8] In Scotland, the SSBC indicated that 67 percent of businesses had intruder alarms, 57 percent special door protection, such as bars, grilles or special locks, 52 percent special protection on windows (e.g. bars or reinforced glass), and 52 percent security lighting.

Burglar alarms are common among both the business community and private households in Britain, but in the former these are predominantly remote signalling alarms, whereas homes tend to have audible-only alarms (Keynote, 2002).

While public funding of improved security for the business sector is rarely an option, in the case of small businesses it has sometimes been available in England and Wales, for example through the *Safer Cities* programme in the 1980s. Tilley (1993) described a number of such initiatives where at least some of the target hardening costs were subsidized, most commonly to provide alarms and shutters. Some *Industrial Watch* projects were also born out of the initiative. A more recent programme in England and Wales was the *Small Retailers in*

Deprived Areas initiative, launched in 2001. Under this initiative, £15 million was made available over three years to improve security in small retail establishments located in particularly deprived areas (Home Office, 2004). Many of the projects supported prioritized enhanced target hardening to reduce burglary.

However, businesses are often reluctant to commit themselves to financing target hardening, even where joint funding is available. For example, in England Bowers (2001) evaluated the Small Business Strategy of the Safer Merseyside Partnership (SMP). This targeted small businesses in the most deprived areas of Merseyside. A victimization survey of businesses was used to identify those at most risk. These were then offered specialist advice from a crime prevention officer. Although some of those visited were also offered grants of up to £1500 towards increased target hardening, take-up was disappointing. Many firms were deterred by the requirement for them to contribute 50 percent towards the additional security.

Our evaluation of a Hotel Burglary Reduction initiative, which also offered matched funding, came to similar conclusions (Mawby and Jones, 2004). Despite grants of up to £2000 being made available, only nine hotels in one major tourist area received the maximum grant and take-up was so poor that the local crime reduction partnership was forced to return a substantial proportion of the grant to the Home Office. Hoteliers generally argued that the scheme was poorly publicized and badly administered, although the police placed more emphasis on the reluctance of hotel owners to make a financial contribution. Many hoteliers accepted this, conceding that in times of financial difficulty burglary was a lower priority than many other problems facing them.

Moreover, the extent to which target hardening acts as a deterrent to reduce commercial burglary, as opposed to residential burglary (Kodz and Pease, 2003), is problematic. Noting a dramatic increase in household ownership of security devices since the late 1980s, authors of the BCS have argued that two findings support a link between improved home security and reduced risk of residential burglary (Dodd *et al.*, 2004). First, homes with better security are more likely to be subjected to attempted (i.e. failed) burglaries rather than completed ones. Second, at the time of the offence burglary victims' security is less extensive than that of nonvictims. These arguments are reiterated for industrial societies as a whole (van Kesteren *et al.*, 2003; Mayhew and van Dijk, 1997: 53–5). Studies of commercial burglary, in contrast, have tended to measure the security effect merely by comparing victims with nonvictims in terms of their security at the time of the survey. Although Hakim and Buck (1993) found that businesses without security in Philadelphia were four times as likely to experience burglary as those with security, most other researchers have been more ambivalent in their findings,[9] probably because those businesses at most risk tend to react by improving their security (Clarke, 2003).

Three English studies provide a more systematic evaluation, albeit with mixed results. On Merseyside, Bowers (2001) found that where small businesses took up the offer of a visit by a crime prevention officer, this led to reduced levels of burglary, and the reduction was even greater where a grant was given for additional target hardening based on this advice. Differences in levels of repeat burglary were also pronounced. The initiative had a greater impact on burglary than other offences. Bowers concluded that, with the exception of security lighting, all additional security measures proved effective, with window locks, other window security, and roller shutters particularly effective. However, where businesses took the advice of Crime Prevention Officers in target hardening their premises, this was far more effective than 'isolated installation of target-hardening measures'. She also found little evidence of displacement. On the other hand, evaluation of the *Small Retailers in Deprived Areas* initiative found no differences in risk between businesses that received funding and those that did not, although among those burgled the number of *subsequent* burglaries was lower for the former (Home Office, 2004). Taylor's (1999) evaluation of the *Leicester Small Business and Crime* initiative produced equally mixed results. In the light of the extent of repeat victimization, burglary victims were provided with either silent alarms or CCTV. However, although the initiative did have some impact upon burglary reduction, it did not produce any increase in arrests.

Evaluation of the effectiveness of CCTV has also been mixed. Brown's (1995) evaluation of CCTV in town centres suggested that this might have a considerable impact on shop burglary rates and also aid detection, where a rapid response is facilitated or the police have visual evidence available, but a widespread review of the literature by Welsh and Farrington (2002) concluded that there was little evidence that CCTV had an impact on burglary.

While target hardening remains a key element of burglary reduction initiatives in England and Wales, in recent years it has been framed in the context of multi-agency partnership working. The 1998 Crime and Disorder Act required local authorities, the police, health authorities, police authorities and probation to work together to address crime and disorder problems in their area. To this end, Crime and Disorder Reduction Partnerships (CDRPs) were created at local government level to produce audits of crime and disorder in the local area on a three-yearly basis and to use these to develop crime and disorder reduction strategies. Although in theory this provides an excellent structure for the involvement of the business community in crime reduction, in practice many CDRPs have failed to engage with businesses. The British Chambers of Commerce (2002) report, for example, notes that CDRPs rarely involve businesses and business crime in their audits, and rarely include business representatives within their partnership structures. The Central and West Lancashire Chamber of Commerce and Industry is cited as one example of this failure to consult:

> Our Chamber covers seven local authority areas and only one has approached us to sit on its crime and disorder partnership. There is little or no business representation on the other partnerships in our area...Based on our experience we agree that local authorities appear reluctant to involve businesses in crime reduction. The emphasis appears to be very much on residential crime, with the perception that businesses can almost expect to be victims of crime (British Chambers of Commerce, 2002: 13).

Similarly, in Cornwall, although audits of the business community were undertaken in 2001 (see Mawby, 2003, 2004), business crime was not considered a strategic priority county-wide, and only one of six mainland CDRPs prioritized it in its strategy document.

Despite the levels of criticism directed at the police and reported earlier, business people tend to see the police as considerably more helpful than their local authorities *vis-à-vis* crime reduction advice (British Chambers of Commerce, 2002). More generally, however, businesses have been less involved in crime reduction partnerships than have statutory authorities (police, probation, local government etc.) or more specialist agencies from the voluntary sector, such as Victim Support. Thus our research on hotel burglary identified the difficulty of managing partnership arrangements when key players (the hotels industry and local tourism) were not routinely integrated into local and established crime reduction partnership structures (Mawby and Jones, 2004). A further partnership glitch involves the difficulty of persuading local businesses to co-operate with each other, where they commonly see their peers as business rivals rather than members of the same community. The *Hotel Burglary Reduction initiative* evaluation, for example, found businesses that had installed security reluctant to co-operate with an initiative that appeared to reward their less committed rivals (Mawby and Jones, 2004). The report on the *Small Retailers in Deprived Areas* initiative similarly noted:

> Indeed, engaging with businesses has proved to be the lynchpin in the relative success or failure of SRDA projects and practitioners should not underestimate how difficult it can be to achieve buy-in from businesses. The interviews with project managers revealed that they frequently found it difficult to get businesses involved, particularly where the schemes required co-operation between businesses. There were varied reasons behind this reluctance, from an entrenched distrust of public bodies to an unwillingness to share information with competitors and fears over data protection (Home Office, 2004: 6–7).

Nevertheless, although in the US Fisher (1991) reported that collective crime reduction measures were uncommon, co-operative ventures, such as 'business watch' type schemes, provide a means of policing business premises that appears fairly common in England and Wales. For example, Taylor (2004) recounts that about half of retailers and nearly a third of manufacturers were taking part in some form of 'co-operative crime prevention activity' in 2002. It may thus be that businesses are willing to sign up to co-operative ventures, but reluctant to fully commit themselves to true partnership working. As the sergeant responsible for the *Hotel Burglary Reduction initiative* put it to me:

> Partnership's probably not quite the right word – most of the involvement, and the same is true to local businesses, the involvement is, is, 'Well, we'd better go along to this, just in case there's something that's going to have a detrimental effect on us.' ...They want something to be done but they feel everyone else should do it.

Given that effective partnership working is one of the key prerequisites of successful crime reduction initiatives (Kodz and Pease, 2003), attitudes like this may go some way to explaining why commercial burglary reduction initiatives have not enjoyed as much success as residential burglary initiatives.

Exploring patterns to commercial burglary

Clearly, not all businesses are equally at risk. Variations have been identified according to two sets of variables: the nature of the business and its location. In terms of the nature of the business, data from the Netherlands indicates that catering and the retail trade experienced particularly high risk (van Dijk and Terlouw, 1996). In England, the CVS also found risk of burglary to be slightly higher in the retail sector than in manufacturing (Taylor, 2004). Similarly, in a study of three Suburban communities in Philadelphia, Hakim and Gaffney (1994) found retail businesses to experience high levels of burglary. In Cornwall, Mawby (2003) also found that retail industries experienced more burglary than manufacturers. On the other hand, the Scottish business survey found the highest risk of break-ins in the manufacturing sector, especially those producing food and beverages.

ICBS data suggest that retailers dealing in tobacco, software and electronics experienced the highest risk (van Dijk and Terlouw, 1996). In Scotland, it also appears that drugs, cigarettes/tobacco, alcohol, computers and expensive electronic equipment are targeted.

Size is also a factor, with larger businesses generally experiencing higher risk (Gill, 1998; Taylor, 2004). Our hotel study also found that burglary was more common in larger hotels. However, the Scottish survey found no relationship between size – measured by turnover or staff numbers – and risk of burglary, a finding the authors suggested was due to the better security enjoyed by larger businesses.

In terms of location, there is clear evidence that businesses sited in rural locations experience least burglary (Taylor, 2004). The Scottish survey also found low risk in agricultural communities. However, area deprivation appears less closely correlated with risk. In England and Wales, risk of burglary was higher in disadvantaged areas among manufacturers, but not amongst retailers (Taylor, 2004). In Scotland, burglary risk was highest in public sector housing estates with older residents or less well off families. However, it was *not* as high in the poorest public sector estates or in the privately rented sector, both areas where household burglary was common. In Philadelphia, Hakim and Gaffney (1994), in contrast, found commercial burglary *more common* in affluent suburbs, suggesting that offenders associated such locations with more valuable items to steal.

In general rural businesses are at low risk of burglary. However, it seems that isolated property, and buildings that are away from main roads, secluded, remote, or near woods, parks etc. experience more break-ins (Hakim and Gaffney, 1994; Mawby, 2003).[10] This relates to the lack of informal surveillance opportunities. Thus Bichler-Robertson and Potchak (2002) found that businesses with low surveillability alley access to the rear were at highest risk. Indeed:

> The contextual analysis indicates that back alley access, with low surveill-ability, is the most important target selection feature. High-crime areas were almost twice as likely to have this feature than low-crime areas (ibid., 51).

Interestingly, while alley-gating is now seen as an effective domestic burglary reduction strategy in England (Johnson and Loxley, 2001; Kodz and Pease, 2003), there is little discussion of it in the context of commercial burglary.

Offenders and offending

Although some research has identified the motives and main characteristics of burglars, the focus of so many studies of burglars (both commercial and domestic) has been on planning, choice of targets, factors which attract or deter them and consequently the implications for crime prevention (Bennett and Wright, 1984; Butler, 1994; Cromwell *et al.*, 1991; Hearnden and Magill, 2004; Nee and Taylor, 1988; Wiersma, 1996; Wright and Logie, 1988). Research is, however, handicapped in that most has been conducted on convicted burglars, especially incarcerated ones (Wright *et al.*, 1992). Since commercial burglary has low detection rates (Clarke, 2003), this suggests that the offender population is skewed towards the least successful criminals. In Britain, Walsh (1986) interviewed 45 prison inmates whose last offence was recorded as commercial burglary and Butler (1994) interviewed small samples of commercial burglars either on probation or in prison. Similarly, the major Dutch study (Kruissink, 1995; Kruissink, 1996; Wiersma, 1996) involved semi-structured interviews with 83 (mainly incarcerated) commercial burglars.

Most of the Dutch sample were male, aged between 20–30, and had had little or no schooling. Commercial burglary was preferred, partly because the offenders could more easily justify crimes where no individual victim was involved, partly because the courts were seen as more severe on residential burglars, and partly because it was more profitable. Nevertheless:

> The majority of the offenders had been active in crime for years, and had certainly not restricted themselves to burglary of businesses (Wiersma, 1996: 218).

Butler (1994), Walsh (1986) and Kruissink (1995) also noted that there was little evidence of much specialization in commercial burglary. Most of their samples had committed household burglaries or other property offences and seemed fairly flexible in their choice of offences.

Paralleling research on domestic burglary (Bennett and Wright, 1984; Hearnden and Magill, 2004; Cromwell, Olson and Avary, 1991), Wiersma (1996) was somewhat ambivalent about the extent of professionalism displayed by his

sample. Many were motivated by the thrill and excitement of the act and proceeds were spent on drugs, alcohol and high living, but most also put a considerable amount of effort into planning the crime. A large majority of his sample
showed cunning and resourcefulness in preparing for and carrying out their burglaries. For example, over 80 percent collected advanced information on access
points, alarms, where valuables were stored etc. Targets were commonly chosen
because of their perceived vulnerability; such as location on a business park or
lack of burglar alarm. He consequently concluded that most could be described
as 'limited reasoning decision makers' rather than professionals.

Ram raiding, in particular, is a crime that is usually well planned and profes-
sionally executed, and tends to be committed by groups of offenders working
together as a team. Donald and Wilson (2000) researched 70 convicted offenders
whose most recent offences involved ram raiding. All were male, with a mean
age of 23. The majority had a previous conviction for vehicle thefts (74 percent),
other theft (67 percent), handling (67 percent), non-dwelling burglary
(63 percent) and thefts from motor vehicles (53 percent), but interestingly rather
less had previous convictions for domestic burglary, robbery or other violent
crimes. The distinctiveness of Donald and Wilson's (2000) approach, though,
was to consider ram raiding groups as 'work groups', with a designated leader,
specialists (such as a driver), and younger members serving apprenticeships, a
distinctly different pattern to that found amongst domestic, and indeed other
commercial, burglars.

Interviews with both commercial and domestic burglars provides additional
evidence on the effectiveness (or otherwise) of increased security.

Occupancy is a good example of a common theme that none the less distinguishes commercial from domestic burglary. Overwhelmingly, burglars prefer
unoccupied premises (Bennett and Wright, 1984; Hearnden and Magill, 2004;
Maguire, 1982). However, whereas in the case of domestic burglary this means
that most offences occur in daylight or evenings (Cromwell, Olson and Avary,
1991; Rengert and Wasilchick, 2000), for commercial burglaries most take place
at night or weekends (Kruissink, 1995; Wiersma, 1996).

In the case of residential burglary, Cromwell, Olson and Avary (1991)
identified two additional types of cues used by burglars in assessing risk:

- Surveillability: the extent to which the premises are overseen by passers-by
  and neighbours.
- Accessibility: including the presence or absence of window locks, an alarm,
  open windows etc.

In England and Wales, however, Hearnden and Magill (2004) reported burglars as
rarely deterred by situational factors (alarms and CCTV being notable exceptions),
and argued that the likely 'yield' from a burglary was the main consideration in
identifying targets.

Maguire (1982) also stressed the potential value of goods, privacy, ease of
access/escape and the presence of burglar alarms (which at that time were rela-

tively rare). Bennett and Wright (1984: 155) considered that 'surveillability' was, alongside 'occupancy' the most important situational cue influencing burglars' choice of targets, including here alarms as 'occupancy proxies'. However, Wright *et al.* (1995), in their comparison of burglars' and a control group's reactions to hypothetical situations, noted that burglars were less likely than controls to be deterred by the fact that the house was occupied or that there were extra door locks.

The commercial burglars interviewed by Walsh (1986) also claimed they were not put off by conventional burglar alarms and similarly Butler's (1994) sample did not overall consider alarms or door or window locks a deterrent, but were more likely to be deterred by a physical presence, whether security staff or members of the public to whom potential targets were visible. In Kruissnik's (1995) Dutch survey, commercial burglars also admitted that they were put off by security staff, by silent alarms wired directly to the police station and by guard dogs, but not by other security equipment. Wiersma (1996) confirms that burglars were not generally deterred by security measures such as 'extra locks and bolts, roll-down shutters, warning lights, cameras, loud alarms and the presence of security personnel' (ibid., 222). On the other hand, just over half *were* deterred by dogs, and silent (as opposed to loud) alarms, and in-house (as opposed to visiting) security guards were considered effective deterrents.

The fact that burglars target premises containing goods that are 'worth' stealing raises the question of how goods are disposed of. Clearly the situation facing an offender who has successfully burgled a home with, normally, one each from a list of household possessions, will be very different from that of a commercial burglar who has stolen large numbers of the same item. In the latter case, stealing to order is more likely and the importance of a fence increases. However, much of the available research on fencing is dated (Mawby, 2001, see also Gill *et al.*, 2004) and little directly addresses differences between commercial and residential burglary. Similarly, discussions of travel patterns, that is, the relationship between residence, everyday lifestyle and choice of targets, almost exclusively relates to domestic burglary (Bottoms and Wiles, 2002; Rengert and Wasilchick, 2000; Wiles and Costello, 2000).

Summary and discussion

Commercial burglary involves someone entering commercial property without permission in order to steal something. This chapter discusses recent research findings under six headings. First, business people's perceptions of and concern about burglary is discussed. The following two sections then address the extent and costs of commercial burglary. Fourth, policy and practice are considered, in terms of policing and crime reduction. Fifth, variations in commercial burglary according to the nature of the business and its location are explored. Finally, research on those who commit commercial burglary is described.

Commercial burglary is particularly common. It is one of the most common, and costly, forms of crime affecting businesses, and businesses experience far more burglary than do residential establishments. Its financial implications are wide, threatening the viability of many businesses, especially small businesses in disadvantaged areas. It may also impact upon staff and clients. However, many business people are ambivalent about crime, and burglary in particular. This, plus some reluctance to get involved in joint action with other businesses and a lack of involvement in local crime reduction partnerships, has tended to restrict participation in joint action and limited the effectiveness of commercial burglary reduction initiatives. Nevertheless, target hardening, incorporating increased door and window security, alarms and CCTV, has become particularly common in recent years. This is somewhat ironic, since the evidence on the effectiveness of target hardening is conflicting. On the other hand, the nature of the business, and its stock, and business location are important in explaining risk.

Combining the findings on risk with those on security and offenders' perspectives, the extent of commercial burglary appears linked to three sets of criteria:

- *Target attractiveness:* what goods are available to steal and how easy they are to fence. Although evidence on fencing *vis-à-vis* commercial burglary is negligible, the greater risk experienced by premises containing drugs, tobacco and electronic goods illustrates the importance of target attractiveness.
- *Accessibility:* how easy it is to break into the property. Here the evidence is less clear-cut. On the one hand, Hakim and Buck (1993) and Bowers (2001) suggest that target hardening may reduce commercial burglary. On the other hand, the (English) Home Office (2004) evaluation of the *Small Retailers in Deprived Areas* initiative reveals little impact, and interviews with burglars provides little evidence that target hardening is an effective deterrent (Butler, 1994; Walsh, 1986; Wiersma, 1996). An exception to this is the deployment of silent alarms, that tend to have been favoured among the business community but rarer among private households.
- *Surveillance:* the possibility of the burglar being spotted. Isolated property (Hakim and Gaffney, 1994; Mawby, 2003; Wiersma, 1996) and buildings that allow the offender to break-in out of sight of passers-by (Bichler-Robertson and Potchak, 2002) appear at high risk. Burglars also admit being deterred if buildings are overseen (Butler, 1994), occupied (Wiersma, 1996) or employ security staff (particularly in-house security) (Butler, 1994; Wiersma, 1996). Higher rates of burglary in larger hotels may also be explained in terms of offenders being more anonymous, and therefore less immediately visible, in such settings.

These criteria can then be directly linked to Clarke's (1997) recommendations for effecting greater security:

- *Target attractiveness* might be reduced by reducing the amount of 'stealable' property when the business is closed and by targeting fences.
- *Accessibility* might be reduced through target hardening, especially silent alarms, and alley-gating.

- *Surveillance* might be increased through increased formal surveillance (in-house security guards), natural surveillance (make access points more visible) and staff training (to increase staff vigilance).

Nevertheless, the business community is often reluctant to increase its spending on security. There are a number of reasons for this. First, burglary is not always considered a problem, and where it is recognized as such may be accorded less priority than other concerns facing businesses. Second, other demands on resources may be prioritized, and even where matched funding is available this may be unattractive. Third, there appears to be a reluctance among businesses to become involved in crime reduction partnerships, and a corresponding reluctance of key local players to incorporate the business sector.

While it seemed clear that businesses experienced a burglary problem, not all business managers are convinced. It is therefore important to use crime statistics and the personal experiences of selected businesses to get home the message that burglary is a problem and that it has a direct impact on business success. However, it is also evident that many businesses, no matter how willing, do not have the financial resources to contribute, even to a matched funding initiative. Therefore, while matched funding may be part of a burglary reduction strategy, it is crucial that low cost alternatives are available to *all* businesses. This should involve video advice and pamphlets that focus specifically on business crime and that are widely circulated, and it might be that using business associations and the internet would be the most effective means for achieving this. Involving businesses in the distribution of advice could incorporate both a 'watch type' scheme and the passing on of practical but low cost advice. Involving businesses in the advice giving and decision making processes might help engender a sense of ownership.

To some extent, multi-agency working is problematic, because many of the key agencies from the business sector are unused to partnership involvement, especially in the context of crime and disorder agendas. This is, however, no excuse. An appreciation that businesses experience high risk, and the adoption of appropriate responses, would seem incontestable, whether the main issues are public disorder, robbery, or burglary. This implies both a commitment on behalf of the police and the inclusion of businesses within local crime reduction partnerships.

Notes

1 The law and criminal procedure in England and Wales are identical, but for convenience the word 'English' is used to encompass both countries.
2 From Western Europe: Netherlands, (West) Germany, France, Switzerland, UK and Italy. From Central and Eastern Europe: Hungary and the Czech Republic.
3 The British Retail Consortium also carries out an annual survey and the British Chambers of Commerce (BCC) conducted a national survey in 2001 (see British Chambers of Commerce 2002). For a smaller scale national survey, see Gill (1998).
4 The findings are also reviewed more extensively at www.scotland.gov.uk/cru/kd01/crime/crime-01.htm. Unless otherwise stated, data from the SSBC included here is derived from this website.
5 This is discussed further in Jones and Mawby (2005) and Mawby and Jones (2004).

6 See also www.scotland.gov.uk/cru/kd01/crime/crime-01.htm.
7 www.scotland.gov.uk/cru/kd01/crime/crime-01.htm.
8 See also Fisher, 1991.
9 See especially www.scotland.gov.uk/cru/kd01/crime/crime-01.htm.
10 See also www.scotland.gov.uk/cru/kd01/crime/crime-01.htm.

Key readings

Surprisingly little written about commercial burglary. Ron Clarke's (2003) short report on burglary in the retail sector (*Burglary of retail establishments*. US Department of Justice, Community Oriented Policing Series, No. 15 (available at www.cops.usdoj.gov), is probably the most comprehensive review of the literature. This acknowledges that, with the exception of the 1994 ICBS (see Dijk, J.J.M. van and Terlouw, G.J. (1996) 'An international perspective of the business community as victims of fraud and crime', *Security Journal, 7*, 157–67), much of the research has been conducted in the UK, with correspondingly little in the US. Surveys of business victimization allow for a comparison of burglary with other offences experienced by the business community. Probably the most comprehensive of these is the Scottish survey, which is covered in detail at www.scotland.gov.uk/cru/kd01/ crime/crime-01.htm. A review of commercial burglary, compared with household burglary, is contained in Mawby, R.I. (2001) *Burglary*. Collumpton: Willan Press. Small scale studies of offence patterns, offending behaviour and burglary reduction policy and practice include: in the US, Bichler-Robertson, G. and Potchak, M.C. (2002) 'Testing the importance of target selection factors associated with commercial burglary using the blended approach', *Security Journal, 15.4*, 41–61; in the Netherlands, Kruissink, M. (1996) 'Commercial burglary: the offender's perspective', *Security Journal, 7.3*, 197–203, and Wiersma, E. (1996) 'Commercial burglars in the Netherlands: reasoning decision-makers?', *International Journal of Risk, Security and Crime Prevention, 1.3*, 217–25; and in the UK, Bowers, K.J. (2001) 'Small business crime: the evaluation of a crime prevention initiative', *Crime prevention and community safety: an international journal, 3.1*, 23–42, and Butler, G. (1994) 'Commercial burglary: what offenders say', pp. 29–41 in M. Gill (ed.) *Crime at work*. Leicester: Perpetuity Press. Again, though, many studies are not exclusive to burglary. Other studies focus on specific targets or techniques, including: ram raiding (Donald, I. and Wilson, A. (2000) 'Ram raiding: criminals working in groups', pp. 191–246 in Canter, D. and Alison, L. (eds) *The social psychology of crime: groups, teams and networks*. Dartmouth: Ashgate); burglary of chemists' shops (Laycock, G. (1985) *Reducing burglary: a study of chemists' shops*. London: Home Office) (Crime Prevention Unit, paper No. 1); and hotel burglary (Jones, C. and Mawby, R.I. (2005) 'Hotel crime: who cares?', *Crime prevention and community safety: an international journal, 7.2*, 19–35).

References

Bayley, D. and Shearing, C. (1996) 'The Future of Policing', *Law and Society Review, 30.3*, 585–606.

Beck, A. and Willis, A. (1991) *Burglary in Currys and Comet: a Comparative Analysis*. Centre for the Study of Public Order, University of Leicester, Leicester.

Bennett, T. and Wright, T. (1984) *Burglars on Burglary*. Aldershot: Gower.

Bichler-Robertson, G. and Potchak, M.C. (2002) 'Testing the Importance of Target Selection Factors Associated with Commercial Burglary Using the Blended Approach', *Security Journal, 15.4*, 41–61.

Bottoms, A.E. and Wiles, P. (2002) 'Environmental Criminology', pp. 620–56 in Maguire, M., Morgan, R. and Reiner, R. (eds) *The Oxford Handbook of Criminology*. Oxford: Oxford University Press.

Bowers, K.J. (2001) 'Small Business Crime: the Evaluation of a Crime Prevention Initiative', *Crime Prevention and Community Safety: An International Journal, 3.1*, 23–42.

British Chambers of Commerce (2002) *Securing Enterprise: a Framework for Tackling Business Crime*. London: BCC.

Brown, B. (1995) *CCTV in Town Centres: Three Case Studies.* London: Home Office (Crime Detection and Prevention Series, paper no. 68).

Burrows, J., Anderson, S., Bamfield, J., Hopkins, M. and Ingram, D. (1999) *Counting the Cost: Crime Against Business in Scotland.* Edinburgh: Scottish Executive Central Research Unit (Crime and Criminal Justice Research Findings no. 35) (see also at: http://www.scotland.gov.uk/cru/resfinds/crffinds/ crf35-00.htm).

Butler, G. (1994) 'Commercial Burglary: What Offenders Say', pp. 29–41 in M. Gill (ed.) *Crime at work.* Leicester: Perpetuity Press.

Clarke, R.V. (2003) *Burglary of Retail Establishments.* US Department of Justice, Community Oriented Policing Series, no. 15 (available at www.cops.usdoj.gov).

Clarke, R.V. (1997) *Situational Crime Prevention: Successful Case Studies (second edition).* New York: Harrow & Heston.

Cromwell, P.F., Olson, J.N. and Avary, D'A. W. (1991) *Breaking and Entering.* Newbury Park, California: Sage.

Dijk, J.J.M. van and Terlouw, G.J. (1996) 'An International Perspective of the Business Community as Victims of Fraud and Crime', *Security Journal, 7,* 157–67.

Distraction Burglary Task Force (2002) *Tackling Distraction Burglary.* (www.crimereduction.gov.uk/ boguscaller8.htm).

Ditton, J. and Farrell, S. (2000) *The Fear of Crime.* Aldershot: Ashgate.

Dodd, T., Nicholas, S., Povey, D. and Walker, A. (2004) (eds) *Crime in England and Wales 2003/2004.* London: Home Office (Research Development Statistics) (also available at www.homeoffice.gov.uk/rds/ crimeew0304.html).

Donald, I. and Wilson, A. (2000) 'Ram Raiding: Criminals Working in Groups', pp. 191–246 in Canter, D. and Alison, L. (eds) *The social psychology of crime: groups, teams and networks.* Dartmouth: Ashgate.

Eckblom, P. and Simon, F. (1988) *Crime Prevention and Racial Harassment in Asian-run Small Shops: The Scope for Prevention.* London: Home Office (Police Research Group Crime Prevention Series, no. 15).

Ellis, C. and Fletcher, G. (2003) 'Antisocial Behaviour and Disorder', pp. 87–99 in Flood-Page, C. and Taylor, J. (eds) *Crime in England and Wales 2001/2002: supplementary volume.* London: HMSO (HO Statistical Bulletin 01/03).

Fisher, B. (1991) 'Neighborhood Business Proprietors' Reactions to Crime (in Minnesota)', *Journal of Security Administration, 14.2,* 23–54.

Gill, M. (1998) 'The Victimisation of Business: Indicators of Risk and the Direction of Future Research', *International Review of Victimology, 6,* 17–28.

Gill, M., Hemming, M. Burns-Howell, T., Hart, J., Hayes, R., Clarke, R. and Wright, A. (2004) The Illicit Market in Stolen Fast-Moving Consumer Goods. Leicester: Perpetuity Research and Consultancy International.

Hakim, S. and Buck, A. (1993) 'Security Systems Cut Business Burglary Risks', *Security Distributing and Marketing, April,* 79–80.

Hakim, S. and Gaffney, M.A. (1994) 'Substantiating Effective Security', *Security Dealer, August,* 148–57.

Hale, C. (1996) 'Fear of Crime: A Review of the Literature', *International Review of Victimology, 4.2,* 79–150.

Hearnden, I. and Magill, C. (2004) 'Decision-making By House Burglars: Offenders' Perspectives', *Home Office Research Findings,* no. 249.

Home Office (2004) *Tackling Crimes Against Small Businesses: Lessons From the Small Retailers in Deprived Areas Initiative.* London: Home Office (Development and Practice Report no. 29) (available at www.homeoffice.gov.uk/rds).

Home Office (2002) *Distraction Burglary Good Practice Guide.* (www.crimereduction.gov.uk/ burglary48.htm).

Hopkins, M. and Ingram, D. (2001) 'Crimes Against Businesses: The First Scottish Business Crime Survey', *Security Journal, 14.3,* 43–58.

Hough, M. (1995) *Anxiety About Crime: Findings From the 1994 British Crime Survey.* London: Home Office (Home Office Research Study no. 147).

Johnston, L. (1992) *The Rebirth of Private Policing*. London: Routledge.
Johnson, S. and Loxley, C. (2001) 'Installing Alley-gates: Practical Lessons from Burglary Prevention Projects', *Home Office Briefing Note 2/01*.
Johnston, V., Leitner, M., Shapland, J. and Wiles, P. (1994) 'Crime, Business and Policing on Industrial Estates: pp. 102–24 in Gill (ed.) *Crime at Work*. Leicester: Perpetuity Press.
Jones, C. and Mawby, R.I. (2005) 'Hotel Crime: Who Cares?', *Crime Prevention and Community Safety: An International Journal*, 7.3, 19–35.
Jones, T. and Newburn, T. (1995) 'How Big is the Private Security Sector?'. *Policing and Society*, 5, 221–32.
Kesteren, J. van, Mayhew, P. and Nieuwbeerta, P. (2003) *Criminal Victimisation in Seventeen Industrialised Countries: Key Findings from the 2000 International Crime Victims Survey*. Netherlands: WODC. (www.minjust.nl/b-organ/wodc/publicaties/rapporten/pubrapp/ob187i.htm)
Keynote (2002) *The Security Industry: Market Review 2002*. Hampton: Keynote Ltd.
Kodz, J. and Pease, K. (2003) 'Reducing Burglary Initiative: Early Findings on Burglary Reduction', *Home Office Research Findings*, no. 204.
Kruissink, M. (1996) 'Commercial Burglary: the Offender's Perspective', *Security Journal*, 7.3, 197–203.
Kruissink, M. (1995) *Inbraak in Bedrijven: Daders, Aangiften en Slachtoffers Onderzocht*. The Hague: Ministry of Justice.
Laycock, G. (1985) *Reducing Burglary: A Study of Chemists' Shops*. London: Home Office (Crime Prevention Unit, paper no. 1).
Maguire, M. (1982) *Burglary in a Dwelling*. London: Heinemann.
Mawby, R.I. (2001) *Burglary*. Collumpton: Willan Press.
Mawby, R.I. (2003) 'Crime and the Business Community: Experiences of Businesses in Cornwall, England', *Security Journal*, 16.4, 45–61.
Mawby, R.I. (2004) 'Crime and Disorder: Perceptions of Business People in Cornwall, England', *International Review of Victimology*, 11.2, 313–32.
Mawby, R.I. and Jones, C. (2004) 'Evaluation of a Hotel Burglary Project', Home Office Online Report 16/04 (www.homeoffice.gov.uk/rds/ pdfs04/rdsolr1604.pdf).
Mayhew, P. and Dijk, J.J.M. van (1997) *Criminal Victimisation in Eleven Industrialised Countries*. Amstelveen, Netherlands: WODC.
Mirrlees-Black, C. and Ross, A. (1995) *Crime Against Retail and Manufacturing Premises: Findings from the 1994 Commercial Victimisation Survey*. Home Office (Home Office Research Study no. 146), London.
Nee, C. and Taylor, M. (1988) 'Residential Burglary in the Republic of Ireland: A Situational Perspective', *Howard Journal*, 27.2, 105–16.
Perrone, S. (2000) *Crimes Against Small Business in Australia: A Preliminary Analysis*. Canberra: Australian Institute of Criminology (Trends and Issues no. 184) (see also www.aic.gov.au)
Redshaw, J. and Mawby, R.I. (1996) 'Commercial Burglary: Victims' Views of the Crime and the Police Response', *International Journal of Risk, Security and Crime Prevention*, 1.3, 185–93.
Rengert, G.F. and Wasilchick, J. (2000) *Suburban Burglary: A Time and a Place for Everything*. Springfield: Thomas.
Simmonds, L. and Mawby, R.I. (2002) 'Addressing Victims' Needs: An Evaluation of Victim Support', paper to British Criminology Conference, Keele, July.
Taylor, G. (1999) 'Using Repeat Victimization to Counter Commercial Burglary: The Leicester Experience', *Security Journal*, 12.1, 41–52.
Taylor, J. (2004) 'Crime Against Retail and Manufacturing Premises: Findings from the 2002 Commercial Victimisation Survey', *Home Office Findings* no. 259.
Thornton, A., Hatton, C., Malone, C., Fryer, T., Walker, D., Cunningham, J. and Durrani, N. (2003) *Distraction Burglary Amongst Older Adults and Ethnic Minority Communities*. London: Home Office (Home Office Research Study no. 269) (www.homeoffice.gov.uk/rds/pdfs2/hors269.pdf).

Tilley, N. (1993) *The Prevention of Crime Against Small Business: The Safer Cities Experience.* Home Office (CPU paper 45), London.

Walker, J. (1996) 'Crime Prevention by Businesses in Australia', *International Journal of Risk, Security and Crime Prevention, 1.4,* 279–91.

Walsh, D. (1986) *Heavy Business.* London: Routledge and Kegan Paul.

Welsh, B.C. and Farrington, D.P. (2002) *Crime Prevention Effects of Closed Circuit Television: A Systematic Review.* London: Home Office (Home Office Research Study no. 252).

Wiersma, E. (1996) 'Commercial Burglars in the Netherlands: Reasoning Decision-makers?', *International Journal of Risk, Security and Crime Prevention, 1.3,* 217–25.

Wiles, P. and Costello, A. (2000) *The 'Road to Nowhere': The Evidence for Travelling Criminals.* London: Home Office (Home Office Research Study no. 207).

Wood, J., Wheelwright, G. and Burrows, J. (1997) *Crime Against Small Businesses: Facing the Challenge.* Swindon: Crime Concern.

Wright, R., Decker, S.H., Redfern, A.K. and Smith, D.L. (1992) 'A snowball's Chance in Hell: Doing Fieldwork with Active Residential Burglars', *Journal of Research in Crime and Delinquency, 29.2,* 148–61.

Wright, R. and Logie, R.H. (1988) 'How Young House Burglars Choose their Targets', *Howard Journal, 27,* 92–104.

13
Shoptheft

Read Hayes and Caroline Cardone

Inventory loss occurs at many points in the retail supply chain: freight shipping, distribution centers, and store backroom areas (Beck, 2004; Beck and Chapman, 2003; Hayes, 2003). But major losses occur on the sales floor (Bamfield, 2004; Hollinger and Langton, 2004; Miller and Kienzien, 2000). For as long as there has been shopping, there has been shoplifting (Edwards, 1976; Walsh, 1978). Also referred to as shopstealing or shoptheft, shoplifting is a specific form of larceny, defined as 'an act of theft from a retailer committed during the hours the store is open to the public by a person who is or appears to be a legitimate customer' (Cleary, 1986; Keckeisen, 1993; Sennewald and Christman, 1992). Shoplifters are not homogeneous, they are of differing ages, races, genders and backgrounds. Their motivations are diverse – many steal apparently out of greed, sometimes for need, at times their acts are seemingly inexplicable (Cameron, 1964; McGuire, 1997; McShane and Noonan, 1993; Moore, 1984). Shoplifting remains a serious social and economic problem in need of more dedicated research on solutions.

Scope, scale and impact

A vital part of our international economy, for instance, retail is second only to the service industry as the largest employer in the United States accounting for over 21 million American jobs. But shoplifting continues to affect this important industry. In 2003, the US retail industry suffered an estimated $11 billion in losses directly due to shoplifters (Hollinger and Langton, 2004). Shoplifting is believed to be the second most significant source of inventory shrinkage, with a $265.30 average dollar value per single incident (Hollinger and Langton, 2004). In 1993–1994, the estimated cost of error and theft in the United States and United Kingdom was over $26 billion – an amount equivalent to one quarter of annual retail profits (Bamfield and Hollinger, 1996; ECR, 2001).

Shoplifting is an international issue. In a 2004 survey of European Theft, retailers estimated 48 percent of shrink was attributable to shoplifting, totaling £1850 million in losses (Bamfield, 2004). Like the US, Canada, Australia, and Mexico also cite shoplifting as second to only employee theft as the most significant source of loss – each attributing approximately 30 percent of their shrinkage to customer theft (Bamfield, 2005). In addition to a national study in the UK (British Retail Consortium, 2004), three recent surveys of retail crime in New Zealand identified shoplifting as the most pervasive cause of retail loss in the country, accounting for 68 percent of losses (Guthrie, 2003).

The impact of shoplifting

When an item is stolen, retailers face both direct and indirect losses. Obviously, the cost of the item and the profit it would have brought is gone. But so too is the capital invested in purchasing, processing, marketing, and displaying that item – as well as the opportunity cost of capital. Significantly, when shoplifters wipe out a popular item, customers become dissatisfied, sometimes turning to rival stores and/or products (Beck, Chapman and Peacock, 2002). Additionally, when retailers become repeated targets of shoplifting and other retail crimes, legitimate shoppers may feel unsafe and demonstrate avoidance behaviors such as reduced shopping activity, limited night-time shopping, shortened shopping visits, and switching to competitors due to the fear of crime (Warr, 2000). Then there are the legal considerations. Prosecuting shoplifters is a costly and time-consuming task (Hayes, 1993a; Sennewald, 2000). Also, in today's litigious society, retailers can be crippled by legal claims should a presumed shoplifter be wrongly accused, or anyone be harmed or mishandled during a crime incident (Hayes, 2003). On a more macro level, shoplifting takes a heavy toll on society, indirectly increasing cost of living, incurring governmental tax losses, and straining social services, courts, jails, and police forces (Farrell and Ferrara, 1985).

Pressure to minimize loss

Some retailers expect and even accept a given amount of loss from theft (usually termed 'shrinkage') as an unfortunate but unavoidable cost of doing business. But theft losses can be so large a retailer's viability is threatened. Johnson and Outcalt (1996) argue the net margins of retail firms are likely to worsen under the pressures of high levels of competition and changes in consumer behavior, making such heavy losses unbearable and in need of focused solutions.

History

In 1164, Henry II complained of 'criminous clerks' stealing money and jewels in the name of God (Hollister, 1994). In Elizabethan times, troupes of thieves roved the streets. The term 'shoplifting' first appeared in the Oxford dictionary in 1673, and few years later Parliament made reference to it as an offense punishable by death. Henry Mayhew, a British sociologist studying London culture in the mid-1800s, reported on the lives of metropolitan shoplifters, especially women, who would stash items under their skirts or in baskets, but who often held surprisingly respectable positions in the city (Klemke, 1992).

The rise of widespread shoplifting as we know it today may not have developed until the late 1800s. Around that time, retailer Frank Woolworth made a simple decision that ultimately changed the face of American retailing: he displayed items outside a glass case. Mr. Woolworth predicated this innovation on the honor system – a fact that, today, shoppers and thieves alike take for granted. Woolworth's groundbreaking marketing decision led to a boom in sales: customers felt empowered, labor costs dropped, and profits soared. This 'self-service' system soon spread from five and dime stores like Woolworth's to grocery stores and others, eventually taking over the entire retail sector. Of course, such an easy-access approach fueled shoplifting. During the turn of the century, shoplifting became rampant in New York, as thieving gangs and delinquent youths grew increasingly brazen in their deviance. In the period of 1870–1900, shoplifting reached epidemic proportions in the US, especially among middle-class women (Klemke, 1992).

The late Victorians had a specific term for his new breed of female shoplifters: 'kleptomaniacs'. It described someone (usually female) who frequently and uncontrollably stole low-priced goods, and was freely interchanged with the term 'shoplifter'. Kleptomania was considered a 'woman's disease' and was closely linked to hysteria and the female menstrual cycle (Abelson, 1992). As such, it became a popular way to excuse a practice that had become quite common amongst middle-class women: 'the diagnosis of kleptomania was socially constructed by key decision-makers to deal with these sensitive cases, thus "legitimizing" the actions of stores and courts to dismiss or acquit those afflicted with this "women's sickness"' (Klemke, 1992).

Later, Freudian-based psychologists began to attribute kleptomania (and shoplifting) to a neurosis spawned by unresolved childhood issues. Some even suggested the condition was an attempt to fill the void left by lost love or sexual frustration (Stekel, 1924). Today, scientists have a discrete definition for kleptomania as a type of impulse control disorder, and the term is no longer synonymous with shoplifting. A rare and misunderstood affliction, kleptomania differs from shoplifting in that the kleptomaniac shoplifts not out of need or desire for items, but to fulfill an impulsive drive to covertly take things (Cupchik, 1997).

Following World War II, the boom in modern merchandising continued. However, this retail success was paralleled by significant increases in theft. The tendency for product manufacturers and retailers to cultivate desire for product certainly contributed to the development of a 'culture of consumption' that persists to this day (Cohen, 2003). Some believe the phenomenon of consumer-based desire itself is at the root of the shoplifting problem (Klemke, 1992). Today's retailers and their product supplier partners thus face a paradoxical challenge: how to heighten product desire for legitimate consumers while simultaneously deterring would-be shoplifters.

Targets

The most popular types of stores to shoplift from are those that carry very desirable items, are readily accessible, and appear vulnerable (Clarke, 1999; Hayes, 1997a).

These types of locations include malls, department stores, discount stores, computer stores, hardware stores, shoe stores, clothing stores, music/video stores, grocery stores, drug stores, and bookstores (Caime and Ghone, 1996; Hayes, 1999a). Modern retailers carry a rich assortment of goods, but a relatively small group of items ('hot products') comprise the majority of theft. The 'hotness' of an item is partially explained by the acronym CRAVED (Concealable, Removable, Available, Valuable, Enjoyable and Disposable), these items are often easier to steal and convert to cash than average products (Clarke, 1999). Examples of current CRAVED items include tobacco products; premium razor blades and face creams; analgesics; smoking cessation products; designer, logo, and leather apparel and shoes (particularly athletic); name brand power tools; vacuum cleaners; printer ink cartridges; steaks; film; coffee; consumer electronics (e.g. DVD players and GPS units); fragrances; infant formula; batteries; music and game DVDs; and over-the-counter medications and test kits (Bamfield, 2004; Clarke, 1999; Hayes, 1999a).

Shoptheft methods

The techniques a shoplifter uses to take merchandise is limited only by the imagination. At the most basic level, there are two approaches: concealment or non-concealment. But beyond that, shoplifting methods vary widely, from the obvious to the outrageous. Many shoplifters prefer to work in teams of two or more. Each participant has a prescribed 'role', and together they approach the task with some type of strategy, either loose or well-formed (Butler, 1994). Shoptheft techniques are widely varied and important for trade readers to learn to spot. In their extensive how-to handbook on the art of shoplifting, Caime and Ghone (1996) detail some of the myriad ways to shoplift:

- *Switch*: Requires a team of at least two shoplifters, one of whom is the 'decoy'. The decoy blatantly takes merchandise, starts asking questions, feigns illness or otherwise creates a scene, thus attracting security's attention. At an opportune moment, the decoy stashes the items. While security continues to focus on the decoy, the other partner grabs the stash and exits.
- *Steaming*: The process by which a large group of shoplifters, perhaps dozens, storm an establishment in unison. The goal is to overwhelm security forces through sheer numbers.
- *Receipt*: Following a legitimate purchase, the shoplifter keeps the receipt, returns to the store, and shoplifts the same item. If questioned, the shoplifter presents the receipt. Some shoplifters comb a store for discarded receipts and use them instead of making a purchase.
- *Buying*: With costly items concealed, the shoplifter proceeds to checkout with the apparent intention of making a legitimate purchase of cheaper 'cover' items. The shoplifter then pretends to have forgotten his/her wallet and exits the store with stolen items. An alternate method involves buying the 'cover' item instead of claiming a lost wallet.
- *Refund*: The shoplifter picks up an item in the store and brings it to the counter for a refund. If a refund is denied, he/she simply exits the store with the item.

- *Tag or Package Switch*: The shoplifter removes the higher price tag, barcode sticker or packaging and replaces it with a less expensive one, thus paying a lower price.
- *Grab and Run or Hit and Git*: Shoplifter quickly grabs product off the shelf and bolts out of the store.
- *Falling:* As shoplifter exits the store, he/she falls, in hopes that staff and security will be too preoccupied with shoplifter's well-being to suspect stolen items.
- *Whole Carting:* Shoplifter casually exits the store with an entire cart full of items or large item, in hopes that the hefty amount of merchandise will reduce suspicion.
- *Buzz-Through Gate:* Two shoplifting partners, one with stolen goods and one decoy, exit through an EAS gate simultaneously. When the alarm sounds, the decoy stays behind to divert security while the actual shoplifter exits the store. Alternately, a single shoplifter may use a legitimate shopper as the decoy, hoping he/she stays behind when the alarm sounds, serving as an unwitting decoy.
- *Dismantling Gates:* The shoplifter somehow disables EAS gates, either by falling on the system, or alternatively unplugging or severing the wires. Another approach involves the shoplifter attaching a small magnet to his/her shoe. This causes the system to set off false alarms, potentially causing management to shut it down altogether.
- *Emergency Exit:* Shoplifter exits with stolen merchandise via the emergency exit.
- *Packing (washroom or otherwise):* Shoplifter retreats to washroom or secluded area, where he/she conceals items before exiting store.
- *Bumping:* Knocking over a display or creating a similar disturbance, the shoplifter distracts store officials, and escapes unnoticed.
- *Distracter*: One shoplifter focuses on stealing goods while the other distracts store employees.
- *Diversions:* Shoplifter employs one of several diversions – such as setting a fire alarm, pretending to be ill, etc. – in order to shift focus away from stolen merchandise.
- *Drop and Collect:* The shoplifter deposits items in a hidden, safe place within the store and returns at a more opportune time to steal them.
- *Shrinker or grazer:* A shoplifter who uses or consumes stolen items while still in the store (i.e. eating grapes in the supermarket). This practice is also called grazing.
- *Dog Food Method:* Shoplifter fills an empty dog food or similar type bag with item while in the store. Tapes or otherwise seals bag shut and pays for 'dog food' at checkout.
- *Double Method:* Taking more than one of the stolen items, when possible.
- *Dressing Up:* Shoplifter simply wears unpaid for items out of a store. Usually involves outerwear.
- *Self-Concealment:* Shoplifter dresses as employee in order to take items from a store. Employee name badges, smocks and other uniform items can sometimes be acquired from former employees, on auction websites or 'on the street'.

- *Clothing/Accessories:* Includes many methods by which shoplifter conceals items in clothing. Some may be more elaborate than others, such as sewing extra pockets into a coat or cutting the seam between pocket and coat lining to create an oversized pocket. Other methods are basic: stashing items under a skirt or dress, in socks or shoes, in elastic girdles, or in a purse, tote, shopping or sports bag.
- *Booster/Magic Box:* Similar to dog food method. Shoplifter acquires a TV or other large box with a receipt, fills the box with goods, and exits the store with receipt as cover. Magic bags or items are bags, purses or boxes lined with layers of foil to reduce the EAS signal.
- *Clerk Exploitation:* Getting employees to inadvertently deactivate EAS tags.
- *Display Case:* If display case is left unmanned, shoplifter steals items directly from it.
- *Walking Out:* A brazen approach, whereby shoplifter nonchalantly walks out of the store (usually with a large item) acting as though it was legitimately purchased.
- *Baby Stroller:* Shoplifter stashes items in baby stroller or under baby before exiting store.
- *Ram-raiding:* Determined thieves crash a motor vehicle through windows or merchandise receiving doors then filling up the automobile with goods before driving away.

Organized Retail Crime (ORC)

A more ominous type of shoplifting has emerged, and appears to be growing termed organized retail crime, or ORC Hayes and Rogers, 2003). The FBI and other experts estimate ORC costs retailers and manufacturers between $12 to 35 billion annually in stolen goods and collateral effects (Cho, 2001; Hayes and Rogers, 2003; USDOJ, 1999). ORC gangs, also called 'booster gangs or crews', usually consist of a group of individuals working separately or together in a crime network to supply local fences. Local fences may then sell upward to mid-level dealers and so on. Often operated by locals and illegal aliens, ORC groups frequently cross both state and international borders to sell stolen goods through small shops, flea markets, fences, truck stops, and newspaper ads (Johns and Hayes, 2003). They sell to individual shoppers, overseas buyers, and even back to legitimate retailers, blending legitimate goods via unknowing or dishonest wholesalers. These groups are also aided by the anonymity and accessibility of Internet auction sites, which provide a fast, easy way of turning stolen merchandise into cash. Currently, the ORC problem shows no sign of abating, and with a continual influx of savvy criminals.

Typologies

It is difficult to define shoplifting demographically, as shoplifters come from all races, socioeconomic levels, genders, ages, and countries. Even large-scale studies have failed to show strong associations between shoplifting and demographic characteristics (Hayes, 1997b). Despite this difficulty, experts continually seek to categorize shoplifters into distinct groups, or typologies in order to better understand the ongoing problem. Most of these classify shoplifting as aberrant, criminal acts, though some tend to view it as a behavior stemming from extreme consumerism and frugality: the ultimate bargain shopper. Either way, classification often yields either very broad or very detailed descriptions of shoplifters. The only agreed-upon generalizations are that most shoplifters range from young to middle age, are likely to be involved in other deviant behaviors, and to be with others at the time of offense (Klemke, 1982, 1992).

Listed typologies have evolved from observation and theory of varying rigor. Most classification systems were developed to either guide offender treatment or deterrence, or both. Cameron (1964), Farrell and Ferrara (1985), Hayes (1993) and Klemke (1992) are not completely derived from specific research, but resulted from systematic observation. All the listed typologies provide utility for retail researchers and asset protection practitioners alike. The psychological classification systems can particularly provide insight for treatment and social worker professionals.

Behavioral and motivational typologies

In 1963, Mary Cameron developed what would become a well-known shoplifting typology: Boosters versus Snitches (Cameron, 1964). The 'Booster' was a professional thief who stole valuable items for resale and was often involved in other criminal behaviors, while the 'Snitch' was an amateur who stole low-value items for personal use. Cameron's typologies, though popular, were in reality overly simplistic. Subsequent recent research has yielded more multi-dimensional typologies.

In 1984, Richard Moore expanded the typology of shoplifting into five categories; *Impulse*: Carries out unplanned theft of low-cost items. *Occasional*: Shoplifts three to six times per year; usually as a result of financial difficulty or peer pressure. *Episodic*: shoplifts because of psychological problems. *Amateur*: Shoplifts weekly for financial purposes. *Semi-Professional*: Shoplifts for high-price items frequently and with technical skill.

Farrell and Ferrara (1985) developed a similar set of typologies, though based on three levels of shoplifter: *First class*: A professional who shoplifts with the intention of reselling the product for profit. *Second class*: Also a professional (meaning skilled theft methods versus for profit theft), but one who shoplifts for personal use, not resale. *Third class*: An amateur shoplifter who steals for personal use. These types will often steal lower-cost items, though potentially in high quantities. Within this group are five subgroups: Expert, Pathological, Impulse, Youthful, and Indigent.

Other classifications have been developed to help retailers better focus prevention efforts on distinctive differences in targeted merchandise, methods and motives. Like Cameron's original 'booster' and 'snitch' typologies, Hayes (1993b) presents a dual classification: professional and amateur. The main distinction between these two is that the professional shoplifts primarily for economic gain by converting stolen items into cash or other valuables, like illegal drugs. He also notes, significantly, that the groups are not mutually exclusive; a given shoplifter may cross from one group to another in accordance with the conditions of the crime. Furthermore, he describes several corresponding sub-groups, based on planning, sophistication, skill, success, financial scope, and frequency: *True Pro*: Approaches shoplifting as a job, routinely stealing items for resale at flea markets or fences. Prefers to work in teams, and may project a sophisticated façade that blends with the retail environment. True pros create high losses for retailers, frequently stealing over $100 in goods in a single incident. This type of thief tends to avoid violence. *Hardcore Pro*: Frequently shoplifts but also participates in a variety of other criminal acts, such as drug dealing, prostitution, auto theft, or burglary, and often has a criminal record. May steal merchandise for cash refund or resale. Sometimes carries weapons, is prone to violence to avoid re-arrest, and employs brazen shoplifting methods like grab-and-runs. *Casual Pro*: Employs methods similar to other types of pros, but does not subsist on shoplifting earnings. This type of offender may be an amateur criminal transitioning into a professional. *Primary Household Shopper*: Occasionally or habitually steals items out of the household budget's range, including cosmetics, high-priced clothing and gifts. Not gender-specific, but is usually the primary caregiver or shopper. Will conceal items in bag or purse, but does not usually incur high losses for the retailer. *Impulsive Shoplifter*: Probably the largest group of shoplifters, this individual steals during a lapse in judgment resulting from greed, stress, impatience, or embarrassment. The dollar amount is usually low, but the frequency of such thefts makes its impact severe. *Juvenile Shoplifter*: There are many reasons behind juvenile theft, including peer pressure to steal, perceived peer pressure or high desire to have an item, but inadequate funds, temporary notoriety, the need to conform, thrill-seeking, the inability to legitimately buy an item, youthful naïveté, and defiance. Juvenile shoplifters often steal relatively low-priced items, and may or may not be violent. *Pathological Shoplifters*: Some deviant behavior is in part caused by pathology, medication, or chemical impairment. This category includes kleptomaniacs – a rare and difficult-to-define condition whereby afflicted persons impulsively (sometimes unknowingly) steal items for no apparent reason.

Based on his review of multiple crime- and sociology-based studies, Klemke (1992) identifies juvenile delinquents, adult middle-class females, and drug abusers as those most likely to shoplift. Klemke acknowledges a fourth group, whom he refers to as the 'atypical shoplifters', as the psychologically disturbed, elderly, antiestablishmentarians, undercover cops, religious leaders, and actresses. The incongruence of this group, and its existence in Klemke's classification system as a catch-all for 'atypical' shoplifters, indicates the inherently difficult nature of grouping shoplifters into prescribed categories. As Klemke states, 'the prestigious social positions and absence of dire financial need make these cases of shoplifting puzzling and presumably rare' (Klemke, 1992: 29).

Psychological typologies

Different types of people shoplift for different reasons. Some shoplift as a way to make a living, selling stolen goods for profit, while others have antiestablishment motivations, believing large retail chains 'deserve' it and can absorb the losses. Some shoplifters steal to support drug habits, while others simply enjoy the 'rush' it gives them. Researchers have explored numerous explanations as to why people shoplift, from pathological acts (Beck and MacIntyre, 1977), to attempt to relieve psychological stresses or societal difficulties (Coid 1984; McShane and Noonan, 1993; Medlicott, 1968). For teenagers, the draw to shoplifting often develops out of peer pressure to offend, the pressure to conform via in-style clothing or entertainment items (without the means to pay for them), or the notoriety they glean from the act (Hayes, 1997b). Moore (1984) identified financial benefit and economic disadvantage as the main motivators behind shoplifting.

Motivation-based typologies facilitate a better understanding of why people steal, assisting retailers with deterrence measures and possibly social workers with rehabilitation efforts. In their study of shoplifting interventions and assessments, Schwartz and Wood (1991) identified five major motivational categories: *Entitlement*: These shoplifters feel they've been treated unfairly, and justify their actions as recompensation, not crime. Examples are anti-corporation or anti-establishment supporters, bitter senior citizens, and inflation opponents. *Addictions*: The behavior of these shoplifters results from addictive disorders; for instance, alcoholics who steal alcohol, drug abusers who shoplift and resell to support a drug habit, or bulimics who steal food. *Peer Pressure*: These juvenile or college-age individuals steal in order to gain acceptance from their peer group. They often shoplift impulsively for low-priced merchandise. *Stress*: Shoplifters in this category exhibit theft behavior as a result with psychosocial stress. Unfortunately, when caught, these shoplifters create even more stress for themselves. *Impulsiveness*: These shoplifters react to a sudden, often inexplicable urges to steal while shopping. The merchandise may or may not be something the shoplifter actually craves. However, Schwartz and Wood distinguish this type of motivation from kleptomania, which they consider a more serious affliction.

Katz (1988) presents another motivation-based typology in his allusion to shoplifting as a type of game, in which the shoplifter's goal is to elude security and 'win' by successfully leaving the store with stolen merchandise. If they're apprehended by security, the 'game' ends in defeat. Many of these shoplifters will, if caught, attempt to pay for the stolen items in an effort to avoid prosecution. Such an approach provides an emotional high if successful, and a corresponding extreme low if caught. Katz also cites other psychological factors – such as depression, stress, senility, peer pressure, and a desire for excitement – as possible shoplifting motivators.

Shoplifting and theories of deviancy

Much of the research on shoplifting derives from the fields of sociology, psychology, and criminology. Similar to criminological research, shoplifting studies tend to explore either individual criminality, or the origin and dynamics of crime events. To that end, it is useful to review some relevant theories of deviancy.

Robert Merton's (1938) research is particularly applicable to shoplifting, in its exploration of deviant behavior as a result of the frustrating disjuncture between a desire for economic success and the lack of means to attain it. This concept, referred to as 'anomie', motivates individuals to seek out goods and material status symbols by any means necessary, and leads to deviant behaviors like shoplifting. A resulting implication is that poorer social groups would be more likely to be deviant, since they lack the means to attain success. Indeed, research supports a modestly inverse relationship between social class and shoplifting (Klemke 1982; Bales 1982). Further studies have expanded Merton's original theory by positing that severe mental disturbance can also lead to anomie, thus positioning it as not merely a result of sociological conditions (McClosky and Schaar, 1965).

Researchers have also applied theories of social control to explain shoplifting. The basic premise was that weak social bonds – such as social disruptions or failures, particularly familial – led to delinquency or deviant behavior. Later studies confirmed a link between weak family structures and delinquency (Belson, 1975; Nye, 1958; Wilkinson, 1980).

Later, socialization theories emerged to explore how what one learns from others affects behavior. This was evidenced in Edwin Sutherland's interactionist theory, which asserted that deviant behavior arose from socialization within certain subcultures (Heimer and Matsueda, 1997). This theory can be applied to organized shoplifting gangs, families, peer groups, or neighborhoods – any situation in which an individual's deviant tendencies result in part from the influences of his/her surrounding subculture. For example, Erikson (1972) found that a high percentage of juvenile delinquency occurs in the presence of other youth, indicating a group influence. Additional studies have linked prostitution and/or drug subcultures with an increase in shoplifting (Kowalski and Faupel, 1990; Miller, 1986), as well as shoplifting among more affluent groups, such as middle-class adolescents (Hoffman, 1971). A more modern makeover of learning theories including social learning theory (Akers, 1998) has had considerable influence on the study of criminality.

Another explanatory theory, neutralization theory, derives from the research of Sykes and Matza (1957), who concluded that although delinquents are relatively committed to social order, they choose to 'neutralize' deviant actions by denying responsibility, injury, or existence of an actual victim. According to this theory, shoplifters see their actions not as criminal, but rather as individual responses to particular situations. Cromwell and Thurman (2003) found shoplifters frequently *a priori* or *ex post facto* neutralize their guilt with a variety of rationalizations.

Other theorists postulate shoplifting is more a form of consumer behavior than strict deviance (Tonglet, 2000). The theory of planned behavior (Ajzen, 2002) applies consumer behavior models to aberrant behavior such as shoplifting. Resulting research has indicated pro-shoplifting attitudes, social factors, apparent shoplifting opportunities, and perceptions of low apprehension risk all contribute to the decision to shoplift, particularly amongst adults and teenagers. Thus, to be effective, the deterrents retailers employ should focus on influencing shoplifter perceptions of the seriousness of theft.

More recently, a growing body of research has sought to explain how crime is related to situational or environmental factors. One such example, rational choice theory, asserts that criminals like shoplifters are in fact frequently normal, reasonable people who weigh the relative risks and rewards associated with a crime before deciding to commit it (Cornish and Clarke, 1986; Felson and Clarke, 1998). In the case of shoplifting, a potential offender might assess how much he/she desires, needs, or will profit from an item against the chance of being caught and resulting punishment.

Another particularly useful theory is routine activity theory (RAT) since it carries beyond individual criminality, and helps researchers and practitioners visualize how crime events occur. RAT describes how likely offenders (such as shoplifters) come to commit a crime partly based on their normal, everyday activities. Routine travel and activities can bring a motivated or likely offender into contact with desirable but vulnerable assets (due to a perceived lack of capable guardianship), resulting in a crime event (Cohen and Felson, 1979; Felson, 1996, 1998).

Complimenting the routine activity model is the work of Brantingham and Brantingham (1993) who developed environmental criminology theory. It contends that criminal activity is most likely to occur when the physical spheres of criminals and victims overlap. That is, a shoplifter's criminal activity will tend to occur in places he visits or that are near paths he/she regularly travels.

The concept of situational crime prevention (Clarke, 1997; Cornish and Clarke, 2003; Smith and Cornish, 2004) combines both routine and rational choice theories in an evolving, evidence-based set of crime prevention techniques. Currently, the theory consists of 25 specific strategies. Situational crime prevention techniques emphasize reducing opportunities, affecting motivations and raising the spector of personal risk for would-be offenders (Felson and Clarke, 1998). The situational approach has in turn spawned study of the direct and collateral effects of crime prevention itself. For example, the phenomenon of crime displacement explains how protective activities may simply displace crime attempts to other locales, times, methods or targets (Clarke, 1997; Hayes, 1997a). An almost opposite effect is diffusion of benefits: this is an umbrella-type theory based on the premise that if some products, areas, or stores are well-protected, potential criminals may be led to believe that all products and places are similarly protected, thus creating a more far-reaching deterrence effect (Smith and Cornish, 2004).

Some theories describe how crime results from an interweaving of many different factors. For example, the theft triangle model focuses on the identification and assimilation of the multiple variables that contribute to a criminal act. Working within the framework of situational crime prevention, the theft triangle recognizes and combines a potential offender's 'background factors' (such as genetic coding, personality traits, cognitive ability, social learning experiences, perceived needs, etc.) with 'foreground factors' (i.e. access to a desirable and vulnerable target) within a specific situation. Some foreground factors an offender may consider before attempting to steal (Hayes, 1997b) are:

- the motive or intention to possess (steal) an item combined with a rationalization of the act such as for personal use, to conform, to convert to cash;
- the perceived level of personal risk of detection and swift and severe sanction for the offender involved;
- the level of opportunity (ease of access and ability to remove the selected assets) within the store setting.

This theory of crime can be used to address specific crime problems as it considers the interactions of offender perceptions and the specifics of a situation to guide focused protective measures (Hayes, 1997b).

Shoplifting data

Specific research on shoplifting is often based on either apprehension case reports or self-report data. Unfortunately like most research, both of these data collection methods are inherently limited by potential sampling, measurement and analytical error.

Apprehension data, collected when the shoplifter is caught and in varying states of mind, can be more indicative of security personnel skill, scheduling, bias, search imaging and workplace practices than shoplifter behavior. Also, the percentage of shoplifters that are actually apprehended is usually very small. In a study of shoplifting in the UK, for example, Buckle and Farrington (1984) found that a disappointing one in 100 to one in 1000 shoplifters were actually apprehended. One must also consider the validity of certain apprehension data; the fact that a shoplifter is facing serious impending legalities may affect the type of information he/she is willing to share (Klemke, 1992).

Self-report data are most often collected via self-administered questionnaires that can produce unreliable data, as results depend on respondents' abilities to recollect – and willingness to share – past events in an honest manner. Sample sizes are again usually small, and participants are often teenagers or young adults. Middle-class adults can be less willing to share past shoplifting experiences, which can lead to the exclusion of a significant portion of the shoplifting demographic (Klemke, 1992). Regardless of data error, and sometimes a lack of theory-informed inquiry, shoplifting research is needed to further enhance preventative efforts.

The sociology of shoplifting

Much shoplifting research has focused on determining a link between deviant behavior and certain demographics. Although many of the resulting conclusions are inconsistent and contradictory, it is nevertheless worthwhile to examine the extent to which research has explored the demographics of the problem.

AGE: Shoplifting appears to be consistent with Gottfredson and Hirschi's (1990) 'invariance thesis', which attests that crime declines with age everywhere and at all times. Most studies support that shoplifting declines with age, although at least one researcher reports there is a spike in occurrences of shoplifting amongst middle-age females (Klemke, 1992). One survey indicated more adult shoplifters than juveniles, though the number of juvenile shoplifters is relatively large when one considers the small percentage of children that actually do their own shopping (Hayes, 1993b; Hayes, 1997b). Dabney, Hollinger and Dugan (2004) found middleaged people shoplifted more frequently in their sample than other groups. It is important to distinguish, however, between shoplifting incidents and shoplifting apprehensions. Juveniles are more likely to be apprehended than adults, and so apprehension data may be misleading (Klemke, 1992).

THE ELDERLY: Early research concluded shoplifters over the age of 60 were least likely to be apprehended. This is possibly explained by the fact that retail personnel were reluctant to observe or apprehend seemingly frail or pitiful senior citizens. However, research has shown an increase in the number of elderly arrests, perhaps due in part to either an increasing average lifespan, or a shift in security personnel attitudes toward apprehension of seniors. Either way, seniors are not the most frequently apprehended age group (Hayes, 1993b; Newman, 1984).

GENDER: Shoplifting is one of the most common female crimes (Bureau of Justice Statistics, 2003). The historic role of the female in society as primary household shopper may give them more opportunities to shoplift than men. While early-era research pointed to females as the main culprits, more recent apprehension report and self-report studies contradict this, showing a slight majority of shoplifters to be male (Cox *et al.*, 1990; Deng, 1994; Flanagan and Maguire, 1990; Hayes, 1999a; Moschis, 1987). However, although females may shoplift less frequently, they are arrested more often in certain venues, and are less likely to report shoplifting acts than males (Deng, 1994). It is important to keep in mind that a particular retailer's merchandise selection greatly dictates the primary sex of its shoplifters (Hayes, 1999a). Women have been found to purchase items while also stealing others, as well as to use certain shoptheft techniques such as price switching more frequently than male thieves (Hayes and Rogers, 2000).

RACE, ETHNICITY, NATIONALITY: Assertions that racial bias drives shoplifter apprehensions is not typically supported by studies since whites are no less likely – and in some cases, more likely – to be apprehended than other races (Cameron, 1964; Dabney, Hollinger and Dugan, 2004; Deng 1994; Hayes, 1999a). However, Murphy (1986) identified blacks, Asians, and other foreigners as types of people security were more likely to suspect and subsequently apprehend – perhaps contributing to an unfortunate self-fulfilling prophecy. Similarly, Deng (1994) found that, despite observed higher frequencies of shoplifting amongst whites, blacks were more likely to be arrested. Dabley, Hollinger and Dugan (2004) found that Hispanic females were more likely to steal than several other race gender categories in a single drugstore observational study. Overall, there is not enough research to determine how, if at all, race, ethnicity and/or nationality affects shoplifting or apprehension behavior. Hayes' (1993) claims of behavior being a more stable and accurate predictor of shoplifting activity that race is supported by the Dabney, Hollinger and Dugan (2004) study.

SOCIAL CLASS and SUBCULTURES: Klemke's research (1992) tentatively concluded that an inverse relationship exists between class and shoplifting; that is, as social class decreases, shoplifting increases (p. 56). Researchers have also examined the connection, between shoplifting and prostitution, drug use, or other crimes. Deng (1994) reports the majority of offenders do not shoplift out of economic need, but conceded that an inverse relationship exists between education and shoplifting. Social class may help explain some shoplifting behavior, but apprehended and otherwise interviewed offenders indicate they come from across the social spectrum (Deng, 1994).

Retailer responses to shoplifting

Effective shoplifting control is a complex challenge requiring ongoing effort (Baumer and Rosenbaum, 1984; Hayes, 1993b; Hayes, 1997b; Johns, Hayes and Scicchitano, 2005; Sennewald, 2000). Most retail responses to shoplifting are designed to discourage or disrupt shoplifting incidents. Unfortunately, when faced with a shoplifting problem, some retailers or store managers react with unfocused 'fast fixes', like removing high-loss products from open sale. Lacking proper analysis, random or un-tested solutions may appear to temporarily decrease theft for a certain product or area. However, they may not significantly reduce the larger, long-term loss problem (Beck, Chapman and Peacock, 2002).

Retail experts believe sustainable, successful loss prevention efforts start at the top of an organization with execution that supports honesty and integrity at every level of operations (Beck, Chapman and Peacock, 2002; Hayes, 1991; Hollinger and Dabney, 1994; Sennewald, 2000). However, before implementing such an approach, it is important that a retailer fully understands the nature and scope of their specific shoplifting problem (Hayes, 1997b). Taking initiative from offenders, a retailer should consider building a profile of its loss, performing targeted analyses of assets, theft, and potential offenders. Video footage review, loss, sales, out of stocks and apprehension data, offender and employee interviews, and store activity audits can all provide insight into the prime causes of loss (Hayes, 2005). In order to address and resolve a shoplifting problem, retailers can strive to create, test, and then refine a tailored combination of operational, managerial, and mechanical loss prevention strategies (Baumer and Rosenbaum, 1984; Shapland, 1995) in specific locations (Eck, 2002).

Operational responses

Store policy and signage

Many retailers have a written shoplifter handling policy and procedure, which details how and when shoplifters will be sanctioned. When made public and visible, such a policy can impact shoplifting since it may be possible to deter some shoplifting incidents by convincing a shoplifter that they will be caught stealing a specific item (Gottlieb, 1982; McNees *et al.*, 1976; Struckman-Johnson, 1978). Legal concerns are reflected in retailers having explicit shoplifting policies specifying which employees are authorized to apprehend shoplifters and how they are to go about it (Cleary, 1986; Keckeisen, 1993; Sennewald, 2000). Such policies help avoid the litigation, publicity, and sanctions that can result from ill-advised detentions, injuries, or excessive force (Sennewald and Christman, 1992). Merchandise return and refund policies are of particular importance to the reduction of shoplifting, as liberal cash refund policies can make shoplifting for return/refund purposes rewarding (Hayes, 1999b; Johns and Hayes, 2003).

Procedure also protect merchandise by making the shipping, receiving, in store storage and selling floor display more secure (Hayes, 1997). Counting high loss merchandise is an example of a product protection procedure, and has been found to be effective in reducing losses (Masuda, 1992).

Fitting rooms

Retailers often employ simple procedures to prevent shoplifters from concealing items in fitting rooms (Hollinger and Langton, 2004). Store employees count the number of items customers bring into the fitting room (which itself is usually limited), and then ensure the same amount makes it back out of the room. Fitting rooms can be systematically cleared to prevent the theft of items left behind in the rooms, and mirrors are caulked to prevent concealing of removed price tags (Hayes, 1993).

Managerial responses

Customer service

Store employees are generally considered the strongest crime controllers (Bamfield and Hollinger, 1996; Hayes, 1991; Hollinger and Dabney, 1994; Langton and Hollinger, 2005). Carter *et al.* (1988) found that descriptive signage in employee break rooms – a list of high-loss items, for example – resulted in reduced losses of those items. When incorporated into a loss prevention strategy, basic customer service skills serve the purpose of improving customer satisfaction and gross sales and profit, while also minimizing shoplifting. Greeting a customer, making eye contact, and offering assistance can all contribute to a sense of monitoring and surveillance that may urge a potential shoplifter to reconsider his/her plans (Sennewald and Christman, 1992). Research on shoplifting deterrents has indicated it is *people*, and specifically the way people interact with potential shoplifters, that most influence the decision to steal (Butler 1994; Carroll and Weaver, 1986; Weaver and Carroll, 1985). Active employees are potential deterrents, and successful retailers take advantage of this, fostering customer interaction throughout the store, from sales managers to stock handlers. Good customer service can endear people to a store (possibly even shoplifters) and prevent frustration-driven impulse shoplifting – the type of theft that sometimes results from a customer's dissatisfaction with the store service (Butler, 1994).

Employee training and incentives

As mentioned before, in order to aid employees in safeguarding the store, managers should stress customer service, visible register location, on-the-job training, and other effective motivators. Not only is employee vigilance an effective approach to preventing shoplifting, it can also be less costly than technological approaches. In a study on retail theft, Lin *et al.* (1994) determined that employee training is one of the retailer's most effective tools in fighting shoplifting. The 2000 Supermarket Shrink Report cited a 9 percent decrease in shoplifting incidents for stores that had a formal loss prevention training program for employees. Store staff can be assigned to work in and protect a select area (zoning) to encourage the employee to feel ownership for that area (Hayes, 1993). Stores that implement targeted training programs, like how to identify shoplifters, often benefit from fewer shoplifting incidents as a result (FMI, 2000). Studies have indicated rewarding employees for workplace efforts can improve task execution (Condly, Clark and Stolovitch, 2003), including contributing to loss prevention (Lin *et al.*, 1994).

Security personnel

Many stores use store-level loss prevention staff to affect shoplifting losses (Hayes, 1997b; Hayes, 2000; Hayes, 2004; Hollinger, Dabney and Hayes, 1999). Uniformed guards or off-duty law enforcement officers are sometimes posted to monitor and be seen by entering and exiting visitors. Plainclothes store detectives are also deployed by some retailers to detect and apprehend shoplifters (see Chapter 17). Proper selection and training of loss prevention personnel is important for any retailer who wishes to mitigate losses and improve safety (Hayes, 2004). Careless hiring procedures can result not only in an unsafe store, but also potential litigation due to negligent hiring (Smith, 2002). Training is equally important; as the process of confronting, detaining, and arresting suspected shoplifters is a physical process. Civil lawsuits resulting from injuries or mishandling are a part of doing business and store management and loss prevention staff must be effectively trained in order to reduce negative situations (Keckeisen, 1993; Sennewald, 2000; Sennewald and Christman, 1992).

In order to cope with the complexity and severity of shoplifting and other retail crimes, many large-scale retailers have a senior-level executive whose sole responsibility is crime and loss control. These specialized professionals co-ordinate the many facets of loss prevention, from safeguarding computer systems to detecting potential shoplifters (Hayes, 1991; Hayes, 2003).

Display and design responses

Store design

Exploring the hypothesis that some retail designs are actually conducive to crime, Francis (1980) concluded that the creation of a too 'welcoming' environment may foster shoplifting. Crime Prevention Through Environmental Design

(CPTED) or Behavior By Design (BBD) provide a set of principles that test how the layout and design of store interiors affect the behaviors of staff and visitors (Moussatche *et al.*, 2004). Unattended counters, high, concealing displays, scarce employees, and easily-accessed items were all cited as signs of a prime target for shoplifting. Simple design changes such as lowered shelf heights, improved lines of sight, or strategic positioning of checkout counters could help decrease shoplifting incidents in these stores. Again, retailers must weigh the benefits of fostering merchandise desirability with the drawbacks of potential shoplifting. The aim of merchandise display is to create temptation, but too much temptation combined with too little safeguarding can lead to devastating losses in certain stores (Sennewald and Christman, 1992).

Mechanical responses

Product packaging

Retailers have long employed product-centric protection concepts. Secured by design concepts include larger packaging, making item concealment, particularly in larger quantities difficult and more obvious, and by using tougher packaging materials and gluing to make packaging more difficult to covertly open, or louder when ripped or cut, in order to tip off nearby employees and others (Hayes and Blackwood, 2005). Likewise, retailers are testing benefit denial techniques such as placing retailer logos or other messages on packaging via stickers, crimping and printing to make stolen goods less desirable or valuable for theft (Hayes and Blackwood, 2005).

Merchandise and area alarms

Some retailers use area alarms based on sensors or closed-circuit television (CCTV) cameras that make audible or covert notification of a customer near or at a display of hot products. Likewise, merchandise such as DVD players can have alarms attached that are activated when an item is removed or the alarm itself is tampered with (Hayes, 1993).

Mirrors

Some retailers employ either a two-way mirror, which is monitored from behind the glass, or a convex mirror, which provides a broad view of the selling floor. Both require active employee surveillance (Hayes, 1993b; Sennewald and Christman, 1992). However, mirrors have a drawback: some offenders have been known to use them to monitor and avoid alert employees.

Cables and protective display fixtures

Mechanical and electric cables are sometimes used for more expensive merchandise. The cable is securely attached to the item at one end and the display rack or stand on the other. This is a particularly effective shoplifting prevention method, as an employee is required to unlock the cable and release the item(s) (Sennewald and Christman, 1992). Many retailers however recognize that reducing access to products can reduce sales as well as loss. Similar to cabling, specially designed product fixtures disrupt shoplifting by requiring the use of two hands, limiting selection to one at a time, or requiring a clerk to open the case. Some fixtures even generate a noise when certain items are selected, creating a sense of risk and alerting staff to would-be offenders.

Electronic tags

EAS, or electronic article surveillance, involves attaching or placing small electronic tags or magnetic strips into or on merchandise, packaging, tickets, or labels. Tags are attached by the manufacturer, a wholesaler, in a distribution center, or by employees in a store. Employees deactivate or remove the tags at checkout for legitimate customers. If an item is removed past detection antennae, an alarm is activated by flashing light and/or sounds. Like most protective technology, EAS requires employee involvement: tags must be affixed, removed, or turned off; and alarm activations require immediate response in order to maintain awareness of and respect for the system. The level of employee involvement required for EAS systems presents the greatest challenge for retailers; in order to provide item protection, the system should be supported by thorough and consistent execution.

Despite the hundreds of millions spent globally on EAS systems, there is relatively little research on its efficacy and/or cost-effectiveness. In Sherman *et al.* (1997) Eck examined five evaluations of EAS and shrinkage reduction. Each study compared shrinkage before and after the installation of EAS in test stores. A single control store measured background trends, analyzing differences between EAS and non-EAS stores. All tests indicated EAS provided some loss reduction. Results varied from 28–32 percent (Bamfield, 1994), to 80 percent reduction (DiLonardo, 1996). Farrington and colleagues (1993) reported even greater reductions in the two stores they examined: 76 to 93 percent. They also found EAS to be more effective than security guards (no improvement), and store redesign (50 to 80 percent temporary improvement) (Farrington *et al.*, 1993). However, due to practical considerations in working with retailers, sampling procedures did not provide for the desired random selection of large samples.

Eck found that only Farrington *et al.* (1993) reported statistical significance tests that determine the probability that the reported reductions were due to chance alone. This multi-study assessment appears in the US Department of Justice publication *Preventing Crime: What Works, What Doesn't, What's Promising*. In the 'Preventing Crime at Places' chapter the author concluded that, 'shoplifting appears to be controllable by the use of EAS technology, and possibly ink tags. If more evaluations had used significance tests we could have classified EAS as "works." In the absence of this information EAS must be placed in the "do not know" category.' Eck also noted that 'limited evaluations of other approaches suggest that there may be alternative approaches as well' (Eck, 1997: 7–19). Thus, there remains much opportunity to conduct robust testing of major loss prevention processes in stores.

Ink-dye tags

These small plastic tags are normally used to protect clothing as a form of 'benefit-denial'. Benefit denial (BD) is an asset protection technique designed to affect an offender's motive (Hayes, 1993, 1997b). When tampered with, a BD like an ink/dye tag expels an ink or dye on the protected garment as well as the tampering hands. The logic behind this is that when the benefit of the BD is removed, that item is inherently less desirable (Hayes, 1993b). Other benefit denial techniques include mechanical and electronic clamps that are attached to jewelry, watches, and other small valuable items. Data indicate strong support for ink tag protection of apparel validating the concept of BD (DiLonardo and Clarke, 1996). Ink tags are also combined with electronic tags to provide simultaneous BD and risk raising protection.

CCTV

CCTV provides a way of detecting, tracking, recording, and hopefully deterring shoplifters. Small cameras or domes are strategically placed around the store, and sometimes monitored by store personnel. Footage from the system can be used to make apprehensions, as evidence in court proceedings, or to study shoplifter habits in order to better prevent future incidents. Some shoplifters are deterred by the cameras, while others fail to see or recognize them. Still others ignore them altogether, assuming (sometimes rightly so) they are unmanned and pose little threat. Offenders concerned about camera surveillance may seek out a 'blind spot' where they can conceal items unobserved. Although not a panacea for shoplifting, CCTV may provide some deterrence effect. In a recent report on supermarket shrink, stores that reviewed CCTV tapes 'regularly' saw a up to a 16 percent decrease in shrink and reported 135 percent more shoplifting apprehensions than stores reviewing tapes just once a month (2000 Supermarket Shrink Survey). Future CCTV systems seem destined to provide more advanced individual human recognition capabilities based on select body and movement characteristics, and may also be able to recognize programmed behaviors of interest such as rapid item removal or approach to a customer in a parking lot (www.IntelliVid.com).

Radio-Frequency Identification (RFID) or electronic price code (EPC) has enormous potential for managing supply chain and store product availability efficiency, as well as helping to reduce losses. The technology uses electronic readers attached to main computers via the Internet to track pallets, cases, and in some cases individual items that have been tagged with a tiny microchip. This process allows retailers to track tagged objects from a supplier, while in transport, in distribution centers, in stores, and eventually may work to help track or recognize stolen items that are being fenced or returned to a retailer fraudulently. Product data may also help determine what items go missing, where and when, even with real-time notification for in-store staff (www.rfidjournal.com/article/articleview/1184/1/1/).

Societal responses

Counseling/Rehabilitation

While some experts stress stricter sanctions for shoplifters, others support broader societal responses such as targeted public service announcements and advertisements, educational programs, and offender counseling and rehabilitation. The latter often involves a twofold approach: short-term crisis intervention to help the offender cope with prosecution and sentencing, then reality-based education efforts that focus on the seriousness of shoplifting as a crime and consequences of future offenses (Moore, 1984). Particularly for non-professional female shoplifters, group therapy can be an effective alternative to sentencing in its ability to address women's needs. It has also shown some effectiveness in reducing future criminal activity (Kolman and Wasserman, 1991).

In another response to shoplifting, some retailers have begun to provide funding for shoplifter rehabilitation programs. Community awareness and support programs such as Shoplifters Alternative and Shoplifters Anonymous work with crowded court systems and retailers in counseling past offenders with the hope that it will curtail future theft. Prosecuting shoplifters in court is a costly endeavor with no guaranteed deterrence effect. In addition to being a difficult process, rehabilitation is not an overall solution since shoplifters must first be apprehended in order to place them in treatment, and shopthieves are rarely caught. Although Shoplifters Alternative maintain they have a low 1.3–2.7 recidivism rate, this is difficult to accurately measure. Few rehabilitation efforts have been supported by sound research, creating yet another arena in which further scholarly attention is warranted (Schultz, 2000).

Laws

Shoplifting's impact on the retail economy has driven the development of stricter penalties for convicted shoplifters and fences (French, 1979; Johns and Hayes, 2003). Some retailers believe increased prosecution for convicted shoplifters, particularly chronic or professional thieves will help diminish the problem (Bellur, 1981). In the 1990s, over half of US states adopted a measure by which retailers could extract fines and payments from apprehended shoplifters, a development which some retailers felt led to a decline in shrinkage (Bamfield, 1998; Farrington and Burrows, 1993; Hayes, 1990). Today, every state in the US has its own retail theft statute, most allowing retailers the opportunity to pursue both civil and criminal sanctions against apprehended shoplifters (Bamfield, 1998; Hayes, 1990). Further, many states have implemented statutes to address more organized forms of retail crime, including current efforts to pass a federal law (www.gmabrands.com/publicpolicy/fedlegis.cfm). Other legal strategies designed to address shoptheft include pre-trial diversion programs where first time (assumed) offenders are referred to community service and offender treatment programs in lieu of formal legal proceedings. Offender rehabilitation and treatment is a complex topic. The efficacy and components of successful rehabilitation programs, as well as the actual impact of diversion programs on nearby retail losses are for later empirical research. Some local court systems have adopted intervention programs in order to reduce offending, as well as to reduce high court caseloads and legal costs.

Discussion

Shoplifting creates tremendous loss and disruption for retailers, while affecting all citizens by reducing product availability, increasing the cost of goods, and creating violence in stores. Shoplifters have been active since the first stores or selling spots appeared, and come from all backgrounds. Demographic factors like age, race, economic background and age have been extensively studied, with age providing the most utility for retailers. Juveniles appear to offend at higher rates than other categories. Researchers have also proposed offender typologies over the years to help understand the psychological reasons for treatment purposes, as well as to classify thieves into groups according to motives, methods and targeted merchandise in order to focus prevention programs.

In addition to typologies, several criminological and consumer behavior theories are being refined to explain individual offending as well as how likely offenders commit retail crimes in order to develop more focused protective efforts. Routine activities, situational crime prevention, planned behavior and theft triangle theories hold much promise for assisting retailers in their quest to sell more and lose less. Like most human phenomenon, external theft losses have been found to cluster in space and time. Certain stores and products are more frequently targeted for theft than others This fact allows retailers to analyze product, location, temporal, offender and other data in order to focus protective efforts.

Currently retailers are using a combination of people, programs and systems to reduce shoplifting frequency and impact. Store staff and managers as well as assigned asset protection employees are trained to provide plenty of customer attention, implement loss prevention procedures and technologies, and to report suspicious people and circumstances, especially in assigned zones. There is opportunity to lay out store interiors to provide for more surveillance with wider aisles, lower shelves, brighter lighting and more visible employee work areas. Hot product packaging protective techniques such as tamper-resistant stickers, crimping and printing, and larger, tougher packaging materials are being tested. Display fixtures are being used to provide more protection by where they're located in relation to employee work stations, as well as by incorporating technologies designed to hinder quiet, rapid product removal. Technologies such as CCTV, electronic detection and BD tagging, merchandise removal alarms increase risk of detection for shopthieves. Locked areas and techniques that reduce access to or the mobility of hot products can provide protection in high loss environments.

Shoptheft reduces item availability and retailer viability while introducing violence into shops. Prior shoplifting research and theory has a richness to it, but despite this, research on shoplifting control remains a rare activity with much opportunity. Of particular need is more extensive study on the dynamics of individual and organized theft, and the main and interactive efficacy of various protective programs and technologies in varied settings.

Six main points

1. Shoptheft profoundly impact retailers, society and individuals by disrupting processes, reducing product availability, and profit – while introducing violence into shops.
2. Offenders come from all backgrounds, both sexes, and all ages and races.
3. Store theft theory and research has focussed on why individuals steal, and how well retailers respond to theft.
4. Retailer response is largely designed to reduce the opportunity for theft, to increase the risk of detection for offenders, and to reduce shoplifting motivations.
5. Asset protection efforts are comprised of people, programs and technologies to promote deterrence and detection.
6. More research and refined theoretical tools are needed to better focus asset protection programs.

Key readings

There is a relatively rich literature on shoplifting. In addition to trade books and articles, there are numerous peer reviewed papers. Cameron (1964) helped get criminologists and others thinking about the types and motivations of shoplifters in a scientific manner. Her concepts came from combining findings from the literature to research in the field. Likewise Klemke (1992) and Shapland (1995) have helped keep research focused and rigorous. Baumer and Rosenbaum (1984) provided descriptions of how retailers can use evidence to guide preventive efforts. Hayes (1993, 1997b, 1999, 2003, 2005) has provided ongoing insight into offender perceptions and behaviors, retailer protective strategies and methods, as well as more rigorous efficacy testing of prevention techniques. Clarke (along with Cornish, Smith and Felson) (1997, 1999, 2001, 2003, 2004) has provided theoretical toolsets to researchers and practitioners alike. Finally, Tonglet (2000) has provided a fresh way to view deviant consumer behavior with implications for theoretical, empirical and practical follow up.

References

Abelson, E.S. (1992) *When Ladies Go A-Thieving: Middle-Class Shoplifters in the Victorian Department Store.* Oxford: Oxford University Press.

Ajzen, I. (2002) 'Perceived Behavioral Control, Self-Efficacy, Locus of Control, and the Theory of Planned Behavior', *Journal of Applied Social Psychology*, 32, 665–83.

Akers, R.L. (1998) *Social Learning and Social Structure: A General Theory of Crime and Deviance.* Boston: Northeastern University Press.

Bales, K.B. (1982) 'Contrast and Complimentarity in Three Theories of Criminal Behavior', *Deviant Behavior*, 3(2), 155–74.

Bamfield, J. (1994) *National Survey of Retail Theft and Security, 1994.* Moulton Park, Northampton: Nene College.

Bamfield, J. (1998) 'Retail Civil Recovery: Filling a Deficit in the Criminal Justice System?' *International Journal of Risk, Security and Crime Prevention*, 3(4), 257–67.

Bamfield, J. (2004) *European Retail Theft Barometer: Monitoring the Costs of Shrinkage and Crime for Europe's Retailers.* Nottingham: Centre for Retail Research.

Bamfield, J. (2005) Retail Crime Overseas. Retrieved March 3, 2005 from website: http://www.chant4.co.uk/retailresearch2003/crime_and_fraud/retail_crime_overseas.php

Bamfield, J. and Hollinger, R.C. (1996) 'Managing Losses in the Retail Store: A Comparison of Loss Prevention Activity in the United States and Great Britain', *Security Journal*, 7(1), 61–70.

Baumer, T.L. and Rosenbaum, D.P. (1984) *Combating Retail Theft: Programs and Strategies.* Boston: Butterworth.

Beck, A.B. and MacIntyre, S. (1977) 'MMPI Patterns of Shoplifters within a College Population', *Psychological Reports, 41*, 1035–40.

Beck, A. (2004) *Shrinkage in Europe: A Survey of Stock Loss in the Fast Moving Consumer Goods Sector*. ECR Europe.

Beck, A. and Chapman, P. (2003) *Hot Spots in the Supply Chain: Developing an Understanding of What Makes Some Retail Stores Vulnerable to Shrinkage*. Brussels: ECR Europe.

Beck, A., Chapman, P. and Peacock, C. (2002) 'A Practical Way to Shrink Shrinkage', *ECR Journal, 2*(2), 59–63.

Bellur, V.V. (1981) 'Shoplifting: Can it be Prevented?, *Journal of the Academy of Marketing Science, 9*(2), 78–87.

Belson, W.A. (1975) *Juvenile Theft: The Causal Factors*. London: Harper and Row.

Brantingham, P.J. and Brantingham, P.L. (1993) 'Environment, Routine, and Situation. Towards a Pattern Theory of Crime', *Advanced Criminology Theory, 5*, 259–94.

Buckle, A., and Farrington, D.P. (1984) 'An Observational Study of Shoplifting', *British Journal of Criminology, 24*(1), 63–73.

Bureau of Justice Statistics (2003) *Sourcebook of Criminal Justice Statistics*. Washington, DC: US Department of Justice.

Butler, G. (1994) 'Shoplifters' Views on Security: Lessons for Crime Prevention'. In M. Gill (ed.) *Crime at Work: Studies in Security and Crime Prevention*. Leicester: Perpetuity Press.

Caime, G. and Ghone, G. (1996) *S(h)elf Help Guide*. Toronto: Trix Publishing.

Cameron, M.O. (1964) *The Booster and the Snitch: Department Store Shoplifting*. NY: Free Press of Glencoe.

Carroll, J. and Weaver, F. (1986) 'Shoplifters' Perceptions of Crime Opportunities: A Process-tracing Study'. In D.B. Cornish and R.V.G. Clarke (eds) *The Reasoning Criminal: Rational Choice Perspectives on Offending*. New York, NY: Springer-Verlag.

Carter, N., Holmstrom, A., Simpanen, M. and Melin, L. (1988) 'Theft Reduction in a Grocery Store through Product Identification and Graphing of Losses for Employees', *Journal of Applied Behavior Analysis, 21*(4), 385–9.

Clarke, R.V. (1997) *Situational Crime Prevention: Successful Case Studies* 2nd edn. Albany, NY: Harrow and Heston.

Clarke, R.V. (1999) *Hot Products: Understanding, Anticipating and Reducing Demand for Stolen Goods*. Police Research Series Paper 112. London, UK: Home Office.

Clarke, R.V. and Felson, M. (eds) (1993) *Routine Activity and Rational Choice. Advances in Criminological Theory*, Vol. 5. New Brunswick, NJ: Transaction Publishers.

Cleary, J. (1986) *Prosecuting the Shoplifter: A Loss Prevention Strategy*. Stoneham, MA: Butterworth-Heinemann.

Cohen, L. (2003) *A Consumers Republic: The Politics of Mass Consumption in Postwar America*. New York: Alfred A. Knopf.

Cohen, L.E. and Felson, M. (1979) 'Social Change and Crime Rate Trends: A Routine Act Approach', *American Sociological Review, 44*, 136–47.

Coid, J. (1984) 'Relief of Diazepam-Withdrawal Syndrome by Shoplifting', *British Journal of Psychiatry, 145*(4), 555–9.

Condly, S.J., Clark, R.E. and Stolovitch, H.D. (2003) 'The Effects of Incentives on Workplace Performance: A Meta-analytic Review of Research Studies', *Performance Quarterly Review, 16*(3), 46–63.

Cornish, G. and Clarke, R.V. (1986) *The Reasoning Criminal: Rational Choice Perspectives on Offending*. New York, NY: Springer-Verlag.

Cornish, D. and Clarke, R. (2003) 'Opportunities, Precipitators and Criminal Decisions: A Reply to Wortley's Critique of Situational Crime Prevention'. In Smith and Cornish (eds) *Theory for Practice In Situational Crime Prevention*, Crime Prevention Studies (series editor Ron Clarke), Vol. 16 (co-published with Criminal Justice Press, New York).

Cox, D., Cox, A. and Moschis, G. (1990) 'When Consumer Behavior Goes Bad: An Investigation of Adolescent Shoplifting', *Journal of Consumer Research, 17*, 149–58.

Cromwell, P. and Thurman, Q. (2003) 'The Devil Made Me Do It: Use Of Neutralizations By Shoplifters', *Deviant Behavior, 24*(6), 535–50.

Cupchick, W. (1997) *Why Honest People Shoplift or Commit Other Acts of Theft*. Toronto: Tagami Communications.

Dabney, D.A., Hollinger, R.C. and Dugan, L. (2004) 'Who Actually Steals? A Study of Covertly Observed Shoplifters', *Justice Quarterly*, 21(4), 693–728.

Deng, X. (1994) *Toward A More Comprehensive Understanding of Crime: An Integrated Model of Self-Control and Rational Choice Theories*. Ann Arbor, Michigan: University of Michigan Dissertation Services.

DiLonardo, R. (1996) 'Defining and Measuring the Economic Benefit of Electronic Article Surveillance', *Security Journal*, 7, 3–9.

DiLonardo, R. and Clarke, R. (1996) 'Reducing the Rewards of Shoplifting: An Evaluation of ink tags', *Security Journal*, 7, 11–14.

Eck, J.E. (1997) *Preventing Crime at Places*. Chapter 7 in Sherman, L.W., Gottfredson, D., MacKenzie, D., Eck, J., Reuter, P. and Bushway, S. (1997) http://www.ncjrs.org/works/index.htm

Eck, J.E. (2002) 'Preventing Crime at Places'. In Sherman, L.W., Farrington, D.P., Welsh, B.C. and MacKenzie, D.L. (2002) *Evidence-Based Crime Prevention*. London: Routledge.

Edwards, L.C. (1976) *Shoplifting and Shrinkage Protection for Stores*, 2nd edn. Springfield, IL: Charles C. Thomas.

Farrell, K., and Farrera, J. (1985) *Shoplifting: The Anti-Shoplifting Guidebook*. New York: Praeger, 87–96.

Farrington, D.P., Bowen, S., Buckle, A., Burns-Howell, T., Burrows, J. and Speed, M. (1993) 'An Experiment on the Prevention of Shoplifting'. In R.V. Clarke (ed.), *Crime Prevention Studies*, Vol. 1. Monsey, NY: Willow Tree Press.

Farrington, D.P. and Burrows, J.N. (1993) 'Did Shoplifting Really Decrease?', *British Journal of Criminology*, 33(1), 57–69.

Felson, M. (1998) *Crime and Everyday Life*, 2nd edn. Thousand Oaks, CA: Pine Forge Press.

Felson, M. (1996) 'Preventing Retail Theft: An Application of Environmental Criminology', *Security Journal*, 7(1), 71–5.

Felson, M. and Clarke, R. (1998) *Opportunity Makes the Thief*. London: The Home Office Policing and Reducing Crime Unit Research, Development and Statistics Directorate.

Flanagan, T.J. and Maguire, K. (eds) (1990) *Sourcebook of Criminal Justice Statistics*. Washington, DC: US Government Printing Office.

FMI (2004) 2004 Supermarket Shrink Survey. National Supermarket Research Group.

Francis, D.B. (1980) *Shoplifting: The Crime Everybody Pays for*. NY: Elsevier/Nelson.

French, J.T. (1979) *Apprehending and Prosecuting Shoplifters and Dishonest Employees*. New York: National Retail Merchants Association.

www.gmabrands.com/publicpolicy/fedlegis.cfm

Gottlieb, J.A. (1982) *Reducing Shoplifting Incidents Through the Use of Signs*. PhD Dissertation, UMI.

Gottfredson, M. and Hirschi, T. (1990) *A General Theory of Crime*. Stanford: Stanford University Press.

Guthrie, J. (2003) New Zealand Centre for Retail Research and Studies. NZ: Dunedin.

Hayes, R. (1990) 'Winning the Civil Recovery War', *Security Management*, 9, 83–4.

Hayes, R. (1991) *Retail Security and Loss Prevention*. Stoneham: Butterworth-Heinemann, 36–45.

Hayes, R. (1993) *Shoplifting Control*. Orlando, FL: Prevention Press.

Hayes, R. (1997a) 'Retail Crime Control: A New Operational Strategy', *Security Journal*, 8, 225–32.

Hayes, R. (1997b) 'Shop Theft: An Analysis of Apprehended Shoplifters', *Security Journal*, 7(1), 11–14.

Hayes, R. (1999a) *Retail Theft Trends Report*. Orlando, FL: Loss Prevention Solutions.

Hayes, R. (1999b) 'Shop Theft: An Analysis of Shoplifter Perceptions and Situational Factors', *Security Journal*, 12(2), 7–118.

Hayes, R. (2000) 'Retail Store Detectives: An Analysis of their Focus, Selection, Training, and Performance Ratings', *Security Journal*, 31(1), 7–20.

Hayes, R. (2003) 'Loss Prevention: Senior Management Views on Current Trends and Issues', *Security Journal, 16*, 7–20.

Hayes, R. (2004) 'Store Detectives: Job Analysis and Workplace Performance', *Security Journal, 17*(3), 10–21.

Hayes, R. (2005) Retail Security and Loss Prevention, 2nd edn. Leicester: Perpetuity Press.

Hayes, R. and Blackwood, R. (2005) Retail Theft Control: Exploring the Effects of Tamper-Resistant Packaging, Removal of Original Packaging, and Product Marking on Item Desirability. In Review.

Hayes, R. and Rogers, K. (2000) Shoplifting and Science: Inside the Mind of the Offender. A paper presented at the National Retail Federation's Annual Loss Prevention Conference.

Hayes, R. and Rogers, K. (2003) 'Catch Them If You Can', *Security Management, 10*.

Hayes, R., and Rogers, K. (2003) *Organized Retail Crime: Describing a Major Problem*. Report for the Grocery Manufacturers Association.

Heimer, K. and Matsueda, L. (1997) A symbolic interactionist theory of motivation and deviance: interpreting psychological research. Nebraska Symposium on Motivation, *44*, 223–76.

Hoffman, A. (1971) *Steal This Book*. NY: Grove Press.

Hollinger, R.C. and Dabney, D. (1994) 'Reducing Shrinkage in the Retail Store: It's Not Just a Job for the Loss Prevention Department', *Security Journal, 5*(1), January, 2–10.

Hollinger, R., Dabney, D., and Hayes, R. (1999) *National Retail Security Survey*. Gainesville, FL: University of Florida.

Hollinger, R. and Langton, L. (2004). 2003 National Retail Security Survey. Gainesville: University of Florida.

Hollister, C.W. (1994) *Medieval Europe: A Short History*. NY: McGraw-Hill.

www.IntelliVid.com (2005) Website.

Johns, T. and Hayes, R. (2003) 'Behind the Fence: Buying and Selling Stolen Merchandise', *Security Journal, 16*, 4.

Johns, T., Hayes, R. and Scicchitano, M. (2005) Professional and Amateur Shoplifter Perceptions: Implications for Prevention (In Review).

Katz, J. (1988) *Seductions of Crime: Moral and Sensual Attractions in Doing Evil*. NY: Basic Books.

Keckeisen, G.L. (1993) *Retail Security Versus the Shoplifter: Confronting the Shoplifter While Protecting the Merchant*. Springfield: Charles C. Thomas, 26–30.

Klemke, L.W. (1982) 'Exploring Juvenile Shopping', *Sociology and Social Research, 67*, 59–75.

Klemke, L.W. (1992) *The Sociology of Shoplifting*. Connecticut: Praeger.

Kolman, A.S. and Wasserman, C. (1991) 'Theft Groups for Women: A Cry for Help', *Federal Probation*, March 1991.

Kowalski, G.S. and Faupel, C.E. (1990) 'Heroin Use, Crime, and the 'Main Hustle', *Deviant Behavior, 11*(1), 1–16.

Langton, L. and Hollinger, R.C. (2005) 'Correlates of Crime Losses in the Retail Industry', *Security Journal, 8*, 27–44.

Lin, B., Hastings, D.A. and Martin, C. (1994) 'Shoplifting in Retail Clothing Outlets', *International Journal of Retail and Distribution Management, 22*(7), 24–30.

Masuda, B. (1992) 'Displacement and Diffusion of Benefits and the Reduction of Inventory Losses in a Retail Environment', *Security Journal, 3*, 131–6.

Mayhew, H. (1968) *London Labour and the London Poor*, Vol. 4. NY: Dove Publications.

McCloskey, H. and Schaar, J. (1965) 'Psychological Dimensions of Anomy', *American Sociological Review, 30*(1), 14–40.

McGuire, J. (1997) 'Irrational Shoplifting and Models of Addiction'. In J. Hodge, M. McMurran and C.R. Hollin (eds), *Addicted to Crime?* Chichester: John Wiley & Sons.

McNees, M.P., Egli, D.S., Marshall, R.S., Schnelle, J.F. and Risley, T.R. (1976) 'Shoplifting Prevention: Providing Information through Signs', *Journal of Applied Behaviour Analysis, 9*, 399–405.

McShane, F.J. and Noonan, B.A. (1993) 'Classification of Shoplifters by Cluster Analysis', *International Journal of Offender Therapy and Comparative Criminology, 37*(1), 30–40.

Medlicott, R.W. (1968) 'Fifty Thieves', *The New Zealand Medical Journal, 67*, 183–8.

Merton, R.K. (1938) 'Social Structure and Anomie', *American Sociological Review, 3*, 672–82.

Miller, E. (1986) *Street Woman*. Philadelphia: Temple University Press.

Miller, L. and Kienzien, M. (2000) 2000 Supermarket Shrink Survey. National Supermarket Research Group.

Moore, R.H. (1984) 'Shoplifting in Middle America: Patterns and Motivational Correlates', *International Journal of Offender Therapy and Comparative Criminology, 28*(1), 53–64.

Moschis, G.P., Cox, D. and Kellaris, J. (1987) 'An Exploratory Study of Adolescent Shoplifting Behavior', *Advances in Consumer Research, 14*. Wallendorf, M. and Anderson, R. (eds) Provo, Utah, Association for Consumer Research, 520–6.

Moussatche, H., Hayes, R., Schneider, R., McLeod, R., Abbott, P. and Kohen, M. (2004) Retailing Best Practices: Reducing Loss through Store Design and Layout. Gainesville, Fl.: University of Florida.

Murphy, D. (1986) *Customers and Thieves: An Ethnography of Shoplifting*. Gower: Aldershot.

Newman, E., Newman, D.J. and Gewirtz, M. (1984) *Elderly Criminals*. Cambridge, MA: Oelgeschlager, Gunn, and Hain.

Nye, F.I. (1958) *Family Relationships and Deviant Behavior*. NY: John Wiley and Sons.

www.Rfidjournal.com/article/articlereview/1184/1/1/

Schultz, D.P. (2000) Retail Chains Cooperate with Shoplifter Group to Curb Repeating Offenders. *STORES*, Dec 2000.

Schwartz, S., and Wood, H.V. (1991) Clinical Assessment and Intervention with Shoplifters. *Social Work, 36*, 234–8.

Sennewald, C. (2000) *Shoplifters Versus Retailers: The Rights of Both*. Chula Vista, CA.

Sennewald, C.A. and Christman, J.H. (1992) *Shoplifting*. Boston: Butterworth-Heinemann.

Shapland, J. (1995) 'Preventing Retail Sector Crimes'. In M. Tonry and D. Farrington (eds) *Building a Safer Society: Strategic Approaches to Crime Prevention*. Chicago: The University of Chicago Press, 320.

Sherman, L., Gottfredson, D., Mackenzie, D. L., Eck, J., Reuter, P. and Bushway, S. (1997) *Preventing Crime: What Works, What Doesn't, What's Promising*. Washington, DC: Office of Justice Programs.

Smith, M.J. and Cornish, D.B. (eds) (2004) *Theory for Practice in Situational Crime Prevention*. New York: Criminal Justice Press.

Smith, S.J. (2002) Workplace Violence. *Professional Safety, 47*(11), 34–44.

Stekel, W. (1924) *Peculiarities of Behavior*. NY: Liverwright.

Struckman-Johnson, C. (1978) *The Effect of Threat Level in Anti-Shoplifitng Signs on Perceptions of Sign Prevention Value and on Shoplifitng*. Ann Arbor, MI: University of Michigan Dissertation Services.

Sykes, G.M. and Matza, D. (1957) 'Techniques of Neutralization: A Theory of Delinquency', *American Sociological Review, 22*(6), 664–70.

Tonglet, M. (2000) 'Consumer Misbehaviour: Consumers' Perceptions of Shoplifting and Shoplifting and Retail Security', *Security Journal, 13*(4), 107–22.

Warr, M. (2000) Fear of Crime in the United States: Avenues for Research and Policy. Measurement and Analysis of Crime and Justice, Vol. 4: Washington, DC: US Department of Justice, Office of Justice Programs.

Weaver, F.M. and Carroll, J.S. (1985) 'Crime Perceptions in a Natural Setting by Expert and Novice Shoplifters', *Social Psychology Quarterly, 48*(4), 349–59.

Wilkinson, K. (1980) 'The Broken Home and Delinquent Behavior.' In T. Hirschi and M. Gottfredson (eds) *Understanding Crime: Current Theory and Research*. Beverly Hills: Sage.

14
Terrorism

Paul Wilkinson

Introduction to the concept

A great deal of unnecessary confusion has been created as a result of the mass media, politicians and others using the term terrorism as a synonym for political violence in general (Schmid, Jongman *et al.*, 1988). Others, seek to ban the word terrorism on the spurious grounds that most of those who use terrorism as weapon prefer to be called 'freedom fighters', 'holy warriors' or 'revolutionaries', depending on the cause they profess to be fighting for. Some so-called 'post-modernists' reject the concept of terrorism on the grounds that it is purely 'subjective', implying that there are no independent objective verifiable criteria to enable us to distinguish terrorism from other forms of activity. The public would be justifiably puzzled if lawyers and criminologists ceased to use terms such as 'murder', 'serial murder', and 'war crime' and 'genocide' simply because those who perpetrate such crimes regard these terms a pejorative.

As for identifying objective criteria for identifying terrorist activity, common sense indicates that the general public in most countries in the world recognize terrorism when they see campaigns of bombings, suicide bombings, shooting attacks, hostage-takings, hijackings and threats of such actions, especially when so many of these actions are deliberately aimed at civilians.

Terrorism can be conceptually and empirically distinguished from other modes of violence and conflict by the following characteristics:

- It is premeditated and designed to create a climate of extreme fear;
- It is directed at a wider target than the immediate victims;
- It inherently involves attacks on random or symbolic targets, including civilians;
- It is considered by the society in which it occurs as 'extra-normal', that is in the literal sense that it violates the norms regulating disputes, protest and dissent; and
- It is used primarily, though not exclusively, to influence the political behaviour of governments, communities or specific social groups. (Wilkinson, 2000: 12–14)

It is true that in the burgeoning of modern international terrorism in the late 1960s and early 1970s many efforts to obtain international agreements and conventions on the prevention and suppression of terrorist crimes were stymied by governments which, for their own political and ideological reasons, wished to block such measures by claiming that there was no internationally accepted definition of terrorism. Since then almost all the major democracies have developed national anti-terrorist legislation and many individuals have been convicted of terrorist offences. We have also seen a considerable amount of international law on terrorist offences developed before and since 9/11, See, *Terrorism: Documents of Local and International Control*, 1979–2005. Moreover, in October 2004 the UN Security Council unanimously passed Resolution 1566 which defines terrorism and declares that in no circumstances can terrorist acts be condoned or excused for political or ideological reasons:

> Criminal acts, including [those] against civilians, committed with the intent to cause death or serious bodily injury, or taking of hostages, with the purpose to provoke a state of terror in the general public or in a group of persons or particular persons, intimidate a population or compel a government or an international organisation to do or to abstain from doing any act, which constitute offences within the scope of and as defined in the international conventions and protocols relating to terrorism, are under no circumstances justifiable by considerations of a political, philosophical, ideological, racial, ethnic, religious or other similar nature ...

It is true that we may have to wait some time before we see a UN General Assembly definition. However, governmental and inter-governmental conferences on problems of terrorism no longer waste days in definitional issues: they have made genuine progress in improving co-operation against terrorism, and those who dismiss the national and international efforts to develop a legal regime to deal with various aspects of terrorism as nugatory are simply wrong. The legal framework to deal with terrorist crimes is far from perfect and very difficult to apply effectively because the more sophisticated and dangerous groups have become more skilled at evading detection, but despite this there have been some major successes in bringing terrorists to justice, (e.g. Ramzi Youssef, Shoko Asahara, Abdullah Ocalan, Abimael Guzman, Carlos the Jackal). Terrorism is not simply a label; it is a concept which has proved indispensable in legal and social science to deal with a complex global phenomenon.

The key statutory definition of terrorism in the UK legislation is contained in the Terrorism Act (2000):

(1) In this Act 'terrorism' means the use or threat of action where –

    (a) the action falls within subsection (2),

    (b) the use or threat is designed to influence the government or to intimidate the public or a section of the public, and

    (c) the use or threat is made for the purpose of advancing a political, religious or ideological cause.

(2) Action falls within this subsection if it –

    (a) involves serious violence against a person,

    (b) involves serious damage to property,

    (c) endangers a person's life, other than that of the person committing the action,

    (d) creates a serious risk to the health or safety of the public or a section of the public, or

    (e) is designed seriously to interfere with or seriously to disrupt an electronic system.

(3) The use or threat of action falling within subsection (2) which involves the use of firearms or explosives is terrorism whether or not subsection (1) (b) is satisfied.

(Terrorism Act 2000, Part 1, (1)–(3))

The US Government has employed the definition contained in US Code Title 22 Section 2656f (d) since 1983 as follows:

The term 'terrorism' means premeditated politically motivated violence perpetrated against noncombatant targets by sub-national groups or clandestine agents, usually intended to influence an audience.

The term 'international terrorism' means terrorism involving citizens or the territory of more than one country.

The term 'terrorist group' means any group practicing, or that has significant sub groups that practice, international terrorism

(US Code Title 22 Section 2656f (d))

Typology, with historical and current examples

Terrorism is an activity or a 'weapon-system' as Brian Jenkins has termed it, which has been used by an enormous variety of non-state groups, regimes and governments. (Historically the use of terror by regimes has been infinitely more lethal than that of non-state groups, because, by definition, regimes/governments are likely to have control of far greater supplies of weapons and manpower to implement their policies of terror in the course of internal repression or foreign conquest).

However, in an operative democracy the major threat of terror is posed by non-state movements or groups seeking to destroy or undermine democratic government and to impose their own agenda by coercive intimidation.

Another basic division is between international terrorism which involved the citizens of jurisdiction of more than one country, and domestic terrorism which is confined within the borders of a single state and involves no foreign citizens or property. This distinction is useful for statistical purposes, but we should bear in mind that almost all protracted domestic terrorist campaigns targeting a specific state develop an important international dimension through their creation of an overseas support network aimed at raising finance, recruits, weapons and other resources for their colleagues leading the struggle against their chosen 'enemy', state authorities and security forces.

One useful way of categorizing non-state terrorist movements or groups is by their political motivation: *Ethno nationalist* groups, for example ETA (Euzkadi Ta Askatasuna or Basque Fatherland and Liberty) which has waged terrorism for 40 years in a struggle to establish an independent Basque state; *Ideological* groups, for example the Red Brigade which waged a campaign against the Italian Republics in the 1970s and 80s with the aim of crating a neo-communist state and socio-economic system; *Religio-political* groups, for example Hamas which aims to create an Islamic Republic of Palestine and ultimately to dismantle the state of Israel; *single issue* groups, such as Animal Rights extremists linked to Animal Liberation Front (ALF) aim to change one aspect of government policy and social behaviour rather than to remodel the political and socio-economic order as a whole. While most members of the Animal Welfare movement are committed to restricting themselves to non-violent protest, the extreme militants are prepared to engage in arson and bomb attacks on the premises of commercial firms they wish to target and to engage in threats and in some cases attacks, on people they describe as animal 'abusers'. It should be borne in mind that campaigns by Animal Rights extremists against specific firms and projects such as the Cambridge animal laboratory have caused industry research labs to lose millions of pounds.

The damage and disruption caused by violent single issue groups should not be underestimated, but so far, at least in the UK, they have not succeeded in killing anyone.

One distinction which is worth adding to our typology is that between potentially *corrigible* terrorism where there is a real possibility of finding a political/diplomatic pathway out of the conflict by addressing its underlying causes, thus very probably reducing if not ending, the terrorist violence spawned by the conflict and *incorrigible* terrorism. In the latter case the movement/group has such absolutist and maximalist aims and poses such a major threat to the lives and wellbeing of civilian communities that the only recourse is to use all possible measures to suppress the group before it can wreak more mayhem.

In order to begin to understand the implications of recent changes in the nature of international terrorism, it is essential to grasp the major differences between the New Terrorism of the al-Qaeda network of networks and more traditional terrorist groups such as the ETA and FARC (see Bergen, 2002 and Gunaratna, 2002). al-Qaeda is not simply another group like ETA but under a different label. ETA has certainly committed hundreds of brutal killings. However, unlike al-Qaeda, ETA did not explicitly adopt a policy of mass killing as an integral part of its strategy. As Brian Jenkins so aptly observed, terrorists in the 1970s and 80s wanted 'a lot of people watching, not a lot of people dead', (Jenkins, 1975: 158)

By contrast al-Qaeda's leader, Osama bin Laden, issued a 'Fatwa' on 23rd February 1998 which announced the setting up of a World Islamic Front for Jihad and declared that 'it is the duty of all Muslims to kill US citizens – civilian or military, and their allies – everywhere'. ('Jihad Against Jews and Crusaders: World Islamic Front: http://www.fas.org/irp/world/para/docs/980223-fatwa.htm). The brutal language of this 'Fatwa' is one way in which the sheer ruthlessness and lethality of this movement is reflected (Lewis, 1998). Their track record of brutal mass-killing in New York, Washington, Kenya, Bali, Casablanca, Saudi Arabia, Iraq and many other places is proof positive of their remorseless use of mass-terror.

Moreover, whereas ETA and other more traditional groups have limited their aims to bringing about radical change in one particular state or region, al-Qaeda has an uncompromising/absolutist commitment to changing the entire international system. The al-Qaeda movement aims to expel the US and other 'infidels' from the Middle East and from Muslim lands generally. They also want to topple Muslim regimes/governments which they accuse of betraying the 'true Islam' and collaboration with the US and its allies. Ultimately their aim is to establish a pan-Islamist Caliphate uniting all Muslims (Gunaratna, 2002). These aims may appear grandiose in the extreme, but we need to bear in mind that bin Laden and his followers fanatically believe that they will prevail in their Jihad because Allah is on their side.

A major difference between the New Terrorism of the al-Qaeda network and more traditional groups is precisely its global network of networks, including affiliates, cells and support. These networks provide the movement with a presence and a capacity to act in at least 60 countries. It is the most widely dispersed non-state terrorist network ever seen and this is what gives the movement 'global reach' (See Aaron Mannes, 2004: 3–112).

'Traditional' terrorist movements generally confine themselves to mounting attacks in one country or region, though in some cases they do develop sophisticated overseas support networks to obtain finance, weapons, recruits, safe haven and the opportunity to enlist wider support for their cause.

In a later section of this chapter, I will assess al-Qaeda's current strategy, modus operandi, targets and tactics and ask to what extent the War on Terrorism can be judged successful in its efforts to crush al-Qaeda.

Assessing the effectiveness and strategic impact of terrorism

Some terrorists appear to believe that terrorism will always 'work' for them in the end, by intimidating their opponents into submitting to the terrorists' 'demands'. In reality the history of modern terrorism campaigns shows that terrorism as a major weapon has only very rarely succeeded in achieving a terrorist group's strategic goals. The clear exceptions to this in recent history occurred in the period of anti-colonial struggles against the British and French after World War II, for example in ending British Mandate Control in Palestine, ending British control of Cyprus, and Aden (Townshend, 1986) and in ending French rule in Algeria (Horne, 1978). However, there were special factors militating in favour of the rebels in all these cases: the public and the government of the colonial power had no real desire to occupy these countries or to sacrifice the lives of young soldiers and colonial police, or to expend their scarce resources, already severely denuded after six years of world war. The anti-colonial movements also had the inestimable advantage of large-scale sympathy among their own population, and the colonial authorities faced a wall of silence when they sought intelligence among the public. But, in the post colonial period there is not a single case of a terrorist movement seizing control in any country. Indeed the use of terrorism as a weapon by insurgents has backfired and alienated the indigenous population (Wilkinson, 1986: 53–68).

There are two other major factors to be considered here. Firstly, historically terrorism has mainly been used as an auxiliary weapon in a conflict involving a much wider repertoire. Secondly, it should be remembered that the use of terror as a weapon of control by dictatorships has been generally much, much more effective that the use of terror as a weapon of insurgency, mainly because dictatorial regimes generally have more ruthless and powerful domestic agencies of repression with which to suppress any incipient opposition (O'Kane, 2000).

However, there is a key difference between terrorists gaining all their strategic goals and terrorists having a strategic impact on macro-political and strategic events and developments. With careful timing and skilful planning terrorists can certainly have a strategic impact on international relations and politics from time to time. There were some clear examples of strategic impact in the 1980s and '90s:

- The 1983 truck bombing of the US marines while they were in barracks in Lebanon compelled President Reagan and his Administration to pull out all US troops out of the multi-national force, and thus sent the message to active or potential terrorists (e.g. bin Laden at that time) that the US could be intimidated into making changes in its foreign policy through the use of terrorism.

Other examples of terrorist attacks having a major strategic impact are:

- In the 1990s the use of suicide bombings against Israeli civilians helped to undermine the peace process between the Israelis and the Palestinians.
- Mass hostage taking by Chechen terrorists in 1996 compelled Russian government to make major concessions to the Chechen leadership.
- The 9/11 suicide hijacking attacks by al-Qaeda on the World Trade Center and the Pentagon had a colossal effect not only on US foreign and security policy and public opinion. They had a major influence on international relations, the US and international economy and on the patterns of conflict in the Middle East (Buckley and Fawn, 2003).

If terrorism rarely gains strategic goals for its perpetrators, why does it remain such a popular mode of struggle for so many groups around the world?

Even when leaders of terrorist groups recognize the fact that they are very unlikely to win their strategic goals, they may be persuaded that the potential tactical benefits to be gained by using terrorism are so attractive that terrorism is a weapon they cannot afford to discard:

- It can help weaken the enemy by a campaign of attrition.
- It is a useful way of inflicting hatred and vengeance on a hated enemy
- It can be used as a means of provoking government security forces into over-reaction, thus driving up support for the insurgents.
- If they can mount spectacular or particularly damaging attacks they will get huge publicity.
- They may gain release of imprisoned terrorists.
- They may get huge cash ransoms.
- Another key factor is that terrorism is a low-cost, potentially high yield and relatively low risk method of struggle for the perpetrators.

How serious is the current threat from the al-Qaeda network? Is the war against terrorism inflicting major damage on al-Qaeda?

Is the 9/11 Commission Report justified in warning that there could be another major terrorist attack by al-Qaeda, perhaps even more lethal and destructive? (9/11 Commission, 2004).

Is the Bush administration justified in claiming that the war against terrorism is being won, or does the evidence in the 9/11 report and arising from other investigations around the world support the opposite conclusion?

Looking at the positive items in the balance sheet, one could be forgiven for assuming that President Bush's optimistic assessment is fully justified. The Coalition Against Terrorism is the largest alliance in the history of international relations and despite the deep disagreements between members of the Coalition over the justifiability and desirability of the invasion of Iraq, it is clear that most members, including the Muslim Coalition states are continuing to share intelligence and co-operate in the wider aspects of counter terrorism. The divisions over the invasion and occupation of Iraq did not result, as some commentators had feared, in weakening the UN Security Council's stance on combating terrorism or undermining its key Resolution (1373) (2001) requiring that 'all states.. c) Deny safe haven to those who finance, plan, support or commit terrorist acts, or provide save havens; d) Prevent those who finance, plan, facilitate or commit terrorist acts from using their respective territories for these purposes against other states or their citizens. 'Nor has the UN abandoned its innovative Counter Terrorism Committee with the proactive role of monitoring member states' compliance with UN resolutions and conventions against terrorism. In an unprecedented step, NATO invoked its collective defence article, Article 5 of the North Atlantic Treaty. Other regional organizations including ANZUS and OSCE have continued to attach high priority to the War Against Terrorism.

The unexpectedly swift toppling of the Taliban regime in Afghanistan by a combination of Northern Alliance and Coalition forces removed al-Qaeda's ability to use Afghanistan as a major base for planning, training, indoctrination and propaganda and caused huge (though by no means fatal) disruption of the al-Qaeda leadership and its communications with its global network of cells, affiliated organizations and support groups.

Hundreds of suspected al-Qaeda militants and members of their support network have been arrested around the globe. Three of those listed by the US as the 22 most wanted terrorist' have been captured or killed (Khalid Sheikh Mohammed, Ahmed Khalfan Ghailani and Muhammad Atef). Some key leaders of al-Qaeda's affiliated organizations, for example in Saudi Arabia, Algeria and Indonesia, have been killed or captured. Although we know that al-Qaeda moves rapidly to replace its losses we also know that some highly experienced and expert operational planners (e.g. Khalid Sheikh Mohammed) are very hard to replace with militants of equivalent experience and capability.

Another significant gain by the Coalition has been the blocking of millions of dollars of terrorist funds in the banking system. This has not resulted in denying al-Qaeda all sources of funds, but it has reduced their ability to finance their global 'holy war' against the US and its allies.

Despite the intensification of al-Qaeda's efforts to destabilize the regimes of the front-line Muslim states, Pakistan, Afghanistan, Saudi Arabia and Iraq, they have not so far succeeded in toppling a single government and replacing it with an al-Qaeda or pro-al-Qaeda regime.

Last but by no means least; al-Qaeda has so far failed, despite repeated efforts since 9/11 in its efforts to carry out a successful attack on the homeland of the US.

On the other side of the balance sheet, it is obvious that there have been some serious failures and mistakes, which help to explain why al-Qaeda remains very much in business and why the Coalition has a long way to go before success in quashing the al-Qaeda threat can be achieved.

First, al-Qaeda's key leaders (Osama bin Laden, Aymanal Zawahiri, Sheikh Said, Abu Musab al-Zarqawi and Saif al-Adel) are still at large. This is a highly significant factor. Bin Laden and his deputy are particularly important as symbols, propagandists and ideologists and provide both general strategic direction and inspirational propaganda. Moreover it is clear that far from being sidelined or rendered powerless by the Coalition's actions, as some commentators have claimed, al-Qaeda's core leadership and its key role as the central hub in the global network has adapted in the face of its setbacks and has survived.

One of the key factors enabling them to survive their major setbacks is their fanatical belief in the ultimate invincibility of their 'holy war'. They believe their setbacks are but temporary reversals in specific countries. In the long term (and they have a totally different perception of the historical calendar from the secular West), they are convinced that Allah is on their side and will bring them victory. Another major factor helps explain the ability of al-Qaeda to adapt and survive in spite of the severe counter-measures taken by the US and the wider international community: bin Laden's network has been able to sustain its campaign by enlisting affiliated groups it has penetrated or hijacked to carry out attacks in the name of al-Qaeda and in pursuit of its wider aims. For example, the major attacks in Bali, Riyadh, Casablanca, Istanbul and Iraq have all been carried out by regional affiliates of the al-Qaeda network, while bin Laden has immediately claimed them as his own (Bergen, 2002; Gunaratna, 2002).

Whatever the rights and wrongs of the invasion of Iraq it could hardly be claimed as a major victory in the War Against Terrorism – on the contrary; it provided a gratuitous propaganda gift to bin Laden, who could portray the invasion as an act of western imperialism against the Muslim world. More recruits could be mobilized for al-Qaeda's 'holy war', and more donations could be obtained from al-Qaeda's wealthy backers. The author warned the House of Commons Foreign Affairs Select Committee of this danger in 2003 (Wilkinson, 2003). In a document leaked to the *New York Times* in July 2005, the UK's Joint Terrorism Analysis Centre (JTAC) warned that: 'Events in Iraq, continue to act as motivation and as a focus for a wide range of terrorist related activities in the UK' (*New York Times*, 2005).

In addition, the post war insurgency, terrorism and general lawlessness, which have resulted from the war, provided a strategic opportunity for al-Qaeda. Thousands of coalition targets (troops and civilians) were suddenly made available in a country without effective border controls, surrounded by Muslim countries with al-Qaeda militants within their populations.

One of the most damaging consequences of the conflict in Iraq has been the deflection of funding and military resources away from Afghanistan. President Karzai is desperately in need of security and economic development. al-Qaeda, in alliance with Taliban and local warlords, is creeping back in alliance with local warlords, especially in the areas bordering Pakistan and in the South East of Afghanistan. The attempt to bring stability and democracy to Iraq is likely to cost billions more US dollars and many more US, British and Iraqi lives. It is of course hugely ironic that many of the American public are still under the illusion that Saddam was involved in the 9/11 attacks and an ally of bin Laden.

Despite the failures of policy and intelligence by the US and its NATO allies and the very real continuing threat of another major attack on the homeland of a Western state, the greater long-term danger to international security and stability is the intensification of efforts by al-Qaeda and its affiliates to destabilize and undermine the governments of some of the front-line Muslim states and to create new lawless zones which they could use as platforms to attack neighbouring states. The fragile interim government of President Karzai is particularly at risk. Pakistan's leader has been the target of repeated assassination attempts and al-Qaeda is undoubtedly trying to exploit what it sees as the golden opportunity to destabilize the new interim government of oil rich Iraq.

In spite of the setback experienced by al-Qaeda network or networks as a result of the War Against Terrorism, the network remained active and dangerous both in the 'front-line' states in the Muslim world where it continues to try to find more secure bases from which it can launch more effective attacks in neighbouring countries, and in western countries where they have established fresh networks, mainly comprising diaspora Muslims, in order to plan terrorist actions within the homelands of the designated enemy. In other words, in the period 2002–2005 the al-Qaeda movement has again morphed, adapting to a situation in which it is forced by circumstances to leave the planning and implementation of terrorist conspiracies to the network affiliates and cell leaders in the relevant region or country. Bin Laden and Zawahiri still provide the ideological leadership and inspiration, but the 'core' leadership is unable to co-ordinate and centrally control actions undertaken in the movement's name. In one sense this is an advantage: it enables them to maintain global reach and exploit vulnerabilities in a wide range of countries simultaneously (Gunaratna, 1999). However, this policy also entails considerable risks of fragmentation and ideological, strategic and tactical divisions between the affiliates and the al-Qaeda leadership. These cracks in the al-Qaeda movement structure are already particularly apparent in South East Asia but are also beginning to emerge elsewhere. An interesting example of the movement's network-building in a European country can be found in the Netherlands. In November 2004 Theo Van Gogh, a Dutch film director and critic of Islam, was assassinated in the Netherlands. The Dutch police investigation discovered that the alleged killer was linked to a larger cell of 15 extremists with links to the al-Qaeda movement. This network, labelled the Hofstad Group by the Police, planned further assassinations. The murder of Van Gogh led to the tit-for-tat burning of places of worship and schools. The Dutch intelligence service, AIVD estimate that there are around 200 extremists liable to commit violence and roughly 1200 who support them. This is a tiny minority of the one million strong Muslim community in the Netherlands, but small numbers of fanatics are fully capable of carrying out deadly and determined terrorist attacks.

The March 2004 train bombings, which killed nearly 200 people and the July 2005 bombings of the London Underground transport system which caused the deaths of 56 people and the ensuing police investigations provided conclusive evidence of the presence of fanatical al-Qaeda networks within major EU countries, comprising extremists recruited within the diaspora Muslim communities, yet linked to international terrorism.

The London bombings, July 2005

The War on Terror came to London on 7th July 2005 when bombs exploded on a Circle line tube train travelling between Aldgate Station and Liverpool Street, on a Piccadilly line train heading from Russell Square to Kings Cross, on another Circle Line train between Edgware Road and Paddington and on a No. 30 double-decker bus en route from Hackney to Marble Arch when it was in Tavistock Place. The bombs killed 52 and injured 700, some critically. The tube bombings caused horrific carnage as the trains were full of commuters travelling to work and the bus bomb blew the top deck off the No. 30 bus.

There was no warning of these co-ordinated attacks which were obviously deliberately aimed at killing large numbers of civilians. The atrocity bore all the hallmarks of an al-Qaeda network attack and the Metropolitan Police investigators swiftly determined that the attacks had been carried our by suicide bombers. The 7th July blasts were the first cases of suicide bombings in Western Europe.

The Police, the Security Service, other counter-terrorism agencies and the emergency services were now in new territory, facing one of the most difficult challenges that they would ever have to confront and which they have long feared. Suicide bombings are notoriously difficult to prevent in an open society, especially when the terrorists pick soft targets where crowds of civilians are gathered. The former Chief of the Metropolitan Police, Lord Stevens and Eliza Manningham Buller, head of the Security Service, had warned the Government and the public that it was not a question of 'if' but 'when' a suicide bombing attack occurred.

There are three aspects of the 7th July attacks which demanded urgent attention by government, the police and the other counter-terrorism agencies:

1. The Police investigations into the attacks concluded the alleged suicide bombers were British citizens. Hence, although the bombings bore all the hallmarks of an al-Qaeda network attack, and Zawahiri, bin Laden's deputy, later claimed 'ownership' of the attacks and threatened further bombings, on a videotape, it is clear that, as terrorism studies specialists had feared, a team of British suicide bomber recruits has been recruited and indoctrinated, and is almost certainly prepared to launch further attacks within the UK. The copy-cat 21st July terrorist operation in which, mercifully, the bombs failed to explode, provide clear evidence of the existence of this wider network, though, as yet (August 2005) no conclusive evidence of a direct operational link between the terrorists involved on the 7th July and those attempting to attack on 21st July has yet been found. However, the fact that the British-born young Muslims, with no known record of terrorist activity and who blended in so perfectly to their own community have been lured into such extreme forms of terrorism confronts the British police, the Security Service, the Government and the public with particularly difficult and complex challenges.
2. A month after the 7th July attacks no arrests of persons suspected of recruiting, planning, bomb-making, or in other ways assisting the 7th July terrorists, had been made. This means there is a real danger of further attacks by other recruits, and that we will not always be fortunate enough to see the bombers fail to explode their devices for some technical reasons not yet disclosed.
3. In light of previous experiences of al-Qaeda network terrorist attacks it is extremely unlikely that the 7th July bombers and the 21st July conspirators had no international links. By early August the Police and Intelligence Services were already investigating possible links to other parts of the al-Qaeda network in Pakistan, Saudi Arabia and East Africa.

In view of the above it would clearly be folly for the authorities to reduce the level of terrorism alert or to suggest to the public that the threat of further suicide bombings by the al-Qaeda network and its affiliates is over. It would also be foolish for other European governments to relax their vigilance. Other countries have been threatened, and the attacks in Madrid and London demonstrate that the al-Qaeda Movement's offshoots within western countries are still very much in business. Only the ill-informed believe the premature obituaries of the movement: al-Qaeda is not like a traditional terrorist organization, but is more of a network of networks, and is going to take time to unravel.

An illustration of the movement's network building in the Middle East came to light following investigations into the March 2005 vehicle bombing in Doha. On the 19th March a vehicle bomb was detonated inside the compound of the Players Theatre in Doha. It killed one British citizen and injured 12 members of the audience. A group calling itself Jund as Sham (Soldiers of the Levant) claimed responsibility for the bombing. The group had emerged in 1995, was based near Sidon in Southern Lebanon, and was a splinter from Asbat al Ansar (League of the Followers), a small group affiliated with al-Qaeda's network. It appears to have developed an Afghan 'branch' by 1999 and then came under the leadership of Abu Musab Zarqawi: members were trained at Zarqawi's camp at Herat, near the frontiers with Iran. Abu Zubeydah and al Zarqawi then began to develop Jund as Sham as an affiliate of al-Qaeda and spreading its network to Lebanon, Jordan, Egypt and Syria. Militants from Jund as Sham were trained in all techniques required for terrorism and political violence. Jund as Sham conspired to commit the Millennium bombings in Jordan in December 1999, but they were prevented by Jordan's Intelligence Directorate. It was assumed that the group were disbanded after the fall of the Taliban regime in fall, 2001. But Jund as Sham, Zarqawi and their network survived as did Zarqawi and Al Tawhid, also one of Zarqawi's groups. This illustrates the network's resilience and durability.

Perhaps the most worrying evidence of further network-building in the Middle East is the emergence of groups of militant Palestinian extremists in Gaza who wish to align themselves with al-Qaeda.

To sum up, the al-Qaeda movement has undoubtedly suffered considerable damage as a result of the War Against Terrorism, but they have kept their network in being and remain a significant threat. It is, to say the least, premature to write their obituary. Ultimately their fate will be determined not only by their leaders' capacity to wage asymmetrical 'holy war', but also by the responses of the governments and publics they are attacking. al-Qaeda's leaders certainly underestimated the backlash from Muslims angered by seeing al-Qaeda murder and injure fellow Muslims in terrorist attacks. The key questions are: Will the Coalition Against Terrorism learn from its failures and mistakes? And will they start to engage more effectively in the battle of ideas against al-Qaeda's cruel absolutist ideology?

The changing relationship between terrorism and warfare

War can be briefly defined as armed conflict between two or more parties, nations or states. The days when international lawyers could claim that the term war only applied to armed conflict between states have surely long gone. The twentieth century and the opening years of the new century are replete with examples of internal wars of all kinds – civil wars, ethnic and tribal wars, religious wars and insurgencies. In common usage the term war is widely used to refer to any conflict relating to war or with the characteristics of war.

Is the Coalition Against Terrorism involved in a war against the al-Qaeda network? It would seem absurd to deny it. al-Qaeda's leaders declared war on the US and its allies. President George W. Bush declared a War on Terrorism after 9/11 attacks. We can hardly claim that the term war is being used purely metaphorically in this context. 9/11 killed more people that the Pearl Harbor bombing. US, British and other troops have been fighting al-Qaeda militants in Afghanistan, Iraq, Yemen and other countries. It is a different kind of war, an asymmetrical war in which one cannot judge success or failure in terms of battlefield or the numbers of tanks and aircraft destroyed or captured. The enemy is largely unseen, hiding among the civilian environment in cities around the world.

The secret intelligence battle, the work of the police and criminal justice systems, the suppression of terrorist finances, measures to prevent proliferation of WMD into the hands of terrorists, sanctions against regimes that assist or sponsor terrorists, and many other methods, in addition to deployment of military forces in counter-terrorism missions, are all part of the multi-pronged struggle to suppress the al-Qaeda network. This does not alter the fact that we are witnessing a kind of warfare, a global war involving the use of terror and counter terror.

Historically terrorism has often been an auxiliary method or weapon in a wider war. Military and paramilitary forces have frequently used systematic terrorism against civilian populations as means of trying to break the will and morale of the enemy's population. Repressive regimes resort to the use of this weapon almost instinctively because they use it to suppress dissent within their own borders, and even among their exiles living overseas (O'Kane, 2000).

Dictators can become addicted to the use of terror and come to believe that it 'works' although there is considerable historical evidence that it is a faulty weapon and that it often has psychological effects which are the reverse of those intended by the perpetrators. Liberal democratic governments, on the other hand, should at all times be conscious of their obligations under the Geneva Convention to avoid deliberate attacks on civilians and to treat captured combatants and those injured in battle humanely. Adoption of the methods of terror to defeat terror leads democracies into a moral and legal quagmire in which they will no longer be perceived by world opinion to be acting in accord with their self-proclaimed democratic values. Their international credibility is undermined (Ranstorp and Wilkinson, 2005; Wilkinson, 2000: 124–36).

The key features of the terror wars which have now become the predominant manifestation of armed conflict are: there are no clear front lines; attacks on civilians become the norm; particularly savage violence is used in 'ethnic cleansing' of whole villages and communities and massacres, mass hostage-takings and mass rapes and destruction of civilian homes become the pattern. Typical examples of 'terror wars' in which terror is used by all sides are the conflicts in the former Yugoslavia, the Chechen conflict with the Russians, and the genocidal ethnic conflicts in Central Africa. One key feature of such conflicts has been that non-state actors (paramilitary and terrorist groups) are often responsible for massive violations of human rights on a scale comparable to, or in excessive of, the war crimes committed by the regular military forces of states (Gilbert, 2003; Wilkinson, 2000: 3–74).

A striking feature of these 'terror wars' is their durability. There is no easy exit from such conflicts. The sheer savagery that characterizes them tends to lead to greater polarization, making efforts at obtaining ceasefires and peace negotiations all the more difficult. Both sides come to see themselves as waging total war. The levels of brutality become particularly intense when the perpetrators of the violence are led or orchestrated by ideologists preaching ethnic or religious hatred. In many of the recent terror wars one side or both obtain assistance from supporters/sympathizers abroad and it helps them to obtain more finance, weapons and recruits to sustain the conflict. Last but not least the UN and regional IGOs are generally either reluctant or unable to attempt peacekeeping or even humanitarian efforts because they know that such commitments may involve them in long-term, costly and dangerous assignments with no prospect of exit, and no help to finance such deployments.

Above all, military forces are inherently handicapped in their efforts to suppress terrorism. Sophisticated modern terrorists of the al-Qaeda network and its affiliates know how to hide and operate covertly in cities around the world, how to melt into their surroundings and to keep communications secret.

To win the struggle against al-Qaeda you need to win the intelligence war and use law enforcement agencies world-wide as well as co-operation in the finance sector, civil aviation industry, private sector and between the public and private sector. The military can be of enormous value when they have specially trained units, equipped and configured for the purposes of counter terrorism for specific operations. An example of this would be the toppling of the Taleban Regime, which had given safe haven to al-Qaeda. But, over-dependence on military operations and heavy-handed use of firepower in civilian areas is likely to cause heavy casualties among innocent civilians and is a huge strategic blunder.

The future of terrorism

In view of the dramatic changes that have taken place with the ending of the Cold War and the aftermath of the 9/11 attacks, it would be foolish to try to predict the future of politics and international relations and the future of terrorism, which is so heavily influenced by the strategic environment. However, it is possible to extrapolate from some of the emerging trends.

It is likely that many of the current terror wars will continue for many years ahead, for the reasons outlined in the previous sections. It is also clear that there will be some fresh outbreaks of this type of warfare in conflict hotspots where it had been hoped that some political resolution had been achieved. Areas which are particularly vulnerable to this reversion to terror war include Central Africa, West Africa, the Horn of Africa, Sudan, Iraq, Afghanistan, Kashmir and Indonesia.

As the author concluded in an earlier section of this chapter, the al-Qaeda movement, though seriously damaged by the extensive international measures against it, seems likely to continue to pose a threat through its global network of networks for some decades ahead. Even if the current leadership is removed from the scene there are likely to be eager successors in the wings ready to pursue the same overall objectives and using the terrorism weapon. Whoever assumes the leadership it seems almost certain that they will retain the key elements of al-Qaeda's ideology and combat doctrine, and hence will continue to wage their Jihad within the front-line countries (Iraq, Afghanistan, Pakistan, Saudi Arabia), and by urging their networks within western countries to launch terrorist attacks on the homelands of the Coalition allies, including, of course, the US and the UK.

The increasing intensity of terrorist violence in Iraq in 2004–2005, combined with the wider insurgency against the US and British troops, and the new Iraqi government and its newly formed police and army units, and against civilians, including deadly attacks on the Shia population, is endangering the efforts to create a more stable and secure Iraq and to make swifter progress of economic reconstruction. It is therefore very clear that whatever one's view may be of the original case for invading Iraq in 2003 and toppling the brutal Saddam regime, the consequences of failure to stabilize the country under its new democratically elected government would have very serious implications, not only for Iraq but for international peace and security throughout the Middle East. If Iraq relapses into complete chaos and civil war it would provide an opportunity for the al-Qaeda-linked terrorists to establish a strong base area within the country to use as a launching pad for further attacks throughout the region. It is therefore in the interests of the international community as a whole to work together to help create a more stable Iraq, as well as to intensify reconstruction efforts in Afghanistan, where the efforts of President Karzai's government are threatened by the efforts of the Taleban and al-Qaeda to re-establish themselves in the areas bordering Pakistan and in the South on the country. There would also be great dangers to the international peace and security if al-Qaeda-linked groups managed to undermine the government of other 'front-line' states, such as Pakistan.

A worrying emerging trend which could confront the international community with significant additional challenges in the next decade is the move on the part of the most extreme militant Palestinian groups in Gaza to align or affiliate with al-Qaeda. Up to the time of writing (Summer 2005) it has been clear that Hamas and the Palestine Islamic Jihad have kept their distance from al-Qaeda, and have concentrated on their own agenda to destroy the state of Israel, to set up an Islamist Republic of Palestine. If some of the militants and suicide bombers begin to collaborate with the al-Qaeda movement there are real dangers that the Israeli-Palestine conflict will be accompanied by acts of international terrorism, and that any effort by the more pragmatic Palestinian leaders and groups to push forward a revival of the peace process with Israel will find their efforts derailed by the 'incorrigibles' aligned to al-Qaeda.

Another growing trend which seems set to continue is the growing collaboration – in some cases partnership – between international organized crime gangs and terrorists. These links are likely to provide much more sophisticated criminal techniques of fundraising for the terrorists leading to much larger sums being made available for the provision of weapons and other resources for terrorist groups such as al-Qaeda. This growing nexus between terrorism and international organized crime is so potentially significant and dangerous for the international community that there is an urgent need to research this aspect of counterterrorism more thoroughly and to introduce tougher international measures not simply to freeze terrorists' existing finances but, more importantly, to dismantle their increasingly sophisticated covert fundraising/organized crime networks (Makarenko, 2002).

The most worrying emerging trend which is likely to have a dramatic effect on the nature and severity of the terrorist threat is the increased interest shown by currently active terrorist groups, especially al-Qaeda and its affiliates, in acquiring WMD materials and expertise.

In view of al-Qaeda's ideology and its declared commitment to mass killing who can seriously doubt that they would not hesitate to use such a weapon? There are numerous reports in the open source literature of al-Qaeda or its affiliate groups attempting to obtain radioactive materials and also uranium. Most experts on nuclear weaponry doubt whether al-Qaeda's network has currently got the necessary expertise and resources to make a nuclear bomb. However, given al-Qaeda's known capabilities in constructing high explosive devices and the ease with which radioactive isotopes can be acquired RDD (Radiological Dispersal Device) attacks are well within their capacity. Documents and video captured from al-Qaeda sites in Afghanistan also demonstrate their ability to construct chemical weapons.

The al-Qaeda training manual captured in Manchester and police investigations in the ricin case also confirm the networks' interest in manufacturing or obtaining poisons. It is only a matter of time before we see such methods being used, though in the next few years we are likely to see the al-Qaeda network continuing to depend heavily on using its weapons of choice; the conventional suicide vehicle bomb, the man portable suicide bomb, mortar attacks and assassinations. However, as they become able to acquire the materials and the expertise to weaponize them, we are likely to see al-Qaeda network experimenting with more exotic and potentially more deadly weapons to increase their capability for mass killing and disruption and damage to economic infrastructure. In the much longer term the danger is that the network will acquire more sophisticated and effective WMD capabilities. Unfortunately, the proliferation of nuclear and other dual use technologies to a wide range of countries increases the danger of illicit acquisition by a terrorist group.

However, there are very good reasons for avoiding overstating the danger of the large-scale terrorist stack. As Richard Guthrie, John Hart and Frida Kuhlan have observed:

> If the threat of large-scale attack should prove to have been overstated, does this matter? After all, even if the threat is low, it is still there, and it is worth taking pains to protect modern societies against their many vulnerabilities to novel types of terror attack. The focus on a large-scale biological and chemical threat could, however, prove to be counterproductive. While small-scale use of hazardous materials is within the technical reach of small organisations, large-scale use such as that required to devastate a large part of a city would require greater resources than most groups possess, or might want to commit. Nevertheless, if such groups hear messages from the Western media based on intelligence information that terrorists are pursuing such methods and could use them easily, the incentive to explore them – at the very least – risks being reinforced. (SIPRI Yearbook, 2005: 628)

General principles of a liberal democratic response to terrorism

It is possible to draw from the recent experience of low-intensity and counter-insurgency operations certain basic ground rules which should be followed by liberal democracies taking a tough line against terrorism.

1. The democratically elected government must proclaim a determination to uphold the Rule of Law and constitutional authority, and must demonstrate this political will in its actions.
2. There must be no resort to general indiscriminate repression. The government must show that its measures against terrorism are solely directed at quelling the terrorists and their active collaborators and defending society against the terrorists. A slide into general repression would destroy individual liberties and political democracy and may indeed bring about a ruthless dictatorship even more implacable than the terrorism and repression was supposed to destroy. Moreover, repressive over-reaction plays into the hands of terrorists by giving credence to the revolutionaries' claim that liberal democracy is a sham or a chimera, and it enables them to pose as defenders of the people.
3. The government must be seen to be doing all in its power to defend the life and limb of citizens. This is a vital prerequisite for public confidence and co-operation. It if is lacking, private armies and vigilante groups will tend to proliferate and will exacerbate civil violence.
4. There must be clear cut and consistent policy of refusing the make any concession to terrorist blackmail. If the terrorist weapon can be shown to pay off against a particular government then that government and its political moderates will find their power and authority undermined. There is abundant evidence that weakness and concession provoke a rapid emulation of terror-

ism by other groups and a dramatic escalation in the price of blackmail demands.

5. All aspects of the anti-terrorist policy and operations should be under the overall control of the civil authorities and, hence, democratically accountable.

6. Special Powers, which may become necessary to deal with a terrorist emergency, should be approved by the legislature only for a fixed and limited period. The maximum should be six months, subject to the legislature's right to revoke or renew the Special Powers should circumstances require. Emergency measures should be clearly and simply drafted, published as widely as possible and administered impartially.

7. Sudden vacillations in security policy should be avoided: they tend to undermine public confidence and encourage the terrorists to exploit rifts in the government and its security forces.

8. Loyal community leaders, official and personnel at all levels of government and security forces must be accorded full backing by the civil authorities.

9. No deals should be made with terrorist organizations behind the backs of elected politicians.

10. Although there are circumstances when it is justifiable for government to engage in secret dialogue with active terrorist groups (for example, to try to secure the release of hostages, or to discover if a terrorist group can be persuaded to adopt a ceasefire and to terminate the terrorist campaign) governments should avoid conceding to demands from groups currently engaged in campaigns of terrorism. Failure to abide by this principle is extremely dangerous. It would send a message to all terrorist groups that 'terrorism pays' and would whet the appetite of the terrorists to use more terror violence to wrest further concessions. It also serves as a powerful propaganda and recruiting boost for the terrorists.

11. Terrorist propaganda and defamation should be countered by full and clear official statements of the government's objectives, policies and problems (Alexander and Latter, 1990).

12. The government and security forces must conduct all anti-terrorist operations within the law. They should do all in their power to ensure that the normal legal processes are maintained, and that those charged with terrorist offences are brought to trial before the courts of law.

13. Terrorists imprisoned for crimes committed and professedly political motives should be treated in the same manner as ordinary criminals. Concessions of special status and other privileges tend to erode respect for the impartiality of the law, arouse false hopes of an amnesty and impose extra strains on the penal system.

14. It is a vital principle that liberal democratic governments should not allow their concern with countering terrorism, even in a serious emergency, to deflect them from their responsibilities for the social and economic welfare of the community. Liberal democratic governments must, by definition, be grounded upon the broad consent of the governed. They are inherently

reformist and ameliorative: it is their citizens' natural and legitimate expectation that their representatives and ministers will respond constructively to the expressed needs and grievances of the people. The business of attending to the public welfare must go on. It is, of course, true that this is one of the greater inner strengths of liberal democracy and, incidentally, one reason why its citizens constitute such a hostile 'sea' for the terrorist to swim in.

It would be the height of folly for a liberal democracy faced with a terrorist emergency to halt its work of amelioration and reform. On the contrary, everything possible should be done to prevent the serious disruption and paralysis of social and economic life so ardently sought by the terrorists. Yet the liberal democratic government should not, on any account, concede a reform or change the policy under terrorist duress. Such grave acts of weakness would only breed contempt for the normal political processes and for the law.

I must emphasize that the above general principles are not meant to be comprehensive. Much qualification and elaboration is needed to relate these ground rules to the actual problems of conducting anti-terrorist operations. Nevertheless, I do believe that these broad principles embody some of the major lessons that have been learned from anti-terrorist campaigns of the past. It is now necessary to outline a more effective strategy for governments and the international community to tackle the threat from the al-Qaeda network. As argued above, al-Qaeda does not display any of the characteristics of a 'corrigible' form of terrorism. Its demands are absolutist and involve nothing less than the reordering of the entire international system on al-Qaeda lines, and its methods of mass killing make it the enemy of the whole civilized world. The strategy must be one of suppression, not appeasement.

Towards an effective strategy to dismantle the al-Qaeda network

Because of the inherently transnational nature of the al-Qaeda movement threat the first prerequisite for an effective strategy against this threat must be that it is genuinely multinational, not only maintaining the solidarity of the existing coalition against terrorism but consolidating and expanding it. Active participation and closest possible collaboration with and between Muslim members of the Coalition is particularly vital because of their greater access to intelligence on the extremist political groups active in their own and neighbouring countries.

Secondly, the strategy must be multi-pronged. Military force is invaluable for certain counter-terrorist tasks, such as hostage rescue, bomb disposal and the physical protection of borders and potential targets but is not a panacea for defeating a terrorist movement dispersed and well hidden and camouflaged in major cities of the world (Kennedy-Pipe and McInnes, 1997; Wilkinson, 2000: 124–36). The multi-pronged strategy must above all be intelligence-led and must utilize to the full all the resources of police and judicial co-operation to apprehend the terrorists and their support networks and to bring them to justice.

It is foolish to underestimate the role of the criminal justice system. If terrorists are convicted after a fair trial on the basis of clear and convincing evidence justice is seen to be done and the democracies continue to occupy the moral high ground. Compromising or circumventing due process only weakens the claims of democracies to be upholding democratic values and principles and gives the terrorists a gratuitous propaganda weapon and recruiting sergeant.

Nor should we neglect the long-term pre-requisites of prevention of terrorism, for example employing the education system, religious and community leaders and the mass media in a battle of ideas to reveal the true face of terrorism and to prevent impatient angry young Muslims from joining the ranks of the terrorist groups and fronts. It is disappointing to discover that the US Government currently spends a mere 0.3 percent of its total defence budget on public information and the battle of ideas. We seem to have already forgotten that this was one of the most effective, perhaps *the* most effective of all the assets the West used to win the Cold War.

Last but by no means least we need to promote far more comprehensive and rigorous counter-proliferation measures to prevent acquisition or use of CBRN weapons and materials by terrorists, and to help protect the public or at least mitigate the effects on the public in the event of a CBRN terrorist attack (SIPRI Yearbook, 2005: 530, 628 and 678).

Public support and the media's role

Strong public support and co-operation with the police is essential in a democracy if the authorities are to be successful in significantly reducing or suppressing threats from terrorist groups. This is not such an impossible task as some writers appear to assume.

Even when confronted with the numerous horrific terrorist atrocities ordinary members of the public continue to show their outrage at brutal attacks on the innocent and demonstrate their humanity and compassion for example by joining emergency service personnel in clawing away the rubble of bombed buildings in the hope of rescuing victims, and by their acts of compassion and practical help to the families of victims. The public do not need special debates on 'what society is for' (Durodie, 2005) to persuade them to rally to the defence or assistance of their neighbours and communities. The vast majority of democratic citizens also know very well that terrorism is the very antithesis of democracy. They know that democracy is far from perfect but they also know that terrorism in democracy is the weapon of the bullies and would-be petty tyrants who try to win by the bomb what they cannot achieve through victory at the ballot box.

The more difficult tasks in relation to public support are (i) how to sustain public vigilance and threat awareness over lengthy periods against a well-armed and resourced terrorist enemy, and (ii) how to help the public identify potentially valuable clues of terrorist activity, and (iii) to persuade members of the public to come forward to act as witnesses or to give evidence in trials involving those accused of terrorist offences. To help overcome the first of these problems more public information should be made available via the mass media and the internet on the terrorist modus operandi and track record highlighting ways in which members of the public might succeed in identifying them. As regards the role of members of the public in courts where terrorists are put on trial, much better witness protection schemes and methods of maintaining witnesses' anonymity when giving evidence would help to encourage more public participation in the judicial process (Clutterbuck, 1975).

It is of course true that in an open society it is the mass media which are the critical source of information about terrorism. Unfortunately the mass media sometimes show gross negligence and irresponsibility in their coverage of terrorism. They can hype terrorist threats, thus playing into the terrorists' hands by magnifying their efforts to create a climate of fear. They can sensationalize and glamorize terrorist activities, thus providing gratuitous publicity and encouragement to the terrorist. Worst of all, the media can occasionally be hijacked and manipulated by the terrorist leaders, as happened to the Italian media in the wake of the kidnapping of Aldo Moro.

As I observed in a recent monograph, 'In an open society with free media it is impossible to guarantee that police anti-terrorist operations will be safeguarded against being compromised or disrupted by irresponsible media activity'. However, a great deal can be achieved by ensuring that expert press liaison and news management are an intrinsic part of the police response to any terrorist campaign, and the contingency planning and crisis management processes. Indeed, in a democratic society a sound and effective public information policy, harnessing the great power of the mass media insofar as this is possible, is a vital element in a successful strategy against terrorism.

This power of the media and the political leadership to mobilize democratic public opinion, so contemptuously ignored by the terrorist movements, reveals a crucial flaw in terrorist strategy. The terrorist assumes that the target group he or she seeks to coerce will always fall victim to intimidation if his or her threatened or actual violence is sufficiently severe. The terrorist believes in the ultimate inevitability of a collapse of will on the part of the adversary. Even on the face of it this is a somewhat naïve assumption. Why should people subjected to threats behave with such docility and weakness? Not only do terrorists frequently score an 'own goal', they also often succeed in hardening society's resistance towards them, and in provoking tougher, more effective counter-measures of a kind which may decimate or permanently debilitate their revolutionary movement.

There are a number of other important ways in which responsible media in a democracy serve to frustrate the aims of terrorists. Terrorists like to present themselves as noble Robin Hoods, champions of the oppressed and downtrodden. By showing the savage cruelty of terrorists' violence and the way in which they violate the rights of the innocent, the media can help to shatter this myth. It is quite easy to show, by plain photographic evidence, how terrorists have failed to observe any laws or rules of war, how they have murdered women and children, the old and the sick, without compunction. For in terrorist practice no one is innocent, no one can be neutral, for all are potentially expendable for the transcendental ends of the terrorist cause.

What else can the media do in a positive way to aid in the struggle against terrorism? There are numerous practical forms of help they can provide. Responsible and accurate reporting of incidents can create a heightened vigilance among the public to observe, for example unusual packages, suspicious persons, or behaviour. At the practical level the media can carry warnings to the public from the police, and instructions as to how they should react in an emergency. Frequently media with international coverage can provide valuable data and leads concerning foreign movements, links between individuals and different terrorist organizations, new types of weaponry and possible future threats, such as planning of an international terrorist 'spectacular' or warning signs of a new threat.

Finally, the media also provide an indispensable forum for informed discussion concerning the social and political implications of terrorism and the development of adequate policies and countermeasures. And media which place a high value on democratic freedoms will, tightly and necessarily, continually remind the authorities of their broader responsibilities to ensure that the response to terrorism is consistent with the role of law, respect for basic rights and demands for social justice.

In sum, it can be argued that these contributions by the media to the war against terrorism are so valuable that they outweigh the disadvantages and risks and the undoubted damage caused by a small minority of irresponsible journalists and broadcasters. The positive work of the media has been either gravely underestimated or ignored. It is always fair game, especially for politicians to attack the media. A more considered assessment suggests that the media in Western liberal states are a weapon that can be used as a major tool in the defeat of terrorism. The media need not become the instrument of the terrorist.

I have examined briefly the perspective of the law enforcement authorities on media coverage of terrorism. I have also noted that although the mass media in an open society are highly vulnerable to manipulation and exploitation by terrorists, they can also make an invaluable contribution to the defeat of terrorism. What are the major policy options for a democratic society in regard to the media's response to terrorism?

First, there is the policy of *laissez-faire*. This assumes that no specific steps should be taken with regards to media coverage of terrorism, however serious the violence or threat of violence may be. The dangers of this approach are fairly obvious: sophisticated and media-wise terrorist organizations will exploit the enormous power of the media to enhance their ability to create a climate of fear and disruption, to amplify their propaganda of the deed to publicize their cause or to force concessions of ransoms out of the government or out of companies or wealthy individuals. At best the *laissez-faire* approach is likely to encourage attack which endanger life and limb and place property at risk. At the most severe end of the spectrum of violence, the tame acquiescence of the mass media as an ally of a terrorist campaign may help to induce a situation of incipient or actual civil war with a concomitant threat to the stability and survival of the democracy in question.

A second policy option on media response to terrorism is for some form of *media censorship or statutory regulation*. In view of the great power wielded by the media, for good or ill, it is hardly surprising to find that, when faced with severe terrorist campaigns, several democratic countries have sought to deny the terrorist direct access to the important platform of the broadcast media. This was clearly the prime concern underlying former Prime Minister Margaret Thatcher's demand that the terrorists should be starved of oxygen of publicity, the British government's ban, since rescinded, on the broadcasting of the voices of terrorist spokespersons.

The closest parallel to the media ban is the use of IRA/Sinn Fein voices in broadcast interviews is the Irish Republic's ban under Section 31 of their 1960 Broadcasting Authority Act, on the carrying of interviews with the IRA, Sinn Fein and other terrorist spokespersons. Sinn Fein protested that it was a legal political party in the Republic of Ireland and therefore had the legal right to broadcasting time. However, the minister who imposed the ban, Conor Cruise O'Brien, said that Sinn Fein was not a legitimate political party but rather a 'public relations agency for a murder gang', (O'Brien, 1976). Predictably, a similar debate surrounded the British ban on Sinn Fein voices.

Students of Irish politics have argued that their media ban (rescinded during the IRA's ceasefire) did actually damage Sinn Fein's efforts to build electoral support and sympathy in the Republic by denying it the aura of legitimacy accorded by television appearances. The angry protests of Sinn Fein in response to the British ban on the voices of their spokespersons, suggests that Sinn Fein leaders were also convinced that the ban damaged them. However, in due course, the British television news programmes became so skilled at providing actors' voices to accompany film footage of Sinn Fein leaders that they turned the voice ban into a farce.

In the wake of the Dunblane and Tasmania massacres of 1996 there was a revival of interest in proposals to curb film and television violence. In July 1996 the Australian government announced new censorship guidelines for films and videos and a requirement that all new television sets be fitted with a V-chip, an electronic locking device that allows parents to block reception of programmes coded as violent or offensive. It is noteworthy that Australia is the only country so far to have introduced these measures, the most far-reaching effort to curb film and television violence, even though its government admits that 'No one pretends to demonstrate a linear connection between electronic violence and real-life violence'. It is also interesting to note that measures of this kind have not been proposed or adopted by states experiencing high levels of politically motivated violence. At the more draconian end of the spectrum of democratic states, efforts to starve terrorists of publicity, the Spanish government introduced a law in 1984 that makes it a criminal offence to support or praise 'the activities typical of a terrorist organization ... Or the deeds or commemorative dates of their members by publishing or broadcasting via the mass media, articles expressing opinion, new reports, graphic illustrations, communiqués, and in general by any other forms of dissemination'. Spanish judges were at one stage even empowered to close down radio stations as an exceptional precautionary measure.

One channel of mass communication which is open to exploitation by terrorist groups, and which the al-Qaeda network of networks uses on a major scale for propaganda, recruitment, and secret communications is the world-wide web. Policing the global internet is a near-impossible task. New websites can be set up at the drop of a hat under new labels; servers in a variety of countries can be used if it becomes impossible to use servers in the terrorists' country of origin. The only saving grace for counter-terrorism agencies is that by vigilant monitoring of the internet they can sometimes obtain valuable insights and information leading to great understanding of the terrorists' mindset and strategic and tactical thinking. (Peter Taylor, 2005).

In general, however, even those democratic states most plagued by terrorism have been reluctant to take the route of comprehensive censorship of the media's coverage of terrorism. It is widely recognized that it is important to avoid the mass media being hijacked and manipulated by terrorists, but if the freedom of the media is sacrificed in the name of combating terrorism one has allowed small groups of terrorists to destroy one of the key foundations of a democratic society. Censorship, in whatever guise, plays into the hands of enemies of democracy. It is also an insult to the intelligence of the general public, and would totally undermine confidence in the veracity of the media if censorship was to be introduced. We should try to uphold the vital principle of free speech so eloquently championed by Thomas Jefferson two centuries ago: 'that truth is great and will prevail if left to herself; that she is the proper and sufficient antagonist to error, and has nothing to fear from the conflict unless disarmed of her natural weapons, free argument and debate'.

However, in any free and responsible society no freedom of expression is totally unlimited. Most of us believe, for example, that pornography should be banned from television and radio. Most decent citizens would also be horrified if the mass media began to provide a platform for race-hate propaganda, or for drug pushers or rapists to come on the screen to boast of their crimes to incite others to commit crimes.

The third option on media policy on terrorism coverage, and the approach most favoured by the more responsible mass media organizations, is *voluntary self-restraint* to try and avoid the dangers of manipulations and exploitation by terrorist groups. Many major media organizations have adopted guidelines for their staff with the aim of helping to prevent the more obvious pitfalls. For example, CBS News' guidelines commit the organization to 'thoughtful, conscientious care and restraint', in its coverage of terrorism, avoiding giving 'an excessive platform for the terrorist/kidnapper', 'no live coverage of the terrorist/kidnapper' (although live on-the-spot reporting by CBS News reporters is not limited thereby), avoiding interference with the authorities' communications (e.g. by telephone lines), using expert advisers in hostage situations to help avoid questions or reports that 'might tend to exacerbate the situation', obeying 'all police instructions' (but reporting to their superiors any instructions that seem to be intended to massage or suppress the news), and attempting to achieve 'such overall balance as to the length' that 'the (terrorist) story does not unduly crowd out other important news of the hour/day'.

The above guidelines are for the most part entirely laudable, and, if properly and consistently implemented, they would help to avoid the worst excesses of media coverage of terrorism. However, one needs to bear in mind that many of those who work in mass media organizations appear blissfully unaware of any guidelines on terrorism news coverage. There is very little evidence of necessary briefing and training of editors and journalists in this sensitive area, and no evidence of any serious effort by media organizations to enforce their own guidelines (Gallimore, 1988). It is governments' frustration over the apparent inadequacy of media self-restraints that leads some to advocate some form of statutory regulation. If the mass media genuinely wish to exercise due care and responsibility in covering the exceedingly sensitive subject of terrorism, in situations where lives may well be at grave risk, they will need to work harder at devising measures of self-restraint that are both appropriate and effective (Schmid and deGraaf, 1982; Wilkinson, 2000: 174–87).

The key contribution of the private sector

Private sector companies engaged in business and industry have every reason to make a useful contribution to preventing, deterring or combating terrorist groups, especially if it is a network such as al-Qaeda which explicitly aims to attack the economic infrastructure. Private sector organizations, especially if they form part of the critical national infrastructure, are potentially direct targets of the terrorists. They may also become direct targets because of the company's country of origin, the nationality of its management or staff or because of the nature of its business and trading links. A firm may also become an indirect target, for example as a result of being located in a business district which offers a particularly attractive soft target for terrorists.

In a broader sense all businesses, even quite small ones, have a vested interest in preventing further major terrorist attacks such as 9/11 or the Madrid train bombings. This is because in the wake of major attacks, causing perhaps hundreds of deaths and injuries, well-informed companies know that there is a serious danger that they will suffer from the knock on effect on the wider commercial sector.

Take for example, the airlines and the aerospace and tourist industries so closely linked with civil aviation. If one sector is hit the others will suffer a sharp downturn. In the event of a spectacular mass-casualty/mass-destruction attack, the value of their stocks and shares may drop dramatically as a result of confidence in the security of their operations and staff ebbing away.

All medium and large-scale private sector organizations located in countries or regions subject to a terrorist threat and which believe themselves to be potential direct or indirect targets need to ensure that they have the full range of measures in place to protect their staff and plant. They need proper crisis management structures, fully trained, briefed and frequently exercised. These need to be able to handle emergencies of a general nature such as bomb threats and attacks as well as threats more specific to their business. For example, companies deploying employees in crisis hotspots around the world need to train and prepare for the possibility of an employee being taken hostage (Jenkins, 1985), and pharmaceutical and food and drink industry companies need to plan and exercise their crisis management capabilities in the event of a product contamination or threat of contamination. Airlines and airports need to plan and rehearse measures to deal with aircraft hijackings and ground attacks on aircraft and airports (Wilkinson and Jenkins, 1998). In relatively quiet times it may be hard to persuade management to keep up with the crisis management and emergency planning activity. They need to be reminded of the appalling potential costs of failure to cope if a crisis strikes.

Government and law enforcement services are clearly unable to protect everything. Firms therefore need to resort to self help, and develop, in close co-operation with the police, sensible measures of physical protection, alarm systems, and appropriate technologies for access control, perimeter security and physical protection of buildings, equipment and stocks. They will also need to develop and exercise the full range of emergency plans, including evacuation, relocation, ensuring business continuity and methods to strengthen resilience and speed long-term recovery. In the UK and other EU countries major companies generally have such plans and procedures in place, but many small and medium-sized businesses have not made contingency plans for major emergencies of this kind. Urgent efforts need to be made to encourage the private sector to take these measures as soon as possible. Many lives could be saved if the measures described above were to be well planned and executed. An inestimable advantage to businesses is that their emergency planning efforts to deal with terrorist attack will also assist them in the event of a major environmental disaster or other potentially catastrophic events. However, there are still many businesses failing to prepare for such emergencies. According to the City of London Police Commissioner, James Hart, only 50 percent of firms in the City had contingency plans in place (BBC News, 2005).

There are two other major assets which the private sector can bring to bear which exploit unique expertise and technical resources in specific sectors, for example in the financial sector, in civil aviation, in the maritime industry, or in the energy industry. One of these strengths is business intelligence which may provide information that is simply unavailable in the public. Partnership between the public and private sector is by no means a one way street of public sector support for the private sector. Take the field of financial intelligence: banks and other companies in the private sector often possess vast amounts of information on suspicious financial activity. Effective measures to suppress terrorist financing require an equal partnership and a readiness to collaborate not only between the public and private sectors but also within them, and across international borders.

A second key asset of the private sector is their development of new and improved technologies which can make a significant contribution to enhancing security (Wilkinson, 1993; Wilkinson and Jenkins, 1998), including biometric techniques for creating forgery-proof passports, security passes etc., explosives detection equipment suitable for use in airport and technical measures to protect airlines against MANPAD attacks and interoperable communications systems for use by emergency services. These are just a few of the potentially invaluable private sector contributions to counter-terrorism. For all these reasons closer partnership with and within the private sector should be developed with much greater urgency.

Conclusion

It would be a serious mistake to exaggerate the importance of the new terrorism of the al-Qaeda movement. There are far greater long-term threats to the security of the human race, dangers also created by human activity: threats to the global environment, for example, should be a far higher priority in the agenda for international co-operation and action. Nor should we overlook the dangers posed by the possibility of interstate warfare between states possessing nuclear weapons. However, the global jihad waged by the al-Qaeda movement is the most dangerous international non-state terrorist threat the world has ever confronted and we should bear in mind that it has had a huge impact on international relations, in addition to the large-scale loss of life and economic disruption it has caused. Nor should we overlook the danger of terrorism triggering a wider conflict. After all, it was a militant supporter of a Balkan terrorist group who triggered the outbreak of World War I by assassinating Archduke Ferdinand.

As I hope to have made clear, the al-Qaeda movement is by far the most serious terrorist threat now faced by the international community. The movement is not like traditional highly centralized terrorist organizations. It has been able to adapt and sustain its campaign of terror through its global network of networks and affiliates, leaving local/regional groups to plan and carry out attacks and to recruit new militants and suicide bombers while providing ideological leadership and general strategic goals and inspirations to its followers around the world. It is therefore just as irresponsible to pretend that the al-Qaeda movement is finished, or that it poses a threat indistinguishable from traditional groups. Last but not least research into the al-Qaeda movement's aims, ideology and track record of terrorist activity shows that it comes into the category of an incorrigible group, i.e. there is no feasible political or diplomatic route to resolving its conflict with the civilized world. Therefore the only sensible way forward is through a co-ordinated, multi-national and multi-pronged approach to unravel the terrorist network and bring it to justice. In the discussion above on the key elements of a successful strategy to counter al-Qaeda I have warned of the dangers of both over-reaction and under-reaction and have stressed the cardinal importance of ensuring that basic civil liberties and the rule of law are upheld even in a severe terrorist emergency. The key roles of high-quality intelligence, public support and co-operation of the mass media and the private sector have been emphasized.

In a general overview chapter it is impossible to provide a comprehensive review of all aspects of the subject. In the wake of major terrorist attacks such as 9/11, the Madrid train bombings and the London Tube suicide bombings there are inevitably demands and proposals for additional anti-terrorism legislation and measures. This is not only understandable, it is often necessary because without a sound framework of laws to deal with terrorist-related crime, one cannot expect the Police and Criminal Justice system to be able to provide effective protection of the public, a strong element of deterrence, or a means of judicial punishment of those found guilty of terrorist crimes.

However, governments should avoid the temptation to bring in new anti-terrorism laws under the illusion the legislation per se would be enough to deal with the problems they wish to address. For example, what is the good of introducing new measures to strengthen border controls if the authorities lack the political will and/or resources to ensure that there are adequate numbers of Special Branch, immigration and customs officers to implement the controls efficiently? And what is the good of having enough staff at airports and seaports if there are no adequate watch lists of persons believed by the security services to be involved in terrorism or serious crime, and no proper recording of those who leave the country? High levels of political will, international co-operation and appropriate use of well proven security technologies, as well as high-quality intelligence and threat assessment will be vital. Moreover, if anti-terrorism legislation is going to work properly it requires the widest possible public support. New proposals for anti-terrorism legislation should be the subject of consultation with all the political parties. Above all, governments should avoid the temptation to rush new legislation through the legislative with inadequate time for consultation and for cross-party agreement to emerge. Anti-terrorism measures are far too important to be treated as part of party political point-scoring and electioneering.

As emphasized earlier, in my discussion of the general principles that should underpin the democracies' response to terrorism, it is not only basic prudence but also a moral responsibility that should impel a democratic government to take full account of deeply felt demands and feelings of injustice felt by the majority or by substantial minorities within the civil society. And this must, of course, necessarily involve taking such feelings and demands into account when they concern the making of foreign policy, especially when passionate opposition is voiced by millions of citizens and when the foreign policy decisions concern peace or war. In this day and age no government claiming to be democratic should treat foreign policy as a *chasse gardée* where only the Prime Minister, Foreign Minister and the cabal of unelected advisers make policy in secret, by-passing the legislature by presenting them with a fait accompli or preempting proper legislative and public debate by manipulating intelligence information to support the policy they have already decided upon. Democratic governments should also be aware that when they do make foreign policy decisions that arouse fanatical hostility from particular religious or ethnic minorities in their society, it is a strong possibility that some groups based within these societies or overseas will exploit this anger to recruit terrorists and launch or intensify terrorist attacks. Of course this does not mean that democratic governments should be deterred from pursuing policies which they believe to be in the national interest in spite of threats or real dangers of terrorist retaliation. It does mean, however, that it would be the height of folly for foreign policy makers to fail to take these considerations into account, and that wise governments should be extremely reluctant to box themselves into a foreign policy venture initiated and controlled by a more powerful ally, and from which it is extremely difficult for the weaker ally to extract themselves.

As I have argued elsewhere (Wilkinson and Gregory, 2005), 'riding pillion' to the foreign policy of a more powerful ally is a high-risk policy. Being a good ally does not necessarily entail falling in with every request made by the more powerful partner. On the contrary, it could be argued that in circumstances where you have a sound basis for believing that your stronger ally is in danger of embarking on a policy that involves dangers that they have underestimated or failed to foresee, it is one's duty to refrain from 'riding pillion' and to warn them of the possible risks. Harold Wilson sensibly declined the US request to join them in the Vietnam War, the US refused to back the UK and France over the Suez venture in 1956. In neither case did this destroy our close alliance.

Last but not least, I have not had the space to deal with the problems of emergency response to mass-casualty terrorist attack in the event of prevention and deterrence failing. The US has rightly undertaken a wide range of measures to strengthen its homeland security following the 9/11 attacks. The UK is not so far advanced but the Police and emergency services have been planning, training and exercising in preparation for a major terrorist emergency. The response of the Metropolitan Police and the London emergency services to the bomb attacks on the 7th July convincingly demonstrated the benefits of intensive emergency planning and preparation. Other countries and major cities will have observed the value of these contingency preparations, and one hopes they too will swiftly develop improved emergency response capabilities. They could save hundreds of lives.

References

Alexander, Y. and Latter, R. (eds) (1990) *Terrorism and the Media*, Mclean, VA: Brassey's.

BBC News: http://news.bbc.co.uk/go/pr/fr/-/1/hi/uk/4137068.stm. City of London Police Commissioner James Hart.

Bergen, P.L. (2002) *Holy War Inc.: Inside the Secret World of Osama bin Laden*, New York: Touchstone.

Buckley, M. and Fawn, R. (eds) (2003) *Global Responses to Terrorism: 9/11, Afghanistan and Beyond*, London: Routledge.

Clutterbuck, R. (1975) *Living with Terrorism*, London: Faber and Faber.

Durodie, B. (2005) 'Terrorism and Community Resilience', *The World Today*.

Gallimore, T. (1988) 'Media Compliance with Voluntary Press Guidelines for Covering Terrorism', paper presented at Terrorism and the Media Research Project Conference.

Gilbert, P. (2003) *Terror Wars*, London: Pluto Press.

Gregory, F. and Wilkinson, P. (June/July 2005) ESRC research briefing, *The World Today*.

Gunaratna, R. (October 1999) *Dynamics of Diaspora-Supported Terrorist Networks: Factors and Conditions Driving and Dampening International Support*. Ph.D thesis, University of St Andrews, Scotland.

Gunaratna, R. (2002) *Inside al-Qaeda: Global Network of Terror*, New York: Columbia University Press.

Horne, A. (1978) *A Savage War of Peace*, New York: Viking Press.

Jenkins (1975) 'International Terrorism: A Balanced Sheet', *Survival*, Vol. 17, No. 4, p. 158.

Jenkins, B. (ed.) (1985) *International Terrorism and Personal Protection*, London: Butterworth.

'Jihad Against Jews and Crusaders: World Islamic Front: http://www.fas.org/irp/world/para/docs/980223-fatwa.htm.

Kennedy-Pipe, C. and McInnes, C. (June 1997) 'The British Army in Northern Ireland', *Journal of Strategic Studies*, 20: 2, 1–24.

Lewis, B. (Nov/Dec 1998) 'License to Kill: Osama bin Laden's Declaration of Jihad, *Foreign Affairs*, Vol. 77, No. 6.

Mannes, A. (2004) *Profiles in Terror: The Guide to Middle East Terrorist Organisations*, Lanham MA: Rowman and Littlefield.

Makarenko, T. (Summer 2002) 'Crime, Terror and the Central Asia Drug Trade', *Harvard Asia Quarterly*, Vol. 6, No. 3.

National Commission on Terrorist Attacks Upon the United States (2004) *9/11 Commission Report*, New York: W.W. Norton.

O'Brien, C.C. reported in *The Times*, 20th October 1976.

O'Kane, R. (2000) 'Post-revolutionary State Building in Ethiopia, Iran and Nicaragua: Lessons from Terror', *Political Studies*, 48, pp. 970–88.

Ranstorp, M. and Wilkinson, P. (eds) (2005) 'Terrorism and Human Rights', *Special Issue of Terrorism and Political Violence*, Vol. 17, No. 1.

Schmid, A.P., Jongman, A.J. with the collaboration of Michael Stohl, Jan Brand, Peter A. Fleming, Angela van der Poel and Rob Thijsse (1988) *Political Terrorism: A New Guide to Actors, Authors, Concepts, Data Bases, Theories and Literature*, Amsterdam: North Holland Publishing Co.

Schmid, A. and de Graaf, J. (1982) *Violence and Communication: Insurgent*.

Stockholm International Peace Research Institute (2005) *SIPRI Yearbook Armaments, Disarmament and International Security*, Oxford: Oxford University Press.

Taylor, P. (July 2005) *The New Al-Qaeda*, BBC2, part 1.

Terrorism and the Western News Media (1982) Beverly Hills: Sage.

Terrorism Act 2000 (2000) Part 1, London: The Stationery Office.

Terrorism: Documents of Local and International Control (1979–2005) Oceana Publications, multi volume series, Dobbs Ferry, New York.

Townshend, C. (1986) *Britain's Civil Wars*, London: Faber and Faber.

US Code Title 22 Section 2656 F (d).

Wilkinson, P. (1986) *Terrorism and the Liberal State*, Basingstoke: Macmillan.

Wilkinson, P. (ed.) (1993) *Technology and Terrorism*, London: Cass.

Wilkinson, P. and Jenkins, B. (eds) (1998) *Aviation Terrorism and Security*, London: Cass.

Wilkinson, P. (2000) *Terrorism Versus Democracy: The Liberal State Response*, London: Cass.

Wilkinson, P. (3rd June 2003) Written Evidence to House of Commons Select Committee on Foreign Affairs, Tenth Report of Session, Qu. 360–7.

15
Information Security

Jason Crampton, Kenneth G. Paterson, Fred Piper and Matthew J. B. Robshaw

Computers and networks dominate the modern world and many aspects of our lives would be impossible without them. In fact, we have become so dependent on computers and networks, be they the Internet, corporate networks, mobile telecommunications networks or special purpose networks for banking or industrial control systems, that we are acutely vulnerable to accidental or malicious system failures. Some questions we might ask about our digital world include the following:

- If I store or transmit sensitive data, then who else can see it or even alter it?
- A compelling Internet presence may be essential for my company, but if someone can see my website, can they alter it too? What is the impact on my company's brand if this happens?
- Can a hacker who gets into my internal network then get access to other resources? Can he use my network as a stepping-off point for further attacks? Am I then liable for damage caused to others?
- To what extent is my business reliant on the availability of networks? What are the impacts if those networks stop working?
- As a consumer, how can I be sure that a particular e-commerce website is that of a reputable company? Are my credit card details adequately protected when doing business with that company?

These are real threats: mobile telephone eavesdropping was a common hobby in the late 1980s; USA Today was a victim of serious web spoofing in 2002; and Google suffered denial of service attacks in 2004 as a side effect of malicious code activity. Indeed, few people will be unaware of the impact to businesses and home users of computer worms and viruses[1] and *information security* has become a vital area of concern. In response to questions like those listed above, three *fundamental threats* to the security of information resources have been identified:

- *Information leakage.* An attacker might be able to recover sensitive information.
- *Integrity violation.* An attacker may be able to replace or manipulate valuable information.

- *Denial of service*. An attacker might make computers and networks unavailable to legitimate users.

Given these threats, there are three matching *fundamental goals* in the field of information security – *Confidentiality*, *Integrity*, and *Availability*. This 'CIA' classification of goals is by no means complete and might be supplemented by goals such as *legitimate use* (the ability to restrict use of a resource to legitimate parties) or *accountability* (holding users to account for their actions or resource usage).

A number of basic *security services* are employed to achieve the three basic goals. A *confidentiality service*, often achieved through the use of encryption, can provide data confidentiality. And while techniques in coding theory can help prevent accidental data corruption, we turn to the field of cryptography for provision of *integrity services* in the face of a malicious adversary. We might also be concerned about authenticating entities rather than just information so we might seek to confirm that a computer or user in some interaction is who they claim to be. More generally, *access control* or *authorization* is a generic term for limiting access to resources within a computer system or network and, in the context of computers, is a feature of all modern operating systems. One other service we wish to highlight is that of *non-repudiation*, which is particularly important in electronic commerce, and prevents one party from denying its participation in some earlier interaction with a second party.

We have divided the chapter into three main sections covering cryptography, network security and computer security. Cryptography provides the fundamental building blocks for information security. We attempt to provide a self-contained and non-mathematical summary of the important features and issues in cryptography. We next address network security, focusing on the main threats to, and security mechanisms employed in, today's TCP/IP-based computer networks. Finally we consider salient issues in computer security, dividing our discussion into physical access control, logical access control, and the subject of vulnerabilities and threats. Our chapter can only provide a brief introduction to the broad topic of information security. Our concluding section, therefore, provides additional insights and reflects on some important trends for the years ahead.

1 Cryptography

To start, we consider a fundamental building block, the *cryptographic algorithm*. Such building blocks are used again and again: sometimes in an obvious and reassuring manner, as in web-based home banking applications, for example; and sometimes transparently and unobtrusively, as in GSM networks.

1.1 Algorithms

Cryptographic algorithms are systematic procedures for establishing some cryptographic goal. There are many different algorithms with different security and performance characteristics. The most natural classification of cryptographic algorithms is based on the nature and usage of the key material, resulting in three important classes of cryptographic algorithm:

- *Symmetric algorithms*: participants in a cryptographic exchange possess the same key material. Examples include *block ciphers, stream ciphers*, and *message authentication codes*.
- *Asymmetric algorithms*: participants in a cryptographic exchange possess different key material. Examples include *key agreement, encryption*, and *digital signature schemes*.
- *Keyless algorithms*: participants in a cryptographic exchange do not use any secret key in these public computations. Examples include *hash functions*.

1.1.1 Symmetric algorithms

In classical cryptography, two participants in a cryptographic exchange share the same secret material or *key*. With such a shared secret key, any messages between the two participants can be encrypted and decrypted, and message confidentiality preserved. Message encryption can be accomplished using either a *block cipher* or a *stream cipher*. For our purposes it is not too important to know much about these; the block cipher encrypts plaintext in fixed-size blocks while the stream cipher encrypts plaintext as it is 'streaming' by. These mechanisms clearly have different properties and they are likely to be deployed in different environments. Suffice it to say that we have very good and well-trusted examples of both ciphers, which we discuss further in Section 1.3.

Two participants can also use shared secret information to authenticate the contents of any messages that they send to one another. To be sure that a message has not been changed or modified *en route* we can use a *message authentication code (MAC)*. There are several prominent examples of MACs in use today and they offer *message integrity*, assurance that a message was not tampered with, as well as *message origin authentication*, assurance that some message was indeed sent by the other party that holds the secret key k. To achieve such authentication the sending party will compute a MAC (also known as an *authentication tag*) using the message and a secret key. This tag is appended to the message. The receiver can also compute the authentication tag on the received message since the receiver possesses the same secret key. This new tag value can be compared to

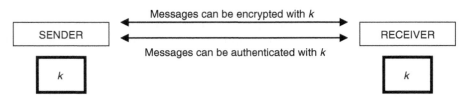

Figure 15.1 With symmetric cryptography both the sender and the receiver share the same secret key k. Messages can be encrypted using k and an encryption algorithm. They can also be authenticated using k and a message authentication code, though in practice a different shared key would be recommended for authentication and encryption.

the received tag value and a matching value implies the message has not been tampered with.

1.1.2 Asymmetric algorithms

The complement to the classical symmetric approach outlined above is provided by *asymmetric* or *public key cryptography*. While work at CESG by Ellis (1970) pre-dated that in the public domain, the classic reference for public key cryptography is the work by Diffie and Hellman (1976). Asymmetric cryptographic techniques are built around hard problems in mathematics such as factoring large numbers. The important feature of a public key cryptographic algorithm is that instead of encryption and decryption being performed with the same key, encryption and decryption are performed with different keys. Not only that, but one of the keys – the encryption key – can be made public and published in a directory. In this way two participants can communicate secretly without agreeing ahead of time on a shared secret key. In principle, they don't even need to know each other and the sender can look up the receiver's public key from the directory and use this public key to send an encrypted message. The receiver possesses the associated secret key and can thereby decrypt the message.

Algorithms that support encryption in this way are referred to as *asymmetric* or *public key encryption* algorithms. But there are public key algorithms that achieve different goals. For instance, one of the first proposals for public key cryptography was as a way of establishing a shared secret between two users; this leads to so-called *public key agreement* algorithms. But it is another goal that can be more interesting; conceptually we can reverse the role of the public and private keys to give what is termed a *digital signature*. When the keys are reversed in this way, the private key is used to perform some calculation involving an electronic version of a document or file. This process cannot be replicated without knowledge of the private key. Then, given a document and associated signature, anyone can look up the relevant public key and use this public key to verify the signature on the document by (essentially) unravelling the signing operation. Thus we have an operation that can only be performed by one entity and yet can be verified by anyone. We have the electronic analogy

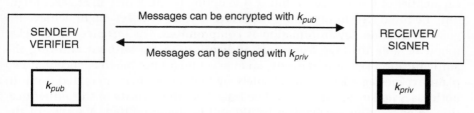

Figure 15.2　With asymmetric cryptography the sender uses a public key k_{pub} while the receiver keeps a related secret key k_{priv}. Without k_{priv} message secrecy is preserved. To form digital signatures, k_{priv} can be used to electronically sign a document with the signature being verified with k_{pub}. In practice a different set of keys would be recommended for encryption and signature.

to the hand-written signature and algorithms that accomplish this are referred to as *public key signature* algorithms. Interestingly, digital signatures were first envisaged by Diffie and Hellman (1976) as being derived directly from a public key encryption scheme by reversing the role of the public and private keys. The most prominent public key algorithm RSA (Rivest, Shamir and Adleman, 1978) can be used for both encryption and digital signatures. However most other public key signature schemes cannot be derived from, or converted to, public key encryption schemes.

Note that for any public key operation the sender needs to be sure that the public key really does belong to the claimed public key holder; thus the public keys need to be authenticated in some way. This is an important and non-trivial issue that we will return to. But it is clear that if the public keys are not authenticated as belonging to the stated individual then the sender of a message cannot be sure a message will be decrypted and read by the intended recipient, and the verifier of a signature cannot be sure of who has signed the message.

1.1.3 Keyless algorithms

The remaining major class of cryptographic algorithms consists of algorithms that do not use any key material. Nevertheless these algorithms perform an important and prominent role in many applications and protocols. These are called *hash functions* or *message digest* algorithms. They have the remarkable property that they generate a fixed length output for an input of *any* length and this forward 'easy' computation is very hard to reverse. That is, given the output from the hash function it is very hard to find an input that could have produced the given output. Furthermore, hash functions have the property that it is hard to find any two inputs that give the same output. This is despite the fact that we know that infinitely many such *collisions* must exist: there are infinitely many possible inputs and yet only a finite number of possible outputs. However a good hash function is designed so that finding even a single example of such a collision is computationally difficult.

1.2 Cryptographic security

When deploying cryptography it is important to consider the likely roles and capabilities of the attacker. While it is tempting to think that an attacker might only be interested in obtaining the secret key, an attacker might achieve his goals even if no key information is compromised. For instance, an attacker might be able to forge a message authentication tag without knowing the authentication key. Alternatively, an attacker might be able to deduce that two plaintext messages are identical solely by looking at their encrypted form. In both cases no key material would be leaked yet the security of the authentication or encryption mechanism would still be compromised. A survey of the potential weaknesses of different cryptographic algorithms and their deployments is beyond our scope here. Suffice to say it is not enough to have good encryption algorithms, and we often appeal to standards to find the best way to use these algorithms.

While it is important to recognize that recovering the secret key is not the only way to compromise a particular deployment, it is also important to recognize that an attacker is always at liberty to try to guess the value of that secret key. It is our goal, therefore, when designing a security infrastructure to ensure that (a) guessing the key requires far more resources than the adversary is willing to invest, and (b) this most basic, *brute force*, attack is the attacker's best option.

For secret-key cryptography the security of the algorithm against brute force attack is clear. If the secret key is n bits in length (that is when written as a string of 0s and 1s it consists of n binary digits or *bits*) then the time required to recover the key by guessing is at most 2^n operations, where an operation is a single encryption operation. While there are some sophisticated models and analysis available, a rule of thumb suggests that anything less than 2^{64} operations is unlikely to offer good security for the future, 2^{80} operations will offer good security and represents the security level of many deployments in the 1990s, while 2^{128} operations should offer good security for the future and provides the benchmark for most contemporary security deployments. These are enormously large numbers; by way of comparison modern cosmology suggests that the age of the universe is around 2^{80} microseconds. Thus, in the absence of any analytical weaknesses, good algorithms in use today are particularly strong and can be suitable for even the most demanding application.

The situation with asymmetric cryptosystems is more complex. We mentioned that these algorithms were built around difficult problems in number theory. Thus the secret keys are not just random strings of bits, but they have some *meaning*. The key material in an asymmetric algorithm is used in a very structured way, and an adversary hoping to recover the secret key can work within the same structured framework. Of course, an adversary shouldn't be able to exploit this structure too efficiently, but attacks better than exhaustive search are available. This means that to obtain a level of security equivalent to that offered by a symmetric algorithm, the keys for asymmetric algorithms need to be longer. For instance, a good block cipher with an 80-bit key provides a security level of 2^{80}. By contrast an asymmetric algorithm built around elliptic curves (NIST, 2000) will typically require a 160-bit key to achieve the same level of security while RSA would require a 1024-bit key. Even though the problem underpinning RSA is hard, it is not as hard as the problem underpinning elliptic curve cryptosystems and RSA keys need to be longer for equivalent security. This can have an impact on the practical suitability of different algorithms. One note of caution; it is not easy to decide whether an algorithm is suitable for deployment without looking at the larger context and deployment environment.

1.3 Cryptographic deployment and infrastructure

As cryptography has moved out of the classified government world many different algorithms have been proposed. Here we mention the most prominent examples and these are likely to be found in the majority of today's deployments. Throughout one should bear in mind that standardized algorithms are typically the most suitable implementation choice.

Block cipher deployment is dominated by DES (NIST, 1997) and Triple-DES (NIST, 2004). These are the most scrutinized and most trusted block ciphers available today. Since the 56-bit key length for DES is too short for many deployments, Triple-DES will often be the encryption algorithm of choice. A new block cipher called the AES (NIST, 2001a) is intended to supersede DES. However it will be some time before it displaces all DES-based ciphers (if ever). The inertia within an installed base should not be under-estimated. The situation for stream ciphers is far more fragmented with many proprietary or individual designs in deployment; for example RC4 can be found in *SSL/TLS*, A5/*n* in *GSM*, E0 in *Bluetooth*, and so on. Most MAC implementations are based around a block cipher (Menezes, van Oorschot and Vanston, 1996) or a hash function (NIST, 2002a). Current hash function recommendations are likely to focus on the SHA-*n* family of hash functions (NIST, 2002b). Within the field of asymmetric cryptography there has been dramatic consolidation with a handful of algorithms in widespread use. Most asymmetric deployments use RSA (NIST, 2000; Rivest, Shamir and Adleman, 1978) though alternatives for digital signatures are provided by the DSA (NIST, 2000) and its elliptic curve variant (NIST, 2000). With regards to performance, it is worth observing that hash functions and symmetric algorithms are generally faster than asymmetric algorithms by some significant degree. Consequently asymmetric algorithms tend to be deployed sparingly, with symmetric algorithms acting as the encryption and authentication workhorses.

Unfortunately, having decided on an appropriate algorithm, our work is really only just beginning. Cryptographic algorithms are rather limited objects and we have to be careful how we implement them. For instance, a block cipher is defined to encrypt a bit-string of a fixed length. How do we use the block cipher in such a way that we can encrypt an arbitrarily long message? Such issues are addressed by defining *modes of use* for a block cipher, and these have been carefully studied and standardized (NIST, 2001b). The use of any cryptographic algorithm can lead to security pitfalls and these concerns need to be addressed in any deployment. We also need to understand how to provide the key material for these algorithms, a consideration which leads us to the idea of a *key life-cycle* that incorporates *key generation, distribution, storage, usage, change*, and finally *key destruction* (Murphy and Piper, 2002). The practice of quantum cryptography allows users to agree on secret key material with an assurance that their quantum communication channel is protected against eavesdropping being given by the fundamental properties of quantum physics. However, the full deployment of such a mechanism is not without its own additional problems. Generally speaking, the provision of an appropriate key generation and distribution network can be particularly difficult, both in theory and in practice.

Public key cryptography is a helpful mechanism in establishing a shared secret between participants for some subsequent cryptographic interaction. However, the introduction of public key techniques is not without its own complications, the most pressing being the need to ensure that a public key does genuinely belong to the stated entity. This association between the key and the entity needs to be authenticated, and the ideal mechanism for doing this is a digital signature created by some trusted authority. This leads us to the concept of a *digital certificate,* a digital signature binding a public key to a given identity. But to check the signature in the certificate, we need the public key of the trusted authority and how can we be sure that the public key we are given is indeed the correct one? The recursive nature of this problem is clear and at some stage we need to authenticate the top-level public key by some other means. This will vary from one deployment to another, but in the case of the world-wide web for instance, the top-level public key for use within SSL/TLS (which we discuss in Section 2.3.2) is embedded within the Internet browser. We therefore trust the browser manufacturer to ensure that this *root key* is correctly authenticated and we trust the development and distribution environments by which the browser ended up on our PC.

2 Network security

Safeguarding the confidentiality, integrity of data carried on networks and the availability of the networks themselves is in many cases essential. Authenticity and accountability can also be important. While Internet security (Oppliger, 2002; Stallings, 2002) often garners much attention, there are often equally serious threats to internal company networks and special-purpose networks such as those required for mobile telecommunications (Mitchell, 2004; Niemi and Nyberg, 2003).

2.1 How networks work

As a basic illustration, consider how a user's web browser retrieves data from a web server. Users invoke applications running on computers connected to a network. The applications (here, the user's web browser and the remote web server application) 'speak' using an application protocol, that is, a set of rules governing communications between applications. In the case of web browsing, the protocol is called Hypertext Transfer Protocol (HTTP). The applications themselves are not responsible for direct communications. Instead, they interact with another piece of software called the *transport layer* to send or receive data. In our example, the transport layer uses a protocol called Transport Control Protocol (TCP) and provides reliable, end-to-end communication between applications. The transport layer divides the stream of application messages into packets and in turn interacts with the *Internet layer* to send or receive data. The Internet layer is yet another sub-system responsible for routing communications between one machine and another. It uses a protocol called the Internet Protocol (IP) and accepts requests from the transport layer to send data to a destination address. It sends data in *IP datagrams* and uses a routing algorithm to decide where to send datagrams. The Internet layer interacts with the network interface layer, which is responsible for transmitting the contents of IP datagrams over specific networks, such as a Local Area Network (LAN) or a wireless LAN. Finally, one can think of the network interface layer as interacting with a physical layer below it, responsible for the transmission of physical signals.

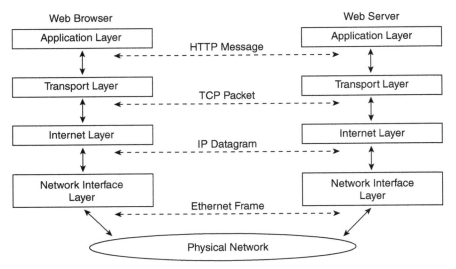

Figure 15.3   Network layering in the TCP/IP protocol stack.

To summarize, in communications networks, a series of protocols are stacked vertically in layers (Figure 15.3). In our example, this structure is known as the *TCP/IP protocol stack*. Actual communication proceeds up and down the protocol stack and via the physical layer. At the same time, one can think of virtual communications as taking place between *peer-processes* using particular protocols at each layer. This approach allows the operation of networks to be studied in digestible pieces and flexibility in the selection of networking technologies. The Internet is just a collection of disparate networks, united by a common addressing scheme based on *IP addresses*, which ensures that data can be transported to any network host. The Internet Engineering Task Force (IETF) is the body responsible for developing Internet standards, known as *Requests For Comments (RFCs)*. An excellent reference for general networking is provided by Comer (2000).

2.2 Security issues – a layer by layer approach

It is instructive to examine the way in which security issues can arise in the different layers of network architecture. We focus on the TCP/IP protocol stack, since it is so prevalent. The general features of the attacks we describe are seen in attacks in many other types of network.

At the physical layer, transmission media of various types (copper cable, optical fibre, wireless and microwave) connects network components together. Hubs are simple devices used to provide a point where data on one cable can be transferred to another. Typical security concerns are: How is access to the network components secured? Is the infrastructure shared with other organizations? Does the networking technology create a signal that can be passively eavesdropped (as is the case with many wireless technologies, for example)?

At the network interface layer, a *network sniffer* is a piece of software running on a network host that reads all the network traffic that it can intercept, regardless of its intended destination. Sniffers can be effective attack tools in networks where data is broadcast to all hosts, for example LANs making use of simple hubs, or wireless LANs. They can be configured to listen for user passwords and other sensitive information. Their effectiveness is curtailed by using switched networking technology in place of broadcast devices, since in this situation data is sent only to the intended destination.

Many security issues come to light at the Internet layer. IP addresses are not authenticated, and so can be *spoofed* by an attacker. Thus, without further protection, one has no guarantees about the origin of data. It can therefore be dangerous to base any access control decisions on IP addresses alone. IP datagrams can also be captured and replayed. Because of the routing mechanisms used by the IP layer, users have few guarantees about the route that will be taken by their data, implying a threat to confidentiality. It may be possible for an attacker to disrupt the routing process and, through this, control the route taken by data. For example, a compromised router could be configured to advertise attractive routes to other routers and so bring interesting traffic its way. Clearly, the security of routing infrastructure is an important consideration in evaluating the overall security of a network.

As a consequence of features of the TCP protocol, *Denial of Service* (DoS) attacks have proven to be a major threat at the transport layer. The basic idea of DoS attacks on TCP is to exhaust the resources available at a host to track pending TCP connections. The effect of this is to deny service to legitimate users who wish to initiate new connections with the attacked host. This attack can be made more powerful by combining it with IP spoofing, so hiding the IP address of the attacker, and by launching it simultaneously from a large number of hosts (in which case the attack is known as a *Distributed Denial of Service*, or DDoS, attack).

At the application layer, attackers typically develop exploits against particular pieces of software and launch those exploits remotely over the network at target machines. Sophisticated attack tools are widely available on the Internet. The objective of such an attack is usually to take control of a target host, so that the information stored there can be harvested or so that it can be used as an attack machine itself. A severe threat is posed by *worms*, which are self-propagating programs that can seek out victim hosts and exploit them in a fully automated way. As a side effect, worms tend to generate very large amounts of network traffic, leading to denial of network service. Viruses, especially those associated with e-mail, typically need some form of user interaction to enable them to spread. Naturally, these types of malicious code pose little threat if an organization's network is carefully isolated from the source of these attacks, the Internet. However, since Internet connectivity is essential for almost all organizations nowadays, this approach is somewhat impractical.

In summary, many security issues can be identified in the TCP/IP protocol stack and its use in supporting Internet-reliant applications. TCP/IP itself offers very little inherent security. Indeed, security simply was not a concern at the design stage.

2.3 Security countermeasures for networks

We now turn to the question of how security can be added to networks. Part of the OSI reference model, ISO7498-2, 1989, discusses network security and lays down much useful terminology. Five main categories of security service relevant to networks can be specified. These are *authentication* (including entity authentication and origin authentication), *access control*, *data confidentiality*, *data integrity*, and *non-repudiation*. Security services are implemented using *security mechanisms*. These can be divided into two classes: specific security mechanisms (including cryptographic mechanisms such as encryption, digital signatures, data integrity mechanisms and authentication exchanges); and non-cryptographic mechanisms (such as traffic padding and routing control) and pervasive security mechanisms, which are not specific to particular services. The latter include *trusted functionality*, *security labeling*, *event detection*, *security audit* trails, and *security recovery*.

2.3.1 Authentication in networks

Entity authentication is a vital security service helping to prevent illegitimate use. This service allows the authentication of the source of a request for access to network resources or to resources on a remote host accessed using the network. Passwords are the most widely used human-centric network authentication method, but these are vulnerable to sniffing and dictionary attacks in open networks. Cryptographic methods can be used to provide stronger solutions. Here, one approach is to have the authenticating party issue a challenge and then the authenticated party provide a response that takes the form of a cryptographically transformed version of the challenge. The authenticating party can check the response for correctness. As an important example, Kerberos (Kohl and Neuman, 1993) provides a fully developed suite of authentication services suitable for network-distributed applications. It uses symmetric key cryptography and has been adopted in the Windows 2000 operating system.

2.3.2 Secure channels

Entity authentication, in fact, provides quite limited security guarantees: it only provides an assurance of identity at a particular moment in time. Perhaps more useful is the ability to build a *secure channel* for communications. Such a channel generally provides confidentiality, data origin authentication and data integrity for data in transit over a network, but not usually any guarantees about the security of data stored on end systems. The general approach to building a secure channel proceeds in three phases. Firstly, the communicating parties engage in a secure protocol, that is, a cryptographically protected exchange of messages. During this exchange, one or both parties is authenticated and some fresh keying material is established. In the second phase, key derivation, the parties each use the keying material from the first phase to set up a set of keys for encryption algorithms and data integrity mechanisms. In the third phase, the parties use these mechanisms to cryptographically protect the traffic passing between them. In this way, a secure communications channel can be built on top of an otherwise insecure network. Three popular approaches to providing secure channels are IPSec, SSL/TLS, and SSH.

IPSec, as defined in IETF RFCs 2401-2412, provides a secure channel by modifying IP datagrams. There are two modes of use: *transport* mode, in which the endpoints of the IP communications must be IPSec enabled, and *tunnel* mode, where IPSec processing is handled on behalf of end hosts by security gateway devices. Through IKE (IPSec key exchange), IPSec provides a highly flexible set of methods for authentication and key establishment. IPSec provides security to IP datagrams irrespective of the higher layer protocols that are in use. It is commonly used for building *Virtual Private Networks (VPNs)* over insecure networks. VPNs can be used to provide a secure connection between offices in different locations or allow remote access for mobile workers.

SSL (Secure Sockets Layer) adds a 'thin' security layer above TCP. SSL is widely supported in web browsers and web servers and is most commonly used in support of electronic commerce and Internet consumer banking providing, for example, a secure channel over which credit card numbers or other authenticating credentials can be transmitted. The SSL Handshake Protocol supports a number of cryptographic methods for authentication and key establishment. In most applications of SSL, the client obtains the server's public key and verifies its authenticity using a chain of public key certificates that links the server's public key and web address to some root public key embedded in the client software. The server is subsequently authenticated via its ability to decrypt some RSA-encrypted material generated by the client. SSL has been adopted by the IETF as TLS (Transport Layer Security) in RFC 2246 (Dierks and Allen, 1999).

SSH (Secure Shell) is an application layer method for building secure channels. It was initially designed to replace insecure remote administration tools such as telnet, but has since been extended to support secure file transfers and e-mail. SSH can be used with the technique of *port forwarding* to allow the construction of general secure channels for network applications.

IPSec, SSL and SSH highlight some general points about the pros and cons of applying security at the different network layers. For example, IPSec is transparent to applications, but can be difficult to deploy and manage because of its complexity and large number of options. SSL relies on TCP and can exploit TCP's in-built reliability; however applications require some modification to use it. Applications generally require more modification to use SSH; at this layer, security can be tuned to individual application requirements but each application must provide its own security. Finally, security is often applied at the Network Interface layer, for example, using link encryptors. Here, all traffic is covered, but only on a single hop between two devices rather than in an end-to-end fashion.

2.3.3 Firewalls and other network security devices

At its simplest level, a *firewall* (Cheswick, Bellovin and Rubin, 2003) is a network security device that inspects network traffic and makes policy-based decisions about whether and where that traffic should be allowed to flow on a network. In a typical configuration, a firewall connects two distinct parts of a network and controls what traffic can flow between them. Often a firewall is placed between an organization's internal networks and its connection to the external Internet. In this configuration, a firewall can limit access to the internal network by outside agencies. Firewalls are also widely used to partition internal networks, for example to separate a personnel department from the remainder of the organization.

Firewalls can also be used to block access from inside the protected network to certain external services. This may be in order to prevent employees downloading and installing untrustworthy software, to enhance employee productivity, or simply to reduce costs by restricting the use of network bandwidth. Firewalls are a common point for enforcing authentication before allowing access to services and as an endpoint of a VPN. As a control point on the network, they can be used to monitor and log network traffic.

Different types of firewalls subject data to different degrees of scrutiny. At one extreme, a simple packet filtering firewall merely examines the IP datagram headers and decides whether to allow or drop the packet based on IP addresses and TCP port numbers. Such a firewall provides a low-to-moderate level of security without much overhead. At the other extreme, an application level proxy provides fine-grained control over traffic by deciding which application protocol is being carried and filtering the traffic for known exploits and vulnerabilities. To be effective, the firewall must always be the single path of communication between the protected and unprotected networks. No firewall can inspect encrypted data (such as SSL traffic) unless it has the appropriate keys. The different firewall types have their strengths and weaknesses, depending on how closely they are able to inspect and interpret data. For example, a simple packet filter cannot detect that a given datagram carries malicious code. A more sophisticated firewall may be able to detect a malicious payload, but this will inevitably be at a cost, either financial or in terms of network performance.

Most firewalls do not *detect* when an attack is underway or has taken place, and most do not *react* to attacks. Rather, they are primarily attack *prevention* devices. Nor do they effectively prevent attacks on systems and networks launched by insiders within the protected network. A number of other network security devices and technologies are of assistance here. An *Intrusion Detection System (IDS)* is a combination of hardware and software that monitors a network and/or network hosts for suspicious activity. Network-based IDS are configured with a selection of *attack signatures* – patterns of network traffic that indicate that an attack is underway. Host-based IDSs are programmed to periodically examine host log files for security sensitive events, such as administrator access to configuration files. Commercial IDS have many shortcomings. They tend to require fine-tuning so as to balance missing genuine attacks and the operator being overwhelmed by reporting. Moreover an IDS is only as good as the signature database it contains. IDSs also tend to have problems processing the large amounts of data flowing in heavily loaded networks.

Recently vendors have launched network security devices combining firewall and IDS features. Known as *Intrusion Prevention Systems (IPS)*, these can, for example, detect that a DoS attack is underway by monitoring traffic at the perimeter of a network and reconfigure a firewall to terminate any suspicious TCP connections immediately. *Vulnerability scanning*, in which vendors provide a diagnostic security service, is another current trend. Here, the vendor is responsible for maintaining all signature databases and attack profiles and the level of security expertise needed by the network operator is reduced. *Honeypots* attempt to set traps for unwary attackers by simulating attractive targets and gathering data on the attacker's behaviour, but are, as yet, unproven commercially.

3 Computer security

The US Department of Defense guidelines on trusted computer systems (often referred to as the Orange Book) state that

> secure systems will control, through use of specific security features, access to information such that only properly authorized individuals, or processes operating on their behalf, will have access to read, write, create, or delete information.
>
> (US Department of Defense, 1983: 9)

In simple terms, computer security is about preserving the *confidentiality* (controlling read access) and *integrity* (controlling write, create and delete access) of information. The *availability* of a computer connected to a network may be vulnerable to DoS attacks, but in this section we focus on the security mechanisms that preserve confidentiality and integrity.

In this section we briefly consider *physical access control* – protecting the confidentiality and integrity of main memory. We also look at *logical access control* – mediating and limiting the interaction between users and computer resources such as files, directories and programs. We conclude the section with a look at the weaknesses in computer systems and how exposure to those weaknesses can be reduced.

3.1 Physical access control

Many data structures and programs vital to the correct operation of the operating system reside in main memory and changes to these structures may lead to unpredictable behaviour and system crashes. The *interrupt vector table*, for example, controls which program is executed when the operating system receives an *interrupt* – an event usually generated by hardware such as a mouse click or the insertion of a floppy disk. The Brain virus infected MS/DOS machines by redirecting the flow of execution to the viral code whenever the interrupt generated by reading the floppy disk drive occurred. In short, physical access control – the protection of locations in main memory – is a particularly important aspect of modern, multi-tasking computer systems.

Computers execute programs, which in turn read and write data stored in main memory. A *process* is a set of resources maintained by the operating system that is used to manage the execution of a computer program. Those resources include one or more regions of main memory used to store the machine instructions that make up the program (and that are executed by the *Central Processing Unit* (CPU) of the computer) and the data used and manipulated by the program. Main memory, then, will be divided into many different regions, each belonging to a different process or the operating system. Each of these regions is protected using *segmentation*.

A *segment* is the basic unit of physical access control. Segments are used to store operating system data structures, such as the interrupt vector table, and data loaded into main memory, such as programs and data files. Each segment has a *segment descriptor* that stores information about the privilege level of the segment, the location of the segment in main memory, the size of the segment, how the segment can be accessed and the purpose of the segment. The descriptor is used to perform certain checks when a computer program attempts to access a segment: Is the program sufficiently privileged to access the segment? Does the memory address belong to the segment? Is the intended access (read or write) permitted for this segment? All modern CPUs, including the Pentium family on which many Unix and Windows operating systems run, provide a number of registers for storing information about the segments in use by a process, and modern operating systems such as Unix and Windows support segmentation.

3.2 Logical access control

In this section we describe how operating systems control access to files and other resources, collectively referred to as *objects*, in a computer system. If we are to differentiate between the level of access given to different users, then we must be able to identify users and processes running on their behalf, collectively referred to as *subjects*. (Of course, if all users are permitted access to all resources, then there is no need for logical access control. Such a situation is rather unlikely in multi-user, commercial computer systems.) Therefore, any operating system that provides access control mechanisms must first identify each user of the system and provide a mechanism for associating the user's identity with any processes that the user initiates. In short, authentication is a prerequisite of access control. The authentication process is used to identify the user, typically by verifying that the username supplied by the user is valid and that the user has correctly entered the password associated with that username.

It goes without saying that the database containing usernames and passwords is an object to which access must be strictly controlled. It is also essential that strong passwords are chosen and that passwords are changed regularly so that attackers cannot guess passwords easily. The number of passwords of length l using characters from an alphabet of a characters is a^l, so passwords should use a variety of different characters sets (such as upper case, lower case, digits and punctuation marks) and be as long as can be conveniently remembered by users.

Many modern operating systems can be configured so that users are forced to choose passwords satisfying these criteria.

If the user is authenticated successfully, the user is associated with a *security context*, which is information that will subsequently be used to identify the processes the user runs and form part of the input to the access control decision function. Typical information included in the security context will be a user security identifier (SID) and SIDs for any security groups to which the user belongs.

Unix (Robbins, 1999) was the most widely used multi-user operating system in the 1980s and the early 1990s, and continues to be extremely popular in commercial organizations. The earliest versions of Unix had a very simple access control mechanism based on group membership. Every object in the system, including devices such as printers and disks, is associated with an owner and an owner group. Access to the object is determined by nine file permissions assigned to the object. The file permissions are arranged in three groups of three and grant read, write and execute access to the owner, the owner group and 'the world', respectively. In this context, 'the world' means any (authenticated) user who was not the owner and did not belong to the owner group. When a request by subject s to access object o is received by the operating system, the reference monitor compares the SIDs of s with those of o, to determine which of the three categories the subject belongs to and then checks whether that category has the desired access right associated with it. Hence a file test.exe with owner alice, owner group research and file permissions rwx r-x - - - would permit read, write and execute requests from alice, read and execute requests from any member of the research group, and deny any requests from any other authenticated user.

Unix was developed in the early 1970s as a lightweight and flexible alternative to the rather complicated Multics operating system, developed by MIT, General Electric and Bell Laboratories. Nevertheless, Multics was a very innovative operating system, being the first operating system to provide per-object access control using *access control lists* and the first to implement *multi-level security* as described by the *Bell-LaPadula model* (Bell and LaPadula, 1976).

The Bell-LaPadula model has had an enormous influence on research into access control. It implements an information flow security policy (Denning, 1976) designed to protect the confidentiality of military documents. Every subject and object is associated with a security level. The set of security levels is ordered and the information flow policy prohibits the transfer of information from a high level to a low level. Conceptually, reading information causes an information flow from the object to the subject, whereas writing information causes an information flow from the subject to the object. Hence the information flow policy requires that a subject s can only read an object o if the security level of s is at least as high as that of o, and s can only write to an object o if the security level of o is at least as high as that of s. The second of these requirements seems rather counterintuitive. However, it prevents a classified user, for example, writing classified information to an unclassified printer. It also prevents *Trojan horse* programs running in the context of a classified user from copying classified

Table 15.1   A fragment of an access control matrix.

	test.exe	sample.txt
alice	{r,w,x}	{r}
research	{r,x}	
bob	{x}	{r,w}
staff	{x}	{r}

information to an unclassified file. (A Trojan horse is a program that appears to be benign, but in fact is performing malicious activities without the user's knowledge.)

The Bell-LaPadula model also includes a *protection matrix* or *access control matrix*. The protection matrix was first introduced in Lampson, 1971, and was studied in great detail in Harrison, Ruzzo and Ullman, 1976. These papers remain among the most widely cited in research papers on access control.

The protection matrix is a table whose rows and columns are indexed by (identifiers for) subjects and objects, respectively. An entry in the table indicates what access is permitted by the subject to the object. On receiving a request from subject s to access object o, a reference monitor based on the access control matrix would match the SIDs in the subject's security context with the SIDs in the matrix and then determine whether the requested access rights were contained in the entries for those SIDs and that object. Table 15.1 illustrates a fragment of an access control matrix. Notice that it provides more control over the allocation of access rights to test.exe than is provided by the group-based access control in Unix. For example, we can limit execute access to the group staff, and we can provide read access to bob without making him a member of either the research or staff groups.

Operating systems rarely implement access control using an access control matrix. Typically such matrices would be sparsely populated, and in a system with hundreds of users and thousands of files the matrix would contain millions of entries, making it rather difficult to administer and inefficient to implement. It is more usual to specify an *Access Control List* (ACL) for each object, which is a list of *Access Control Entries* (ACEs). Each ACE specifies a subject and the access rights that subject has for the object. In short, an ACL comprises the non-empty entries in a column of the access control matrix. ACLs continue to be widely used in operating system security and form part of the access control mechanism in Windows 2000 (Solomon and Russinovich, 2000).[2]

3.3 Vulnerabilities and attacks

It is well known that computer security is often undermined by weaknesses (usually referred to as *vulnerabilities*) in a computer system. Most vulnerabilities are due to human error, arising from incorrect program design, poor programming practice, incorrect or incomplete configuration of security features or disregard for security policy. In this section we consider how they can be exploited, how the number of vulnerabilities can be reduced, and how the impact of exploits can be reduced.

Many exploits in recent years have taken advantage of *buffer overflows*. A buffer is an area of computer memory of fixed size that may be used to store user input. If the size of the input is not checked before entering it in the buffer, it is possible for the input to exceed the size of the buffer and overwrite adjacent memory locations. This may simply cause the machine to crash, but far more dangerous are attacks that exploit a buffer overflow in order to redirect the flow of execution.

The stack is a particularly important data structure that is used when a program calls a second program. The stack stores parameters passed to the new program and a *return address*, which identifies the address of the next machine instruction in the calling program enabling the CPU to return control to the appropriate point when the called program has finished executing. If the size of the parameters passed to the called program are not checked, an attacker can engineer a parameter designed to overwrite the return address on the stack (exploiting the buffer overflow) with an address of the attacker's choosing, causing arbitrary attack code to be executed instead of returning control to the calling program.

A comprehensive, albeit rather technical, account of how to exploit stack overflows is given by Aleph One (1996). Buffer overflow vulnerabilities are particularly common in programs written in C and C++. Unfortunately, most commercial operating systems, including Unix and Windows, are written in these languages. Newer programming languages such as Java and C++ have been designed to eradicate some of the programming errors that lead to buffer overflows.

The Internet worm is a famous early example of malicious code which exploited a stack overflow vulnerability in the Unix sendmail program (Spafford, 1989). More recently, the MSBlast worm exploited a buffer overflow in Windows to run a program on the vulnerable machine that then downloaded further attack code. This enabled the infected machine to scan the Internet searching for other vulnerable computers to attack and thus propagate the worm. It should be noted that software vendors regularly release 'patches' that can be applied to protect vulnerable computer systems from malicious code. Countermeasures to the threats posed by malicious code include the installation of firewalls (in order to prevent an attacker using network traffic to probe the computer system for information); the regular patching of systems (in order to replace or repair vulnerable programs); and the installation of anti-virus software (in order to identify and neutralize malicious code).

Inadequate or incorrect input validation may lead to other vulnerabilities in computer software. Many attacks on web-based systems, such as the 'dot dot attack', the 'Unicode exploit' and 'SQL injection attack', make use of the fact that data supplied by a user as input to a web form or as part of a URL are not correctly validated. These vulnerabilities can only be removed by ensuring programmers are aware of the dangers and that they program 'defensively' so that programs only accept input that conforms to certain acceptable patterns.

Many computer systems have a number of default user accounts. It is very easy to obtain the default passwords for many of these accounts from the web.[3] However, a significant number of computer systems are used 'out-of-the-box' leaving powerful administrative accounts with their default passwords, thereby allowing attackers to log on to and take control of a vulnerable system. A simple countermeasure is to rename and to use very strong passwords for such accounts.

An important concept in computer security is the *principle of least privilege* (Saltzer and Schroeder, 1975), which means only giving each user account the minimal set of access rights required by that user. Unfortunately, many computer systems do not obey this principle: default user accounts have too many access rights; ACLs give users access to objects that is not required; and web servers have redundant services running and unused ports open. All of these configuration errors are weaknesses that can be exploited by an experienced attacker. Poor configuration of security-related data structures and poor password policies are known to be responsible for many vulnerabilities in computer systems (Anderson, 2001).

Further details on all types of vulnerabilities and exploits can be found on the CERT web pages.[4] CERT stands for *computer emergency response team* and was formed in 1988 at Carnegie Mellon University, partly as a response to the Internet worm. It provides information about vulnerabilities, exploits and best practice for computer security. There are a number of other organizations offering similar information, including SANS[5] and Bugtraq.[6]

4 Information security in context

It is impossible in a chapter of this length to discuss all the important issues in information security. Indeed, many books of considerable length appear each year and Anderson (2001) and Schneier (2004) both provide accessible accounts of some issues and solutions in information security.

While we began our survey with cryptographic algorithms, it should be clear that these are only a small part of information security. Thankfully the current state of cryptographic research is such that, barring major developments such as factoring large numbers efficiently or the invention of a (functioning) quantum computer, we should feel safe in choosing cryptographic algorithms from the small – but adequate – pool of standardized and trusted algorithms. And once that choice is made, we typically use the algorithm as a black box and show little interest in what goes on inside.

We next provided an introduction to network security, with an emphasis on the security of TCP/IP networks and the Internet. But many topics in network security were not considered in this brief survey. As we hinted, the security of core network infrastructure and naming services such as DNS is an issue of immediate relevance and interest. The security of network management (rather than management of network security) has traditionally been quite poor. We omitted wireless networking technologies such as Bluetooth and IEEE 802.11 standards, as well as mobile telecommunications networks, ranging from the largely insecure first generation, through to GSM and on to third generation networks. Nor did we cover the security issues faced within special purpose networks, such as military, banking and fixed-line telecommunications networks, where the operating environment and threats can be quite different from those on the Internet. The advent of distributed systems technologies such as utility and GRID computing and web services will almost certainly bring additional security issues to light.

Computer security was covered in the final section. The field is so large that it was not possible to consider many issues that arise from poor design and implementation of security protocols and other programs. Many of the vulnerabilities in modern operating systems arise because of the programming language in which those systems are written. Constant patching, new releases of software and changes in modern programming language design mean that fewer program bugs can now be exploited, but the bugs that remain are all potential points of attack. The cost of an effective patch management and anti-virus programme can consume a significant portion of an organization's information security budget.

An area outside the scope of this chapter, yet of great importance, is that of *information security management*. With an effective programme of management in place, an organization can ensure that controls are driven by an *information security policy* developed by an appropriate body after an assessment of the information security *risks* facing the organization. By contrast, if an organization focuses solely on technical security controls, the best it can hope to achieve is an uncoordinated patchwork of countermeasures that may not be adequate or appropriate. Information security management properly encompasses security training and awareness programmes which can be important in combating threats that have no effective technical solution (such as *social engineering* whereby an attacker exploits human behaviour to extract valuable information about an organization or individual). Examples include *phishing attacks* where the attacker combines *spam* e-mail (purporting to come from a victim's bank) and *web spoofing* (creating a fake bank website) to obtain access to consumers' on-line bank accounts.

Looking to the future, the lines between cryptography, network security and computer security are likely to become increasingly blurred. Already, network-reliant applications such as e-mail or peer-to-peer technology have led to difficulties with spam as well as the illegal distribution of copyrighted material (particularly music and video files). Potential solutions to these problems seem to encompass many different technical and legal measures. Indeed, the *Trusted Computing Group* is developing specifications for hardware and software that use cryptographic techniques to provide certain assurances about the integrity of the platform and the software running on it. The *trusted platform module*, which stores hash values of various software components, is expected to become a central hardware component in trusted computing systems. As another example, Web services security is a generic term for a variety of security services designed to protect e-commerce transactions and open up computer systems, in a controlled fashion, over the Internet (Crampton, 2004). These services are based on a number of standards, typically using XML, the *de facto* format for document-based information interchange.

Regardless of future trends in information security, two things are certain: there will always be a need for information security and there will always be people interested in circumventing that security. Information security has come a long way in the last 50 years. While the goal of providing appropriate security is a difficult one to achieve, it is attainable the vast majority of the time. Nevertheless, new techniques will almost certainly be required to ensure that computers, networks, and the data they carry are adequately protected in the years to come.

Notes

1 *Computer Economics* estimated that the 2001 outbreak of the 'I Love You' virus cost global business $8.75 billion.
2 Equally, it is possible to define a *capability list* for each subject, where each entry in the list specifies an object and the access rights the subject has to that object. A capability list comprises the non-empty entries in a row of the access control matrix. Capability lists have been less widely used in commercial operating systems, but there is increasing interest in their use in distributed systems.
3 See http://www.phenoelit.de/dpl/dpl.html, for example.
4 http://www.cert.org/
5 http://www.sans.org/
6 http://www.securityfocus.com/

Key readings

A highly readable and informative survey of cryptography and its place in today's applications is given by Murphy, S. and Piper, F. (2002) *Cryptography: A Very Short Introduction*, Oxford University Press. An excellent resource for those interested in the design and technical foundations of cryptographic algorithms is provided by Menezes, A., Van Oorschot, P. and Vanstone, S. (1996) *The Handbook of Applied Cryptography*, CRC Press. For a general introduction to modern computer networking, Comer, D. (2000) *Internetworking with TCP/IP Vol.1*, 4th Edition, Prentice Hall, is indispensable. A taster of the broad set of concerns in network security can be found in Oppliger, R. (2002) *Internet and Intranet Security*, 2nd edition, Artech House or in Stallings, W. (2002) *Network Security Essentials (International Edition)*, Pearson. A comprehensive introduction to the topic of computer security is provided by Bishop, M. (2003), *Computer Security: Art and Science*, Addison Wesley Professional.

References

Aleph One (1996) 'Smashing the stack for fun and profit', *Phrack Online*. 7(49), File 14 of 16. This article can be found at: http://www.insecure.org/stf/smashstack.txt
Anderson, R. (2001) *Security Engineering: A Guide to Building Dependable Distributed Systems*. New York: Wiley.
Bell, D.E. and LaPadula, L.J. (1976) Secure Computer Systems: Unified Exposition and Multics Interpretation. Mitre Technical Report MTR-2997.
Bishop, M. (2003) *Computer Security: Art and Science*, Boston: Addison Wesley Professional.
Cheswick, W.R., Bellovin, S.M. and Rubin, A.D. (2003) *Firewalls and Internet Security: Repelling the Wily Hacker*, 2nd edn, Boston: Addison Wesley.
Comer, D.E. (2000) *Internetworking with TCP/IP Vol.1*, 4th edn, Upper Saddle River: Prentice Hall.

Crampton, J. (ed.) (2004) 'XML'. *Information Security Technical Report*, 9(3), Elsevier and Royal Holloway.

Denning, D.E. (1976) 'A Lattice Model of Information Flow', *Communications of the ACM*, 19(5), 236–43.

Dierks, T. and Allen, C. (1999) RFC 2246 – The TLS Protocol Version 1.0.

Diffie, W. and Hellman, M. (1976) 'New Directions in Cryptography', *IEEE Transactions on Information Theory*, IT-22(6), 644–54.

Ellis, J.H. (1970) The Possibility of Secure Non-secret Digital Encryption. Available via http://www.cesg.gov.uk.

Harrison, M., Ruzzo, W., and Ullman, J. (1976) 'Protection in Operating Systems', *Communications of the ACM*, 19(8), 461–71.

ISO/IEC 7498-2 (1989) Information processing systems – Open Systems Interconnection – Basic Reference Model – Part 2: Security Architecture.

Kohl, J. and Neuman, C. (1993) RFC 1510 – The Kerberos Network Authentication Service (v5).

Lampson, B. (1971) 'Protection', *Proceedings of the 5th Annual Princeton Conference on Information Sciences and Systems*, pp. 437–43.

Mitchell, C.J. (ed.) (2004) *Security for Mobility*, London: IEE Press.

Menezes, A., van Oorschot, P. and Vanstone, S. (1996) *The Handbook of Applied Cryptography*. Boca Raton: CRC Press.

Murphy, S. and Piper, F. (2002) *Cryptography: A Very Short Introduction*. Oxford: Oxford University Press.

NIST (1997) *The Data Encryption Standard (DES)*. FIPS 46.

NIST (2000) *The Digital Signature Standard (DSS)*. FIPS 186-2. Available via http://csrc.nist.gov/publications/fips/.

NIST (2001a) *The Advanced Encryption Standard (AES)*. FIPS 197. Available via http://www.nist.gov/aes/.

NIST (2001b) Recommendation for Block Cipher Modes of Operation – Methods and Techniques, SP 800-38A. Available via http://csrc.nist.gov/publications/nistpubs/.

NIST (2002a). The Keyed-Hash Message Authentication Code (HMAC). FIPS 198. Available via http://csrc.nist.gov/publications/fips/.

NIST (2002b) *Secure Hash Standard (SHS)*. FIPS 180-2. Available via http://csrc.nist.gov/publications/fips/.

NIST (2004) Recommendation for the Triple Data Encryption Algorithm (TDEA) Block Cipher, SP 800-67. Available via http://csrc.nist.gov/publications/nistpubs/.

Niemi, V. and Nyberg, K. (2003) *UMTS Security*, New York: John Wiley.

Oppliger, R. (2002) *Internet and Intranet Security*, 2nd edn, Boston: Artech House.

Robbins, A. (1999) *UNIX in a Nutshell: System V Edition*, 3rd edn, Cambridge: O'Reilly & Associates.

Rivest, R., Shamir, A. and Adleman, L. (1978) 'A method for obtaining digital signatures and public-key cryptosystems', *Communications of the ACM*, 21(2), 120–6.

Schneier, B. (2004) *Secret and Lies: Digital Security in a Networked World*, New York: Wiley.

Spafford, E. (1989) 'The Internet Worm: Crisis and Aftermath', *Communications of the ACM*, 32(6), 678–87.

Solomon, D.A. and Russinovich, M.A. (2000) *Inside Windows 2000*, 3rd edn, Microsoft Press International.

Saltzer, J.H. and Schroeder, M.D. (1975) 'The protection of information in computer systems', *Proceedings of the IEEE*, 63(9), 1278–308.

Stallings, W. (2002) *Network Security Essentials (International Edition)*, Upper Saddle River: Pearson.

US Department of Defense (1983) *Trusted Computer Systems Evaluation Criteria*. Department of Defense Computer Security Center, Number CSC-STD-001-83. Available at http://www.radium.ncsc.mil/tpep/library/rainbow/5200.28-STD.h

Part III
Security Services

16
The Security Officer

Alison Wakefield

Introduction

What makes the role of the contemporary security officer so fascinating? Internationally, the private security industry has grown remarkably in size and profile so that, for the city dweller, regular contact with security personnel has become almost a daily ritual as one enters and exits one's workplace, seeks directions in a shopping mall, or submits to a baggage or body search when entering a tourist venue or progressing through an airport. We place our trust in those individuals who supervise our office or apartment blocks, employ technologies to survey us as we move through shopping malls and other large complexes, maintain order in the busy social venues we sometimes frequent, or even patrol our neighbourhoods. The visibility and status of security personnel has increased steadily and subtly, so it is important that we know who they are, what they do and why they do it.

The aim of this chapter, therefore, is to illuminate our picture of the contemporary security officer. It is centred around the questions 'how many security officers are there?', 'what do they do?', 'what sorts of people are they?' and 'what are their working conditions like?' It also asks 'what sort of relationship do they have with the police?' in recognition of the security officer's growing involvement in many law enforcement functions. These five questions are responded to in turn, with reference to the international research literature including a recent study by the author.

What is a 'security officer'?

It is helpful first to set out a definition of the term 'security officer'. The private security industry is extremely broad in scope and its 'manned' or 'personnel' sectors encompass a host of services. These include the provision of guards and mobile patrols, private investigators, store detectives, door supervisors ('bouncers'), bodyguards and mercenaries, as well as services such as security consultative work, private custodial services and the transport of cash. The focus of this chapter is those persons supplied by the 'manned guarding' sector of the private security industry, providing uniformed officers to protect distinct territorial areas, as well as those 'in-house' operatives fulfilling similar security roles as employees of the end user organizations. A definition provided by the international professional security association ASIS International offers further clarification of the term, seen to refer to:

> An individual ... employed part or full time, in uniform or plain clothes, hired to protect the employing party's assets, ranging from human lives to physical property (the premises and contents). The definition excludes individuals who are not employed in the capacity of a security officer. (2004: 10)

The emphasis on assets as opposed to territories within this definition better reflects private security's explicit connection with organizational loss prevention. In excluding individuals not officially employed as security personnel, it also signifies a clear functional separation from those occupational roles in which security functions are undertaken but do not constitute the defining aspects of the work, as in the case of caretakers and receptionists for example.

How many security officers are there?

Attempts to calculate the number of security officers operating internationally have been inconsistent, although they remain useful in demonstrating the global scale of the manned guarding sector, and the size of countries' security industries in relation to their populations. They also allow for national comparisons with the numbers of police officers employed in each country, giving a sense of the extent to which security personnel are engaging in law enforcement functions. Although ratios of police officers to security officers in different nations are not provided in this chapter, readers may wish to consult the recent EU-wide estimates produced by CoESS and UNI-Europa (2004), readily available on the web.

To date, the most extensive contribution to the global measurement of the manned guarding sector has been the work of de Waard (1999). Reporting findings from an international survey undertaken in 1997, he compared various features of the industry in 27 countries, including its personnel. While advising that his figures should be seen as approximations rather than exact measures, taking account of the measurement problems associated with a lack of official industry data and functional diversification within the industry into areas other than simply 'security', de Waard estimated that in 1996 some 592,050 security officers were operating across the 15 member states making up the European Union (EU) at that time. He found that security personnel were most prevalent in the United Kingdom, with 275 personnel per 100,000 inhabitants, translating into one security officer for every 364 citizens. This compared with one officer per 5184 citizens in Greece at the other end of the scale, in which the average ratio across the EU was one security officer per 1028 citizens.

Subsequent EU studies have produced different findings, however. When comparing de Waard's (1999) research with a study of the 15 member states by the

Institut des Sciences du Travail (2003), and a survey of the expanded EU (25 states as of 1 May 2004) by CoESS and UNI-Europa, the estimated total numbers of security personnel are reasonably consistent for some of those states (Austria, Germany, Italy, Luxembourg and the United Kingdom). Yet there are wild variations between the three surveys in the estimates relating to other countries and particularly Greece, with its one security officer per 428 citizens according to CoESS and UNI-Europa representing a marked difference to de Waard's estimate. In the CoESS and UNI-Europa survey (2004), the estimate for the UK of one security officer per 401 citizens is just a little above the average for the newly expanded EU – one security officer per 497 citizens – suggesting that the UK may not be as heavy a user of private security personnel as de Waard had previously indicated.

Variations between the three surveys in the *total* number of security officers working in EU countries are less extreme. These figures, which relate to the 15 states making up the EU before its expansion, range from 592,050 in 1996/97 (de Waard, 1999), to 709,875 in 2002 (based on Institut des Sciences du Travail, 2003) and 733,010 in 2004 (based on CoESS and UNI-Europa, 2004). The estimated total for the whole EU (covering all 25 states), according to CoESS and UNI-Europa, is 1,008,550.

Also of interest is the contrast between the EU picture and that of certain new world countries as identified by de Waard (1999). Calculations of the ratio of citizens per security officer based on de Waard's figures show a much greater prevalence of security personnel in Canada in which, he estimated, there is one officer for every 231 citizens; and in Australia, the US and South Africa for which the ratios were respectively one to 194, 172 and 111. Only New Zealand was found to have a higher ratio, of one officer to approximately 652 citizens.

The vast discrepancies between the three surveys indicate that the figures need to be treated with great caution. The reasons for the differences are likely to include not only a lack of official industry data and functional differentiation within the 'manned' security industry as highlighted by de Waard, but also the absence of a standard definition of the industry to take account of such counting dilemmas as whether to include or exclude the 'in-house' security sector or the management personnel. The different counting rules employed in the three surveys render any comparisons between them almost meaningless, so they can provide no sense of the growth in the number of security personnel from 1996/97 (the reference date of de Waard's data) onwards. The considerable size of the security industry internationally, however, is indisputable, and the estimate by CoESS and UNI-Europa (2004) of the total number of security personnel operating across the EU is evidence of a powerful international industry and the fact that security personnel are now a common feature of most countries' systems of order maintenance and protection.

Many reasons have been put forward for the security industry's expanding size and profile, and a pan-European study by Cortese *et al.* (2003) set out a number of reasons for the sector's considerable growth across Europe. These were seen to include increased safety concerns on the part of companies, public institutions and private individuals; the expansion of privately controlled, publicly accessible spaces ranging from hypermarkets to airports; public spending restrictions leading to increased outsourcing of non-core tasks to the private sector; and a general growth in the sub-contracting of security functions within both the public and private sectors. In a global society that is increasingly preoccupied by risk, there is no reason why such trends – and the industry's global expansion – should not continue.

What do security officers do?

The development of the security industry has included the emergence of new and increasingly sophisticated opportunities for security personnel, so that the security officer's role is no longer synonymous with that of the night-watch guard which epitomized private security after the Second World War. There has been a rapid expansion, for example, in security positions which bring officers into continuous contact with the public, or which require sufficient levels of technological competence for officers to be entrusted with operating increasingly advanced closed circuit television (CCTV) and other electronic security systems.

There is, therefore, considerable variation in security roles between jurisdictions, markets and clients or employers. According to Cortese *et al.* (2003), three of the EU countries (Belgium, Spain and the Netherlands) in their study have adopted a functional grouping of security roles for the purpose of setting national wage scales, and this illustrates the diversity of positions. The groupings used in the Netherlands, for example, include 'valuable objects guard/receptionist', 'mobile surveillance guard', 'in-store security guard' and 'control centre operative'. Research studies which refer to the various tasks undertaken by security personnel have tended to focus on particular functional groupings rather than those tasks applying across the industry as a whole (e.g. McManus, 1995 and Rigakos, 2002, in relation to neighbourhood security; Shapland, 1999 and Wakefield, 2003, on the security of shopping malls and other publicly accessible spaces under private control; and Gill, 2004, with regard to uniformed store detectives).

One exception, however, is the Canadian study undertaken by Shearing *et al.* in 1980, whose survey of 10,338 security officers provided a detailed account of the day-to-day responsibilities of security personnel in a wide range of roles. Common security functions across a range of client sites, such as office buildings, warehouses, shops, shopping centres, educational establishments and residential complexes, included foot patrol, the screening and/or escorting of visitors and traffic control. Their roles were found also to include responding to problems, whether these were of a criminal or non-criminal nature, and caused by human or natural factors; report-writing; and non-security tasks including rubbish disposal, snow-shovelling, flag-raising, general maintenance and administering first aid (Shearing *et al.*, 1980). The authors noted of the latter, 'These tasks fall to the security guard not because they are regarded as security tasks, but because the security guard can conveniently undertake them, because he is present in a situation requiring this skill' (1980: 170).

My research (detailed in Wakefield, 2003) uncovered a similar diversity of duties, and attempted to situate them in a functional framework. The study included an investigation of the functions of security personnel within three privately controlled, publicly accessible leisure venues in England: a cultural centre (the 'Arts Plaza'), a shopping mall (the 'Quayside Centre') and a retail and leisure complex (the 'City Mall'). In these centres, the teams of security personnel fulfilled a broad set of functions whereby they effectively 'governed' the privately controlled territories according to the expectations and standards of their organizational clients, simultaneously acting as caretaker, police officer, public relations representative and perhaps more. Six core security functions, common to all three sites, were identified, described as 'housekeeping', 'customer care', 'preventing crime and anti-social behaviour', 'enforcing rules and administering sanctions', 'responding to emergencies and offences in progress', and 'gathering and sharing information'. The limitations of the analysis are that it does not provide a weighting to the functions and tasks, either in relation to the proportion of officers' time devoted to them, or the priority afforded to the tasks by their clients, managers or the officers themselves. The analysis does, however, offer a detailed picture of security work in three settings, as well as a functional breakdown that offers a means of comparing the findings from other studies.

Thus, in Table 16.1 the security tasks set out by Wakefield (2003) are compared with the key training areas for security personnel recently recommended by the Security Industry Authority for England and Wales after a period of consultation with the industry and its clients (SIA, 2004), as well as three other research studies. These studies are concerned respectively with store detectives (Brough and Brown, 1989), retail security (Gill, 2004) and assorted security roles in one London borough located at a market, supermarkets, shopping centres, colleges, pubs, nightclubs and a residential neighbourhood (Jones and Newburn, 1998).

The security officers' 'housekeeping' duties, as identified by Wakefield (2003), afforded them a central role in the day-to-day upkeep of the three centres in the study. The purpose was to maintain the fabric of the buildings, to ensure that the centres operated safely and smoothly, and in so doing, to promote a pleasant and well-kept environment that would encourage members of the public to visit. Such duties included monitoring the centres for safety risks such as the threat of fire or flood (through foot patrols and the monitoring of CCTV systems), closing windows, reporting spillages and storing keys. Preventing corporate losses by maintaining a safe environment was the key objective behind these housekeeping duties, exemplified in the emphasis on fire safety highlighted by Brough and Brown (1989), Jones and Newburn (1998) and Gill (2004), and the priority afforded to health and safety guidance in the training curriculum proposed by the SIA (2004).

'Customer care' duties were seen by Wakefield (2003) to be carried out in the interests of public relations, with the security officers usually acting as the first point of contact for customers needing assistance. Common requests related to

Table 16.1 A functional breakdown of security roles

	Brough and Brown (1989) Store detectives	Jones and Newburn (1998) Assorted security roles	Wakefield (2003) Security of leisure venues	Gill (2004) Retail security officers	SIA (2004) Recommended training topics
Housekeeping	• Prevention of losses from carelessness, fire, poor safety policies and/or outdated or inoperative alarm systems	• Performing fire safety checks	• Foot patrols • Storage and control of keys • Energy-saving e.g. turning off lights • Keeping access roads clear • Reporting of breakages and hazards • Deployment of cleaning and maintenance staff • Performing fire drills • Control of background music • Management of car park and collection of payments • Setting up and dismantling of displays	• Testing fire alarms • Ensuring empty boxes are flat packed • Checking rubbish bins	• Health and safety at work
Customer care		• Staffing entrance booths and taking money from customers • Giving first aid • Assisting with inquiries such as directions	• Provision of information, in person or by public address • Recording and storage of lost and found property • Reception duties • Stewarding of special events	• Finding and reuniting lost children	• Customer care and social skills

389

Table 16.1 A functional breakdown of security roles – *continued*

	Brough and Brown (1989)	Jones and Newburn (1998)	Wakefield (2003)	Gill (2004)	SIA (2004)
	Store detectives	**Assorted security roles**	**Security of leisure venues**	**Retail security officers**	**Recommended training topics**
Preventing crime and anti-social behaviour	• Preventing crimes such as shoplifting, internal theft and cheque fraud • Surveillance of offenders • Seeking out dishonest employees	• Locking and unlocking gates and doors • Access control • Foot patrol • Vehicle patrol • CCTV monitoring • Undercover surveillance • Dispersing crowds of youths • Routine searching of customers on entry	• Provision of wheelchairs to customers • Dressing as Centre mascot • Responding to other customer requests • Foot patrols and maintaining a visible presence • Locking and unlocking of premises • Reporting/securing insecure tenant property • Access control • Setting and unsetting of alarms • CCTV monitoring • Cash escort duties • VIP protection	• Opening and closing stores • Patrolling shop floor • Providing visible presence • Guarding entrances and exits • Checking goods match receipts • Identifying and reporting of suspicious staff • Conducting staff searches • CCTV monitoring • Checking tagging equipment • Carrying out perimeter checks	• Patrolling • Access control • Searching • Security systems

Table 16.1 A functional breakdown of security roles – *continued*

	Brough and Brown (1989)	Jones and Newburn (1998)	Wakefield (2003)	Gill (2004)	SIA (2004)
	Store detectives	Assorted security roles	Security of leisure venues	Retail security officers	Recommended training topics
Enforcing rules and administering sanctions	• Reporting to management regarding lax store policies	• Enforcing rules against smoking, noise, inappropriate attire • Enforcing parking regulations • Ejecting banned people	• Asking people to desist from 'anti-social' behaviour • Exclusion of persons from the centres • Imposition of bans or injunctions	• Ejecting undesirables/ banned people	• Conflict management
Responding to emergencies and offences in progress	• Dealing with people who are emotionally disturbed, under the influence of alcohol or drugs, violent or carrying weapons • Arresting offenders	• Responding to calls for assistance • Responding to alarm activations • Guiding emergency services • Responding to criminal incidents, including arrest and detention of offenders	• Responding to fire and burglar alarms • Evacuating building • Summoning of and liaison with emergency services • Provision of first aid/ alerting ambulance • Arresting offenders • Searching for lost children • Responding to abandoned bags/suspicious packages • Responding to incidents of nuisance behaviour • Responding to other non-crime incidents • Responding to crime incidents or security risks	• Assisting with conflict/violent situations • Assisting with bomb evacuation • Attending to activated alarms	• Emergency systems • Emergencies • Conflict management

Table 16.1 A functional breakdown of security roles – *continued*

	Brough and Brown (1989) Store detectives	Jones and Newburn (1998) Assorted security roles	Wakefield (2003) Security of leisure venues	Gill (2004) Retail security officers	SIA (2004) Recommended training topics
Gathering and sharing information	• Seizing and preserving exhibits • Preparing reports for police and court officials • Presenting evidence and exhibits in court • Maintaining a filing system • Liaising with police, courts and other agencies	• Initial investigation of crimes including gathering evidence • Reporting offences under by-laws • Joint operations with the police	• CCTV monitoring • Form-filling • Security networks within the centres • Informal liaison with the police • Providing information to police investigations	• Investigating and detecting malpractice	• Communications and reporting
Other	• Employee education/training				

the provision of directions around the centres, information about events or details of opening times, the taking note of complaints, or the arranging or administering of first aid. Customer care responsibilities such as providing first aid, giving directions and looking for lost children were also described by Jones and Newburn (1998) and Gill (2004), but were not identified in Brough and Brown's (1989) research on the role of the plain clothes store detective. The perceived importance of customer care skills is indicated in the SIA (2004) report.

According to Wakefield (2003), the officers' duties in 'preventing crime and anti-social behaviour' were fulfilled by means of proactive patrols and CCTV monitoring. They maintained the security of the centres by ensuring that doors and windows were locked as appropriate, controlling the access of people and vehicles to certain areas of the centres, escorting employees who were carrying cash, and remaining vigilant to the threat of terrorism by being alert to abandoned packages and bags. The officers also monitored the centre visitors for potential criminal and anti-social behaviour, targeting persons thought to be behaving in an 'anti-social' manner, those who fitted 'risk profiles' in their manner or appearance, and those considered to be 'known offenders'. The studies by Brough and Brown (1989), Jones and Newburn (1998) and Gill (2004) identified a similar range of duties, showing the emphasis placed on surveillance by means of foot patrol and CCTV monitoring. Relevant training needs identified by the SIA (2004) included the topics of patrolling, access control, searching of persons and vehicles and operating security systems.

The officers observed by Wakefield (2003) became involved in 'enforcing rules and administering sanctions' in circumstances when visitors to the centres were seen to be behaving in ways that might discourage the custom of other visitors. Their approach was to ask visitors to desist from the behaviour that was causing offence, and if they failed to comply, to insist that they leave the property (resorting to assistance from the police if the visitors refused to leave). According to the other three studies, the sorts of rules found to be enforced by security personnel included restrictions on smoking and noise by college students, on the attire of pub/nightclub customers, or on parking (Jones and Newburn, 1998), and adherence to company security policies by staff (Brough and Brown, 1989). Furthermore, both Jones and Newburn (1998) and Gill (2004) noted that the retail security officers in their studies became involved in ejecting banned individuals from premises. The SIA (2004) recommend training in conflict management for security officers in recognition of the fact that such roles may require officers to confront members of the public about unacceptable forms of behaviour.

Wakefield (2003) found that 'responding to emergencies or offences in progress' occurred when criminal incidents and non-criminal emergencies had been identified by means of surveillance by the security staff or through reports from visitors, other centre employees or staff from the tenant companies. The most common offence type was theft, followed by public order problems of varying degrees of severity. Non-criminal emergencies that were observed during the research included four (false) fire alarms, a small fire, several water leaks, discoveries of unattended packages and bags (treated as potential terrorist threats) and a number of occasions when first-aid was administered to patrons who had been taken ill on the premises, or ambulances were summoned. The findings reported by Brough and Brown (1989), Jones and Newburn (1998) and Gill (2004) similarly reflected the variety of criminal and non-criminal emergencies that a security officer might be called upon to deal with, including evacuations of premises due to bomb threats or alarm activations. Appropriately, the SIA (2004) recommend training in emergency systems, dealing with emergencies as well as the conflict management skills already mentioned.

The term 'gathering and sharing information' was adopted by Wakefield (2003) to encompass five related duties: CCTV monitoring, form-filling, participating in security networks, engaging in informal liaison with the police and providing information to police investigations. By recording information about incidents, the officers ensured that evidence was available if needed in the future; and in their exchange of information the security personnel and local police officers were able to co-ordinate their activities and enhance the quality of their working relationships. The studies by Brough and Brown (1989), Jones and Newburn (1998) and Gill (2004) noted similar duties but placed a particular emphasis on investigation and evidence gathering. The training curriculum recommended by the SIA (2004) takes account of these duties in its recommendations for instruction in communications and reporting.

Taking account of the vast range of security duties, as outlined in Table 16.1, Shearing and Stenning (1981) see 'surveillance' as being the central characteristic of security work, and the functional breakdown presented in this analysis supports their observation. In the research by Wakefield (2003) the security officers' foot patrol and CCTV surveillance duties placed them at the centre of social life within their organizations, and their continuous presence ensured that they were ready to respond quickly to any safety breaches or emergencies, requests for assistance by the public, or incidents of criminal or anti-social behaviour. These duties also illustrate very clearly the prominence that the contemporary security officer has achieved within public life, with the required skill levels indicating how far security roles have developed from that of the post-war nightwatchman.

What sorts of people are they?

With security personnel now carrying out such prominent roles as those detailed by Jones and Newburn (1988) and Wakefield (2003), it is useful to know something about the types of people in whom such trust is placed. The most detailed studies to date relate to security personnel in Canada (Farnell and Shearing, 1977; Shearing *et al.*, 1980; Erickson, 1993; Rigakos, 2002), the United States (Kakalik and Wildhorn, 1971), Singapore (Nalla and Hoffman, 1996) and Britain (Michael, 1999; Wakefield, 2003). Their findings are reviewed with respect to three categories: personal characteristics, working backgrounds and aspirations.

Personal characteristics

A survey of security officers conducted in the United States in the 1970s presented an unfavourable picture of the industry's personnel:

> The typical private guard is an aging white male who is poorly educated and poorly paid. His average age is between 40 and 55; he has had little education beyond the ninth grade; he has had a few years of experience in private security; he earns a marginal wage ... and often works 48 to 56 hours a week to make ends meet. (Kakalik and Wildhorn, 1971, vol. II: 67)

The personnel of the Singaporean security industry displayed similar characteristics, according to Nalla and Hoffman (1996). They found that only 13 percent of the 271 security officers in their sample were 40 years of age or younger, with two-thirds aged 51 or older, and only 3 percent found to be female. The educational level was variable: 23 percent of respondents had been educated only to primary level, 71 percent had gained a secondary education, and 1 percent had attended university.

The earlier research of Shearing *et al.* (1980) on the security industry in Canada presented a more positive picture. Comparing data collected in 1976 with findings from a similar survey undertaken in 1971 (Farnell and Shearing, 1977), the researchers found that the security officers in their sample reflected a broad spread of ages in which 54 percent were aged 40 years or younger, the average age having fallen to 38 from 51; and 9 percent of officers were female compared with 3 percent in 1971. Many of the Canadian security officers were well-educated: 45 percent had completed or gone beyond high school education (compared with 29 percent in 1971), and some of the more educated were recent immigrants or students working part-time. Shearing *et al.* found evidence of major change within the industry between 1971 and 1976, and predicted that if these trends continued, the workforce of contract security by the mid-1980s would be very different from the picture painted by the Rand Corporation. They did not, however, conduct a further follow-up study.

In his study of a Canadian security firm called 'Intelligarde', Rigakos (2002) found that a typical officer in the company was a young, white male with some college training in law enforcement or security and just under two years of security experience. The average age of an Intelligarde officer was found to be 26.2, contrasting with the mean age among Toronto security officers of 37 found by Erickson (1993); and 77 percent of Intelligarde staff were found to have been born in Canada, with the second most common country of birth being Jamaica (4 percent). On the matter of gender, Rigakos found that 92 percent of the Intelligarde staff were male, contrasting with Erickson's figure of 66 percent. Rigakos hypothesized that the high proportion of male officers at Intelligarde may have been due to the dangerous nature of the work, the macho culture it cultivated, or general recruiting practices. Finally, Rigakos found that nearly 70 percent of the Intelligarde officers were enrolled in, or had completed college law enforcement or criminal justice training; and 67 percent had (or were close to receiving) college diplomas or university degrees. Nearly 10 percent had been to university.

In my study of three leisure venues in England (Wakefield, 2003), the overall sample reflected a broad range of age groups, with the youngest officers at each site aged in their late teens or early twenties and the oldest in their sixties. The spread of ages was most even at the Quayside Centre, while the majority of security officers at the Arts Plaza were under 30 years of age, and those at the City Mall were over 30 years of age in all but one case. The proportion of female security officers employed at the three sites was also variable: at the Arts Plaza, ten out of the 28 officers (35.7 percent) were women, including one inspector and one control room operator. Three female officers were employed at the Quayside Centre (12.5 percent), with one holding the rank of supervisor, while no women were employed as security officers at the City Mall.

The security officers were British in all cases at the Quayside Centre, and in all but one case in the City Mall team, which included a Hungarian officer. The Arts Plaza security team, by contrast, comprised 14 South Africans, ten Britons, two Zimbabweans and one Moroccan. Many of the South African security officers had chosen to work in the security industry as a stop-gap prior to travelling round the world, and had heard through word-of-mouth of the contract security company that employed them. Finally, while the officers' levels of educational attainment were not investigated, questioning about their working backgrounds revealed that three of the South African security officers interviewed at the Arts Plaza had studied for university degrees.

Working backgrounds

Several studies have explored the extent to which security officers had prior experience in security, the armed forces and the police. In Britain, Michael (1999) interviewed 50 officers and found that 33 (66 percent) had previously worked in one or more of these professions. Specifically, six security officers had work experience in the police service, six had been members of the army, six had experience in the navy and seven had served in the Royal Air Force. In Singapore, by contrast, just 10 percent had prior military experience, and 28 percent had prior law enforcement experience (Nalla and Hoffman, 1996), and an even lower proportion (22.8 percent) of the officers in Rigakos' (2002) Canadian study had backgrounds in the policing or military sectors. In a small survey undertaken in Saudi Arabia among security officers employed by banks (de Jong, 2002), it was found that, of the 22 officers who answered the question on their previous job, three had come from the armed forces, whereas the remainder had joined directly from school (8), been unemployed (5), or worked in one of an assortment of other jobs (6) including a shepherd, a taxi driver and a salesman.

My research (Wakefield, 2003) took account of the security officers' lengths of service as well as their working backgrounds. At the beginning of the two-month research periods at each centre, just one officer in a team of 24 at the Quayside Centre, and one officer in a team of ten at the City Mall, had less than six months' service, while the new joiners at the Arts Plaza numbered six out of a team of 28. During the research periods, seven officers resigned from the Arts Plaza, and six were appointed in their place while another returned from extended leave; and two officers resigned from the Quayside Centre, one of whom was replaced. The higher turnover of staff at the Arts Plaza was due in part to the contract security company's recruitment of South Africans who chose to work temporarily in security to finance their world travel, as well as the larger size of the team at the Plaza, although it is recognized that staff turnover levels in contract security are typically high. According to the security manager at the Plaza, '... someone will move around [the industry] for an extra two pence per hour'.

A number of officers at the three sites had worked for their employers for many years. One officer at the Arts Plaza had been employed there for 26 years, while two had seven years' service. Two of the contract security staff at the Quayside Centre had been employed there for eight and nine years respectively, and one of the in-house security staff had served for nine years. The City Mall security team included one officer with ten years' service, two who had served for 24 years and one who had been there for 26 years. With only ten security officers working at the City Mall, the proportion of long-serving officers was considerable, once again highlighting the lower turnover of its in-house team. More typically, however, the security officers had been employed at their respective sites for less than two years.

The career backgrounds of the security officers were wide-ranging. Nine of the security officers who were interviewed had prior experience of working in security: three at the Arts Plaza, two at the Quayside Centre and three at the City Mall. Just two of the interviewed officers, based at the Arts Plaza and City Mall, had served in the armed forces (although three of those who had declined to be interviewed also had military backgrounds – one based at the Quayside Centre and two at the City Mall). Many of the officers had previously worked in other 'unskilled' roles, ranging from factory work to waitering, retail and cleaning. Some officers had been employed in skilled manual roles, including joinery, mechanics and case making; and a number had held managerial positions in such fields as the gold mining, pub and funerals trades.

Aspirations

Rigakos (2002) identified a 'wannabe' culture within Intelligarde. In other words, the officers in his study were seen to be striving for 'professional and well-paying careers in public law enforcement' (p. 104). Almost all were 'young, energetic, and eager to be hired by public policing agencies', factors which instilled 'a sense of collective purpose' whereby 'everyone wants law enforcement experience' (p. 126).

In my study (Wakefield, 2003) there appeared to be four main reasons why the officers had chosen to work in security: money, redundancy, familiarity with the work or an interest in the job. One officer at the Arts Plaza reported, 'most of them look at it short term. They're here for the money.' Despite modest hourly wages, working in security provided an opportunity to save money as a result of the long working hours and overtime opportunities. This, combined with the international strength of the UK pound, had attracted the South African back-packers at the Arts Plaza to the job, as one of them reported: 'they told us it's best to be in security because it's long hours, seven days a week. You can get as much work, as many hours on the one side and on the other side you haven't got time off to spend all your money'.

Two officers, one at the Arts Plaza and the other at the Quayside Centre, had moved into security after periods of redundancy. The latter recounted: 'I was actually made redundant ... when they closed the factory ... I applied thinking I was a bit too old for it but I wasn't, got the job, two years later I'm still here'. Three officers had applied to the City Mall after previous experience of security roles. It was likely that previous experience of security-related roles also accounted for the movement of ex-armed forces personnel into the industry, although since most of the ex-forces officers were among those who had not con-sented to be interviewed, their reasons for choosing to work in security were not explored.

At the Quayside Centre, more of the staff described the nature of the work itself as having attracted them to their roles. One officer described the work as, 'bit of a challenge ... meet loads of new people', and a colleague reported similar reasons for his attraction to the job: 'it was something new. I enjoyed it ... nice to meet loads of people ...'. Another officer from the Centre who lacked the qualifications for joining the police explained: 'It's something like the police, ain't it, and you're still dealing with crime – I don't like sitting down all day'.

A recent Canadian study (Taylor-Butts, 2004) found a fairly even spread of ages working in the industry, with a much higher percentage of personnel under the age of 25 and over the age of 54 than was typical in public policing; as well as discovering that women had a higher representation in private security than public policing, making up around 25 percent of security personnel but only 17 percent of police officers. Educational differentials were also apparent: 96 percent of police officers had attained at least a high school diploma, com-pared with 76 percent of security officers, and 55 percent of police officers had completed a college certificate/diploma or university degree, compared with 28 percent of security officers.

Thus to summarize, recent studies seem to suggest that there is no 'typical' security officer, challenging the depiction of a stereotypical 'aging white male' presented by Kakalik and Wildhorn (1971). Research findings by Rigakos (2002), Wakefield (2003) and Taylor-Butts (2004) suggest that stereotypes of unskilled, uneducated security personnel may have become less relevant as the industry has moved into more demanding and prominent areas of work.

What are their working conditions like?

Having focused on the types of people working in security roles, a fuller sense of the experience of working in security as well as the quality of service likely to be provided can be gained from exploring the remuneration, working hours and training that are typical within the industry. Although a sense of what is 'typical', particularly with respect to training provisions, is not particularly clear in relation to the limited body of literature available, there remain some useful literature sources to consider.

Pay and conditions

Shearing *et al.*, writing in 1980, discovered that pay levels in security remained low despite growing skill levels. The average hourly wage paid to security officers at the time of their research was found to be $3.10, with many reporting earning the minimum wage at that time of $2.65, and their benefits were reported scarcely to exceed those required in law. In Britain, although there has been no detailed research into security officers' pay and conditions, the Low Pay Unit has campaigned about the levels of pay for security staff (Williams *et al.*, 1984). South (1988) argued that, with its low pay levels and the anti-social and long hours of the shift system, the private security industry is unlikely to attract high-calibre employees. As he explained, the intensely competitive nature of the market makes the problem difficult to fix, as pay levels are driven down in a market where the major costs are the wage bills, and hours remain long because two 12-hour shifts in 24 hours are more cost-effective than three shifts of eight hours. Consequently, the industry suffers an ongoing problem of high turnover (Kakalik and Wildhorn, 1971; Wiles and McClintock, 1972; Shearing *et al.*, 1980; South, 1988).

My research (Wakefield, 2003) was conducted before the implementation in the UK of EU Working Time Regulations and the National Minimum Wage. For the security officers in the study, their earnings were low and their hours were long. The hourly wages of the security staff at the Arts Plaza at the time of the case studies was £5.11, while at the Quayside Centre, the contract security staff and in-house security staff received £3.50 and around £5.00 respectively. The wage at the City Mall was £5.10, and the staff received 50 percent additional pay for each hour of overtime and 100 percent extra for hours worked on public holidays. Officers at each of the centres reported that their wage rates exceeded local averages for the security industry, however.

There were no fringe benefits for contract security officers. The director from the security company employed at the Arts Plaza acknowledged:

> ... until the individual reaches or completes his first year, his terms and conditions of employment don't really improve that much. I am talking about holiday pay and so on – you are working in an industry where there is no sick pay or guaranteed sick pay. We all base ourselves on, and I speak for the majority here, statutory sick pay conditions ...

At the City Mall, by contrast, the higher pay levels were supplemented by sick pay, three weeks' paid holiday, free parking, company pension arrangements and shares in the company after a year's service. It was likely that these generous provisions, far from typical of the British security industry, were a key factor in the low turnover of staff at the Mall and the long service of some of the officers.

The shift systems varied between the three research sites. Most of the security officers at the Arts Plaza performed 12-hour day and night shifts with shift changes at 7 am and 7 pm, working an average of 60 hours per week. In addition, a number of officers covered the opening hours on 11 am to 11 pm shifts, working up to seven days a week. Many of the security officers on the day shift were the transient workers, seeking to save as much money as possible, and usually grateful for the extra shifts. At the Quayside Centre, the security officers who patrolled the malls worked an average of 50 hours per week made up of ten- and 12-hour shifts. The control room staff worked fewer hours per week, with the supervisor working a 40-hour week of eight to four shifts, and his two colleagues performing blocks of five 12-hour day shifts (averaging 42 hours a week according to one of the control room staff). A contract security officer from the night shift team looked after the control room outside the opening hours of the Centre. At the City Mall, the four officers on the day shift worked 40-hour weeks and took turns in carrying out additional Sunday shifts, while the night security officers performed 13-hour shifts in three-day blocks interspersed with three rest days, working an average of 40 hours a week. There was, therefore, a marked difference in the total working hours of the security officers at the three sites, with the in-house staff at the Quayside Centre and City Mall working considerably fewer hours than their counterparts in contract security.

The survey by Cortese *et al.* (2003) reveals marked differences in average working times between the six EU countries in the study. This was due to variations in the weekly working time ranging from 35 hours in France to 48 hours in the UK, the establishment of daily and weekly maximums in some countries such as Belgium (12 hours and 60 hours respectively) or Spain (9 hours), and strict limits on overtime being applied in certain countries including Spain (80 hours a year), the Netherlands (176 hours a year) and France (180 hours a year). The report found 12-hour shifts to be the most common work period for security officers, however, which remained the most practical solution in view of the round-the-clock nature of guarding operations. The CoESS and UNI-Europa (2004) study provides a more detailed breakdown of daily, weekly and overtime maximums for all 25 EU member states. It finds the UK security market to be one of the least regulated in this respect with average working hours in the industry exceeding 60 per week, and overtime regularly being worked across all sectors of the industry.

Recent research from the United States provides evidence of poor pay at a time when the country's emphasis on security has never been greater. Parfomak (2004) reports that contract security officer annual salaries averaged $19,400 in 2003, less than half the average salary for the police. A study of 100 security officers in New York (Gotbaum, 2005) revealed a variation in wages from the federal minimum of $5.15 to $16.25 per hour, with an average of $9.86.

Training

Little has been written about the training of private security personnel. Writing in 1980, Shearing *et al.* noted that in the Canadian industry formal training was limited, although they found that security officers themselves largely believed that their training was adequate. As many security jobs were found to involve only basic skills such as talking, reading and writing, Shearing and his colleagues argued that there appeared to be no need for more that a brief period of orientation for new officers, while conceding that they had not taken account of client perspectives on training requirements. Clearly, the security market has changed considerably since the publication of their findings, however, with security personnel fulfilling so many new areas of responsibility. In the UK, for example, this has been recognized in the establishment of a 'Sector Skills Strategy Group' by the new Security Industry Authority, tasked with undertaking a comprehensive consultation with the industry relating to training and skills requirements as well as overall standards, and taking account of new legislation in the form of the Police Reform Act 2002 which offers scope for limited new powers to be conferred on security personnel within police-run accreditation schemes.

In my study (Wakefield, 2003), there was a considerable difference in the training fulfilled by the security personnel supplied by contract security companies, and those employed in-house, since the officers from the contract security firms were required to follow the training curriculum laid down in BS7499. This involved two days' classroom training, and two days' instruction at the client site. A director of the security company employed at the Quayside Centre described the content of the training curriculum:

> [they cover] the notebooks, incident reports, the basics of law, powers of arrest ... the on-site training is local knowledge of the centre, obviously the people, radio procedures ... handling lost and found property, health and safety ... the various forms that they use ... the car park situation, the fire fighting, vehicle log, the radio codes ... This is all the law at the back, squatters, trespass, indecency offences, crimes of violence, arson, criminal damage, use of force ... and so on. And the emergency procedures, the fire rendezvous, the areas of evacuation for bombs or fires ... the different types of extinguishers ...

The scope of the training, covering a wide range of procedures, form-filling and the basics of law, illustrated the breadth of responsibility held by the security officers. With a minimum of four days devoted to training, and an established curriculum that covered all of the areas identified as being essential by the industry's major professional associations in conjunction with the BSI, it was evident that new contract security staff received a basic grounding in a standard set of core skills before they were permitted to work alone at their client sites. The quality of the programmes was, however, not evaluated as part of the research.

By contrast, the in-house security team at the City Mall were trained by their colleagues while working, in practices and procedures that had been developed on site, and were not associated with any formal industry standards. One officer described the nature and format of the training: 'I was already qualified as far as they were concerned, but there was three months' probation, learning cameras

... keys, alarm code settings, control of the general public ...'. A colleague reported:

> ... you are expected to use your common sense ... I went straight onto nights. I was shown the alarms, etcetera by [the supervisor] at 6pm. Also the two other lads you work with show you what to do for a month, and you work the 6pm shift for that time with the other lads bringing you up on the CCTV ...

The in-house control room staff at the Quayside Centre had also trained 'on the job'. One officer who had been the first person appointed to work in the control room, reported, 'I received, if not none, very little [training]. You know, mine was self-taught ... I was in a position that I was here when all the systems were being put in'. His colleague confirmed, 'It was ongoing, actually, 'cause I got flung in the deep end'.

The research also revealed how, in the case of the two contract security teams in the study, formal training requirements were exceeded through the provision of additional courses run by the client organizations. At the Arts Plaza and the Quayside Centre, the majority of officers had completed courses in customer care, and several officers at each of the two centres had achieved basic first aid qualifications. Other initiatives included fire prevention training at the Arts Plaza, and disability awareness courses at the Quayside Centre. Future plans to develop training in legal powers, with the assistance of local police officers, were also reported at both centres.

A further dimension to the training provision at the Arts Plaza, in this case sponsored by the contract security company which employed the officers, was the provision for longer serving officers to undertake National Vocational Qualifications (NVQ) courses in 'manned guarding'. The opportunity to study for these qualifications enabled the security officers to improve their promotion prospects if they so desired, showing that career advancement was possible within contract security. The management support for the qualifications demonstrated a view that there would be organizational gains in having better-qualified staff, possibly associated with the company's transition into more sophisticated security roles. The NVQ training was also actively supported by the local police force, which provided instruction in relation to certain areas of the syllabus such as citizen powers of arrest.

The study by CoESS and Uni-Europa (2004) offers limited information on the training requirements in most of the 25 EU member countries, including in most cases the minimum number of training hours which each security officer must complete. This varies considerably across Europe, from the basic two days' classroom (plus on the job) training that officers in UK-based security companies working to the British Standards Institution (BSI) standard BS7499 must undertake, to the 320, 250 and 217 hours that security officers working in Hungary, Poland and Sweden, respectively, must undertake. The data reveals nothing of the qualitative nature of the training, however. Finally, Parfomak (2004) contrasts the European figures with the generally lower training requirements for

American security officers (ranging from zero to 48 hours according to the state); and Gotbaum (2005) revealed that 12 percent of the 100 officers in her New York study reported having received no training at all.

To sum up, the body of available research literature on the working conditions and training of security personnel around the world has traditionally been very limited. There is likely to be truth, however, in South's (1988) claim that the industry is unlikely to attract high-calibre employees in view of the working conditions and wage levels that are typically found, and that the problem is not specific to the UK (in which his research was based). In my study, the relatively low pay and challenging working conditions of the contract security staff differed markedly from those enjoyed by the in-house officers, while paradoxically it was only the contract security personnel who received structured and comprehensive training. This was alarming in view of the range of security officers' responsibilities, demonstrated earlier, and reflects the need for regulatory structures for the security industry to take account of the in-house sector. Yet such a negative picture is not always typical: recent studies by Cortese *et al.* (2003) and CoESS and UNI-Europa (2004) have revealed enormous variations in standards across Europe, indicating that jurisdictions such as the UK and many US states in which working conditions are particularly challenging may be able to learn lessons from some of their European counterparts.

What sort of relationship do they have with the police?

The overwhelming focus of criminological attention to the security industry has related to its relationship with public policing, and expansion into law enforcement functions on behalf of both the public and commercial sectors. Arguably this has served to misrepresent the industry in terms of its core functions and loss prevention objectives, since much of security officers' work occurs away from public view, and is made up of a collection of tasks fulfilling a far greater set of objectives than simply security. Yet the relationship between security personnel and the police *is* relevant to this chapter for several reasons.

A key trend in the contemporary development of cities across the globe has been the privatization of urban space, to produce large tracts of privately controlled property for public use, such as the shopping centre, business park or gated residential community. Such developments have raised substantially the profile of the security industry in policing, as property owners have frequently drawn on private security services in exercising their legal rights to determine how their territories are policed (Shearing and Stenning, 1981, 1983). A second social trend which has promoted the involvement of security personnel in law enforcement functions is the growth in outsourcing of security functions within the public as well as the private sector so that, in the UK, contract security personnel may be employed to run the control rooms of municipal CCTV control rooms, or fulfil 'neighbourhood warden' roles in patrolling areas of social housing. Third, these new types of role have increasingly brought security personnel into day-to-day contact with the police, encouraging the exchange of information and intelligence between the two sectors, sometimes (as in the case of the UK) with active governmental encouragement (see Wakefield, 2003). Finally, the subsequent increase in the exercising of formal legal powers and authority (e.g. access to personal data) by security personnel has made it more important than ever for the security industry to present an image of utmost respectability and legitimacy. In this final section, therefore, attention is directed to the research evidence on the mutual perceptions of security and police personnel, and the nature and quality of day-to-day contact and collaborative working. These are explored in turn.

Studies in the United States and Singapore have investigated the perceptions of private security and police personnel of the relationship between the two sectors, showing evidence of some police hostility towards security staff. The Hallcrest Report provided findings from a national survey in the United States of the views of police chiefs and security supervisors, indicating that security supervisors rated the relationship as good to excellent, while the police regarded it as poor to good (Cunningham and Taylor, 1985). Nalla and Hoffman's (1996) survey of 271 Singaporean security officers found that 71 percent agreed or strongly agreed with the assertion, 'Security guards have a positive view of police officers'; while 75 percent of respondents disagreed or strongly disagreed with the statement, 'Police officers generally have a positive opinion of security guards', suggesting that many may have had personal experience of police hostility. A subsequent study by Nalla and Hummer (1999) surveyed samples of US 'security professionals' (as opposed to front-line officers) and police officers of assorted ranks, finding that police perceptions of security officers and the two sectors' co-operative efforts were broadly positive, and more so (in both cases) than estimated by the security professionals.

A further body of relevant research has focused on the nature and quality of collaborative working between the police and private security personnel. The two sectors inevitably come into contact with each other as a result of day-to-day eventualities, with the police often being dependent on other agencies for information about crime, and at other times being obliged to assist other bodies lacking the authority to deal with problems independently. A study by Jones and Newburn (1998) of the various policing bodies operating within the London Borough of Wandsworth found evidence of co-operative working between the police and the larger private security operations in the Borough. This included exchanging general advice and information, intelligence-sharing about specific cases, sharing of equipment or facilities, handing over of cases, joint operations, social contacts and police responses to emergency calls by private security staff. From this survey, the authors concluded that although private security teams and other alternative forms of policing were taking an increasing role in policing the Borough, for many, their activities were partially underwritten by London's Metropolitan Police.

McManus' (1995) case studies of three residential areas patrolled by private security teams found evidence of 'regular and high quality co-operation' between the security officers and the police in two of the areas (Moston and Bridton), while there was little contact between the agencies in the third (Becton). McManus found that in Moston the police often asked the security officers to look out for stolen vehicles or vehicles suspected of being used in crime, and the two agencies regularly communicated by means of radio and telephone communication. In Bridton, patrolled by a security officer operating alone, police officers regularly updated the officer on local crime incidents and he passed details to them of any individuals or vehicles that he regarded as suspicious.

Shapland's (1999) study provided an insight into co-operative working between the police and private security teams in two shopping centres. At her first centre, plain-clothes operations against shop theft were mounted in partnership with the police; and tenant retailers within the centre, along with the centre managers and the police, had instigated a pre-trial diversion scheme for juveniles arrested for shop theft in the centre. A small police station staffed by two police officers was located alongside the private security team in her second centre, in which a sense of partnership between the two agencies was less evident. Shapland found that almost all crimes coming to the attention of security personnel at the second centre seemed to be being reported to the police, and that the police were expected to shoulder the responsibility in dealing with offenders. In these two examples, the working relationships and co-operative working practices between the police and private security teams were negotiated locally, raising the possibility that the nature of inter-agency collaboration may be distinctive to every partnership in every location.

A detailed study of a Toronto based contract security company was undertaken by Rigakos (2002). 'Intelligarde International', also detailed in McLeod (2002) from the perspective of its CEO, is a firm that is 'actively extending private policing into the public domain' (Rigakos, 2002: 26), operating within residential districts, car parks and harbour and beach areas, and possibly almost unique in its involvement in such law enforcement activities as 'clearing crack houses, processing evictions and even disrupting the business of "drug gangs"' (p. 27). With most of its security personnel striving for law enforcement careers, as Rigakos reports, the opportunities for officers to undertake placements in public police agencies appeared to help foster a positive relationship between the security personnel and the police, to 'buttress the organization's commitment to law enforcement and send a message to security officers that their efforts are supported' (p. 126). Yet Rigakos describes a working relationship of varying character and quality, not devoid of conflict and perceptions by security personnel that they are seen as inferior by many police officers, but also mutually beneficial at times. Examples are provided of security personnel reporting sightings of drunk drivers on public roads to the police, and the police in one division proving to be consistently prompt in responding to requests for help with arrests. Rigakos notes how Intelligarde officers' varying relations with police officers often reflected the different histories of the company's relationship with the various police divisions, but found some examples of close personal ties developing.

In my research (Wakefield, 2003) it was evident that each of the three security teams was integrated in local policing networks in a variety of ways. The quality and extent of the working relationships varied between the sites, however, and a strong pattern seemed to emerge whereby, in cases where key representatives within the police organization had taken the initiative personally to invest time in cultivating relationships with the security teams, these had been fostered easily. Five categories of regular collaborative working were identified, described as 'responding to crimes in progress', 'investigating crime', 'intelligence sharing', 'knowledge sharing' and 'partnership working' (whereby 'intelligence sharing' refers to the exchange of locally generated offender information, and 'knowledge sharing' is the provision of expert knowledge in an advisory capacity).

These studies demonstrate the important practical benefits for security officers of achieving a positive relationship with the police, although my study highlights the importance of key individuals within the police service being able to steer such working arrangements by acting as ambassadors for their organizations and facilitators of productive collaboration. For security personnel, their reliance on the police for assistance with arrests and other emergencies underlies the most crucial need for good working relationships, but the need is not one sided. This is demonstrated in the variety of reasons for contact between the two sectors, including a two-way flow of information and instances of joint operations.

Conclusion

This chapter has demonstrated the considerable international scope of 'manned' private security, and the breadth of functions undertaken by the contemporary security officer as security roles have become more and more sophisticated. With security personnel now frequently placed in routine contact with the public, or tasked with operating complex security systems, the low skill levels, low pay and long hours which remain typical of the industry in many jurisdictions cannot be regarded as acceptable, leading to service limitations such as high turnover and poor standards. Recent research efforts (e.g. Cortese *et al.*, 2003 and CoESS and UNI-Europa, 2004) to demonstrate industry variations across Europe must be commended for highlighting these discrepancies, as well as providing examples of national good practice from which lessons might be learned.

In a global society that is increasingly preoccupied with the management of risk, a continuing expansion in the scope of the industry – and the prominence of the security officer – is certain, and an area that is especially ripe for continued growth is the involvement of security personnel in law enforcement. The privatization of urban space has rendered security personnel responsible for the policing of large, privately controlled territories to which the public routinely have access, in which they have many functions in common with the public police officer. Similarly, the outsourcing of security functions within the public sector has, in many cases, bestowed new law enforcement responsibilities on security personnel. In such roles, the cultivation of positive relationships with the public and the police is as essential as the need to overcome service limitations. The growth in such opportunities, which are raising expectations of security officers in terms of responsibilities, skill sets and required service standards, must be seen as one of the key drivers for improvement in the manned guarding industry.

Key readings

An excellent introduction to the structure of the security industry in Britain, the nature and impact of its post-war expansion and the issues presented by the industry's growing role in law enforcement are provided in Jones, T. and Newburn, T. (1998) *Private Security and Public Policing*, Oxford: Clarendon. More detailed analyses of the delivery of security, in terms of the day-to-day activities of security personnel, are offered in studies by Wakefield and Rigakos (Wakefield, A., 2003, *Selling Security: The Private Policing of Public Space*, Cullompton, Devon: Willan Publishing; Rigakos, G., 2002, *The New Parapolice*, Toronto: University of Toronto Press), and a useful companion to Rigakos' academic text is a book written by its CEO about the very same 'law enforcement company': McLeod, R. (2002) *Parapolice: A Revolution in the Business of Law Enforcement*, Toronto: Boheme Press. Finally, for a set of useful factsheets on the security industry in each of the 25 states of the EU, accessible on the web, see CoESS and UNI-Europa (2004) *Panoramic Overview of Private Security Industry in the 25 Member States of the European Union*, Wemmel, Belgium: Confederation of European Security Services (CoESS) and UNI-Europa (available at http://www.coess.org/stats.htm).

References

ASIS International (2004) *Private Security Officer Selection and Training Guideline*, Alexandria, Virginia: ASIS International, http://www.asisonline.org/guidelines/guidelines.htm (accessed 28 February 2005).

Brough, M. and Brown, D. (1989) *Every Retailer's Guide to Loss Prevention*, North Vancouver: Self-Counsel Press.

CoESS and UNI-Europa (2004) *Panoramic Overview of Private Security Industry in the 25 Member States of the European Union*, Wemmel, Belgium: Confederation of European Security Services (CoESS) and UNI-Europa, http://www.coess.org/stats.htm (accessed 28 February 2005).

Cortese, V., Dryon, P. and Valkeneers, A. (2003) *Private Security and Work Organisation*, Brussels: Centre de Sociologie du Travail, de l'Emploi et de la Formation de l'Université Libre de Bruxelles, http://homepages.ulb.ac.be/~vcortese/RapportSPOT_EN.PDF (accessed 28 February 2005).

Cunningham, W.C. and Taylor, T. (1985) *Private Security and Police in America: The Hallcrest Report I*, Stoneham, MA: Butterworth-Heinemann.

de Jong, M. (2002) 'Peace of Mind? Perceptions of Contractual Security Guarding at Commercial Banks in Saudi Arabia', *Security Journal*, Vol. 5, No. 1.

de Waard, J. (1999) 'The Private Security Industry in International Perspective', *European Journal on Criminal Policy and Research*, Vol. 7, No. 2.

Erickson, B. (1993) *People Working in the Toronto Private Contract Security Industry*, Ottawa: Police Policy and Research Division, Solicitor General of Canada.

Farnell, M. and Shearing, C.D. (1977) *Private Security: An Examination of Canadian Statistics*, Toronto: Centre of Criminology, University of Toronto.

Gill (2004) *Uniformed Retail Security Officers*, Leicester: Perpetuity Research and Consultancy International.

Gotbaum, B. (2005) *Undertrained, Underpaid, and Unprepared: Security Officers Report Deficient Safety Standards in Manhattan Office Buildings*, New York: Public Advocate for the City of New York, http://pubadvocate.nyc.gov/policy/pdfs/securityofficersreport.pdf (accessed 28 February 2005).

Institut des Sciences du Travail (2003) *Sectoral Unions and Employers Organisations in the Private Security Sector in the EU*, Project VT/2002/0215, Louvain, Belgium: Louvain,

Belgium: Institut des Sciences du Travail, Universite Catholique de Louvain, http://www.trav.ucl.ac.be/research/presentation.html (accessed 28 February 2005).

Jones, T. and Newburn, T. (1998) *Private Security and Public Policing*, Oxford: Clarendon.

Kakalik, J.S. and Wildhorn, S. (1971) *Private Security in the United States*, Santa Monica, CA: RAND Corporation (five vols.).

McLeod, R. (2002) *Parapolice: A Revolution in the Business of Law Enforcement*, Toronto: Boheme Press.

McManus, M. (1995) *From Fate to Choice: Private Bobbies, Public Beats*, Aldershot: Avebury.

Michael, D. (1999) 'The Levels of Orientation Security Officers have towards a Public Policing Function', *Security Journal*, Vol. 12, No. 4.

Nalla, M.K. and Hoffman, V.J. (1996) 'Security Training Needs: A Study of the Perceptions of Security Guards in Singapore', *Security Journal*, Vol. 7, No. 4.

Nalla, M.K. and Hummer, D. (1999) 'Relations between Police Officers and Security Professionals: A Study of Perceptions', *Security Journal*, Vol. 12, No. 3.

Parfomak, P.W. (2004) *Guarding America: Security Guards and US Critical Infrastructure Protection*, Washington: Congressional Research Service, http://www.fas.org/sgp/crs/RL32670.pdf (accessed 28 February 2005).

Rigakos, G. (2002) *The New Parapolice*, Toronto: University of Toronto Press.

Shapland, J. (1999) 'Private Worlds: Social Control and Security in Britain', in J. Shapland and L. van Outrive (eds) *Police et Sécurité: Contrôle Social et l'Interaction Publique-Privé* (Policing and Security: Social Control and the Public-Private Divide), Paris: L'Harmattan.

Shearing, C.D., Farnell, M.B. and Stenning, P.C. (1980) *Contract Security in Ontario*, Toronto: Centre of Criminology, University of Toronto.

Shearing, C.D. and Stenning, P.C. (1981) 'Modern Private Security: Its Growth and Implications', in M. Tonry and N. Morris (eds) *Crime and Justice: An Annual Review of Research Vol. 3*, Chicago: University of Chicago Press.

Shearing, C.D. and Stenning, P.C. (1983) 'Private Security: Implications for Social Control', *Social Problems*, Vol. 30, No. 5.

SIA (2004) *Specification for Core Competency Training and Qualifications for Security Guarding*, London: Security Industry Authority.

South, N. (1988) *Policing for Profit*, London: Sage.

Taylor-Butts, A. (2004) 'Private Security and Public Policing in Canada, 2001', *Statistics Canada*, Vol. 24, No. 7, http://www.statcan.ca/english/preview/85-002-XIE/P0070485-002-XIE.pdf (accessed 28 February 2005).

Wakefield, A. (2003) *Selling Security: The Private Policing of Public Space*, Cullompton, Devon: Willan Publishing.

Wiles, P. and McClintock, F.H. (1972) *The Security Industry in the United Kingdom: Papers presented to the Cropwood Round Table Conference, July 1971*, Cambridge: Institute of Criminology, University of Cambridge.

Williams, D., George, B. and MacLennan, E. (1984) *Guarding Against Low Pay*, Low Pay Pamphlet 29, London: Low Pay Unit.

17
Store Detectives and Loss Prevention

Read Hayes

Introduction

Retailers the world over suffer store-level crime and losses. Many retail businesses employ in-store loss prevention or asset protection staff to help control theft and other problems. However, this has been a largely neglected area of study. This chapter provides some background on store detectives including how they fit into crime prevention strategies, their training, and routine protective methods and tasks. The main focus of this chapter is a discussion on improving retail store performance through the recruitment, development and deployment of store detectives. This chapter discusses and describes retail crime and loss, how retailers attempt to control loss and the important role store detectives have in this process. This is done by reviewing the peer reviewed and trade literature. Also covered is the training many detectives receive, and the types of job decisions they must routinely make. This discussion provides insight into store detective job tasks.

Retail crime and loss in perspective

The need for store security is believed to have increased after 1879 when Utica, New York merchant Frank W. Woolworth, determined to increase sales while reducing his labour costs, began the practice of openly displaying merchandise. The results were as Woolworth expected, sales rose; but presumably so did shop theft (Edwards, 1976).

Retailers the world over suffer theft and loss. While on average, retail companies universally lose approximately 1–2 percent of their sales, and almost a quarter of their profit annually (Bamfield and Hollinger, 1996); their responses to losses and theft vary widely (British Retail Consortium, 2004; Speed *et al.*, 1995). Some businesses rely on combinations of procedures, staff training and customer service, and prevention technologies such as electronic tag systems and cameras (Hayes, 1991). Many retailers attack theft with store detectives who patrol the store on foot or with video camera systems searching for theft activity (Hayes, 1993; Jones, 1998).

Before the large push into national chains, earlier retailers were often better positioned to deal with the financial fallout from store theft since there was less intense or national (and well-financed) competition. Retail businesses were typically focused locally with less incentive to match each other's pricing. Now retail, like most business segments, has consolidated into regional and national power sellers. Volume merchandise and advertising buying means customers can benefit from lower pricing. Major mass retailers such as Wal-Mart and Target, large department stores such as Macys, and 'category killers' like The Sports Authority and Home Depot are now battling for dominant market share in most significant US markets. Other major retailers across the globe use the same tactics. Customers are often won over by retailers offering lower and lower prices. This struggle for customers means retailers are less able to raise prices to offset large inventory and cash losses (Hayes, 1997a). Meanwhile company shareowners, such as investors, demand continued earnings growth. Earnings and share price growth result from profitable performance (usually the result of increased sales and tight expense control). The equation also includes the insistence of good customers and employees on relatively safe and crime-free stores. This dynamic may compel retail organizations to increasingly confront retail crime and the annual billions in annual inventory losses (British Retail Consortium, 2004; Hayes, 1997a; Hollinger and Langton, 2005). Retailers spend approximately 0.5 percent of their annual sales on loss prevention efforts (Hollinger and Hayes, 2000).

Responses to retail crime and loss

Retailers facing pervasive crime and loss attempt to control their problems by applying some basic principles (Bamfield and Hollinger, 1996; Felson, 1996, 1998; Hayes, 1997a). In order to maximize shareowner value, companies must increase sales while reducing operating and merchandise costs (Hayes, 1997a, 2000). Sound loss prevention helps these businesses accomplish both objectives. Effective loss prevention provides direct impact on a retailer's top-line (revenue), as much as bottom-line (profits). Properly protected items mean more desirable assets remain available for sale, since thieves do not tend to target undesirable items (Hayes, 1997c) and tend to prefer Fast Moving Consumer Goods (Gill et al., 2004) or craved items (Clarke, 1999). On-shelf availability (the opposite of out of stocks) means more sales revenue, and satisfied customers.

Protected cash receipts means hard-earned money can be leveraged to improve the organization, and likewise reward investors and staff. Another critical role for many loss prevention departments is in increasing perceived 'safeness' or the reverse of the fear of crime and victimization. A safe shopping and work atmosphere means customers and staff feel comfortable spending time, and money, or being productive, on company property. These actions are part of situational crime prevention.

Store detectives and asset protection

Crime prevention can be described as a large set of actions and interventions designed to prevent crime events. One proposed model for crime control involves three major emphases: primary, secondary, and tertiary prevention (United Nations, 1999). Some crime prevention efforts are focused on the community as a whole; or specific places. These include programmes such as public advertising, Neighbourhood Watch, efforts to install better lighting in parks or alleys, the use of CCTV surveillance in high-crime areas, and policing, and efforts to provide community support to families and youth believed to be most at risk of offending and victimization. These are often called 'primary prevention' activities (Sherman *et al.*, 1997; United Nations, 1999), or prevention efforts in Zones 1–5 (Hayes, 1997a).

'Secondary prevention' targets potential offenders. School dropouts, abused children, and chronically needy people can be hooked up with appropriate services to reduce risk/need, thereby ultimately reducing crime (United Nations, 1999).

'Tertiary prevention' is similar to specific deterrence (mentioned later), and comprises efforts to prevent further crime(s) by someone who has been charged or convicted. This includes everything from diversion programmes for first time offenders, to rehabilitation efforts aimed at more persistent offenders, to intensive surveillance of high-rate offenders (United Nations, 1999).

Generally, store detectives can be considered a part of primary prevention (within Zone 2 according to Hayes, 1997a), and are assigned to reduce crime events or attempts within a given location or store group. Some store detectives are assigned to track and affect the crime activities of high-rate, high-impact offenders ('boosters'), also working into the tertiary prevention mode.

As mentioned previously, in order to reduce loss, merchants strive to first reduce crime attempts. Several negative outcomes can flow from crime attempts or events (e.g. injury, physical damage, asset loss, bad publicity, civil and criminal liability, trauma, investor concern). In order to suppress crime activities, we need to better understand how and why they occur. Criminological theories provide explanatory tools for retailers to use for controlling crime events on their properties. A particularly useful theory for understanding crime in retail settings, termed routine activities, combines human ecology, rational choice and deterrence components (Cohen and Felson, 1979; Felson, 1998; Hollinger and Dabney, 1994). Routine activities theory, in its simplest form, contains three primary elements: (1) a likely or motivated offender; (2) a suitable target (or desirable asset), and finally, (3) the absence of a capable guardian or place manager against the offence (Felson, 1998). A capable guardian can be described as a person or object, other than the victim, that is able to keep a watchful eye on a potential victim or asset, and may also act as a deterrent to offenders (Felson, 1998). Store detectives serve in the role of an organization's primary capable guardians, charged with actively reducing the opportunities for theft of merchandise in their assigned store(s). These detectives primarily reduce crime attempts by promoting deterrence (Hayes, 2000).

To reduce crime attempts, a sense of control, or deterrence, must be established (Clarke, 1997; Hollinger and Dabney, 1994). Like many loss prevention tactics used by retailers to reduce unexplained losses of merchandise, store detectives are expected to deter would-be thieves by convincing them that stealing merchandise will result in their apprehension and sanction. The offender's sense of personal risk of detection, punishment and humiliation, should be compelling enough to overcome their desire and ability to steal (Bamfield, 1994; Hayes, 1993).

Deterrence is believed to result from this perceived risk through both personal and vicarious observations (Piquero and Paternoster, 1998). Would-be shop thieves in part learn to avoid deviant behaviours such as stealing through direct positive, negative, or neutral experiences with their parents, police or other authorities before, during, and after an attempted negative behaviour. Some of an offender's activities are detected and acted on, while some were either not detected, or not acted on. A person's own experiences and perceptions can combine with those related by others, or the media, to provide a general sense of actual risk (Stafford and Warr, 1993). Some deterrence can be gained through specific crime disruption or suppression tactics. These tactics can be segmented based on how they affect an offender's perceptions and behaviours (Hayes, 1997a, 2000; Jones, 1998).

Cornish and Clarke (2003) focus on the concepts of deterrence and routine activities in the context of situational crime prevention. They postulate 25 crime opportunity-reducing techniques, which includes **formal surveillance**. Store detectives are included under this technique. Detectives patrol stores on foot, or by using CCTV surveillance systems, searching for clusters of behaviours they believe indicate theft activity. Behaviours that can suggest theft activity include: standing very close to item display fixtures, hunching over items, keeping hands down to remove tags and packages while concealing, and eyes looking more for cameras and employees than at the products themselves (Hayes, 1993). If theft behaviour is observed, the detectives often attempt a non-violent apprehension of the offender(s) or make his/her presence known to the 'offender' in the hopes of getting him/her to leave the premises.

The detention, processing, and financial and restrictive sanctions that should follow, are hypothesized to specifically deter the offender (specific deterrence), while demonstrating to others that observe or hear about the detention (general deterrence) the fruitlessness and risks of dishonesty in the store (Hayes, 2000). Just as crime can be displaced in time, geographically, to other targets, and even in intensity or type by situational protection efforts (Clarke, 1997), specific items or locations might be protected by crime prevention initiatives applied elsewhere. This proposed phenomenon is termed diffusion of benefits (Clarke, 1997), and implies that a loss prevention effort to protect one object, space or place, may help protect a nearby or similar thing, which is not actually protected. Store detectives help promote diffusion of benefits (or a 'halo effect') by apprehending thieves, and gaining general deterrence when other would-be thieves see or hear about the detentions, and alter their behaviour for fear that the level of protection (and risk to them) exists in another location or time (Clarke, 1997; Scherdin, 1992).

It is hoped that deterrence is gained by convincing potential shop thieves that stealing from their intended victim is too difficult, too risky (in this case *via* the clear and present danger of detection and apprehension by store detectives), or is a fruitless exercise. Secondly, companies endeavour to reduce the amount of loss incurred from those theft attempts that do take place. Merchants attempt to reduce their average, or cumulative, loss amounts by increasing their ability to quickly detect theft, as well as the ability to quickly respond, apprehend offenders, and recover their assets in saleable or merchantable condition. Finally, retailers try to reduce the financial or emotional impact of their losses on the company. Businesses can reduce the negative impact of incurred loss by tax write-offs, insurance claims, asset recovery, rebates, and some civil actions such as theft damages recovery (Bamfield, 1998; Hayes, 1997a, 1990).

The tactical role of store detectives

As mentioned, part of a retailer's response to high loss problems, and pressure to control them, is the deployment of special loss prevention or asset protection employees. While all company employees are expected to help control and report crime and loss, as designated capable guardians or situational place managers, the primary role of loss prevention employees is generally to focus exclusively on asset protection. The term loss prevention, as opposed to loss reaction, implies that the role of loss prevention personnel is a combination of preventive and reactive activities; with a focus on prevention. As well as investigating crimes, loss prevention employees typically are solely charged with reducing crime and loss, although some companies also combine safety, procedural audit, or other similar functions into a loss control department. Loss prevention employees are expected to reduce organizational loss by continually auditing loss prevention procedural compliance, creating employee loss prevention awareness at all corporate levels, and specifying and maintaining loss control programmes and systems in their assigned store(s) (Hayes, 1991). Many prevention personnel also investigate theft incidents and apprehend suspected internal and external offenders (Hayes, 1991).

Like most organizations, retailers have hierarchical employee structures. In loss prevention, these positions are often defined by degrees of responsibility, store dispersion, geography, and actual job function (Brough and Brown, 1989; Hayes, 1991, 2000; Jones, 1998). At the top of the structure, some companies have vice presidents or directors of loss prevention (LP) who act as the primary security decision-makers. In the 'field' (non headquarters-based loss prevention managers) regional and district loss prevention executives implement asset protection initiatives. Dishonest employees are often investigated by district or regional loss prevention managers, and by designated internal investigators.

Many companies (35 percent) with large store formats, and a variety of loss prevention problems, also employ store detectives (also referred to as agents, operatives or specialists) to operationalize loss prevention initiatives in individual or small groups of stores (Hollinger *et al.*, 1996). Companies with small store formats (often less than 10,000 square feet) tend to rely more on the store selling staff and managers to control theft foregoing the use of loss prevention detectives.

The role of most store-level loss prevention personnel is to focus primarily on controlling losses from external or non-employee sources, with a particular emphasis on shoplifting suppression. Detectives are expected to devote most of their time to detecting and apprehending thieves, but they also spend considerable time working with other employees, and loss prevention systems, to reduce theft opportunities. Retailers generally consider apprehension to be part of a comprehensive prevention programme. Apprehension may appear to be reactive, but some general and specific deterrence may be gained through aggressive apprehension (Hayes, 1991).

Because of their role in deterring and apprehending dishonest customers, store detectives can either add-value to an organization, or create serious liability making detective selection, training and management very important. The more competent employees are at handling assigned job tasks, routine job situations, and dynamic workplace demands and cultures in general, the better their performance. Job performance in today's highly competitive workplace environment is changing. Many jobs are becoming increasingly more complex. Employees are required to show more initiative, provide better customer service, and work in teams. It has been proposed that an individual's unique mixture of underlying traits such as cognitive ability and personality makes certain people better suited for certain positions. Because different jobs require differing abilities and propensities, it is important to better define the store detective position.

Store detectives in the literature

One important aspect of store detectives is the amount of autonomy they exercise on a daily basis (Hayes, 2000; May, 1978). Due to this freedom, store detectives, working within company guidelines, are free to creatively reduce theft and loss. Alternatively, these semi-autonomous loss prevention detectives may create tremendous liability by apprehending individuals who did not actually steal anything or by botching the apprehension and processing of suspected thieves (Keckeisen, 1993).

Although there are thousands of retail companies, many employing store detectives in the US, they have not been a frequent topic of empirical research. Only rarely does the scholarly literature discuss store detectives and then usually only as a part of the research project and not as the subject of the study (Axelrod and Elkind, 1976; Bamfield and Hollinger, 1996; Baumer and Rosenbaum, 1984; Blankenburg, 1976; Beck and Willis, 1998; Brodt, 1994; Buckle and Farrington, 1984; Butler, 1994; Carter *et al.*, 1988; Cupchik, 1997; Farrell and Ferrara, 1986; Farrington and Burrows, 1993; Feuerverger and Shearing, 1982; Hayes, 1997a, 1997b; Hollinger and Dabney, 1994; Keckeisen, 1993; Klemke, 1992; May, 1978;

Murphy, 1986; Ray, 1987; Walsh, 1978). A few of these academic projects provide some useful insight into the role of store detectives.

Axelrod and Elkind (1976), briefly discuss store detectives and their role in large stores. The researchers observed that store detectives seem to react to shoplifting by apprehending offenders rather than otherwise deterring them from stealing. The authors also noted that many retailers did not allow their non-security staff to apprehend shoplifters due to civil liability concerns. This observation supports the idea that where employed, detectives are often used as the primary capable guardians of a company's assets since other store employees and even many uniformed security guards (often provided by third party companies or off-duty law enforcement officers) generally lack the training and temperament needed to handle risky theft situations (Felson, 1998). Eck (1995) describes employees that exercise surveillance and control over a specific location (such as a store) as place managers.

Feuerverger and Shearing (1982) analyse the decision processes of store detectives regarding sanctioning of apprehended store thieves. The authors point out that the decisions of store security personnel are primarily shaped by the desire to maximize company profitability. Due to this motivation, their actions may tend to support this end game by focusing more heavily on more costly theft situations (high cost merchandise rather than trivial items, etc.) An exception to this prioritization tends to be that any 'professional' shoplifter is considered very important.

Klemke (1992) briefly mentions store security agents, and that the agent's role often lies primarily in detecting and apprehending shoplifters. The author provides advice to security personnel on detection cues to look for such as booster boxes that enable the concealment of goods while in a store. He also comments on May's (1978) study that implies that security agents 'create' shoplifting statistics by targeting juveniles for close surveillance since they are most prone to stealing. Klemke (1992) also points out Murphy's (1986) support for May's ideas about 'manufacturing' shoplifting incidents. Finally, Klemke notes that most apprehensions result from store staff reports or detective surveillance, rather than from customer reports.

Davis *et al.* (1991) discuss store detectives (described as private police) as a tool for demanding civil damages from apprehended shoplifters for their employers. The authors claim the detectives are agents of their organizations that skim money from affluent shop thieves, while turning over poor offenders to the police. As a note, 49 of 50 US states have specific statutes that allow victimized retailers to recover civil damages from apprehended shoplifters, but retailers report the amount they recover in damages does not come close to covering protection costs, much less the cost of lost merchandise (Hayes, 1990).

As mentioned, another study (May, 1978) examines store detectives and their role in curbing juvenile theft. The author discusses the large amount of autonomy enjoyed by store detectives. The article discusses that this independence can work well if detectives are disciplined and focused on protecting high-loss, high-impact merchandise (high wholesale cost with little profit margin), but may be a problem if they concentrate on surveilling inexpensive, high-margin, high-loss items in order to catch elevated numbers of offenders (possibly ignoring the fact that high theft, regardless of what the items are, can create serious problems in a store and needs to be addressed).

Murphy (1986) discusses two companies that use store detectives provided by an outside supplier to apprehend shoplifters. Murphy (1986) describes the utility of non-uniformed detectives to gain some additional deterrence over obvious staff or uniformed guards since they can create an impression that there is always someone surveilling the sales floor. He also points out that the Home Office (UK) issued a statement in support of the use of plainclothes store detectives to supplement uniformed personnel to aid in the control of professional thieves.

The trade or lay literature, which primarily includes 'how to' retail security books or manuals, includes references to store detectives (Brough and Brown, 1989; Cohen, 1981; Copeland, 2000; Curtis, 1960, 1983; Defranco, 2003; Edwards, 1976; French, 1979; Ganton, 1990; Hayes, 1991, 1993; Horan, 1996; Jones, 1998; Kimiecik, 1995; Manley, 2003; Miller, 1993; Neill, 1981; O'Brien, 1996; Purpura, 1993; Rapp, 1989; Sandler, 1985; Sennewald, 2003; Sklar, 1982; Walker, 1996; Van Maanenberg, 1995). The most useful work for this study, Brough and Brown (1989: 9–10), seems to summarize the non-academic or trade perspective, and lists the primary responsibilities of store detectives. According to their analyses, store detectives are responsible for the prevention of such crimes within the company as shoplifting, internal (employee) theft, cheque and refund fraud, use of stolen credit cards, robbery, purse snatching, pick-pocketing, indecent acts of various sorts, vandalism, and use of counterfeit money. The researchers add that store detectives are also responsible for dealing with people who are emotionally disturbed, under the influence of alcohol or drugs, violent, or who are carrying weapons. In addition, these personnel should be in charge of preventative measures – that is, prevention of losses from carelessness, fire, poor safety policies, and/or outdated or inoperative alarm systems. Many retailers do not let their in-store loss prevention personnel deal with non-shoplifting-related events, violence or weapons.

Store detective responsibilities

In order to more precisely focus on store detective training, research was conducted with two large US retailers. Hayes (2001) found during interviews, focus groups and periods of observations with two large US retailers that store detective job tasks and work situations could be classified into a working taxonomy. Specifically, interview and observation notes suggested that job tasks and work situations could be classified into five primary domains and labeled the 'Five A's'.

1 *Apprehension* – internal and external theft resolutions such as apprehending, deterring, and processing employee and non-employee thieves.
2 *Awareness* – training and motivating non-loss prevention employees on asset protection issues.
3 *Auditing* – checking for, and following up on store risk levels, and loss prevention procedural compliance.

4 *Area focus* – collecting and analysing local crime and loss event, offender interview data and demographic data for systematic patterns such as high-loss items and locations, and theft techniques in order to focus their work efforts.
5 *Additional responsibilities* – other tasks and situations store detectives deal with such as escorting bank deposits, securing a store during a storm or riot, or helping a store manager with a non-loss prevention task such as processing a freight delivery or cleaning up spilled liquid.

A number of other detective responsibilities may be considered either primary or secondary in the view of Brough and Brown (1989). These include surveillance of criminals within the store and its attached parking lots, warehouses, etc.; arresting offenders; seizing and preserving exhibits; maintaining a filing system and preparing reports for police and court officials as well as maintaining a liaison with police, courts, and other agencies; presenting evidence and exhibits in court; investigating cases involving employees and seeking out dishonest employees; and reporting to management regarding lax store policy execution. It is not unusual for store detectives to also be asked to present educational programmes to employees. These may consist of films, brochures and lectures on a variety of topics such as customer and employee theft, cheque fraud, stolen credit cards, counterfeit money, suspicious refunds, fire safety, general store policies and systems, and emergency measures such as bomb threats, civil disturbance, robberies, floods and blackouts, just to mention a few.

Of the greatest importance, however, is the primary duty of the store detective to act as a liaison between employees and management and between the company, the police and court officials. From the above discussion, it is clear that the store detective's job responsibilities are varied and can be relatively complicated. In order to carry out their responsibilities successfully, they must develop job-critical skills. These should include the following:

- Auditing of loss prevention programmes, loss prevention training initiatives, and loss prevention systems for compliance to company operating standards. This process is supposed to be used as a tool for store managers;
- Training store staff on daily loss prevention tasks (and motivating them to carry them out);
- Developing a mental search image of potentially harmful situations, events and people so that these threats may be dealt with and diminished; and
- Thorough, safe investigative, and apprehension techniques.

The primary focus of store detectives

How senior loss prevention decision-makers currently view the role of their store detectives versus how they want to evolve the store detective programme heading in the new century has been studied as well. There has been a long debate in loss prevention regarding what actions constitute preventing problems and which are purely reactive (e.g. Axelrod and Elkind, 1976). Detecting and apprehending shop thieves is certainly reacting to a situation, but the apprehension of offenders and resulting formal and informal sanctions should generate at least some general and specific deterrence (Stafford and Warr, 1993). While most store detectives are plain clothed (without uniforms or identifying items), some retail companies are experimenting with having all or some detectives work in distinctive blazers in order to more broadly advertise a security presence. The question for senior loss prevention decision-makers is whether having their detectives stand at the store entrance/exit overtly identified as a member of loss prevention staff prevents more theft attempts than does apprehending shop thieves after covertly observing their theft activities.

Regardless of the form of their primary role, in order for store detectives to perform their loss prevention tasks, some training must take place. The next section addresses the topics senior loss prevention decision-makers feel their training programme should emphasize in order to meet the loss prevention department's mission and goals.

Training store detectives

The issue of training store detectives is covered albeit not extensively in the lay literature; mostly the topic is a small section in security and loss prevention books (Curtis, 1983; Edwards, 1976; French, 1979; Ganton, 1990; Hayes, 1991, 1993; Jones, 1998; Keckeisen, 1993; Miller, 1993; Murphy, 1986; Neill, 1981; Purpura, 1993; Rapp, 1989; Sandler, 1985; Van Maanenberg, 1995; Walker, 1996).

Training topics are often designed to address tasks store detectives are supposed to perform. Neill (1981: 49–50) lists some training topics he believes most important to store detectives, regardless of their company's country of origin or merchandise mix:

...They should be trained in and have a sound knowledge of:

- modern loss prevention techniques;
- the physical security of premises;
- the relevant laws of arrest, search and court procedure, including the laws of evidence and defamation;
- general retail security systems and procedures;
- report writing and the giving of evidence;
- cash register operating procedures;
- retail procedures peculiar to the type of store in which they are operating and the type of merchandise to be protected;
- company loss prevention policy as laid down by higher authority;
- up to date alarm systems and retail security protection devices;
- the protection of cash on premises and cash in transit;
- a reasonable understanding of fire prevention methods, the use of fire extinguishers and evacuation of customers and staff to safety in the event of fire or other catastrophe.

The list of training topics provided by Jones (1998) highlights the wide variety of tasks detectives perform. Hayes (1997b) further focuses training recommendations on the handling of shop thieves based on a series of decisions, which must be made by the store detective:

1   *Detection of a suspected shop thief* (Decision point 1 – 'Should I watch the suspects or not? Are they exhibiting suspicious behaviours (a) theft actions such as moving close to articles or counter surveillance movement such as repeatedly visually scanning the area, (b) reactions to anxiety and adrenaline release and are they physically capable of theft?')

2   *Evaluation of the multiple 'suspicious' subjects* (Decision point 2 – 'Which subject is my priority, based on the probability (and financial impact) of their committing a theft?')

3   *Surveillance of the subject(s)* (Decision point 3 – 'How should the subject(s) be watched – overtly in order to deter them right now, or covertly in order to detain them and gain longer term and possibly broader general deterrence?')

4   *Determination of theft act* (Decision point 4 – 'Did (is) a theft (going to) take place, did I personally see the subject (a) approach our product, (b) select our product, (c) take or conceal our product, (d) without losing sight of them, and (e) pass the last point of sale without paying for our product without permission?')

5   *Employee's response to a Theft Act* (Decision point 5 – 'I saw the subject take an item. What action should I take (a) terminate my surveillance, (b) try to get them to put our products back without an apprehension (bluff them), or (c) apprehend the subject?)

6   *Customer contact* (Decision point 6 – 'If the customer resists my lawful apprehension attempt, should I (a) just let them go, or (b) attempt to physically restrain them?')

7   *Safety measures* (Decision point 7 – 'Should I search the suspect for weapons in order to protect myself and others?') The employee attempts to reduce the possibility of a lethal attack by removing potential weapons from the area and if necessary, the detained subject.

8   *Employee processes the incident and interviews and debriefs the subject and witnesses* – The employee writes the report, processes any evidence and if they are called, waits for the police to arrive.

9   *Deterrent action* (Decision point 8 – 'What sanctioning action against the offender should I take for best future deterrence of this offender and others (a) release the subject, (b) press criminal action, (c) take civil action, or (d) a combination of (b) and (c)?')

10 *Detention duration of suspects* (Decision point 9 – 'When I do detain a suspect, how long should they be detained while being processed and held for the police?')

Based on the number and complexity of situational decisions a store detective must make when dealing with shop theft alone, careful selection of individuals capable of consistently making them in fast-paced situations appears very important. Innovativeness, discipline and mental toughness are requirements for the store detective today.

Discussion

Store detectives are viewed by many large retailers as an important part of a larger crime and loss control strategy by playing a vital role in suppressing customer theft and asset losses. In-store loss prevention agents tend to focus their work roles into at least five work domains: apprehension of shoplifters and dishonest employees, non-security employee asset protection awareness training, auditing of protective measures and their usage, collecting data to focus protective efforts, and other duties as assigned by their supervisors. Detectives by nature of their being widely dispersed in large retail chains can exercise considerable autonomy, and make serious decisions such as detaining persons they believe have stolen, or dealing with violent customers. Liability and safety concerns therefore move retailers to more carefully select, train and supervise store detectives. These factors make research-informed, focused selection, training, deployment and management of store-level protective staff very important. Despite some coverage of in-store security personnel in the research literature, more emphasis is needed on selection, training, deployment and supervision of store detectives, along with work on measuring the impact of store detectives on actual loss levels.

Key readings

Literature on retail store detectives is sparse, consisting mostly of trade books, with a sprinkling of peer reviewed work. No single work has yet been found that discusses store detectives in-depth until this chapter was produced largely from Hayes (2001) *US Store Detectives: The Relationship between Individual Characteristics and Job Performance*. Unpublished PhD thesis, Leicester: University of Leicester. General books by loss prevention practitioners have long provided some insight into what store detectives do including Curtis, B. (1983) *Retail Security: Controlling Loss for Profit*, Boston: Butterworth-Heinemann, Edwards, L.C. (1976) *Shoplifting and Shrinkage Protection for Stores 2ⁿᵈ edn*, Springfield, IL: Charles C. Thomas and Hayes, R. (1991) *Retail Security and Loss Prevention*, Boston: Butterworth-Heinemann, Axelrod, A.D. and Elkind, T. (1976) 'Merchants' Responses to Shoplifting: An Empirical Study', *Stanford Law Review*, 28, 589, 596, 609–12 and Feuerverger, A. and Shearing, C.D. (1982) 'An Analysis of the Prosecution of Shoplifters', *Criminology*, 20(2) 273–89 highlight how store detectives can be controversial in who and why they detain for shop stealing. Finally, two papers Hayes, R. (1997b) 'Crime and Loss Control Training: U. S. Retailers' Response to Rising Theft, Competition and Risk', *International Journal of Risk, Security and Crime Prevention*, 2(4) 267, Hayes, R. (2000) 'Retail Store Detectives: An Analysis of their Focus, Selection, Training, and Performance Ratings', *Security Journal*, 31(1) 7–20 discuss the focus and training of retail store detectives.

References

Axelrod, A.D. and Elkind, T. (1976) 'Merchants' Responses to Shoplifting: An Empirical Study', *Stanford Law Review*, 28, 589, 596, 609–12.
Bamfield, J. (1994) *National Survey of Retail Theft and Security*, Moulton Park, Northampton: Nene College.

Bamfield, J. (1998) 'Retail Civil Recovery: Filling a Deficit in the Criminal Justice System?', *International Journal of Risk, Security and Crime Prevention*, 3(4) 257–67.

Bamfield, J. and Hollinger, R.C. (1996) 'Managing Losses in the Retail Store: A Comparison of Loss Prevention Activity in the United States and Great Britain', *Security Journal*, 7(1) 61–70.

Baumer, T.L. and Rosenbaum, D.P. (1984) *Combating Retail Theft: Programs and Strategies*, Stoneham, MA: Butterworth, 115–24.

Beck, A. and Willis, A. (1998) 'Sales and Security: Striking the Balance', in M. Gill (ed.) *Crime at Work: Increasing the Risk for Offenders Volume II*, Leicester: Perpetuity Press, 95–106.

Blankenburg, E. (1976) 'The Selectivity of Legal Sanction: An Empirical Investigation of Shoplifting', *Law and Society*, 109–30.

British Retail Consortium (2004) *2003 British Retail Crime Survey*.

Brodt, S.J. (1994) 'Shoplifting and Amateur Shoplifters In the 90's: A Case Study', *Journal of Security Administration*, 17(2) 11–20.

Brough, M. and Brown, D. (1989) *Every Retailer's Guide to Loss Prevention*, North Vancouver: Self-Counsel Press, 90–2.

Buckle, A. and Farrington, D.P. (1984) 'An Observational Study of Shoplifting', *British Journal of Criminology*, 24(1) 63–73.

Butler, G. (1994) 'Shoplifters Views on Security: Lessons for Crime Prevention', in M. Gill. (ed.), *Crime at Work: Studies in Security and Crime Prevention*, Leicester: Perpetuity Press.

Carter, N., Holmstrom, A., Simpanen, M., and Melin, L. (1988) 'Theft Reduction in a Grocery Store through Product Identification and Graphing of Losses for Employees', *Journal of Applied Behavior Analysis*, 21(4) 385–9.

Clarke, R.V. (1997) *Situational Crime Prevention: Successful Case Studies 2nd edn*, Albany, NY: Harrow and Heston.

Clarke, R. (1999) *Hot Products: Understanding, Anticipating and Reducing the Demand for Stolen Goods*, Police Research Series, Paper 112, London: Home Office.

Cohen, H. (1981) 'Loss Prevention: A Management Guide to Improving Retail Security', New York: Progressive Grocer.

Cohen, L.E. and Felson, M. (1979) 'Social Change and Crime Rate Trends: A Routine Activities Approach', *American Sociological Review*, 44, 588–608.

Copeland, W. (2000) *Absolutely Complete Retail Loss Prevention Guide*, Phoenix, AZ: Absolutely Zero Loss.

Cornish and Clarke (2003) 'Opportunities, Precipitators and Criminal Decisions: A Reply to Wortley's Critique of Situational Crime Prevention', in M. Smith and D. Cornish (ed.) *Theory for Practice in Situational Crime Prevention*, NSW, Australia: Federation Press.

Cupchick, W. (1997) *Why Honest People Shoplift or Commit Other Acts of Theft*, Toronto: Tagami Communications.

Curtis, B. (1960) *Modern Retail Security*, Chicago: Charles C. Thomas.

Curtis, B. (1983) *Retail Security: Controlling Loss for Profit*, Boston: Butterworth-Heinemann.

Davis, M.G., Lundman, R.J. and Martinez, R. (1991) 'Private Corporate Justice: Store Police, Shoplifters, and Civil Recovery', *Social Problems*, 38, 395–411.

Defranco, L.M. (2003) *Retail Manager's Guide to Crime and Loss Prevention: Protecting Your Business from Theft, Fraud and Violence*, Flushing, NY: Loose Leaf Law Publications.

Eck, J.E. (1995) 'A General Model of Geography of Illicit Retail Marketplaces', in D. Weisburd and J. Eck (eds) *Crime and Place, Crime Prevention Studies*, 4, Monsey, NY: Criminal Justice Press.

Edwards, L.C. (1976) *Shoplifting and Shrinkage Protection for Stores 2nd edn*, Springfield, IL: Charles C. Thomas.

Farrell, K. and Farrera, J. (1985) *Shoplifting: The AntiShoplifting Guidebook*, New York: Praeger, 87–96.

Farrington, D.P. and Burrows, J.N. (1993) 'Did Shoplifting Really Decrease?', *British Journal of Criminology*, 33(1) 57–69.

Felson, M. (1996) 'Preventing Retail Theft: An Application of Environmental Criminology', *Security Journal*, 7(1) 71–5.
Felson, M. (1998) *Crime and Everyday Life 2ⁿᵈ edn*, Thousand Oaks, CA: Pine Forge Press.
Feuerverger, A. and Shearing, C.D. (1982) 'An Analysis of the Prosecution of Shoplifters', *Criminology*, 20(2) 273–89.
French, J.T. (1979) *Apprehending and Prosecuting Shoplifters and Dishonest Employees*, New York: National Retail Merchants Association.
Ganton, L.C. (1990) 'Training: The Best Buy in Retail Security', in S.M. Gallery (ed.), *Security Training: Readings from Security Management*, Stoneham, MA: Butterworth's.
Gill, M., Henning, M., Hart, J., Burns-Howell, A., Hayes, R. and Clarke, R. (2004) *The Illicit Market in Fast-Moving Consumer Goods*, Leicester: PRCI.
Hayes, R. (1990) 'Winning the Civil Recovery War', *Security Management*, 9, 83–4.
Hayes, R. (1991) *Retail Security and Loss Prevention*, Stoneham: Butterworth-Heinemann, 36–45.
Hayes, R. (1993) *Shoplifting Control*, Orlando, FL: Prevention Press.
Hayes, R. (1997a) 'Retail Crime Control: A New Operational Strategy', *Security Journal*, 8, 225–32.
Hayes, R. (1997b) 'Crime and Loss Control Training: U. S. Retailers' Response to Rising Theft, Competition and Risk', *International Journal of Risk, Security and Crime Prevention*, 2(4) 267–78.
Hayes, R. (1997c) 'Shop Theft: An Analysis of Apprehended Shoplifters', *Security Journal*, 7(1) 11–14.
Hayes, R. (2000) 'Retail Store Detectives: An Analysis of their Focus, Selection, Training, and Performance Ratings', *Security Journal*, 31(1) 7–20.
Hayes, R. (2001) *US Store Detectives: The Relationship Between Characteristics and Job Performance*, Unpublished PhD Thesis, University of Leicester.
Hollinger, R.C. and Dabney, D. (1994) 'Reducing Shrinkage in the Retail Store: It's Not Just a Job for the Loss Prevention Department', *Security Journal*, 5(1) January 2–10.
Hollinger, R., Dabney, D. and Hayes, R. (1996) *National Retail Security Survey*, Gainesville, FL: University of Florida.
Hollinger, R. and Hayes, R. (2000) *National Retail Security Survey*, Gainesville, FL: University of Florida.
Hollinger, R. and Langton, L. (2005) *2004 National Retail Security Survey*, Gainsville, FL: University of Florida.
Horan, D.J. (1996) *Retailer's Guide to Loss Prevention and Security*, Boca Raton, FL: CRC Press.
Jones, P.H. (1998) *Retail Loss Control 2ⁿᵈ edn*, Oxford: Butterworth & Co. Ltd., 21–4.
Keckeisen, G.L. (1993) *Retail Security Versus the Shoplifter: Confronting the Shoplifter While Protecting the Merchant*, Springfield: Charles C. Thomas, 26–30.
Kimiecik, R.C. (1995) *Loss Prevention Guide for Retail Businesses*, New York: John Wiley and Sons.
Klemke, L.W. (1992) *The Sociology of Shoplifting: Boosters and Snitches Today*, New York: Praeger.
Manley, A.D. (2003) *The Retail Loss Prevention Officer: Elements of Retail Security*, Upper Saddle River, NJ: Pearson Higher Education.
May, D. (1978) 'Juvenile Shoplifters and the Organization of Store Security: A Case Study in the Social Construction of Delinquency', *International Journal of Criminology and Penology*, 6, 137–60.
Miller, C.I. (1993) *Supermarket Security Manual*, Washington, DC: Food Marketing Institute.
Murphy, D.J.I. (1986) *Customers and Thieves: An Ethnography of Shoplifting*, Gower: Aldershot.
Neill, W.J. (1981) *Modern Retail Risk Management*, Sydney, Australia: Butterworth's.
O'Brien, K. (1996) *Cut Your Losses!: A Smart Retailer's Guide to Loss Prevention*, Kansas City, KS: Midpoint Trade Books.

Piquero, A. and Paternoster, R. (1998) 'An Application of Stafford and Warr's Reconceptualization of Deterrence to Drinking and Driving', *Journal of Research in Crime and Delinquency*, 35, 3–39.

Purpura, P.P. (1993) *Retail Security and Shrinkage Protection*, Stoneham, MA: Butterworth-Heinemann.

Rapp, B. (1989) *Shoplifting and Employee Theft Investigations*, Port Townsend, WA: Loompanics Unlimited.

Ray, J. (1987) 'Every Twelfth Shopper: Who Shoplifts and Why?', *Social Casework*, 68, 234–9.

Sandler, N.W. (1985) *How to Protect your Business*, Elmsford, NY: The Benjamin Company.

Scherdin, M.J. (1992) 'The Halo Effect: Psychological Deterrence of Electronic Security Systems', in R.V. Clarke (ed.) *Situational Crime Prevention: Successful Case Studies*, Albany, NY: Harrow and Heston.

Sennewald, C.A. (2003) *Shoplifters Versus Retailers: The Rights of Both*, Chula Vista, CA: New Century Press.

Sherman, L., Gottfredson, D., Mackenzie, D.L., Eck, J., Reuter, P. and Bushway, S. (1997) *Preventing Crime: What Works, What Doesn't, What's Promising*, Washington, DC: Office of Justice Programs.

Sklar, S.L. (1982) *Shoplifting: What You Need to Know About the Law*, New York: Fairchild Publications.

Speed, M., Burrows, J. and Bamfield, J. (1995) *Retail Crime Costs 1993/94 Survey: The Impact of Crime and Retail Response*, London: British Retail Consortium.

Stafford, M.C. and Warr, M. (1993) 'A Reconceptualization of General and Specific Deterrence', *Journal of Research in Crime and Delinquency*, 30, 123–35.

United Nations (1999) 'Strategies for Crime Prevention: Discussion Paper on the Theme of the Eighth Session of the Commission on Crime Prevention and Criminal Justice', UN Commission on Crime Prevention and Criminal Justice.

Van Maanenberg, D. (1995) *Effective Retail Security: Protecting the Bottom Line*, Port Melbourne Australia: Butterworth-Heinemann, 191.

Walker, J. (1996) *Retail Detective Training Manual: How to Conduct the Observation, Surveillance & Apprehension of Shoplifters*, Austin, TX: Thomas Investigative Publications, 8–24.

Walsh, D.P. (1978) *Shoplifting: Controlling a Major Crime*, London: Macmillan.

18

Private Investigators

Tim Prenzler

Private investigators represent an important component of modern justice systems. This chapter examines the evolving nature of their work, alongside issues of ethics and conduct, law and regulation, cultural representations, and the social impact associated with the expansion and diversification of the sector. A major argument of the chapter is that private investigators in many countries serve an essential function in supplying a demand for law enforcement and crime prevention that is not adequately met by the public sector. Government regulation is necessary to minimize unethical practices, but there is also a case for giving licensed investigators special powers to access information and obtain evidence in the pursuit of justice for their clients.

Definitions

What is a private investigator? The answer depends on the context in which the term is used. The most common usage refers to an individual operating a business that conducts inquiries for a client for a fee, or an employee of such a firm. Colloquial usage includes 'PI', 'private eye', 'private detective' or 'gumshoe'. (The latter refers to a type of soft-soled shoe worn by detectives in the 19th century.) The idea of a private investigator can be extended to include private sector 'in-house' investigators. These are employees of a regular company who conduct investigations or engage in forms of crime prevention against customers or staff. Examples include 'store detectives' (see Chapter 17) and fraud investigators.

The term also overlaps with a broader field of work that is covered by the generic term 'enquiry agent'. The enquiry process is frequently directed at serving legal notices or repossessing property after locating a person. In government licensing systems, these categories are sometimes distinguished from 'private investigators' by the use of terms such as 'commercial agents', 'process servers' or 'bailiffs'. Often, however, such activities merge into one another. For example a 'private investigator' might be engaged to both locate a person and serve a summons. 'Investigation services' or 'enquiry services' are useful terms to describe this broader industry sector.

Historical background

Various forms of private and public provision of crime prevention and law enforcement have existed throughout recorded history (see Chapter 1). The modern period of public policing is most closely associated with the formation of the 'New Police' in London in 1829. But even after that time, and as government police organizations spread around the world, people continued to seek justice and protection outside the state. Public policing appeared as the primary form of law enforcement in many countries from the latter part of the 19th century up until the 1970s and 1980s, when the growth of private security became a major phenomenon. The prominence of private security is not, however, new, as indicated by the title of a book on the subject, *The Rebirth of Private Policing* (Johnston, 1992). In his historical survey, Johnston emphasizes how the modern criminal justice system, in which police take the initiative in investigations and prosecutions, was not the norm in the past. Governments:

> made little or no attempt at criminal detection. Crime was brought to the courts when victims prosecuted offenders. Officials did not go out to find it. Justices dealt with the evidence, but detection and apprehension of suspects was left to victims, who often went to great lengths to regain stolen property (1992: 9).

This vacuum of government provision created a market for private investigators and, in Britain, spawned various forms of 'thief taker' organizations, and co-operative 'felons associations' concerned with recovery of stolen property and prosecution of suspects for a reward. Frontier societies created by colonial settlement, especially in the 19th century in north America, also spawned both in-house security services ('company police'), with investigative functions, and private contract security firms, also with investigative functions (Johnston, 1992). Wide-scale problems with theft of horses and cattle-rustling created a market for recovery agents. Banks and railways were vulnerable to armed hold-ups, and counter-measures included attempted recoveries of stolen valuables and location of offenders. Bounty hunters stepped in and became a feature of the frontier, but conditions also led to the establishment of large and well-known firms including Brinks (1859) and Pinkertons (1850). The latter became particularly powerful, providing services to both companies and government, including espionage activities against the Confederate side during the Civil War; and infiltrating labour unions during the Great Depression (Gill and Hart, 1996).

Johnston (1992) observes that the enormous growth in security services in the post-World War Two period was marked by a predominance of guarding services, to the extent that private 'protection' was seen to have largely displaced private 'detection'. Nonetheless, detection and recovery regained some ground, especially from the 1980s, when corporations placed more resources into investigations of illegal business competition. The massive growth in easy personal credit also contributed to the growth of debt recovery services. Other changes have contributed to the growth of private investigation work. For example, there appears to have been a resurgence in the demand for fidelity checks in the 1990s following the AIDS epidemic (Miall and McDonald, 1993). Attempts to wind back the welfare state and a trend towards privatization of government services were evidenced in attempts to curb benefit fraud in association with the out-sourcing of surveillance work to private operators (George and Button, 2000).

Industry dimensions

One common way of measuring the size of the security industry is in relation to police numbers. This varies considerably from country to country but can be as high as 2.5 or more security providers for every police officer (Jones and Newburn, 1998). Within the security sector, the enquiry sub-sector can also vary considerably. In the United States, the comprehensive *Hallcrest Report* estimated that in 1990 there were about 70,000 private investigator employees and about 15,000 companies, taking about 10 percent of security market revenues. Within the whole security sector, guards made up 54 percent of personnel, alarm installers 12 percent, manufacturing personnel 9 percent, locksmiths 7 percent and investigators 7 percent (Cunningham *et al.*, 1990: 216–39). In Britain, one of the more comprehensive studies from the mid-1990s found that of 8259 security firms listed with Telecom, in terms of their main service, detective agencies made up 9 percent, bailiffs 1.9 percent, credit investigations 1.9 percent and debt col-lectors 5.2 percent (Jones and Newburn, 1998: 75). One recent study found that in the state of New South Wales, Australia, in 2001 there were more licence holders in the enquiry sector alone (15,800) than police (13,614) (Prenzler and King, 2002).

The *Hallcrest Report* found that most investigator companies were small, with an average size of about 2.5 investigators. This would seem a typical profile for the sector in advanced industrial societies (Newburn and Jones, 1998; Gill and Hart, 1997c). Sole operators and partnerships are still very much a feature. A major reason for the small scale of enterprises is the extensive use of sub-contracting of 'operative' work, usually to single operators. Sub-contracting allows firms that deal directly with clients considerable flexibility in managing their workflow and it means they can avoid administering a large workforce. It enables firms to engage specialists as required, and to extend their reach geographically (George and Button, 2000). The sector is a traditional male domain, with women typically making up less than 10 percent of investigators. But this is slowly changing. Female agents are just as capable and successful as men, as demonstrated in Val McDermid's (1995) book *A Suitable Job for a Woman: Inside the World of Women Private Eyes*.

Limited regulation of the industry means that in many countries, private investigation is one of the easiest businesses to set up, although establishing a client base can be difficult (George and Button, 2000). Employees have tradition-ally received limited on-the-job training with only a few short courses available in the private training field (Gill and Hart, 1997c). One British study (Jones and Newburn 1998: 89) found that 30 percent of private investigators were ex-police. Another study (Gill and Hart, 1997c: 133) found that 43.6 percent of investigators preferred to employ staff with a police background. However, views are frequently divided on the value of police experience. Where ex-police may be frustrated by more limited powers in private practice, they also tend to have a better knowledge of the investigative process and evidence. The number of ex-police in the industry facilitates communication and co-operation with police (Gill and Hart, 1997b). Larger investigations can involve a range of private and public sector specialists. For example, George and Button refer to specialists engaged to recover the £26 million lost in the Brinks Mat robbery in the 1990s. After £22 million was recovered the celebratory party included 'solicitors, barristers, accountants, police, private investigators, bankers and loss adjustors' (2000: 90).

Work profile

There is a popular image of the private investigator as a lone operator whose clients are private individuals that 'walk in off the street'. The main task requested is to discover whether or not a partner is having an affair. Associated tasks include discretely investigating a suspected fraud or theft, or locating an heir or a missing person. The role of private investigators in 'fidelity checks' was driven by strict divorce laws that required evidence of infidelity. The modus operandi of such investigations involved obtaining material evidence, such as photographs or letters, often by illegal means such as trespass or theft. Some evidence would be admissible in court. However, with illegal evidence it was best to threaten the guilty parties with exposure of the material through means that could not be traced to the investigator nor their client. If all went to plan, the errant partner would then plead guilty to adultery. Hence the negative image of 'The man in the dirty raincoat with upturned collar, watching lights go off in bedrooms and storming in with camera and flashbulb at the ready' (Draper, 1978: 26).

Since the 1960s and the introduction of 'no fault' divorce in many countries, personal work of this nature has become a minor part of the work of most private investigators. Two key developments have been apparent (Gill and Hart, 1997b, 1997c; Jones and Newburn, 1998; Prenzler and King, 2002; Reichman, 1987; South, 1988). The first was a major shift, over the period from the 1970s to the 1990s, away from personal work towards insurance fraud, legal work and other commercial work. Increasing competition and frustration with the growth of insurance fraud led to a well-organized system of claims assessment and referral of suspect claims to investigators. The second major change was the uptake of video camera surveillance. The compact camera was a major technical innovation that greatly enhanced the capacity for covert surveillance and production of legal evidence that could be reproduced in court.

Private Investigator work can be categorized in different ways. The following provides a four-part set of types of work.

1 **Anti-fraud work** is conducted mainly for large insurance firms but also for some self-insured private companies and government insurance agencies. The work includes 'factual' or surveillance work. For factual matters, the process usually begins with interviewing the claimant, establishing a record of interview, and then making further enquiries if necessary. With surveillance, the investigator usually contracts to do a standard number of hours observation on the person making a suspect claim. Many of these cases involve a claim of physical disability, and agents will try to discover contrary evidence – mainly evidence of physical mobility. Insurance work is a very broad classification, which includes arson and false claims of accidents. Welfare fraud includes understating income or claiming unemployment benefits when working.

2 **Legal work** is a mainstay of much private investigation. This 'background' or factual work for lawyers in civil, and some criminal cases, includes locating and interviewing witnesses or claimants. The law firm may also request surveillance on a party to gather evidence in relation to the defence or instigation of litigation. In some cases, agents will locate and analyse forensic evidence, such as documents or scenes of traffic accidents, or investigate the financial condition of people in terms of their capacity to pay court-ordered compensation. Another aspect of legal work is the service of legal summons – process service.

3 **Commercial enquiry** relates primarily to business competition, and entails liability investigations, workplace investigations into theft or harassment, pre-employment checks, and electronic counter-measures (de-bugging). A business that keeps losing contracts might be subject to undercutting by rivals using eavesdropping equipment to obtain tender information (George and Button, 2000: 89). Liability investigations relate to questions such as amounts of money owing to parties in a contract. Pre-employment checks involve interviewing persons who can attest to a job applicant's character or checking educational qualifications or previous work experience. Another area is trademark and copyright investigations in cases where traders are suspected of using a copyrighted logo without permission or selling pirated music, for example. Some investigators may also undertake risk and security assessments, theft recoveries, forensic accounting, and investigation of computer-based attacks on businesses. An associated, and large, area of work is that of repossessions and debt collection to enforce legal contracts and obligations. 'Due diligence' enquiries involve checking the bona fides of potential clients or business partners. This is especially important with the growth of a business beyond national borders and the potential for businesses to be left with unpaid invoices or saddled with business partners with criminal records intent on fraud.

4 The final area is **domestic investigations or personal work**. This can include checking partner fidelity, checking for teenage drug use, searching for missing

persons, abducted child recoveries, and private legal matters. The latter might include such things as checking on the likely income of an estranged spouse who is suspected of avoiding child maintenance payments. In some cases, modern partner checks extend to 'integrity checks', where an undercover operator tries to tempt a partner into beginning an affair (George and Button, 2000: 89).

A study of investigation firms in Britain in the 1990s found that solicitors made up about 61 percent of customers, banks 33 percent, private companies 20 percent and private individuals 14 percent (Jones and Newburn, 1998: 86). An Australian study found that 70 percent of firms sampled did insurance work, 65 percent did legal work, 60 percent did commercial work and 35 percent did domestic work (Prenzler and King, 2002; see also Gill and Hart, 1997b). Information is the product of private investigators. How to get information is the challenge. Their craft knowledge and skills allow them to obtain information that their clients cannot, or do not want to, obtain themselves. An investigation will often begin with information supplied by the client, such as company records or addresses of customers. The investigator may then follow these sources to other leads, including interviewing associates or neighbours of the target. A range of publicly accessible legal data sources is also usually available. These include telephone books, electoral rolls and property records. Governments or private firms may also provide access for a fee to specialist databases such as lists of bankrupts, insurance claimants or credit histories. Many of these are now in electronic form online or on disc. In some cases, government departments, such as transport departments, may allow conditional access to information such as details of traffic accidents (Prenzler and King, 2002).

Despite the utility of many modern information sources, there is a group of people who disappear off these databases and become extremely difficult if not impossible to trace. 'Skip tracing' is a term used for this type of work. Investigators in this area, and those concerned with background checking, cast an envious eye at databases usually closed to them, such as registers of births, deaths and marriages; rental property information; adoption records; criminal histories; and immigration records (to see if a person has left the country or to locate a place where they may be hiding assets). Direct undercover work is occasionally practiced by agents infiltrating protest groups, for example, or working in a business as a regular employee to check on employee crime (see Chapter 8) (Gill *et al.*, 1996; South, 1988).

Most private investigators maintain a comfortable living or average income, with a few becoming wealthy. Differences in earnings appear to depend in part on the nature of work, clients and location. There can be considerable competition and attempted undercutting in tendering between firms but, once established, most investigators seem to stay in the business until retirement. Normally, investigators charge an hourly rate, plus additional costs, such as petrol or accommodation. Only a few investigation firms bill on results only, although 'no serve-no fee' is practiced by some process serving firms (Gill and Hart, 1997b, 1997c).

Most investigation work appears not to be dangerous, especially if agents have good verbal skills. But process serving and debt recovery can be extremely dangerous, with the main risk coming from assaults. This work involves direct confrontation with people who are often under stress in extreme financial difficulty. Repossessions of vehicles and furniture can at times lead to heated confrontations. Surveillance carries some dangers, such as being accosted by the other party. Discovery can lead to threats and attempted assault. But, overall, job satisfaction appears fairly high. Personal autonomy is a major factor.

Ethics and conduct

Just as private investigators operate in something of a shadow land adjoining the public justice system, they are also frequently portrayed as inhabiting a shadowy realm of morality. In some media representations they are shown as willing to engage in any kind of deceitful practice. This stereotype is not without some basis in fact. Like policing, security work has a high opportunity factor and strong pressures for misconduct. This results from the possession of privileged knowledge about clients' assets and vulnerabilities, and from the potential 'Dirty Harry'-style conflict between noble ends and legal constraints – as with police detectives.

Illegal or unethical conduct includes trespassing, theft, intercepting and opening mail, eavesdropping, obtaining confidential information, deceptive conduct (such as obtaining entry under false pretences), or using threats or inducements. It can include practices such as staging incidents to provoke surveillance targets into letting down their guard (by deflating a car tyre or tipping over a rubbish bin) or conducting inappropriate surveillance (such as at a funeral). Advances in the range, power and compactness of electronic surveillance equipment have greatly expanded the scope for invasions of privacy. The scale of illicit practices in reality is difficult to assess. Some forms of malpractice, such as purchasing confidential information, have in modern times developed into corrupt networks involving public servants and police, and have been exposed in detail by official inquiries (King and Prenzler, 2003). A major source of information corruption is an 'old boys network' of police and ex-police turned investigators (Jones and Newburn, 1998).

In contrast to this negative image, research also suggests that many private investigators see themselves as gatekeepers of legitimate privacy and safety (King and Prenzler, 2003). In this regard, there appears to be a marked difference between corporate and private clients. Corporate clients typically do not request breaches of law. Concern with reputation is a major factor, and government clients often verge on paranoia about adverse publicity. With insurance work, there is always a chance that evidence may end up in court and therefore it needs to be obtained legally. But the more private agents deal with the general public, the more they are subject to enquiries regarding illegal or unethical services. A private investigator can expect a trickle of requests for actions such as placement of listening devices in homes or offices, service of threats, breaking and entering to search for evidence, and location of people who enquirers want to harass or assault. A small sub-category of this group is men on domestic violence protection orders seeking spouses who have gone into hiding, stalkers or even organized crime groups with murder contracts to execute (Button, 1998: 9). Private investigators claim to filter and reject such requests. In other cases, they will moderate clients' requests and try to find a legal compromise. For example, an enquirer who travels for work may suspect their partner is having an affair and requests bugs be placed in the house and telephone. The investigator will explain this is illegal but suggest that legal surveillance would be equally effective in discovering the truth.

Some investigators will defend deceptive tactics – such as leaving a dead cat outside a front door to induce a person to make an appearance (Miall and McDonald, 1993) or using an attractive woman to knock on a target's door under the pretext of door-to-door sales and asking questions that will involve checking the target's identity (King and Prenzler, 2003). One interviewee in a British study recalled growing up in the business and helping his father with similar 'pretext enquiries':

> We've been going out on surveillance operations since the age of ten ... Dad would be taking the family out to the seaside for the day, then he'd stop the car for a while and ask us to play football in front of someone's garden. He would then take a picture of whoever came out to complain, probably to check who lived at that address (in Gill and Hart, 1997c: 131).

Such practices are defended by the argument that the aim of finding a person evading a legal obligation outweighs the ethically questionable means of deception. In the words of a recovery agent:

> [Bending the rules] is usually to right a civil wrong ... We may be looking at a debt that's owed to a client on the verge of bankruptcy. If he is owed £20,000 and I find that the debtor has £20,000 and can get enforcement against the creditor and a bank, it is surely more moral to do this than to protect the privacy of the debtor (in Gill *et al.*, 1996: 313).

Regulation

There is a trend in many countries towards governments taking a greater role in controlling the security industry through a variety of regulatory mechanisms, and this trend has included the enquiry sector. The main aims of regulation are to ensure entry-level competency and integrity, and ensure that standards are maintained (see Chapter 24). The primary mechanism is occupational licensing. Compulsory pre-entry training is used in an attempt to ensure the skill basis is sufficient to start work; and personal referees and a criminal history check are used to try to exclude persons who may be disposed towards corrupt or criminal conduct. A licensee who commits such an offence loses their licence for a period, and clients or members of the public who feel they have been subjected to malpractice may complain to the regulator and have the matter investigated. Regulation may also include specific codes of conduct or enforceable guidelines on particular aspects of security work. Debt recovery agents, for example, often have restrictions placed on them about the time of day when they can approach a debtor and the type of language they must use – excluding intimidating behaviour and threats of violence.

Misconduct problems and the inherent ethical risks of private investigator work have been recognized by governments and enhanced regulation appears to be largely supported by professional bodies that represent investigators (Jones and Newburn, 1998: 92). However, effective regulation is a problematic task because of the difficulties in monitoring conduct. Many victims, for example, may not even be aware that their privacy has been violated. Investigators and surveillance operatives are highly mobile and could be engaging in misconduct that regulators are unable to detect. In addition, pre-entry training levels in many jurisdictions remain minimalist and questionable – one week of training is not untypical (Prenzler and King, 2002). A common contradiction in regulation is that bugging devices are often freely available for sale that are illegal to apply in most circumstances (Button, 1998). Industry self-regulation is a supplementary form of control by which professional bodies aim to represent a quality membership. However, despite these strategies, clients of investigators and members of the public are still heavily dependent on trust and on individual investigators self-regulating their conduct.

Legal powers and responsibilities

The law as it relates to private investigators varies, of course, between jurisdictions, but there are some common principles that tend to apply, especially in liberal democracies. One important point is that a licence does not usually confer any special powers or rights. Consequently, in the course of their work, investigators are subject to criminal and civil laws in the same way as any other citizen. Generally speaking, the critical areas of law that relate to private investigators cover contract law, property access and trespass, nuisance, defamation, privacy and eavesdropping.

Investigators have contractual obligations to their clients that come under common law or commercial statute law provisions (Sarre, 2003). The investigator is acting as an 'agent' of the client and therefore has a duty to follow instructions that are legal and to generally act in the interest of the client. There may be specific contract requirements such as acting in person, or there may be an explicit or implied agreement that the work can be passed to employees or subcontractors. There is also likely to be a responsibility to account for time and costs, through time sheets or receipts. If the private investigator acts outside the client's instructions, they will be in breach of contract and may be liable to pay damages. But, generally, the investigator must exercise discretion in pursuing lines of enquiry, and acts by way of an implied authority of the client on many operational decisions.

Law commonly reflects the saying that 'one's home is one's castle'. Normally, a police officer or a private citizen cannot enter another person's property or conduct a search without expressed or implied consent, unless under special circumstances such as to prevent a criminal act. An entrant upon land for a lawful purpose (such as delivering a parcel) is assumed to have consent unless notified to the contrary by the occupier (Sarre, 2003). An investigator commits trespass if they enter a property where it is clear there is no consent (for example, a 'private property – do not enter' sign), or remains on the property after being asked to leave or is found there 'without lawful excuse'. If the investigator enters the property by a misrepresentation this will negate any consent. Thus the law empowers a private agent to enter property and approach occupiers in some circumstances, but largely restricts their capacity to covertly obtain material evidence or identify or contact someone trying to hide. This can make process serving very challenging, as direct delivery of a legal notice into the hands of the nominated person is usually required. In the case of repossession, an agent's ability to enter and seize property without permission is also usually restricted. Together with forcible entry, this could lead to a charge of 'break, enter and steal'. Where resistance is anticipated, repossessors may obtain a court order, but this is unlikely to authorize any use of force. As a last resort, the police may be able to attend and assist. Of course, if an agent is attacked, they would be allowed to use reasonable force to protect themselves. Outside private property, there may not be any legal restriction on seizing goods. This can include forcibly breaking into a car parked in a public location in order to repossess the car (Hardy and Prenzler, 2004).

Common legal rights facilitate surveillance work in public places. It is usually not illegal to tail or photograph someone. But if the surveillance becomes too overt it could be become an act of nuisance or harassment. The same may apply to 'overzealous' investigations, with repeated questioning of person's colleagues or acquaintances. Similarly, 'stings' or 'set ups' designed to expose fraudulent disability claimants might be legal unless they become too overt. Additionally, any action that leads to harm is likely be open to an action for 'tort'. In many cases it is also possible that the law allows investigators to act deceptively in approaching people, although fair trading legislation might make some actions illegal. An example would be where an investigator claims they are employed by a market research company in order to access a person's property (Hardy and Prenzler, 2004).

When acting on private property on behalf of the owner, investigators often have enormous power that follows from the right to place conditions on entry to premises (Rigakos and Greener, 2000; Sarre, 2003). This gives authority to in-house investigators in the public or private sector who can require a person to attend an interview, answer questions or have their locker or bags searched. If a subject refuses to co-operate, they may have their employment terminated or be expelled from a premise. Targets of enquiries receive some protection from defamation laws. Investigators need to be careful that in questions they ask, and statements they make, they do not wrongfully impute anything that may be harmful to a person's reputation.

Listening devices have typically been subject to some form of regulation long before privacy laws were introduced. Investigators may be allowed to covertly record conversations they are party to, but it is unlikely in most jurisdictions that they will be allowed to listen in on, or record, conversations as a third party – although this might be possible in certain circumstances such as extreme threat. Intercepting or opening mail is also typically an offence that restricts private investigators.

Often laws related to privacy have been scattered across a variety of sources, such as telecommunications intercept law and acts governing government departments. However, there has been a trend in many countries to more clearly define and protect people's privacy in specific legislation (Gill and Hart, 1997b). Typically, this legislation will stipulate that information can only be used for the purpose for which it was gathered. This prohibits private investigator access in many cases. However, the evolution of the law is not necessarily all bad news for private investigators. Privacy legislation can allow voluntary disclosure of information to agencies involved in law enforcement, including private enquiry agents, in some circumstances (King and Prenzler, 2003).

Cultural images

Private investigators have a high profile in the murder mystery and suspense genre in novels, films and television dramas. Most readers would be familiar with fictional private detective figures such as Arthur Conan Doyle's Sherlock Holmes or Agatha Christie's Poirot, or with films such as *The Maltese Falcon* or *Chinatown*. Stories about private detectives have contributed to an image of the cynical lone operator in a seedy second floor office, taking the occasional case from a private client. As enquiry work has become more routinized and commercial, the cultural image persists because of its narrative value and intrigue.

The cultural image is also typically dualistic: both 'glamorous and sinister' (George and Button, 2000: 87) and with investigators either 'knaves' or 'knights' (Gill and Hart, 1997a). What is usually certain is that the classical detective novel will end with a reassuring and satisfying resolution of the mystery by the protagonist. Although the intervention of the fictional private eye might bring the miscreant before the courts, the story is likely to include the realization of 'private justice' or 'real justice'. Gill and Hart (1997a: 636) cite as an example the ending of the 1970s' film version of Raymond Chandler's *Farewell My Lovely*, when the investigator, Philip Marlowe, kills a murderer who has faked his own death and escaped justice by bribing the police.

Of some interest is an Atlantic divide in the genre. Gill and Hart (1997a) identify an English preference for the gentlemen amateur detective – with upper class clients, a leisurely plot, and reassurances for the reader of restored social order and hierarchy. The counterpoint to the detective hero is the bumbling local constable. The American version displays a more gritty realism, with a more action-oriented and violent depiction of mean streets, and a more pessimistic message about the need for the heroic individual to continuously struggle against crime and corruption. The counterpoint is the corrupt or indifferent city police.

Social impact

The last 20–30 years have seen a substantial increase in the use of private agents to counteract fraud and assist lawyers and businesses in other work related to crime reduction and the pursuit of justice. There is, however, very little research measuring the achievements of investigators, whether for their clients or indirectly for the 'public good'. Private investigators interviewed for an Australian study claimed very high success rates for clients. They generally estimated their ability to obtain concrete results in the range of 70–90 percent (Prenzler and King, 2002). This was assessed in terms of recovery of losses, dropping of suspect insurance claims, criminal convictions or employment termination of offenders. Respondents claimed an approximate minimum saving of between $3 and $6 for every $1 spent on a case. Significant reductions in government payments have also resulted from the deployment of private surveillance agents against suspected fraudulent welfare claimants (Prenzler and King, 2002: 2). Anecdotally, many investigators claim satisfaction from helping private clients in difficult circumstances: by stopping long-term stalking for example, or providing assurances about the safety of a runaway teenager. These achievements are sometimes contrasted with an under-resourced or indifferent criminal justice system. Many investigators also have very positive views of the wider contribution they make to society, primarily as champions of the honest worker by keeping down costs affected by fraud and debt evasion (Prenzler and King, 2002).

Although under-resourcing of government services is a likely factor in the demand for private enquiry work, confidentiality is another factor. For example, if police discovered on behalf of concerned parents that a teenager was using drugs there would probably be an obligation to lay charges. A private investigator could simply reveal their findings, and parents could then try to get their child into a treatment programme. More generally, private investigators can provide a personal service, and continuity of case management and communication, not usually available from even the best police department. In the case of debt recovery, in many countries this is treated as a civil matter that must be pursued by the wronged party. Debt recovery agents are therefore involved in a response to a type of hidden crime. Tracing and interviewing witnesses is also an essential component of the delivery of justice in cases of a civil, but often criminal, standing. Here there is also a role to be played by private investigators in the defence of civil liberties and prevention of miscarriages of justice. Much of the legal work in relation to criminal justice is for the defence; in part because 'once the police have decided to press charges, their efforts are generally geared towards gathering evidence for the prosecution' (Gill and Hart, 1997b: 557). Hence, private investigations play a vital role in balancing the power of the state in the courts.

One downside, however, for many theorists, is the potential injustice associated with the growth of 'private justice'. This involves two dimensions. A 'social justice critique' (Prenzler, 2004) emphasizes how a 'mixed economy' of law enforcement and crime prevention favours the rich, resulting in unequal security and unequal access to justice (Loader, 1997). The second dimension – more narrowly defined as a 'justice critique' (Prenzler, 2004) – focuses on the impacts on due process of privatized justice (Shearing and Stenning, 1983). Offenders dealt with 'privately' may benefit unfairly from decisions not to enforce the law and not to inform police of an offence. At the same time, suspects may suffer from the denial of due process. Where, for example, police would prosecute a suspect in a case of employee theft, a firm might take the easier option of dismissing them, thereby denying the suspect the presumption of innocence and the protection of the court process. Allied with this is fear of a 'new surveillance' (Marx, 1986), 'widening webs of surveillance' (Reichman, 1987) and the 'dispersal of social control' away from democratic government (Hoogenboom, 1991). This follows from the new technologies of CCTV, listening devices, x-ray scanning, and computerized access to personal records. Theorists such as Hoogenboom acknowledge, nonetheless, that the growth of security services and new technologies do not pose a direct threat to democracy and civil liberties. They do, however, pose a challenge to improved accountability and the appropriate regulation of security technology. It is also unlikely that governments are going to address inequalities in access to justice with large increases in expenditure on public justice systems. It is important therefore that there is more public debate about how regulation and policy can address these vital issues of 'liberty, privacy and equity' (Stenning, 2000: 347).

Conclusion

Private investigators provide a wide range of services to their clients. Some of these services are essential to the business operations of insurance companies, legal firms and other businesses. Investigation services also provide a public benefit in the fight to reduce the cost of fraud and to facilitate justice for aggrieved parties who are the victims of crimes and other wrongs. However, there are potential large-scale inequalities and injustices that can result from the expansion of such forms of 'private justice'. There are also powerful pressures on private agents to breach the law in pursuit of legitimate goals; and there are pressures to pursue ends that are not justifiable, such as assisting with revenge or harassment. This potential for misconduct means that regulation is essential to protect clients and innocent third parties from breaches of privacy or other violations of liberties, and to maximize the benefits of private agent work. Many investigators argue that increased controls on their conduct through government regulation should be matched by enhanced powers for licence holders, such as access to information under strictly controlled conditions. This is potentially a future direction for private agent work, entailing enlarged interactions with government agencies, and contributing to the greater acceptance of private investigators as a legitimate part of the complex network of justice services.

Key readings

Draper, H. (1978) *Private Police*, Sussex: Harvester Press is an easy-to-read early qualitative study on the work of private investigators in Britain, with an extensive exploration of types of occupational deviance. Gill, M. and Hart, J. (1997a) 'Private Investigators in Britain and America: Perspectives on the Impact of Popular Culture'. *Policing: An International Journal of Police Strategy and Management*, Vol. 20, pp. 631–40 is a particularly good study for devotees of the private detective novel with a summary of cross-Atlantic perspectives on how the genre works differently in the US and Britain. Similarly, Gill, M. and Hart, J. (1997b) 'Exploring Investigative Policing: A Study of Private Detectives in Britain', *British Journal of Criminology*, Vol. 37, pp. 549–67 is based on questionnaires completed by private detectives in Britain. It makes a close examination of the changing work profile of private investigators with an emphasis on commercial work and a section on potential conflicts with ethical standards. Jones, T. and Newburn, T. (1998) *Private Security and Public Policing*, Oxford: Clarendon Press combines quantitative and qualitative data sources to show the diverse range of types of work now done by private investigators. McDermid, V. (1995) *A Suitable Job for a Woman: Inside the World of Women Private Eyes*, London: HarperCollins is a very interesting read based on interviews with female detectives. It highlights both the capability of women private detectives and the often amusing and difficult situations in which private investigators can find themselves in. Miall, T. and McDonald, M. (1993) *Gumshoe*, Sydney: screened on ABC TV is a fascinating documentary that includes interviews with investigators and extended re-enactments of aspects of their working days. It puts the viewer right in the scene and oscillates between the hilarious and the tragic. See also, Prenzler, T. and King M. (2002) 'The Role of Private Investigators and Commercial Agents in Law Enforcement', *Trends and Issues in Crime and Criminal Justice*, No. 234, pp. 1–6, based on interviews with 40 private detectives. This study explores the evolving nature of their work and clientele, explores the types of ethical issues they face and how they seek to resolve them, and includes attention to ways of assessing the benefits of private agency work.

References

Button, M. (1998) 'Beyond the Public Gaze – The Exclusion of Private Investigators from the British Debate over Regulating Private Security', *International Journal of the Sociology of Law*, Vol. 26, pp. 1–16.
Cunningham, W., Strauchs, J. and van Meter, C. (1990) *Hallcrest II: Private Security Trends 1970–2000*, Stoneham, MA: Butterworth-Heinemann.
Draper, H. (1978) *Private Police*, Sussex: Harvester Press.
George, B. and Button, M. (2000) *Private Security*, Leicester: Perpetuity Press.
Gill, M. and Hart, J. (1996) 'Historical Perspectives on Private Investigation in Britain and the US', *Security Journal*, Vol. 7, pp. 273–80.
Gill, M. and Hart, J. (1997a) 'Private Investigators in Britain and America: Perspectives on the Impact of Popular Culture', *Policing: An International Journal of Police Strategy and Management*, Vol. 20, pp. 631–40.
Gill, M. and Hart, J. (1997b) 'Exploring Investigative Policing: A Study of Private Detectives in Britain', *British Journal of Criminology*, Vol. 37, pp. 549–67.
Gill, M. and Hart, J. (1997c) 'Policing as a Business: The Organisation and Structure of Private Investigation', *Policing and Society*, Vol. 7, pp. 117–41.
Gill, M., Hart, J. and Stevens, J. (1996) 'Private Investigators: Under-researched, Under-estimated and Under-used?', *International Journal of Risk, Security and Crime Prevention*, Vol. 1, pp. 305–14.
Hardy, S. and Prenzler, T. (2004) 'Legal Control of Private Investigators and Associated Private Agents', *Australian Journal of Law and Society*, Vol. 18: in press.
Hoogenboom, R. (1991) 'Grey Policing: A Theoretical Framework', *Policing and Society*, Vol. 2, pp. 17–30.
Johnston, L. (1992) *The Rebirth of Private Policing*, London: Routledge.
Jones, T. and Newburn, T. (1998) *Private Security and Public Policing*, Oxford: Clarendon Press.
King, M. and Prenzler, T. (2003) 'Private Inquiry Agents: Ethical Challenges and Accountability', *Security Journal*, Vol. 16, pp. 7–17.

Loader, I. (1997) 'Private Security and the Demand for Protection in Contemporary Britain', *Policing and Society*, Vol. 7, pp. 143–62.

Marx, G. (1986) 'The Iron Fist and the Velvet Glove: Totalitarian Potentials within Democratic Structures', in J. Short (ed.) *The Social Fabric: Dimensions and Issues*, Beverly Hills, CA: Sage.

McDermid, V. (1995) *A Suitable Job for a Woman: Inside the World of Women Private Eyes*, London: HarperCollins.

Miall, T. and McDonald, M. (1993) *Gumshoe*, Sydney: screened on ABC TV.

Prenzler, T. (2004) 'The Privatisation of Policing', in R. Sarre and J. Tomaino (eds) *Key Issues in Criminal Justice*, Adelaide: Australian Humanities Press.

Prenzler, T. and King M. (2002) 'The Role of Private Investigators and Commercial Agents in Law Enforcement', *Trends and Issues in Crime and Criminal Justice*, No. 234, pp. 1–6.

Reichman, N. (1987) 'The Widening Webs of Surveillance: Private Police Unravelling Deceptive Claims', in C. Shearing and P. Stenning (eds) *Private Policing*, Newbury Park, CA: Sage.

Rigakos, G. and Greener, D. (2000) 'Bubbles of Governance: Private Policing and the Law in Canada', *Canadian Journal of Law and Society*, Vol. 15, pp. 145–85.

Sarre, R. (2003) 'Legal Sources of Private Security Powers', *Canberra Law Review*, Vol. 7, pp. 109–28.

Shearing, C. and Stenning, P. (1983) *Private Security and Private Justice: The Challenge of the 80s*, Montreal: Institute for Research on Public Policy.

South, N. (1988) *Policing for Profit*, London: Sage.

Stenning, P. (2000) 'Powers and Accountability of Private Police', *European Journal on Criminal Policy and Research*, Vol. 8, pp. 325–52.

19
CCTV: Is it Effective?

Martin Gill

Introduction

Closed Circuit Television Cameras (CCTV) have in some countries become a major weapon in the fight against crime and the promotion of public safety, and their use appears to be expanding. Indeed, at the time of writing nowhere does there appear to be a cut back in the use of CCTV. Those that have systems are keeping them and trying to keep apace with developments in the technology, those that do not are often monitoring developments closely.

Locating cameras strategically around locales affords the opportunity to surveille those scenes remotely. Images that are captured are transmitted in a variety of ways where they can be monitored and recorded for post event analysis. CCTV systems are what criminologists consider to be a 'situational measure', in that by conducting surveillance, cameras increase risks for offenders who are deterred and/or are more likely to get caught, and as a consequence people feel and are safer. Those responsible for law enforcement, and often this is private security personnel, gain in other ways too. They are able to allocate the right amount of resource to incidents as and when needed, have the potential to be monitored while they deal with the incident, enabling additional help to be allocated if required, and conduct post event investigation and analysis.

However, it would be a mistake to assume that CCTV is an unqualified good. There are two powerful drivers that provide a check against its further adoption and which form much of the focus of this chapter. The first concerns the effectiveness of CCTV, and no less importantly its cost effectiveness. There is now a rich body of literature on the effectiveness of CCTV but the findings are conflicting. Some suggest that CCTV works according to a range of criteria, some suggest it does not or that the effect is neutral. The second major concern is that CCTV represents 'big brother', impacts negatively on people's civil liberties through an invasion of personal privacy (as is the case with other situational measures, see von Hirsch *et al.*, 2000) and challenges the balance of power and the nature of the relationship between individual and state.

These twin concerns are not trivial and the aim of this chapter is to discuss them in more detail and it does so by separating the discussion into four parts.

The first part focuses on the extent of CCTV. Discussions about both effectiveness and the impact on privacy will depend on the amount of CCTV installed. The second part is concerned with the uses of CCTV. Similarly, just how CCTV is used offers important insights into its effectiveness and claims that it is intrusive. The third part looks at effectiveness and specifically addresses questions such as: does it reduce crime, does it make people feel safer, and does it displace offending? The fourth part looks at privacy issues and the 'big brother' claims are assessed. Here the work of a range of scholars is referred to and supplemented with data derived from surveys that highlight public views. Finally the chapter will end with a summary discussion.

The extent of CCTV

It is tempting, but a mistake, to discuss CCTV systems as if they are the same or similar, they are not. Cameras differ markedly in their capacity to see in different conditions and are used in different ways. Static cameras will typically have a different function to cameras that can pan, tilt and zoom (PTL), to those that are portable and redeployable at speed (Gill *et al.*, 2005a), which at least one author views as the future of CCTV (Cameron, 2004). Some have a specialist function. Automatic number plate recognition can be linked to a range of databases (such as the stolen vehicle register) and guide law enforcers to vehicles that merit stopping. Facial recognition systems – which are still evolving not least because the ease with which people can be identified varies with circumstance (Givens *et al.*, 2003) – offer the opportunity to identify individuals which can be helpful in controlling access to locations, and in a different way can help identify those who are wanted for offences. Although the most common view of a CCTV system is one in which cameras capture images that are sent to a monitor which are then interpreted by operators, the latest generation of cameras are much more intelligent because they are supported by software programmes. For example, they can identify exceptional behaviour or objects/individuals and send this to a screen. This way the operators only need to look at images that have been identified as being exceptional and are sent to a monitor for that purpose, rather than continuous monitoring of what is mostly an uneventful scene.

The problem is that these systems are new; they have not been subjected to much independent research. Indeed, most of what has been undertaken has focused on the first generation of cameras, used overtly, and they form the focus of what is being discussed here. The heavy investment in these types of cameras means that they are likely to be here for years, and a temptation to invest in alternative new technologies needs to be tempered with the fact that their effectiveness is not proven and they are still emerging technologies. Unsuspecting customers have previously suffered from being guinea pigs for the latest CCTV innovation (Gill *et al.*, 2003, 2005a; Smith *et al.*, 2003).

Not all countries have adopted CCTV with the same degree of enthusiasm. The US has been traditionally sceptical about CCTV (Nieto, 1997), but this technology is now commonplace and installing CCTV was spurred on by the terrorist attacks of September 11 (Nieto *et al.*, 2002). The UK remains distinctly enthusiastic and it has been estimated that there are well over four million cameras in place (McCahill and Norris, 2003a; see also Phillips, 1999) although five million cameras will be a closer estimate today. Elsewhere cameras are becoming common and more acceptable and this includes Australia (Wilson and Sutton, 2003a, b), Austria (Ney and Pichler, 2002), France (Martinais and Bétin, 2004), Germany (Helten and Fischer, 2003, 2004; Toepfer *et al.*, 2003), Scandinavia (Lomell *et al.*, 2003; Rudinow *et al.*, 2004; Wiecek and Sætnan, 2002; Winge and Knutsson, 2003), Switzerland (Klauser, 2004; Müller and Boos, 2004; Ruegg *et al.*, 2004), as well as in Russia, the Middle East and beyond (Norris *et al.*, 2004).

Uses of CCTV

Although CCTV is generally viewed and justified as a crime prevention measure, it has a range of other uses. Indeed, even when the apparent aim of CCTV is to reduce crime there is a need to look behind the explanations given since research has shown that it has a role to play in economic regeneration and general management of town centres (Mackay, 2003). It can serve a range of management functions relating for example to traffic (Ney and Pichler, 2002) and street cleaning (Norris and McCahill, 2003: 5). Where crowds gather, and this includes customers, it can be a useful management tool although even here the value of CCTV may be questioned. For example, Dixon *et al.* (forthcoming) found that over a quarter of respondents considered that public places CCTV cameras reduced people's sense of personal responsibility for others, and Ditton (2000) makes the point that CCTV can undermine people's commitment to watching the street. The same can also be true of the workplace (Beck and Willis, 1995). Certainly a small proportion of police officers surveyed by Gill and Hemming (2004) supported this view.

As will be shown, monitoring of individuals is a double-edged sword. On the one hand CCTV can monitor individuals, for example in the UK, police officers, social workers, housing officers and noise abatement officers can be monitored when attending 'difficult' areas covered by CCTV and thereby promote their safety. Some companies favour CCTV because it affords them protection. At least one major retailer and a major bus operator have justified the cost of CCTV on that basis that it provides independent evidence to protect them against malicious claims. Where customers say they 'slipped over' or were 'pushed' cameras provide a form of independent evidence enabling them to admit liability and avoid an expensive court case when they are wrong, and defend themselves when they are not shown to be at fault. Some companies claim to have negotiated lower insurance claims as a consequence.

On the other hand, and more controversially CCTV can be used within workplaces to assess staff. Cameras provide a way of checking whether staff are complying with procedures, and whether their behaviour is consistent with company policies. Some have viewed this as spying and the main problem, which underlines the civil liberty concerns which are discussed later, is that sometimes CCTV is introduced for one purpose and used for another. For example, McCahill (2002: 187) notes from his review of systems:

> while the stated aims of the vast majority of CCTV systems were related to crime control, once in play they were used for entirely different purposes. In the commercial retail sector the CCTV system was used also to check whether staff were meeting company requirements – for example compliance with till procedures or rules relating to refunds and exchanges. On some sites the cameras were used to monitor the body language of the shop staff to make sure they were being 'polite' and 'friendly' with customers. Other security managers explained how the cameras could be used to monitor the productivity of the shop worker.

Concerns that cameras may be used to spy on people (Honess and Charman, 1992) have long fuelled civil liberty concerns. There can be no doubt that workers are becoming more visible and this potentially changes the nature of the relationship between people and particularly between the observed and observers. For McCahill (2002) it would be no surprise if cameras became the cause of crime as employees sabotaged them, and some public cameras have already been vandalized (Gill and Spriggs, 2005). Certainly companies have used images to support disciplinary action against staff, croupiers, cashiers and product delivery staff have all been caught stealing on camera and punished as a consequence.

Clearly, the same cameras will have different purposes in the same contexts and their value will vary with context. As Lomell *et al.* (2003: 49) concluded from their work in Scandinavia:

> It came as no surprise that video surveillance in shops was directed primarily at shoplifting, in the open street system at a broader spectrum of crimes, in railway stations at service and safety functions, in the cultural institution at access control and theft of artifacts etc.

CCTV cameras have a wide variety of uses (see Gill and Turbin, 1998, 1999; Gill *et al.*, 2005c; Tilley, 1993), and it is important to recognize this. First to ensure that assessments about effectiveness can be made of the uses to which they are put. Second, to facilitate the implementation of procedures to safeguard against abuses. More on these points later.

Is CCTV effective? Does it reduce crime, and make people feel safer, does it help the police, does it deter, does it displace?

Does it reduce crime?

The issue of effectiveness is central to discussions about CCTV. To recap, the logic of CCTV, put simply, is that because offenders know they are being watched they will decide not to risk committing offences, and if they do there will be an image of them that can help identify them and be used to support a prosecution. Because there are increased risks to offenders it renders places safer and people fear crime less as a consequence.

There are a range of CCTV evaluations. Studies using an experimental design (Farrington and Painter, 2003) have facilitated assessment of effect, while those adopting a scientific realism approach have added to the understanding as to why effects have or have not occurred with a particular focus on the 'mechanisms' by which CCTV has an impact (Pawson and Tilley, 1997; see also Gill and Spriggs, 2005; Gill and Turbin, 1998, 1999).

Evidence of effectiveness from the reviews of CCTV paint a somewhat mixed picture (e.g. Eck, 2002; NACRO, 2002; Phillips, 1999), in that some studies show that CCTV has had an effect of some sort, others show a negative effect, others suggest the effects are neutral. For example, Ditton's (2000: 699) work in Glasgow invite CCTV advocates to consider striking research findings:

> Comparing responses before and after the CCTV cameras were installed, preparedness to use the city centre has not increased, feelings of safety are lower in the city centre than in the two control locations and have not improved. The city centre is more likely to be avoided than are the other two locations, and this has increased. Worries about being a victim remain greater in the city centre.

Thus there are several ways of measuring success. Welsh and Farrington (2002) have summarized the findings from a range of studies, initially for the British Home Office but later under the umbrella of the Campbell Collaboration (see Welsh and Farrington, 2003). They utilize strict criteria to include all worldwide studies that they define as rigorous. The reviews are distinguished by being systematic, using explicit methods to first identify, then collect and thereafter to assess previous research. A meta analysis is included which uses statistical techniques to assess the results from different studies and provide a summary of overall effect. The process of collecting data to meet the requirements of the Campbell Collaboration can be onerous (see Gill *et al.*, 2005d).

So what did Welsh and Farrington (2002) find? Their assessment criteria meant that just 22 studies were included, 11 had a desirable effect on crime, while in five the effect was undesirable and in another five there was no clear evidence of effect, while in one case it was not possible to tell. The meta analysis provided a little more detail, of the 18 studies that were included again half showed a desirable effect (all from the UK), while nine did not (and all five north American studies were in this group). More detailed analysis revealed no effect on crimes of violence but a significant impact on vehicle crime (see also Skinns, 1998).

Looking closely at location revealed some trends. They combined, somewhat oddly, studies of the city centre and public housing and found that CCTV had a small positive effect (although none of the north American studies showed an effect). For advocates of CCTV the findings on effectiveness from studies of public transport were disappointing. Indeed, only in car parks there was a 41 percent reduction in car crimes was the impact clearly positive but, as the authors recognize, this needs careful interpretation:

> ... the success of the CCTV schemes in car parks was limited to a reduction in vehicle crimes (the only crime type measured) and all five schemes included other interventions, such as improved street lighting and notices about CCTV cameras. Conversely, the evaluations of CCTV schemes in city centres and public housing measured a much larger range of crime types and the schemes did not involve, with one exception, other interventions. These CCTV schemes, and those focused on public transport, had only a small effect on crime. Could it be that a package of interventions focused on a specific crime type is what made the CCTV-led schemes in car parks effective?

There are however important limits to these types of reviews. For example, they exclude those studies where CCTV was not the main intervention, when clearly it is possible that CCTV can play an important supporting role for example, to policing operations. Also only crime rate outcomes were assessed, not others such as usability of public space, feeling of public safety or those relating to non-crime uses such as transport management. Moreover, they did not include any qualitative research to help put the quantitative data in perspective. Thus the research conclusion is that CCTV works in some places but not others and we are not sure why. As Painter and Tilley (1999: 4) note:

> No-one should ever believe that any individual crime prevention measure (including CCTV) will always reduce crime. The potential effectiveness of measure depends on their suitability to the circumstances in which a given crime problem manifests itself.

Of course, what makes a measure work or not will depend on a host of influences affecting the context in which CCTV is introduced. It is therefore perhaps not surprising that the findings on effectiveness are mixed. There are many things that can impact on whether a CCTV scheme works or not; the way it is designed, whether it is implemented well, whether it is managed effectively, the nature of the relationship with the police (see, Gill and Spriggs, 2005; Gill *et al.*, 2003; Smith *et al.*, 2003). There is also the quality of the evaluation, and as noted above not all evaluations are considered robust. This is not always the fault of the evaluators, clients are often prescriptive and sometimes budgets do not allow for scientifically reliable studies. Also evaluations are problematic, often full implementation does not take place (Gill and Spriggs, 2005; Smith *et al.*, 2003) or there are no clear objectives to measure against. As Ditton and Short (1999: 215) noted from their work in Scotland:

> there seem to have been a succession of goals, and with the benefit of hindsight, it is now clear that the original objectives have been regularly replaced to the point here, in a two year period, current goals bear no resemblance to initial ones.

By far the most comprehensive review of CCTV has been conducted by Gill and Spriggs (2005, and see Gill *et al.*, 2005a, b, c, d, e, f, g). They evaluated CCTV projects across the UK in different settings and came to a range of conclusions. On a general level, while six of the 14 systems analysed showed a reduction in all relevant crime, in only two of these did the target area perform statistically significantly better than their respective control area following the introduction of CCTV. And in one of these crime trends and confounding factors could have accounted for the result. So the somewhat striking conclusion was that in only one of 14 CCTV schemes that were evaluated was there a change that could be due to CCTV, and that was in a scheme devoted to reducing vehicle crime in car parks. In this case the reduction in vehicle crime was greater (80 percent) for those car parks that had the highest ratio of crimes per parking space before the cameras were installed, and this was statistically significant. These tended to be the larger car parks, which suffered greater absolute levels of crime. Medium and low risk car parks showed smaller, but nevertheless marked decreases (34 percent and 37 percent respectively) (see Gill *et al.*, 2005f). The general conclusion, following Welsh and Farrington, was that impulsive crimes (e.g. alcohol-related crimes) were less likely to be reduced than premeditated crime (e.g. theft of motor vehicles).

Neither of the redeployable schemes showed a reduction in long-term crime levels although they were principally intended to address short-term crime problems, so this is less surprising (Gill *et al.*, 2005c). An assessment of camera coverage showed that those systems with a larger viewshed (that is they could surveille large parts of the area) tended to reduce crime more than those with a smaller one. While a marked positive correlation of 0.51 between viewshed area and effect size was found, this was not significant. So while there was a generally positive relationship between density and crime reduction, installing extortionately large amounts of cameras provided no additional benefits.

The authors are cautious about the interpretations that can and should be placed on the findings. They note that overall crime reduction may not be the best measure, not least because in some cases an increase in crime was due to the public reporting more offences. Moreover, some CCTV schemes reduced specific offences (see, Gill *et al.*, 2005g). And a part from a range of implementation issues which impacted upon effectiveness (see Gill and Spriggs, 2005; Gill *et al.*, 2003; Smith *et al.*, 2003), CCTV can be made more effective when it becomes intelligent. On a practical level this typically meant benefiting from observations made by various 'watch' or radio links schemes (see Gill *et al.*, 2005e), and the link with the police was crucial (see below).

Overall, the public views after CCTV had been installed were less positive than they had been beforehand. Moreover, the public were less likely to think that people reported more incidents to the police, less likely to think that the police responded more quickly to incidents, and less likely to think that crime was lower (Gill and Spriggs, 2005).

Moreover, it was difficult to conclude that CCTV is effective on cost grounds. In summary, CCTV produced few cost benefits. This needs to be put in context, given that the schemes had little impact on crime rates, alongside which it must be noted that the cost of setting up schemes was high. Even in the car park scheme the cost benefits were low because although vehicle crime was reduced it has a comparatively low monetary value. This fuels the view of the authors that CCTV should not be judged on its ability to reduce crime, there are many other uses and benefits to CCTV as the above discussion has noted (and see, Gill and Spriggs, 2005).

Does it make people feel safe?

Just as the findings on effectiveness of CCTV in reducing crime are mixed, so are findings from research on whether it makes the public feel safer. When asked before it is introduced whether CCTV will make people safer and/or fear crime less most answer in the affirmative (Chainey, 1999), although this is not always seen as one of its main beneficial effects (Honess and Charman, 1992). And while some studies have found that CCTV has made people feel safe (Sarno *et al.*, 1999), especially women (Brooks, 2005) it is not always the case that people's fears are reduced as Ditton (2000: 699) notes:

> ... the three sweeps of the survey have uncovered no evidence that the instal-
> lation of CCTV cameras in Glasgow's city centre has positively had an effect
> on what is generally known as the fear of crime.

Moreover, when Ditton asked about the value of street cameras over half said they would feel safer, but even here a caveat is necessary since CCTV 'is not making the unsafe feel safe; it is making the already safe feel safer' (p. 702).

The real benefit of making people feel safer is if, as a consequence, they use areas they did not do so before. Here the findings are optimistic for CCTV. Bennett and Gelthsthorpe (1996) found that respondents in Cambridge claimed they would use the city centre more if CCTV was installed, especially after dark (22 percent) compared with during the day (8 percent). Similarly, Ditton (2000) found that 15 percent of respondents said they would use the street more if CCTV was installed, and those feeling unsafe were especially likely to, but Ditton, understandably, is sceptical of such claims unless they can be post-tested and backed up by experience. Gill and Spriggs (2005) found that the proportion of respondents who visited places they had previously avoided following CCTV installation ranged from just 2 percent to 7 percent. This contrasts markedly with the percentage of respondents interviewed before CCTV was installed who thought that they *would* visit places that they avoided once CCTV was installed. On average, 15 percent of pre-implementation respondents thought CCTV would permit them to visit places they avoided, with figures ranging from 6 percent to 23 percent for individual projects.

There are potentially a range of factors that can help explain why and whether CCTV makes people feel safe. Prime amongst them is being sure those being asked have noticed the cameras. For example, Dixon *et al.* (forthcoming) noted that only 40 percent of respondents stated they had noticed the cameras and

54 percent stated that they had not. Honess and Charman (1992) who found that less than 35 percent of street respondents were aware of CCTV (although the publicity was not high because of the desire not to fuel civil liberty worries). Other studies have found awareness to be higher amongst the public (67 percent) and businesses (95 percent) (Sarno *et al.*, 1999). Ditton (2000: 704) noted:

> Three months after installation, only 33 per cent of those in the city centre knew cameras were in operation; 15 months after installation, this had only risen to 41 per cent ... There were no differences in awareness of CCTV between those who felt safe in the city centre and those who didn't; between those who would sometimes avoid the location and those who wouldn't; and between those who worried about being a crime victim and those who didn't. Victims were slightly more likely to be aware of the CCTV cameras than were non-victims.

Similarly, Sarno *et al.* (1999: 30) found that:

> Sixty-three percent of the public who were aware of cameras said they felt safer as a result ..... Those who did not know there were cameras present were asked if they are likely to feel safer in the future. Sixty-six percent believed they would feel safer.

Gill and Spriggs' (2005) work was conducted from 2002–04 and they found awareness varied but was generally high (ranging from 61 percent to 97 percent awareness). Overall, there was a positive correlation (0.32) between awareness levels and camera density, although it was non-significant. That there was less awareness of CCTV in large city centre areas where perhaps the cameras are but a small part of the large amounts of street furniture already present is predictable. Not that greater awareness should be viewed as an indication of more positive attitudes. The authors found that, generally, the proportion of respondents happy or very happy about the presence of CCTV cameras declined over the evaluation period, although it still remained quite high with results ranging from 69 percent to 96 percent. Nor was there much evidence that people felt safer. Overall while feelings of safety increased after CCTV installations (in all but one area) in only three (of 12) areas was the increase greater than in control and in none was this statistically significant.

Of greater significance was the finding that awareness of cameras increased fear about becoming a victim of crime compared to those who were unaware of them. Overall, people's perceptions about the impact of CCTV on safety are often linked to their beliefs about other matters. For example, Bennett and Gelthsthorpe (1996) and Dixon *et al.* (forthcoming) are amongst those who found that positive attitudes towards CCTV generally included positive views about tackling crime. Gill and Spriggs (2005) found some evidence to show a reduction in fear of crime following the installation of CCTV but little to suggest that this could be attributable to CCTV not least because there were no major differences between experimental and control areas. They suggest that a better explanation for lower levels of fear was a reduction in the level of reported victimization within the areas.

When considering that individuals did not significantly change their behaviour once the cameras were installed, even though they believed they would, and support for CCTV reduced, there is a suggestion that the idea of CCTV was far more appealing in theory than it actually proved in practice. As will be discussed below this does not seem to be due to civil liberties, since the findings seem to indicate that residents do not consider the cameras as intrusive once installed as they may have previously thought.

It is more likely that the concern was about effectiveness since it was in areas where effectiveness was perceived to be low that the biggest reduction in support occurred. The authors had a major focus on residential areas and here survey respondents were clearly sceptical about the effectiveness of cameras. When presented with a list of statements about CCTV fewer agreed with those that suggested the effect of CCTV was positive than did when surveyed before CCTV was installed. Indeed, across all areas surveyed, and in response to each of the statements, there was a reduction in perceived effectiveness of CCTV. There was a 12 to 55 percentage point drop in the proportion of respondents who agreed with the statement 'with CCTV, level of crime has got lower'.

Does CCTV help the police?

It has been argued that CCTV has not had much impact on policing and is unlikely to do so (Goold, 2004), and although the police have often been viewed as obvious supporters of CCTV this is not always the case in practice (see, Coleman, 2004; Norris and McCahill, 2003). Similarly, Sarno *et al.* (1999: 18) found that not many incidents are captured on camera and the liaison with the police can be patchy:

> Operators spend much of their time scanning target areas looking for suspicious behaviour and incidents. This is their main means of gathering information and evidence ... Little direct intelligence information appears to be passed to operators from the police.

Certainly law enforcement has some cause to feel threatened by CCTV since in the early days of public space, there was concern that CCTV in the UK might be used as a substitute for the police (Honess and Charman, 1992), and there is still some residual concern today (Coleman, 2004: 204). Bennett and Gelthsthorpe (1996) found that when the public were asked their preferences for different types of prevention measures the most popular was more police patrols, followed by more or brighter street lights, CCTV and then more private security patrols. However, Dixon *et al.* (forthcoming) found higher levels of public support for CCTV than for street drinking measures and Gill and Hemming (2004) found, albeit on a small sample, that a large majority of officers agreed that town centre CCTV reassures the public (73 percent) and that it makes town centres safer at night (66 percent).

Early research work suggested, at least as far as interrogations were concerned, that the police had more to gain than suspects from the video-taping of interviews (McConville, 1992). Other more recent work of the use of CCTV in the custody suite has suggested more positive benefits to both sides (Newburn and Hayman, 2002). Gill and Hemming's (2004) work revealed that almost half of the officers surveyed had made use of CCTV footage either by showing it to suspects during interviews or by producing it as evidence in prosecutions. Officers reported that use of the images had resulted in a positive outcome in the majority of the prosecutions where it had been used, and the effectiveness was even more marked in interviews. Similarly, Chainey (1999) found that in Hackney, CCTV camera footage directly helped to make 42 arrests involving 73 persons between April–July 1998.

Control room

The control room is the place where images are observed and recorded. They can be managed or owned by either the police which is common in the US (Brinkley, 2004), or by local authorities which is more common in the UK (Gill *et al.*, 2005b). While the former facilitates strong links between the control room and the police it fuels concerns about 'big brother'. Local authorities reduce this threat but distance operators from law and rule enforcers. There are then advantages and disadvantages to each.

The control room is the hub of a CCTV scheme and its effectiveness can be affected by a wide range of issues including the quality of equipment, the number of operators and ratio of operators to screens, the amount and level of training operators receive as well as the management and organization of work there (see, Gill *et al.*, 2005b; see also Smith, 2004). Particularly important for the impact of CCTV is the relationship between the CCTV control room and those who respond to calls (McCahill and Norris, 2003), be that the police on the streets or security officers in private space. Indeed, Gill and Hemming (2004) found that police officers viewed the staff in the control room as the main weaknesses of CCTV (see also Goold, 2004).

The issues affecting the control room have been discussed fully elsewhere (see, Gill *et al.*, 2005b; see also Helten and Fischer, 2004) but the issue of staffing is crucial and worth highlighting here. Part of the difficulty is that much of the operators' work is mundane, one senior police officer referred to it as 'mind numbing monotony'. Engaging security officers in other duties to vary the routine is a technique that can be used to break that monotony (Gill, 2004) – such as managing alarms (Lomell *et al.*, 2003) – but this can also be a distraction. Loveday and Gill (2003) found that where operators were not distracted they were more successful.

Moreover, the quality of recruits has not always been high, not being native speakers (Norris and McCahill, 2003), lacking both basic skills (Helten and Fischer, 2003) and training (e.g. Sarno *et al.*, 1999) – which can greatly impact on effectiveness (Rudinow *et al.*, 2004) – suffering poor working conditions (Loveday and Gill, 2003) has resulted in a lack of commitment to the job (Wilson and

Sutton, 2003b). It is perhaps not surprising then that operators have often not always been viewed as a success (see, Gill *et al.*, 2005b; Loveday and Gill, 2003; McCahill, 2002; Norris and Armstrong, 1999; Smith, 2004).

Certainly they do not pass on information about all the incidents they identify to the police. On average it seems that 24 percent of the incidents observed by researchers were logged by operators with a range from 5 percent to 72 percent across 13 different control rooms, and the police, much to the chagrin of operators, did not respond to all incidents notified to them (Gill *et al.*, 2005b). Indeed, there is a danger of the police being 'imaged out' (Gill and Spriggs, 2005) because of the sheer amount of footage being made available to them. There is a real danger that rather than viewing CCTV as a means of saving on police officers time they become a primary justification by the police of the need for more staff.

Part of the problem has been in underestimating the skill involved in being an effective CCTV operator. They need, amongst other things, to be able to communicate with police and other third parties including private security (hence the importance of being able to speak the local language); be able to work the technical equipment to monitor cameras and this includes tracking suspects, to be able to review images and identify key information. They also need local knowledge which has encouraged some to highlight the benefits of recruiting locals.

And at this point it is perhaps poignant to recall just some of the successes that have been identified. For example, Norris and McCahill (2003) found that within the shopping mall they studied, 22 out of 84 (26 percent) of the targeted surveillance incidents resulted in someone being deployed, usually a mall security officer. They provide further details on 21 of these deployments and report that in nine there was at least one arrest or an ejection from the mall (mostly for shop theft). Meanwhile, Loveday and Gill (2003) found that where monitoring led to a further course of action other members of staff were called on for assistance in 19 percent (26) of cases, the police were called in 26 percent (37) of cases and arrests were made in 19 percent (27). This further action led to stock being recovered in 81 percent (67) of incident reports. Moreover, during the 3-month research period the 12 operators studied reported being involved in detections which resulted in recovering goods worth a total of £7447.30.

Does CCTV deter?

Phillips (1999) has underlined the need to continually demonstrate the deterrent effect of CCTV by publicizing the risk it poses to offenders. Much of the work on offender decision-making has suggested that for any measure to be effective offenders have to believe that it will result in them getting caught and the research about CCTV in this respect is not overly encouraging. Wright and Decker (1997) found armed commercial robbers to be sceptical of the value of CCTV. Gill and Loveday (2003) found that while more than seven in ten offenders interviewed believed CCTV would encourage police attendance, they did not generally believe it would increase the chances of them getting caught. Those who were the most aware and positive about the crime prevention effect of CCTV were those who had previously been caught on camera, which may perhaps offer some optimism for the potential effectiveness of CCTV in the future. However, the picture quality will have to be good otherwise it will merely encourage the view that the threat from CCTV is not real.

There was also some encouraging news from the work of Short and Ditton (1998). They found that some offenders were deterred, or said they were. However, for the most part CCTV merely changed the way they said they committed their offences. For example, there was evidence that some offenders carried on albeit more cautiously, yet the authors note some benign displacement in that more serious assaults became less serious ones.

Does it displace?

Displacement has long been viewed as an endemic drawback of situational measures and CCTV is no exception (see, Armstrong and Giulianotti, 1998; Flight *et al.*, 2003; Waples *et al.*, forthcoming). There is evidence that CCTV does displace offences but this does not always mean that the effects overall have been negative (Burrows, 1979; Skinns, 1998). Commonly, there will be displacement of some crime and not others. For example, Chainey (1999) found no displacement for street robberies but there was for motor vehicles. Offenders' accounts confirm that there may be displacement into areas not covered by CCTV (Short and Ditton, 1998). Sometimes though the displacement is to less serious offences and to that extent is benign.

Waples *et al.* (forthcoming; see also, Gill and Spriggs, 2005) confirmed these somewhat mixed findings. They found that overall spatial displacement occurred infrequently in their evaluated projects. However, two of the three cases of spatial displacement they did find were attributed solely to the installation of CCTV, as no other explanatory confounding factors were present. There was one possible case of diffusion of benefits, but this could also be explained by confounding factors present in the area. There was some internal displacement within areas covered by the project where, for example, vehicle crime was displaced from areas covered by cameras to areas where there was no CCTV coverage. These findings tend to suggest that while spatial displacement, and indeed other types may occur, including within project areas, and there may be diffusion of benefits, the former can hardly be considered a major drawback nor the latter a common advantage.

Privacy and civil liberties

CCTV has come to prominence at a time when privacy issues are at the forefront of public debate, and CCTV has great potential to intrude to the point of impinging on people's privacy. There are essentially two main perspectives that emerge from the work, the view of scholars who have outlined a range of potential threats, and those of the public that can be derived from surveys that have been conducted (mostly in the UK).

Theorists have long been concerned with explaining the dangers of too much surveillance. McCahill and Norris (2002) have reviewed what they consider to be the three main theoretical approaches to the study of visual surveillance, from sociology (to assess the impact of the extended generation of information on surveillance), critical criminology (to discuss the central role of CCTV in the development of different risk-based strategies to control crime), and urban geography (to discuss the market forces that are extending the use of CCTV). The central issue for those who are concerned about civil liberties threats is essentially one about power relationships.

Commonly, frameworks derived from both Focault's (1977) panoptican and Marxism to explain how CCTV is or can be used to reinforce class divisions with the (economically) powerful surveilling the marginalized or underclass (see, Fussey, 2004; Lyon, 1994; Norris and Armstrong, 1999). Some scholars have raised concerns about the ethics of using CCTV (e.g., von Hirsch, 2000, also Shapland, 2000). Some see CCTV as a divisive measure reflecting (and then causing) a lack of trust between members of societies (Duff and Marshall, 2000).[1] The problem is fuelled by the belief that managing or regulating CCTV is fraught with difficulties not least because definitions of privacy vary (Gallagher, 2004). As Gras (2004: 12) has noted legal regulation requires that privacy issues are given due prominence – this is one of the few ways that the greater priority of security over privacy can be checked – and this is much more problematic when CCTV is already commonplace:

> If we are not only to witness an ever increasing proliferation of CCTV, the authorities permitting installation must not only have the right to dismantle on the grounds that the cameras are no longer necessary to achieve the aim for which they were installed but also because the area in which they are installed now has so many cameras that issues of consent and possibly the nature of the privacy rights of those under surveillance has changed. This of course requires the political will to define and confer such powers.

Additional concerns focus on CCTV being used alongside other technologies (Pierce, 2002, see also Chapter 26), for example RFID to pose an even greater threat (Cameron, 2004; not least because they can be used discriminately (Introna and Wood, 2004, see also Chapter 20). And digitalization has merely increased the intrusive capacities of CCTV (Graham and Wood, 2003). Since 2000 in Switzerland a 'Big Brother' award has been made to organizations and individuals who are perceived as violating human rights, these are viewed as ironic political statements against intrusions of privacy (Müller and Boos, 2004). For McCahill (2002) the challenge to civil liberties is tied up in the development of '*The Surveillance Web*'. His work, based on original research, illustrates how different systems can combine to produce a powerful network of surveillance with far-reaching implications (p. 95):

> the construction and operation of CCTV surveillance systems has given rise to a whole new range of human linkages. This has brought together the police,

private security managers, department store and shopping centre managers and store detectives. These developments are increasing the integration of police and private security CCTV systems and facilitating information-sharing and liaison between those responsible for managing those systems.

The problem for McCahill is that *The Surveillance Web* is not always as positive as security practitioners tend to assume. He finds that 'known' people are subject to intensive surveillance even though they have not been found guilty; that children are excluded from shopping malls in school hours and ponders whether they are displaced to less safe streets; and people are banned from areas where there are services they may need. A particular problem is that commercial image of areas such as shopping malls means that groups are excluded 'before they have shown they can behave properly' (p. 146) and therefore their human rights are infringed (see also Coleman, 2004; von Hirsch and Shearing, 2000). Indeed, as Lyon (2003) has noted the real power of CCTV is not that it can see people but that it can sort people and categorize them. Similarly, Reeve (1998: 79) concluded:

> Findings from the research also suggest that within the move towards using the town centre as a commercial entity there are powerful pressures to exclude certain forms of behaviour and, by implication, to limit access to certain groups.

CCTV seen from this perspective is a means of disenfranchising certain groups (Bannister *et al.*, 1998), and leads to divided communities (Davis, 1990; Boddy, 1992). At least part of the argument here is that an attempt to eliminate activities that do not conform to the norm has negative implications for cultural development (see, Coleman, 2004; Fyfe and Bannister, 1998). Norris *et al.* (1998a: 271) have summarized the implications:

> if the growing divide between those who have and have not and those who are included and excluded is intensified through the use of new technology, there is a real danger that our cities will come to resemble the dystopian vision so beloved by futuristic film makers. Fortified, armed and electronically protected pockets of privilege will be surrounded by the ever increasing presence of poverty, resentment and hostility.

This divisiveness is driven by the commercial imperative. It is important not to overlook the commercial aspects that CCTV and the wider process of regeneration present. As McCahill (2002: 12) has noted:

> town centre manages and 'image makers' are promoting the use of city-centre CCTV surveillance systems as a means of providing a 'risk free' environment designed to attract consumers and tourists.

And CCTV can be instrumental in reducing insurance premiums, in making areas more attractive to businesses and shoppers and in offering other services.

Sarno *et al.* (1999) found that while businesses representatives accepted that the main aim of CCTV was to reduce or deter crime, they appreciated its potential to increase customer trade. Indeed, 46 of 132 respondents felt that there had been an increase in trade after CCTV, about a third cited reduced levels of shoplifting and burglaries. Approaching a half felt more secure at work as a result – and about a third more secure going to and from work.

But to return to the point, the fact that CCTV can be divisive has fuelled concerns about the 'big brother' effect that for some CCTV represents. Davies (1998a: 254; see also Davies, 1998b) has long highlighted the threats posed by CCTV which he feels marks:

> a fundamental shift in the balance of power between citizen and state, an increase in surveillance, a diminution of individual autonomy, and the creation of rigidity within the machinery of government.

But the privacy concerns are not just about the consequences for the disadvantaged or the changing relationship between individual and the state. There is a real concern that those doing the observing are not easily held accountable, and there is growing evidence that there are genuine reasons to be troubled about the behaviour of some operators (see, Gill *et al.*, 2005b; Lomell *et al.*, 2003; McCahill, 2002; Norris and Armstrong, 1999; Norris and McCahill, 2003). Part of the issue here is who is watching who and precisely for what purpose? Brown (1998: 218) for example has noted:

> More men, sitting in front of camera screens, add visibility. It does not necessarily add security. The kinds of behaviour which CCTV can monitor and ostensibly provide a basis for action on are the rare and spectacular acts of physical assaults on women in the high street. It cannot monitor the alcohol fuelled male gaze nor the alcohol fuelled male display: indeed, in one sense it is a part of the male gaze, and therefore part of the problem rather than the solution.

It is important to understand the nature of people's concern on this point, and they can be ascertained from a range of surveys. Honess and Charman (1992) found that respondents expressed concerns about CCTV either because they viewed it as an invasion of privacy or because they distrusted CCTV operators. Bennett and Gelthsthorpe's (1996) concluded that worries about civil liberties related to a general dislike about being watched, followed by concerns about growing state control, followed by the control and monitoring of CCTV. Spriggs *et al.* (2005) found that those who thought crime was a problem were less likely to consider CCTV cameras an invasion of privacy while Bennett and Gelthsthorpe's (1996: 87) reported that those who felt 'very safe' were much more concerned about civil liberties, they also concluded that:

> the majority of people who were worried about CCTV did not believe that CCTV was a bad idea. In other words, public concerns about civil rights issues

were not strong enough to make them believe that CCTV should not be installed.

Survey findings put public views about CCTV in perspective. For example, Chainey's (1999) study in Hackney, London, found that 76 percent disagreed that 'CCTV infringes civil liberty' but this statistic was 'agreed' markedly more by respondents in areas where CCTV covered residential properties (e.g. housing estates) a point that will discussed below. Similarly Dixon *et al.* (forthcoming) found that 10 percent felt CCTV infringed their individual rights, and the more people agreed that CCTV increased feelings of safety and the less concerned they were about CCTV impinging on their individual rights. Moreover, two-thirds of people felt that the more CCTV cameras there were the better, principally because they felt that anyone obeying the law had nothing to fear. Gill and Spriggs (2005) found that the experience of CCTV reduced concerns about the invasion of privacy. An interesting study was conducted by Newburn and Hayman (2002) in police custody suites. They found that CCTV was valued by both police officers and detainees and the authors conclude that the willingness of the latter, 'to trade privacy for protection, is compelling evidence in support of the use of CCTV in this way' (p. 169). Typically it is funding issues rather than concern about civil liberties that prevents schemes evolving (McCahill, 2002, see also Smith *et al.*, 2003), although a desire not to be left out can also be important (Gill and Hemming, 2004).

Concern about the potential threat to privacy that CCTV poses varies with circumstance. Ditton (2000) found that men minded more than women, and younger more than older people as did Spriggs *et al.* (2005) who also found that non-whites were more likely than whites to consider CCTV to be an invasion of privacy. Location was also important in that 33 percent mind being watched in the street, although only 14 percent in a car park. There had been a long held view (noted above) that those in residential areas would be viewed as especially intrusive, but that is not borne out by the evidence. Spriggs *et al.* (2005) found that about a sixth of residential respondents felt that CCTV would be an invasion of privacy. There was not much difference when all the nine areas they studied (including town and city centres) were considered, around 17 percent of all respondents either agreed or strongly agreed that the introduction of CCTV would be an invasion of people's privacy (with a range of 12 percent to 23 percent). Gill and Spriggs (2005) found that the presence of CCTV did not generally discourage people from visiting places in that only 1 percent of respondents said they avoided places after the installation of CCTV.

In some cases the concern about the intrusive impact of CCTV has guided how it will be used. For example, one bus company in the UK introduced CCTV to its vehicles, but the drivers were suspicious, principally that they might be monitored at work which they claimed was an infringement of their civil liberties. The Union gave support and as a consequence it was agreed that while the cameras would be used as a crime prevention measure they would never be used in disciplinary cases against drivers. Indeed, serious concerns about the intrusive potential of CCTV have led to the introduction of regulations to guide its use in various codes of practice that need to take account of various privacy-related laws. However, having well written codes, and ensuring that these are used in practice remain a challenge. Indeed, in Europe, in both London (McCahill and Norris, 2003a) and Berlin (Toepfer *et al.*, 2003) some systems have not complied with the law.

Discussion

CCTV has long been viewed as controversial but it is a much more complex measure than is often realised. There is a lot to consider in making CCTV work. Specifying and installing a CCTV system requires the skills of photography, information technology, mechanical engineering, electronics and civil engineering. And the design itself has to take account of a whole range of possibilities. The communication system, that is the method of transferring images from a camera to a recorder can be achieved by a using a computer and Internet Protocol (IP), via cables (co-ax, twisted pair, fibre optic), or by wireless (e.g. microwave or infrared) while G3 is an alternative method of transferring pictures from a remote site. Then there is the decision about whether to have an analogue or digital system or, as many systems are in reality, a mixture of the two. Intelligence can be added by using algorithms. All these are examples of some of the technical possibilities and they all have different implications for the types of systems that can evolve and the effectiveness of them. Then on top of this are all the management issues that can impact on whether a system works. Indeed, all systems require human interaction and it is readily apparent to even the most causal observers of the CCTV scene that the pace of development in humans' use of CCTV has fallen some way behind the pace in technological progress (see for example, Gill *et al.*, 2005a).

More effort is needed to change buyers' behaviour. Too often buyers get advice about security from sales personnel. Customers believe they want CCTV and they call up a seller of CCTV. The seller arrives and gives the clients what they want, but it is not necessarily what they need to provide a solution in the most cost effective and practical way. What is less in evidence, and much needed, is a clear identification of the problem, a prerequisite to deciding which of a range of measures are appropriate in that context. It is naive to expect a seller of CCTV – especially one paid on commission – to advise the client that a security officer or an intruder alarm is a better bet. Companies may well claim that they provide end-users with what they ask for but they do not always provide what end-users need and that responsibility needs to rest with end-users.

Indeed, end-user and public education are crucial. At present many people have a high expectation of CCTV and an unrealistic one. If unchallenged it could lead to disenchantment and fuel concerns about civil liberties. After all, people will typically accept some intrusion into their lives if a greater good can result, and thus they need to be clear that there is a greater good. There are warning signs already in that people are less positive about CCTV when they have experience of it. At present they still remain largely positive but complacency here is unwise. Moreover, widespread police support cannot be assumed; the police are in danger of becoming imaged out. As there become more cameras so logically there become more images but it is far from clear there is a well-developed strategy for dealing with them. Going forward a strategy, at both the national and local level, is a must.

Thought needs to be given to the types of measures used alongside CCTV. Just as CCTV is a developing technology, so there are other technologies which present threats to privacy. If the public begin to believe that the balance between privacy and security has gone too far so then their faith in technological measures may be questioned. It is incumbent on the security world, and Government too, to show that the benefits of security outweigh the costs and at present too much is assumed and too little independently evaluated.

That CCTV has a future in security and crime prevention is unquestioned, but it is neither easy to use nor uncomplicated to manage. And how it will be used will affect how it will be perceived (Norris and McCahill, 2006). Moreover, the growing amount of potentially intrusive measures, of which CCTV is but one example, marks a gradual a shift in the balance of the relationship between individual and state, this trend needs to be monitored. On a practical level instead of starting with the solution, we need to start with the problem and correctly define it. This is a skilled task but a good security risk assessment should be the basis of all good security strategies and this should incorporate a security audit to ensure that the right measurers are implemented and are properly integrated into a broader security strategy. On a strategic level (at least regionally and nationally) there needs to be a specific CCTV strategy highlighting its main functions, the resources needed to make it work and highlighting the role of different parties in that process. CCTV will often have a role to play in enhancing security, and a crucial one at that, but given the findings from independent research available to us at present, it is clear that we still have a lot to learn about how to use it to best advantage.

Note

1 Private security generally is divisive in that it offers protection to those who can afford to pay (see South, 1988).

Key readings

For a discussion of the effectiveness of CCTV there are perhaps two key references: see Gill, M. and Spriggs, A. (2005) *Assessing the Impact of CCTV*, Home Office Research Study (292), London: Home Office (http://www.homeoffice.gov.uk/rds/pdfs05/hors292.pdf.) and Welsh, B. and Farrington, D. (2003) *Effects of Closed Circuit Television Surveillance on Crime: Protocol for a Systematic Review*, Campbell Collaboration Crime and Justice Group Third revision: November 4, http://www.aic.gov.au/campbellcj/reviews/2003-11-CCTV.pdf. Different types of surveillance studies are contributing considerably to our understanding of CCTV, good references include: McCahill, M. (2002) *The Surveillance Web: The Rise of Visual Surveillance in an English City*, Collumpton: Willan and Norris, C. and Armstrong, G. (1999) *The Maximum Surveillance Society: The Rise of Closed Circuit Television*, Oxford: Berg. See also: The Politics of CCTV in Europe and Beyond, Special Issue, *Surveillance and Society*, 2(2/3) http://www.surveillance-and-society, and Nieto, M., Johnston-Dodds, K. and Simmons, C. (2002) *Public and Private Applications of Video Surveillance and Biometric Technologies*, Sacramento:

Californian Research Bureau. The Urban Eye project which looked at CCTV in different European countries produced some useful findings, see http://www.library.ca.gov/crb/02/06/ 02-006.pdf. http://www.urbaneye.net/results/results.htm. There are a number of books and edited collections that have generated important insights for theory and/or policy, and these include: Gill, M. (ed.) (2003) *CCTV*, Leicester: Perpetuity Press, Lyon, D. (ed.) (2003) *Surveillance as Social Sorting: Privacy Risk and Digital Discrimination*, London: Routledge, Norris, C., Moran, J. and Armstrong, G. (eds) (1998) *Surveillance, Closed Circuit Television and Social Control*, Aldershot: Ashgate and Painter, K. and Tilley, N. (eds), *Surveillance of public space: CCTV, Street Lighting and Crime Prevention*, CPS 10, Mounsey: Criminal Justice Press.

References

Armstrong, G. and Giulianotti, R. (1998) 'From Another Angle: Police Surveillance and Football Supporters', in C. Norris, J. Moran and G. Armstrong (eds), *Surveillance, Close Circuit Television and Social Control*, Aldershot: Ashgate.

Bannister, J. Fyfe, N. and Kearns, A. (1998) 'Closed Circuit Television and the City', in C. Norris, J. Moran and G. Armstrong (eds), *Surveillance, Close Circuit Television and Social Control*, Aldershot: Ashgate.

Beck, A. and Willis, A. (1995) *Crime and Security: Managing the Risk to Safe Shopping*, Leicester: Perpetuity Press.

Bennett, T. and Gelthsthorpe, L. (1996) 'Public Attitudes to CCTV in Public Places', *Studies on Crime and Crime Prevention*, 5(1), 72–90.

Boddy, T. (1992) 'Underground and Overhead: Building the Analogous City', in M. Sorkin (ed.), *Variations on a Theme Park*, New York: Hill and Wang.

Brinkley, S. (2004) 'Video Surveillance and Privacy in the US', CCTV User Group Conference, 19–21 April, Manchester.

Brooks, D. (2005) 'Is CCTV a Social Benefit? A Psychometric Study on Perceived Social Risk', *Security Journal*, 18(2), 19–30.

Brown, S. (1998) 'What's the Problem Girls? CCTV and the Gendering Public Safety', in C. Norris, J. Moran and G. Armstrong (eds), *Surveillance, Close Circuit Television and Social Control*, Aldershot: Ashgate.

Burrows, J. (1979) 'Closed Circuit Television on the London Underground', in P. Mayhew, R. Clarke, J. Burrows, M. Hough and S. Winchester (eds), *Crime in Public View*, Home Office Research Study 49, London: HMSO, 21–59.

Cameron, H. (2004) 'CCTV and (In)dividuation', *Surveillance and Society*, Special Issue: The Politics of CCTV in Europe and Beyond, 2(2/3), http://www.surveillance-and-society.

Chainey, S. (1999) *Crime Mapping Case Studies Volume 2: Successes in the Field*, United States Institute of Justice, Washington DC.

Coleman, R. (2004) *Reclaiming the Street: Surveillance, Social Control and the City*, Collumpton: Willan.

Davis, M. (1990) *City of Quartz*, London: Vintage.

Davies, S. (1998a) 'CCTV: A New Battleground for Privacy', in C. Norris, J. Moran and G. Armstrong (eds), *Surveillance, Close Circuit Television and Social Control*, Aldershot: Ashgate.

Davies, S. (1998b) *Big Brother: Britain's Web of Surveillance and the New Technological Order*, London: Pan Books.

Ditton, J. (2000) 'Crime and the City: Public Attitudes Towards Open-Street CCTV in Glasgow', *British Journal of Criminology*, 40(4), 692–709.

Ditton, J. and Short, E. (1999) 'Yes, It Works, No, It Doesn't: Comparing The Effects of Open-Street CCTV in Two Adjacent Scottish Towns', in K. Painter and N. Tilley (eds), *Surveillance of Public Space: CCTV, Street Lighting and Crime Prevention*, CPS 10, Mounsey Criminal Justice Press.

Dixon, J., Levine, M. and McAuley, R. (forthcoming) *Street Drinking Legislation, CCTV and Public Space: Exploring Attitudes Towards Public Order Measures*, Home Office.

Duff, R. and Marshall, S. (2000) 'Benefits, Burdens and Responsibilities: Some Ethical Dimensions of Situational Crime Prevention', in A. von Hirsch, D. Garland and

A. Wakefield (eds), *Ethical and Social Perspectives on Situational Crime Prevention*, Oxford: Hart Publishing.

Eck, J.E. (2002) 'Preventing Crime at Places', in L.W. Sherman, D.P. Farrington, B.C. Welsh and D.L. MacKenzie (eds), *Evidence-Based Crime Prevention*, 241–94, London: Routledge.

Farrington, D. and Painter, K. (2003) 'How to Evaluate the Impact of CCTV on Crime', in M. Gill (ed.), *CCTV*, Leicester: Perpetuity Press.

Flight, S., Heerwaarden, Y. and van Soomeran, P. (2003) 'Does CCTV Displace Crime? An Evaluation of the Evidence and a Case-Study from Amsterdam', in M. Gill (ed.), *CCTV*, Leicester: Perpetuity Press.

Foucault, M. (1977) *Discipline and Punish: The Birth of the Prison*, London: Allen Lane.

Fussey, P. (2004) 'New Labour and New Surveillance: Theoretical and Political Ramifications of CCTV Implementation in the UK', *Surveillance and Society*, Special Issue: The Politics of CCTV in Europe and Beyond, 2(2/3), http://www.surveillance-and-society.

Fyfe, N. and Bannister, J. (1998) 'The Eyes Upon the Street: Closed Circuit Television Surveillance and the City', in N. Fyfe (ed.), *Images of the Street*, London: Routledge.

Gallagher, C. (2004) 'The CCTV and Human Rights: the Fish and the Bicycle? An Examination of *Peck V. United Kingdom* (2003) 36 E.H.R.R. 41', *Surveillance and Society*, Special Issue: The Politics of CCTV in Europe and Beyond, 2(2/3), http://www.surveillance-and-society.

Gill, M. (ed.) (2003) *CCTV*, Leicester: Perpetuity Press.

Gill, M. (2004) *Retail Security Officers*, Leicester: Perpetuity Research and Consultancy International.

Gill, M. and Hemming, M. (2004) 'The Evaluation of CCTV in the London Borough of Lewisham: a report, Leceister: Perpetuity Research and Consultancy International, http://www.perpetuitygroup.com/prci/publications.html#lewishamcctv.

Gill, M. and Loveday, K. (2003) 'What Do Offenders Think About CCTV?', in M. Gill (ed.), *CCTV*, Leicester: Perpetuity Press.

Gill, M. and Turbin, V. (1999) 'Evaluating "Realistic Evaluation": Evidence from a Study of CCTV', in K. Painter and N. Tilley (eds), *Surveillance of Public Space: CCTV, Street Lighting and Crime Prevention, Crime Prevention Studies*, 10, Monsey, NY: Criminal Justice Press.

Gill, M.L. and Turbin, V. (1998) 'CCTV and Shop Theft: Towards a Realistic Evaluation', in C. Norris, G. Armstrong and J. Moran (eds), *Surveillance, Order and Social Control*, Aldershot: Gower.

Gill, M., Smith, P., Spriggs, A., Argomaniz, J., Allen, J., Follett, M., Jessiman, P., Kara, D., Little, R. and Swain, D. (2003) *National Evaluation of CCTV: Early Findings on Scheme Implementation, Effective Practice Guide*, Home Office Development and Practice Report, (7), London: HMSO.

Gill, M. and Spriggs, A. (2005) *Assessing the Impact of CCTV*, Home Office Research Study (292), London: Home Office, http://www.homeoffice.gov.uk/rds/pdfs05/hors292.pdf.

Gill, M., Collins, K., Hemming, M. and Rose, A. (2005a) *A Good Practice Guide for the Implementation of Redeployable CCTV*, Home Office Development and Practice Report, London: Home Office, http://www.homeoffice.gov.uk/rds/pdfs05/rdsolr1605.pdf.

Gill, M., Spriggs, A., Allen, J., Hemming, M., Jessiman, P., Kara, D., Kilworth, J., Little, R. and Swain, D. (2005b): *Control Rooms: Findings from Control Room Observations*, Home Office Online Report, London: Home Office, http://www.homeoffice.gov.uk/rds/pdfs05/rdsolr1405.pdf.

Gill, M., Spriggs, A., Allen, J., Argomaniz, J., Bryan, J., Hemming, M., Jessiman, P., Kara, D., Kilworth, J., Little, R., Swain, D. and Waples, S. (2005c) *The Impact of CCTV: Fourteen Case Studies*, Home Office Online Report, London: Home Office, http://www.homeoffice.gov.uk/rds/pdfs05/rdsolr1505.pdf.

Gill, M., Spriggs, A., Allen, J., Argomaniz, J., Bryan, J., Jessiman, P., Kara, D., Kilworth, J., Little, R., Swain, D. and Waples, S. (2005d) *Technical Annex: Methods Used in Assessing the Impact of CCTV*, Home Office Online Report, London: Home Office, http://www.homeoffice.gov.uk/rds/pdfs05/rdsolr1705.pdf.

Gill, M., Swain, D., Spriggs, A., Allen, J., Argomaniz, J. and Waples, S. (2005e) *Assessing the Impact of CCTV – The South City Case Study*, Home Office Online Report, London: Home Office, http://www.homeoffice.gov.uk/rds/pdfs05/rdsolr1105.pdf.

Gill, M., Little, R., Spriggs, A., Allen, J., Argomaniz, J. and Waples, S. (2005f) *Assessing the Impact of CCTV – The Hawkeye Case Study*, Home Office Online Report, London: Home Office, http://www.homeoffice.gov.uk/rds/pdfs05/rdsolr1205.pdf.

Gill, M., Allen, J., Spriggs, A., Argomaniz, J. and Waples, S. (2005g) *Assessing the Impact of CCTV – The Northern Estate Case Study*, Home Office Online Report, London: Home Office, http://www.homeoffice.gov.uk/rds/pdfs05/rdsolr1305.pdf.

Givens, G., Beveridge, J.R., Draper B.A. and Bolme, D. (2003) *A Statistical Assessment of Subject Factors in the PCA Recognition of Human Faces*, http://www.cs.colostate.edu/evalfacerec/papers/csusacv03.pdf.

Goold, B.J. (2004) *CCTV and Policing: Public Area Surveillance and Police Practices in Britain*, Oxford: Oxford University Press.

Graham, S. (1998) 'Towards the Fifth Utility? On Extension and Normalisation of Public CCTV', in C. Norris, J. Moran and G. Armstrong (eds), *Surveillance, Close Circuit Television and Social Control*, Aldershot: Ashgate.

Graham, S. and Wood, D. (2003) 'Digitizing Surveillance: Categorization, Space and Inequality', *Critical Social Policy*, 20(2), 227–48.

Gras, M.L. (2004) 'The Legal Regulation of CCTV in Europe', *Surveillance and Society*, Special Issue: The Politics of CCTV in Europe and Beyond, 2(2/3), http://www.surveillance-and-society.

Helten, F. and Fischer, B. (2003) *Video Surveillance on Demand for Various Purposes. Berlin Shopping Malls as Socio-Technical Testbeds for CCTV*, UrbanEye Working Paper No, 11, http://www.urbaneye.net/results/ue_wp11.pdf.

Helten, F. and Fischer, B. (2004) 'Reactive Attention: Video Surveillance in Berlin Shopping Malls', *Surveillance & Society*, 2(2/3), 323–46, http://www.surveillance-and-society.org/articles2(2)/berlin.pdf.

Honess, T. and Charman, E. (1992) *Closed Circuit Television in Public Spaces: Its Acceptability and Perceived Effectiveness*, Crime Prevention Unit Paper 35, London: Home Office.

Introna, L.D. and Wood, D. (2004) 'Picturing Algorithmic Surveillance: The Politics of Facial Recognition Systems', *Surveillance and Society*, Special Issue: The Politics of CCTV in Europe and Beyond, 2(2/3), http://www.surveillance-and-society.

Klauser, F. (2004) 'A Comparison of the Impact of Protective and Preservative Video Surveillance on Urban Territoriality: the Case of Switzerland', *Surveillance & Society*, 2(2/3), 145–60, http://www.surveillance-and-society.org/articles2(2)/switzerland.pdf.

Lomell, H.M., Sætnan, A.R. and Wiecek, C. (2003) 'Flexible Technology, Structured Practices: Surveillance Operation in 14 Norwegian and Danish organizations', UrbanEye Working Paper No. 9, http://www.urbaneye.net/results/ue_wp9.pdf.

Loveday, K. and Gill, M. (2003) *CCTV*, in M. Gill (ed.), Leicester: Perpetuity Press.

Lyon, D. (1994) *The Electronic Eye: the Rise of the Surveillance Society*, Oxford: Polity.

Lyon, D. (ed.) (2003) *Surveillance as Social Sorting: Privacy Risk and Digital Discrimination*, London: Routledge.

Mackay, D. (2003) 'Multiple Targets: The Reasons to Support Town-centre CCTV Systems', in M. Gill (ed.), *CCTV*, Leicester: Perpetuity Press.

Martinais, E. and Bétin, C. (2004) 'Social Aspects of CCTV in France: the Case of the City Centre of Lyons', *Surveillance and Society*, Special Issue: The Politics of CCTV in Europe and Beyond, 2(2/3), http://www.surveillance-and-society.

McCahill, M. (2002) *The Surveillance Web: The Rise of Visual Surveillance in an English City*, Collumpton: Willan.

McCahill, M. and Norris, C. (2002) 'Literature Review', UrbanEye Working Paper No. 2, http://www.urbaneye.net/results/ue_wp2.pdf.

McCahill, M. and Norris, C. (2003) 'Four CCTV Systems in London', UrbanEye Working Paper No. 10, http://www.urbaneye.net/results/ue_wp10.pdf.

McCahill, M. and Norris, C. (2003a) 'Estimating the Extent, Sophistication and Legality of CCTV in London', in M. Gill (ed.), *CCTV*, Leicester: Perpetuity Press.

McConville, M. (1992) 'Videoing Interrogations: Police Behaviour On and Off Camera', *Criminal Law Review*, August, 532–48.

Müller, C. and Boos, D. (2004) 'Zurich Main Railway Station: A Typology of Public CCTV Systems', *Surveillance and Society*, Special Issue: The Politics of CCTV in Europe and Beyond, 2(2/3), http://www.surveillance-and-society.

NACRO (2002) *To CCTV or Not to CCTV? A Review of Current Research into the Effectiveness of CCTV Systems in Reducing Crime*, London: National Association for the Care and Resettlement of Offenders.

Newburn, T. and Hayman, S. (2002) *Policing, Surveillance, and Social Control: CCTV and Police Monitoring of Suspects*, Cullompton: Willan.

Ney, S. and Pichler, K. (2002) 'Video Surveillance in Austria', UrbanEye Working Paper No. 7, http://www.urbaneye.net/results/ue_wp7.pdf.

Nieto, M. (1997) *Public Video Surveillance: Is It an Effective Crime Prevention Tool?*, Sacramento: California Research Bureau, California State Library.

Nieto, M., Johnston-Dodds, K. and Simmons, C. (2002) *Public and Private Applications of Video Surveillance and Biometric Technologies*, Sacramento: Californian Research Bureau, http://www.library.ca.gov/crb/02/06/02-006.pdf.

Norris, C. and Armstrong, G. (1999) *The Maximum Surveillance Society: The Rise of Closed Circuit Television*, Oxford: Berg.

Norris, C., Moran, J. and Armstrong, G. (eds) (1998) *Surveillance, Close Circuit Television and Social Control*, Aldershot: Ashgate.

Norris, C., Moran, J. and Armstrong, G. (1998a) 'Algorithmic Surveillance: The Future of Automated Visual Surveillance', in C. Norris, J. Moran and G. Armstrong (eds), *Surveillance, Close Circuit Television and Social Control*, Aldershot: Ashgate.

Norris, C. and McCahill, M. (2003) *On the Threshold to the Urban Panoptican: Analysing the Employment of Closed Circuit Television (CCTV) in European Cities and Assessing its Social and Political Impacts*, Work Package IV: CCTV Systems: Their Structures and Practices, Centre for Criminology and Criminal Justice, University of Hull, Hull HU6 7RX, March.

Norris, C. and McCahill, M. (2006) 'CCTV: Beyond Penal Modernism', *British Journal of Criminology*, 46(1), January, 97–118.

Norris, C., McCahill, M. and Wood, D. (eds) (2004) 'The Growth of CCTV: A Global Perspective on the International Diffusion of Video Surveillance in Publicly Accessible Space', The Politics of CCTV In Europe and Beyond, Special Issue, *Surveillance and Society*, 2(2/3), http://www.surveillance-and-society.

Painter, K. and Tilly, N. (1999) 'Surveillance of Public Space: CCTV, Street Lighting and Crime Prevention', *Crime Prevention Studies*, 10, New York: Criminal Justice Press.

Pawson, R. and Tilley, N. (1997) *Realistic Evaluation*, London: Sage Publications.

Pierce, C. (2002) *The Professional's Guide to CCTV*, Boston: Butterworth-Heinemann.

Phillips, C. (1999) 'A Review of CCTV Evaluations: Crime Reduction Effects and Attitudes Towards its Use', in K. Painter and N. Tilley (eds), *Surveillance of Public Space: CCTV, Street Lighting and Crime Prevention*, CPS 10, 123–55, Mounsey: Criminal Justice Press.

Reeve, A. (1998) 'The Panopticisation of Shopping: CCTV and Leisure Consumption', in C. Norris, J. Moran and G. Armstrong (eds), *Surveillance, Close Circuit Television and Social Control*, Aldershot: Ashgate.

Rudinow, A. Sætnan, H. Lomell, M. and Carsten, W. (2004) 'Controlling CCTV in Public Spaces: Is Privacy the (Only) Issue? Reflections on Norwegian and Danish Observations', *Surveillance and Society*, Special Issue: The Politics of CCTV in Europe and Beyond, 2(2/3), http://www.surveillance-and-society.

Ruegg, J., November, V. and Klauser, F. (2004) 'CCTV, Risk Management and Regulation Mechanisms in Publicly-Used Places: A Discussion Based on Swiss Examples', *Surveillance and Society*, Special Issue: The Politics of CCTV in Europe and Beyond, 2(2/3), http://www.surveillance-and-society.

Sarno, C., Hough, M. and Bulos, M. (1999) *Developing a Picture of CCTV in Southwark Town Centres: Final Report*, Crime Policy Research Unit, South Bank University.

Shapland, J. (2000) 'Situational Prevention: Social Values and Social Viewpoints', in A. von Hirsch, D. Garland and A. Wakefield (eds), *Ethical and Social Perspectives on Situational Crime Prevention*, Oxford: Hart Publishing.

Short, E. and Ditton, J. (1998) 'Seen and Now Heard', *British Journal of Criminology*, 38(3), Summer, 404–28.

Skinns, D. (1998) 'Crime Reduction, Diffusion and Displacement: Evaluating the Effectiveness of CCTV', in C. Norris, J. Moran and G. Armstrong (eds), *Surveillance, Close Circuit Television and Social Control*, Aldershot: Ashgate.

Smith, G.J.D. (2004) 'Behind the Screens: Examining Constructions of Deviance and Informal Practices among CCTV Control Room Operators in the UK', *Surveillance and Society*, Special Issue: The Politics of CCTV in Europe and Beyond, 2(2/3), http://www.surveillance-and-society.

Smith, P., Spriggs, A., Argomaniz, J., Allen, J., Jessiman, P., Kara, D., Little, R., Swain, D., Follett, M. and Gill, M. (2003) 'Lessons in Implementing CCTV Schemes: An Early Review', in M. Gill (ed.), *CCTV*, Leicester: Perpetuity Press.

South, N. (1988) *Policing for Profit*, London: Sage.

Spriggs, A., Gill, M., Argomaniz, J. and Bryan, J. (2005) *Public Attitudes Towards CCTV: Results from the Pre-Intervention Public Attitude Survey Carried Out in Areas Implementing CCTV*, Home Office Online Report, London: Home Office, http://www.homeoffice.gov.uk/rds/pdfs05/rdsolr1005.pdf.

von Hirsch, A. (2000) 'The Ethic of Public Television Surveillance', in A. von Hirsch, D. Garland and A. Wakefield (eds), *Ethical and Social Perspectives on Situational Crime Prevention*, Oxford: Hart Publishing.

von Hirsch, A. and Shearing, C. (2000) 'Exclusion from Public Space', in A. von Hirsch, D. Garland, and A. Wakefield (eds), *Ethical and Social Perspectives on Situational Crime Prevention*, Oxford: Hart Publishing.

von Hirsch, A., Garland, D. and Wakefield, A. (eds) (2000) *Ethical and Social Perspectives on Situational Crime Prevention*, Oxford: Hart Publishing.

Tilley, N. (1993) *Understanding Car Parks, Crime and CCTV: Evaluation Lessons From Safer Cities*, Crime Prevention Unit, Paper No. 42, London: HMSO.

Toepfer, E., Hempel, L. and Cameron, H. (2003) *Watching the Bear. Islands and Networks of Visual Surveillance in Berlin*, UrbanEye, Working Paper No. 8, http://www.urbaneye.net/results/ue_wp8.pdf.

Waples, S., Fisher, P. and Gill, M. (forthcoming) *CCTV and Displacement: Evidence from a National Evaluation*.

Welsh, B. and Farrington, D. (2002) *Crime Prevention Effects of Closed Circuit Television: A Systematic Review*, Home Office Research Study, No. 252, London: Home Office.

Welsh, B. and Farrington, D. (2003) *Effects of Closed Circuit Television Surveillance on Crime: Protocol for a Systematic Review*, Campbell Collaboration Crime and Justice Group Third revision: November 4, http://www.aic.gov.au/campbellcj/reviews/2003-11-CCTV.pdf.

Wiecek, C. Sætnan, A.R. (2002) Geographies of Visibility. Zooming in on Video Surveillance Systems in Oslo and Copenhagen, Working Paper No. 5, http://www.urbaneye.net/results/ue_wp5.pdf.

Wilson, D. and Sutton, A. (2003a) *Open-Street CCTV in Australia, Australian Institute of Criminology*, Trends and Issues in Criminal Justice No. 271, Canberra, Australia.

Wilson, D. and Sutton, A. (2003b) *Open Street CCTV in Australia: A Comparative Study of Establishment and Operation*, A report to the Australian Criminology Research Council (CRC Grant 26/01-02), Melbourne, Australia.

Winge, S. and Knutsson, J. (2003) 'An Evaluation of the CCTV System at Oslo Central Railway Station', in M. Gill (ed.), *CCTV*, Leicester: Perpetuity Press.

Wright, R. and Docker, S. (1997) *Armed Robbers in Action*, Boston: Northeastern University Press.

20
Shrinkage and Radio Frequency Identification (RFID): Prospects, Problems and Practicalities

Adrian Beck

Introduction

In a promotional video for the work of the Auto ID Centre in Boston Mass-achusetts, the then Executive Director Kevin Ashton commented that: 'this is as significant a technology as certainly the Internet, and possibly the invention of the computer itself' (AutoID Centre, 2005). He pronounced it as the dawn of the next 50 years of computing. Bold statements indeed. This chapter intends to explore this apparently revolutionary new technology and consider its implica-tions for dealing with the problem of stock loss. It will begin by mapping out precisely what this new technology is and how developers and the business com-munity intend to use it. It will go on to briefly outline the problem of shrinkage in the retail sector and some of the issues relating to its control and management to date. This is important because without a clear understanding of the context within which RFID is intended to operate, then its potential impact cannot be properly identified. The chapter will then consider how the current challenges of shrinkage might be addressed through the use of RFID (taking the premise that all items in a retail supply chain have been tagged). Finally, the chapter will con-sider some of the obstacles to its introduction, including concerns about con-sumer privacy, which has become a growing concern for implementers and consumer groups alike. The chapter is partly based upon original research carried out with European retailers and manufacturers, technology providers and deve-lopers, standards agencies and academics, as part of an ECR Europe project on the potential of Radio Frequency Identification (RFID) to tackle shrinkage in the Fast Moving Consumer Goods sector (FMCG).[1]

While reading this chapter, it must be borne in mind that the pace of change in technologies in this area is extremely fast – as these words are being written, numerous organizations are hard at work to make the comments and conclu-sions presented here both outdated and potentially inaccurate. Therefore, this chapter provides a relatively generalized review focusing on the key issues as they currently prevail.

Developments in Product Identification and RFID

Putting tags on items in order to either 'learn' something about them or enable them to 'interact' in some way with other 'things' is nothing new. Electronic article surveillance tags have been around for about 40 years and have been used primarily by the retail sector to try and counter the problem of shop theft. Other systems have also been developed, most notably the barcode and the associated Universal Product Code (UPC), which have revolutionized the identification of products in the supply chain (Haberman, 2000). Through the Uniform Code Council (UCC) and the International Article Numbering Association (EAN International), barcodes have become a universally accepted standard and also a ubiquitous part of product packaging. The UPC enables types of products to be identified optically and for these products to be linked to databases that provide further information about them, primarily their price. UPC has had a major impact upon the commercial world through the degree of global consensus it has required and achieved (Haberman, 2000).

However, what the current barcode system does not do is identify each product uniquely – one bottle of shampoo is not distinguishable from another. It also relies upon line-of-sight to gather the information and the consequent human intervention to normally achieve this (members of staff have to normally handle the items to register the barcode). These and other limitations have led to developments in RFID and the associated technologies relating to the means of carrying data (tags).

What is radio frequency identification?

Like a barcode, a radio frequency tag is a data carrier. While a barcode carries data in a visible symbol and is read at optical or infrared wavelengths, an RFID device (or tag) carries data programmed into a chip and operates at various radio frequencies.[2]

All RFID systems have three main components, see Figure 20.1:

- The RFID tag with its own data, functions and physical characteristics. Broadly speaking, all tags comprise a semiconductor chip with memory processing

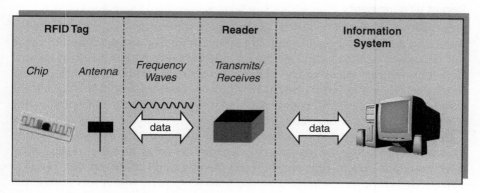

Figure 20.1 Radio frequency identification

capability and a transmitter connected to an antenna (aerial). The great majority of tags used within the retail environment are passive, taking their energy
from the electromagnetic field emitted by readers.
- The reader with its own functions and physical characteristics. It comprises
an antenna and a controller, which codes, decodes, checks and stores the
data, manages communications with the tags and communicates with the
management system.
- The management system with its own hardware and software. This is the
nerve centre for the application and forms part of the RFID user's information
technology system. It is responsible for using the data received from and sent
to the RFID tags for logistics and commercial management.

The perceived general benefits of RFID

As RFID systems use radio waves, they can do things that optical technology
cannot do, including:

- *Line of sight*: you do not have to be able to see a tag to be able to read it, a tag
must merely pass through the electromagnetic field emitted by the reader.
- *Range*: tags can be read at very long range – many hundreds of metres in the
case of very specialized tags. RFID devices used in mass logistic applications
are thought to need a range of around one to five metres.
- *Bulk read*: many tags can be read in a short space of time. For example the
GTAG specification is designed to read 250 tags in less than three seconds.
- *Selectivity*: potentially, specific data can be read from a tag.
- *Durability*: tags can be hidden from the elements or placed in a plastic
casing.
- *Read/write (RW)*: RFID tags can be updated after the original data has been
loaded. This might be a simple change in status: 'paid for'/'not paid for' in the
case of a tag used in conjunction with retail electronic article surveillance
(EAS). It could however, involve much more complex data such as warranty
and service history in the case of, for instance, a car or microwave oven.

Recent developments

The application of radio frequency technology is nothing new – it has been used in
numerous applications for the past 30 years or more. For instance, motor vehicle
drivers may be familiar with their use for tollbooth automation, while its integration into security access badges is now increasingly common. The significant
restriction on its widespread use has traditionally been the cost of the tag and the
associated technology, with battery powered tags with read/write capability costing
as much as €24 each (Homs, 2004).

However, in the last 5–6 years significant developments have been achieved in
dramatically reducing the cost and size of computer chips, and the creation of an
open standard system that can be used for any application on any physical
object. This work was pioneered by the Auto ID Centre, which was founded at
the Massachusetts Institute of Technology (MIT) in 1999. Its mission was to

'merge the physical world with the information world to form a single, seamless network, using the latest technology developments embracing electro-magnetic identification, computer modelling and networking' (AutoID Centre, 2002). Funded primarily by major retailers and their suppliers, the Auto ID Centre set about developing a system which they believed would eventually replace the barcode as the means by which objects would be identified. One of the key developments of the Auto ID Centre was the creation of the Electronic Product Code (EPC) – a numbering system that would enable all objects to be given a unique number that could be stored on a low cost chip and could be used to link an object to various other data sources, often through the use of the Internet. Many have described this as a 'licence plate' for objects (EPC Global, 2005). In October 2003, the Auto ID Centre was officially closed and its intellectual property and technology was transferred to EPCglobal Inc, a joint venture between EAN International and the UCC.

EPCglobal Inc describes itself as: 'a not-for-profit organisation entrusted by industry to establish and support the Electronic Product Code (EPC) Network as the global standard for immediate, automatic, and accurate identification of any item in the supply chain of any company, in any industry, anywhere in the world. Our objective is to drive global adoption of the EPCglobal Network' (EPC Global, 2005). In addition, the closure of the Auto ID Centre also spawned the creation of 'Auto-ID Labs' – a federation of universities that continue to research and develop new technologies and applications relating to RFID and EPC integration.[3] Their research covers a wide range of RFID-related issues including: the placement and application of tags to consumer products; the exchange of large volumes of data over the Internet; product lifecycle management; the use of readers and antennas in retailer environments; and issues of security and privacy.

While the Auto ID Centre and its off shoots have played a crucial role in establishing the parameters for how the 'new generation barcode' will operate, including developing and testing some of the technology required to make it work, a significant fillip to the greater use of RFID has recently come from the US mega retailer Wal-Mart. With more than $200 billion annual sales, this hugely powerful retailer, with considerable influence over its suppliers, announced that it wanted its top 100 suppliers to begin fitting all their cases and pallets with RFID tags that can transmit automatically information about their contents by the beginning of 2005. Suppliers such as Unilever, Proctor and Gamble and Gillette have had to quickly begin to develop their RFID capabilities in order to meet this demand, and where Wal-Mart lead, many other retailers are usually quick to follow.

The 'tagged world'

The growth in RFID is certainly not without its critics – some see the vision of the 'tagged world' as unrealistic and unnecessary – the technological steps necessary and the degree of collaboration are formidable, and many of the problems it is designed to address can already be effectively tackled with existing technologies and better management systems.[4] Others see it as potentially having a significant impact upon consumer privacy and opposition groups have sprung up in the US, UK, Germany and elsewhere, highlighting what they see as the promotion of 'spy' chips on consumer products.[5] While the final section of this chapter will consider some of these issues, the next part will take the vision of where all things (be they pallets, cases or items) have an RFID tag attached, and that these tags are capable of being effectively tracked along the entire supply chain[6] (through the use of widely distributed readers), and the resultant information is then capable of being analysed in real or near real time. It does recognize that there are many potential benefits to organizations from this technology[7] and that there may be considerable overlap between them, but the emphasis of the next part of this chapter will be its impact as it relates to the problems of shrinkage only (see definition below).

The problem of shrinkage

The rather euphemistic term 'shrinkage' is used by the business world to describe the losses that occur while they attempt to complete the deceptively simple task of producing, distributing and eventually selling goods to consumers. The term covers an enormous gamut of events, which can for the most part be broken down into two types: malicious and non-malicious. Malicious events represent those activities that are carried out to intentionally divest an organization of goods, cash, services and ultimately profit. Non-malicious events occur within and between organizations that unintentionally cause loss, through poor processes, mistakes, bad design and so on. Like the former, this has a dramatic impact upon the profitability of an organization.

The importance of perceiving the intentionality is the impact it has upon the approach adopted to tackle it. As the word implies, intentional presumes deliberateness and a degree of forethought. It also presumes to a certain extent that existing systems have been found to be vulnerable – sometimes by accident, often by 'probing' – and duly 'defeated' by the offender. As such, remedial action to deal with some types of malicious activity will have a shelf life or period of effectiveness that deteriorates as offenders find new ways to overcome them. It could also lead to displacement – offenders target different products, locations, times or methods, or change the type of offence they commit (Clarke, 1995 and 1997). On the other hand, unintentional shrinkage is usually less dynamic and more susceptible to lasting ameliorative actions. While they may require similar levels of vigilance (for instance to ensure staff continue to follow procedures) they are less liable to be anything like as evolutionary in nature as their malicious counterparts.

Shrinkage in retailing

Opinions vary on a definition for shrinkage. Some take a very narrow perspective and limit it to the loss of stock only, choosing to exclude the loss of cash from an organization, or consider it to relate only to the losses that cannot be explained – 'unknown losses' as they are usually referred to (Masuda, 1992). At the other end of the spectrum, some argue for a much more inclusive, broad ranging definition which encompasses both stock and cash, as well as the losses that result from shrinkage events – 'indirect losses' – such as out of stocks[8] caused by shop theft, the sale of stolen goods on the 'non-retail' market[9] or the production of counterfeit products.

Recent research has once again demonstrated the extent of the problem of shrinkage for retailers and their suppliers throughout the world. In 2004, research sponsored by ECR Europe on behalf of the FMCG sector[10] calculated that the annual bill for shrinkage was €24.17 billion, based upon an annual turnover of €1004 billion (M+M Euro Trade, 2004). This equated to 2.41 percent of turnover – 1.84 percent for retailers and 0.57 percent for manufacturers (Beck, 2004). A similar study in Australasia, using the same methodology found that losses from shrinkage accounted for 1.73 percent, and amounted to $A942 million (Phelps, 2002). In the US, work by Hollinger has estimated that shrinkage costs the retail sector $33.6 billion a year (Hollinger, 2004).

Non-malicious shrinkage: process failures

The 2004 ECR survey found that for retailers, process failures accounted for 27 percent of all losses or €5 billion a year or nearly €14 million a day. In the US, it has been estimated that for every $100 of shrinkage, $17.50 could be due to process failures (Hollinger and Hayes, 2000). This is a significant price to pay for organizations not getting it right.

The key elements that contribute to process failures (Paper Shrink) are: stock going out of date; price reductions; damage to stock; delivery errors; pricing errors; scanning errors; incorrect inventory checks; product promotion errors; master file errors; and returns. Common to most process failures is that they are a consequence of two related types of failure: a failure to *collect* and a failure to *communicate* information accurately and timely about the products currently within the supply chain. Process failures occur when two deceptively simple questions cannot be fully answered: 'what products do we have?' and 'where are they?' Answers to these questions then enable the key questions of 'what products do we need?', 'where do we need them to be?' and 'what price should we be charging for them?' to be answered.

Malicious shrinkage: internal and external theft, and inter-company fraud

The ECR survey estimated that for retailers 28 percent of all losses were due to internal theft, which accounts for just over €5 billion of loss each year. Despite this, companies, stock loss practitioners and indeed researchers have continued to largely ignore it as an area of concern, choosing to focus more on the other problems affecting the sector, particularly external theft (Mars, 1982; Beck and Willis, 1993; Hollinger *et al.*, 1996; Bamfield, 1998). This seems to happen for four reasons. First, because organizations generally lack reliable, timely and detailed data on stock loss, incidents of staff theft are rarely recorded compared with other forms of theft. Second, there is a tendency for unknown losses to be apportioned to offenders outside the company because it perceived to be more palatable and politically expedient to do so. Third, by its very nature, staff theft can be a difficult crime to detect and investigate and hence security practitioners are likely to focus on more visible forms of criminality. Finally, targeting staff theft is often seen as bad for morale.

In stark contrast to internal theft, external theft has for the most part dominated the stock loss agenda. Despite numerous studies showing that it is not the single most significant threat to organizations, it continues to receive the lion's share of stock loss expenditure (Buckle and Farrington, 1984). Partly this is because of some of the factors outlined above, but also because security service providers have played a significant part in setting the agenda and promising quick fix technological panaceas.

The 2004 ECR Europe study on stock loss identified that for retailers 7 percent of all losses were thought to be due to inter-company fraud, which equates to €1.3 billion a year. Inter-company fraud is defined as the losses due to suppliers or their agents deliberately delivering less goods than retailers are eventually charged for by them, or retailers deliberately returning fewer goods to manufacturers/suppliers than agreed/specified. The critical aspect of many of the approaches adopted by suppliers to defraud retailers at the point of delivery, is that they exploit two key factors: the inability of most retailers to accurately check the delivery of items to a distribution centre or store and the 'distance' between the point of delivery and the administrative/ordering function of the retail organization. The sheer scale of deliveries to retail organizations means that it is almost impossible to check, certainly at item level, that what a supplier claims they have delivered has actually arrived. In addition, suppliers can exploit any disjunction between point of order and invoicing, and place of delivery. Likewise, retailers can also exploit these difficulties when returning stock to suppliers or when making false claims about under/non-delivery of ordered stock.

Responding to malicious shrinkage

As detailed earlier, the three types of malicious shrinkage outlined above, and the specific threats associated with each of them, present a significant challenge to stock loss practitioners. In particular, and of direct relevance to the use of RFID, is the evolutionary nature of the approaches adopted by offenders – for some a new crime prevention strategy is perceived as less of a problem and more of a challenge. In addition, internal thieves are often in an ideal position to 'probe' new and existing processes and procedures to find loopholes that will enable them to increase their opportunities and reduce their risks. Recognizing the organic nature of the approaches adopted to carry out malicious shrinkage is important in developing reduction strategies that are both realistic and responsive to this constantly changing offending environment.

Of particular interest to the RFID debate is the use of EAS because it has been seen as a possible replacement/enhancement of this technology. As noted earlier, these technologies have been in use for about 40 years and are designed to increase the perceived risk of the offender being caught. This is normally done by overtly marketing the presence of the system in the store. This is done in four ways: overt tags on products; the positioning of 'gates' at the entrances of stores; an audible alarm should the system be activated; and in-store notices alerting customers to the use of the system. The offender must then believe that the system will detect a tagged item leaving the store, that a member of staff will respond and apprehend the offender, and that the store will then proceed with some form of sanction (handing them over to the civil police for prosecution and so on).

In theory this is an excellent form of crime prevention for dealing with the specific problem of shop theft.[11] However, many difficulties have arisen, which have undermined the deterrent impact of these systems. One of the key problems has been the high level of false alarms (the system being activated by a non-theft event). Some studies have found that as many as 93–96 percent of activations are false (Handford, 1994; Beck and Willis, 1995a). False activations of alarms can be caused by a wide range of factors, including: customers leaving the store with a tag that has not been properly de-activated by store staff; customers entering the store with a non-de-activated tag from another location; tags reactivating themselves after de-activation; and electrical items carried by customers triggering the system (bleepers, laptop computers, etc).[12]

The impact of this has been to markedly reduce the confidence store staff have in the system and create a massive credibility gap (the crying wolf syndrome (Handford, 1994; Shapland, 1995). This in turn has an impact upon the thought processes of the would-be offender: the likelihood of apprehension is perceived as much lower and hence increases the rationale to offend. In addition, professional shoplifters have become accustomed to finding ways to defeat the system. Once again, there are many methods adopted, including: removing the tag,[13] bending the tag, enclosing the tag within a substance that prevents it from sending a signal (aluminium foil lined shopping bags for instance), or purposefully activating the system to enable others to leave with stolen goods while store staff are responding to the intentional system activation (or resetting it).

Current EAS systems also suffer from a lack of compatibility between competing proprietary technologies. There are currently four main types: Acousto-Magnetic (AM), Radio Frequency (RF), Electromagnetic, and Microwave. Each has positive and negative aspects, depending upon the circumstances in which they are used.[14] However, the overall lack of standardization and considerable variation in sectoral and geographical adoption has created real problems for retailers and manufacturers alike. For instance, in the retail store environment some types of tags from one system can inadvertently trigger alarms in another system, while some products are unsuited to the application of tags (such as batteries or other metallic items). For manufacturers, meeting competing demands from numerous retailers to source tag products with a multitude of different types of EAS tag technologies[15] can add dramatically to production costs, not only through the initial cost of the tag, but also because of the impact of applying the tag can have on rates of productivity.[16]

Evidence on the effect of EAS on levels of loss is mixed, with some studies suggesting it is very effective (particularly concerning the use of 'hard' tags), while others conclude it is of limited value (Sherman *et al.*, 1997; Wanke, 2002). Most of the studies, however, suffer from a lack of rigour in the way they have been carried out, undermining the extent to which lessons can be drawn from them. What would seem clear, is that for certain types of offender (particularly the opportunist) the deterrent impact of tagging systems, if properly managed, is evident. The impact of EAS on the more determined offender is much less certain. Hence, the significant cost of installing and maintaining many such systems are unlikely to be justified on the grounds of savings in reduced losses from theft. Above all, the limited scope of what the current EAS technologies are designed to achieve (deal with shop theft only and simply notify staff when a tagged product has left the store without being de-activated)[17] should mean that their future role in stock loss management remains limited.

Meeting the challenges – what role for RFID?

If the technology providers and standards agencies can deliver the concept of a supply chain where each product can be uniquely identified and tracked as it makes its way from the point of production through the distribution network and into the retail stores and beyond, then the potential benefits for stock loss management are dramatic and far reaching. Hence, the purpose of this section of the chapter is to take the vision of 'a supply chain where all objects can be identified and tracked automatically' and consider how it may impact upon the problems of shrinkage and its management.

Process failures

Process failures are an area where RFID could have a dramatic and profound effect. As detailed earlier, process failures are for the most part a non-malicious unintentional outcome of a breakdown in the management of the movement of products through the supply chain. They are mainly caused by a lack of transparency in knowing where things are. The RFID scenario directly tackles this problem by providing a mechanism for tracking products automatically. It will provide accurate and timely answers to the key questions: what products do we have and where are they? By doing this, it will eliminate many of the problems outlined earlier. In particular, errors in inventory should become a thing of the past. Because product recognition and recording will be automated, the problems associated with accuracy (staff not counting stock properly) and timeliness (the physical and cost limitations of carrying out stock audits) will be dramatically reduced (Hayes, 1991). In effect, organizations would be able to maintain real time inventories of their stock.

In addition, because staff will know exactly at any moment in time what stock is currently out on the shelves, they will be able to better manage the rotation and replenishment of stock (hence reduce the amount that goes out of date or has to be reduced in price). Errors in delivery should also be reduced – receiving staff will know precisely what stock has arrived as it crosses the threshold of the building (this is particularly important for mixed pallet deliveries to stores). This information can then be automatically cross-checked with original order requests and any discrepancies noted.

RFID should also markedly reduce the scanning errors made by till operators. Indeed, they could simply become product identification authenticators – providing a visual check between what has been read and what appears on the customer's receipt (this may be a reassuring middle ground between the current system and the future vision of a checkout-less shopping environment) – and the receivers of payment (not too dissimilar to the self-scan systems used by some supermarket chains).

Inter-company fraud

Like process failures, inter-company fraud could also be radically reduced through the introduction of RFID. The majority of supplier fraud occurs because the recipient of the goods is usually unable to physically check that the items claiming to be delivered have in fact arrived or are those that were ordered in the first place. Once again, the transparency and visibility of product provided by RFID is the key. Recipients of arriving tagged stock will be able to immediately cross check the delivery note with the original order and the goods presented at the point of delivery. Any overages and underages can be quickly identified and reconciled. Similarly, the authentication of each of the arriving products could be cross-checked with the manufacturer's database of products to check the credibility of the delivered stock. Likewise, such levels of transparency will also counter problems of retailers attempting to defraud suppliers by claiming that stock deliveries were incomplete or not returning stock as indicated – suppliers will be able to use the same technology to validate any reverse logistics.

Internal theft

Because of the nature of this type of shrinkage, as outlined earlier, it is a difficult problem to solve, but RFID could play a role in a number of different ways.

Theft by staff

Most staff theft in retail stores is considered to take place in the back room areas, where staff have the greatest opportunity for removing goods and remaining unobserved. They then have a number of options as to how the product is removed from the premises. There are four main ways: consume it; secrete it in their personal belongings and then carry it out as they leave; place it outside the store, usually in a garbage receptacle for recovery at a later date; or use the internal post to have the items delivered to their home or some other 'safe' location.

The first is difficult to combat, and there is an argument that the normal physical limits on what staff can consume in a day preclude the need for such a problem to be prioritized. Carrying items out (either directly by staff or being dumped for later recovery) could be countered by tag readers being placed at all staff exits. Likewise, internal post boxes could either be located within known reader areas, or alternatively, a reader could be attached to the post box itself. Either way, the existence of product within the post box will be detectable. The readers could then either activate an audible alarm and or inform security staff of the illicit movement of goods outside the accepted boundaries. In this respect, it would act very much like the existing EAS tagging systems, but with the added benefit of security staff knowing the identity of the product that has triggered the alarm.[18]

Collusion

Staff colluding with shoplifters, particularly at the point of purchase is notoriously difficult to detect. In the 'checkout less' scenario,[19] the opportunity for this type of activity would be completely removed. The system would automatically 'detect' each and every product as it moves through the checkout area, nullifying any attempts to either not scan the product in the first place or, 'fool' the system into thinking that one product was in fact another, cheaper item. Even if checkouts remain, then the ability to intentionally 'mis-scan' a product would be dramatically reduced, as the item information would be transferred independently of the till operator.

Smart management: deterring dishonesty in the workplace

Perhaps one of the biggest impacts RFID may have on internal theft is through the deterrent impact of the information it can provide to managers and loss prevention staff. Internal theft is a function of opportunity and a lack of disincentives. By radically improving the visibility of product and its movement throughout the working environment (including if it leaves through exits at the back of the building), not only should staff have less opportunity to remove goods, but also security managers should be able to respond more quickly and effectively to incidents as they occur. These two factors (supported by judicious advertising of the system by the company, reinforced with a tough policy for those caught stealing and carefully planned access control) will act as a powerful deterrent to all staff.

External theft

Intelligent Electronic Article Surveillance (IEAS)?

As detailed earlier, current strategies for responding to shop theft have focused on the use of EAS technologies – usually based upon tags activating an audible alarm at the point of exit. This strategy requires a reaction from a member of staff to either apprehend the offender or confirm that goods have been legitimately purchased and that the tag has either not been removed or deactivated. As research has shown, the level of false alarms on current EAS systems has resulted in extremely poor levels of confidence in the system by staff and a resultant low-level response to alarm activations at store exits. Dedicated shop thieves know this too and regularly rely upon store staff apathy and disbelief in the system to defeat EAS systems. For example, shoplifters working as part of a team will purposefully trigger the system to enable other members of the team to then exit the store while the system is either activated or being reset by store staff.

One of the real dangers in the 'all item' tagged world, if the tags are used in the same way as current EAS tags (i.e. to trigger an alarm if the tag has not been deactivated at the point of sale), is that the level of reliability at the point of deactivation needs to be dramatically and consistently higher than currently achieved. If it is not, then the shopping mall of the future will resonate to a constant cacophony of alarms as a proportion of the many millions of tagged items moving from the point of sale to the store exit falsely trigger the security gates. This would not only irritate and embarrass honest customers, but also further reduce the confidence staff have in the system and provide yet more 'background noise' for shoplifters to exploit.

Dynamic hot product lists

What is perhaps more realistic, is to be product sensitive in the activation of the 'EAS component' of the tag. The notion of hot products is now a familiar concept within shrinkage management, where particular items are highlighted as being far more at risk of theft than others and hence deserve greater attention (Clarke, 1999). In addition, by having access to better quality information on the products being targeted (through the greater visibility of products in the supply chain), stock loss managers could develop a much more dynamic, context driven hot product list, enabling them to decide which products should be EAS active given the local circumstances (such as store location).

Sweep thefts

Sweep thefts are a major problem for retailers, as they can result in significant losses through offenders taking large numbers of products at one go from the shelf. Developing a proactive response to this problem requires raising the risk of apprehension to the potential offender. This can be done in two interrelated ways. First, making the offender 'aware' that the 'system' has noted the number of products that have been removed from the shelf. This could be done through innovative active on-shelf displays with remarks such as 'thank you for purchasing x number of x product' being shown. Secondly, through alerting in-store staff that a multiple number of pre-defined 'risky products' have been removed at once. They in turn could then be provided with additional information to enable them to either track the offender (for instance through linking the activation to in-store CCTV), and or be better prepared when the multiple stolen items eventually activate a store exit alarm. If this level of risk awareness and response can be achieved, then it could send a powerful deterrent message to the offender community and further reduce the threat.

Tag visibility and deterrence

For the opportunistic shop thief at least, the deterrent impact of overt security measures has been found to be relatively successful. Overt security tags, the presence of CCTV, security signs and the presence of security guards can all act to 'put off' the casual offender. In order to maximize the 'security potential' of a tagged product, the prospective offender needs to know that it has been tagged in the first place.[20] Much of the technological drive of RFID is to make the chips and antennae as small as possible, principally to enable them to be embedded in the product or the packaging, so that they are virtually invisible to the consumer. The danger with this is that any deterrent impact may be as small as the eventual chip! Therefore, careful consideration needs to be given as to how the tags will be advertised. This can be done at three levels: at the micro level through notices on the product packaging; at the mezzo level through the use of displays in the shopping environment; and at the macro level through raising general public awareness through the media.

Removing tags

One of the problems with existing tagging systems, is that the applied tag is vulnerable to removal by the committed and wily shop thief. Certainly some of the proposed ideas on embedding the tag within the product or the packaging will overcome many of the current tag removal strategies, but it may not necessarily stop those offenders who use other methods to nullify the ability of the chip to communicate with readers (such as placing the tagged product within an aluminium foil lined bag). The tracking capabilities of the proposed RFID system may, however help with this problem too. For instance, the 'disappearance' of a tagged item between the shelf and the till could alert store staff to its possible theft. This would obviously, however, require a very dynamic and interactive information management system together with an extremely prompt response from security staff for it to be a realistic proposition.

Returning stolen goods

A common method adopted by shop thieves is to return stolen goods in order to try and get a cash refund. There are many variants of this, including: the purchase of the same product as the one stolen and then using the genuine receipt to refund the stolen item; using a stolen or invalid cheque book/credit card to purchase items and then returning the goods and getting a cash refund; intimidating store staff, claiming that receipt-less items were genuinely purchased. Whatever the method adopted, they rely upon the same factor – store staff are unable to tell whether the particular item being returned was ever purchased in the first place. By being able to uniquely identify each product and whether it has legitimately passed through a checkout, store staff will be able to quickly verify the status of a product. In the situation where a stolen or invalid cheque book/credit card has been used, then store staff should be able to link the item to the payment and either return the cheque (if it is still within the store), or cancel the financial transaction. In turn, they should be able to better link the offender and the item through the transaction. Either way, the ability to identify individual products and their status (legitimately purchased or not) could be a powerful tool in reducing the losses created by refund fraud.

Developing an information-led strategic approach to shrinkage management

As detailed earlier, stock loss management is blighted by a number of key problems, not least the dearth of reliable data on how, when and where shrinkage occurs throughout the supply chain. RFID offers the very real prospect of providing shrinkage managers with a window on real stock loss. It could for the first time enable an accurate understanding of what percentage each of the shrinkage factors (internal and external theft, process failures and supplier fraud) actually make up of the whole. This would be a dramatic breakthrough, enabling stock loss managers to begin to develop a much more strategic approach to managing the problem.

By making the supply chain considerably more visible and transparent through the unique identification of all products, RFID could open up a whole series of opportunities for stock loss practitioners to significantly impact upon the current losses attributed to shrinkage. As detailed above, process failures and inter-company fraud are particular areas that could be effectively targeted through the information made available by RFID. In Europe alone and just within the FMCG sector, this could be a saving of over €6 billion.

Within the areas of external and internal thefts, the impact may be less dramatic, but there are certainly considerable benefits to be gained. With both problems, stock loss practitioners are disadvantaged by the delay between the incident occurring and the event being detected (if at all). This time lag is particularly exploited by offenders within organizations, who quickly recognize the opportunities presented by complex, unwieldy and poorly managed stock inventories. Once again stock visibility data will provide a powerful lever for shrinkage managers to develop more effective and lasting processes and procedures to tackle the malicious theft of stock from throughout the supply chain. This will be done not least because of the ability to create accurate and auditable records of accountability, increasingly connecting the movements of goods to people. Irrespective of the detection capabilities offered by this, the deterrent impact on staff could be significant, providing a truly proactive and lasting solution to the problem (providing it is regularly reinforced).

In terms of external theft, particularly shop theft, simply considering RFID as a replacement for current EAS technologies would be a mistake – it is a concept currently low on credibility. However, the opportunities provided by the information made available about the movement of products and their relationship with other products could enable stock loss practitioners to begin to target their resources much more effectively in dealing with this problem. Certainly relating to returns fraud and sweep thefts, it could play a key role.

Indirect shrinkage

In the transparent supply chain, where stock loss managers can uniquely identify each product and provide an auditable trail of where it has been, they can begin to challenge some of the problems that have been previously perceived as beyond their remit/capabilities. The two key areas are counterfeiting and the sale of stolen goods in the 'non-retail' market. Counterfeiting of goods cost the business community in the UK £250 billion a year, while the figure for the US is estimated to be $600 billion (Alliance Against Counterfeiting and Piracy, 2005; Business Action to Stop Counterfeiting and Piracy, 2005). In addition to this enormous loss of potential sales, it can also have a detrimental impact upon the reputation of a company, by inadvertently associating it with products that are sub-standard or dangerous. Manufacturers and their customers could, through the ability to uniquely identify all genuine products, quickly identify fake products entering the supply chain. Security managers could then collaborate with the policing agencies, through providing auditable and evidential-quality records, and help in investigations to bring the organizations producing the counterfeit products to account.[21]

Similarly, security managers could liaise with the public police to begin to address the sale of stolen goods. Car boot sales or flea markets have frequently been seen as an opportunity for recipients of stolen goods to sell them in the open market. Once again, the problem has been the inability to provide evidence that the goods on 'sale' have been stolen (in the same way as items being returned for a refund at a retail store, as detailed above). The police could be provided with readers that enable them to gather data on the goods being sold. This information would then be linked directly to the manufacturer/retailer database and the 'status' of the items quickly established.

In both instances, the traceability of product is once again the key. But it also highlights the way in which the security manager of the future could take on a more expansive role, targeting problems that are seen as beyond their current remit but are malicious in nature and directly impact upon the bottom line profitability of organizations.

Prospects, problems and practicalities

Technicalities and cost

Without doubt there are considerable technological hurdles to be overcome before the 'vision' of a completely tagged world is ever to be realized. Indeed, the majority of retail and supplier respondents to a survey conducted by Homs (2004) thought that item level tagging was unlikely within the next six years, or indeed ever. One of the supplier respondents is quoted as saying: 'we don't think there will be significant uptake of item-level tagging. The benefits are still unclear. And it will take many years for all our customers to handle RFID tags for inventory management, so in the near term, there's no point in us implementing them on a wide scale' (Homs, 2004). Problems with read range, reader interoperability, working with products containing fluids and the perennial difficulty of RFID and metal, will continue to tax developers over the next decade (RFID Journal, 2005b).

Issues of cost have also slowed the expansion of RFID, and early claims by groups such as the Auto ID Centre that a 5 cent tag is inevitable and likely within a few years have been questioned. Homs argues that even by 2012, the most basic tag will still cost €0.26 each – six times more than the price at which most consider it economically viable to consider item level tagging on a large scale (Homs, 2004). In addition, for some the price of the tag is only a small part of the cost equation and RFID implementers will have to face up to huge infrastructure and IT costs to enable the system to work, estimated at tens or hundreds of millions of dollars for a large company. In addition, server and network infra-structures would also need fortifying to handle the thousands of additional data transactions per product (Niemeyer *et al.*, 2003).

Perhaps what is much more realistic, and is being evidenced by the approach being adopted by large retailers such as Wal-Mart is a phased introduction, focus-ing initially on pallets and cases and possibly high priced individual items or those perceived to be particularly vulnerable to stock loss (hot products).

In addition, the RFID vision is dependent upon manufacturers and suppliers tagging their products at source and ultimately paying for this in the first instance. The current debate on EAS source tagging is instructive on this issue. As detailed earlier in this chapter, EAS tags are designed to deal only with the problem of shop theft and only really advantage those at the very end of the supply chain – they are uni-dimensional in purpose and prospective beneficiary. Quite rightly, manufacturers have difficulty in justifying a business case to support this strategy. However, the proposed RFID approach has many more potential benefits to offer the manufacturer community as it can be used to directly tackle some of *their* key shrinkage problems. In other words, because RFID can be used to address a range of shrinkage issues throughout the supply chain, it is multi-dimensional both in terms of prospective beneficiaries and problems addressed. Given this, then the arguments against this type of source tagging become less persuasive.

Concerns about consumer privacy – 'the mark of the Beast'[22]

For the most part, the pioneers of recent developments in RFID and the EPC were almost exclusively focused on how to make the technology work and designing the systems and processes that would enable their vision of the 'Internet of Things' to become a reality.[23] Little if any attention was given to what the public might think about potentially having microscopic RFID chips embedded in all the products they were purchasing from their local retailer and then residing for ever in their homes and indeed the clothes they wear. Even when it was consid-ered, it was generally discussed in terms of how useful they would be to the con-sumer – such as enabling them to interact with their domestic appliances or getting rid of checkout queues in supermarkets. And so when stories began to emerge in the media that focused more on the 'big brother' characteristics of RFID than the miraculous benefits to supply chain efficiency of large multina-tional companies, the advocates were totally unprepared. Retailers and their sup-pliers are extremely sensitive to adverse publicity, and pictures of demonstrators picketing outside retail stores and pressure groups organizing campaigns to boycott particular branded products, were no doubt met with horror in most boardrooms.[24]

Consumer concerns seem to be focused on the possibility that RFID chips may be used to monitor their movements, identify the products they have purchased and allow organizations to gather and share information about them without their knowledge (Parliamentary Office of Science and Tech-nology, 2004). Pressure groups such as CASPIAN[25] have not been slow to use the media to promulgate these albeit currently impossible uses of the types of RFID tags envisioned for use within supply chains – current statutory limitations on the amount of power readers can emit make the tracking of RFID tags beyond a few feet currently impossible, while limitations on the sharing of personal information are covered in the UK by the Data Protection Act.

One of the reasons why there has been a lack of generalized consumer support for the use of RFID on products has been a perceived lack of benefit. A useful analogy can be drawn with mobile phones. Modern mobile phones have tremendous capacity for monitoring the movements and location of users, while telecom providers routinely log phone usage (who has called who and when) and store text messages sent by users (Green and Smith, 2004). As a means of 'spying' on the public, this type of technology is way ahead of anything that current developments in RFID tags on consumer products can achieve. The critical difference, however, is that users of mobile phones recognize the benefits of owning and using this technology and are prepared to forfeit some of their privacy to enable them to continue to use them. When it comes to RFID-enabled tags on consumer goods, they are unclear what they gain from their use – why should they give up yet more of their privacy for no apparent benefit? Promoters of this technology need to address this issue – how will it benefit the customer? A recent consumer survey found that the public were particularly interested in its use to: recover stolen goods more quickly; improve the security of motor vehicles; reduce the cost of consumer goods; improve the security of prescription drugs; enable faster and more reliable product recalls to take place; and help to improve the quality and safety of food products (National Retail Federation, 2004). Those looking to implement RFID need to think carefully about how they manage consumer and media representations of this technology otherwise the concept may never get beyond its use on pallets and cases.

Conclusion

It is important not to see RFID as a panacea to the problems of shrinkage, as it clearly is not, but more as a potentially powerful *tool* to enable stock loss practitioners to manage the problem much more effectively. Current stock loss prevention practice is characterized by a paucity of knowledge that generates responses that are piecemeal, partial, unsystematic and reactionary in nature, fuelled by parts of the security sector committed to championing the use of proprietary technologies. RFID, by giving access to unparalleled levels of product information, could empower shrinkage managers to enable them to collaborate more successfully with the rest of their company and other organizations across the supply chain and develop solutions that are effectively targeted, sustainable and receptive to the constantly changing threats presented by shrinkage. In this respect, it fits neatly with much of the shrinkage reduction 'philosophy' developed by ECR Europe, including the use of the 'Stock Loss Reduction Road Map' and the emphasis upon developing approaches that are systematic, systemic and based upon inter- and intra-company collaboration throughout the supply chain

(Beck *et al.*, 2001). RFID could play a pivotal role in enabling this approach to be both easier to adopt and more successful in achieving the desired outcome – reducing stock loss.

Notes

1 Efficient Consumer Response Europe is an organization that aims to facilitate better collaboration between retailers and their suppliers in order to improve their ability to reduce costs, improve efficiency and provide consumers with a better shopping experience. As part of their work, they regularly sponsor research on a wide range of issues including shrinkage, data synchronization, and supply chain management. For further details: http://www.ecrnet.org/. For a copy of the ECR report entitled: *Automatic Product Identification and Shrinkage: Scoping the Potential*, contact the author at: bna@le.ac.uk.

2 Typically 125 KHz, 13.56 MHz, 2.45 GHz and around 900 MHz.

3 The universities involved in the Auto-ID Labs network are: MIT, University of Cambridge, University of Adelaide, Keio University, Fudan University and University of St Gallen. They currently rely upon funding from EAN.UCC, governments and industry to support their work.

4 There are also many other concerns about the impact such a system may have on a range of other issues, not least the environment and the privacy of those who come into contact with tagged items.

5 An organization called CASPIAN (Consumers Against Supermarket Privacy Invasion and Numbering) has been particularly active in the US (http://www.nocards.org), but demonstrations have also been held in Germany (http://www.spychips.com/) and the UK (http://www.spy.org.uk/cgi-bin/rfid.pl#mands).

6 In this context, the supply chain is considered to be from the point of production, through transportation and warehousing, on to the retail outlet and reverse logistics (in the case of goods being returned). It also includes those items that enter the supply chain illegally (counterfeit) and leave the supply chain prematurely (for instance for sale in the 'non-retail' market).

7 A whole host of potential uses have been identified, including: soft sensing of product freshness; faster product recalls; streamlined supply chains; improved compliance checking; interaction warnings; easier logistics for custom products; automatic recall; medication validation, etc.

8 One study has suggested that between 7 to 10 percent of product may be out of stock at any one time (ECR Europe, 2003).

9 Such as car boot sales or flea markets.

10 The term Fast Moving Consumer Goods sector is used here to mean those retailers and their suppliers who provide a range of goods sold primarily through supermarkets and hypermarkets. The core of their business is providing 'essentials' such as various fresh and processed foodstuffs, but they also stock a wide selection of other goods as well including health and beauty products, tobacco, alcohol, clothing, some electrical items, baby products and more general household items. Examples of FMCG retailers include Auchen, Carrefour, Coop Italia, ICA, Interspar, Tesco and Wal-Mart. Examples of FMCG manufacturers include Allied Domecq, Gillette, Johnson & Johnson, Proctor and Gamble and Unilever. In the US, this sector is also referred to as the Consumer Packaged Goods sector.

11 It should be noted that EAS technologies are not designed to deal with many of the other problems faced by retailers such as burglary, robbery, internal theft, process failures or inter-company fraud.

12 The list of objects that can activate different types of EAS system is almost legion, ranging from pacemakers and metal legs, to personal identity cards and library books.

13 Some retailers have argued that source tagging would reduce this problem, enabling manufacturers to more effectively incorporate the tag into the product or its packaging.

While this would be true, there are considerable difficulties in implementing EAS source tagging, not least the lack of agreement on a standard global system (what type of tag should manufacturers adopt, will it have to vary around the world, will it have to vary depending upon the retailer being supplied?). Such matters can have a dramatic effect upon the production costs for manufacturers, with companies such as Gillette estimating that applying EAS tags to their products slows down their production lines by as much as 35 percent. In addition, who pays for the tag is a thorny issue, particularly given that the sole purpose of EAS is to deal only with shop theft. Not surprisingly, manufacturers are reticent about investing in a technology that has a dubious track record and will deliver little real value to their businesses.

14 There appears to be little consensus within the EAS industry about which technology is most suited to use in the retail environment, although there has been some recent discussion of creating a single industry standard security tag for the US market (IDTechEx Limited, 2002).

15 Some companies have resorted to applying more than one type of tag to a product.

16 Methods to deal with the impact upon production rates have included 'fractionalization', whereby goods are selectively tagged at point of production (for instance every third item). This approach clearly relies upon the deterrent aspect of the tags being very clearly 'advertised' to would-be offenders.

17 The author recognizes that some EAS management systems are now slightly more sophisticated, and can interact with EPOS systems and record what caused tag activations. However, their scope is still considered to be relatively limited.

18 This works on the assumption that staff have not been able to remove the tag. If the stolen products were for future re-sale, then overly damaging the packaging (in order to remove or de-activate the tag) would be counter-productive. However, many of the problems highlighted earlier, concerning professional shop thieves and their attempts to counter EAS tags may also apply for members of staff engaged in stealing from the company.

19 One of the elements of the 'vision' put forward by the Auto ID Centre was that in the future, stores may not need tills, as customers would be billed automatically once the products have passed through the store exit.

20 A study by Beck and Willis (1995b) found that only 13.4 percent of customers were aware of the presence of EAS tags, while Hayes and Rogers (2002) found that 86 percent of apprehended shoplifters were unaware products were EAS tagged (quoted in Hayes, R. [unpublished] EAS Impact Analysis: A White Paper).

21 For instance, in the US, RFID is seen as a potential solution to the growing problem of counterfeit medicine (RFID Journal, 2005a).

22 https://secure.endtime.com/apstore/prod_det_2.asp?ProdID=79247.

23 It is not clear who originally coined this term, although Kevin Ashton the former Executive Director of the Auto ID Centre is regularly quoted saying it (See http://www.forbes.com/technology/forbes/2002/0318/155.html).

24 Some have argued that the apparent U-turn by clothing retailer Benetton to attach RFID tags to its Sisley line of clothing was a consequence of adverse media publicity (http://networks.silicon.com/lans/0,39024663,10003640,00.htm). Similarly, the sudden decision by Wal-Mart to cancel a planned smart shelf project using item level tagging has also been claimed by anti-tag pressure groups as a consequence of their actions (http://www.nocards.org/).

25 http://www.nocards.org/.

Key readings

It is difficult to recommend texts on this subject because it is such a new and emerging area in the field of security and stock loss prevention. The Auto ID Centre MIT in Massachusetts produced a wide range of White Papers covering a host of topics relating to RFID (see http://www.autoidlabs.org/whitepapers/) For a generalized overview on how the technology works including issues such as standardization, and legislation governing the use of radio frequencies, see Hodges, S. and Harrison, M. (2003) *Demystifying RFID: Principles & Practicalities, An Auto ID Centre White Paper*. In the same series is a paper looking particularly at stock loss, see Alexander, K., Gilliam, T., Gramling, K., Grubelic, C., Kleinberger, H., Leng, S., Moogimane, D. and Sheedy, C. (2002) *Applying Auto-ID to Reduce Losses Associated with Shrink, An Auto ID Centre White Paper*. For a relatively brief review of the background, uses, future developments and limitations on the use of RFID, see Parliamentary Office of Science and Technology (2004) *Radio Frequency Identification (RFID), Postnote*, London: Parliamentary Office of Science and Technology. For a relatively up-to-date review on the difficulties of producing low cost chips and the impact this may have upon the use of RFID technologies in the short term, see Homs, C. (2004) *Exposing the Myth of the 5-Cent Tag*, Cambridge, MA: Forrester. The cost and IT implications of retailers using this technology are reviewed in Niemeyer, A., Pak, M. and Ramaswamy, S. (2003) 'Smart Tags for Your Supply Chain', *The McKinsey Quarterly*, No. 4. Finally, the *RFID Journal* is a useful source for topical reviews on developments in this field (http://www.rfidjournal.com/).

References

Alliance Against Counterfeiting and Piracy (2005) http://www.aacp.org.uk/, retrieved 11th April.

AutoID Centre (2002) http://www.autoidcenter.org/home_vision.asp, retrieved 10th January.

AutoID Centre (2005) http://www.ccgd.ca/en/secure/MITVideo.asp, retrieved 11th April.

Bamfield, J. (1998) 'A Breach of Trust: Employee Collusion and Theft from Major Retailers', in M. Gill (ed.) *Crime at Work: Increasing the Risk for Offenders*, Leicester: Perpetuity Press, pp. 123–42.

Beck, A. (2002) Automatic Product Identification and Shrinkage: Scoping the Potential, *A White Paper for ECR Europe*, Brussels: ECR Europe.

Beck, A. (2004) *Shrinkage in Europe 2004: A Survey of Stock Loss in the Fast Moving Consumer Goods Sector*, An ECR Europe White Paper, Brussels: ECR Europe.

Beck, A. and Willis, A. (1993) 'Employee Theft: A Profile of Staff Dishonesty in the Retail Sector', *Journal of Asset Protection & Financial Crime*, Vol. 1, May, pp. 45–57.

Beck, A. and Willis, A. (1995a) *An Evaluation of Security Hardware*, Vol. 4, Leicester: University of Leicester.

Beck, A. and Willis, A. (1995b) 'Enemy Within', *Security Management Today*, Vol. 4, No. 9, pp. 16–17.

Beck, A., Bilby, C., Chapman, P. and Harrison, A. (2001) *Shrinkage: Introducing a Collaborative Approach to Reducing Stock Loss in the Supply Chain*, ECR Europe: Brussels.

Buckle, A. and Farrington, D. (1984) 'An Observational Study of Shoplifting', *British Journal of Criminology*, Vol. 24, No. 1, pp. 63–73.

Business Action to Stop Counterfeiting and Piracy (2005) http://www.iccwbo.org/home/BASCAP/menu.asp, retrieved 11th April.

Clarke, R.V. (1995) 'Opportunity-Reducing Crime Prevention Strategies and the Role of Motivation', in P. Wilkstrom, R.V. Clarke and J. McCord (eds) *Integrating Crime Prevention Strategies: Propensity and Opportunity*, Stockholm: National Council for Crime Prevention.

Clarke, R.V. (1997) *Situational Crime Prevention: Successful Case Studies*, Albany, NY: Harrow and Heston.

Clarke, R.V. (1999) *Hot Products: Understanding, Anticipating and Reducing Demand for Stolen Goods*, Police Research Series Paper, No. 112, London: Home Office.

ECR Europe (2003) *Optimal Shelf Availability – Increasing Shopper Satisfaction at the Moment of Truth*, Brussels: ECR Europe.

EPC Global (2005) http://www.epcglobalinc.org/about/faqs.html#1, retrieved 11th April.

Green, N. and Smith, S. (2004) 'A Spy in Your Pocket? The Regulation of Mobile Data in the UK', *Surveillance and Society*, Vol. 1, No. 4, pp. 573–87.

Haberman, A. (ed.) (2000) *A Life Behind Bars*, Cambridge, MA: Harvard University.

Handford, M. (1994) 'Electronic Tagging in Action: A Case Study in Retailing', in M. Gill (ed.) *Crime at Work: Studies in Security and Crime Prevention*, Leicester: Perpetuity Press.

Hayes, R. [unpublished] *EAS Impact Analysis: A White Paper*.

Hayes, R. (1991) *Retail Security and Loss Prevention*, Stoneham: Butterworth-Heinemann.

Hayes, R. and Rogers, K. (2000) *Shoplifting and Science: Inside the Mind of the Offender*, A paper presented at the National Retail Federation's Annual Loss Prevention Conference.

Hollinger, R. (2004) *National Retail Security Survey*, Gainesville, FL: University of Florida.

Hollinger, R. and Hayes, R. (2000) *National Retail Security Survey*, Gainesville, FL: University of Florida.

Hollinger, R., Greenberg, J. and Scott, K. (1996) 'Why Do Workers Bite the Hands That Feed Them? Employee Theft as a Social Exchange Process', *Research into Organisational Behaviour*, Vol. 1, pp. 111–56.

Homs, C. (2004) *Exposing the Myth of the 5-Cent Tag*, Cambridge, MA: Forrester.

IDTechEx Limited (2002) 'EAS Defeated in the US', *Smart Label Analyst*, No. 15, April.

M+M Euro Trade (2004) *Trade Structures and the Top Retailers in the European Food Business*, Frankfurt: M+M Euro Trade.

Mars, G. (1982) *Cheats at Work: Anthropology of Workplace Crime*, London: Unwin.

Masuda, B. (1992) 'Displacement vs Diffusion of Benefits and the Reduction of Inventory Losses in a Retail Environment', *Security Journal*, Vol. 3, No. 3, pp. 131–6.

National Retail Federation (2004) *RFID and Consumers: Understanding Their Mindset: A US Study Examining Consumer Awareness and Perceptions of Radio Frequency Identification Technology*, Washington: National Retail Federation.

Niemeyer, A., Pak, M. and Ramaswamy, S. (2003) 'Smart Tags for Your Supply Chain', *The McKinsey Quarterly*, No. 4.

Parliamentary Office of Science and Technology (2004) *Radio Frequency Identification (RFID)*, *Postnote*, London: Parliamentary Office of Science and Technology.

Phelps, D. (2002) *ECR Australasia Loss Prevention Survey (Preliminary) Highlights*, Kingston ACT: ECR Australasia.

RFID Journal (2005a) http://www.rfidjournal.com/article/articleview/611/1/1/, retrieved 11th April.

RFID Journal (2005b) http://www.rfidjournal.com/article/articleview/1056/1/82/, retrieved 11th April.

Shapland, J. (1995) 'Preventing Retail Sector Crimes', in M. Tonry and D. Farrington (eds) *Building a Safer Society: Strategic Approaches to Crime Prevention*, Chicago: The University of Chicago Press.

Sherman, L., Gottfredson, D., Mackenzie, D., Eck, J., Reuter, P. and Bushway, S. (1997) *Preventing Crime: What Works, What Doesn't, What's Promising*, Washington, DC: Office of Justice Programs.

Wanke, E. (2002) 'How EAS Source Tagging Rewrote Shrinkage History in the Music and Video Sector', *Loss Prevention*, May–June.

Part IV

Security Management

21
Management
Joshua Bamfield

Introduction

This chapter views security as a management function and analyses its main activities in the context of current management thinking. Since the beginning of the 20th century, a considerable literature has been produced assessing managerial work and effectiveness. This research, carried out by academics and practising managers, has concerned analysing what managers do, assessing the outcomes from different management actions, and producing theories of management designed to have a general applicability.

Management thinking gave birth to several specialisms including operations management, logistics, human resource management (HRM), and strategic management. Whilst there can be no doubt that 'security management' is a branch of management, security itself has been the subject of very little research or comment by management specialists. Many management texts on 'security' tend to be technical guides rather than discussions of different management approaches, Kovacich and Halibozek (2003) being a recent exception. Compared, for example, with policing, which now has a significant literature on its management, culture and politics, there has been relatively little discussion about how corporate security should be resourced, managed, and empowered.

This chapter deals with the work of the security manager in determining the purpose or mission of the security department, setting objectives, organizing, planning, leading, and communicating in order to achieve the goals of the security department and the security objectives of the organization.

The business of management

Managing security involves a range of tasks including: running a department with staff (possibly on several different sites); planning future outcomes; budgeting; controlling outcomes and monitoring performance; interacting with other departments and corporate senior executives; making department policy; and working with other people and organizations outside the corporation such as the police, the prosecution services, and other security officers.

Mary Follett, one of the pioneers of management thought, defined 'management' simply as, a process of 'getting activities completed efficiently with and through other people' (Brecht, 1963: 34). The manager has to act in a wide variety of roles. The key management functions, according to the work of Henri Fayol, required managers to undertake a wide number and range of activities to support seven management roles: *planning, leading, organizing, controlling, staffing, co-ordinating* and *motivating* (see Brecht, 1963). These roles are often termed the 'classical' management functions and they describe the main tasks of management. The early Management researchers such as Mary Follett, Fayol, and F.W. Taylor believed they were establishing a new science of Management. They endeavoured to find what successors called 'the one right way' to accomplish every productive task, whether using a shovel or designing a factory (Robbins *et al.*, 2004). This early view that management thinking was a science that would demonstrate the ultimate 'right way' to accomplish any business activity has been replaced by a succession of theories of management, which emphasize that there may be several 'right ways' to manage. The final choice would depend on a range of factors reflecting an organization's leadership style, structure, culture, workforce skills, and the organization's environment. This approach is known as *contingency theory* – that the situation should determine the most appropriate action (Hannagan, 2005). However, there is still an unslakable thirst for 'magic solutions' in management: management 'fads' meet a natural human need for the latest fix for problems. Kennedy (2002) argues that simple (and usually effective) ideas which may work in some situations but not all are oversold as 'complete business solutions' and include corporate planning, management by objectives, the McKinsey 7S Excellence approach, quality circles, business process re-engineering, and matrix management.

The 'scientific' view that managerial work at any level consists of being an analytical planner, strategist and decision maker, who impartially guides his or her department, team or organization in accordance with its rationally-set goals has been undermined by a number of writers from Mintzberg (1973) onwards. Mintzberg studied the actual content of managerial work carried out by executives. He found that the manager spent most of his or her time reactively, in responsive mode, dealing with problems, communicating with subordinates and colleagues in other parts of the business, and learning subconsciously from a multiplicity of experiences rather than being a detached reflective thinker, rational organizer and analytical planner. Hales' (1999) summary of recent research on this area supported Mintzberg's original conclusions.

For Kovacich and Halibozek (2003), much corporate security management work is purely responsive to day-to-day issues. A 2003 study by Hayes (2003) found that US retail security managers spent most of the time engaged in tactical activities rather than in strategic analysis and planning. The most significant role for the security managers was 'responding to, rather than preventing issues such as large employee theft incidents or violence' with 'loss prevention personnel/ staff matters' a close second. Other key tasks were investigations management and building working partnerships: the analytical and 'deeper' work of *long-term planning* and *loss-prevention budget planning and management* were fifth and sixth respectively. Whilst this might seem to be a failure to perform at the appropriate level, it is a normal feature of the reality of managerial work. Planning, leading, organizing still have to be done, but needed to be inserted somehow into a context of constantly challenging operational demands.

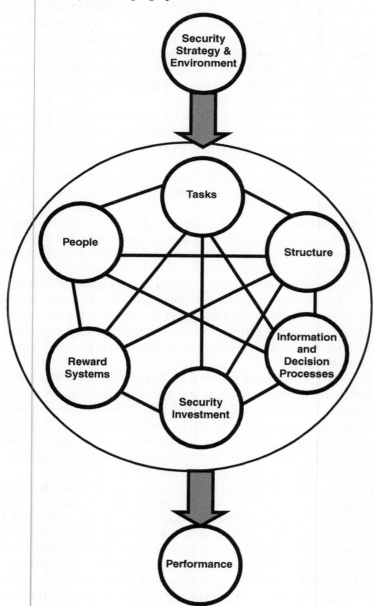

Figure 21.1   Security department organizational design variables
Source: Adapted from Galbraith, J. (1977) *Organizational Design*

Like all managers, the security manager is faced with uncertainty and a changing set of problems caused both by internal issues, tensions and strategies and by external environmental changes. The security manager, as the leader of one of many teams within an organization, needs to configure his or her security operations and plans using several key design variables. The main ones are shown in Figure 21.1, adapted from Galbraith (1977). The variables are *tasks, structure, information and decision processes, security investment, reward systems* and *people*. These variables are all interconnected, shown in Figure 21.1 by the connections between every variable. The manager's success (or otherwise) in achieving congruence between these variables and the security strategy will determine the level of security performance that is achieved.

The department's *tasks* comprise its plans, policies, and priorities, which give effect to its strategy. Many of these are described in the department's plan, but others may be implicit in the way the department works. The preparation of strategies is discussed later.

Structure describes the way the department divides up the work: how it is organized, the supervision of employees, the chains of command, and the use of teamwork.

Information and Decision Processes are reporting systems, audit information, and the way security decisions are made. Major issues are whether the information provided is timely, relevant and accurate and the use of adequate co-ordinating technologies to help staff work together.

Security Investment includes a range of electronic technologies (including CCTV and electronic surveillance and access control), security barriers, vehicles, safes, locks and other equipment. Key concerns are whether the technologies and the level of investment are sufficient to meet department *tasks* (including protection, investigation and intelligence) and whether these provide a good balance between different needs.

Reward Systems show whether there is an incentive to do all that needs doing. The term denotes payment methods and pay rates, and systems of promotion, recommendation and congratulation, but also includes what happens, if anything, to personnel and teams who fail to perform effectively. People are motivated to work not only by financial considerations, but also by their evaluation of the worth of the job. Reward Systems are a potential problem for security, because the sector suffers from low wages and low productivity.

People consist of the staff of the Department, including third-party employees and also specialists (in IT for example) from other Departments. This will involve issues such as the numbers of staff, their training and their development plans, and their experience of security and of the rest of the business. The Department needs a wide mix of staff, including more junior staff capable of taking over management positions when they have sufficient experience, specialist investigators and IT experts as well as people with good project management experience. The security manager needs to be assured that there is no mismatch between the Tasks facing the Department and the human resources that are available to it.

Purpose: an ever expanding remit

The basic purpose of the security department in an organization is often summarized in a Statement of Mission, such as 'to protect company assets and ensure a safe and secure environment for our customers and our staff'.

The security department will have some involvement with most other departments. Business executives and company employees may welcome the existence of a security department to provide advice and support when required, but frequently find it difficult to appreciate the role of security in adding value to the business in a similar way to other departments such as finance, purchasing, IT, or operations. Kovacich and Halibozek (2003) call security 'a *necessary evil*. You are there because they really have no choice' (p. 63).

In addition to the security department's original role of protection through guarding, other roles have developed with new statutory regulations covering areas such as fire, health and safety, the physical protection of any people on the company's premises or using its products, data protection, anti money-laundering requirements, curbs on organized crime, and counter-terrorism. It has created wide-ranging needs for risk assessments, policies and procedures, and compliance audits to be undertaken. Kovacich and Halibozek (2003) and Manley (2004) indicate that conducting risk assessments and security audits are an essential part of the work of security not only because they can be the basis of developing improved security strategies, but simply because employers are required to carry out objective risk assessments to meet their legal obligations or inhibit legal challenges in the event of loss or injury.

Hayes' (2003) survey of US retail loss prevention managers showed that many were responsible for other 'security' areas including safety (72 percent of the sample), internal audit (45 percent), inventory control (38 percent), and insurance claims management (25 percent). Other responsibilities included price changes, transportation, and employee screening. A dated summary of security managers' other roles in the UK (Hearndon, 1993) included staff training (24 percent), customer liaison (23 percent), safety (22 percent), fire (22 percent), recruitment (21 percent) and site office and cleaning (6 percent).

There are many different dimensions to 'security'. Figure 21.2 shows key business issues affecting asset protection and some of the main threats to which they are exposed by illegal or wrongful activities. These are all security *issues*, but it is unlikely that all of them will be the sole responsibility of the security manager. One reason is to avoid overloading the security manager with excessive responsibilities, the second is that many of these issues overlap with other functional areas. In many large organizations, IT security, finance, fire, health and safety, and wastage may be the responsibility of other specialist departments.

Although the security manager may not be directly responsible for security in these other areas, many firms regard them as being part of the *domain* of security. The domain, or extended area of operation, covers more than the security manager's strict area of responsibility. In terms of IT security, for example, although the security manager may not report to the Head of IT, he or she may

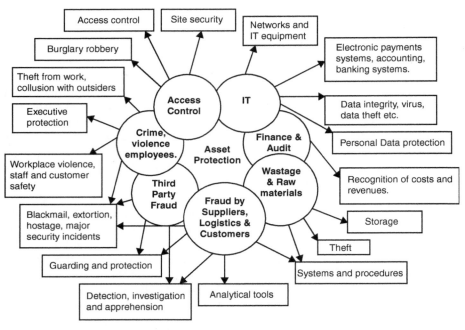

Figure 21.2   Security issues in a business organization

provide support and advice to the IT department in one or more ways: specific training, coaching key staff in security approaches, help in drawing up security procedures, playing a significant part in investigating security incidents, being responsible for apprehending and interviewing staff wrongdoers (as the Company's experts on how to arrest people without creating legal liabilities for the employer), and liaising with police and national security bodies about IT security or specific security breaches. IT security is a particular issue for organizations. IT crime and malware present severe problems and could become great threats to organizational survival (Schneier, 2003), yet the question of how IT security should be handled in organizations is rarely satisfactorily resolved.

In this way, the security manager *embeds* security into the systems, processes and working practices of other departments as well as carrying out its visible work of investigating serious criminal threats, risk controls, guarding, and safeguarding business continuity. Obviously there can be issues if the work of the security manager in a wider domain leads to blurred accountability or uses significant resources.

The security manager needs to change the perceptions of his or her role from that of 'a necessary evil' to being seen as part of the organization's value chain, a significant contributor to the process of producing goods and services safely and economically (and thereby 'adding value'). To make this case, the security manager needs to have a clear idea of what security adds to the business. The dangers of complacency and under-investment in relation to security may be equally as serious as failing to update the Company's production methods, its products or the IT system. Security benefits should include being able to operate more safely in all business areas, lower inventory costs, reductions in required safety levels for inventory, and less disruption to the business owing to missing product or equipment. A current example is the success of major European retailers in reducing shrinkage (stockloss) from 1.45 percent of turnover (sales) in 2002 to 1.25 percent in 2005, saving the industry a total of €4181 billion annually (Bamfield, 2005). The security department needs to be *pro-active* rather than *re-active*, anticipating security issues from emerging external threats or changes in corporate strategy. The result of 'embedding' security within corporate systems, procedures and processes should further promote changed attitudes. The combined effect of security benefits can be estimated through a security impact analysis that measures the security effect through its impact upon sales and turnover, net profit, gross profit margins, and in lowering costs.

The security strategy

Strategy is the name for the significant plans that allow the organization's objectives to be achieved by aligning the enterprise with its environment (Johnson *et al.*, 2005). New product-market objectives may require different technologies, new ways of doing business and changes in the workforce. The word 'strategy' may be reserved solely for enterprise-wide corporate plans and the use of the title 'Security Business Plan' may be preferable.

The security strategy must support the organization's corporate strategy (Kovacich and Halibozek, 2003; Fisher and Green, 2003). The security manager needs to audit the organization and the environments in which it operates. This audit will incorporate any risk assessments that are desirable or necessary for the organization. A security audit consists of two main features. One feature audits the current *security strengths and weaknesses* of managers, staff, technologies, equipment, methods of working, reporting systems, procedures and other factors that impact upon the effectiveness of the department. The audit should also cover 'other' areas regarded as actually or potentially within the domain of the security manager. The second feature examines the *security opportunities and threats* facing the department, the organization and its actual and intended environment over the longer term. It must include the security implications (favourable and unfavourable) of new strategies, environments (for example new markets), technologies, social trends (e.g. part-time work), economic changes (such as increases in local unemployment), and political and legislative changes (including changes in fraud legislation or changes in the regulation of security employees). Possible methods of analysis are discussed in Johnson *et al.*, (2005) and Kovacich and Halibozek (2003).

The security audit will, almost inevitably, show a mismatch between the capability of the security department and what is required to support the strategic direction of the organization. Over time, changes in the business environment,

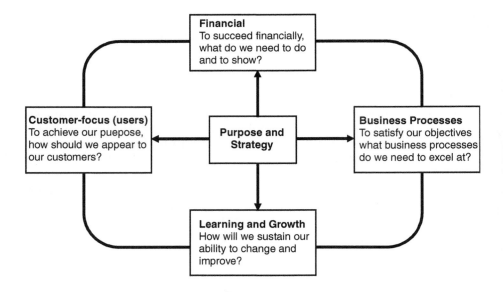

Figure 21.3   The balanced scorecard approach
Source: Adapted from Kaplan, R.S. and Norton, D.P. (1996) *The Balanced Scorecard: Translating Strategy into Action*

crime trends, new technologies and the need to cut costs create a widening gap between the company's current security situation and what it ought to be. This difference may be termed the *security gap*. The security strategy should indicate the policies and investments required to reduce or eliminate the organization's 'security gap'. Inevitably, of course, the world changes and yesterday's key security priority may become less critical as successful defensive measures are introduced and new threats are perceived. Eliminating the security gap completely is probably impossible. The security strategy adopted should not be so rigid as to prevent the department being able to respond to new types of security provision or new security threats. Indeed it must be seen as an ongoing process in which the department is constantly rethinking the strategic threats and the strategic resources it needs to provide security for the organization.

Instead of concentrating on only a few areas of security problems, the security manager needs to adopt what has been termed the 'Balanced Scorecard' approach (Kaplan and Norton, 1996) as shown in Figure 21.3. This view argues that organizations must adopt a range of targets and strategies; they need to monitor the different objectives set, but also map the key drivers and the relationships between the organizational variables (Figure 21.1) and the performance outcomes for every part of the business.

The Balanced Scorecard, used as a management system, allows the security department to clarify how its purpose and strategy translates into action (Trompenaars, 2003). Activities need to occur within each of the boxes, and not just one or two. *Learning and Growth* should include not only training, but also the use of mentoring, tutoring and coaching to help staff development. *Business Processes* should identify which processes need amendment to ensure consistency across the organization. *Financial* is important because security is seen as a cost and not a profit centre. Activities in this box should be directed towards ensuring that accurate and timely data is generated which shows the current position and what managers need to do to ensure that financial outcomes are as planned. Lastly, *Customer-focus* (or user-focus) incorporates the concept that security needs to have a positive relationship with its users. It is not necessary that they should *like* the security department, but it is vital they should respect what it is doing and have an honest interchange of views if anything is wrong.

The security strategy itself is broken down into periodic Business Plans showing what is intended over the next six months or 12 months to achieve that intended new security position.

Security department objectives

Galford and Drapeau (2003) argue that setting objectives which stretch people and departments without being unrealistic is one of the most important business functions. It provides *focus* for the next period by indicating the key goals that are to be achieved. Hannagan (2005) shows that objectives are expected to be SMART: *specific* about what is to be accomplished, *measurable*, *attainable*, *result*-oriented, and *time-specific* (to occur within an allotted time frame). Otherwise performance cannot readily be tested. An objective meeting these criteria might be: 'to reduce stockloss (at selling price) from 1.4 percent of turnover to 1.1 percent within the next 12 months'. This objective is measurable in ways that 'to reduce our stock losses' is not (McCrie, 2001). Objectives that are *non-specific* are often regarded as statements of intent rather than practical objectives.

A security department operates within a budget-constrained environment. It is not a police force dedicated to applying sanctions for infractions of the criminal legal code. The department needs to ensure it uses resources cost-effectively. It needs to support the strategic objectives of the organization and contributes most to organization effectiveness when it ensures it gets the greatest security results from a given security expenditure.

Objective setting indicates what is to be achieved in the next period, states the priorities of the business, and implicitly shows what changes are required (in equipment, strategy, procedures, training, and product) to achieve the new goals. Some caveats are required; at its worst, objective setting may involve a conspiracy to set undemanding goals because the chief security manager is ineffective or is unambitious (perhaps near to retirement) or to 'buy off' powerful department heads. Minimalist target setting of this kind is likely to mean that necessary changes are not introduced to the security department, whilst staff themselves may not be comfortable working in an undemanding environment.

Security departments have particular problems when attempting to test their department against challenging specific and measurable objectives. Security is a service department, which carries out many activities directly and achieves others by assisting and supporting other departments. The security department cannot measure its output in sales or profit, in physical quantities such as the number of washing machines produced or tonne/miles that have been shipped, patients seen, or students enrolled. Security is an input rather than an output. There is no simple yardstick to measure security: stockloss, attacks on vehicles, employee fraud, and the successful clear-up rate of incidents are all dimensions of 'security' but cannot be combined into a single measure. It may be possible, however, to develop a *series* of measures that show the impact of security. Moreover security data are of variable quality, often not timely (Howell and Lehockey, 1997) and may not directly measure the work of security.

In these circumstances, the security department sets a range of objectives or *key performance indicators* (KPIs) that measure both department activity and the impact of activity upon the organization. There are generally about four kinds.

1 The integrity of stock, equipment and other assets.
2 The activity rate of security staff and equipment use. These measure only part of the work done by security departments and ignore, for example, the support provided to other parts of the business. The productivity of security equipment (including 'down time') is an important measure of the quality of the investment as well as revealing some of its hidden costs.
3 The trend and impact of crime incidents. The security department may also measure its effectiveness in terms of its ability to lessen the impact of specific crime incidents, for example by showing a reduction in the amount stolen per burglary.
4 The financial performance of the department against budgets and the corporate financial planning system.

Decision making

Effective decision-making is at the heart of good security management. The manager is under increasing decision-making pressures. The quality of decisions made are increasingly important to the organization's success; the manager has reduced time to make decisions; the situations and issues that require decisions are increasingly complex; and there are increasingly adverse consequences of inappropriate decisions being made. Even apparently routine, day-to-day decisions may have longer-term consequences.

Decision-making is a process which starts from a recognition that a decision is needed, includes the need to define the problem, clarify the objectives that the successful decision must meet, collecting evidence or data, generating alternatives, evaluating these alternatives, and then making the decision. The decision then must be implemented and its results monitored. The outcomes achieved and the ultimate conclusions reached about the decision process may affect future decision processes, so managers are constantly learning from what they do. There are many techniques that deal with the decision process (Chapter 13 of Hannagan, 2005: 391–423, provides a good review).

There are three major types of decision: *strategic, administrative* and *operational*. A *strategic* decision, as we have seen, is concerned with corporate aims and objectives and often results from lengthy deliberation. The results may be felt immediately (as in the case to close down part of the business) or it may take several years before it is known whether the right decision has been made. An *administrative* decision is typically concerned with establishing systems and procedures or rules to be followed when dealing with particular situations. *Operational* decisions are normally routine decisions about how to deal with an individual case of fraud, whether to upgrade CCTV in a particular location this year or next year, or recruiting another data analyst.

Because it is difficult for managers and their staff to approach every decision as though it were unique, organizations and individuals develop decision-making rules to save time and to encourage consistency in decisions. These rules, some of which may be legal requirements (for example relating to recruitment policy), are incorporated into organizational procedures that may be published as formal administrative procedures. At another level, rules-of-thumb (or *heuristics*) are developed to deal with a wide range of events. Heuristics may be used to determine how many suppliers are shortlisted or how to apply company procedures to a range of 'difficult' cases, such as which customer thieves should be reported to the police. Rules-of-thumb provide a quick decision which is 'good enough' in the circumstances, rather than having to agonize over every incident. Obviously, if this approach is merely a cover for prejudice or incompetence, then it is highly inappropriate.

Security investment decisions about the purchase of new CCTV equipment or analytical software have to be based upon a calculation of whether the *benefits* (such as reductions in losses, lower staffing costs and better information) exceed the investment *costs* (the capital costs, maintenance and service costs). Rational investment appraisal of this type is the basis of virtually all investment decisions within organizations today. Because the choice of appraisal method or assumptions made about future interest rates or wage rates can affect the results of the calculation, it is normal for the organization to specify in detail exactly how investment appraisals will be carried out.

Rational decisions do not only require that there should be realistic decision criteria, sufficient evidence or information, and that the objectively-correct decision method is used. Security managers, in common with all decision makers within organizations, have to guard against making a particular decision simply because every one else seems to be making it. Janis (1982) has shown that groups of managers with similar backgrounds can be susceptible to accepting uncritically a common viewpoint or decision and ignoring any contrary evidence. The common mindset that gives rise to this is termed *groupthink* by Janis. Economists talk in terms of *information cascades* (Bikhchandani *et al.*, 1998) whereby so much information and 'evidence' becomes available to managers both formally (through the media, books and reports) and informally from colleagues and opinion leaders that a particular investment decision is seen as logical and inevitable. It takes a brave person to take a contrary view. Yet this process led to the *dot.com* fiasco at the beginning of this century. Security managers may be subject to the same pressures to conform and make similar investment decisions to security managers in other businesses even though there may not be much evidence that the organization requires this new project apart from the *information cascade*.

The reporting relationships of the security manager

As a service department with cross-organizational functions, there is no natural 'home' for the security department. It can be placed almost anywhere. Most commonly, security managers report to the Finance or Operations Director and less frequently to the IT director, Company Secretary/Legal Department, or HR director. My own research into retail security indicates that if a Director has a particular interest in Security, or is perhaps less encumbered with reporting relationships than other Directors, he or she may become responsible for the security manager. If Facilities (buildings, land, lighting, cleaning, parking, access, maintenance, and architects) are separately organized in a single silo with a Facilities Manager, then security may be made the responsibility of that Department. This is common in public agencies and not-for-profit organizations including private hospitals, although it is criticized as emphasizing guarding/ protection and underrating investigations or pro-active security work (Sims, 2004a, 2004b). Much will depend upon such matters as: the quality of the relationship between the security manager and his or her superior, how interested the superior is in security issues, how much time they can give to security matters (and make reasoned decisions about security), and how effectively the superior represents the security department on the Main Board.

French (2004) argues that security needs to be involved with strategy rather than the question of 'who stole that tin of peas?' In turn this requires security managers to be fully involved with the Board of Directors and senior executives and learning how to deal with issues at that level. They have to be able to make reasoned arguments relating security messages to investors, the board and the workforce. Kovacich and Halibozek (2003) suggest the optimal reporting relationship involves the security manager having his Managing Director or Chief Executive Officer (CEO) as the immediate line manager. Whilst this *may* provide the security manager with ready access to the senior people in the organization and assist in making a strategic contribution, the actual time allotted by the CEO to security issues may be severely curtailed. The CEO is responsible for strategy, managing relationships with stakeholders, and a large number of key functional areas, including Finance, IT, Operations and Marketing. Culver (2005) argues that security is now so important that the security manager should sit on the Board of Directors, although this relates primarily to crisis response and to risk mitigation for penalties resulting from breaches of *duty of care*. A security manager who is a member of the Board will need to be able to make an effective contribution to business discussions across most facets of the business. Many security managers possess these skills and are moving into directorial or Vice-President positions, but there are other security managers who are unlikely to be able to meet the challenges of a board-level position. Beck *et al.* (2002) provide some partial support for the idea that security managers should report directly to the CEO. They found that retail security departments that reported to the Board of Directors achieved significantly lower stockloss than security managers who reported lower down the hierarchy. Even if the direction of causation is the other way round (perhaps good security managers can convince their superiors that it is best if they report to the Board) it may demonstrate that security managers attempting to make a strategic contribution need ready access to the CEO and senior directors, which may result from a reporting relationship to the CEO or possibly a seat on the Board.

Structure

Organizational structure describes the extent of complexity, formalization and centralization in organizational design (Hannagan, 2005). It answers questions such as 'How do we divide up the work?', 'Who is responsible to whom and for what?' and 'How are employees expected to work together to achieve their objectives?' In security departments as in most other departments, the relationship between different grades of staff is normally that of a pyramid; the lower levels report to more senior staff, who report to their superiors until the ultimate level of authority and responsibility is reached.

Figure 21.4 shows the main areas of responsibility of a medium-sized security department, although this should not be regarded as the best or only way to structure security operations. The security manager is responsible for a number of distinctive security sub-areas from 'Security Equipment' to 'Investigations and Specialists'. In addition to the people, systems, and equipment directly under the security manager's control, his or her advisory and support relationships with the managers and directors in other functional areas of the business (such as operations, procurement, sales, or HRM) is indicated by a dotted line to all these other groups. The term a 'dotted-line' relationship is one where there is some responsibility but no direct reporting or command relationship (Robbins *et al.*, 2004).

The security department must develop a relationship with external organizations including the local police, local and national security managers, and national security and crime-prevention organizations. These external organizations are an essential part of the security department's constituency and can be a source of information about emerging trends, new security ideas, the effectiveness of security suppliers, as well as providing support for pro-active local or regional crime fighting.

Within the security department, every sub-area, division or zone will have a manager or supervisor in control. Figure 21.4 implies that every sub-area is on an equal footing with the other sub-areas, but this is unlikely. A map of power

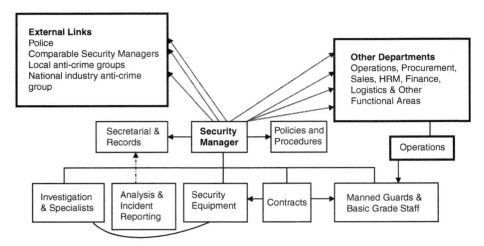

Figure 21.4   Main divisions and areas of responsibility of the security department, The Anywhere Corporation

relationships would probably look very different from this organizational chart. *Investigations and Specialists* provides some support for *Security Equipment* with staff taking on project work for different security equipment. *Contracts Group* supports and advises *Security Equipment* and *Manned Guards and Basic Staff* on negotiating and agreeing contracts and auditing contract compliance. This contract specialism may, of course, be placed within the two different sub-groups. If the basic grade staff or uniformed staff are all contracted from third-party suppliers, as happens with many companies, the *Contract Group* itself may take over the functions of *Manned Guards and Basic Staff*. Thus there may be many different ways of organizing security.

Smaller organizations will have fewer distinct sub-groups and may even be a small team of only three or four people, although the security functions outlined in Figure 21.4 will usually still need to be performed.

The 'cost centre' approach to business control involves charging every conceivable cost at a local level instead of recovering these costs through overheads. Organizations that operate in more than one location are likely to charge the cost of security equipment or staff to the location's cost centre. This approach has two major implications for the structure of the security department. Firstly, as individual locations are now paying these costs, they will expect to have a say in the use of equipment and to have control over 'their' employees. Secondly, as the manager or budget holder in each location is responsible for financial outcomes (or performance against budget) he or she will expect to decide their use of security and not to have their security costs determined for them by the organization's security manager. The usual outcomes of this approach are that security investment decisions are made in partnership (not necessarily equal partners) with the individual locations and that the security staff report to and take orders from their superior at each location with recruitment, standards, training, procedures, and personal development being managed by the organization's security department.

Although the security manager will expect to control how the department's organizational structure is determined, structure has to reflect strategy. As noted earlier, even changes in accountancy policy can have a significant influence on structure, decision-making, and the number of staff ultimately reporting to the security manager and how they are controlled. The impact of strategy becomes even more apparent as the organization grows; it may decentralize and set up divisions. Each division becomes a mini-company with considerable autonomy and is responsible for its own operations (discussed further by Johnson *et al.*, 2005). Divisions may even be different countries (where, for example, a retailer may operate in three countries, each country being a separate division), markets (a manufacturer may have divisions for coffee, confectionary, and canned fruit), or production stages (such as mining, refining, and component manufacture). In Figure 21.5 each division has its own security operation, which reports to the chief officer or managing director of that division. The heads of division report to the group at group Head Office. In response to the new divisional structure, the company's security manager has become the 'Group Security Manager'. He or she is normally supported by a small team with three main functions. It supports the divisional security managers (a dotted-line relationship), provides quality assurance, and ensures consistent security standards across the corporation. It advises the CEO and the Board on security matters, helps set corporate security policy, and may provide executive protection for the Board and headquarters. Lastly, Group security will provide specialist services for the Group and divisions concerning high-impact crimes, kidnaps, extortion and business continuity.

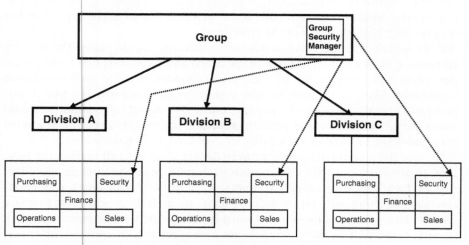

Figure 21.5 Security manager's roles in multi-divisional corporation

In addition to specialist departments, most organizations use a network of inter-department committees to co-ordinate matters covering areas such as health and safety, capital expenditure, trading, systems, operations and other sectors. If the security manager is to play a significant part in embedding security within the organization, he or she would expect to have some involvement with committees concerned with facilities, new developments, safety, trading, logistics and storage and audit. It is true, however, that some security managers feel that to be involved in 'policy' is a diversion from their primary purpose. An alternative may be for the security manager to be invited to attend committees, when a relevant topic occurs on the agenda.

Another model involves creating an inter-departmental security committee or, in retailing, a 'Shrinkage Action Committee' with representatives from those relevant departments such as procurement, security, logistics, trading, and HRM. It is important, also, that the security department advises on new projects, new facilities or stores, and new products. The security committee normally has an enterprise-wide remit and attempts to work outside departmental boundaries by identifying security issues and what needs to be done corporately to overcome them. This form of joint problem solving can be a very powerful method of operation, although if the committee is perceived to be primarily a means by which security complains about other departments, the committee's future may be limited. In retailing, the committee might attempt to reduce in-store damage to merchandise by persuading procurement to specify improved packaging and reducing theft by making packages more difficult to open, by strapping more expensive items (such as computer software or power tools), or source tagging at time of manufacture. Normally the job of the buyer or merchandiser is simply to buy specified items at an economic price; he or she is often unaware of losses in stores caused by damage or by theft. The quality of the work of the security committee will reflect the quality of its members – their seniority, experience and authority within the organization. A strong security committee may be able to provide the security manager with additional leverage in achieving his or her security objectives throughout the enterprise.

If the security manager were a Board member, one would expect the security committee to be a sub-committee of the Board and have as its role to set priorities, plans and expenditure. In these circumstances, detailed implementation would most likely be through an inter-departmental group which would implement and manage these plans and expenditure. The Board sub-committee would assess the performance of the security group and the security department against plan and deliver assurance on security to shareholders or stakeholders.

Because the security department has to deliver services to all parts of the business, its structure will reflect its location strategy through the number and diversity of locations from which it operates. A multi-site business can create considerable complexity for the security department. In large-scale sites that face security issues, there is likely to be considerable security investment and small security teams may be based on each site with specialists (such as investigators) brought in from head office or the local region when required. Smaller sites and those where security issues are infrequent may have only limited security invest-ment and may not have any security presence, their staffing requirements being met by a regional or national team. In cases where the number of staff required at each location is relatively small, the security department can face considerable problems in ensuring that the location is constantly staffed for the agreed hours, in supervising staff effectively, and providing personal development.

Outsourcing

An important issue for security is the use of 'outsourcing'. Businesses in all coun-tries have adopted a practice of using third-party firms to provide business ser-vices that are not regarded as 'core' to the organization and security is just one of many departments that have been so affected. One possible conclusion of out-sourcing would be to contract out the whole of the security operation (including management); this occurs in a minority of organizations. Security equipment can also be outsourced, CCTV or electronic surveillance systems being rented from a third-party provider who configures and maintains them. Outsourcing can mean that the security department becomes a relatively small unit of directly-employed staff who are IT specialists, investigators, supervisors and consultants. The size of the security department may drop from 90 staff to ten and a key thrust of the security department can become procurement, negotiating, contract formalities, and monitoring contract compliance.

The rationale for security outsourcing relates to cost (it is usually cheaper to employ contract workers), flexibility (it is easier to meet fluctuating staffing needs), and certainty (cover for illness and holidays). With outsourcing, a range of operational issues can be passed to the supplier organization, enabling the secu-rity department to concentrate on higher-level issues. However outsourcing may also be associated with a range of problems, such as quality (inconsistent staffing may make it hard to raise standards), control (third-party staff may have less com-mitment), and inflexibility (third-party staff may be unwilling to undertake addi-tional duties). Kakabadse and Kakabadse (2000) have shown that organizational experiences of outsourcing have often not fulfilled the hopes of their originators. But although some organizations have gone through a cycle of complete out-sourcing followed by bringing certain functions back, it seems likely that out-sourcing in security is here to stay. The management issues include: how to outsource without loss of control; determining which types of operations should stay with the security department rather than being outsourced; how to motivate and develop staff who work for other people; and, how to select and manage the optimum number of suppliers. Security managers need to learn how to make out-sourcing work in their organization. The signs are hopeful. Many security contrac-tors, attempting to escape from dog-eat-dog price competition for uniformed employees, are starting to provide comprehensive managed services for specific security issues rather than generic manpower as they may have done in the past.

Outsourcing is one of several changes that have swept over how businesses are organized and co-ordinated in response to new management thinking, new technologies, and changed economic circumstances (Hamel and Prahalad, 1994). Key themes include: decentralizing business decisions so that more decisions than before are made locally rather than having to pass up the chain of command; 'de-layering' organizational structures so that there are fewer levels of responsibility (supervision) between the shop floor or lowest grade staff and the chief executive; wider 'spans of control' (a supervisor is responsible for more people); 'job enrichment' intended to expand the role of the individual's job, providing additional responsibility; and 'lean' and 'flexible' systems based on small teams, joint decision-making supported by technology, and the ability to change the work being done quickly (Hamel and Prahalad, 1994).

The security department has responded to these changes by outsourcing lower grade staff, especially uniformed security staff; staff numbers have been reduced; one or more supervisory layers in the security department have been eliminated; and team work is encouraged where possible with delegated responsibility rather than a unitary chain of command in which most decisions are taken by the security manager. There has been increased use of technology to replace staff, to aid staff (for example, CCTV and cellphones), technologies to assist supervision (such as remote monitoring), and technologies that produce better-quality and faster information so that the security teams can work more effectively (including internet protocol, expert systems, and messaging systems).

The security manager as leader

Leadership, like sex appeal, is a quality everybody wishes they possessed. Drucker (1989) argues that 'leadership is not itself good or desirable. Leadership is a means. Leadership to what end is the crucial question'. He condemns what he terms *mis*leaders – over-confident people, charismatic, convinced of their own infallibility, unable to change, and *wrong*. He argues that they betray their followers.

Leadership is the process of motivating other people to act in certain ways to achieve organizational goals. The nature of leadership will depend upon several contingent factors. One is the type of organization, its culture, formality, and style (autocratic or democratic). A more formal environment may require leaders who understand the rationale for formality rather than those who reject it out of hand (Hannagan, 2005). An effective leader in a sales environment might fail in a security department.

Second, subordinates will expect their leaders to be expert at some, if not all, aspects of the department's purpose and can regard managers with suspicion that have no previous experience of their area. Labich (1988) argues that the leader needs to be an expert: 'from boardroom to mailroom, everyone had better understand that you know what you are talking about'. Third, leadership will also depend upon the maturity of the subordinates. Hersey *et al.* (1996) argue that less-experienced or less committed subordinates require a more directive style of leadership than mature, confident, trained and experienced subordinates, who might prefer a more hands-off approach based on delegation.

Fourth, Galford and Drapeau (2003) show that leaders need to trust their subordinates, they need to be seen as trustworthy, and be credible and reliable if they are to win the support of their subordinates. Fifth, subordinates will expect leaders to take an interest in them as people, their need for personal development and new skills, the equipment they are able to use on the job, and the roles they fulfil within the organization. Finally the followers expect their leaders to be successful: successful in gaining resources, in resolving conflict and dealing with problems, and successful in anticipating new threats and changing priorities for the business.

The security manager needs to lead in respect to codes of conduct and standards. The security department, because of its purpose, needs to act (and to be known to act) according to ethical standards. There is a natural danger that, because security tends to deal with human weaknesses, staff can develop a corporate culture which is aggressive, contemptuous of others, or which is prepared to profit from the poor behaviour of others by misbehaving themselves. The security manager has to ensure that the values, beliefs, and assumptions of staff are part of a culture which is open in its dealings and meets high ethical standards (Drucker, 1989).

An assumption behind much management thinking is that the appropriate leadership style, skills, and good decision-making can overcome most problems experienced in the workplace. Rieple and Vyakarnam (1996) show that management ruthlessness can also be an effective leadership style in fast-growing companies. Ruthlessness is defined as dismissing or disciplining poorly-performing staff and is frequently supported by well-performing staff. Argenti (1997) makes a similar critique of stakeholder thinking as being 'all things to all men' rather than being decisive about performance- and profit-oriented actions.

Contingency ideas of leadership such as those proposed by House (1971) suggest that a leader's behaviour is motivational when subordinates understand that they need to perform and they receive coaching, guidance, support and rewards that are necessary for them to perform at an acceptable level. Sharply directional (controlling) leadership is more satisfactory where tasks are ambiguous or stressful or where there is substantial conflict within the workgroup or where subordinates are inexperienced. More participative styles of leadership will be effective where staff have high perceived ability or considerable experience or are more self-directed. The nature of the decision and the situation are also important. Vroom and Jago (1988) suggest that autocratic leadership will work best where problems are structured, subordinates share the objectives behind decision-making, and are likely to accept the leader's decision, once it is made. Otherwise more participative decision-making would produce better results. However where decisions have to be made quickly due to limited time and the manager has sufficient skills to make a satisfactory decision an autocratic style may in fact satisfy everybody. The assumption behind different theories of leadership style is that the manager can alter his or her stance to fit the situation. This is actually quite difficult and it may be necessary to change to a manager with a different style.

Communication with others

Successful communication is important for all managers; for security it is essential. As noted earlier, the security department needs active support from executives and staff in other departments as well as its own if it is to do its work successfully.

'Communication' is defined by Jablin *et al.* (1987) as transference and understanding of meaning. Shannon and Weaver's model of communication (cited in Hannagan, 2005) is widely used to describe communication issues – based on how telephones work. They argued that communication involves a Message that passes from an Information Source to a Receiver. It needs to be *encoded* (converted into a signal), move through a Communication Channel, and then *decoded* back again to create the same message for the Receiver. The signal passing through the Communication Channel is subject to interference termed Noise that can affect whether the message can be understood by the Receiver or its meaning distorted.

Thus many things can go wrong with the communication, for example it may not be received, it may not be understood or it may be altered so that its meaning is changed. A number of writers have also drawn attention to 'conceptual filters' that affect how people react to messages and change the meaning of the communication from that originally sent (Jablin *et al.*, 1987). A formal letter drawing attention to a breach of company procedures and warning of further action if there were a repetition would normally be seen as much more serious than the same words spoken by the same participants in a brief conversation walking along a corridor after a meeting. This is not necessarily how the manager may have perceived the communication.

Difficulties in interpreting communications are even more likely where different nationalities or cultures are involved. Trompenaars (2003) describes how attempts by American managers to delegate responsibility to others may be seen not as a sign of trust, but for people from more formal backgrounds as a form of trick.

De-coding communications (to discover what they mean to the originator) does not only involve language; non-verbal communication (body language) can be just as powerful. My research into shop crime showed that young tourists or students from Greece and Italy when apprehended as shoplifters in central London would immediately take out their wallets and offer high-value notes. Small-scale customer theft in those countries is a civil misdemeanour. They were showing they understood the situation and that they were prepared to pay for the goods and any other penalty the shop required. However what this meant to UK security staff was: they are showing they are guilty and they are probably trying to bribe their way out of being reported to the police, which in itself is an offence.

The message can be communicated in a spoken, written, visual (pictures), or non-verbal form. There are a variety of ways in which each form of communication can be used: a memorandum, a notice on the office noticeboard, formal letter, e-mail, post-it note, or scribbled comment on scrap paper can all suggest different things about the importance of the communication, about the message originator as well as possibly about the originator's feelings about the recipient. In addition to the content of the message, our conceptual filters resulting from previous experience, self-perception, power, and situation will affect how we interpret messages.

If people do not share the values of the security manager, they may give little weight to his or her messages. It is important to see communication as a two-way process affecting the recipient of the message, not only its sender. The effective manager recognizes that there will be communication breakdowns and emphasizes the need to relate the communication to the values and ideas of the people receiving them (rather than to Security's own needs). A variety of methods of communication need to be used, for example, a spoken message followed up by a note of what was said would be better than either on its own. Using too many communications create problems of its own: they become a form of 'noise' and recipients may be unwilling to commit the time necessary to understand the different messages or to sift through them so they may concentrate upon the most important ones. The same is true if the security message is constantly shrill or aggressive. There may also be hidden agendas and distrust of the security department, which influences how people understand the messages it attempts to send. The manager needs to obtain feedback (formal or informal) from the people for whom the message is designed. There is also evidence that the perceived content of messages becomes distorted as the situation changes. Messages that are disruptive – for example that an important project is not going to plan – may be filtered out or disregarded because they do not conform to the shared values of the organization, a form of *groupthink*.

Hollinger and Langton's (2004) survey of retail crime in the United States gives information about how US retail loss prevention departments communicate crime-prevention messages to company employees. The key methods are shown in Table 21.1. A multiple set of methods are used, the most important being staff newsletters, a telephone hotline, posters and noticeboard publicity, and regular presentations to staff.

Table 21.1   Crime-prevention communication by US retailers, 2003

	Percentage Use By Respondents, %
Newsletters	92.2
Anonymous telephone hotline	88.3
Bulletin boards/posters	86.4
Periodic programmes/lectures	82.5
Video tapes	63.1
Honesty incentives (cash gifts)	60.2
In-store LP employee committees	32.0
Internet web-based communication	24.3
Training audiotape/announcements	11.7

Source: Derived from Hollinger and Langton (2004) *National Retail Security Survey 2003: Final Report*

In these circumstances, the security department should try to avoid swamping recipients with messages. It may decide to focus on only a few key ideas. It can use several channels of communication to get them across, depending on the nature of what needs to be communicated: methods could include a presentation at department meetings, posters, notices, leaflets, memoranda, an article in the staff newspaper, and enclosures in pay packets. Redundancy can be useful in communications, by helping to remind people that there is a message and what its content is. The security message can be reinforced by repeating the whole communication process again, by altering its appearance without changing the content (for example, by using different posters and leaflets), by attempting to embed the message by asking managers in the different functional areas to deliver the message, or by asking for feedback. Feedback will show whether the message has been understood and accepted.

Conclusions

This chapter has attempted to show that the modern security department needs to move away from a pre-occupation with guarding and low-level crime to see itself as having a key strategic impact upon the organization. Security managers have to challenge misconceived views about security held within the organization: one way of doing this is by attempting to develop a realistic calculation of the contribution security makes to the organization's productivity, profitability, safety, and sense of well-being. To be able to deal with the range of organizational security issues, internal and external, that need to be addressed, the security manager has to develop sophisticated planning skills and be capable of configuring the different variables of *task, structure, information and decision processes, security investment, reward systems* and *people*. This means that the effective security manager has to be a good strategist, able to relate current and future resources to changing organizational requirements and to combat developing external threats. Relationships with other departments are critical because much of the work of security is normally carried out in other functional areas rather than by security staff, highlighting the importance of good inter-department communications and the need to embed security processes within the organization's systems and procedures.

There are a number of options covering the way the security department is led, and the manager will need to ensure there is a good fit between the workforce, its skills and self-confidence and the leadership style he or she chooses to use.

If the department's strategic vision is to be accomplished, the security manager will need access to the Board and to be seen as a senior figure with authority and understanding. The skills, training and expertise of the security manager (and how much he or she can learn on the job) will determine whether security's shift to a more strategic approach can be successfully made.

Key readings

A good security text based on the tasks facing a newly-appointed manager is Kovacich, G.L. and Halibozek, E.P. (2003) *The Manager's Handbook For Corporate Security: Establishing and Managing a Successful Assets Protection Program*, New York: Butterworth-Heinemann. Good, well-grounded texts on general management issues are Hannagan, T. (2005) *Management Concepts and Practices*, Harlow, Essex: Pearson Education and Robbins, S.P., Coulter, M. and Langton, N. (2004) *Management*, Englewood Cliffs, NJ: Pearson Prentice Hall, 8th edn. A useful evaluation of security issues can be found in Fischer, R.J. and Green, G. (2003) *Introduction to Security*, Newton, MA: Butterworth-Heinemann, 7th edn and the more operational aspects in McCrie, R.D. (2001) *Security Operations Management*, Boston, MA: Butterworth-Heinemann.

References

Argenti, J. (1997) 'All Things to All Men: The Surest Route to Perdition', *Strategy*, March, pp. 4–5.

Bamfield, J. (2005) *European Retail Theft Barometer V: Monitoring the Costs of Shrinkage and Crime for Europe's Retailers*, Nottingham: Centre for Retail Research.

Beck, A., Bilby, C. and Chapman, P. (2002) 'Shrinkage in Europe: Stock Loss in the Fast-moving Consumer Goods Sector', *Security Journal*, Vol. 15, No. 4, pp. 25–39.

Bikhchandani, S., Hirshleifer, D., Welch, I. (1998) 'Learning from the Behaviour of Others: Conformity, Fads, and Information Cascades', *Journal of Economic Perspectives*, Vol. 12, pp. 151–70.

Brecht, E.F.L. (1963) *The Principles and Practice of Management*, London: Longmans.

Culver, R. (2005) 'Are You on Board?', *SMT*, May, pp. 32–3.

Drucker, P. (1989) *The Practice of Management*, Oxford: Heinemann Professional Publishing.

Fisher, R.J. and Green, G. (2003) *Introduction to Security*, Newton, MA: Butterworth-Heinemann, 7th edn.

French, P. (2004) 'Only Connect', *Professional Security*, October, p. 60.

Galbraith, J. (1977) *Organizational Design*, Menlo Park, CA: Addison Wesley.

Galford, R. and Drapeau, A.S. (2003) *The Trusted Leader*, London: Simon and Schuster.

Hales, C. (1999) 'Why Do Managers Do What They Do? Reconciling Evidence and Theory in Accounts of Managerial Work', *British Journal of Management*, Vol. 10, pp. 335–50.

Hamel, G. and Prahalad, C.K. (1994) *Competing for the Future*, Boston, MA: Harvard Business School Press.

Hannagan, T. (2005) *Management Concepts and Practices*, Harlow, Essex: Pearson Education.

Hayes, R. (2003) 'Loss Prevention: Senior Management Views on Current Trends and Issues', *The Security Journal*, Vol. 16, No. 2, pp. 7–20.

Hearndon, K. (1993) 'Profile of The Security Manager', *Security Handbook*, London: Kluwer.

Hersey, P., Blanchard, K.H. and Johnson, D.E. (1996) *Management Of Organizational Behavior: Utilizing Human Resources*, Upper Saddle River, NJ: Prentice Hall.

Hollinger, R.C. and Langton, L. (2004) *National Retail Security Survey 2003: Final Report*, Center for Studies in Criminology and Law, Gainsville, FL: University of Florida.

House, R.J. (1971) 'A Path-Goal Theory of Leader Effectiveness', *Administrative Science Quarterly*, Vol. 16, pp. 321–38.

Howell, S. and Lehockey, M. (1997) 'Pattern Analysis for Control System Diagnosis', *European Management Journal*, Vol. 15, No. 2, pp. 167–73.

Jablin, F., Putnam, L., Roberts, K. and Porter, L. (1987) *Handbook of Organisational Communication: An Interdisciplinary Perspective*, Newbury Park, CA: Sage.

Janis, I. (1982) *Groupthink: Psychological Studies of Policy Decisions and Fiascos*, Boston: Houghton Mifflin.

Johnson, G., Scholes, K. and Whittington, R. (2005) *Exploring Corporate Strategy: Text and Cases*, Harlow: Prentice Hall International.

Kakabadse, N. and Kakabadse, A. (2000) 'Outsourcing: A Paradigm Shift', *The Journal of Management Development*, Vol. 19, No. 8, September, pp. 670–728.

Kaplan, R.S. and Norton, D.P. (1996) *The Balanced Scorecard: Translating Strategy into Action*, Cambridge, MA: Harvard Business School Press.

Kennedy, C. (2002) *Guide to the Management Gurus*, London: Random House, 2nd edn, p. 16.

Kovacich, G.L. and Halibozek, E.P. (2003) *The Managers Handbook For Corporate Security: Establishing and Managing a Successful Assets Protection Program*, New York: Butterworth-Heinemann.

Labich, K. (1988) 'The Seven Keys to Business Leadership', *Fortune*, October 24, pp. 54–62.

Manley, A.D. (2004) *The Retail Loss Prevention Officer: The Fundamental Elements of Retail Security and Safety*, Englewood Cliffs, NJ: Pearson Prentice Hall.

McCrie, R.D. (2001) *Security Operations Management*, Boston, MA: Butterworth-Heinemann.

Mintzberg, H. (1973) *The Nature of Managerial Work*, New York: Harper and Row.

Rieple, A. and Vyakarnam, S. (1996) 'The Case for Managerial Ruthlessness', *British Journal of Management*, Vol. 7, pp. 17–33.

Robbins, S.P., Coulter, M. and Langton, N. (2004) *Management*, Englewood Cliffs, NJ: Pearson Prentice Hall, 8th edn.

Schneier, B. (2003) *Beyond Fear: Thinking Sensibly about Security in an Uncertain World*, Mountain View, CA: Copernicus Books.

Sims, B. (2004a) 'The SMT Forum', *SMT*, Nov., pp. 18–21.

Sims, B. (2004b) 'The SMT Forum', *SMT*, Dec., pp. 18–21.

Trompenaars, F. (2003) *Did The Pedestrian Die? Insights From the Greatest Culture Guru*, Oxford: Capstone Publishing.

Vroom, V.H. and Jago, A.G. (1988) *The New Leadership: Managing Participation in Organizations*, Englewood Cliffs, NJ: Prentice-Hall.

22
Risk Management

Mary Lynn Garcia[1]

Introduction

It is a standard practice in most businesses to manage the risk of undesirable events on critical operations, processes or facilities in order to ensure that negative impacts towards the overall enterprise are minimized. For example, most companies monitor their compensation and liability risks periodically to be sure that there are no unacceptable exposures to loss. Similarly, corporate assets must be protected from damage or loss resulting from adversary attacks, which is the function of the security organization. To accomplish this, security professionals must assess the risk to corporate assets and recommend security systems that reduce risk to an acceptable level.

This chapter will address the use of risk management principles and processes in security system evaluation. Security is only one aspect of organizational risk and therefore must be considered in the context of holistic risk management across the enterprise, along with other aspects such as financial risk management, liability and property/net income financing, employee benefits, environmental health and safety, and property engineering. For the sake of clarity, we will use the term enterprise to include organizations, companies, agencies, governments, or any other entity with the need to manage security risks. We will also use the term assets to include people, property, information or any other aspect of an enterprise that has value.

The chapter is organized into several sections, beginning with definitions and then reviewing risk management in business. Subsequent sections discuss risk management in security; risk assessment techniques; measuring risk and vulnerability assessment. Experienced security practitioners may see this chapter as a review, while students or those outside the security profession can use this as an introduction to security risk management.

Definitions

One problem inherent to the discipline of security today is the lack of common terms and definitions that are accepted by the security community. As the reader will note from the citations, this is a long-standing problem in security. Risk, risk management, risk assessment, and risk analysis are terms used throughout the security industry, but without common definitions. For example, risk management is defined differently in four commonly used security textbooks (Burstein, 1994; Fisher and Green, 1998; Hess and Wrobleski, 1996; Timm and Christian, 1991) despite the fact that risk management is a mature discipline in its own right. Some of these definitions are included below to emphasize this point, to show that there is flexibility in interpretation, and to establish the definitions used in this discussion.

Merkhofer (1987) defines risk as an uncertain situation in which a number of possible outcomes might occur, one or more of which is undesirable. Another definition comes from Haimes (1999), who defines risk as the measure of probability and severity of adverse effects. Kumamoto and Henley (1996) define risk as a collection of pairs of likelihoods and outcomes. A dictionary definition of risk is exposure to injury or loss (American Heritage Dictionaries, 2000). There is no great distinction among these definitions, and so the Haimes definition will be used because it appears to capture the intent of security risk management while leaving room for a rigorous treatment of risk. The key point is that there are undesirable situations that may occur, and that security systems exist to reduce a subset of these occurrences.

Another source writes that security hazards are defined as acts or conditions which may result in the compromise of information, loss of life, damage, loss, or destruction of property, or disruption of the mission of the installation or facility (Schultz, 1978). Schultz believes that the existence of security hazards constitutes a security risk and the degree of risk depends on the probability of adverse effects occurring as a direct result of the hazard and the extent to which the enterprise will be affected by such hazard. Schultz describes two types of security hazards – natural and manmade. Natural hazards are the result of natural phenomena and include floods, storms, earthquakes, winds, snow and ice, and fires. Manmade hazards involve the state of mind, attitude, weakness, or other traits of one or more persons. These include intentional acts against the operation or mission of an enterprise. Other examples include industrial accidents, civil disturbances, sabotage, pilferage, carelessness, and accidents. This characterization of security hazards is widely held in the security industry; however, we believe that this view is flawed.

At Sandia National Laboratories, we have found it useful to differentiate security from safety. We generally define safety as the measures (people, procedures or equipment), used to prevent or detect an abnormal condition that can endanger people, property or the enterprise. These abnormal conditions are the same as those described by Schultz as natural security hazards, but also include accidents caused by human carelessness, inattentiveness, lack of training or other unintentional events. Security, on the other hand, includes the measures used to protect people, property, or the enterprise from malevolent human threats. This includes Schultz's civil disturbances, sabotage, and pilferage, as well as theft of critical property or information, workplace violence, extortion, or other intentional attacks on assets by a human. While we agree that a good security risk management program will consider safety events since they can have the same consequence, we separate the two because they are caused by different initiating events – i.e. abnormal conditions versus malevolent, intentional human-caused event. The differences are important enough to note when considering security and risk management. An excellent paper comparing security and safety assessments that shows the theoretical basis for performing them differently was written by Snell (2002).

Because both safety and security systems address the threat (i.e. the initiating event) to assets, they are similar in their approach; however, fires, hurricanes, and accidents are not intentional events, they are the result of physical conditions or human errors. Safety systems are implemented to prevent these events by including sprinklers in buildings to fight fires or by hardening a structure in a hurricane-prone area. When fires or 'accidents' are intentional, they become malevolent attacks against assets and are defined as sabotage incidents. These assets require additional protection in the form of security measures, such as detection of unauthorized access to critical areas or equipment, background checks of employees, and tamper protection of equipment. Some safety measures will help in detection and response to security events (sprinklers will fight fires, regardless of the cause), but some attacks require additional detection and response capability. For example, a disgruntled employee can sabotage critical manufacturing equipment and reduce production to a significant extent. Without security controls, it could be difficult to determine quickly enough whether this is an intentional act of sabotage and prevent a significant loss of revenue.

This brings us to the more complicated problem of defining risk management. As before, there are many sources of definitions, and a few from different disciplines will be cited. Fisher and Green (1998), authors of a leading security textbook, define risk management as making the most efficient before-the-loss arrangement for an after-the-loss continuation of business. They further define the 'security risk management program as having four steps':

- Identification of risks or specific vulnerabilities
- Analysis and study of risks, including the likelihood and degree of danger of an event
- Optimization of risk management alternatives (avoidance, reduction, spreading, transfer, acceptance, any combination of all)
- Ongoing study of security programs

Related to this, they suggest that risk analysis includes identifying threats and vulnerabilities, and that threat assessment identifies the risk, while threat evaluation determines the criticality and dollar cost of risk. Their definition also introduces the idea of risk management alternatives. Risk management may take one of several different forms. Good risk management programs should include a combination of risk financing (insurance) and risk control tools to treat the risk.

The risk approaches used include avoidance, reduction, spreading, transfer, and acceptance (Grose, 1987).

Risk avoidance is accomplished by eliminating the source of the risk. For example, a company may choose to buy a critical component from another company, rather than manufacture it. This removes the production line as a sabotage target. Risk reduction is achieved by taking some actions to lower risk to the enterprise to reduce the severity of the loss. This is the goal of many security programs – lower risk by implementing at least some security measures. Risk can also be spread among multiple locations, perhaps by having similar production capability at more than one enterprise site. Then, loss of capability at one site might be managed by increasing production at the other locations. Another example of risk spreading might be the distribution of assets across a large industrial site. By separating the assets, fewer assets may be at risk during any given adversary attack. Risk transfer is the use of insurance to cover the replacement or other costs incurred as a result of the loss. This is an important tool in many security systems. Risk acceptance is the recognition that there will always be some residual risk. The key is in knowingly determining a level that is acceptable to the enterprise, rather than unwittingly accepting it. In most risk management programs, a mix of these approaches is used to address identified risks.

Another definition of risk management used in security comes from Hess and Wrobleski (1996), who define it as anticipating, recognizing, and analysing risks; taking steps to reduce or prevent such risks and evaluating the results. In their view, the risk management process has five steps:

- Asset valuation and judgment about consequences of loss
- Identify and characterize threats to assets, in as much detail as possible based on needs of a customer
- Identify and characterize the vulnerability of specific assets
- Identify countermeasures, costs and tradeoffs
- Risk assessment considers asset valuation, threat analysis, and vulnerability assessment, along with acceptable level of risk and any uncertainties

They state that risk analysis includes vulnerability, probability, and criticality. Vulnerability is equated to identifying threats, i.e. vulnerability to kidnapping, arson, bombs, burglary, and natural disasters and accidents. Probability involves analysing the factors that favor loss, such as crime rate in the area, effectiveness of physical security, records of past losses, where losses are occurring, and whether or not the site is a likely target. Criticality is a measure of the consequence of loss, assuming there is a loss. This is not limited to the dollar cost of the items lost, but can include recovery time, increased insurance costs, and loss of life. This definition compares favorably to Fisher and Green's (1998), with the addition of some specifics about the process.

In contrast to the two previous definitions of risk management, consider one used in engineering provided by Kaplan and Garrick (1981), who state that in risk assessment, the analyst attempts to answer the three questions: What can go wrong? What is the likelihood that it would go wrong? What are the consequences? The answers to these questions help identify, measure, quantify, and evaluate risks. Then, risk management builds on risk assessment by answering a second set of questions: What can be done? What options are available? And what are their associated tradeoffs in terms of costs, benefits, and risks? What are the impacts of current management decisions on future options? The answer to the last question is what provides the optimal solution. Total risk management results from this process, where total risk management is defined as a systematic, statistically-based, holistic process that builds on a formal risk assessment and management by answering the two sets of questions and addressing the sources of system failures.

It should be noted that Kaplan and Garrick devised their approach for engineered systems, which can use quantified measures for many aspects of their operation. In security systems, all components may not be statistically-based, especially considering that we do not know the probability of attacks by all human adversaries in a statistically meaningful sense. It is likely that a retail store knows the frequency with which shoplifters attack each store in the enterprise, in which case reliable data is available and can be used. On the other hand, there are no similar numbers for terrorist attacks, even though there is evidence that high value or high profile assets are in danger (US Department of State, 2004). Awareness of this has been heightened since the attacks on New York and Washington DC on 9/11 and the Madrid train bombings. There are also ways to measure the value of an asset to an enterprise, and to assess the performance of security technology using qualitative or quantitative techniques. These topics will be discussed in more detail in the sections on Risk assessment techniques, and Measuring risk.

Because the Kaplan and Garrick definition seems to encompass the others in their intent and explicitly introduces the use of tradeoffs to facilitate the process, we will use their definition of risk management to frame the remaining discussion. In this way we can combine the elements of risk management together in a coherent, flexible, and structured manner.

We can summarize these varying definitions by noting that there is general agreement among these definitions that risk management, using one or a combination of alternatives, relies on risk assessment, which in turn relies on vulnerability assessment. In addition, each definition includes threat, asset value, and vulnerability as a part of their overall risk management process. This flow provides the basic outline of risk management, where the questions posed by Kaplan and Garrick are answered in their respective phases. This focuses attention on providing the appropriate information to senior managers or the Board of Directors of the enterprise so that they can make informed risk management decisions.

Risk management in business

A common theme of customers and security professionals alike is that the business case for security must be made in order to acquire the resources necessary to protect assets. It is agreed that this is a necessary step, but there appears to be a lack of preparation by many security professionals in making this case, particularly as compared to their peers in other divisions across the enterprise (see Chapter 25). The following is an overview of risk management from a business perspective, along with notes about which areas lend themselves best to security risk management. Experienced practitioners will already be familiar with these methods, but students or those new to the industry may find this useful.

In enterprise business risk management, there are a number of ways that risk types are categorized. A few commonly used categories include market, credit, operational, strategic, liquidity, and hazard risks (Miccolis, 2002). Of these, hazard risk, or exposure to loss arising from damage to property that typically includes the perils covered by property/casualty insurance, is most applicable to security risk.

There are four ways of measuring risk in business risk management: solvency-related measures, performance-related measures, covariance, and covariance matrix (Miccolis, 2002). Of these, performance-related measures are best suited for security applications. Techniques for measuring performance include variance, standard deviation, and below-target-risk. Of these, variance and standard deviation are most suited to security applications, where variance is used for dollars and standard deviation can be used in financial analysis, as well as in measuring some security technology, such as delay times of barriers, which can be represented by a time delay plus or minus a standard deviation.

The techniques and measures above are used in various combinations to assist enterprise risk management decision-making in the following areas (Miccolis, 2002):

- Capital management, including capital adequacy, capital structure, capital attribution, and capital allocation, all of which address the amount, mix, assignment and deployment of capital across the enterprise.
- Asset allocation which is the determination of the optimal mix of assets by asset class (usually to maximize expected reward within risk constraints). In advanced applications, the analysis reflects the nature and structure of both assets and liabilities.
- Reinsurance/hedging strategy optimization, which reflects program costs and risk reduction capability; usually conducted through candidate analysis. The risk reduction capability includes both reduction in required economic capital and reduction in the cost of capital or required rate of return.
- Crisis management, the proactive response of an organization to a severe event that could potentially impair its ability to meet its performance objectives. Crisis management would be applicable to security events.
- Contingency planning, the process of developing and embedding in the organization crisis management protocols in advance of crisis conditions. Contingency planning would be applicable to security events. A good example of the use of both crisis management and contingency planning is the development of business continuity plans to address the enterprise

response to natural disasters, loss of senior executives, security incidents, or other events that disrupt enterprise operation to a significant degree.

It is interesting to note that Miccolis' descriptions of crisis management and contingency planning are the opposite of their use in by some security professionals. For example, many security professionals use crisis management as the description of protocols during a safety or security incident. In a similar manner, they consider contingency planning to be implementation of a security system. This may be an example of the difficulties created by the lack of common terminology and practice.

Risk management in security

As noted above, some aspects of business risk management can be applied to security. An awareness of and practice in these methods can help security professionals speak to senior management in a language that is meaningful to them and show how the security function supports enterprise success. In this section, we will review some responsibilities of senior managers in an enterprise and try to place security operations in the larger context of the enterprise.

A corporate officer's responsibilities include protecting corporate assets. A variety of issues can affect senior management's decisions on making security upgrades including corporate politics, budgeting issues, liability, opportunity costs, profit motive, and return on investment. Politics come into play in corporate decisions everywhere. The best way to limit politics in security decisions is to work closely with senior management in keeping them informed of meaningful risks and potential liabilities and the losses associated with them. Regarding budgeting issues, all security measures have costs to acquire, implement, and maintain. There are also costs associated with the limitations imposed on enterprise operations and its employees by these security measures. Many security programs create excessive costs or limitations that conflict with the core business. The best approach is to develop a sensible security plan that manages risk relating to identified security vulnerabilities and achieves protection goals with a minimum of cost. It is also important that the security program design balances both security controls and business requirements.

Liability is an important aspect of senior management's security decisions, but it is not the only or most important aspect. Unless an enterprise makes some effort at due diligence, they may be liable for the resulting damages based on negligence.

In law, due diligence is defined as a measure of prudence or activity, as properly exercised by a reasonable and prudent man under the particular circumstances, that is not measured by any absolute standard, but depends on the relative facts of the case (Garner, 2004). In business, due diligence is defined as the process whereby a potential business buyer makes sure that they fully understand, to the maximum extent possible, the anatomy of the company they are considering buying or merging (Brown, 2003). Related to crime and security, due diligence is generally defined as the process of protecting a company from commercial crime by evaluating and reducing the risk of a criminal event occurring.

A corporation must exercise a degree of due diligence to avoid the appearance of culpability or negligence and to provide itself with a degree of legal or regulatory protection. A form of due diligence can be found in corporate security policies that define the procedures, guidelines and practices for configuring and managing security in the work environment. By enforcing their corporations' security policy, senior management can minimize enterprise risks and show due diligence to their customers and shareholders. Due diligence can also be maintained through processes including vetting, authentication, and database tracking services, such as those used in background investigations.

Although senior management is not directly involved in the collection of due diligence information, security professionals must keep them informed of security issues, prove to them the value of implementing security upgrades, and keep them engaged with the process in order to get their buy-in and support. Security professionals must also understand the corporation's business and effectively communicate with senior management in a non-technical, business-focused way. Likewise, because senior management is ultimately responsible for securing their corporation's assets, it is in their best interest to not simply delegate that function to the security organization and forget about it – they must be able to give their shareholders and customers every assurance that due diligence has been performed.

The differing definitions of due diligence seem to set up a conflicting set of conditions, particularly for security managers. On one hand, the legal definition seems to leave room for enterprises to anticipate reasonable malevolent attacks on assets and take reasonable protective actions. Over the past several years, we have seen this term used more and more in the security context. If we allow that due diligence is indeed part of the security function, then it would seem logical that enterprises have a duty to protect assets to meet the legal definition. If this is true, it seems reasonable to ask why so many security directors report that they cannot get the resources required to protect critical assets. In fact, it is a common occurrence that enterprises do not see security as a value-added activity. This could appear to be an intentional decision on the part of senior managers of an enterprise not to reasonably protect at least critical assets from defined threats, which in turn could appear as though they are exposing the enterprise to more risk than necessary. Certainly, the definition of reasonable leaves room for interpretation, but in the context of risk management for security, it seems as though a duty falls to the enterprise to conduct a risk assessment that will support informed risk management decisions and implementation. It does not take much imagination to consider the liability this exposes the enterprise to in the event of a serious attack on critical assets.

This point is illustrated by an example in 2004, concerning threats to Las Vegas casinos in the US. Based on information received by US intelligence agencies, there were indications that Las Vegas was a target of Islamic terrorists.[2] In an effort to be proactive, the US Federal Bureau of Investigation (FBI), called a meeting in Las

Vegas and invited the security directors of all major casinos to attend and be briefed on the information. Only two police officers attended. The article cites Justice Department memos that allege that the desire to avoid liability by casinos was one reason that no casino security directors attended. There are conflicting versions of the story in the aftermath of the original report, but if true, this is a remarkable assertion, although one we repeatedly hear when discussing asset protection with security directors of many commercial enterprises. This seems to be at odds with the due diligence discussion above; a reasonable person might expect that threats would be updated periodically and that the security system might have to change as a result. There will be enterprise liability whether assets are protected or not, and the desire to avoid this state by ignoring threats seems inconsistent with risk management in general and the security function specifically. As noted in the risk management discussion above, threats and the value of assets need to be considered, and then risk management decisions need to be made, all within the due diligence domain. This statement is generally met with the argument that if a security event is a low probability, even if there is a high consequence of loss, there is no need to address the possibility. The attacks of 9/11 are good examples of the error of this argument. A low probability is not zero and every enterprise has some consequences that are unacceptably high (Garcia, 2000).

Opportunity cost is another way for senior management of a corporation to view an investment in security upgrades. The definition of opportunity cost from microeconomics is what must be given up or changed in order to reach the desired outcomes (Bach, 1971). Another definition is that whatever is given up or allowed to pass are the opportunity costs associated with achieving goals or the cost of a lost opportunity.[3] For example, if a corporation has a choice to fund an expansion of their product line or perform a security upgrade and they choose the security upgrade, they will be missing out on a potentially lucrative business opportunity for that year in order to reduce corporate liability.

In evaluating decisions on whether or not to make security upgrades, senior management must also evaluate the effect that the cost of the upgrades will have on profit, and the return on investment (ROI). In business, return on investment is broadly defined as net income divided by investment. ROI can also be looked at as the combined effect of two factors: profitability and investment. ROI measures how effectively the firm uses its capital to generate profit; the higher the ROI, the better. More generally, ROI is the income that an investment provides in a year (Anthony *et al.*, 1995). A thorough description of ROI in security is provided in Chapter 25.

Senior management will likely give up some other corporate priority in order to fund a security upgrade. Therefore, it is imperative that the security upgrade achieves its goals with the best investment value. A case can also be made to senior management that the proposed security investment will increase profitability by increasing shareholder and customer confidence that the organization has performed due diligence by appropriately addressing these potential liabilities. This is related to the previous discussion on due diligence.

Getting the support of senior management on security initiatives is a difficult but necessary task. The key is getting senior management to understand why they should pay for security upgrades. Beaver (2002) has summarized a variety of techniques that can be used by security professionals to convince senior management that security upgrades are value-added activities that effectively reduce risk to the enterprise.

Risk assessment techniques

As discussed above under Definitions, risk assessment is a necessary part of risk management. Risk assessment is the process of defining how big the risk is. This section describes a number of techniques that exist to support risk assessments in many different areas, such as safety, operations, economics, or business. It is not meant to be an exhaustive review of techniques, but is an overview that can be used to select credible approaches to security risk assessments. Any one or a combination of the tools may be appropriate for a security risk assessment for a particular enterprise, depending on the threat, the consequence of loss of the asset, and the risk tolerance of the enterprise. An overview of risk assessment in general is available through a new guideline (ASIS International, 2003), and on risk assessment for dams in particular (Matalucci, 2002). In addition, most introductory security textbooks discuss how to conduct risk assessments.

Risk assessment techniques fall into one of three categories: heuristic (*ad hoc*), inductive, or deductive means. Another way of stating this is that some methods are more qualitative in nature, while others are more quantitative. Each method has its strengths and weaknesses, with the major difference being that a quantitative technique requires measurable data. One benefit of a quantifiable approach is that correlation between security system performance and cost can be easily made (i.e. ROI can be demonstrated). Contrast this with qualitative *ad hoc* techniques that are often list-based and are limited to the way the analysts feel about the solution. The following information is based on an overview written by Wyss (2000).

Inductive techniques use a bottom-up approach, where risks are identified at the beginning of the analysis rather than as a result of a systematic deductive top-down approach. An example of an inductive approach is the use of event trees, which specify an undesirable occurrence as a sequence of events, and uses inductive logic to infer its results. An event tree traces an initiating event through a sequence with different possible outcomes. While event trees are useful, they are difficult to use to represent feedback loops within the system. Inductive analyses can be incomplete, since the analyst may not have considered all the possible scenarios because the list is the starting point, not the end result. They may also neglect multiple concurrent attacks.

Deductive risk assessment is generally represented by the use of fault tree analysis, and uses logic diagrams to represent deductive reasoning, to determine how a particular undesired event may occur. Fault trees are often used in conjunction with event trees to determine the most basic causes of individual events. Conditional probabilities are assigned to different locations that give the probability of an event occurring given that specific conditions exist at other locations. Using probabilistic risk assessment is more formal, scientific, technical, quantitative and objective when compared to risk management, which involves value judgment and heuristics, and is more subjective, qualitative, societal, and political. Ideally, the use of probabilities is based on objective likelihoods, but in security it is common to use more subjective likelihoods based on intuition, expertise, partial, defective, or erroneous data and occasionally, dubious theories. This is important because these are major sources of uncertainty, and uncertainty is a major element of risk. Additionally, these techniques can reduce the credibility of the security risk assessment for senior management who regularly see documented data in standard analysis models. In security systems, this uncertainty is even larger than normal, due to the lack of dependable (i.e. quantifiable) data for all types of adversary attacks (Kumamoto and Henley, 1996). The likelihood of an event, as well as the significance of the outcome can be evaluated more easily when causal scenarios for the outcome are used; however, this approach is limited as noted above. We can use fault trees and event trees, when probabilities are known, or these tools can be used qualitatively to show the relationships between and among components in the trees. In this way, valuable information about locations of critical components that need security protection can be identified and used to support the business case for necessary security upgrades. Kumamoto and Henley (1996) have written a detailed description of how to create and use both event trees and fault trees. A shorter description of the use of fault trees and logic diagrams is given in Garcia (2001).

Simulation tools, often in the form of software, are used to complement logical models. The simulation tool is used to evaluate scenarios that are created as a result of the logical model. Often, these scenarios are combined into related groups to reduce the number of scenarios to a manageable number. Scenarios may be provided by regulatory groups, based on the judgment of subject matter experts, selected using previous incidents, or derived from the results of logical models. Examples of simulation tools used in physical security include EASI, ASSESS, and JCATS (Garcia, 2001). More complex simulation tools may use automatic generation of the scenarios to be evaluated.

Risk assessment addresses the outcome of a successful adversary attack, the likelihood it will occur, the attack scenario, and the population affected. Recall the three questions that we are trying to answer in risk assessment: What can go wrong? What is the likelihood that it would go wrong? What are the consequences? Population size is an important risk factor that is also included in the risk assessment. When a population as a whole is at risk, it is called a societal risk. If the risk is reduced to a particular individual in the population, risk is reduced to a single person. This is why security risk assessments often use the number of people injured or killed as a result of an attack as one criterion in the risk assessment (Kumamoto and Henley, 1996).

Measuring risk

A common equation that is used in measuring risk is:

$$R = P_O * C$$

where R is the risk, P_O is the probability of occurrence of the event, and C represents the consequence of a successful event. In security use, P_O is often replaced with the frequency or likelihood of the event and consequence is referred to as criticality. This method of assessing the risk of a successful adversary attack can be used in a qualitative or quantitative manner. While this is a traditional form of the risk equation, and can be used quite successfully in business, it may not be sufficient for use in security. The question comes down to: how do we show senior managers a difference in security system effectiveness before and after upgrades if these are the only two terms that are used?

A method to address this problem for physical security systems was developed in the early 1970s. The newly formed US Department of Energy (DOE), which replaced the Atomic Energy Commission, began to move away from prescriptive physical security standards and towards a performance-based philosophy in which, rather than meeting a list of regulatory mandates (feature or compliance-based approaches), sites were required to implement a physical security system meeting a defined level of performance. This approach was welcomed by the nuclear industry, which understood the value of using sound systems engineering principles instead of prescriptive checklists to develop successful systems. This was due to the expectation that these sites would be safe, secure, and reliable and that any loss was unacceptable. In support of this concept, facility representatives stated:

> Recently proposed physical security performance criteria appear to be a significant step ... the 'cookbook' approach to regulations should be replaced with system performance requirements (Bishop *et al.*, 1976)

> [security] based on performance criteria can provide a more direct measure of effectiveness than the traditional approach of [security] by regulation ... What is believed by many to be a superior system is a set of performance objectives and criteria from which a licensee can optimize his plant and [security] system design to suit his circumstances ... (Hansen *et al.*, 1977)

The fundamental principles of designing and evaluating physical security systems using a performance criteria process were based on defining objectives for a system, and then determining whether or not the system achieved those objectives. These objectives included facility characterization, threat definition, and asset identification. Component testing was considered to be an essential part of this process, since historical reliance on expert opinion and a feature-based approach had proven so problematic and unreliable. A significant effort was devoted to the development of analysis tools to aid in the assessment process and researchers also emphasized the need to focus on collecting the most accurate data available to use in the models. They stated:

> It can be argued that even a fully refined technique will be complex and possibly even misleading because of the problems associated with obtaining credible input data. Recognizing this possibility, it was elected to undertake a program which stresses the need for data and for simplified analytical techniques to give insight into the problems of physical security (Todd and Nickell, 1975)

By applying accepted statistical methods to results of physical security component performance testing, the effectiveness of a system can be expressed quantitatively as the probability that the system will achieve its objectives. This is defined as the probability of system effectiveness. If a system meets an acceptable probability of system effectiveness, it is judged as satisfactory. If it fails to meet an acceptable probability of system effectiveness, an analysis will show vulnerabilities and aid in the development of solutions to enhance the effectiveness of the system. Since the methodology involves testing, the results can be used to quickly and efficiently pinpoint the cause of failures, and test the effect of possible solutions.

As a result of this work, two important techniques for analysing potential adversary actions were developed for physical security systems with the goal of preventing theft or sabotage of a high consequence asset. These include analysing both potential adversary paths to an asset (adversary path analysis), and exploitable vulnerabilities in a physical security system (scenario analysis). In addition, over time, continued testing and refinement of these basic principles yielded the following expanded form of the traditional risk equation:

$$R = P_A * (1 - P_E) * C$$

Where:

P_A = the probability of adversary attack. For critical assets, we can assume there will be an attack, which establishes a conditional risk (where the condition is that there will be an attack). Note that this does not mean we are saying that P_A will be one, only that the asset value is so high it will be protected, regardless of the likelihood of the attack.

$P_E = P_I * P_N$, and P_E is the probability of security system effectiveness, P_I is the probability of interruption by responders, and P_N is the probability of neutralization of the adversary, given interruption. P_N can include a range of tactics from verbal commands up through deadly force. The appropriate response will depend on the defined threat and consequence of loss of the asset. P_E quantifies the effectiveness of the security system versus the defined threat. The more effective the system, the less vulnerable it is to the defined threat.

C = consequence of loss of the target.

An initial risk value is calculated to establish a baseline measure of the current security system, and then calculated again to show reduction in risk as a result of any proposed upgrades. This allows a method of comparing various cost/performance options for specific threats, which will support implementation decisions. Since the 1970s, this equation has been applied to cyber security, critical infrastructure protection, personnel and transportation security, and other security applications.

The major difference between this equation and the more traditional form is that this version separates security system effectiveness (P_E) from P_A, which allows the contribution of the security system to overall risk reduction to be demonstrated as a discrete term. In effect this allows us to decompose the P_O term (probability of occurrence of a successful attack) into two parts – the likelihood the site is attacked, and the likelihood this attack is successful.[4] This seems more consistent with the intent of the risk management and assessment definitions above, which all agreed that threat, criticality, and vulnerability assessments are required to make risk management decisions. As a result, presentation of security risk assessment results to senior management become clearer because it uses the same techniques they are accustomed to seeing from other divisions within the enterprise.

It is true that this approach is not mathematically rigorous due to the difficulty of determining P_A, as noted by Rasmussen (1976) and Manunta (2002), but that does not eliminate the use of this approach to develop insights. It remains to this day the best method we have seen to represent security system effectiveness in a way that facilitates cost/benefit tradeoffs using similar assumptions (i.e. defined threats and identified assets). And, as noted by Manunta, the aspect that lends itself most to mathematical analysis is the equipment used in the protection system, which is a large part of the vulnerability assessment. One method used to avoid the problem of determining P_A for critical assets is to use a conditional risk, as noted above under the definition of P_A. For other assets, data likely exists to determine the probability of attack by lower threats.

This risk equation can be used in a quantitative or qualitative analysis because it relates the three accepted elements of risk assessment (threat, criticality, and vulnerability) to each other, and shows how risk will vary with each term. Even a qualitative analysis can show that if the likelihood of attack is high, and the consequence of loss is high, high system effectiveness is needed, or there is a high risk. If risk is not reduced to an acceptable level, we iterate between security upgrades and analysis until we are satisfied that risk has been reduced to an acceptable level. In addition, this equation allows the security solution (system effectiveness) to be scaled to the magnitude of the problem (likelihood of attack and consequence of loss) and helps senior management understand what they receive for their investment (i.e. ROI) and why upgrades are necessary. Use of this performance-based technique eliminates a common problem we see in many security systems – no improvement in system effectiveness despite a considerable dollar investment.

Each element of the risk equation can be influenced through the use of different risk management alternatives. For example, implementation of security measures, including physical, information, or personnel protection, are really risk reduction techniques that operate on the P_E term. The likelihood of attack (P_A) can be addressed through elimination of the risk by outsourcing a product or service. Consequence of loss (C) can be addressed by spreading risk through use of redundant production lines at different sites, or by elimination.

An additional use of this risk equation is that the security risk lifecycle can be viewed in context. When considering security systems and the attack timeline, we can break the attack into three discrete phases. Pre-attack, which is the time the adversary takes to plan the attack, the attack phase, when the adversary actually attacks the site, and post-attack, when the adversary has completed the attack, and the consequences of a successful attack occur. If the problem is approached this way, each term in the equation is of primary importance during different phases of the attack. As such, P_A is most useful during the pre-attack phase. This is where intelligence agencies and deterrence have their biggest effect. Intelligence agencies gather information concerning threats and provide assessments about their likelihood of attack. These agencies may even develop enough information to disrupt an attack by collecting enough legal evidence to arrest the adversary, through tips from inside sources, or by alerting targeted enterprises, allowing them to increase security protection. All of these activities will have an effect on P_A. An excellent example of this occurred in 2004, when intelligence agencies acquired information indicating that Citibank in New York and the World Bank in Washington, DC were terrorist targets, which led to increased security at these locations.[5]

At some point, the adversary attacks and the likelihood of attack is no longer in doubt. In this phase P_E, which represents vulnerability of the site to the defined threat, is the dominant term. P_E answers the question: How likely is the security system to prevent completion of a successful attack by the defined threat? This is the focus of the vulnerability assessment that is performed to support the risk assessment.

After a successful attack (if the security system prevents adversary success, this stage may not occur), when the adversary has completed a theft or sabotage path and initiated an event that can cause either immediate or delayed consequences, the C term becomes the predominant measure of risk. Thus we can put the three terms together, quantitatively or qualitatively, to represent risk for the overall protection system or for a specific subsystem, such as physical security.

If a quantitative approach is used, the P_A and C terms can be calculated using historical data and consequence criteria. In a qualitative analysis, these terms can be represented by using descriptors such as likely, very likely, or not likely for P_A, and critical, severe, or minimal for the C term. This determination will be based on the capability of the threat and the consequence of loss of the asset. If the likelihood of attack is high, but the consequence is low (think about shoplifting at one store in an enterprise), the problem to be solved is easier than if both P_A and C are high. The cumulative effects of losses across the enterprise must also be considered. Many thefts of low-value items can add up to a high overall impact. This is part of the consequence analysis.

In addition to determining the likelihood of an adversary attack, a threat definition for the enterprise must be created during the risk assessment and specific information must be collected about the adversary. Adversaries can be separated into three classes – outsiders, insiders, and outsiders in collusion with insiders. For each class of adversary, the full range of tactics (deceit, force, stealth, or combinations of these) should be defined. Deceit is the attempted defeat of a security system by using false authorization and identification; force is the overt, forcible attempt to overcome a security system, and stealth is any attempt to defeat the detection system and enter the facility covertly. For any given facility in an enterprise, there may be several threats such as a criminal outsider, a disgruntled employee, competitors, or some combination of the above, and the security system must protect assets against all of these threats.

Other threat characteristics that should be considered include capabilities such as weapons, tools, or explosives they may use, and their motivation (US Department of State, 2004). Adversaries may be motivated by ideological, financial, or personal reasons and this can make a big difference in the protection system that is needed. For example, a highly motivated adversary who is willing to die for a cause is much different from vandals who will flee when discovered. It can also be helpful to consider the number of adversaries expected as part of the threat definition. This can be non-specific, such as a small group, or more detailed, as in 2–4 individuals. Choosing the most likely threat or threats, and then verifying system performance against these threats is the basis of vulnerability assessment.

Asset identification for the enterprise or facility is also a part of risk assessment. Assets may include critical assets or information, people, or critical areas and processes. A thorough review of the facility and its assets should be conducted. Questions such as: What losses will be incurred in the event of sabotage of this equipment? What undesirable events exceed the enterprise risk tolerance? will help identify the assets or equipment that are most vulnerable or that create an unacceptable consequence of loss. Assets are usually identified using some sort of consequence analysis, where criteria are created to screen all assets and prioritize their value. Criteria such as number of people at risk of injury or death, dollar impact to the enterprise, damage to reputation, loss of market share or position, and environmental damage are commonly used. We recommend the use of objective criteria and that monetary value is not the only measure of loss, although we would agree that all criteria can be assessed using monetary value. There is a certain point where monetary value may not have as much meaning, such as the attacks of 9/11. The loss of so many lives can be represented by dollars (US Department of Justice, 2002), but the cost to rebuild property cannot be compared to the cost of 3000 lost lives.

The form of the asset will also be a consideration in asset identification. If a particular piece of critical or private information must be protected, and the information exists in both paper and electronic forms, both forms must be equally protected. It would do little good to implement very tight physical security for the information if the information is stored on a vulnerable network. This is an example of the security principle of balance, which means that all paths to the asset are equally difficult for the adversary. If the protection systems are not balanced, there is additional risk. Due to the different forms of information, some attack methods are difficult to prevent. For example, an insider can memorize a sentence of critical information each day and write it down when they leave the site, or could fax the information offsite to an accomplice. This is another aspect of risk assessment.

The process of determining these objectives will be somewhat recursive. That is, definition of the threat will depend on target identification, and vice versa. This recursion should be expected and is indicative of the complex relationships among protection system objectives. The overall risk assessment process is summarized in Figure 22.1. This process includes threat definition and estimation of likelihood of attack, a consequence analysis to prioritize assets (criticality), a vulnerability assessment to evaluate how effective the security system is in protecting assets from defined threats, and the qualitative or quantitative assessment of risk using these factors. If risk is not acceptable, security system upgrades or other risk management alternatives must be implemented.

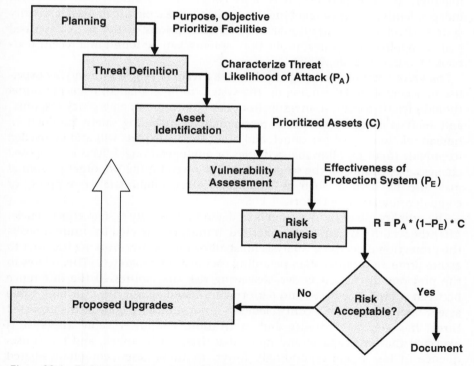

Figure 22.1 Risk assessment process. The process includes planning of which sites will be evaluated, defining the threats and identifying assets, and determining system effectiveness in protecting the assets from the defined threats. Once these aspects are understood, the determination of risk can be made. System effectiveness may be determined qualitatively or quantitatively and will vary based on the capability of the threat.

Vulnerability assessment

As defined above, risk assessment provides the information that answers the three questions: What can go wrong? What is the likelihood that it would go wrong? What are the consequences? A vulnerability assessment (VA) is used to support the risk assessment by answering the first question: What can go wrong? Although threats and assets to be protected are generally identified prior to a VA, we often see enterprises include these steps in their VA. Understanding the enterprise (or the specific facility that is part of the enterprise), defining the expected threat, and identifying key assets are objectives that the VA team needs to understand before they can conduct a thorough and meaningful assessment. These objectives establish the level of protection required and serve as the underlying assumptions necessary to support the VA. The following discussion summarizes the process and techniques used in a VA to effectively assess the security system. The security system in this case may be a subsystem of the overall protection scheme, such as physical, cyber- or executive protection, or it may be the overall protection afforded by all of the subsystems working together. In our experience, it is more common to evaluate each subsystem independently, and then combine the results to give a picture of overall security system effectiveness. Additional detailed descriptions of the steps described here, as applied to physical protection systems, can be found in a recent textbook by Garcia (Garcia, 2005).

The VA of a security system generally takes a team of people with varying expertise to accomplish. Depending on the system to be evaluated, team personnel should include technical, investigation, law enforcement, emergency response, and analysis experts. Operations representatives including safety, production, human relations, legal personnel, and other facility experts will also be needed to provide input on allowable activities or any operational effects of proposed changes. Depending on the scope and time allowed for the VA, other personnel may also be needed, such as technical writers, administrative support, or computer simulation operators.

The primary job of the VA team is to determine security system effectiveness. After the security system is characterized, it must be analysed to ensure it meets the protection objectives. Analysis must allow for features working together to assure protection rather than regarding each feature separately. This relates to the previous discussion under Measuring risk that addressed the difference between compliance-based and performance-based approaches. For high value assets, mere presence of security elements is not sufficient, because the expected threat has greater capability and motivation. For lower value assets, it is expected that less capable and motivated threats will attack, and the consequence of loss is correspondingly lower. In these cases, compliance-based approaches might work, but one might question what the ROI is on a security system that does not protect assets even from less capable adversaries. Due to the complexity of protection systems, an analysis usually requires the use of modeling techniques. If any vulnerabilities are found, upgrades must be proposed to correct the vulnerabilities and a new analysis must be performed to verify that the vulnerabilities have been addressed.

The purpose of a security system is to prevent an adversary from successful completion of a malevolent action against an enterprise. The primary security system functions are detection, delay, and response. For a system to be effective there must be awareness there is an attack (detection) and slowing of adversary progress to the targets (delay), thus allowing responders time to interrupt or stop the adversary from completing the attack (response). The VA team must determine if individual security elements are installed, operated, and maintained properly, if procedures are followed, and if personnel are trained appropriately to provide an effective and integrated system that accomplishes this purpose. The process described below is explained in more detail in Garcia (2001).

Detection is the discovery of an adversary action. It includes sensing of covert or overt actions using physical or network intrusion sensors or observation by personnel. Once an alarm is initiated and reported, alarm assessment begins. The faster the alarm source is assessed, the faster any appropriate response will be, resulting in a more effective system. In physical security, the fastest way to assess an alarm is through the use of video images using closed circuit television (CCTV) cameras; on networks, alarm assessment is much harder. Video assessment of alarms should not be confused with video surveillance. Video assessment is defined as the integration of a sensor with a video image showing the cause of the alarm, while video surveillance is the use of CCTV cameras to scan and possibly record images, without benefit of sensors. Depending on the threat and consequence of loss of the asset, either technique can be used, but if the asset is high-value and cannot be lost, surveillance would not be effective. Surveillance systems depend either on human operators to sense an adversary attack, which is not effective (Tickner and Poulton, 1973), or on after-the-fact review of video images. If the enterprise is prepared to lose the asset, after-the-fact review is acceptable. If, on the other hand, the asset cannot be lost, the system is not effective, and the risk is much higher. Key indicators of detection effectiveness include the probability of detection (expressed quantitatively or qualitatively), nuisance alarm rate, camera resolution, light-to-dark ratio, recording of integrated alarm and video data at the appropriate resolution, and effective operation under all weather conditions and facility states, such as open or closed, emergencies, or day and night.

Entry control is part of the detection function. Entry control refers to equipment used to allow entry to authorized personnel and detect the attempted entry of unauthorized personnel and material. Access control is used to represent the procedures and databases that support the equipment that is used. Entry control can be implemented through physical means such as card readers at turnstiles or fingerprint readers at computer keyboards. Access controls include the use of personal identification numbers, passwords, and visitor control procedures. Key indicators of entry control effectiveness are throughput, ease of entry using deceit tactics, and false accept and reject rates of equipment.

Delay is the second function of a security system and is the slowing down of adversary progress. Delay can be accomplished by personnel, barriers, locks, and activated delays in physical systems, and through encryption and honeypots in networks. The measure of delay effectiveness is the time required by the adversary (after detection) to bypass each delay element. Although the adversary may be delayed prior to detection, this delay does not contribute to system effectiveness because the site is not aware of an attack. Without this awareness, the site cannot respond, and the asset will be lost. Delay before detection is primarily a deterrent. The key indicator for delay elements is time to defeat the element. The delay time will depend on adversary tools and the barrier material.

The response function consists of the actions taken by guards, law enforcement, or other responders to prevent adversary success and includes interruption and neutralization. Response does not necessarily refer only to immediate armed response to a security event. For example, other responses may be to sound a horn to evacuate a building or a delayed response might be to record legally admissible video information to use in prosecuting an adversary. This assumes that the asset can be lost, at least temporarily. Network responses include disconnecting the adversary from the network or paging the network administrator. The capability and goal of the threat, value of asset, and legal constraints will determine the appropriate response. The key indicator of response effectiveness is time to respond.

The more the deployed system deviates from the functional integration of detection, delay and response, and the more key indicators that are degraded, the more vulnerable the enterprise. This in turn increases the risk to the enterprise. There are some factors that indicate a degree of risk acceptance (knowingly or not), such as the lack of an immediate response to attacks on critical assets, delay with no detection, detection of intrusions with no integrated alarm assessment, or lack of integration of multiple layers of security. The amount of protection required is a function of the value of the asset and the risk tolerance of the enterprise.

Once all the appropriate data has been collected, a risk analysis is conducted to establish the effectiveness of the security system in protecting assets against a defined threat. Analysis techniques are based on the use of adversary paths and scenarios, which assume that a sequence of adversary actions is required to complete an attack on an asset. Outsider attacks (paths) will start outside the facility; insider paths will start inside the facility (i.e. past some layers of security). The specific steps in the attack and threat capabilities are considered for this analysis. Paths that are not likely to be used by the defined threat are not considered. Thus, if the defined threat is two vandals with a can of spray paint and no tools, they will not cut fences, break through locked steel doors, or attack networks. It is important to note that system effectiveness will vary with the threat. As the threat capability increases, performance of individual security elements or the system as a whole will decrease. This is why risk analysis must be performed for each defined threat.

System effectiveness (P_E), which is a measure of system vulnerability, is combined with threat (P_A) and asset value (C) as described above to determine the baseline risk. If the risk is acceptable, the VA team documents the results and archives the report for future reference. If the risk is not acceptable, options must be proposed to address the identified risk. Risk may be addressed through the use of avoidance, reduction, spreading, transfer, and acceptance alternatives. At this point, the VA team proposes options that lower risk to an acceptable level, and provides the cost of each option. The goal is to achieve the best risk management for the cost (i.e. maximize ROI). These options and their associated costs are presented to senior management, who make the final decision about which option will be implemented. Using our definition, risk management builds on risk assessment by answering the questions: What can be done? What options are available? and What are their associated tradeoffs in terms of costs, benefits, and risks? What are the impacts of current management decisions on future options? The answer to the last question is what provides the optimal solution. The process continues through the ongoing review of threats, assets, and vulnerabilities to ensure that risk is managed to an acceptable level.

Summary

This chapter discussed the use of risk management in security. It presented some basic definitions in order to establish a common language, and introduced techniques used in business risk management. A description of how risk assessment fits into risk management was provided, along with an overview of risk assessment techniques. Risk assessment includes an understanding of the threat to the enterprise, the value of assets that are to be protected from the threats, and a vulnerability assessment based on threats and assets. The chapter included a description of the use of a risk equation that is used to relate threats, assets, and vulnerabilities and to place the risk terms in the context of an adversary attack lifecycle. The chapter also discussed vulnerability assessment and how security functions must work together to be effective in meeting protection system objectives. Analysis of risk and how this supports risk management was also discussed.

Notes

1 Mary Lynn Garcia gratefully acknowledges the assistance of Carole Lojek, John Wirsbinski, Greg Wyss, Joe Sandoval, and Tommy Woodall. This chapter was authored by Sandia Corporation under contract with the US Government. Accordingly, the US Government retains a non-exclusive royalty-free license to publish or reproduce the published form of this contribution, or allow others to do so, for US Government purposes.

2 San Diego Union Tribune 8/11/04, story available at http://www.signonsandiego.com/uniontrib/20040811/news_1n11vegas.html.

3 Investorwords (2004) Definition can be found at: http://www.investorwords.com/cgi-bin/getword.cgi?4250.

4 Note that these two likelihoods are not independent. P_A is higher for scenarios where P_E is lower because adversaries are more likely to attack weak systems, where they are more likely to be successful. This is really the crux of vulnerability assessment – to determine if the security system is sufficient to prevent successful attacks by defined threats.

5 Washington Post 2004. This article can be found at http://www.washingtonpost.com/ac2/wp-dyn/A32900-2004Aug1.

Key readings

For a practical text that reviews the procedures and technologies used in risk management in a narrative form that limits statistical jargon, see Koller G. (2000) *Risk Modeling for Determining Value and Decision Making in Business and Industry*, Boca Raton, FL: Chapman & Hall/CRC. For a rigorous but introductory discussion of probability theory, see Ross, S.M. (1997) *Introduction to Probability Models 6th edn*, San Diego: Academic Press. An excellent review of the systems engineering processes and principles used in designing and evaluating integrated systems that appeals to both technical and non-technical readers is provided in Martin, J.N. (2003) Systems Engineering Guidebook, *A Process for Developing Systems and Products*, Boca Raton, FL: CRC and for an engaging overview of project management techniques that should be used to manage the administrative aspects of risk and vulnerability assessment, see Mochal T. and Mochal J. (2003) *Lessons in Project Management*, New York: Apress/Springer.

References

American Heritage Dictionaries (2000) *American Heritage Dictionary of the English Language 4th edn*, Boston: Houghton Mifflin Company.

Anthony, R.N., Reece, J.S. and Hertenstein, J.H. (1995) *Accounting: Text and Cases 9th edn*, Chicago: Irwin.

ASIS, International (2003) *General Security Risk Assessment*, available at: http://www.asisonline.org/guidelines/guidelines.htm.

Bach, G.L. (1971) *Economics an Introduction to Analysis and Policy 7th edn*, Englewood Cliffs: Prentice-Hall, pp. 336–7.

Beaver, K. (2002) *Selling Security to Upper Management*. This article can be found at: http://searchsecurity.techtarget.com/tip/1,289483,sid14_gci837832,00.html.

Bishop, D.M., Wilson, D.W. and Shaver, J.W. (1976) 'Accountancy, Physical Control and Security: A Question of Balance', *J Nuc Matl Mgmt*, Vol. 5, No. 3, p. 577.

Brown, R.L. (2003) *Publication R106: Accomplishing Due Diligence: 125 Details to Examine Before Buying a Business*, Niantic, CT: Business Book Press, available at: http://www.businessbookpress.com/catalog/cat7.htm.

Burstein H. (1994) *Introduction to Security 1st edn*, Englewood Cliffs: Prentice Hall.

Fisher, R.J. and Green, G. (1998) *Introduction to Security 6th edn*, Boston: Butterworth-Heinemann, pp. 168–9.

Garcia M.L. (2000) 'Truth and Consequences', *Security Management*, Vol. 44, No. 6, pp. 44–8.

Garcia, M.L. (2001) *The Design and Evaluation of Physical Protection Systems*, Boston: Butterworth-Heinemann.

Garcia, M.L. (2005) *Vulnerability Assessment of Physical Protection Systems*, Boston: Elsevier.

Garner, B.A. (2004) *Black's Law Dictionary 8th edn*, St Paul: West Publishing.

Grose, V.L. (1987) *Managing Risk: Systematic Loss Prevention for Executives 1st edn*, Arlington, VA: Omega Systems Group, pp. 47–8.

Haimes, Y.Y. (1999) 'Risk Management', in A. Sage and W. Rouse (eds) *Handbook of Systems Engineering and Management*, New York: John Wiley and Sons, pp. 137–73.

Hansen, L.E., Nilson, R. and Schneider, R.A. (1977) 'An Approach to the Use of Performance Criteria in Safeguards', *J Nuc Matl Mgmt*, Vol. 6, No. 3, p. 277.

Hess, K. and Wrobleski, H. (1996) *Introduction to Private Security 4th edn*, Minneapolis/St Paul: West Publishing, pp. 423–9.

Kaplan, S. and Garrick, B.J. (1981) 'On the Quantitative Definition of Risk', *Risk Analysis*, Vol. 1, No. 1, pp. 11–27.

Kumamoto, H. and Henley, E.J. (1996) *Probabilistic Risk Assessment and Management for Engineers and Scientists 2nd edn*, Piscataway, NJ: IEEE Press, pp. 17–20.

Matalucci, R.V. (2002) 'Risk Assessment Methodology for Dams (RAM-D)', *Proc 6th International Conference on Probabilistic Safety Assessment and Management (PSAM6)*, Vol. 1, pp. 169–76.

Miccolis, J. (2002) 'The Language of Enterprise Risk Management: A Practical Glossary and Discussion of Relevant Terms, Concepts, Models, and Measures', Expert Commentary, *International Risk Management Institute (IRMI)*, available at: http://www.irmi.com/expert/articles/miccolis007.asp, May.

Manunta, G. (2002) 'Risk and Security: Are They Compatible Concepts?', *Security Journal*, Vol. 15, No. 2, pp. 43–55.

Merkhofer, M.W. (1987) *Decision Science and Social Risk Management*, Holland: Kluwer Academic Publishers Group.

Rasmussen, N.C. (1976) 'Probabilistic Risk Analysis: Its Possible Use in Safeguards Problems', *J Nuc Matl Mgmt*, Vol. 5, No. 3, pp. 66–8.

Schultz, D.O. (1978) *Principles of Physical Security*, Houston: Gulf Publishing Company.

Snell, M.K. (2002) 'Probabilistic Security Assessments: How They Differ from Safety Assessments', *Proc 6th International Conference on Probabilistic Safety Assessment and Management (PSAM6)*, Vol. 1, pp. 123–8.

Tickner, A.H. and Poulton, E.C. (1973) 'Monitoring up to 16 Television Pictures Showing a Great Deal of Movement', *Ergonomics*, Vol. 16, No. 4, pp. 381–401.

Timm, H.W. and Christian, K.E. (1991) *Introduction to Private Security*, Pacific Grove: Brooks-Cole Publishing.

Todd, J.L. and Nickell, W.C. (1975) 'Physical Security Effectiveness Evaluation', *J Nuc Matl Mgmt*, Vol. 4, No. 3, p. 391.

US Department of Justice (2002) *September 11 Victim Compensation Fund of 2001. Explanation of Process for Computing Presumed Economic Loss*, Washington DC: Government Printing Office, also available at: http://www.usdoj.gov/victimcompensation/vc_matrices.pdf.

US Department of State (2004) *Patterns of Global Terrorism*, Washington DC: Government Printing Office, also available at: http://www.state.gov/s/ct/rls/pgtrpt/2003/c12108.htm.

Wyss, G.D. (2000) 'Risk Assessment and Risk Management for Energy Applications', in P. Catania (ed.) *Energy 2000: State of the Art*, L'Aquila, Italy: Balaban Publishers, pp. 163–84.

23

Disaster and Crisis Management

Dominic Elliott

Many organizations, and populations, are vulnerable to the threat of catastrophic events – the seemingly unthinkable can happen and yet it seems that organizations remain ill prepared for such events. Although many countries around the Pacific Rim have tsunami warning systems in place, none were available when the South East Asian tsunami struck in late 2004. Estimates of loss of life exceed 150,000 and the true costs are inestimable. A few months earlier, with fewer deaths, Hurricane Charley struck the coasts of Cuba and Florida, causing an estimated $5–11 billion of damages to property. One concern of crisis management is the managerial response to such disasters, and the efforts which may be made to limit the impact of such events through investment in more resilient infrastructure. The scope of crisis management has extended, since the 1970s to include so called manmade disasters (see Turner, 1976; Perrow, 1984, for example). These include industrial accidents (e.g. Bhopal), major power failures (such as those of 2003 which affected millions in the North East US and others in London, Rome and New Zealand), and, a growing category, major terrorist incidents (New York, Bali, Madrid, Istanbul, Baghdad and Beslan). The scope of a crisis management approach is one which encompasses the full range of major systems failure impacting upon organizations, from tornadoes to terrorism. In Chapter 22, Garcia distinguished between 'safety' and 'security'. The former relates to a potentially dangerous abnormal condition and the latter to the measures used to protect people, property, or organizations from malevolent human threats. Motivation appears to be the key different characteristic between defining a measure as safety or security focused. Although the events which trigger a 'crisis' may differ, the extent to which they interrupt organizational activity will be determined by pre-crisis preparedness and managerial responses. There is also the question of at what point does careless behaviour (safety) become wilful negligence (security).

The purpose of this chapter is to provide an overview of a crisis management approach. The chapter begins with a brief review of a disaster versus crisis management approach, including a definition of key terms. It proceeds to provide a suggested structure for business continuity management – a process for identifying potential threats and organizational vulnerabilities through to risk assessment. The chapter concludes with a review of an extensive case of two similar crises, namely the contaminations of Perrier (1990) and Coca-Cola (1999) respectively. Although these were not, so far as is known, the result of any malevolent action, they illustrate many of the problems associated with effective crisis management and learning.

Disaster management approach

The terms disaster and crisis are used so frequently and interchangeably that in common language there is little difference between the two. Yet the terms reflect different approaches to similar phenomena. The root of the word 'disaster' lies in the Latin definition for 'bad star,' reflecting an almost fatalistic view of an event. The term is often used to describe a natural event such as flood or tsunami. The means to prevent such 'acts of God' are clearly beyond us at present, although it is possible to build defences against floods or tsunami warning systems. The primary concern of disaster studies has been with the response of organizations to the economic and human consequences of natural events. However, in an investigation of the deaths of some 500,000 people, following a cyclone in East Bengal, Hardin (1971) criticized the view that the cyclone was the cause of death as too simplistic. An alternative explanation identified the underlying cause as systemic, including a combination of inadequate infrastructure, overpopulation and the decision to locate people in a hazardous area. The term disaster refers to the human impact rather than the flood that triggered it, a subtle but key distinction.

Researchers, who primarily use the term disaster, tend to focus upon the responses of organizations to catastrophic events and, especially, threats from natural hazards. Within this literature, the term 'crisis management' has invariably been equated with the processes of 'emergency managing' – with the management of resources and personnel to deal with the task demands of a disaster (see for example, Quarantelli, 1988). Contingency planning and emergency preparedness are particular concerns, as are the processes by which *post*-disaster communications and co-ordination are achieved. The underlying causality of crises has not, in general, been considered in detail by this school reflecting, in part, its primary concern with 'naturally occurring disasters'.

Crisis management approach

An alternative approach, termed the 'Industrial Crisis School', uses the term 'crisis management' to refer to organizational activity before, during and after a specific crisis incident. For example, the accident at Bhopal in 1984, which killed more than 2500 people, challenged the widely held views of many working within the global chemical industry that numerous layers of defence are adequate to prevent any plant failure from occurring. There were suggestions, although never proven, that the toxic release was the result of sabotage (Shrivastava, 1987). The manner in which contingency plans failed to cope with the demands of the event, the behaviour of people under conditions of crisis, the process of risk communication and the speed with which the event escalated are all hallmarks of a crisis event.

A defining characteristic of crises, distinguishing them from other events, is that a crisis has a symbolic importance beyond its physical properties. This leads managers and other personnel to question critically, and fundamentally, existing methods of operation:

> To some extent this is what distinguishes *crisis management*, where both the physical and symbolic dimensions of a crisis are addressed before and after a crisis, from *security management* which is limited to the technical side of safety, and *crash management* which is limited to reactive actions (Pauchant and Mitroff, 1992: 18).

As Turner (1976) argues:

> there is little need for a re-evaluation of culturally accepted devices when accidents, even on a large scale, occur in situations recognized as hazardous. When a trawler is lost in Arctic fishing grounds, or when a wall collapses onto a firefighting team, there is much less comment than when an accident kills passengers on a suburban commuter train (p. 380).

Billings *et al.* (1980) critique of Hermann's (1971) 'classical' model that had identified three dimensions to crisis, 'degree of threat, surprise and limited time for decision making':

> Two actors may be in precisely the same situation, yet one may feel uncertainty, time pressure etc. and define the situation as crisis, while the other may see it as a routine decision-making situation. Crisis resides in the person as well as in the situation. (Billings *et al.*, 1980: 306).

The psychological dimension of crisis was also identified by Eberwein (1978):

> structural concepts of crisis stress the objective aspect of the phenomenon that is a specific state of affairs independent from the fact of being perceived or not ... while psychological concepts are those defining the subjective or perceptual aspect of a specific state of affairs ... irrespective of the fact whether such a state of affairs exists or not outside ... perception. (p. 126).

It follows from this discussion that two identical events may be perceived in different ways, one as a crisis, and another as an accident. That is, one challenges core organizational assumptions and provides a first step towards full cultural readjustment; alternatively, the other (an accident) is treated as a 'structural' failure only (Pauchant and Mitroff, 1992). Crises are defined, therefore, as events which challenge core values and assumptions. They are non-routine interruptions and indicate that the assumptions underpinning operating practices are flawed.

Although 'symbolism' has been identified as the defining characteristic of crises, a second characteristic concerns their impact upon a wide range of stakeholders. As Smith and Elliott (2005) reported, when Firestone tyres, fitted to Ford's Explorer motor vehicle, were implicated in a large number of fatal accidents, both Bridgestone and Ford sought to deflect blame for the event away from themselves. On 6th August 2000 a US Federal agency raised concerns about the safety of the tyres and the Ford Explorer. Sears Roebuck, a distributor, immediately stopped sales of suspect tyres. Ford announced a voluntary recall on August 9th, some three days after the official concerns on August 11th. Ford identified a range of possible causes including, an earlier strike in the plant where Firestone tyres were produced and design flaws in the rubber coating on the tyres; firmly placing responsibility for the failure upon Firestone. The United Steel Workers Union threatened Firestone with strike action, selecting a moment of peak vulnerability for the employer. Lawyers were quick to offer their services on a no-win no-fee basis. Goodyear, a competitor of Bridgestone, was quick to exploit their vulnerability with a number of tactical movements of stock and prices. The media was quick to highlight the conflict between Ford and Firestone and to provide coverage of consumer and consumer group concerns. In this example there was no single event as is often assumed; this escalation resulted from the accumulation of many incidents which combined to create crises for the organizations concerned. The crisis unfolded through many interactions between diverse stakeholders, the term 'creeping crisis' might be more apt. An objective of some terrorist activity is to create a form of creeping crisis that undermines the *status quo*. This may be directed against an organization, as the concerted attacks on the Huntingdon Life Sciences laboratory have been, or against government as the current insurgency in Iraq and Sri Lanka illustrates. Crises involve many different stakeholders and it may not always be clear which are the key ones. Any crisis response must also take into consideration the diversity of stakeholder involvement and need if management efforts are to be effective (see for example, Mitchell *et al.*, 1997).

A third characteristic of crisis is that whatever the trigger, the impact is held largely determined by the actions and inactions of managers (Pauchant and Mitroff, 1988, 1992; Smith, 1990). This may encourage a simplistic approach to any attempts to understand the underlying causes of crisis. As a result organizations often search for technical solutions to problems that are human in origin. Crises possess social and technical characteristics and any strategies for prevention or cure must take this into consideration (see for example, Elliott and Smith, 1993). This socio-technical view of crises also assumes that managerial attention must be placed, not only upon the focal crisis incident but, upon a preceding 'crisis of management' and the subsequent post-crisis phase. In summary, a crisis management approach is defined here as one that:

- Recognizes the impact, potential or realized, of crisis events upon a wide range of stakeholders

- Acknowledges that crisis events possess both social and technical dimensions
- Identifies the roles played by managers and organizational processes in incubating the potential for crisis
- Assumes that managers may develop resilience to business interruptions through processes and changes to operating norms and practices

Three stages of crisis

A crisis management approach recognizes a minimum of three distinct phases of crisis, as depicted in Figure 23.1 (see for example, Smith, 1990)

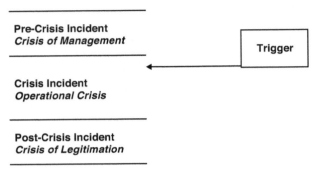

Figure 23.1   Stages of crisis model
Source: Adapted from Smith, D. (1990)

Pre-crisis of management

The pre-crisis stage refers to the period in which the potential for failure is incubated. In the extended period before an incident occurs, decisions will be made that make the organization more or less vulnerable to crises. Such decisions might include (in)appropriate staffing levels, the discrediting or ignoring of internal and external safety reviews, or an ignoring of intelligence concerning the potential threat from illegal or malevolent behaviour. This period may occur over many years as managers and organizations are frequently predisposed to resist change, even when incidents indicate systemic and procedural inadequacies. For example, Harold Shipman the British general practitioner, was able to murder more than 200 of his patients during a suspected 20-year period, because despite growing evidence, the belief that medics preserve life rather than remove it acted as a protective screen (see Elliott and Smith, 2006). As Turner (1976, 1978) observed:

> Common causal features are rigidities in institutional beliefs, distracting decoy phenomena, neglect of outside complaints, multiple information handling difficulties, exacerbation of the hazards by strangers, failure to comply with regulations and a tendency to minimise emergent danger. (Turner, 1976: 378).

In the Shipman case, external complaints that emerged from non-medics were viewed as too incredible to be acted upon; the systems of regulating medical behaviours were overseen by fellow medics; monitoring information was gathered; most significant was the view that a doctor murdering patients was as incredible as Father Christmas stealing presents. The interplay between factors, argued Turner, might lead to a 'failure of foresight' as staff and systems are unable to identify potential risks. Toft and Reynolds (1992) developed this argument into the notion of 'failures of hindsight', whereby organizations failed to learn effectively from crisis events leading to the recurrence of similar crisis incidents. Even with the benefit of hindsight, these rigidities of belief, information handling difficulties, etc. act to prevent effective learning. This argument is central to the contribution of later authors including Shrivastava (1987) Pauchant and Mitroff (1988, 1992), Miller (1990) and Reason (1990, 1995) who, whilst not dismissing the relevance of environmental factors, argued that crises can often be better explained in terms of internal (i.e. organizational) factors than external ones. That is, the propensity to crisis resides within organizations. For example, a study of the effects of the IRA bombing of the City of London identified that:

> The particular organizational crises triggered by the City of London bombings were largely determined by internal factors – the degree of centralisation, hardware and software backup routines and out of hours staff communications. A gas explosion or earthquake might have had similar effects. Following the City's Bishopsgate bombing, the Nat West's data transfer routines were cited as a key factor in its ability to maintain operations. Conversely, the routines of the Hong Kong and Shanghai Bank Corporation did not facilitate a quick return to normality. (Swartz *et al.*, 1995: 19).

Crisis management, thus, is not simply concerned event management but with the entire three stage process.

Operational crisis

The second stage refers to the immediate organizational handling of an incident. Clearly, this period will vary according to the nature of the crisis itself and the ability of the organization to respond. Fitzgerald (1995) describes the period following the triggering incident as a 'glide path'; this metaphor reflects the differing abilities of an aircraft to glide based upon environmental conditions and other factors such as design, load and pilot skills. Organizations will also differ in their abilities to continue their operations in the aftermath of a crisis event. As the example from the City of London highlighted, the presence of business continuity plans and the processes with which to activate and implement them are key success factors in ensuring the ability to resume business. Of course a catastrophe the scale of 9/11 may overwhelm all but the largest or best-prepared organizations. A simple analogy may be drawn with personal health. An individual may increase his/her probability of longevity by eating and drinking sensibly, taking exercise and by avoiding smoking and pollutants. A healthy lifestyle may also increase an individual's chances of recovering from an accident. However, should such an individual be crushed by a meteorite they will still, in all probability, die instantly. Effective preparations increase the chances of longevity and may, to return to our earlier metaphor, lengthen the distance of the so-called 'glide path'. A number of suggestions are made in a later section concerning how this stage may be effectively managed.

Post-crisis of legitimation

The third stage refers to the period in which an organization seeks to consolidate and then reposition itself. Of course, stage three feeds back into stage one as organizations may or may not learn from their experiences. Smith and Sipika (1993), drawing upon the case of Union Carbide following the Bhopal disaster, argued that the removal of senior decision makers (scapegoats) provided a platform for cultural adjustment and reconfiguration. This may occur in some cases but not in all. A review of safety systems at the Bradford Football Stadium some eight years following a fire indicated the continuance of the lax safety culture that predated the disaster despite the removal of those held to be at fault (Elliott and Smith, 1997).

A crisis management approach has evolved from considering how to manage crisis incidents (i.e. phases two and three), to considering how the potential for crisis may be incubated by organizations themselves (see Pauchant and Mitroff, 1992; Elliott and Smith, 1993 for a detailed case study). Thus, although Risk management describes the process as undertaken by organizations, a crisis management approach denotes a frame of reference in which incidents occur in three stages and in which organizations, themselves, incubate the potential for failure. This chapter now turns to consider a process for business continuity management (BCM).

Business continuity management

In an organizational context, business continuity management (BCM) has evolved into a process that identifies an organization's exposure to internal and external threats by synthesizing hard and soft assets to provide effective prevention and recovery (Elliott *et al.*, 2002). Essential to the success of BCM is a meticulous understanding of the wide range of threats (internal and external) facing an organization. Figure 23.2 identifies one possible process for BCM; it provides a starting point for considering crisis management in practice.

The scope of risk and crisis management can be focused or broad, reflecting the managerial mindset of an organization. One classification of categories of risk may be seen in Jones and Sutherland's (1999) guidance notes, appended to Turnbull Report (1999), it identifies four broad areas of risk. It is clear from Table 23.1 that some categories of risk have a greater relevance to security issues, particularly compliance and operations.

Identify Objectives and Scope
Identify Causes of Crises
Business Impact Analysis
Internal Analysis
Products/services
Activities & resources
Dependencies
External Analysis
Market environment
Stakeholder analysis
Supply chain analysis
Business Impact Evaluation
Objectives
Risks
Priorities
Scenarios
Generating the Plan

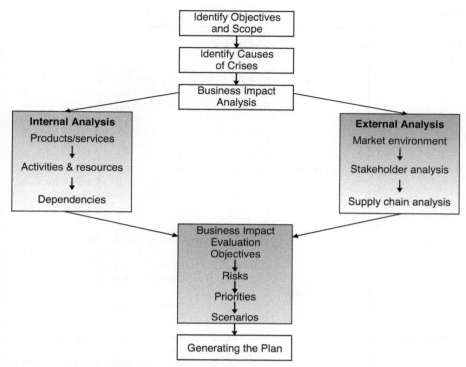

Figure 23.2 A process for business continuity management
Source: Elliott *et al.* (2002)

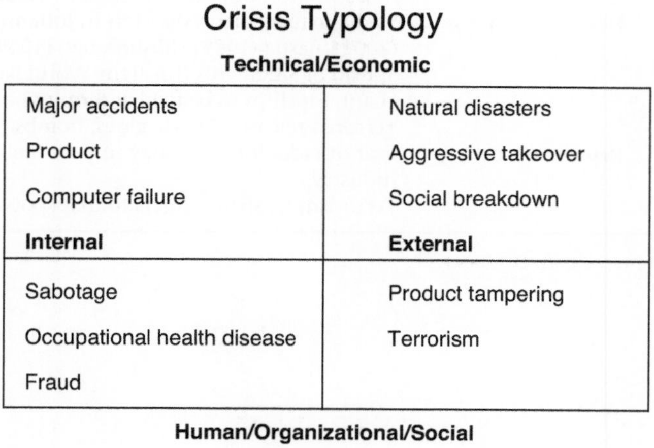

Crisis Typology
Technical/Economic
Major accidents
Product
Computer failure
Internal
Natural disasters
Aggressive takeover
Social breakdown
External
Sabotage
Occupational health disease
Fraud
Product tampering
Terrorism
Human/Organizational/Social

Figure 23.3 Crisis typology
Source: Shrivastava, P. and Mitroff, I. (1987)

Table 23.1   Risk matrix

Category of risk	Example	Illustration
Business	Wrong business strategy	In early 1970s Adidas dominated the running shoes industry. It underestimated the growth in demand for running shoes and the aggression of new rival, Nike. With relatively low barriers to entry, stronger promotion, sharper pricing and ongoing research and development it might have built barriers to entry (Hartley, 1995).
	Industry in decline	Landline telephones. Border currency exchange posts around European Union following creation of single currency.
	Too slow to innovate	EMI resist Compact Disc technology during early 1980s.
Financial	Liquidity risk	Greater air travel during summer months creates cashflow difficulties during quieter, winter months.
	Credit risk	Leicester City borrowed £50 million to build new stadium and is relegated, losing key revenue stream.
	Misuse of financial resources	Insider dealing. Targeting of electronic banking systems for fraudulent purposes.
Compliance	Tax penalties	Silvio Berlusconi subjected to on-going enquiries concerning tax evasion.
	Breaches of professional guidelines/ Companies Act	Self-regulation of financial institutions may prevent identification of common malpractice. Harold Shipman persistently broke protocols but method of compliance monitoring depended upon trust.
Operational & others	Succession problems	Inspirational CEO moves on with no obvious successor. Assassination of political religious leader.
	Health and safety	Stadia management, disasters in Johannesburg (2001), Bastia (1989) Hillsborough (1989). Spread of SARS virus threatens World Badminton championships to be held at Birmingham, UK, 2003. Terrorist release of toxic gases, bombs.
	Reputation risk	Fear of radiation risks may impact mobile phone industry. Terrorism in Spain targets tourist spots.

Source: Adapted from Elliott, D. (2004)

Another framework developed to identify the range of threats facing an organization was developed by Shrivastava and Mitroff (1987), see Figure 23.3. The
framework classifies crises by determining where they are generated (internal/
external) and which systems (technical versus social) are the primary causes. This
matrix may be used as the starting point for considering the range of potential
interruptions that might occur. Given that developing contingency for every
eventuality may be impractical, the matrix provides the basis for clustering 'families' of crises together so that preparations for each group may be attempted; this
obviates the need to attempt to plan for each type of triggering incident. The first
task is to consider all the potential causes of interruptions before proceeding to a
consideration of the impact upon business objectives for each of these. This is
undertaken through the business impact analysis (BIA).

Business impact analysis

The BIA is a vital element of the BCM process. Meredith (1999: 139) identifies
this analysis as the 'backbone of the entire business continuity exercise'. It determines priorities and therefore, many of the financial commitments to business
continuity. The BIA involves assessing the likely financial and operational consequences of a crisis. The focus of the BIA is upon a specific business process, which
might be defined as a group of business activities undertaken within an organization. Such activities may occur within or between departments. For a fuller
discussion of how a BIA might be undertaken see Elliott *et al.*, 2002). In brief, it
should identify the range of potential crises, organizational objectives, an outline
of key processes and the identification of (flowcharts, etc.) linkages and dependencies with other business units, suppliers, customers and other agencies, etc.
(Elliott *et al.*, 2002). The aim of the process is to stimulate a consideration of
threats and their likely impact upon business processes. Overall, the BIA offers a
preliminary analysis of some of the idiosyncrasies of an organization's resources,
systems and operations.

The BIA should also include an organization's product or service portfolio. As
such, it should fit closely with an organization's strategic analysis. The results
should clearly identify organizational and business unit dependencies. For example, the growing use of web-based service provision in sectors such as insurance, banking, and mobile phone support has increased their dependency upon
information and communication technologies. Other dependencies might
include reliance upon key suppliers, or customers. The power cuts of the past
three years indicate the dependence of many businesses upon utility suppliers.
Rail crashes in the UK during 1999–2000 seriously disrupted rail services and
consistently delayed key personnel from reaching their desks in the city of
London. From a marketing perspective, extended brands mean that threats to
one product may have an impact upon the full brand family. Rumours around
Persil products, for example, impacted upon sales across the entire brand family.
The commercial benefits of consolidating brand names and lines may create new
vulnerabilities.

Complementing the internal review is an examination of an organization's environment through external analysis. As Shrivastava and Mitroff's (1987) typology of crises identifies, the external environment is a significant, potential cause of crises. Moreover, Smith's (1990) crisis of legitimation implies that the response of an organization facing an interruption, and the way that it is perceived (or otherwise) to act appropriately by rivals, customers, regulators, and other observant parties is key to its successful management of crisis. As our earlier example of the Ford–Firestone case highlights, crises involve multiple stakeholders, each with their own agenda, priorities and perceptions.

The position of a company's product or service in a market will also influence the impact of an interruption. A product with a low market share and few dependencies will suffer a lesser impact from a crisis than one with a high market share and high degree of dependency. Conversely, there is some evidence that high market share, combined with a strong reputation and high levels of consumer trust may aid the crisis recovery process. Tylenol remains a market leader despite the deaths of more than ten customers in two separate incidents during the 1980s, when the capsule form of the drug was injected with cyanide. This contrasts sharply, as we shall see, with the Perrier and Coca-Cola crises in which no one died. Next, those involved in the planning process should consider how the market position (market share and image) could be affected by the onset of a disaster. Could it delay a new product launch, erode the company's market position or adversely change the company's image? In terms of the effect on company performance, these products/services and their dependencies should be a priority for business continuity protection.

As identified in the introduction, an understanding of stakeholders is key to effective crisis management. It makes good business sense for organizations to be aware of their stakeholders as their interests and the satisfaction of their needs may determine business success. The objectives of an organization will be circumscribed by the extent to which relationships with stakeholders such as suppliers, distributors, shareholders, and customers are successfully managed, as indicated earlier in the case of Ford and Firestone. Nowhere is this more important than in BCM, since their response to the organization in the post-crisis phase will have an impact on the success of recovery efforts and, ultimately, survival of the company.

Stakeholders are those individuals, groups or organizations who have an interest in an organization. Stakeholders possess power that can be wielded to support or to thwart organizational change. This is typically linked to the urgency they feel about an issue and the legitimacy with which they are held to have the right to speak (Mitchell *et al.*, 1997). An organization's stakeholders may be divided into 'primary' and 'secondary' groups. Primary stakeholders are those who enable the organization to produce its goods and services. The involvement with primary stakeholders usually involves an economic transaction. Secondary stakeholders include those organizations or individuals who are affected, indirectly by the activities of the organization. Professional bodies, the general public, pressure groups, local authorities all form part of this group of stakeholders. Clearly, they all have their own objectives and their influence over the organization will also differ greatly. The use of the term 'secondary' is not meant to indicate that these groups have a lesser impact on organizations. Government agencies, for example, wield much power over where businesses might be sited and the green movement have in recent years been very successful in getting corporations to consider environmental issues.

As Elliott *et al.* (2002) have suggested, any framework for a stakeholder analysis, should consider:

- Identifying who an organization's stakeholders are
- Identifying the goals of stakeholders with regard to the organization
- Identifying the likely impact of an interruption upon each stakeholder and their likely reaction towards it
- The ways in which stakeholder relationships can be managed during an interruption

The concept of stakeholders and its value for effective crisis management is not a distant and abstract one. No organization is self-sufficient and each organization will depend to a greater or lesser extent upon a range of different stakeholder groups. Potentially important stakeholders may not immediately be apparent. The circumstances of crisis may change power relationships. For example, Shell discovered, when they sought to dispose of the Brent Spar oil rig in the North Sea, that it may be the least obvious stakeholder groups that can exert tremendous power. Green Peace, through clever use of media images and an essentially emotional argument, forced the giant Shell, and the UK Government, to back down over the issue of oil rig disposal. An environmental activist now advises the Shell board on environmental matters. From a political perspective, the attack by a relatively small group of terrorists upon the World Trade Center on September 11th 2001 has triggered significant military efforts in the Middle East as well as major changes in US Homeland Security.

Planning for supply chain interruptions

Supply chain issues, such as purchasing and product development, have traditionally fallen under the remit of purchasing and procurement departments. However, consideration of the role of the supply chain in business continuity has grown given that the tight integration of companies along a supply chain often comes to form a source of competitive advantage (Chadwick and Rajagopal, 1995). A stark illustration of this can be seen in following a fire at the Longford natural gas processing plant in Australia. The 1998 incident cut supplies for over a week and restrictions lasted for several months. As a consequence, both Toyota and Ford were forced to close their plants with Toyota estimating losses of AUS$10 million for each day of non-production. In addition, we have previously noted that as stakeholders suppliers are clearly influential to the degree to which they can exert their bargaining power over customers downstream in the supply chain (Porter, 1980). Thus, planners' attention should also be directed to the potential risks that their organizations face from ill-prepared suppliers, whatever the state of their own, internal business continuity management preparations. Similarly, an interruption to a key customer may interrupt demand for a supplier's goods and/or services. Such supply chain analysis should look upstream as well as downstream.

Business impact evaluation

The business impact evaluation (BIE) constitutes the final step in the planning process. It seeks to pull together the preceding analyses into a cohesive whole as a prelude to drafting the business continuity plan. The BIE re-evaluates the initial objectives, set at the outset of the BCP process and assesses the risk against those objectives. It determines the priorities for business resumption and appropriate investments. Key considerations are an assessment of the resources that each business unit and function requires to resume at an appropriate time. This may result from a reflection upon a range of alternative 'resumption scenarios'. According to Elliott *et al.* (2002) the BIE comprises of four analyses. First, a refining of the business continuity objectives. Second, an evaluation of the risks. Third, the establishment of priorities for business recovery, and fourth the development of business interruption scenarios.

Objectives

In order to have practical and 'testable' objectives, those which have been identified prior to the BIA should be refined in order to elucidate the minimum required level at which each function or business process can operate. These amended objectives may include reference to temporal issues. For example:

- Customer contact must be re-established within two hours
- Invoicing must be resumed within one week for major customers and return to normal within two weeks
- Deliveries from suppliers must recommence within four hours
- Level 1 ICT systems must be operational within 45 minutes

Through the incorporation of greater detail into these objectives, a further sequence of events and timings can be devised and incorporated into the draft business continuity plan.

Risk assessment

The term risk assessment describes the process of gauging the most likely outcomes of a set of events and the consequences of those outcomes. At a personal level, informal assessments of risk are more or less a continual mental process from when to pull out from a junction in a car, judging when to compliment a colleague on their appearance through to purchasing decisions and so forth. The risk management discipline has sought to formalize risk assessment in an attempt to reduce the effects of personal bias. However, a limitation where complex systems are concerned is that identifying all possible outcomes and consequences is problematic. It has been argued that any attempt to quantify risk will fail because no matter the degree of mathematics sophistication, all risk assessment is inherently value laden (Toft and Reynolds, 1992). Nevertheless, a structured approach to risk assessment may be better than none. But, a good understanding of the aims and objectives of such a process is more important than a detailed statistical knowledge. A simple matrix, with axes depicting the degree of threat against the likelihood (probability) of occurrence, is commonly used to categorize risks and hence to prioritize remedial actions (Figure 23.4).

Although providing a useful rule of thumb it does not take into account the extent to which an organization has the potential to control an incident, nor for any assessment of the extent to which certain 'risks' might be deemed acceptable to an organization or to other stakeholders. For example, Johnson & Johnson might have deemed that the public would treat them sympathetically if they suffered from a repeated malicious product tampering episode. In many instances the tradeoffs will not be as extreme as in the case of the Tylenol poisonings and organizations must themselves balance investment in preparations against what the public or other groups may consider that they should do.

The outcome of this process should be to provide a rich understanding of the threats and hazards facing an organization. The next stage, once priorities have been determined, is to translate the knowledge into a series of plans. A fuller discussion of this process may be seen in Elliott *et al*. 2002. For the purpose of this chapter we proceed to a necessarily brief consideration of how incidents might be managed.

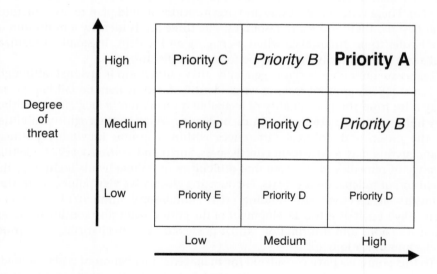

Figure 23.4   Risk priority matrix

Incident management, levels of response, communications and decision making

A key component of effective incident management is the crisis management team. In addition to the day-to-day structures required to implement risk management, a command and control structure for managing crisis incidents is needed. A commonly used format is a three-tier structure, as advocated by the Home Office (1997a, 1997b), mimicking the structure used by the British Police Service who label the three levels bronze, silver and gold system (operational, tactical and strategic respectively). This structure emerged from an attempt to encourage consistency between the emergency services and thereby minimize confusion when dealing with an incident (Flin, 1996).

The purpose of the three levels is to ensure that an organization's response to an incident is effectively co-ordinated. Bronze (operational) corresponds to the normal operational response provided by the emergency services where the management is of routine tasks. The immediate response to an incident is likely to be managed at this level. When the emergency services deal with a major incident, the 'bronze commander' is likely to lead a front line team. Silver (tactical) refers to the command level, which seeks to identify priorities and allocate resources accordingly. During a major incident, it is likely that the 'silver commander' will take charge of managing the incident itself. The role of the Gold (strategic) group and commander is to take an overview, to arbitrate between any conflicts at silver level and to assume responsibility for liaising with the media and key stakeholder groups. The 'gold commander' is not expected to participate in the detailed management of an incident (adapted from the Home Office, 1997a, 1997b). There is no one best way and organizations should plan to use structures that best fits their needs and resources. The three levels identify a minimum of three roles to be undertaken when managing an incident. In smaller organizations one team or individual may perform these distinct roles.

Teams are important because, generally, they outperform individuals although, as Janis' (1983) groundbreaking work identified, teams may be fallible. Errors may arise from the poor quality of available information, a lack of monitoring key indicators (e.g. accident statistics, budgetary controls) the cognitive abilities of the group and political differences within a group. Inevitably political manoeuvring may reduce team effectiveness. Smart and Vertinsky (1977) identify a range of remedies to the potential difficulties of fallible teams including, the inclusion of independent experts, encouraging alternative viewpoints, protecting minority perspectives and holding crisis simulations. Implicit in Smart and Vertinsky's analysis is the development of the critical team that continually questions decisions and information whilst possessing the mechanisms, personnel and communication.

To this point, we have considered the managerial incubation of crises, immediate crisis response and the post-crisis stage. The chapter has outlined a practical process by which organizations may better prepare themselves for managing interruptions effectively. The central aim here is to prevent an incident escalating into a full-blown crisis. It is however, beyond the remit of any chapter to provide anything more than a brief overview of current thinking and advice. Further reading is identified at the end of the chapter. However, crisis management theory has emerged from a consideration of practice and the next section provides a detailed account of two, similar crises. Although separated by nearly ten years there are common elements to the experiences of Perrier and Coca-Cola. Although, for a variety of reasons the impact upon Perrier was far greater than that upon Coca-Cola. The cases highlight how organizations may incubate the potential for crisis, the involvement of multiple stakeholders and the importance of learning from crisis.

Perrier and Coca-Cola: making a drama out of a crisis?

In 1989 the Perrier Group was the world's leading producer of mineral waters. It had built its market share on the basis of its attributes of purity and natural health, so much so that Perrier Water was used as a control in tests by many research laboratories (Butler, 1990). With global sales turnover of Ffr15.15 billion in 1989, Perrier was the generic name for sparkling mineral water (Betts, 1988). Despite this success, during the late 1980s major shareholders and media commentators began to question Perrier's 'curious' diversifications; a widely held view was that these reflected Perrier's Chairman, Gustav Leven, low boredom threshold. Leven, and Perrier, were perceived of as difficult and secretive (Financial Times, 1990). Warnings of an operational crisis were also identified during 1989, with production difficulties, dock strikes and rumours that the source had been contaminated (Pitcher, 1990). During the later half of 1989 Perrier was operating at the limit of its resources. In February 1990, tests in an American laboratory identified the presence of benzene, a known carcinogenic, within US supplies of Perrier water (Friedman, 1990). A total recall of bottles of the Perrier brand was eventually instigated, although the company's initial response was slow.

The 1990 recall: a chronology of events

The key events of this crisis period are shown in Table 23.2.

Table 23.2   Chronology of Perrier's contamination crisis

Date 1990	Description of Perrier's product recall crisis
February 2nd	US Food and Drugs Administration suspect contamination, Perrier Group notified.
February 5–10th	Increase in trading in Perrier Stock suggests spread of rumours.
February 12th	Public announcement in US of benzene contamination. Recall of 72 million bottles announced. Problem perceived as American only. Human error in French plants suggested as cause of contamination by Perrier US. Sabotage mentioned. UK supermarkets clear shelves of Perrier Water.

Table 23.2   Chronology of Perrier's contamination crisis – *continued*

Date 1990	Description of Perrier's product recall crisis
February 13th	Perrier market value falls by 15 percent on Paris Bourse. Perrier Group announce that they have identified the cause of the problem and that normal production would resume within days. Source Perrier identify cause of incident as an employee using the wrong cleaning fluid.
February 14th	a.m. Perrier UK aware of contamination in own supplies. Perrier Group prevents any announcement of UK recall. UK retailers begin removing bottles from shelves. p.m. Source Perrier announce worldwide recall of Perrier Water products. First 'Perrier Group' press conference.
February 15th	Perrier Group identifies the cause as failure to change filters indicating that benzene occurred naturally in the Perrier Spring.
February 16th	Perrier's claim of naturally occurring benzene refuted by scientists at the Water Research Centre.
February 24th	Perrier Group of America receives first lawsuit for knowingly selling contaminated water.
March 7th	Perrier relaunched to French market.
March 30th	Perrier sell soft drinks division to Cadbury-Schweppes for £150 million.
May 11th	£43 million provision made in accounts for handling the crisis.
June 30th	Additional £41 million provision made in accounts for handling the crisis. Leven announces his retirement.
1992	
March 25th	Nestle purchases Perrier for Ffr15 billion (£1.6 billion).

United States

Although neither the US nor the UK government considered the contamination posed a risk to health, Perrier US eventually announced a recall of 72 million bottles. The absence of batch identification numbers made it difficult to identify potentially contaminated batches (Friedman, 1990). Although slow to start Perrier portrayed its crisis response as a super effort which may, if portrayed effectively, demonstrate an organization's overriding concern for its customers regardless of cost to itself (Shrivastava and Siomkos, 1989). This approach was mirrored in the UK, where it was stated that: 'While the slightest doubt exists about the future of Perrier, we cannot continue to sell it' (Rawstorne, 1990).

Uncertain of the contamination's cause, Perrier speculated that human error at the source spring was to blame; media coverage highlighted the automated processing of mineral water, far removed from the image of ancient springs and natural purity that figured so highly in corporate communications. A 24-hour

emergency telephone hotline was set up for worried customers and the communication's budget was increased to $25 million. Newspapers and radio were targeted
because they were the quickest media 'to get into and prepare for (Friedman, 1990).

Although seen initially as a US difficulty only, some UK supermarkets began
removing Perrier from their shelves. Group Perrier's silence created a global communication's vacuum, which was filled with speculation and rumour. The
financial costs of the crisis at this point were estimated to include $40 million
lost sales alone. Already disenchanted, financial investors were further dismayed
when on February 13th the news of the contamination was greeted with a drop in
share values of 15 percent (Dawkins, 1990).

France

Viewed initially as a US crisis, the crisis response from the Paris headquarters
focused upon reassuring investors. This led to negative comparisons with Union
Carbide's handling of the Bhopal disaster in which thousands had died
(Rawstorne, 1990). The cause of the contamination was now identified as a care-
less employee spilling cleaning fluid at the bottling plant (Dawkins, 1990).
However, Perrier made no comment about which stocks had been affected
(Rawstorne, 1990). This encouraged media speculation about the causes of the
contamination with reports of industrial sabotage and terrorist activity emerging
(Crumley, 1990). In all of this Perrier appeared to be an organization that was
not in control of the crisis but was, rather, being controlled by the event itself.
The Perrier Group came under increasing pressure from its own subsidiaries, suggesting poor internal communications. Perrier UK informed the Group that they
were testing their stocks with a view to a product recall if necessary. Perrier
Group vetoed any unilateral product recall, instructing Perrier UK to wait for
further announcements. Eventually, on February 14th, a worldwide recall was
announced, but as the Financial Times commented:

> the problem is that it may be too late. Beyond putting out brief announce-
> ments through subsidiaries affected in the US this press conference was the
> first time Perrier had made any attempt to explain to the world what it was
> doing about the crisis (Financial Times 1990: 19).

A new explanation of the contamination's cause emerged when Zimmer, Source
Perrier's CEO, contradicted previous accounts, he explained that filters, which
removed impurities such as benzene from the natural gas that gave Perrier its
fizz, had not been replaced according to routine maintenance procedures
(Dawkins, 1990). This was the first indication that the 'contamination' was due
to a naturally occurring constituent of the mineral water. The implication was
that Perrier had been negligent (Dawkins, 1990; Crumley, 1990).

Further controversy was triggered as conflicting scientific evidence speculated
about whether there was such a compound as 'naturally' occurring benzene
(Souster, 1990) and thus raised the question of whether the source might have
been contaminated by industrial pollutant (Souster, 1990).

Until this point each national subsidiary was defending its own corner indicating the absence of any global continuity plan, a view supported by Perrier's vice president of marketing:

> We'd just spent 18 months working out a crisis plan that was just complete ... But the plan would only take us through the first week. We never imagined something this big (Booth, 1995: 22).

The lack of a consistent crisis plan for each market ensured that varying causal theories were put forward. The group, as a collective, was forced to deal with a range of issues at the same time and seemed unable to provide a unified response. As a consequence, consumer confidence was eroded further as the media exposed the inconsistencies in the response. In the US, however, the distributor demonstrated greater awareness of the implications of the contamination and the need to protect its own customers. The early announcement of a product recall was its only viable course of action and projected the correct image to its audience (Rawsthorne, 1990).

Post-crisis recovery

Perrier's relaunch was supported with a global advertising campaign aimed to regain its pre-crisis market share (Graham, 1990). The central message was a reassurance that Perrier was (still) pure and safe. The UK CEO stated, 'I don't like to call it a re-launch, Its a welcome back campaign' (Olins, 1990). Perrier's plan was to supply the French market within three weeks of the crisis, followed by the main European markets before relaunching in the United States within eight weeks (Graham, 1990). In each market the relaunch was preceded by intensive television and billboard advertising. Labels on the distinctive green bottle identified them as 'new production' to ensure that there was no confusion with old stocks.

Further tests by the FDA investigated Perrier's claims that its mineral water was 'naturally sparkling'. Although carbon dioxide was naturally present in the Vergeze spring, it was removed and replaced during the bottling process (Harris, 1990). In the UK, J. Sainsbury, then the UK's largest retailer, refused to restock the product. J. Sainsbury insisted that Perrier remove the word 'naturally' from its labels and that its bottling practises at the Vergeze plant be improved (Butler, 1990). Clearly these concerns posed a continuing threat to Perrier's brand image and represented a potential disaster for Perrier's repositioning strategy. Perrier's initial response was one of bullishness and a refusal to accept such interference in its activities (Butler, 1990). To fund the relaunch, Perrier sold its soft drink distribution business to Cadbury-Schweppes, at half the original asking price (Buckingham, 1989; Dawkins, 1990). An £84 million provision was set aside to cover the costs of managing the crisis. Investors were informed that dividend payments would be maintained, despite the cost of handling the contamination. Funding of the product recall, the repositioning strategy and a continued dividend payment was secured by the divestments. Leven, whose management style was seen as inept for a global business, announced his retirement from the company (Dawkins, 1990). This, as Slatter (1984) has observed, is often the case as successful turnaround frequently requires a new management team.

The Perrier case has frequently been cited as an example of poor crisis management and there are certainly many lessons to learn. Fast forwarding through history to 1999, another soft drinks company experienced a crisis providing an opportunity to gauge the effectiveness of learning from crisis.

Coca-Cola

During 1999, fears of contaminated soft drinks prompted the largest product recall in Coca-Cola's history. Although the 'contamination' affected much of Western Europe, the events were centred on Belgium. Unfortunately for Coca-Cola, fears of contamination occurred in the midst of a major health scare for the Belgian government and public. Criticisms of the Belgian Government's handling of the dioxin contamination of chicken and eggs had led to the resignations of the Ministers for Agriculture and Public Health on 1st June, little more than a week before news of Coca-Cola's difficulties emerged. An appreciation of this context is vital to any understanding of the Coca-Cola product ban and recall crisis. Key events of the Coca-Cola crisis are shown in Table 23.3.

Approaching 200 people reported feeling ill after drinking Coca-Cola. Although the symptoms were limited to consumers in France and Belgium the

Table 23.3   Chronology of Coca-Cola's European contamination crisis

Date 1999	Description of Coca-Cola product ban and recall crisis
June 8th	Reports of Belgian school children falling ill after drinking Coca-Cola. Coincides with dioxin contamination of Belgian poultry produce.
June 9th	Coca-Cola issues press statements that its products are safe.
June 11th	Fifty people have complained of stomachaches, nausea and headaches. Coca-Cola Belgium recalls 2.5 million bottles with a use by date of 2nd, 3rd and 4th of December (suggests difficulties in batch identification).
June 14th	Belgian Health Ministry bans all Coca-Cola products.
June 15th	One hundred complaints and eight people in hospital. Luxembourg bans all Coca-Cola products. France bans all Coca-Cola products made in Dunkirk plant. Carrefour removes all Coca-Cola products from shelves. Coca-Cola voluntarily withdraws all Belgian-made products from The Netherlands. Coca-Cola announces that sub-standard carbon dioxide at the Antwerp plant would cause an off taste and that a fungicide used on wooden plants at the Dunkirk plant would cause an offensive odour.
June 16th	Eighty people in Northern France reported ill. French consumer affairs Ministry orders removal of entire stock of 50 million cans because of difficulties in identifying Belgian sourced produce. Coca-Cola Chairman expresses regret for difficulties.

Table 23.3   Chronology of Coca-Cola's European contamination crisis – *continued*

Date 1999	Description of Coca-Cola product ban and recall crisis
June 17th	Coca-Cola offers to reimburse medical costs of anyone taken ill after drinking one of their products. Lenfant, director-general of the Belgian subsidiary, reports that causes of illness were, with absolute certainty, the bad carbon dioxide. Other spokespersons reported that there was no proven connection between Coca-Cola products and the illnesses.Independent analysts identify the illness as resulting from a mass hysteria connected with the earlier problems with dioxin contaminated poultry products. Aga, supplier of carbon dioxide, announces that it can find no evidence of sub-standard carbon dioxide. French Consumer Affairs Ministry reports evidence indicating that the fungicide explanation was practically impossible.
June 18th	390,000 bottles of Coca-Cola removed by Spanish authorities. Swiss Cantons impound imported Coca-Cola. Coca-Cola announces that hydrogen sulphide and Carbonyl sulphite were the two harmless contaminants not to have been filtered out.
June 19th	Utrecht University based, Coca-Cola sponsored toxicologist reports that impurities could not explain the reported health problems.
June 21st	Belgian Health Ministry refuses to lift ban.
June 22nd	Coca-Cola places full-page advertisements in Belgian, French, Spanish and Greek newspapers apologizing for the contamination.
June 23rd	Ban on production in Belgium lifted. Dunkirk plant remains closed with inspection for possible 'rat poison' contamination. 28,000 Coca-Cola owned vending machines in Belgium remained closed.
June 24th	French ban lifted.
June 25th	Dutch and Luxembourg bans lifted.
June 30th	Coca-Cola warns that unit sales in Europe were down by 6–7 percent during the second quarter.
July 13th	Fourteen million cases of soft drinks withdrawn. Estimated cost of US$60 million.

suspect plants supplied to The Netherlands, Germany, Luxembourg, Spain and Switzerland. Government bans, across North Western Europe, created the impression that Coca-Cola was reluctant to act. Control of the crisis passed to government agencies created an impression that Coca-Cola was uncaring. The coincidence of the contamination scare with the unrelated dioxin contamination of Belgian poultry produce had raised the profile of such incidents within Belgium (Kielmas, 1999). Intense media coverage and criticism had lead to the resignation of Belgian government ministers and a highly sensitized public. This was a potentially hostile environment for any suspected product contamination.

Defective carbon dioxide and a fungicide were identified, initially, as the immediate causes of the contamination, although the evidence for this was mixed (see Table 23.3). Most important was that the identification of these 'causes' was interpreted as an attempt by Coca-Cola to deflect blame for the contamination onto two suppliers. Coca-Cola's crisis response received extensive criticisms. For example, highlighting a perceived slow response to the difficulties:

> Coke must get out in front and give the impression of openness – and only a top guy can do it. Until that happens, even if the company succeeds in solving quality control problems at its plants, Coke may still have a lot of work to do to win back European consumers (Worms, 1999: 48).

From a spokesperson from the AXA group: 'Coca-Cola threw away the book on risk management. They refused to acknowledge that there was a crisis' (Kielmas, 1999: 32). For The Economist (1999):

> Coca-Cola's public-relations error is to have seemed keener to protect its own back than to ally the understandable fears of consumers ... the firms legal sounding insistence that there were no 'health or safety issues' and that the drinks 'might make you feel sick, but are not harmful' were hardly going to reassure people ... A statement on June 16 from Douglas Ivester, the firm's chairman, expressing his regret, arrived hopelessly late (Economist, 1999: 62).

With hindsight it appears that Coca-Cola failed to fully appreciate the sensitivity of the Belgian public and government, and neighbouring countries, to such product contaminations. Timing is of the essence, following as it did the dioxin contamination of the preceding six months. It is likely that analysts at Coca-Cola's Atlanta headquarters were not fully aware of this recent history and thus of the likely strength of concerns. The quick introduction of government bans may have been excessive in the light of the real hazard to health, as identified later. However, given resignations less than two weeks earlier it would be a brave politician who failed to act quickly and assertively. It seems that, as with Perrier ten years previously, Coca-Cola did not fully appreciate the implications of the potential for damage associated with an alleged contamination. How did Coca-Cola's response compare with Perrier's?

Case analysis

These cases both demonstrate the importance of understanding context and stakeholders. Coca-Cola was unaware of the Belgian sensitivity to product contaminations at that particular time. In a similar way Perrier had failed to see the threat posed by contamination to a brand associated with natural purity and health. Neither organization fully understood the complex web of relationships between stakeholders which quickly permitted the two crises to go beyond the control of the both.

In both cases there was a time gap between identifying the problem and action. Each crisis was pushed through public and media pressure placing Perrier and Coca-Cola, respectively, on the defensive. Although Perrier's UK and US responses were largely consumer-focused, that of Source Perrier was focused upon attempts to reassure investors. There is little evidence of the development of a communications strategy to meet the needs of a diverse and complex group of stakeholders. Indeed, despite the favourable view of Perrier UK's media response, the Group as a whole received extensive criticism. Perrier's handling of the disaster was described as:

> uneven at best, ranging from head in the sand refusal to talk, to announce-
> ments in arch corporatese, to bursts of pique. Another commentator called it
> 'the caveman approach to public relations' (Crumley, 1990: 5)

Coca-Cola's response appears to have concerned identification of the causes and, importantly, external perpetrators. The needs of its diverse stakeholders, retailers (e.g. Carrefour) Government and consumers (medical expenses), were not taken account of until later. This was interpreted as an attempt by the company to protect its own back rather than expressing an immediate concern for its customers. That the reported illnesses appear to have been unrelated to the consumption of Coca-Cola mattered little; it was what consumers believed to be true.

While Perrier had no experience of similar crises, it had ignored the warnings of contamination that had circulated for some six months preceding the crisis. There was no clear view of who the key stakeholders were at each stage of the crisis or the message that should be targeted towards each group. While Coca-Cola also failed to perceive the conditions peculiar to Belgium and much of Western Europe at that time. It is possible that with its global interests, Coca-Cola failed to comprehend local sensitivities. Had news of Belgium's dioxin contamination reached Atlanta?

There was evidence of significant differences in opinion regarding the strategic direction of the Perrier Group, between key shareholders and the management team, personified in Leven. Such division may cause problems for an organiza-tion at the best of times. During a crisis it may of course create a common sense of purpose or, alternatively, one party may exploit the troubles to meet their own objectives. There is no evidence that this was the case for Coca-Cola. This pro-duct contamination, unfortunate though it was, did not threaten the entire orga-nization as was the case with Perrier. This is partly because of the differences in size between the two companies and the fact that the contamination cut deep into Perrier's branding of natural purity. As Raymond Perrier (no relation) pointed out, 'The images of peasants filling empty bottles from gushing springs was destroyed' (Economist, 1999).

There is much evidence that the behaviour of the different divisions of the Perrier Group was unco-ordinated. This added to the potential for contradiction, and reinforced, in the minds of the media and financial institutions, the view that Perrier was poorly managed. The lack of a proper business continuity plan was clear. Finally, the evolution of the crisis indicates the lack of a co-ordinated response on the part of Coca-Cola with the Company's subsidiaries responding to government bans introduced over a ten-day period. Coca-Cola was caught off guard and whilst the costs of the interruption were relatively minor for such a large company it might indicate some flaws in its preparations for business continuity. Fortunately for Coca-Cola the financial impact was small as the countries affected accounted for less than 2 percent of its total annual, global sales. For some stock analysts the scare represented a buying opportunity, given long-term confidence in the Coca-Cola brand (Financial Times, 1999). In this way a reputation built up over a long period of time may help an organization overcome a crisis.

Finally, would the crisis management response have been very different had the incidents been the result of sabotage or criminal behaviour? The example of Johnson & Johnson's Tylenol crisis, in which a number of customers died in two separate incidents when the painkiller capsules were laced with cyanide, suggests that when a company in crisis is perceived of as the victim, public sympathy may emerge. However, Elliott *et al.* (2002) have argued that the pre-crisis efforts of Johnson & Johnson to build a strong caring image and good links with the media, in addition to their response, combined to make their efforts a great success. Certainly events which result from malevolent activity may provide a convenient scapegoat, but should organizations be demonstrated to have ignored previous warnings or to be seen as having failed to take sufficient precautions, then the cause may not be seen to be as important as an organization's own behaviour.

In summary, these two cases of contamination provide us with insights into the crisis management process and offer some important lessons. In the first instance, it is clear that organizations need to communicate in an open and consistent manner. Disjointed communications, without any sense of a common strategy, can create serious problems for a company. Communications should be clear, unambiguous and free from attempts at the projection of blame elsewhere. The scapegoating process is often viewed with considerable suspicion by the media and other observers. A second issue to emerge from these events concerns the development and utilization of contingency/crisis plans. Developing such plans without testing them or providing training for staff will severely inhibit the plan's effectiveness. A core element of such a planning process should involve media training for key staff and the creation of media friendly background information which can be given out in the early stages of the crisis. There was little evidence of such plans in the responses of either Perrier or Coca-Cola. It seems inconceivable that Coca-Cola does not possess such plans suggesting that it was a failure in their implementation that lay behind the poor crisis response. A third issue concerns the role of trust in stakeholder management. Organizations that appear to prioritize profit over safety will find that their attempts to manage their image will be plagued by the persistent lack of trust amongst stakeholders. This process is not something that can be established during a crisis but should be an integral part of a company's strategy. Organizations must be aware of the variety of stakeholder groups, interests and power in planning for and when managing crisis events. Some utility companies maintain databases of vulnerable groups who might require special attention should there be an interruption in supply (e.g. hospitals, residential care homes, etc.). Politicians or vociferous pressure groups may also be listed in order that potentially embarrassing media coverage can be anticipated. Since the Brent Spar difficulties, Shell has employed environmental activists as consultants to provide input at board level.

Closely linked to stakeholder management is historical context. On the one hand there is the history of media relations, perceived openness and ongoing marketing communications. Certain product attributes may be more vulnerable to threat, such as 'natural purity'. Alternatively, there is the context in which an incident occurs. For Perrier the disenchantment of key investors and lack of good links with the media removed potential allies during the crisis. Media support for Johnson & Johnson was vital for their recovery from the Tylenol incidents. For Coca-Cola the coincidence of the contamination with the high profile dioxin problems created an ultra-sensitive environment for their own difficulties. Continuity plans; including crisis communication blueprints can only assist an organization's crisis response. Effective crisis response requires ongoing environmental scanning in order that such plans can be used in a flexible manner and adapt to the particular circumstances of each incident. For the global company there are likely to be many local difficulties that have the potential to trip them up. Finally, the recognition of a company's intangible assets is an important, but neglected aspect of the strategic management process. All too often, organizations fail to take account of their intangible asset base when developing contingency plans for crisis events. As the cases discussed here illustrate, the reputational costs of a crisis can be considerable.

Conclusion

As we indicated in our introduction, as individuals we are increasingly dependent upon one another and upon the organizations that meet our needs. This interdependence is reflected at an inter-organizational level too. Systems failures, the impacts of natural hazards and the effects of terrorist activity appear to be increasing in intensity and in their occurrence. This chapter has sought to demonstrate that crisis and business continuity management approaches are applicable to a wide range of events including those triggered by security breaches. Although the nature of the trigger has some importance, organizations may retain much control through developing resilience and business continuity plans.

Key readings

There is a wealth of information and knowledge surrounding crisis, disaster and business continuity management, some of it summarized here. A good, clear introduction, not biased honestly, Elliott, D., Swartz, E. and Herbane, B. (2002) *Business Continuity Management: A Crisis Management Approach*, London: Routledge combines an academic reader with much guidance to practical business continuity management. Pauchant, T. and Mitroff, I. (1992) *Transforming the Crisis Prone Organisation*, San Francisco: Jossey Bass Publishers provides a good review of the relevant literature as well as a tool for diagnosing an organization's predisposition to crisis. Smith, D. (1990) 'Beyond Contingency Planning: Towards a Model of Crisis Management', *Industrial Crisis Quarterly*, Vol. 4, No. 4, pp. 263–75 provides a good summary of alternative models of the crisis management process. Smith, D. and Sipika, C. (1993) 'Back from the Brink: Post Crisis Management', *Long Range Planning*, Vol. 26, No. 1, pp. 28–38 is widely cited and provides insights into the process of managing effective turnaround. The seminal work of Turner, B.A. (1976) 'The Organizational And Interorganizational Development Of Disasters', *Administrative Science Quarterly*, Vol. 21, pp. 378–97 shows where the field of study really started. Finally, Waring, A. and Glendon, I. (1998) *Managing Risk*, London: Thomson Business Press is a highly readable, academically rigorous, but practically useful, guide to risk management.

References

Betts, P. (1988) 'Bubbling Over in a Healthy Market', *Financial Times*, Wednesday, January 13th, p. 22.

Billings, R., Milburn, T. and Schaalman, M. (1980) 'A Model of Crisis Perception', *Administrative Science Quarterly*, Vol. 25, pp. 300–16.

Booth, S. (1995) *Crisis Management Strategy*, London: Routledge.

Buckingham, L. (1989) 'Perrier in £250m Soft Drinks Sale', *The Guardian*, Wednesday, November 8th, p. 16.

Butler, D. (1990) 'Perrier's Painful Period', *Management Today*, August, pp. 72–3.

Chadwick, T. and Rajagopal, S. (1995) *Strategic Supply Management*, London: Butterworth-Heinemann.

Crumley, B. (1990) 'Fizzzzz Went the Crisis', *International Management*, April, Vol. 45, No. 3, p. 5.

Dawkins, W. (1990) 'Perrier Price Falls by 12%', *Financial Times*, Tuesday, February 13th, pp. 1 and 32.

Dynes, R. and Aguirre, B. (1979) 'Organisational Adaptations to Crises: Mechanisms of Co-Ordination and Structural Change', *Disasters*, Vol. 3, No. 1, pp. 71–4.

Eberwein (1978) 'Crisis Research – The State Of The Art: A Western View', in D. De Frei (1978) *International Crises And Crisis Management*, Conference Proceedings, University of Zurich, pp. 126–43.

Economist (1999) 'Coca-Cola: Bad for You?', *The Economist*, June (US) 19, p. 62.

Elliott, D. (2004) 'Risk Management', in J. Beech and S. Chadwick, *The Business of Sports Management*, London: Pearson Education.

Elliott, D. and Smith, D. (1993) 'Learning from Tragedy: Sports Stadia Disasters in the UK', *Industrial and Environmental Crisis Quarterly*, Vol. 7, No. 3, pp. 205–30.

Elliott, D. and Smith, D. (1997) 'Waiting for the Next One: Management Attitudes to Safety in the UK Football Industry', in S. Frosdick and L. Whalley (1997) *Sport and Safety Management*, Oxford: Butterworth-Heinemann.

Elliott, D. and Smith, D. (2006) 'Patterns of Regulatory Behaviour in the UK Football Industry', *Journal of Management Studies*, Vol. 43, No. 2, pp. 289–316.

Elliott, D. Swartz, E. and Herbane, B. (2002) *Business Continuity Management: A Crisis Management Approach*, London: Routledge.

Financial Times (1999) 'Perrier's Architect', *Financial Times*, Thursday, March 1st, p. 19.

Fitzgerald, K.J. (1995) 'Establishing an Effective Continuity Strategy', *Information Management and Computer Security*, Vol. 3, No. 3, pp. 20–4.

Flin, R. (1996) *Sitting in the Hot Seat*, London: John Wiley.

Friedman, A. (1990) 'Perrier Faces Lawsuit from US Customers', *Financial Times*, Saturday, February 24th, p. 12.

Graham, G. (1990) 'Perrier on the Shelves Again', *Financial Times*, March 7th, p. 34.

Hardin, G. (1971) 'Nobody Ever Dies of Overpopulation', *Science*, Vol. 171, pp. 524–32.

Harris, C. (1990) 'Sainsbury Refuses Perrier', *Financial Times*, April 24th, p. 34.

Hartley, R.F. (1995) *Management Mistakes and Successes 4th edn*, New York: John Wiley.

Hermann, C.F. (1971) *International Crisis*, New York: Free Press.

Home Office (1997a) *Business as Usual: Maximising Business Resilience to Terrorist Bombings*, London: Home Office.

Home Office (1997b) *Bombs, Protecting People and Property 3rd edn*, London: Home Office.

Janis, I.L. (1983) *Victims of Groupthink 2nd edn*, Boston, MA: Houghton Mifflin.

Jones, M.E. and Sutherland, G. (1999) *Implementing Turnbull: A Boardroom Briefing*, London: Institute of Chartered Accountants of England and Wales.

Kielmas, M. (1999) 'Interest in Recall Covers Rises: Coca-Cola Scare Fuels Awareness of Risks', *Business Insurance*, Vol. 33, No. 28, pp. 18–22.

Meredith, W. (1999) 'Business Impact Analysis', in A. Hiles and P. Barnes (1999) *The Definitive Handbook of Business Continuity Management*, Chichester: John Wiley.

Miller, D. (1990) *The Icarus Paradox*, New York: Harper Business.

Mitchell, R.K., Agle, B.R. and Wood, D.J. (1997) 'Toward a Theory of Stakeholder Identification and Salience: Defining the Principle of Who and What Really Counts', *Academy of Management Review*, Vol. 22, No. 4, pp. 853–86.

Olins, R. (1990) 'Perrier Moved Fast to Keep its Sparkle', *The Sunday Times*, March 4th, p. D10.

Pauchant, T.C. and Mitroff, I.I. (1988) 'Crisis Prone Versus Crisis Avoiding Organizations: Is Your Company's Culture its Own Worst Enemy in Creating Crises?', *Industrial Crisis Quarterly*, Vol. 2, pp. 53–63.

Pauchant, T.C. and Mitroff, I.I. (1992) *Transforming The Crisis Prone Organisation*, San Francisco: Jossey Bass Publishers.

Perrow, C. (1984) *Normal Accidents*, New York: Free Press.

Pitcher, G. (1990) 'The Day the Bubbles Went Burst', *The Observer*, Sunday, February 18th, p. 60.

Porter, M.E. (1980) *Competitive Strategy*, New York: Free Press.

Quarantelli, E. (1988) 'Disaster Crisis Management: A Summary of Research Findings', *Journal of Management Studies*, Vol. 25, No. 4, July.

Rawstorne, P. (1990) 'If One Green Bottle Should Accidentally Fall', *Financial Times*, Friday, February 16th, p. 5.

Reason, J.T. (1990) *Human Error*, Oxford: Oxford University Press.

Reason, J.T. (1995) 'A Systems Approach to Organizational Error', *Ergonomics*, Vol. 38, No. 8, pp. 1708–21.

Shrivastava, P. (1987) *Bhopal*, Cambridge, MA: Ballinger.

Shrivastava, P., Mitroff, I., Miller, D. and Miglani, A. (1988) 'Understanding Industrial Crises', *Journal Of Management Studies*, Vol. 25, No. 4, July.

Shrivastava, P. and Siomkos, G. (1989) 'Disaster Containment Strategies', *The Journal of Business Strategy*, September/October, pp. 26–30.

Shrivastava, P. and Mitroff, I. (1987) 'Strategic Management of Corporate Crises', *Columbia Journal of World Business*, Vol. 22, No. 1, pp. 5–11.

Slatter, S. (1984) *Corporate Recovery*, London: Penguin Books.

Smart, C. and Vertinsky, I. (1977) 'Designs for Crisis Decision Units', *Administrative Science Quarterly*, Vol. 22, pp. 640–57.

Smith, D. (1990) 'Beyond Contingency Planning; Towards a Model of Crisis Management', *Industrial Crisis Quarterly*, Vol. 4, No. 4, pp. 263–76.

Smith, D. and Elliott, D. (2005) 'Learning from Crisis', *Management Learning*, in press.

Smith, D. and Sipika, C. (1993) 'Back From The Brink: Post Crisis Management', *Long Range Planning*, Vol. 26, No. 1, pp. 28–38.

Souster, M. (1990) 'Doubts over Perrier's line on benzene source', *The Times*, Friday February 16th, p. 1.

Swartz, E., Elliott, D. and Herbane, B. (1995) 'Out of Sight Out of Mind: The Limitations of Traditional Information Systems Planning', *Facilities*, Vol. 13, No. 9/10.

Toft, B. and Reynolds, S. (1992) *Learning from Disasters*, Butterworth-Heinemann.

Turnbull, N. (1999) The Internal Control: Guidance for Directors on the Combined Code Internal Control Working Party of the Institute of Chartered Accountants.

Turner, B. (1976) 'The Organisational and Interorganisational Development of Disasters', *Administrative Science Quarterly*, Vol. 21, pp. 378–97.

Turner, B. (1978) *Man-Made Disasters*, London: Wykeham.

Waring, A. and Glendon, I. (1998) *Managing Risk*, London: Thomson Business Press.

Worms, P. (1999) 'Things Aren't Going to Get Better', *Business Week*, No. 3635, p. 48.

Part V
Issues in Security

24
Regulation of Private Security: Models for Analysis

Mark Button and the Rt Hon Bruce George MP[1]

Introduction

The growth in size and role of the private security industry in most countries has lead to numerous portrayals of these changes, but probably the most pertinent is Stenning and Shearing's (1980) description of them as a 'quiet revolution'. In most industrial countries there are more people employed in the security industry than the public police (De Waard, 1999; Campbell and Reingold, 1994; Cunningham *et al.*, 1990). Studies in some countries have also revealed almost every major function of the police being carried out by the private sector (Jones and Newburn, 1998; Rigakos, 2002; Crawford and Lister, 2004). These dramatic changes in the size and role of private security have been accompanied in most jurisdictions by the introduction of legal measures to improve the governance of private security or reform often long-standing regimes (Moore, 1987, 1990). A growing body of research reveals the purpose and effectiveness of these regulatory measures have varied significantly and this chapter will explore some of the findings and issues raised in the research. In doing so it will focus upon the licensing/standards related regulatory measures of conventional security operatives and firms, rather than accountablity/ complaints issues or transnational/mercenary related activities (for overview of these see, Sarre and Prenzler, 1999; Stenning, 2000; George and Cooper, 2002; Brodeur *et al.*, 2003). It will begin by exploring the debate over regulation with the rationale for intervention and some of the arguments raised against. The chapter will then move on to outline and update the model of regulation we have advocated, before exploring on a regional basis throughout the world some of the most salient aspects of regulatory systems and identifying best practice. Finally the chapter will assess more radical approaches for regulation of private security with other policing provision.

Before we embark upon this analysis, however, it is important to note some caveats. The information on regulation in this chapter was secured through a variety of methods. This included primary sources such as copies of legislation/ regulations, official publications, official websites and letters from persons attached to regulatory bodies or subject to regulation in different jurisdictions.

Secondary sources through various reports and articles in various journals were also consulted. Regulations are constantly changing and consequently many of the sources consulted are soon out of date. Some of these resources are also based upon questionable sources and frequently poor methodologies. Thus publications that were used for this chapter may be out of date or contain errors. Even an official website with legislation and regulations linked to it might also be of limited use because it is not regularly updated. Thus exploring different systems of regulation can be viewed as a snapshot in time, based in part on opaque images. As soon as that picture has been taken things change and the image of certain parts may also not be clear. As such this chapter must be considered as one snapshot in time based upon the best image available at the time of writing.

Regulation and its rationale?

It is important to define what is meant by regulation as it is a term that is often misunderstood. Regulation is a broad concept encompassing any state laws, regulations or stipulations of bodies with statutory force, which affect individuals and organizations. According to Francis (1993: 5) regulation can be defined as, 'state intervention in private spheres of activity to realize public purposes'. When advocates call for statutory regulation of the private security industry they usually envisage some form of statutory licensing or registration, rather than general regulation. It will be illustrated later that in virtually every country some form of statutory licensing or registration applied to the private security industry. Such measures, however, have provoked lively debates and it is important to understand some of the arguments for and against statutory intervention.

The case for

Different forms of regulation are not the only policy option for the private security industry. Another option would be to prohibit it, as was and still is the case in hardline communist countries like North Korea. At a lesser level, however, certain activities in the private security industry might be prohibited, such as the in-house security sector in Spain (Gimenez-Salinas, 2004). The reality of a modern economy, however, means that this is not really an option for the wider industry. So why do governments regulate security sectors?

In some countries the regulation that exists for private security was introduced for a completely different reason. In Belgium and the Netherlands original legislation (passed in the 1930s and reformed more recently) was passed to control fascist militias. Some states in the US use regulation for nothing more than a means to raise revenue. The strongest argument advocated, however, is that because of the position of trust security employees are placed in, they should be required to be of a certain character. People with certain criminal records or known links with criminal organizations are therefore argued not to deserve the right to work in the private security industry. There has been much anecdotal evidence presented of private security staff abusing their positions of trust and many exposes of criminals and/or those with links to criminal gangs operating in unregulated industries/sectors. For instance the Association of Chief Police Officers (ACPO) in England and Wales published research illustrating over 2500 offences committed annually by private security staff (ACPO, 1995). In Japan there has been evidence of security firms linked to, or even owned by criminal organizations. In 1971 of the 321 companies that existed 20 presidents were convicted criminals, including two with links to organized criminals (Miyazawa, 1991). There was also evidence of security staff committing crimes. In 1982, 362 ordinary and 371 special penal offences were committed by security guards of which, 55 and 92 respectively, were committed while on duty (Yoshida, 1999). In some jurisdictions the focus upon regulation has been aimed more on preventing terrorists or those with links to them gaining employment in the industry, as was the case in Northern Ireland.

The second most common strand to the arguments put forward for regulation has been the poor standards of performance of the industry in general. It has been argued that private security is not like any ordinary product or service, as its effectiveness has an impact on safety and crime prevention. Some of the evidence that has been provided includes security officers scared of the dark (House of Commons Defence Committee, 1990), using excessive force (House of Commons Home Affairs Committee, 1995), misusing firearms (Kakalik and Wildhorn, 1971b) to name a few. Poor standards of performance was also a major issue in the decision to regulate the Spanish (Gimenez-Salinas, 2004) and Japanese security industry (Yoshida, 1999).

The final strand of the arguments for regulation has been the least debated and explored and this is the accountability of the industry. Central to this aspect of the debate is whether private security staff are considered to undertake special duties. As Stenning and Shearing (1979: 263) have argued:

If private security personnel are in reality no different from ordinary citizens, a law which treats them alike seems most appropriate. But if in reality they are not, and the law still treats them as they are, it becomes inappropriate ...

The overwhelming evidence that has began to emerge on private security illustrates they do undertake special functions, have access to privileged information, exercise power, use force and conduct many functions comparable to the police (Jones and Newburn, 1998; Gill and Hart, 1997; Button, 1998; Rigakos, 2002; Wakefield, 2003). Therefore to treat such personnel as ordinary citizens would not seem appropriate. Advocates of regulation argue for mechanisms to control their activities and ensure appropriate structures of governance exist. Indeed in many countries there have been examples of the abuse of power by security officers. For instance in Japan guards have been used to hit protesters, end industrial action by force and have worn uniforms similar to the police (Yoshida, 1999).

The case against

The case against regulation in recent years has largely revolved around debates concerning the market and the effectiveness of government intervention

(Murray, 1996; Home Office, 1996). In the past, however, arguments have also been raised relating to the legitimacy regulation might bring to the private security industry. Some of these arguments will now be considered.

The most recent opposition to regulation in the UK has centred on the free market ideology of the last Conservative government. An integral element of this policy was to pursue deregulation wherever possible and where there were calls for statutory intervention, voluntary measures were encouraged instead. It was argued that the choice of security products and services were a matter for the buyer and the principle of *caveat emptor* (buyer beware) applied. If a buyer selected a poor quality security service or product that was their problem. In essence advocates of this line of argument maintain security is no different from a dry cleaning service or the purchase of a television set. Linked to this argument opponents believe that regulation would only increase the burdens on business and ultimately increase costs (Home Office, 1991; Murray 1996). Indeed in the US some private security companies have used their lobbying muscle to prevent and where not possible minimize regulation upon their activities for this reason (Jaksa, 2004).

During the late 1960s and early 1970s the arguments against regulation in the UK followed a very different line. Initially there was a concern that regulation might give the industry a legitimacy and authority it did not deserve (Home Office, 1979). Proposals for the regulation of private investigators were rejected on the grounds it might give them a 'licence to pry' (*Hansard*, 13 July 1973: col 1966). Similarly in 1981 Lord Willis' Security Officers Control Bill was opposed by some Lords on the grounds it might give the public the impression they have 'special powers', like those of the police (*House of Lords Report*, 3 December 1981: col 1166).

Private security regulation

The debate over whether parts of the private security industry should be subjected to regulation in terms of a licensing or registration scheme masks, however, the fact that many parts of the industry in most countries are subjected to special regulation (Button and George, 2001). For instance aviation, port and nuclear security are the subject of international agreements, which set out obligations on signatory countries to implement minimum standards of security. Countries also frequently expand through national intervention upon this international framework. However, the focus of this chapter will be upon general licensing/registration schemes for the wider private security industry.

The nature of private security regulation usually reflects the political structures of a country. In most federal systems of government, for instance, private security licensing is the responsibility of state governments as in the US, Canada and Australia. In most unitary countries regulation is the responsibility of the national government and applies to the whole country. For instance in France, New Zealand and Sweden in this case. This does mask some anomalies, however, for in the UK, which is also a unitary state, there is devolution to Scotland and Northern Ireland and differences exist in the regulatory system that applies to them as is the case in Spain with the Basque and Catalan regions. There are also frequently Federal attempts to address the problems of reciprocity for security firms and operatives operating across borders. For instance the 1993 Armoured Car Reciprocity Act enabled security officers to carry their weapons across state borders. There have also been attempts to establish federal minimum standards in the broader private security industry in the US by Congressmen from both parties, which have all failed so far.

Comparing regulatory systems

In earlier work we identified three broad characteristics which to compare and contrast regulatory systems (George and Button, 1997). These were the width of regulation, which is the extent to which the different sectors of the private security industry are regulated. Second was the depth of regulation, which was the number and type of regulations to be met by security firms and employees. Finally the organization responsible for regulation could be differentiated. Debate over this model and further research has enabled us to refine and add to this model. Some of these issues will now be explored.

Width of private security regulation

Definitions of private security and what sectors constitute the industry have been the subject of much debate (George and Button, 2000; Manunta, 1999). The private security industry consists of a wide range of distinct sectors, including: contract static guarding; in-house static guarding; armed guarding; armoured car operators; door supervisors (or bouncers, as they are commonly known); bodyguards; private investigators; security consultants; security systems installers; locksmiths; security shredders; manufacturers and distributors of security equipment; and security storage, to name most, but not all, sectors (Cunningham *et al.*, 1990 identify 26 segments of the service and manufacturing sectors, including guard dogs and forensic analysis, for instance). Some sectors deny they are part of the security industry or are not perceived as such. Regulatory systems vary on which of these sectors are regulated. However, in terms of most systems Figure 24.1 below distinguishes the sectors that in our view warrant debate in terms of this model. There are other sectors of the private security industry, some of which are also frequently regulated. They are, however, either very small, peculiar to a particular country or the arguments for regulation do not really apply to them as much (such as manufacturers of security equipment).

Narrow		Wide	
Private Investigators	Manned Security Services	Security Consultants	Installers of Security Equipment

Figure 24.1   The width of regulation
Source: Adapted from George, B. and Button, M. (1997: 191–2)

568   *The Handbook of Security*

Thus the principle of the model is that if manned security services (a significant part of it) and private investigators are regulated, along with at least security consultants it would be classed as wide. The reality of regulation means that in some cases this does not quite work, for instance in some systems private investigators are not, but all the others are. In these cases the broader features of the width of the system is applied.

Depth of regulation

Regulatory systems can also be distinguished on the depth of regulation that is applied to the private security industry. Figure 24.2 outlines the main types of regulations that could be applied to the private security industry. There are regulations that seek to address character of employees, owners, etc and then there are regulations that seek to enhance the quality of security provision through minimum standards of training and operation. Second there is the distinction between licensing requirements for employees and for firms. For a *Comprehensive*

A. Entrance Requirements for Firms to Enter Industry

i. Payment of Fee for License

ii. Restrictions on Background of Owner/Qualifying Agent

iii. Minimum Experience/Qualifications of Owner/Qualifying Agent

iv. Minimum Training for Owner/Qualifying Agent

v. Passing of Examination by Owner/Qualifying Agent

B. Entrance Requirements for Individuals to Work in Industry

i. Payment of Fee for License/Registration

ii. Restrictions on Background of Employees

iii. Minimum Training for Employees

iv. Passing of Examination by Employees

v. Requirement for Refresher/Specialist Training

C. Minimum Standards of Operation

i. Bonding/Insurance

ii. Facilities/Equipment

iii. Other Standards

Figure 24.2 A comprehensive regulatory system
Source: Adapted from George, B. and Button, M. (1997: 193)

classification there would need to be regulations applying to both firms and employees that not only address character, but also seek to enhance the quality of security. There would therefore need to be regulation in all three categories A, B and C in Figure 24.2. Thus there must be minimum standards of entrance for both firms and individuals, and there must be minimum standards of operation for them. The second characteristic is regulation that goes beyond background requirements which attempt, however strongly, to ensure the competence of firms and individuals. The test, then, would be on experience requirements for owners/qualifying agents and minimum standards of training for employees. Hence the further down the list of criteria in categories A, B and C in Figure 24.2 the more comprehensive the system. Anything less than the above would result in a *Minimal* classification.

In many jurisdictions where there are no or in some, sitting under statutory requirements, are voluntary and/or self-regulatatory standards. These are based upon associations, standards and the demands of clients. These may have an important impact upon sectors of the private security industry frequently using 'sticks' other than legislation to ensure compliance. For instance in the UK the National Approval Council for Security Systems through pressures from the police and insurers is able to regulate over 90 percent of commercial intruder alarm installations (George and Button, 2000). In Canada research has also illustrated how the demands of clients is also increasingly impacting upon the standards of firms (O'Conner *et al.*, 2004).

Compliance with regulation

Another important distinction that was under-developed in our original paper was the degree of compliance towards the regulation. There are significant differences in the culture of compliance and degree of enforcement in different jurisdictions and amongst different occupations (Hyde, 2003; Lister *et al.*, 2001). Therefore what on paper might seem like a Comprehensive Wide system when analysed in terms of the degree of compliance might be much less effective.

In Canada, Hyde (2003) has explored this issue in depth. Some of his findings included low numbers of staff employed in regulatory agencies with some struggling to cope with the large number of licence applications. Limited or no strategies to uncover non-compliance was also found in many of the provinces, with a tendency to focus upon reactive investigation of complaints, rather than proactive random inspections. Finally Hyde found sanctions that were in some cases very low and unlikely to act as a significant deterrent. Similar problems were illustrated by Kakalik and Wildhorn (1971a) in their study of regulatory bodies during the late 1960s and early 1970s. They found some states where no denials to applicants had occurred and they even found one regulatory body where one policeman was responsible for regulation in the whole state in addition to his police duties! Research by the National Advisory Committee on Criminal Justice Standards and Goals (1976) also illustrated the limited resources of regulatory agencies. For instance in California at the time there were ten staff dealing with 1633 licence applications and 75,000 registrations. This would mean each

Model	Description
Non-Interventionist	There is no statutory licensing system for the private security industry (although there might be some special regulatory measures).
Minimum Narrow	Minimal regulations apply such as character requirements and they only extend to the manned guarding and/or private investigator sectors.
Minimum Wide	Regulation applies to the wider private security industry but only with minimum requirements.
Comprehensive Narrow	There are regulations that seek to raise the quality of the industry such as training standards for employees and for firms, but they only apply to the manned guarding and/or private investigators.
Comprehensive Wide	There are quality enhancing regulations that are applied to employees and firms across the wider private security industry.

Figure 24.3   Five models of regulation
Source: Adapted from George, B. and Button, M. (1997: 195–6)

member of staff dealing with around 30 registrations per day without allowing for holidays or personnel dedicated to other functions.

As some of the states surveyed have not changed their legislation since this period and the budgetary climate for public organizations has deteriorated over the last 30 years, there seems little evidence to suggest that regulatory bodies have become more efficient with larger budgets and more staff. This is a fundamental problem because no matter how high the standards, if there are insufficient resources and staff to operate and police the system then those standards are of little worth. Thus, when classifying the different states in terms of enforcement there was not enough available evidence or time to research this issue further. Nevertheless, this is an important area that requires further research. In the absence of such research all we can outline is whether compliance is 'High' or 'Low' where in the latter there is significant evidence of non-compliance with the legislation.

Responsibility for regulation

In our discussion of our model in 1997 probably the least developed part was the responsibility for regulation. Revisiting this aspect of regulation we can now propose the following distinctions. In terms of responsibility there are three categories. First of all there are *Monopoly* systems, where all parts of the private security industry that are regulated are subject to one body. Second there are *Divided* systems which can be further divided between *Functional* and *Territorial*. As the name suggests in a *Divided* system there is more than one organization responsible for regulation. In the *Functional* version different organizations take on responsibility for regulating different parts of the private security industry and in the *Territorial* model responsibility is shared for the same sectors but certain responsibilities are devolved to another body in a defined geographical location.

Five models revisited

From the original research on regulation based upon the width and depth criteria we were able to identify five models. These are set out in Figure 24.3. These still provide – in our view – the best basis to distinguish regulatory systems. Some of the other factors will be added to in the discussions from the regions later in this chapter. Additionally one can add a 'High' or 'Low' compliance orientation to the four models as well as distinguish whether it is a 'Monopoly' or 'Divided Functional' or 'Divided Territorial'.

Regional review

To gain a deeper insight into the nature of regulation of the private security industry this chapter will now examine in greater depth some of the different systems that exist from a regional perspective. It will begin by reviewing the experience of Western and Eastern Europe, before examining the US and briefly Canada and Australia. In doing so the aim is to illustrate some of the significant differences in regulation, demonstrate how the models identified earlier apply and also elucidate some of their positive and negative experience of regulation. The review is clearly biased towards the industrialized 'western' countries, but space constrains and lack of publicly available data made this inevitable for this paper. Observations on the most effective system will be left to the concluding part of this chapter after considering Loader's more radical proposals for regulation.

Western Europe

Despite some initiatives for European Union (EU) level regulation (see George and Button, 2000; COESS, 2004) the primary basis for regulation of the private security industry in EU countries are national regulatory systems (see Allen, 1991; De Waard and Van Der Hoek, 1991; De Waard, 1993; SITO, 1994; Hakala, 1998; De Waard, 1999; Weber, 2002). Most countries in Western Europe can be classified as Comprehensive. There are, however, a few members of a diminishing club that still follow the Non-Interventionist model such as Cyprus, Ireland and Scotland. In Ireland, however, legislation has recently been passed which will address this and in Scotland the devolved government has signalled its intention to opt into the English and Welsh system.

The Minimum Narrow model of regulating private security is diminishing in Europe as countries gradually develop more comprehensive models of regulation. The jurisdictions that fit this model include Austria, Greece, Luxembourg and Northern Ireland. There are, however, wide variations amongst these countries in the depth of regulation. In Greece *Law 2518 on Private Security Undertakings of 1997* created a basic licensing system for owners, managers and employees in the contract-guarding sector, based upon character requirements. In Austria to establish a security firm, an individual needs relevant experience and/or to pass an exam, as well as to meet certain background requirements. There are no standards for employees, although firms are obliged to check with the police if they have a criminal record – which they can do. Similarly in Luxembourg firms require authorization from the Ministry of Justice to operate, but there are few standards for employees.

The most popular form of regulatory system in Western Europe is the Comprehensive model. Those countries with a Comprehensive Narrow regulatory system only generally regulate the contract guarding (armed and unarmed), cash-in-transit (CIT) and private investigation sectors. In Belgium and the Netherlands the regulations are probably the widest and most comprehensive in the world. In the former they cover contract and in-house security guards, CIT guards, private investigators and installers of intruder alarm systems; and the latter, these plus locksmiths and security consultants.

The mandatory minimum standards of training in Western Europe are some of the most stringent in the world. The standards set in some countries are such that they rival the introductory training courses of the police. For instance in Spain 260 hours of training is required and in Sweden it is 217 hours. Some countries also set other minimum standards of training for roles other than ordinary security officers. In Belgium for instance different standards of minimum training are also set for managers, CIT guards, dog handlers to name a few. The Figure below also illustrates that the most common means of regulation is through a minimum number of hours. The Netherlands is distinct from this in setting a standard exam that must be passed within 12 months or the ID card is withdrawn. The full range of training standards are set out in Figure 24.4.

Country	Statutory Minimum Training Standards
Belgium	Security officers 130 hours and must pass test. Additional specialist training of 42 hours (weapons), 66 hours (protection of people), transportation of valuables 78 hours, 40 hours (middle managers) amongst various others.
Denmark	Security officers 120 hours to commence within two weeks and be completed within six months. No exam.
England and Wales	Security officers 30 hours (22 ½ theory 7 ½ practical).
Finland	Security officers 40 hours basic training (with plans to increase to 100 hours). Specialist training for use of weapons and guard dogs mandated.
Germany	Security officers 24 hours basic training and 40 hours for managers.
Netherlands	Three weeks basic training and then additional training that leads to Basic Security Diploma which must be passed in 12 months, otherwise guard loses ID card and therefore job.
Portugal	Security officers required to undergo 58 hours training and those engaged in transport of valuables, persons an additional 42 hours, those using firearms 30 hours and those in pubs/clubs 30 hours.
Spain	Security officers required to undergo 240 hours theoretical and 20 practical.
Sweden	Security officers 217 hours (97 hours classes, 120 hours on the job). Additional specialist training of 25 hours (security officers in public areas), 40 hours (CIT), 40 hours (guard dog services), 21 hours and annual test with further 4 hours (armed guards), and 80 hours (bodyguards).

Figure 24.4 Training standards for security officers in selected comprehensive European nations

Sources: Confederation of European Security Services (2004); CoESS/UNI Europa (2004); Weber, T. (2002: 31–6); and (SIA, u.d.) Security Guarding – Required Training, retrieved from http://www.the-sia.org.uk/home/licensing/security-guarding/training/training_sg.htm on 17 January 2006
Notes:
1 In Denmark courses are laid down by the police, educational authorities and the Labour Ministry also has a role; and in Sweden training is set by National Police Board.
2 In Spain training is carried out at regional centres and in-house by accredited companies. Exam set by National Police and must be passed. Ministry of Education responsible for training of private investigators, Institute of Criminology organizes courses.

Russia and Eastern Europe

Before discussing the private security industry of Russia and some countries in Eastern Europe it is appropriate to reiterate the caveats outlined at the beginning of this chapter. It is all but impossible to give anything more than a snapshot of the situation that exists in the region as it is in continual upheaval. Although there was discernibly a guarding profession before the rise of communism the relative absence of private property and the state monopoly on the provision of services meant that for most of the communist era activity resembling private security as it is now recognized was limited, with only factory guards and militia (police) guarding property. The collapse of communism and the rise of the free market generated an unprecedented growth in private security activity. However, in countries such as Russia it quickly became clear that many of the major players in the emerging private security industry were of dubious character and that left unchecked, the private security industry threatened to add to lawlessness rather than provide relief from it.

Russia's response came in the form of the Federal law on *Private Detective and Protection Activity* in the Russian Federation. Adopted on 11th March 1992 it formally recognized the private security industry and the right of firms involved in the industry to 'protect legal rights and interests of their clients'. The law covers a wide range of activities stretching from the exercise of physical protection of property and individuals to the collection of data and the protection of trademarks. While the law was broad in the range of activities it recognized as reasonable security activities, it was not ambitious in seeking to regulate them. Included was the requirement that in order to gain a licence from the regional Commission for Licences and Permission the head of perspective agencies must be able to demonstrate a special qualification or a minimum of three years experience with a state law enforcement or security agency. Stipulations such as these were few in number and were included in legislation to guarantee work for former state security officials rather than ensure the quality of personnel (Volkov, 2001).

Thus Russia's initial efforts at legislation could be categorized as Wide, but with little depth as Russia's legislative institutions, themselves in relative infancy, sought to recognize various activities as legitimate rather than closely regulate the carrying out of them. Regulation, however, remains highly decentralized and there is evasion of the law on a large scale compounded by inefficient enforcement. In the period since 1992 the limitations of the initial legislation have became increasingly apparent. The relative lack of checks outside those mentioned above has facilitated the continued presence of corrupt, criminal and even terrorist elements in the Russian private security industry (Ivanov, 2004). While efforts to add depth to Russia's legislative framework have been occasionally productive, such as the legislation in 1997 regulating the use of weapons. Efforts at more Comprehensive legislation have stalled as international private security firms lobby against protectionist elements to proposed legislation.

Eastern and Central Europe have seen a similarly impressive expansion in private security activity in the last decade. In many instances the industry and regulation of it has matured much more quickly than could have been expected, for countries that less than two decades ago had little in the way of private enterprise and as such little need for private security.

An example of a broad and relatively in-depth legislative arrangement can be found in Poland where the sector's origins can be traced back to the 1980s. Although legislation did not emerge until 1997, the *Protection of Persons and Property Act* was representative of the sophisticated thinking, which surrounded the Polish security sector. Initially relating to static guarding, close protection for the transfer of money and hazardous items as well as the assembly, installation and maintenance of intruder alarms, the legislation was supplemented in 2001 with provisions to regulate the private detection industry. The Polish private security industry now consists of some 3600 firms employing 200,000 people. Acquiring a licence requires 146 hours of theoretical training as well as 114 hours of practical training and acquiring a Second degree licence requires over 300 hours of training.

Similarly in Hungary where the industry is estimated to employ 80,000 people, could be categorized in legislative terms as Comprehensive Wide. In addition to legislation currently being prepared, Hungary's industry is covered by 1998 legislation relating to numerous activities including static guarding, CIT, events management, body guarding, electronic surveillance, private investigation and dog handling. Hungary's regulation has both breadth and depth with certification to enter the industry involving mandatory psychological examination and 320 hours of training encompassing legal, theoretical and professional knowledge.

However, while rapid expansion of the private security industry can be seen consistently through the various states of Eastern and Central Europe, regulatory arrangements with the breadth and depth of Poland and Hungary's are not uniform. The Czech Republic is a clear example of a market that has undergone expansion similar in size to either Poland or Hungary's, but has for a variety of reasons not reached the same level of maturity in regulatory terms. Private security firms in the Czech Republic are governed by general laws that apply to small businesses. There has been no legislation or regulatory codes relating specifically to private security. Despite the fact that the industry now employs over 30,000 people training for personnel takes place on an *ad hoc* in-house basis and firms are obliged only to make the Police Presidium aware of the uniforms they intend to use.

North America

US

In the US regulation of the private security industry is a state responsibility and as a consequence there are a wide range of systems in operation. There have been a number of studies over the last 30 years assessing the different regulatory systems. These have included Hemmens *et al.*, (2001), Culligan (1992), Hamil

(1991), Kakalik and Wildhorn (1971a), the National Advisory Committee on Criminal Justice Standards and Goals (1976), Buikema and Horvath (1984), Moore (1987), Elig (1993), McCrie (1993), Fischer and Green (1992) and NBFAA (u.d.). These studies of regulation of the private security industry in the US reveal only a handful of states not regulating the private security industry. Hemmens *et al.* (2001) have identified Alabama, Idaho, Kentucky, Mississippi, Montana, North Dakota and South Dakota as Non-Interventionist. Our research, however, suggests there is regulation in Montana and North Dakota. Nevertheless most states do regulate, but generally the standards of regulation are not high and apply to the manned guarding and private investigator sectors. Unlike continental Europe these two activities are usually regulated together by the same regime. In terms of responsibility there are Monopoly regulators such as Texas, which regulates the wider industry through the Board of Private Investigator and Security Agencies. There are also a number of states that are Divided Functional regulators *vis-à-vis* intruder alarm installers. In Florida the Department of State, Division of Licensing regulates the manned guarding and private investigator sectors and the Department of Business and Professional Regulation is responsible for alarm installers.

Most states have a Minimum Narrow or Wide system based upon licensing of owners and/or employees. The licensing requirements usually relate to minimum standards of character and other operational requirements. There are also a large number of states that set training standards for armed security officers. If every regulatory system was compared on every standard and issue contained in the regulations this analysis would run to several hundred pages. There are standards on uniforms, what words must be shown on badges, vehicles, fees, information required on application forms and ID cards, grounds for revocation, how board members are chosen, general procedures and the ethics expected of security personnel to name some. Several states even go as far as mandating appearance standards for security officers. For instance Alaska mandates several conditions for appearance.

> Natural hair must be clean, neat and combed. Hair must not extend below the top of the shirt collar at the back of the neck when standing with the head in normal posture. The bulk of the rest of the hair must not interfere with the normal wearing of all standard headgear (Alaska Statutes Section 13 AAC 65.010).

The standard also details how wigs or hairpieces should be worn, the length of sideburns and moustaches and the standards of clean shaveness. In light of space constraints the wide variety of such requirements will not be considered. Perhaps of more relevance is to consider the Comprehensive regulating states as there are only a minority of states that can be regarded as fitting this model and even those that fit this, have very basic standards in comparison to those regimes in Western Europe. This is illustrated in Figure 24.5 and the state training standards for security officers.

State	Unarmed Training Standards
Alaska	Eight hours pre-assignment training; 40 hours further training within 180 days and must pass annual refresher course.
Arizona	Agency licensee responsible for providing training for security guards before expiration of provisional registration certificate. Amount not specified.
Arkansas	Eight hours pre-assignment training and exam; and four hours training before the expiration of each pocket book.
California	Two hours pre-assignment training (different mandatory training for certain specialized roles).
Florida	Sixteen hours classroom training and exam. With provisions for the length of the course to increase by four hours every two years up to a maximum of 40 hours.
Georgia	Eight hours classroom training.
Illinois	Twenty hours classroom training within 180 days.
Louisiana	Eight hours classroom training within 30 days.
New York	Eight hours preassignment training and 16 hours on the job.
North Carolina	Four hours within 80 days.
North Dakota	Three levels of training: Apprentice Level 16 hours off the job and 16 hours on the job; Security Officer Level after 1000 hours and before 2000 hours and includes 32 hours off the job training; and Commissioned Security Officer after 4000 hours service another 80 hours off the job training.
Oklahoma	Three levels of training: Basic 22 hours off the job; Security Guard 18 hours off the job training; and third phase relates to firearms training.
Oregon	Eight hours pre-assignment classroom training and four hours annual refresher training.
South Carolina	Must complete a satisfactory training course.
Tennessee	Four hours training within 30 days of employment and pass exam.
Utah	Twelve training and exam.
Virginia	Sixteen hours training basic, but different categories of training for different personnel.
Washington	Four hours pre-assignment training.

Figure 24.5 Minimum training standards for unarmed security officers in states with Comprehensive regulatory systems
Sources: Various statutes and Hemmens *et al.* (2001)

There is much to be learnt from the US private security industry given the long history of regulation of certain sectors and the wide range of different systems. The minimal nature of these systems, as well as the numerous problems associated with them, is underlined when one compares the US regulatory experience with some Western European countries explored earlier. Most of the states have minimal regulation based upon character and of those with comprehensive regulation, only Alaska mandates minimum training for unarmed security officers above a week (40 hours). This encompasses eight hours of pre-assignment training followed by a further 40 hours within 180 days. The fact that many US states only effectively mandate a single day pre-assignment training for unarmed security officers illustrates the low standards of even the more stringently regulating states.

This leads one to the conclusion that despite the significant minority of states with a comprehensive approach, if one had to classify the US as a whole, the minimal model would be the most appropriate. This definition is reinforced when the US states are compared with the comprehensive regulating Western European countries where mandated training is often in the hundreds of hours.

Canada

Across the border in Canada a similar federal structure exists where regulation is the responsibility of the provincial and territorial governments. As in the US there have been a number of studies of regulation in Canada and include Hyde (2003), Gerden (1995), Leclair and Long (1996), Mollard *et al.* (1993), Oppal (1994) and Shearing and Stenning (1981).

The common approach in the Canadian provinces is also the Minimum Narrow approach with only the static contract guarding and private investigation sectors regulated. The regulation standards only apply to character requirements for owners, managers and employees. There are, however, provinces such as British Columbia and New Brunswick that regulate the wider industry. One of the most notable sectors which is not regulated in most Canadian provinces or territories is the in-house sector. The Canadian Corps of Commissionaires is also exempted from regulation in many of the provinces and territories.

However, there is a trend in Canada towards wider regulation with Shearing and Stenning (1981) noting expansion of regulation to other services beyond contract guarding and investigation services. More recently the Oppal Commission of Inquiry into policing in British Columbia recommended that regulation should be extended to in-house security employers and employees, the Canadian Corps of Commissionaires, the employees of armoured car operators, bouncers, bodyguards and guard dog operators. The Commission also recommended that the legislation should be made more flexible so that security services can be included when required (Oppal, 1994). Research by Hyde (2003) has highlighted that apart from Newfoundland, mandatory training standards are relatively new with a 64-hour training course introduced for security officers in British Columbia and mandatory approved training in Saskatchewan.

Australia

Australia is also a federal state with responsibility for regulation at the state and territorial level (Prenzler and Sarre, 1999). The only federal intervention in Australia facilitates mutual recognition of different states' regulatory requirements. Under the Commonwealth Mutual Recognition Act 1992 an individual licensed in one state to operate in the private security industry is entitled to the same licence in another, except Western Australia (Northern Territory Security Industry Working Party, 1995). However, difficulties have emerged over the issue because of the different training standards in the respective states.

Legislation in some states dates to the 1950s, in others have only recently been enacted and in some, old legislation has been amended or consolidated. Prenzler and Sarre (1999) have undertaken a detailed study of the regulatory systems in operation. Analysis of this research suggests most of the states (and territories) pursue a Minimal Narrow or Wide system of regulation with only Queensland clearly pursuing a Comprehensive system of the Narrow variety, regulating contract guards, crowd controllers (or door supervisors) and private investigators. New South Wales has the widest system with in addition to the sectors Queensland regulates alarm installers, locksmiths and trainers too.

In all the states in Australia there are licensing conditions for employers and employees in regulated sector based upon character requirements. For employers and companies there are additional requirements based upon financial position. The character requirements in all cases are based primarily upon absence of a criminal record. In most cases the offences acting as a disqualification are listed in the legislation. In some of the states there is also a ten-year rule. This states that individuals who have not been convicted of any of the listed offences in the last decade could be licensed, subject to meeting the other requirements. Such requirements in some states also go beyond criminal convictions. In Queensland *inter alia* associating with known criminals, taking advantage of the bankruptcy laws or having been a patient under the Mental Health Act are also used to disqualify potential applicants (Prenzler *et al.*, 1998).

In some of the states there are provisions for the standards to be set that would enhance the quality of service, although the practicalities of their implementation do not always live up to the legislation. For example in South Australia and Tasmania there are provisions in the legislation for prescribing the standard of education, practical skill and experience, but no detailed training standards. In the Northern Territory and Victoria there are minimum standards of training for crowd controllers (Prenzler and Sarre, 1999). In Queensland there is a minimum of 35 hours training for private investigators, 37 hours for security officers and 24 hours for crowd controllers (Prenzler *et al.*, 1998). In New South Wales and Western Australia the National Security Competency Standards for Security Officers have been adopted, but these lack a minimum number of training hours and key subjects such as conflict resolution and the use of force (Prenzler and Sarre, 1999). In New South Wales installers of security equipment – physical and electronic – must meet the prescribed qualifications and security consultants must be able to demonstrate to the Commissioner of Police they have the qualifications and experience to operate.

The plural model of regulation

The realization that private security is part of a broader process of 'fragmentation' or 'pluralization' of policing has led to some more radical ideas for regulating the new policing order. This chapter has focused largely upon the debate and experience of regulating private security using schemes focused solely upon the private security industry. Beyond the police and private security, however, there are other agencies from the public, hybrid, private and voluntary sectors. Loader (2000) recognizing the growing complexity of policing has criticized the existing models of control based upon specific sectors of policing and sought to resurrect and redevelop the ideas of Jefferson and Grimshaw (1984) of police commissions. Loader proposes the establishment of policing commissions at local, regional and national levels whose aim would be:

> ... to formulate policies and coordinate service delivery across the policing network, and to bring to democratic account the public, municipal, commercial and voluntary agencies that comprise it (Loader, 2000: 337).

The commissions would consist of elected and appointed members to ensure social representativeness and would have three broad functions. First they would be responsible for policy formulation and strategic co-ordination. This would encompass setting policies and targets for the state police and developing policing plans, largely at the local and regional levels. The second set of functions would relate to the authorizing, licensing and subsidizing of policing. This would involve operating a licensing system for private security firms and staff as well as setting standards on human rights, anti-discriminatory and equal opportunities policies. The commission would also issue tenders inviting voluntary, private and municipal bodies to provide policing services. Linked to this they would also seek to make good inequities in policing provision in specific areas by allocating state provision or by contracting in additional provision. The final set of functions of the policing commissions would relate to monitoring, inspection and evaluation. These would include bringing the different forms of policing to democratic account, through the provision of information, inspection of policing agencies, and monitoring the extent to which the different agencies achieve their objectives. Similar ideas have also emerged with Johnston and Shearing's (2003) model of Nodal Governance.

It is not the place to debate these radical models in depth here. However, a number of questions and issues do arise that should be considered in future discourses (Jones, 2003). There might be a risk that giving the commissions the responsibility for a wider range of policing organizations, beyond the public police, might actually risk a greater centralization of power? Questions also arise over what will happen to much of the existing infrastructure of police governance? Are they to be abolished or remain under the new system? Another issue that would need to be considered is the extent to which the policing commissions applied to the extended policing community. Would they stretch to cover the responsibilities of organizations such as the Royal Society for the Prevention of Cruelty to Animals (RSPCA), benefit fraud investigators and health and safety inspectors, or would the scope be more restricted? Thus such proposals represent radical and innovative ideas to confront the growing plurality of policing, but require much more debate and consideration.

The most effective model and concluding comments

This chapter has examined the international experience of regulation and in doing so applied it to models of regulation we have updated for this chapter, but which were first outlined in 1997. In the brief space available in the conclusion we would like to outline in our view some of the key issues *vis-à-vis* regulation. Our view of the private security industry is what Jones and Newburn (1998) describe as a 'liberal democratic' perspective, in that it has a significant and positive contribution to play in policing. To achieve this effectively, however, we believe a strong system of regulation that provides good governance for the private security industry is necessary.

Research has suggested that the highest quality security industries in Europe are in Sweden, the Netherlands and Belgium (Berglund, u.d.) and it is no surprise to find them pursuing Comprehensive Wide systems. This is compared to Britain and Germany near the bottom who at the time pursued the Non-Interventionist and Minimum Narrow models respectively (De Waard, 1999). In the US model statutes and influential Government reports have advocated both Comprehensive and Wide models of regulation (George and Button, 1997) and research on the states overall illustrated a trend towards more regulation, although not necessarily Comprehensive or Wide versions (Hemmens *et al.*, 2001). The trend of reforming systems to enhance the quality of the private security industry can also be found elsewhere. In Canada the reform of British Columbia's system to Comprehensive Wide, as well as other quality enhancing reforms in Newfoundland and Saskatchewan illustrate this trend (Oppal, 1994; Hyde, 2003). Reforms have also been pursued in several of the Australian states to enhance quality, through the introduction of or modifications towards what could be described as more Comprehensive Wide models of regulation (Prenzler *et al.*, 1998; Prenzler and Sarre, 1999), as has been the case in Japan with reform of the original Minimal regulation (Yoshida, 1999).

It is also clearly important to have a 'High' level of compliance and this can only be achieved through appropriate enforcement strategies and structures. We are less prescriptive about the best organizational structure, but the 'Monopoly' system would be our preference because it avoids problems of delegation, duplication and differences emerging between different bodies. The changing structure of policing with increasing 'fragmentation' and delivery of services pose significant challenges in establishing the most efficient form of regulation. As the new patchwork of policing unfolds with the growing position of the private security industry, it is vital that the growing body of research continues to inform policy-makers to ensure the effectiveness of regulation is not compromised, so that private security can play a full and effective role in policing.

Note

1   The authors would like to thank Anthony McGee and COESS for their help in producing this chapter.

Key readings

For a detailed analysis of the different regulatory systems in most of the European Union countries see De Waard, J. (1999) 'The Private Security Industry in International Perspective', *European Journal of Criminal Policy and Research*, Vol. 7, No. 2, pp. 143–74; and Weber, T. (2002) *A Comparative Overview of Legislation Governing the Private Security Industry in the European Union*. Retrieved from http://www.coess.org/pdf/final-study.PDF on 24th November, 2004. For some very interesting overviews of specific countries, the following are worth looking at Yoshida, N. (1999) 'The Taming of the Japanese Private Security Industry', *Policing and Society*, Vol. 9, No. 3, pp. 241–61; Prenzler, T. and Sarre, R. (1999) 'A Survey of Security Legislation and Regulatory Strategies in Australia', *Security Journal*, Vol. 12, No. 3, pp. 7–17; and for the US see Hemmens, C., Maahs, J., Scarborough, K.E. and Collins, P.A. (2001) 'Watching the Watchmen: State Regulation of Private Security 1982–1998', *Security Journal*, Vol. 14, No. 4, pp. 17–28. If you would like to examine the debates over more radical measures to govern security in the broader patchwork of policing see Loader, I. (2000) 'Plural Policing and Democratic Governance', *Social and Legal Studies*, Vol. 9, No. 3, pp. 323–45 and Johnston, L. and Shearing, C.D. (2003) *Governing Security*, London: Routledge. For those interested in the accountability of security officers see, Stenning, P.C. (2000) 'Powers and Accountability of the Private Police', *European Journal on Criminal Policy and Research*, Vol. 8, No. 3, pp. 325–52.

References

ACPO (1995) Memorandum of Evidence. In, House of Commons Home Affairs Committee (1995) *The Private Security Industry*, Vol. II, London: HMSO.

Allen, S. (1991) *The A-Z Guide to European Manned Guarding*, London: Network Security Management Ltd.

Berglund, T. (u.d.) *The Security Industry in Europe – How to Act and React Towards Europe*, Unpublished Paper Presented to the Confederation of European Security Services.

Brodeur, J.-P., Gill, P. and Töllborg, D. (2003) 'Introduction', in J.-P. Brodeur, P. Gill and D. Töllborg (eds) *Democracy, Law and Security: Internal Security Services in Contemporary Europe*, Aldershot: Ashgate.

Buikema, C. and Horvath, F. (1984) 'Security Regulation: A State-by-State Update', *Security Management*, January.

Button, M. (1998) '"Beyond the Public Gaze", The Exclusion of Private Investigators from the British Debate Over Regulating Private Security', *International Journal of the Sociology of Law*, Vol. 26, No. 1, pp. 1–16.

Button, M. and George, B. (2001) 'Government Regulation in the United Kingdom Private Security Industry: The Myth of Non-Regulation', *Security Journal*, Vol. 14, No. 1, pp. 55–66.

Campbell, G. and Reingold, B. (1994) 'Private Security and Public Policing in Canada', *Juristat Service Bulletin*, Ottawa: Canadian Centre for Justice Statistics.

Confederation of European Security Services (COESS) (2004) *Towards a European Model of Private Security*, retrieved from http://www.coess.org/documents/coess-uni-joint-final-en.pdf on 25th November, 2004.

CoESS/UNI Europa (2004) *Panaromic Overview of the Private Security Industry in the 25 Member States of the European Union*, retrieved from http://www.coess.org/pdf/panorama1.pdf

Crawford, A. and Lister, S. (2004) *The Extended Policing Family*, York: Joseph Rowntree Foundation.

Culligan, J.J. (1993) *Requirements to Become a PI in the 50 states and Elsewhere: A Reference Manual*, USA: Research Investigative Services.

Cunningham, W.C., Strauchs, J.J. and Van Meter, C.W. (1990) *Private Security Trends 1970–2000*, Hallcrest Report II, Stoneham (US): Butterworth-Heinemann.

De Waard, J. (1993) 'The Private Security Sector in Fifteen European Countries: Size, Rules and Legislation', *Security Journal*, Vol. 4, No. 2, pp. 58–62.

De Waard, J. (1999) 'The Private Security Industry in International Perspective', *European Journal of Criminal Policy and Research*, Vol. 7, No. 2, pp. 143–74.

De Waard, J. and Van Der Hoek, J. (1991) *Private Security Size and Legislation in the Netherlands and Europe*, The Hague: Dutch Ministry of Justice.

Elig, G. (1993) 'Private Security Quality Assurance', *Security Concepts*, August.

Fischer, R.J. and Green, G. (1992) *Introduction to Security*, Boston: Butterworth-Heinemann.

Francis, J. (1993) *The Politics of Regulation*, Oxford: Blackwell.

George, B. and Button, M. (1997) 'Private Security Regulation – Lessons from Abroad for the United Kingdom', *International Journal of Risk Security and Crime Prevention*, Vol. 2, No. 3, pp. 109–21.

George, B. and Button, M. (2000) *Private Security*, Leicester: Perpetuity Press.

George, B. and Cooper, S. (2002) *The Regulation of Private Military Companies: A Reaction to the Foreign Office Green Paper*, Unpublished Submission to Foreign and Commonwealth Office Green Paper on 'Private Military Companies: Options for Regulation'.

Gerden, R. (1995) *Private Security Review, Unpublished Report for the Ministry of Solicitor General and Correctional Services*, Ontario: Canada.

Gill, M. and Hart, J. (1997) 'Exploring Investigative Policing', *British Journal of Criminology*, Vol. 37, No. 4, pp. 549–67.

Gimenez-Salinas, A. (2004) 'New Approaches Regarding Private/Public Security', *Policing and Society*, Vol. 14, No. 2, pp. 158–74.

Hakala, J. (1998) *A Comparison of Statutory Regulation and Controls as They Concern the Private Security Industry in Four Nordic Countries*, MSc Thesis, Leicester: University of Leicester.

Hamil, W. (1991) *National Laws and Statutes for Private Investigators and Security Guard Agencies*, Oklahoma: Oklahoma Investigations.

Hemmens, C., Maahs, J., Scarborough, K.E. and Collins, P.A. (2001) 'Watching the Watchmen: State Regulation of Private Security 1982–1998', *Security Journal*, Vol. 14, No. 4, pp. 17–28.

Home Office (1979) *The Private Security Industry: A Discussion Paper*, London: HMSO.

Home Office (1991) *Private Security Industry Background Paper*, Unpublished paper.

Home Office (1996) *Regulation of the Contract Guarding Sector of the Private Security Industry*, London: Home Office.

House of Commons Defence Committee (1990) 'Sixth Report', *The Physical Security of Military Installations in the United Kingdom*, HC 171, London: HMSO.

House of Commons Home Affairs Committee (HAC) (1995) *The Private Security Industry*, Vols. I and II, HC 17, London: HMSO.

Hyde, D. (2003) *The Role of 'Government' in Regulating, Auditing and Facilitating Private Policing in Late Modernity: The Canadian Experience*, Paper presented to In Search of Security Conference, Montreal, Quebec, February.

Ivanov, V. (2004) Speaking at the 4th Annual International East-West Security Conference, London, September 2004.

Jaksa, J.J. (2004) 'Is the Guard Trained or Not? The Attempt to Legislate Security Guard Training in Michigan', *Security Journal*, Vol. 17, No. 4, pp. 67–76.

Jefferson, T. and Grimshaw, R. (1984) *Controlling the Constable: Police Accountability in England and Wales*, London: Cobden Trust.

Johnston, L. and Shearing, C.D. (2003) *Governing Security*, London: Routledge.

Jones, T. (2003) 'The Governance and Accountability of Policing', in T. Newburn (ed.) *Handbook of Policing*, Cullompton: Willan.

Jones, T. and Newburn, T. (1998) *Private Security and Public Policing*, Oxford: Clarendon Press.

Kakalik, J. and Wildhorn, S. (1971a) *Current Regulation of Private Police: Regulatory Agency Experience and Views*, Vol. 3, Washington DC: Government Printing Office.

Kakalik, J. and Wildhorn, S. (1971b) *The Law and Private Police*, Vol. 4, Washington DC: Government Printing Office.

Leclair, C. and Long, S. (1996) *The Canadian Security Sector: An Overview*, Unpublished Report.

Lister, S., Hadfield, P., Hobbs, D. and Winlow, S. (2001) 'Accounting for Bouncers: Occupational Licensing as a Mechanism for Regulation', *Criminal Justice*, Vol. 1, No. 4, pp. 363–84.

Loader, I. (2000) 'Plural Policing and Democratic Governance', *Social and Legal Studies*, Vol. 9, No. 3, pp. 323–45.

McCrie, R.D. (ed.) (1993) *Security Letter Source Book*, New York: The City University of New York.

Manunta, G. (1999) 'What is Security?', *Security Journal*, Vol. 12, pp. 57–66.

Miyazawa, S. (1991) 'The Private Sector and Law Enforcement in Japan', in W.T. Gormley (ed.) *Privatisation and its Alternative*, Madison: University of Wisconsin Press.

Mollard, M.J., Mackay, R.C. and Taylor, A.T. (1993) *Report on the Regulation of the Private Security Industry in British Columbia*, submission to the Commission of Inquiry – Policing in British Columbia.

Moore, R.H. (1987) 'Licensing and Regulation of Private Security', *Journal of Security Administration*, Vol. 10, No. 1, pp. 10–15.

Moore, R.H. (1990) 'Licensing and Regulation of the Private Security Industry: A Historic View of the Court's Role', *Journal of Security Administration*, Vol. 13, No. 1 and 2, pp. 37–61.

Murray, C. (1996) 'The Case Against Regulation', *International Journal of Risk, Security and Crime Prevention*, Vol. 1, No. 1, pp. 59–62.

National Advisory Committee on Criminal Standards and Goals (1976) *Private Security. Report of the Task Force on Private Security*, Washington, DC: Government Printing Office.

National Burglar and Fire Alarm Association (NBFAA) (u.d.) *Alarm Company State Licensing Requirements*, Bethesda, MD: NBFAA.

Northern Territory Security Industry Working Group (1995) Regulation of the Private Security in the Northern Territory, Discussion Paper.

O'Conner, D., Lippert, R., Greenfield, K. and Boyle, P. (2004) 'After the "Quiet Revolution": The Self-Regulation of Ontario Contract Security Agencies', *Policing and Society*, Vol. 14, No. 2, pp. 138–57.

Oppal, W.T. (1994) Closing the Gap – Policing and the Community. Use of Non-Police Personnel Excerpts, The Report of Policing in British Columbia Commission of Inquiry.

Prenzler, T., Baxter, T. and Draper, R. (1998) 'Special Legislation for the Security Industry: A Case Study', *International Journal of Risk, Security and Crime Prevention*, Vol. 3, No. 1, pp. 21–33.

Prenzler, T. and Sarre, R. (1999) 'A Survey of Security Legislation and Regulatory Strategies in Australia', *Security Journal*, Vol. 12, No. 3, pp. 7–17.

Rigakos, G.S. (2002) *The New Parapolice*, Toronto: University of Toronto Press.

Sarre, R. and Prenzler, T. (1999) 'The Regulation of Private Policing: Reviewing Mechanisms of Accountability', *Crime Prevention and Community Safety: An International Journal*, Vol. 1, No. 3, pp. 17–28.

Shearing, C.D. and Stenning, P.C. (1981) 'Modern Private Security: Its Growth and Implications', in M. Tonry and N. Morris (eds) *Crime and Justice An Annual Review of Research*, Vol. 3, Chicago: University of Chicago Press.

SITO (1994) *The European Study – Training and Qualifications Within the European Security Industry*, Worcester: SITO.

Stenning, P.C. (2000) 'Powers and Accountability of the Private Police', *European Journal on Criminal Policy and Research*, Vol. 8, No. 3, pp. 325–52.

Stenning, P.C. and Shearing, C.D. (1979) 'Private Security and Private Justice', *British Journal of Law and Society*, Vol. 6, No. 2, pp. 261–71.

Stenning, P.C. and Shearing, C.D. (1980) 'The Quiet Revolution: The Nature, Development and General Legal Implications of Private Security in Canada', *Criminal Law Quarterly*, Vol. 22, No. 2, pp. 220–48.

Volkov, V. (2001) 'Security and Enforcement as Private Business: The Conversion of Russia's Power Ministries and it's Institutional Consequences', in V. Bonnell (ed.) *New Entrepreneurs in Russia and China*, Boulder (US): Westview Press.

Wakefield, A. (2003) *Selling Security – The Private Policing of Public Space*, Cullompton: Willan.

Weber, T. (2002) *A Comparative Overview of Legislation Governing the Private Security Industry in the European Union*, retrieved from http://www.coess.org/pdf/final-study.PDF on 24th November, 2004.

Yoshida, N. (1999) 'The Taming of the Japanese Private Security Industry', *Policing and Society*, Vol. 9, No. 3, pp. 241–61.

25

Corporate Security: A Cost or Contributor to the Bottom Line?

Dennis Challinger

1 Security – a given in the corporate world

Every business corporation understands that security is an inevitable expense – the fact that they all keep their premises physically secure is evidence of that. However not every corporation would embrace Dalton's recent view 'that security management is not an odd-but-necessary back-lot function, but is instead a vital business function that is essential to any organisation's continued viability' (Dalton, 2003: xii). More likely they would agree that security is a 'necessary evil (and they) really have no choice' (Kovacich and Halibozek, 2003: 63).

In this chapter, a corporation is defined as any organization that employs a number of people to achieve a common purpose, whether as a commercial company or a government instrumentality. The word corporation therefore subsumes retailers, manufacturers, banks and hotels as well as hospitals, schools, universities and public transport, etc.

While quite different in output, all these corporations must operate in a financially responsible way and obviously that includes protecting their assets. In this chapter it will be assumed that is done through what will be called a corporate security department (although in practice a small corporation may not need a separate department). At a minimum, the corporate security department will implement measures to physically secure business premises and assets. However any further security measures that may be implemented within a corporation will usually result from further internal corporate decision-making.

Regrettably, internal decision-making about security may lack the careful consideration that is taken when other issues – most notably income-generating activities – are considered. Some security decisions appear to be made after a breach of security has occurred. Some are made when it is simplistically assumed that continued security is no longer needed. Some are made when it is feared that business will be lost if security is not in place to reassure customers or clients. Some may be made when management observe that a competitor has some security equipment in place that they do not have. And fortunately, some are made on the recommendation of the head of corporate security.

In some corporations the head of corporate security does not have a lot of influence. However there are others where the role of corporate security is openly acknowledged. One example of the latter is Wal-Mart, the world's largest retailer, where the head of their corporate security department – the Vice President of loss prevention – reports directly to the CEO. As the CEO has put it:

> Politics being what they are, it's too easy for decisions (about security) to be misguided when you allow internal politics to enter in. With loss prevention reporting to me, that allows me to set the tone, the discipline, about what effective loss prevention is. (Lee, 2002: 17)

However in general much corporate decision-making about security does not appear to be soundly or evidence-based. That is not sensible as corporate management should want to ensure their security is the best possible for their corporation.

The difficulty is that some corporate managers still hold entrenched views regarding security, its funding and its impact. There are also problems appreciating what a corporate security department does, what it is capable of, and how it contributes to the corporation's bottom line. These are the topics which will be discussed in this chapter.

2 Deciding the best security for a corporation

The best security keeps all the corporation's assets secure – and therein lies a paradox. The success of corporate security is measured by the absence of activities which would have negative effects on the corporation if they occurred. Put another way, a highly-effective security manager may become the victim of his or her own success.

It can be hard for the head of corporate security to acquire further necessary funds within the corporation because, if the department has been doing a really good job, its achievements are effectively invisible and a need for more resources seems unwarranted. On the other hand, if the security has been poor and there have been many incidents causing loss to the company, a stronger case can be made for more funds to prevent further losses (that is, if the head of corporate security withstands the accusations that he or she is a bad performer).

Within a corporation there are other departments that also measure fewer incidents as signs of success. Occupational Health and Safety is seen as successful when there are reductions in workplace accidents and fewer worker's compensation claims. Facilities managers are doing a great job when there are no losses due to fires because fire prevention equipment is installed and working.

However each of those departments has an advantage over security in that there is generally legislation in place requiring their continued existence. By law, workplace environments must be made safe and buildings must have the correct fire fighting equipment in place.

In general then security is not legally mandated. However the absence of workplace sabotage or workplace theft is as beneficial to the corporation as, or even more beneficial than, an absence of workplace accidents. The difficulty is that the absence of thefts is based on an assumption that many (more) would have occurred if security measures had not been in place.

Long-time security consultant Dalton has stated that:

> (the security) profession ... is largely based on assumptions. We make management and financial decisions based on a great number of unproven assumptions. Ours is a profession that is both uncodified and largely unproven. We assume that security officers provide some deterrent value. We assume that state-of-the-art technologies are effective in preventing loss of assets and life ... (Dalton, 2003: xxviii)

If corporate decision makers do not also accept assumptions such as these then there is plainly going to be problems deciding on the best security. If for instance they do not accept the assumption that internal thefts are a likely activity then their view of what may be the best security is not going to accord with the views of their corporate security head. They may end up making decisions based on views about corporate security that are simply wrong.

3 Corporate management's view of security

Management has a number of views of corporate security that are generally erroneous and which can be said to place the security function at a disadvantage. They include the following:

Security is not a major corporate priority

The bulk of effort in most corporations goes to generating more business to make more profit. That can mean that insufficient time is given to consideration of security requirements and they are not as rigorously considered as they should be. Yates (2003) points out:

> many organizations have not integrated security into their culture. For many, it has been addressed by simplistic measures such as employing a former police officer as a security guard or putting out a memo. Specifically there has been a major failure

- to enhance security rather than simply overlaying security onto existing practices
- to identify and incorporate best security practice
- of visible CEO leadership on security
- to implement reinforcing behaviour in organizations such as regular security updates, security education and reward system for security conscious behaviour

- to provide security training, education and competence
- to prepare the groundwork for effective local law enforcement co-operation (Yates, 2003: 75)

Security is not worth doing

There are some activities conducted by the corporate security department which may not be seen by other parts of the corporation as necessary or worth doing. One pointed example of this is the matter of internal theft or fraud which some management may not see as issues for them, still believing myths about the prevalence of that behaviour (Albrecht and Searcy, 2001).

On the other hand, some corporations may 'consider employee theft as an unpreventable, unpleasant situation which is part of doing business (and) ... expect employees to steal' (Oliphant and Oliphant, 2001: 443). But because the extent of employee theft is unknown, management cannot decide 'which costs are greater – to catch a thief or accept it as the inevitable' (*ibid.*: 443). If then they accept the inevitability of internal theft – tantamount to an encouragement for staff to steal – it follows that they do not wish corporate security to pursue such deviance. In their opinion that would not be worthwhile, however that position would simply condone theft by workers.

Security is a nuisance

Some management view security as an impediment to good business and efficiency. If for instance a business meeting is delayed because of security requirements to access a particular part of a building, then security may be said to be jeopardizing business. The fact that the security requirements are well publicized and the majority of corporation staff have no trouble organizing their schedules around those requirements may be disregarded by a complainer.

Security procedures may also require that accurate and current records are kept of corporate assets so that, in the event of theft, an investigation will be expedited. But if those requirements are seen as onerous, or just a nuisance, they too may be ignored.

The alleged nuisance value of security is sometimes used by staff who develop a mindset that causes them to go out of their way to not abide by security requirements – they may decline to wear their corporation ID badge, or argue about signing in a visitor. Support for corporate security from senior management is vital to create a security-aware workplace.

Security is the enemy

In some cases a view may be held by part of the workforce that the security department is their enemy. Such sentiments may arise when the result of security activity has been to identify some staff engaging in inappropriate behaviour that has led to their being disciplined (or even dismissed). This can particularly arise where management sends mixed messages about behaviour as illustrated by the discussion of internal theft above.

The situation may be made even more difficult in instances where undercover security operatives may have been employed to deal with dishonesty amongst staff. The use of an undercover operative posing as a patient in a hospital to identify the staff member stealing patients' money is an example. (Healthcare Risk Management, 2002). It might be thought that honest staff would not be at all concerned at this practice given that it removes a thief from the workplace but this approach by the security department may be seen by them as underhand and acting in a way that doubts the honesty and trustworthiness of all staff (Ironically the undercover staff who were used in the cited example also had roles in auditing and monitoring the security staff to ensure they were performing effectively).

Even the implementation of security systems aimed at protecting staff can be seen as invasive and confirming that corporate security is the enemy. An example of this is the radio frequency-based tracking systems that can locate any worker at a corporation's facility. As an example, one such system has been installed in a Las Vegas hospital to ensure the safety of hospital staff and to keep out intruders and prevent infant abductions (Taylor, 2002).

However because the system is also

> capable of logging in when employees arrive for work and leave the hospital as well as tracking when they go into a restroom or step out for a smoke … (some staff) fear the intrusion of an unseen Big Brother (Taylor, 2002: 14).

Such attitudes could possibly lead to those staff adopting a negative stance towards security in general.

Security is an unskilled occupation

Many in a corporation appear to believe that anyone can 'do' security and that it needs no particular training or aptitude. It is therefore seen as a corporate function of no great merit. This view probably comes from observations or interactions with base-grade, often uniformed, security staff who operate access points or guard property.

It is plainly inappropriate to judge the security function on those staff alone but they are the 'front line' for the corporate security department. The reality is that those staff may be lowly paid and may sometimes be unimpressive. But they have issues to deal with that others may find exceedingly uncomfortable and be unwilling to do. For instance, Button (2003) reports high levels of verbal abuse and threats of violence experienced by security staff at a British shopping and leisure complex where '40 per cent had experienced assault (slight bruising/ bleeding) in the past year' (Button, 2003: 235). It is a credit to those who train, or skill-up, these staff that major problems arise only infrequently.

Correcting management misunderstandings

The above clearly indicate possible sources of real strain between security and others in the corporation. Many managers do not seem to understand the value of, or contribution to the corporation from the security department. They see security as a burden or a cost. However such managers should think about the consequences there might be for the corporation if it did not have a sound level of security.

On the other hand, the corporate security department must ensure that the reasons for the various security requirements are explained. Somerson (2003) puts this elegantly with respect to access control,

> employees need to be told that the ID card is not intended to unduly inhibit their ingress or egress, nor is it intended to identify their presence or otherwise invade their privacy. Instead, the purpose of the ID card is to signify clearly that staff is authorized to be at the facility and to discourage anyone else from entering. (Somerson, 2003: 158)

The corporate security department must change the corporation's mindset about security and remove any lack of understanding of the role and activities of the department. It may be that at present, many security professionals are not good communicators, or lack the commercial awareness to see that they need to 'sell' their function.

4 What corporate security does

The corporate security smorgasbord

The range of activities undertaken by corporate security varies from corporation to corporation – a typical list appears in Kovacich and Halibozek (2003: 161). However the only real exposure to security for many staff relates to access control and ID passes, and those activities can lead to strains if not aggravation, as catalogued above.

While not a complete list, the following outlines many of the activities that a corporate security department undertakes in a typical corporation.

- controlling ID pass issue and access (including reward programmes for staff compliance)
- managing a security control room monitoring CCTV and alarms
- recommending and managing physical security hardware for corporation sites
- managing on-site parking (including after-hours escorts and citations)
- managing uniformed manpower (including after-hours patrols)
- co-ordinating emergency evacuations
- responding to on-site incidents
- writing and publishing corporate security policies
- developing and delivering security awareness programmes for employees
- developing workplace violence prevention procedures
- developing and maintaining fraud prevention strategies
- providing executive protection services for management (including travel briefings)
- implementing security at residences of senior executives

- providing personal and domestic security guides for staff
- overseeing security for off-site events such as AGMs
- dealing with public demonstrations impacting on corporation sites
- collaborating with Information Technology security counterparts
- collaborating with Occupational Health and Safety practitioners
- dealing with information leaks
- investigating criminal incidents (including thefts by and from staff)
- investigating harmful external activities like product counterfeiting
- maintaining and analysing incident and intelligence databases
- liaising with local law enforcement (when necessary)

This list more than adequately demonstrates the considerable contribution that corporate security makes to the corporation. Yet the list is not, and should not be, static. Indeed it should change as potential threats to the corporation change.

For instance, since the 9/11 terrorist attack in New York, corporate security departments in many corporations have been tasked with developing particular plans for dealing with the risk of random and targeted acts of terrorism. Such plans should result from continuous assessment of security risk, the other main activity of corporate security.

Security risk assessment

Any corporate security department should be proficient at undertaking security risk assessments so that they can target their activities to address the greatest risks to the interests of the corporation. Having identified the risks to the corporation it is necessary to develop countermeasures or options to mitigate them. They include reducing the risk (for instance by installing security equipment or implementing new policies), transferring the risk (for instance by insuring against it or contracting others to manage it), or 'simply accepting the risk as a cost of doing business' (ASIS International, 2003: 14).

Security risk assessment comprises a particularly important contribution to the corporation from the corporate security department. The risk assessment process provides a way of prioritizing threats faced by the corporation. That requires some necessarily subjective qualitative judgements to be made of the likelihood of the threat and its impact on the corporation if it were to occur.

The corporate security manager is clearly in the best position to make those judgements as they 'belong' to the corporation and in their day-to-day working life are exposed to the range of the corporation's activities. Those managers have a real advantage over an outside security consultant who may, and in practice often does, recommend a broad raft of security solutions that may be unnecessary because they are geared towards problems that the corporation does not have, or which are relatively unimportant.

The standard risk assessment approach has long been used in financial management (e.g. by banks in assessing foreign exchange trading) and engineering (e.g.

assessing the level of reinforcement needed in a high-rise building) but in many respects is in its infancy in the (corporate) security area (but see Chapter 22). Arguably 9/11 has much to do with this new focus on the risk assessment process. Now corporations are aware that security risks must be part of their future risk assessment activities and that good security is essential.

In the US corporate risk assessment has actually been mandated by the Sarbanes Oxley Act of 2002 which was a legislative response to the accounting scandals caused by the fall of some publicly held companies like Enron and WorldCom. The Act requires compliance with a comprehensive reform of accounting procedures for publicly held corporations to promote and improve the quality and transparency of financial reporting by both internal and external independent auditors.

The Act aims to minimize the risk of corporate malfeasance, but

> there are several links between Sarbanes-Oxley requirements and a company's security program. They include: ensuring appropriate awareness of company security policies and commitment by management; designing and implementing appropriate security controls; and documenting and auditing security policies and making sure they are understood by management and end-users. (Williams, 2003).

5 Impact of good corporate security

Commercial impact

The immediate impact of good security on the commercial health of a corporation is that it keeps the corporation's assets secure. The assets are therefore able to be utilized, the additional expenses involved in replacing them are avoided, and the possibly greater losses through loss of business or inability to service clients are forestalled.

Good security may actually increase business opportunities for a corporation. For instance a shopping mall which is known to have good security in place can actually attract customers from other malls where customers may feel less safe. These intangible sorts of benefits are picked up by Yates (2003) with what he has termed the 'security dividend'.

The concept of a security dividend

As Yates puts it '(t)he key to making security sustainable is to ensure that all stakeholders get a dividend for their security investment' (Yates, 2003: 100). Yates is an engineer who has reviewed the issue of security of Australia's critical infrastructure. His concern is seeing security embedded more formally in business operations, and for that to happen he suggests there needs to be a good return on any investment in security. Good corporate security will deliver a dividend for all stakeholders, in this case particularly the corporation and its staff and customers (who are part of the public at large).

The security dividend for the corporation

The security dividend from good security in a corporation includes the following (adapted from Yates, 2003: 101)

- The corporation's business efficiency increases because good security is geared towards preventing incidents that may cause loss. Indeed the change of title in retailing from security to loss prevention was to emphasize the focus on preventing bad events occurring – a far more desirable outcome than addressing the results of those bad events later on.
- The corporation becomes more attractive to customers leading to an increase in business. The converse of this is the loss of business that can occur in the absence of security. In one English city it was 'estimated that 650 jobs were lost within the retail and leisure sectors and turnover was reduced by £24 million (in 1990) as a result of avoidance behaviour which was caused by the public's concern about crime in that city' (Holden and Stafford, 1997: 5). Indeed the impact of crime on shopping habits can be profound and include postponement of purchases, less recreational shopping, and less shopping at night (see Halverson, 1996).
- The corporation increases its employee retention rate because people prefer to work in a safe workplace. The financial benefit of reducing employee turnover in a corporation cannot be understated. One study in 2000 found that the 'annual cost of employee turnover in the supermarket industry exceeds industry profits by more than 40%' (Meyer, 2000: 40) so increased retention in that industry would be most beneficial.
- The corporation demonstrates that it is a good corporate citizen, partly because its investment in security reduces the demand on police services allowing them to deal with more urgent matters. In a time when corporate citizenship and 'ethical investing' are becoming important considerations, such a corporation becomes more attractive to investors and may increase its shareholder loyalty.
- The corporation's exposure to legal liability claims is reduced when it is able to show that it had taken care to incorporate appropriate security measures into its business practices.

The security dividend for the public at large

The security dividend for the public from good corporate security takes a number of forms but is very much related to the way in which that security impinges on the public sphere. The use of attractive planter boxes on paths at the local shopping centre as security against ram raids can contribute to the amenity of the area. The installation of graffiti-proof surfacing on new buildings can ensure a more pleasant environment and greater use by the public while creating less attractive sites for offenders. The re-design, installation of security lighting and employment of attendants in public carparks have been shown to reassure users and deter thieves (Oc and Tiesdell, 1998). And the employment of uniformed safety officers on public transport has been shown to make an 'important contribution to cutting petty crime' (van Andel, 1989: 55).

However, there is always the possibility that somehow introduced security measures will lead to a negative public reaction, and therefore a negative security dividend. For instance, the widespread use of opaque roll-down security shutters can turn a strip shopping centre into a 'hostile environment and can convey a message that the area is prone to crime' (Beck and Willis, 1995: 206).

And recent research concerning young people in public places noted that

> the *cumulative impact* of adverse interactions with police, security guards or teachers can leave youth with a sense of betrayal by adults and powerless to challenge such behaviour ... it may be that the long-term price of aggressive policing and other *forms of surveillance* is a less cohesive community (Fine *et al.*, 2003: 155, emphasis added).

In turn that could lead to negative attitudes towards CCTV, at least from this section of the public.

When a head of corporate security installs some surveillance at their workplace which does overlook a public area, they would not normally consider the possibility that it would add to the cumulative impact mentioned above. They would be even more unlikely to consider their security approach as possibly contributing to a less cohesive community in the future.

The impact of private security on the community at large is seriously discussed by Zedner (2003) who writes 'whilst security is posited as a public good, its pursuit is inimical to the good society' (Zedner, 2003: 171). This is not the place to deal with that argument but it is obviously important to consider the possibility of deleterious effects on the public from corporate security initiatives. Apart from anything else, not being sensitive to the local community could lead to the corporation losing business.

6 Impact of bad corporate security

The impact of bad security on a corporation can be swift, immediate and telling and can arise in the following three ways.

Direct losses

The direct losses that affect the corporation commence with the financial costs associated with an incident, however even they may not be accurately counted. Consider the burglary of a warehouse on a rainy night. The thieves remove roofing and drive off with stolen products in a corporation truck. Management in many corporations would record the losses from that incident as comprising the cost of the stolen product, the truck and repairs to the roof.

However the costs are considerably more than that, and it is incumbent on corporate security to ensure that management appreciates the full extent of damage to the corporation. The full costs are even more important to report accurately and completely when it is time to consider financial measures relating to corporate security (to be discussed later).

In the above burglary, the losses to the corporation do of course commence with the value of the stock, the truck, and repairing the damages. In addition there is:

- the cost of lost business because (the stolen) stock cannot be provided to customers (who then go elsewhere);
- the value of stock damaged by being left exposed to rain coming through the hole in the roof the burglars left;
- the cost of hiring a truck to enable deliveries to continue;
- the cost of employee and management time spent clearing up, dealing with the police, ordering replacement stock, etc instead of performing their usual duties;
- the cost of buying a new truck and fitting it out in the corporation's livery; and so on.

Over and above the immediate costs resulting from a criminal incident, there are other sources of increased costs. First, there are costs for increased security as invariably management will decide to increase security at the site of the incident (and sometimes adopt recommendations from corporate security's earlier security risk review of the site). And further direct costs may arise when the corporation's insurance premiums are increased after a claim is lodged for the incident.

Indirect losses

The most serious indirect losses occur because of damage to the corporation's image or reputation. Plainly a hotel that is known to be frequented by drug dealers and is the scene of drug overdoses will become unpopular. A hospital which has suffered (even) one infant abduction, or has a record of thefts from patients, will not be the first choice for many patients. A shopping centre which was the scene of an armed robbery where bystanders were shot may well be avoided by many shoppers.

The negative media coverage that such incidents attract can fuel a long-term negative consumer perception of the corporation and its brand. That can lead to considerable public relations costs by the corporation in an effort to overcome poor image problems.

But apart from the public, the corporation's employees can also be gravely affected by incidents occurring as a result of failed security. Stress or trauma-related workers' compensation claims may be made, and morale (thus productivity) may drop. Staff turnover may increase and industrial action may involve strikes or working-to-rule, possibly generating even more damaging publicity. It might also be necessary to offer higher wages in order to attract future employees because of general negative perceptions of the workplace.

Legal action against the corporation

Corporations get involved in more than their fair share of litigation and bad security can add to that burden. Public or premises liability cases are a major source of cost for corporations.[1] While investigations by corporate security identify some of these as fraudulent – slip-and-fall cases in supermarkets are a good example – expensive payouts do occur, often due to a lack of duty of care.

Retailing corporations in particular are fairly frequent recipients of liability writs. Some years ago it was said that 'the moment a retailer invites a customer to park his car and enter their doors, that they are essentially creating entrapment, and are therefore liable in case something happens to that shopper' (Cockerham, 1994: 38).

Today,

> the courts throughout North America have made it clear that property and business owners have a duty to provide appropriate security and safety measures at each site. Because we live in a strong data-centric economic and business environment, demonstrating this due regard almost invariably requires providing credible documentation ... (Dalton, 2003: 580).

Most importantly, that documentation has to show that reasonable measures to keep people safe and secure had been implemented by the defendant corporation.

To ensure that the measures are reasonable, the corporation needs professional advice from its corporate security department. It is not only incumbent on the department to do that, it should be an objective of theirs 'to substantially limit general liability exposure and the associated cost of premises liability litigation' (Figlio, 2002: 57). Figlio suggests that this is the second major objective of a corporate security department after the establishment of a good return on investment for the corporation (an issue to be discussed later).

Even with good security in place some litigants will 'try it on' in the hope that the corporation might fold and settle, rather than run the risk of bad publicity. If the security in place is 'bad' they always stand a chance. That is why it is essential that corporate security provide the very best advice and their operatives always conduct themselves efficiently.

Of course there will always be bizarre liability claims. One was initiated in connection with the rape of an American hospital patient, a 44-year-old woman suffering from cerebral palsy, in hospital for chemotherapy and unable to defend herself. The rapist was sentenced to ten years imprisonment. But he is now suing the hospital for $2 million for its 'inadequate security in protecting visitors as well as their patients', as that caused him pain and suffering.[2]

Liability matters aside, another raft of litigation arises from defective security practices. Most notable are false arrest or false imprisonment cases that result from members of the public being erroneously apprehended for shoplifting. A recent survey of 235 such lawsuits found that 'nearly all the suits were filed for justifiable reasons' (Patrick and Gabbidon, 2004: 49).

Many large judgements have been made to false-arrest plaintiffs who have been inappropriately dealt with, or in some cases have actually died, after what is often appalling behaviour by store security staff. There is not a better example of the necessity for security operatives to be comprehensively trained and to comply with the corporation's security policy and procedures.

A final area of litigation is action for defamation. A recent Australian case involved two contractors who were dismissed for stealing from a corporation which incidentally had listed its 'impeccable reputation' on its website as a key 'value for success'.[3] After dismissing the men, notices had been posted at corporation locations saying they had been dismissed for stealing. The notice also read in part 'theft of any kind is unacceptable, is deemed serious conduct (*sic*) and will result in instant dismissal'. The men had not faced any criminal action. A jury found they had been defamed and they were awarded $500,000.

7 How can corporate security demonstrate its value?

The above sections have given a good indication of the extent of corporate security's activities and outlined why it is important that they engage in good practices. But measuring the corporate security department's actual value to the whole corporation is not straightforward.

Separating out security's impact

In many corporate settings, separating out the impact of security is difficult. As an example consider a factory where the theft of workers' personal property has dropped over the past year. While corporate security had introduced awareness programmes and had new lockers installed for staff, those actions alone may not explain the drop. It may be that new staff rosters had been introduced along with a new time-keeping system which could accurately list workers on-site at any time. Perhaps an employee assistance programme with counselling for drug abuse and gambling had been commenced. And the new factory manager with his habit of walking around the factory daily may have had particular impact. It would have to be said that at best corporate security could claim only some of the credit.

Worse, if workers in that factory had decided to stop reporting personal thefts because they simply did not want to draw more management attention to themselves, the actual number of thefts may not even have dropped. This illustrates how difficult it is to measure the very thing that corporate security is trying to address.

The retail sector provides the best example of being able to measure the effect of security on its operations. Regular six-monthly stocktakes provide a measure of losses the retail corporation has suffered. But as with the above example, corporate security cannot claim all the credit, though invariably they are blamed for any increase in shrinkage that might have occurred.

A further complication arises if security decisions are actually made by others. DiLonardo's (1997) study of the use of electronic article surveillance (EAS) systems in retail stores provides a good example. It shows that reductions in store shrinkage occurred when EAS was introduced and sustained. It also shows the experience in stores where, after shrinkage had reduced, management decided to remove the EAS systems because the shrinkage had been achieved (and they wanted to put the equipment in other stores which now had greater shrinkage). It is an important finding that shrinkage in those stores increased after the EAS equipment was removed, and reduced again when the equipment was re-installed.

That episode also proved that the security measure did work and although the decisions to withdraw it were not made by the security department, at the end of the day the result reflected well on them.

Evaluating corporate security's preventive impact

It is a central tenet of corporate security that many of the security solutions it implements will prevent incidents from occurring. But in broad terms there is a paucity of hard data to support that belief.

Take one of the mainstays of corporate security, the uniformed security operative, found on corporation reception counters or access points worldwide. Dalton wonders

> (w)hat, if any, is the crime prevention value of a uniformed security officer? ... Preventative value has been a long-standing issue, even in law enforcement. From studies that have been done, it would appear that the presence of uniformed personnel has little deterrent value (Dalton, 2003: 284).

This is perhaps a little harsh (see Gill, 2004). Intuitively, some people trying to enter a corporation's offices without authority are going to be unsettled by a uniformed operative who they must pass. Not that in reality that operative is necessarily going to physically attempt to stop them, the mere presence of the operative may cause the potential intruder to leave.

It is interesting that even without firm validation of the impact of uniformed staff, one of the knee-jerk reactions to intruder problems is often for management to insist on more uniformed operatives being deployed.

It may well be that uniformed or private security staff have an even wider impact on the public. One recent study by econometricians found that private security does produce some 'general deterrence impact' on the incidence of crime in the community at large, but statistically only for rape (Benson and Mast, 2001: 741). That research does however caution that obvious uniformed security guards, signs and noticeable video cameras may simply displace some crime, leading to a fall in the local crime statistics.

Mainstream research into crime prevention is not all that more convincing. In one review of 13 physically-based (or situational) crime prevention programmes Welsh and Farrington (1999) found that only eight of them returned clear-cut benefit-cost ratios. That is, the value of such activities as surveillance or target-hardening was able to be demonstrated in some cases. Note however that programmes aimed at employee theft, fraud or shoplifting were excluded from their review because 'the primary victim ... was a business, not a person or household' (Welsh and Farrington, 1999: 346).

Value to government

In discussion of the security dividend it was pointed out that government received a benefit from the presence of corporate security because it could free up police resources for more serious or urgent matters. That would certainly arise when there was a risk of a corporation being subject to some sort of political protest and minimal police resources were necessary to complement private security resources on-site. This demonstrates the value of corporate security in a broader sense.

The complementary nature of the relationship between police and corporate security is also apparent when police take advantage of corporate assets, for instance using a corporation's security cameras to monitor activity on a public street outside their premises.

This relationship between police and corporate security might be expected to flourish in the future because as Sarre and Prenzler (1999) point out 'traditional police (are now) very much secondary players in responding to crime' because security resources in most western countries outnumber traditional police by at least two to one (Sarre and Prenzler, 1999: 17).

8 Funding corporate security

The return on investment (ROI) in corporate security

According to Figlio the first fundamental objective of a loss prevention programme is 'to demonstrate convincingly the return on investment of the organisation's security programs'. (Figlio, 2002: 57) This is achievable when a particular security solution is to be assessed for dealing with a particular problem, even though that may still require acceptance of the sort of assumptions referred to earlier.

As a case in point, PricewaterhouseCoopers established that EAS systems installed in retail stores to lower shrinkage, have a sound ROI. But that was based on acceptance of inventory shortage figures as a sound and reliable measure of in-store thefts (DiLonardo, 2003).

Demonstrating a sound ROI for a total corporate security department with all the activities listed in section 4 is however a real challenge. It also sits awkwardly with the measure of a successful corporate security department – the absence of problems.

Figlio is right however, modern management requires return on investment (ROI) figures or some such to allocate funding within the corporation. Ultimately all departments receive funding on the basis of that sort of financial evaluation, but the corporate security department is at a real disadvantage.

What the department has to do is to somehow convert the previously described security dividend into dollars and then use them in its ROI calculation. Once again that will require acceptance of a number of assumptions.

If those assumptions are not accepted by management, it is well nigh impossible to present a ROI for most of the security department's activities. Consider the access control system which has successfully prevented strangers from entering the corporation's premises. Assumptions would have to be made about the number of intruders there would have been without that access control. And further assumptions would have to be made about what those intruders would have done while they were on corporation premises. Would they have stolen corporation assets or worse, assaulted corporation workers? And what would the value of the losses to the corporation have likely been?

Or what of the fact that no burglaries have occurred on the corporation's premises, surely a clear sign that the security in place was effective. Here at least there may be local police statistics showing the numbers of similar buildings in the neighbourhood have been burgled. However any number of reasons could be put forward to explain why those police figures do not provide a suitable benchmark – those other buildings store different assets, they are unoccupied for longer periods, etc.

And what of the factory burglary previously described? As discussed the total costs associated with it were far greater than the value of the stolen property and the damage done. If the corporate security department had faithfully costed all recent burglaries, how relevant would that data be as a basis for ROI calculations? What if the burglary had occurred on a fine rather than a rainy night?

In all likelihood, the finance department would be reluctant to accept an ROI based on either the police statistics or detailed incident costs calculated by corporate security. So a corporate security head might take refuge in mounting a scare campaign indicating the dire consequences that might follow if sufficient funding is not provided. This move is a double-edged sword insofar as management might see this as a sign of professional inability to protect corporate assets and look for another director.

Even where relevant data is available there may be difficulties using it to calculate an ROI. As described earlier, in retailing, the levels of shrinkage revealed after the six-monthly stocktake provide a metric that reflects the activities of the security (or loss prevention) department. Even here, however, there are any number of internal and external factors that could have impacted upon the losses suffered in a store (the new store layout makes it harder for thieves to get out without payment, local police have clamped down on undesirable activity in the local shopping precinct, etc).

But a greater difficulty is that because the stocktakes are only conducted every six months, the security department is trying to prove the value of having done something six months previously. In the following months other things may have happened to mitigate the impact of the security team.

It is not only the expenditure side of the ROI model where assumptions and predictions need to be made. The corporate security head may have to forecast changing patterns of offending against the corporation which will introduce new costs. For instance, it may be that an increase on attacks on un-reinforced vending machines on railway stations is predicted on the basis of recent target hardening of vending machines in shopping centres.

The assumption that thieves will likely move to the soft targets, and that funds would therefore need to be available to prevent losses from that, makes sense to corporate security. However the finance department may again not be impressed by the lack of hard data.

All is not lost however. The key thing is to make sure the corporation, and particularly its finance department, appreciate the range of activities undertaken by corporate security and appreciate the ways in which it makes sense to calculate benefits. The ROI task is hard but can be achieved with goodwill and understanding.

Outsourcing corporate security

Invariably corporations are looking for ways to reduce the costs of running their business. In particular they look at internal departments – such as corporate security – whose functions could be outsourced because that would be cheaper.

But focusing on the issue of cost while ignoring performance is short-sighted. Security professionals are split on whether outsourced security operatives perform poorly. Dalton dispenses with myths about outsourced security staff, he says 'they come from the same labour pool (as internally employed staff), they can be loyal as loyalty is fostered by trust and acceptance, (and) higher turnover has not been proved' (Dalton, 2003: 81). Nevertheless, if outsourced security staff are actually paid less – and how else can they be cheaper? – they may simply be disinclined or unwilling to do the job well.

In practice it is usually base-grade security services that are outsourced. In their discussion of contract (outsourced) security Button and George (1998) focused on corporations' use of contract static guards. They found that the majority of their small sample of British corporations did outsource guard services, but they also found that over four to five years about 30 percent of the sample had changed their mix of in-house and contract guards over time. This indicates that continuous oversight of the performance – and value – of the contract guards is undertaken.

The major hidden cost of outsourcing lies in the burden of managing the contract relating to those staff. Without close management, the contractor providing the security operatives can get away with providing a lesser service than that set down in the contractual agreement.

The potential risk of a 'bad' incident occurring as a result of that lesser service delivery is a real concern. If litigation were to arise as a result of that incident, the fact that the corporation had tolerated poor or sub-standard service delivery would be particularly damaging.

The inclusion of performance-based payments and punitive clauses in a contract would assist in more rigorously dealing with shortfalls in performance. But that requires close contract management, and there is a direct cost to the corporation in doing that. Indeed the costs of doing so may well be greater than any notional savings from using contract staff rather than in-house staff.

At the end of the day, the decision about using contract security staff is not a simple matter of comparing costs. Hidden costs and risks need to be considered. But more importantly there is a judgement to be made about the sort of security resource that a corporation wants. A dedicated in-house security staff which is professional, well-managed and part of the corporation's culture has an inherent value beyond the apparent cost-savings from using contract labour, however many corporations 'can best be served by an appropriate blend of full- and part-time and in-house and contract security personnel' (Sennewald, 2003: 157).

Re-organization of corporate security

Another model for funding the corporate security department can be found where a corporation has made all of its departments independent but with each charging the others for their services. This shared services model may be good in theory but in practice can lead to fragmentation of the corporate culture.

Consider what might occur in practice. Senior executives from one of the business units in the corporation are going overseas and the corporation security policy requires them to receive a security travel briefing. When they learn that they have to pay (usually less than market) internal fees for this briefing, they decide to forego it because their expenses would increase if they did so.

Now corporate security is faced with a policy breach, as well as their own budget shortfall. The business unit has acted in a way that is not in the best interests of the corporation as a whole. After all if those executives were to come to grief on their trip, the corporation might appear badly in the eyes of the public and would also have to meet any unbudgeted expenses.

Another example of re-organizing corporate security is provided by the 5200 independently owned and operated Ace Hardware stores in the US. That group created a wholly owned subsidiary company to provide loss prevention services to their members – it effectively privatized its corporate security department. 'The nine-person (subsidiary) staff offers Ace retailers a variety of security services on a voluntary fee-for-service basis. The program has succeeded not only in reducing shrinkage but also in generating revenues' (Falk, 1996: 47).

Again, the re-organization occurred to fund the operation of the corporate security department. It appears in the Ace case, member stores were keen to buy security expertise (and may have done so from a private supplier in the absence of their own subsidiary). The risk in a big and formalized corporation is that security will be relegated to nice-to-have rather than the essential service that it is.

9 Corporate security as a contributor to the bottom line

The discussion to date has clearly indicated the many ways in which corporate security adds value to the corporation. Its actual contribution to the financial bottom line are necessarily indirect. For example preventing losses avoids stripping money directly from the bottom line. And providing a secure and safe workplace which reduces staff turnover and minimizes poor (and unproductive) morale, averts unnecessary expenses for the corporation.

However the challenge for corporate security is presenting such contributions in a way that modern management accepts. The difficulty in doing that in a financial framework has been discussed in the context of establishing an ROI for the corporate security department as a whole. And it is from the financial perspective that the notion of corporate security being seen as a profit centre has emerged.

The fundamental feature of a profit centre is that it is capable of generating revenue which exceeds its operating costs. This is not a traditional role of a security department and it would be a mistake to require it, as it could readily divert the department from its important role of preventing other revenue in the corporation from being lost. In any event, actual revenue generators in a corporate security setting are few.

One revenue generator could be the revenue from car-parking violations where it is the corporate security department's task to manage car-parking. Another could be the sale of access control tokens, especially replacement tokens for which a surcharge might apply. In each case the security department would be engaging in an 'unpopular' enforcement-type role and it is plain that the damage that could be done to the standing of corporate security within the corporation could be substantial.

It has been suggested that civil recovery could act as a revenue source, but that is a programme for the corporate victim of an offence to recoup some of the funds they expended in dealing with a particular offender. While most frequently used for shop thieves, civil recovery is also used by some corporations when dealing with internal thefts. While civil recovery procedures can contribute 'revenue' to the organization they should never be used as a means of generating a profit. In any event as Bamfield points out, 'the proper role of private profit in crime prevention and in dealing with offenders is a vexatious issue' (Bamfield, 1998: 263).

In summary then, there are three positions impacting the bottom line that a corporate security department can adopt within a corporation.

- If corporate security remains as a department within the corporation charged with minimizing losses to the corporation as a whole, then it cannot operate as a profit centre. In strict terms it remains a cost centre but as Millwee has pointed out, '(w)hat was once considered by some to be a cost center has become a business benefit center, as the safety and security of our co-workers has redefined the mission of security practitioners all over the world.' (Millwee, 2002: 122).
- If corporate security becomes part of a shared service model, then by selling its services within the organization it becomes a cost-recovery department. It should not be expected to raise revenue over and above its actual costs, from its internal clients. Imagine the internal outcry if in order to increase its revenue stream the department increased the price of ID passes because that was one of the few revenue raising devices it had.
- If corporate security becomes an arms-length supplier of security advice to the corporation it would cease to be part of, or tied to, the corporation. The risk is that business units in the corporation might go elsewhere or decline to use its, or any other, services. The good news is that with the Ace Hardware example described above: 'Originally, the board of directors wanted to break even with the company, but *the service has paid for itself over the past year and surpassed its financial expectations*' (Falk, 1996: 47, emphasis added).

Overall, corporate security must gain recognition for its contribution to the bottom line. It can do that if it can 'convince employees and executives that security matters to them, to the company, and to the community; that it helps to protect the bottom line and, thus, their jobs' (Somerson, 2003: 158).

10 Corporate security moving forward

Embedding security in the corporation

Corporate security in the past has often been seen as somehow separate from the rest of the corporation. In part this may have been caused by the enforcement role the department had. But often their role was unappreciated and their contribution to the fiscal value of the corporation was seen as a negative – a cost.

There is no doubt that 'security professionals have missed important opportunities to make security an integral part of the corporate team' (Millwee, 1999: 118). And it is certainly true that the time is here for corporate security departments to 'break away from what has become the conventional approach to asset protection and seek new venues for value added contributions.' (Dalton, 2003: xxvi).

In some corporations, management are not aware, and do not consider, ways in which security might contribute to the business of the corporation. A fine exception to this is provided by American retailer Wal-Mart whose CEO states that the VP of loss prevention is

> required to sit in on every single management meeting that we have. They are a part of that management group's core decisions that are made about what's right for the business. They have to look at anything that we're doing as the first line of thought from a loss prevention standpoint, because most merchants and operators aren't given to go there first (Lee, 2002: 20).

One example of where corporate security can make a valuable contribution relates to proposals for new business initiatives or new products. Corporate security is able to identify ways in which the new initiative might be compromised and lead to loss for the corporation. That would allow modifications or safeguards to be built into the proposal to prevent those losses from happening in the first place.

Playing that role can sometimes support and give weight to new proposals. For instance when an Australian supermarket corporation was planning to introduce EFTPOS facilities for customers, corporate security was able to point out that increasing the use of 'plastic card' payment at store checkouts would have real security benefits. Customers paying with 'plastic' and being able to make cash withdrawals would reduce the amount of cash in checkout tills thus making them far less attractive targets for snatch thieves. Additionally the need for deliveries of cash to stores by armoured cars would reduce and the likelihood of armed robberies in and around stores would decrease. Both of these were strong points in favour of introduction of EFTPOS not foreseen by store operations.

Corporate security's involvement in mainstream corporate activities is most important. Joining with HR, safety teams and operations groups is part of that. But the key is to become a versatile player.

> (S)ecurity professionals must develop, refine and adopt a broader managerial outlook. They must practice the same managerial competencies required by general managers running their respective businesses.[4]

They must also become thoughtful and clever communicators to ensure that management understands the benefits of security for the corporation.

Can't measure – can't manage

The difficulties of providing hard data that would be accepted by the corporation to justify funding corporate security have been discussed above. But of course having hard data also allows corporate security to make sensible decisions about its own activities. Figlio gives examples of the range of data that a retail loss prevention manager might use to make 'future data-driven decisions truly possible' (Figlio, 2002: 57). He suggests that site-specific data is necessary including neighbourhood crime vulnerability, specific detailed shortage (shrinkage) data and details of security measures and programmes in use at the site.

But not only should hard security-related data be collected where possible, it should not be kept hidden away. Yates suggests that corporations should report on their security performance in their Annual Reports in addition to the commentaries on their social, economic and environmental performance – the commonly referred to triple bottom line. He notes that 'the advantage of integrating security into the triple bottom line reporting approach is that security is seen in the context of the other main business drivers, rather than isolated and unconnected' (Yates, 2003: 106).

Yates also suggests that corporate security needs a suite of measuring devices including security impact statements, minimum security standards and other benchmarks. That would leave the way open for insurance companies to offer discounts off premiums for corporations whose security practices, especially those related to terrorism, meet the standards.

The more corporate security can measure its activities the more it can illustrate its value to the corporation. But more than that, it can use the data it collects to better manage its day-to-day activities and to confirm that its security programmes are efficient and meeting the corporation's needs.

A new corporate security focus

In his appraisal of the security world since 9/11 Dalton asks 'what is a corporation's most valuable asset?' because obviously that should be the focus for corporate security. Somewhat surprisingly he opts not for its employees or its customer base. He suggests:

> that in terms of the survivability of a corporation, the most valued asset is the company's intellectual property, that which positions them in the marketplace and allows them to remain competitive. Employees serve as the catalyst for assuring that this asset – intellectual property – is developed, used and protected. IP ... defines the organisation's ability to stay profitable ... Only with profitability comes the assurance of continuity, which translates into job security ... Employees, including the most senior executives, are replaceable. This does not mean that they are not important, and perhaps even critical ... security's role is not to abandon the protection of people and tangible assets (Dalton, 2003: 72).

That position leads Dalton to suggest a new model for a global security function which would be largely advisory and have the following three pillars:

1 Business Risk analysis comprising: current business risks; new partner product and market due diligence; major fraud investigations; data security investigations; strategic fraud prevention; special request enquiries; competitive intelligence protection; intellectual property protection; e-commerce threat management and geo-political business profiling.
2 Human Resource Security comprising: strategic partner qualification; security awareness and ownership; international HR security; new hire qualifications and orientation; executive protection; workplace violence prevention; ethical business practices.
3 Global Operations support comprising: corporate policy development; security standards and guidelines; uniformed security services; site compliance and quality assurance; systems design and research; special projects management and special events management. (pp. 174–5)

The activities listed under those headings encompass the corporate security of old, but place them in a new perspective which may resonate with modern corporation management. This is an example of weaving corporate security into the corporation culture (Millwee, 1999).

This does not overcome the difficulty of making a financial case for the corporate security department. Nor does it overcome the need to develop metrics of success. However it does clearly indicate the valuable contribution that corporate security makes to the continued business success of any corporation.

Notes
1 See Chapter 6 by Dan Kennedy.
2 'What, me, responsible?' (2002) *The American Enterprise*, July–August, Vol. 13, No. 5, p. 10.
3 'Employees Win $500,000 in Defamation Case' (2003) *The Age*, 21 November, p. 4.
4 'A Discontinuity in the Security Field' (2002) *POA Bulletin*, August, pp. 1–5.

Key readings
For a good security text which canvasses the issues in an uncomplicated way see Kovacich, G.L. and Halibozek, E.P. (2003) *The Manager's Handbook For Corporate Security: Establishing and Managing a Successful Assets Protection Program*, New York: Butterworth-Heinemann. For a good and accessible example of the sort of hard data needed to make a case for security, see Figlio, R. (2002) 'Using Data to Measure the Effectiveness of LP Programs and Limit Your Liability', *LossPrevention*, May–June, pp. 57–8. A more academic piece demonstrating reductions in employee theft has been written by Oliphant, B.J. and Oliphant, G.C. (2001) 'Using a Behavior-Based Method to Identify and Reduce Employee Theft', *International Journal of Retail and Distribution Management*, Vol. 29, No. 10, pp. 442–51. While for a critique of security which should get most practitioners thinking see Zedner, L. (2003) 'Too Much Security', *International Journal of the Sociology of Law*, Vol. 31, No. 3, pp. 155–84.

References
Albrecht, W.S. and Searcy, D. (2001) 'Top 10 Reasons Why Fraud is Increasing in the U.S.', *Strategic Finance*, Vol. 82, No. 11, pp. 58–61.

ASIS International (2003) *General Security Risk Assessment Guideline*, Alexandria Virginia.

Bamfield, J. (1998) 'Retail Civil Recovery: Filling a Deficit in the Criminal Justice System', *International Journal of Risk, Security and Crime Prevention*, Vol. 2, No. 4, pp. 257–67.

Beck, A. and Willis, A. (1995) *Crime and Security: Managing The Risk to Safe Shopping*, Leicester: Perpetuity Press.

Benson, B.L. and Mast, B.D. (2001) 'Privately Produced General Deterrence', *Journal of Law and Economics*, Vol. 44, No. 2(2), pp. 725–46.

Button, M. (2003) 'Private Security and the Policing of Quasi-Public Space', *International Journal of the Sociology of Law*, Vol. 31, No. 3, pp. 227–37.

Button, M. and George, B. (1998) 'Why Some Organisations Prefer Contract to In-House Security Staff', in M. Gill (ed.), *Crime At Work Vol 2*, Leicester: Perpetuity Press, pp. 201–14.

Cockerham, P.W. (1994) 'Safe Shopping', *Stores*, June, pp. 38–9.

Dalton, D.R. (2003) *Rethinking Corporate Security in the Post 9/11 Era*, New York: Butterworth-Heinemann.

DiLonardo, R.L. (1997) 'The Economic Benefit of Electronic Article Surveillance', in R.V. Clarke (ed.), *Situational Crime Prevention*, New York: Harrow and Heston, pp. 122–31.

DiLonardo, R.L. (2003) 'The Economics of EAS: Rethinking Cost Justification for Apparel Retailers', *LossPrevention*, November–December, pp. 20–6.

Falk, J.P. (1996) 'Nailing Down Hardware Store Security', *Security Management*, December, pp. 46–51.

Figlio, R. (2002) 'Using Data to Measure the Effectiveness of LP Programs and Limit Your Liability', *LossPrevention*, May–June, pp. 57–8.

Fine, M., Freudenberg, N., Payne, Y., Perkins, T., Smith, K. and Wanzer, K. (2003) 'Anything Can Happen With Police Around: Urban Youth Evaluate Strategies of Surveillance in Public Places', *Journal of Social Issues*, Vol. 59, No. 1, pp. 141–58.

Gill, M. (2004) *Uniformed Retail Security Officers*, Leicester: Perpetuity Research and Consultancy International.

Halverson, R. (1996) 'Crime Steals Shoppers' Confidence', *Discount Store News*, Vol. 35, No. 9, pp. 70, 72.

Holden, T. and Stafford, J. (1997) *Safe And Secure Town Centres: A Good Practice Guide*, Westminster: Association of Town Centre Management.

Kovacich, G.L. and Halibozek, E.P. (2003) *The Manager's Handbook for Corporate Security: Establishing and Managing a Successful Assets Protection Program*, New York: Butterworth-Heinemann.

Lee, J. (2002) 'The View From The Top', *LossPrevention*, March–April, pp. 17–20, 56–8.

Meyer, S. (2000) 'Employee Turnover: It's Big…It's There', *MMR*, March 20, p. 40.

Millwee, S. (1999) 'How Can Security Get Inside the Door?', *Security Management*, December, pp. 116–18.

Millwee, S. (2002) 'Focus on ASIS', *Security Management*, February, p. 122.

Oc, T. and Tiesdell, S. (1998) 'City Centre Management and Safer City Centres: Approaches in Coventry and Nottingham', *Cities*, Vol. 15, No. 2, pp. 85–103.

Oliphant, B.J. and Oliphant, G.C. (2001) 'Using a Behavior-Based Method to Identify and Reduce Employee Theft', *International Journal of Retail and Distribution Management*, Vol. 29, No. 10, pp. 442–51.

Patrick, P.A. and Gabbidon, S.L. (2004) 'What's True About False Arrests', *Security Management*, October, pp. 49–56.

'Private Security Firms Go Undercover in Your Hospital' (2002) *Healthcare Risk Management*, June, pp. 67–8.

Sarre, R. and Prenzler, T. (1999) 'The Regulation of Private Policing: Reviewing Mechanisms of Accountability', *Crime Prevention and Community Safety*, Vol. 1, No. 1, pp. 17–28.

Sennewald, C.A. (2003) *Effective Security Management 4th edn*, New York: Butterworth-Heinemann.

Somerson, I.S. (2003) 'Are Security Awareness Programs Undervalued?', *Security Management*, August, pp. 175–8.

Taylor, M. (2002) 'Systems Help Hospitals Ensure Patient, Staff Security', *Business Insurance*, December 16, pp. 14–16.

van Andel, H. (1989) 'Crime Prevention That Works: The Case of Public Transport in the Netherlands', *British Journal of Criminology*, Vol. 29, No. 1, pp. 47–56.

Welsh, B.C. and Farrington, D.P. (1999) 'Value for Money? A Review of the Costs and Benefits of Situational Crime Prevention', *British Journal of Criminology*, Vol. 39, No. 3, pp. 345–68.

Williams, F. (2003) 'Sarbanes, Oxley and You', *CSO Magazine*, October, at http://www.csoonline.com/read/100103/counsel.html.

Yates, A. (2003) *Engineering a Safer Australia: Securing Critical Infrastructure and the Built Environment*, Engineers Australia, Barton ACT.

Zedner, L. (2003) 'Too Much Security', *International Journal of the Sociology of Law*, Vol. 31, No. 3, pp. 155–84.

26

Trends in the Development of Security Technology

Clifton Smith

Introduction

The goal of crime reduction is to moderate the inclination for persons to commit crimes in the community and the workplace. However, crime prevention strategies appear to have only a moderate effect on the frequency of crime (e.g. see Chapter 19 by Gill on CCTV), and so there is a need for better ways of protecting assets of the community and workplace. Communities and individuals have used design strategies (e.g. CPTED) and physical security target hardening methods (e.g. defence in depth) to secure and protect their assets. However, as the techniques and devices available to criminal elements become more sophisticated, then law enforcement agencies and security professionals need to have a comprehensive knowledge and understanding of security technology principles and practices. This can be achieved through maintenance of current knowledge of the latest security technology and systems for the protection of assets of an organization.

Physical security is the term used to describe the physical measures designed to safeguard people, to prevent unauthorized access to property, and to the protection of assets against sabotage, damage and theft. The physical security of the organization prevents access to places such as premises, buildings, rooms, vaults, laboratories, and car parks. The security design principles of *Defence in Depth (DiD)* and *Crime Prevention Through Environmental Design (CPTED)* probably represent the two near extremes of a continuum of approaches for the protection of assets (see Chapter 5 by Schneider). However, the principle of *target hardening* through the application of security technology can be applied to most approaches to security design; that is, target hardening can be applied to DiD and CPTED and to intermediary security models. The form of the target hardening can range from strength of materials in barriers in DiD to covert surveillance in CPTED. Examples of target hardening of a security design providing substantial strength to resist access to a facility are:

- Perimeter fences provide a physical barrier against unauthorized access to a facility

- Laminated glass in window frames prevents breaking for entry, or damage through vandalism
- Locking devices on doors and windows provide a measure of access control according to the authorization of keys
- High security containers such as fire proof cabinets and safes have the capacity to protect valuable assets and information against determined attacks

The foundation for the continued development of security technology and its applications for the protection of assets at the national and industrial levels of security will depend upon understanding of the principles and concepts of the technologies. Because security technology has a vital role in a nation's security, economy and growth, then technological advances will depend upon the quality of learning and understanding of security systems and their applications.

This chapter will discuss the relevance of security technology to security principles for the protection of assets, and will emphasize the role of security technology in the management of a security protection strategy. A description of trends in the development and applications of security technology will be presented, and as a consequence provide an understanding of the principles and concepts necessary for effective asset protection. An emphasis on the context of the security is necessary for technology to be applied will be discussed, together with an understanding of the place of technology in security theories. Finally, it is necessary to understand the purpose of security technology when applied in a security management strategy.

The purpose of security technology

In order to achieve a condition of security for a facility or organization, it is necessary to consider the application of the Campbell Triangle (Campbell, 2003) which proposes the components of *planning and design, the security management plan*, and *the security technology* to support the security strategy. It is important to emphasize that the security technology installed within a facility is a function of the security management plan (Purpura, 2002), and in this capacity the security technology supports the management plan. There is no place for reactive decisions to install security systems outside the security management plan, as the plan should be self-sustaining and reactive decisions will inflate the cost of security in a facility.

The assets for protection in an organization are considered to be the *people*, the *information*, and the *property* in and at the facility (Fischer and Green, 2004). The people of an organization are usually considered to be its most valuable asset for both strategic and ethical reasons. Thus the *people* include the management, the employees, delivery personnel, clients in the organization's facility, and visitors to the building. The people are considered as assets to the organization in different and varying ways, with each category having a contribution to the well-being of the organization. A security management plan is an essential component of the asset protection strategy, as it stipulates policies and procedures for the security of an organization (Walsh and Healy, 2004: 19-I-1). The validity of incorporating security technology into the security plan will be a management decision and will depend upon the objectives of the organization. Both the management strategy and the risk model applied to the development of the security management plan incorporate feedback loops in the evaluation phases of the processes. Thus there will be a continuous review of the performance of security technology within the security management plan.

The level of security to be invoked will be determined by the *criticality* and the *vulnerability* of the people, information, and property of the organization. The role of security technology is to support the security management plan of the organization. The interdependence of the three components of the protection of assets strategy with the planning and design phase preceding the development of the security management plan, which is then supported by security technology.

Justification for security technologies

Security technology is applied in a security protection strategy to prevent damage or removal of assets through unauthorized intrusion. However, it should not be assumed that security technology is the key to asset protection, but rather should be considered as a component of the security protection strategy. As effective security consists of the three major components of *security design and planning, security technology*, and *security management*, the function of technology in the security protection strategy is to support the management of the protection of assets (Fischer and Green, 2004; Fay, 2002; McCrie, 2001). Security technology, as a stand-alone component of the security strategy, cannot successfully prevent asset attack, but rather its function is to enhance the management of asset protection. The professional skill of the security manager or security analyst is to achieve the optimum mix of the components of design and planning, technology and management for a particular risk and threat assessment of a facility.

The inclusion of security technology in a security management strategy can be justified in a theoretical context through the application of security asset protection principles to a facility or location. The theoretical principles that are generally applied by professional security managers are:

- Defence in Depth (DiD) (Smith, 2003)
- Crime Prevention Through Environmental Design (CPTED) (Crowe, 2000)

Defence in Depth

The purpose of physical security is to delay a *determined* intruder for sufficient time until a response team arrives to apprehend the trespasser. This delay is best achieved by a series of barriers, rather than a single strong barrier (as we acknowledge that any barrier can be breached given sufficient time and resources). The principle of *Defence in Depth* imposes a succession of barriers, which require access, between the public and asset to be protected. This principle has been developed to gain time for a response from police or other organizations for the protection of a facility, and has been employed for thousands of years.

The physical security afforded by the Defence in Depth strategy is achieved through the security functions of: *deterrence, delay, detection*, and *response*. (Smith and Robinson, 1999; Walsh and Healy, 2004: 19-I-4). The classes of barriers that provide these functions are:

- Psychological barriers such as signs, security lighting, and low fences on boundaries provide deterrence at a location.
- Physical barriers such as fences and walls, shutters, locks of all descriptions, and safes and security cabinets through strength of materials provide a delay function for penetration (Walsh and Healy, 2004: 3-I-2; Berger, 1999).
- Electronic barriers detect the presence of intruders in restricted areas and include: optical and infrared beams, CCTV, volumetric detection systems such as passive infrared and microwave systems, linear detection systems such as microphonic cable and laser infrared beams, and point detection systems such as break glass and magnetic reed detectors.
- Procedural barriers in security management through procedures can place barriers to impede the progress of an intruder into a facility. Such procedures can include key management systems, static and mobile guards, and identification badges.

The number of layers of barriers in a defence in depth strategy for the protection of an asset will be determined by the perceived level of threat, the criticality of the asset, and the value of the asset. Thus the selection of appropriate barriers for the defence in depth strategy will depend upon the assets to be protected and the strategic importance of the facility (Walsh and Healy, 2004: 19-I-5). The application of security technology as barriers in layers of protection is an essential component in the protection of assets according to the defence in depth principle. The selection of appropriate technology will be determined by the *criticality, consequence*, and *likelihood* of an attack on the facility under protection (Walsh and Healy, 2004: 3-I-2).

Crime Prevention Through Environmental Design

Architects and urban planners use design and space management concepts to manipulate human behaviour. The strategy of *Crime Prevention Through Environmental Design (CPTED)* has been described by Crowe:

> the proper design and effective use of the built environment can lead to a reduction in the fear of crime and the incidence of crime, and to an improvement in the quality of life. (Crowe, 2000; Fennelly, 1997)

The CPTED crime prevention strategy involves the three overlaying strategies of natural access control, natural surveillance, and territorial reinforcement as approaches to reduce crime in a locality (Walsh and Healy, 2004: 19-VIII-3; also see Chapter 5 by Schneider).

The emphasis of design in CPTED differs from the traditional target hardening method used in a defence in depth situation. Target hardening is aimed at denying or limiting access to a potential crime target through the application of artificial or physical barriers. The traditional approach has tended to overlook the opportunities available for natural access control and natural surveillance. However, alternately CPTED has been developed to apply pure target hardening tactics where the application will support the effective use of the environment.

Although the design and planning components of CPTED are crucial and essential, the introduction of technology to target hardening has the effect of resisting determined intruders who are resilient to the principles of CPTED. Thus security technology can enhance the CPTED strategy natural access control, natural surveillance and territoriality.

Function of security technology

Security technology is a component of a security strategy for the protection of assets. Hence the function of security technology in an access control function is to detect the presence or activities of people who provide the threat to the assets of an organization. Without the presence or activities of people, there is no security problem (however safety and environmental problems may exist). The security associated with access control is concerned with the authorization, identification, and detection of people in situations that may present a threat to the organization. Then the purpose of security technology is to operationalize the security management plan of the organization, by detecting the presence or activities of people either from within the organization or as an external threat to the organization. The level of risk presented by the threat will determine the level of sophistication of the technology to protect the assets.

Some instances of detection by appropriate technology of the presence and activities of people will include:

- Identification for authorization through verification of the credentials of an authorized person
- The detection of trespassers in a restricted area in an art gallery when persons move too close to works of art
- The detection of intruders into a high security area, whether authorized or unauthorized
- Environmental conditions in an intelligent building by sensing the number of people in zones in the building and controlling these environmental conditions
- Duress signals from distressed persons such as prison guards in a threatening situation
- Access control monitoring to know which persons have passed a control point
- Authorized person in a *control* situation such as a registered driver in control of a vehicle

The ability of security technology to detect the presence of unauthorized people in a facility will significantly reduce the risk to the assets of the organization. Conversely, if the establishment is aware of the occupancy by a person at a location and the identity of the person in that location through access control technology, then an enhanced reduction in crime and an improvement in safety will result.

However, the actions of people have also a detrimental effect on security threat to an organization. That is, people may be authorized to be present in a location but are not authorized to engage in particular activities. These actions may breach security policy and protocol. Thus it is necessary for the security of an organization to detect the activities of persons which may be adverse to the interests of the organization and the assets of the facility.

Actions of people that threaten the security of organizations or even nations through unlawful activities could include:

- Importing prohibited drugs by smuggling through airports
- The abuse of information by computer hacking and information theft
- Industrial espionage through communications eavesdropping and data interceptions
- The theft of assets of an organization with commodity shrinkage through retail crime

Because the activities of people are a major threat to the assets and safety of an organization, the detection of these actions is an important barrier in a defence in depth strategy. Effective access control of actions by authorized people is necessary to control breaches of security protocols and policies and will reduce the potential risk to corporations and community groups.

Principles of detection

The security management plan of an organization determines the extent and application of security technology in the protection of assets in a facility. However, as the application of crime becomes more highly developed so is the necessity for increased sophistication of technology to support the security management plan. It is the security management plan of the organization that protects the assets of its community, and the function of the security technology is to support this plan through the enhancement of its barriers of defence.

If the purpose of security technology is to detect the presence and activities of people, then the detection methods must be devised to respond to these stimuli. The development of appropriate sensors to detect the presence of people and the range of activities of people is a prolific applied scientific endeavour in security science. A schematic approach to the development of security technology for the detection of people and their actions requires the following components:

- A *signal* must be produced from the person, either from their presence or their actions. The signal could be reflected light from the person being captured by a CCD camera to enable identification of the person. Also, infrared radiation emitted through body heat could be detected by a passive infrared (PIR) detector device. Similarly, the signal could be produced by movement caused by a person touching a microphonic cable on a fence. Alternatively, the detection of molecular vapour from a package of drugs in a suitcase characterizes a signal for detection.

- A *sensor* is the component in a security detection system that responds to the presence of the emitted signal. As a consequence, the sensor is usually capable of detecting the source that produced the signal in the security context. The application of the sensor, and hence the detector, is in accordance with the security management plan so that rings of defence of the DiD strategy are not breached. There is a wide range of sensors in security technology systems for the detection of people and their activities. These sensors range from *break glass* detectors that are microphones tuned to the frequencies of breaking glass, through to X-ray detectors for the presence of explosives in cargo. Other examples of detectors with sensors include CCD chips in cameras to detect low levels of light, and the disturbances in magnetic fields caused by the presence of ferromagnetic metals.

- Usually the signal produced has low amplitude, so that an *amplifier* is used to increase the effect of the signal when compared to the noise in the system. The signal-to-noise ratio (SNR) is increased by the amplifier in order to detect a change in the signal with the presence of a person or the activity of a person. The amplifier increases the sensitivity of the security technology to detect small changes in signal strength, and so is able to sense subtle effects of intrusion within the sensing domain. Depending upon the type and style of sensor used in the security technology, the amplifier will possess functions to increase the signal strength. Light intensifiers will use opto-electronic solid state amplifiers, and fibre optic cable could use laser amplification. However, most sensors convert the input signal to electrical energy, so that the amplification of the signal in the sensor output most often employs relatively standard electronic amplifier technology.

- The function of the *analyser* is to determine whether a signal has been detected, or not! Often the signal, even after amplification, is still weak so that it must be detected above background noise in the electronic system. Logic and comparison circuits are engaged to determine if a genuine signal has been received. An improvement in the signal-to-noise ratio (SNR) translates to a lower false alarm rate (FAR) and hence a higher probability of detection (Pd). Discriminant analysis is often included in the circuitry to determine if the immediate signal is any different to the previous signal sample. Current development in analysers incorporates *intelligence* into the system to enable better discrimination between active signals and background noise. Intelligent circuitry can also improve the validity of the detection. This circuitry will decide whether the detection from a signal is a *wanted* or *unwanted* incident. That is, the discrimination of signals against predetermined criteria will accept or reject the signal.

- The purpose of the *alarm* in the security technology detection system is to indicate that an anomalous incident has been detected. The alarm signifies the detection of a signal from an unauthorized presence or action, and indicates that a response is necessary to investigate the phenomena. The authenticity of the alarm condition must be confirmed, so that the intruders can be apprehended if they had caused the alarm to function. The response may take the form of a mobile patrol team, or an armed response force, or the local police force. However, the initial response may be intensive surveillance through CCTV cameras in the locality of the triggered alarm condition.

The issue of *unwanted alarms* is still with us, as security technology systems respond to spurious signals generated by sources other than actual intruders or unwanted actions. However, a marked improvement is evident over the past few years, with both reliability and validity of the systems being enhanced. Here the reliability of the system is the continued alarm condition from repeated identical instances where signals have been generated from unauthorized presence or activities. This situation may be illustrated by the instance of the same corrupted magnetic card failing to open the door in an access control system. The validity of the system is the detection and alarm condition from an authentic attempt to breach the security of a facility. The discrimination between an actual attack on the security technology and a spurious signal from the environment or other natural causes will determine the level of validation of the system. A trend in security system design is the incorporation of further intelligence into the discrimination function to reduce unwanted alarms.

Hierarchy of intrusion detection systems

Security technology for the detection of intrusion can be applied to perimeters on fences and walls, on open ground or sterile zones, buried beneath the ground surface, inside buildings on doorways, on walls, in rooms and under floors. Garcia (2001) indicates that the ideal intrusion protection boundary is a sphere enclosing the asset to be protected. The function of intrusion detection systems is to detect the presence of unauthorized persons or vehicles, usually in locations that may pose a threat to the organization (Garcia, 2001). Because intrusion detection technology is based on a sensor detecting a signal, there are strengths and weaknesses of performance for all types and forms of detection systems. The *standard*, or well-developed, security detection technologies continue to be modified to increase sensitivity and reduce false detection rates in order to improve performance (Honey, 2000). These standard intrusion detection systems can be categorized as single or many-dimensional in function (Cumming, 1992).

Point detectors

One-dimensional detectors in a security technology system are *point* detectors that operate at a particular location such as access control usually to respond to unauthorized entry. Some examples of point detectors are reed switches that are located on doors to detect opening, and pressure pads beneath surfaces to detect the removal of a work of art.

Linear detectors

Security technology systems that can detect signals from a linear detection structure will include the group of sensors applied to monitor fences, walls, and doorways. These detectors include visible and infrared laser beams such as *tripwires*, microphonic cables mounted on fences, optic fibre cables on fences and under surfaces, E-field systems on fences, and leaky cable detectors buried underground.

Area detectors

The application of detection systems that monitor a horizontal or vertical area in two-dimensions will detect the intrusion of unauthorized persons into the detection field. Examples of these area detectors will include vibration detectors on walls, break glass detectors on windows, and motion detection systems. These detectors provide a two-dimensional detection field of signals from disturbances on the surfaces.

Volumetric detectors

Volumetric detectors monitor the presence or movement of individuals either in an exterior environment or within the confines of a building or facility. These three-dimensional detection systems have the facility to detect movement through the Doppler Effect, attenuation of a beam, or receiving a signal from the presence of the intruder. Again, some examples of volumetric detection systems include microwave, ultrasonic, active infrared detection, and passive infrared detection systems. The limits or boundaries of exterior application of volumetric detection systems will be determined by the strength of the signal generated, and the sensitivity of the receiving element in the system. Interior limits are placed on the extent of the radiating field by the physical surfaces in the building such as walls, panels and doors. However, some radiating fields penetrate the boundary surfaces and cause unwanted alarms.

Trends in detection systems

The security industry is currently experiencing a massive transformation as many of the traditional analogue technologies that have been applied to the protection of assets, are replaced by the digital innovation. The conversion of analogue signalling from sensors to digital outputs allows comprehensive signal processing with the quantum step in level of intelligence that can be incorporated in the system. This transformation has set the scene for future major improvements in quality of processing of signals from sensors, providing levels of intelligence in the capacity of system to discriminate intruder from an unwanted alarm condition.

All modes and types of security systems have and will benefit from fundamental improvements in the applications of physics and engineering on the detection of objects, the transmission of signals, and processing of the signals for an anomalous output. These security systems include internal and external intrusion detection systems, access control systems, integrated systems, smart buildings and information security systems. The improvement in quality and performance of security systems is increasing exponentially (Smith, 2004) with exceptional performance currently delivered by a selection of systems (Cano, 2004). This chapter will discuss the foreseeable trends for a selection of security systems being applied to the protection of assets. Indicative of trends that can be expected, the types of systems to be discussed will be CCTV, security imaging, intrusion detection systems, and biometrics within the domain of access control (Rolf and Cullity, 1997).

Intelligent CCTV

Over the past decade, the Closed Circuit Television (CCTV) industry has changed dramatically, particularly with the availability of enhanced equipment and features (Kreugle, 1995; Damjanovski, 2000; Garcia, 2001; Coretta, 1999; see also Chapter 19 by Gill) The enhancement of CCTV systems has contributed to a relative decline in equipment prices, and provided an increased and more effective service component, and hence a demand for value in CCTV systems (Matchett, 2003; Murphy, 1999). The development of enhanced CCTV systems through automation and intelligence has converted these systems into powerful and responsive management tools. There is a trend for CCTV to be further integrated with other surveillance and access control technologies to provide an effective multi-functional security system (Pierce, 2002). The integration of CCTV images and computer processing is developing a powerful tool for the detection of intruders (STAN Insight, 2000; Walsh and Healy, 2004: 38-III-17).

This trend in computer vision technology is revolutionizing the concepts, applications, and products in video surveillance and CCTV (Lipton and Heartwell, 2002). This approach to intelligent vision technology is highly relevant to large outdoor facilities such as airfields, refineries, power plants, and industrial facilities. These types of facilities generally require constant surveillance due to the strategic nature of their functions, and so the capacity of computer vision technology to maintain valid surveillance of the locality appeals to cost structure of the organization.

A form of intelligent CCTV is the video motion detection (VMD) application that uses a camera system as a means of intruder detection. The earliest intruder image processing algorithms employed frame differencing, where the previous frame is compared with the current frame, is a technique that still forms the cornerstone of many of the current sophisticated surveillance systems. The technique requires stored sample frames from the camera input which are compared to subsequent frames of the camera to identify changes in picture detail. Some problems that occur with this approach in VMD are:

- No concept of image understanding, with all pixels in the image having equal importance

- No exploitation of domain knowledge, with no ability to take advantage of the image information in the comparison of frames
- No knowledge of the target and its movement as only a difference in image structure is detected
- Susceptible to camera movement and weather effects, as these can be interpreted as motion in the field of view of the scene

However, a VMD system has the capability of presenting several detection zones simultaneously on screen. A change in one or more of these zones can activate an alarm and cause the system to commence recording. Although VMD is more suitable to indoor applications as changes in light, shadows or small moving objects in the internal application, as the exterior applications have a tendency to cause false alarms (Cieszynski, 2001). However, exterior applications have been developed to minimize the negative features of VMD by filtering out unwanted alarm conditions (Meyer *et al.*, 1998).

The Advanced Exterior Sensor (AES) system (Ashby and Pritchard, 2004) integrates the three sensor technologies of thermal infrared imaging, visible light imaging, and microwave radar in a system that scans a full rotation in about a second. Surveillance of wide areas is possible from the three sensors, with images from the infrared and visible detectors and the radar range data being upgraded each rotation. The range information has a resolution of about a metre, and the panoramic imagery is examined for change. This system has the capacity to be applied at airport runways, oil refineries and gas facilities, and other infrastructure locations where large open areas are present.

Multiple video camera surveillance systems are applied to monitor an environment using the perceptual functions of a human observer, through detection and identification of objects moving within the field of view of the cameras. As there is a limit to the perceptions of human observers, the application of automated systems require the development of image processing and computer vision to detect, locate, and track a target as it moves through the field of view (Ellis, 2002). Multiple cameras can be applied in several ways to the surveillance of the locality by:

- Spatially adjacent cameras extend the coverage of the surveillance
- Overlapping views provide redundancy of the images, so as to minimize the ambiguities of occlusion, and maximize the accuracy of position determination

Tracking objects that appear simultaneously as images in two or more cameras can be used to minimize the effects of occlusion (unlikely to occur in both views at the same time). A mapping function relates the location of a pixel in one view with the same pixel in the view from the other camera. This pixel mapping function is called homography (Ellis, 2002) and can be determined by locating a minimum of four equivalent points in two views. However, the points must lie in the same plane, but this condition is often satisfied for surveillance systems in constructed environments, where tracked objects will share a common ground plane.

The trend to develop specialized video surveillance tools has seen a range of approaches being applied to the detection of people. A single or multi-camera system has the capacity to detect, identify, classify, and track objects moving through a surveillance field. Particularly, the system has the capacity to detect people travelling the wrong way in crowded environments, such as airport security exits. The intelligence in the system has the ability to distinguish between potentially threatening activities and environmental events such as trees blowing in the wind, waves on the shore, water reflections, and tidal movements.

Another approach in intelligent CCTV has been developed in the domain of detection systems represented by the AMETHYST (AutoMatic Event auTHentication sYSTem) system (Thiel, 1999; Horner *et al.*, 2000). This approach is a trend to automate the guarding function in secure facilities through the application of intelligent CCTV. The AMETHYST system differs from VMD through the intelligence applied monitoring of camera channels for alarm conditions. The VMD system continues to monitor every channel connected to each camera all of the time that it is active. Thus the VMD would alarm if there were suspicious movement detected by any of the cameras. Possible detection would include movement of shadows, animals, and lighting glare ensuring a high unwanted (false) alarm rate.

However AMETHYST has the capacity to assess the status of an alarm generated by an external intrusion detection system (for example optic fibre cable, microphonic cable, microwave, leaky cable, and active infrared). AMETHYST analyses the images from just before, and at the time of alarming, from an existing intrusion detection system. The cameras of AMETHYST are all active all of the time, but the system only considers images from the *active* or *near active* cameras according to the location of the alarm. Because the system is camera specific by targeting individual alarms, it allows a more sophisticated analysis of the images in the location of the alarm. While VMD will partially compensate for camera shake or lighting variations by adjusting the sensitivity, AMETHYST can correct for these changes before the images are analysed.

The trend of CCTV towards a management information system (MIS) is in progress, where CCTV is considered as a multi-purpose tool in the management of an organization. (Brooks and Smith, 2002; Norris and Armstrong, 1999a, 1999b). These applications of intelligent CCTV include:

- real time surveillance of objects and persons in the field of view
- multiple tracking features including the detection of movement against the normal flow of movement
- dormant systems that activate on detection of the presence of a threat
- radio links for detection systems allows remote area monitoring with intelligent CCTV

Intelligent imaging

Intelligent CCTV with charged couple device (CCD) cameras has the capability to detect in the infrared region of the electromagnetic spectrum. An advantage of multi-spectral imaging in near or short-wave infrared wavelengths is an ability to detect camouflaged targets. The reflectivity from camouflaged surfaces in infrared radiation produces images very different from those produced by visible light. Because the purpose of camouflage is to disguise or confuse the image in visible light, IR images will not suffer this disadvantage as does visible radiation.

This trend towards multi-spectral imaging will produce a wider spectral detection range as solid state detection continues to progress. The technique of analysis of infrared reflectivity will also produce information on chemical and structural properties of materials to assist the identification of objects in the field of view. However, where most CCD camera measurements and data are logged against time, it is also possible to log these data against changes in status. Measurements associated with a physical process can be described in the time domain (quantity s as a function of time t, that is $s(t)$). However, the measurements can also be described in the frequency domain by the amplitudes and phases of component frequencies of the time domain measurements. Measuring data in the frequency domain is the equivalent of obtaining multi-spectral data from the same image. Thus if the image processing was adapted from the time domain to the frequency domain, a wider selection of image information will become available for systems that can scan over the wavelength spectrum.

The application of near infrared spectroscopy (NIRS) to security issues and problems has been enhanced by the development of solid state surfaces in CCD cameras that are sensitive to these spectral ranges. The identification and detection of objects and persons by using near infrared radiation are included in applications such as:

- The identification of materials such as plastics and polymers in order to disclose counterfeit objects. These materials are included in ID cards, bank cards, drivers licenses, credit cards, and some currencies (Toriumi *et al.*, 1997).
- The authentication of wood and paper in forensic testing of specimens from crime scenes, and antique objects that may be forgeries
- Again, the NIRS forensic examination of textiles will identify the fibre and colour characteristics of the material
- The analyses of images with camouflaged targets can exploit the property of the reflectivity of infrared radiation from materials as it is drastically different from the images in visible light (Norton *et al.*, 1997). The detection of illicit crops secreted in natural undergrowth can be achieved with NIRS technology (Smith and Ballard, 1999)
- The forensic application of NIRS to human tissue to identify skin pigment, hair and hair follicles, skull thickness, and scar tissue is being developed

The trend towards the analysis of reflectance radiation from the surfaces of objects indicates the potential for NIRS as an enhancement to security imaging for surveillance, detection, identification, and observation.

Barrier and open ground detection systems

Fences and walls as barriers and open ground detection systems generally have sensors that respond to movement, vibration, or intrusion into magnetic and electrical fields. These sensor systems can include:

- Microphonic sensor cable: mounted on fences and vertical surfaces to sense the movement of the fabric of the fence
- Optical fibre cable: mounted on fences to detect movement through attenuation of the beam strength through flexing of the cable. Similarly, can be buried beneath the ground to detect the presence of an intruder's weight on the cable to change its shape or configuration
- Leaky cable: buried co-axial cable with some of the shielding removed to produce a field that extends above the surface of the ground. The presence of an intruder into this field will distort the field and register an alarm condition
- Seismic detection: a string of geophones consisting of conducting coils and permanent magnets can be mounted on surfaces or buried under the ground. The geophones are very sensitive to movement or vibration, and have the capacity to detect the presence of intruders through disturbance.

The movement and vibration sensor detection systems detect intrusion by converting mechanical vibrations caused by intruder related activities to electrical signals. These signals are processed by the intelligence of the system, and classified as hostile by producing an alarm, or benign from a non-threatening source. The proper functioning of the sensor relies on its placement on the barrier or structure so that a strong mechanical link is made between the sensor and the barrier.

Trends in movement and vibration detection systems are towards universality of mechanical coupling between the sensors and the fabric of the surface (Macalindin, 2001), so that the detection system will bond to all forms of materials. Also, the application of considerable intelligence into the analysis component of the system to filter unwanted signals producing false alarms (Backx and Harman, 2002; Maki *et al.*, 2002).

The biometric-smart card interface

Smart cards have at last begun to gain acceptance by the community, and as such will have a direct impact on applications to security and safety. More than 2.03 billion smart cards were shipped in 2003 according to a report from industry analyst Frost and Sullivan. They indicate that enterprise security accounts for most of the growth, with most interest from Europe, Asia, Latin America, and South America. Although banks and shared card applications is a significant area of growth, there will be considerable demand for government ID applications such as passports and drivers licenses (Dreifus and Monk, 1998).

The weakness in smart card authentication is the absence of a link from the person presenting the card to the true owner of the card. The traditional and readily accepted techniques for linking the person to the card (Walsh and Healy, 2004: 8-I-2) are by:

- Photograph identification
- Personal identification number (PIN)
- Password

However, none of these methods truly identifies the cardholder as the authorized owner of the information stored on the card. Systems are being developed that link-authorized user of the smart card to the card and its contents through the registration of a biometric signature stored on the card. The debate whether it is better to store the biometric signature on a database addressed by the card reader (comparing one to many), or to store the signature on the smart card itself (comparing one to one) has been concluded. The strong weight of evidence falls in favour of the storage of the biometric identification signature on the smart card provides the most rapid response for access control and most effective security of the biometric signature (Most, 2002; Sanchez-Reillo, 2000).

The application of access control to a barrier whether it is a doorway, a computer network, or a bank account provides a means of ensuring that only authorized persons or users can pass the barrier (Konicek and Little, 1997). The traditional approach to access control is through tokens such as keys and tickets, and knowledge such as PINs and passwords. However the application of biometric signatures, such as fingerprint, iris, face and hand geometry have the potential to uniquely identify persons for access through a barrier (Walsh and Healy, 2004: 8-II-10). The biometric characteristic is the *true* identifier of a person as it is linked by a one-to-one correspondence with a particular individual. That is, the biometric feature is unique to that person.

The two classes of biometric characteristics are those of *physical* (physiological) characteristics and *behavioural* characteristics (Smith *et al.*, 1993). Examples of physiological characteristics include facial features, vein patterns in the retina, the personal characteristics of body odour, and fingerprints; while examples of behavioural characteristics include voice analysis, signature dynamics, movement gaits, and keyboard typing rhythms (Van Renesse, 1998).

The biometric signature produced by the individual can be compared to a library for biometric signatures seeking a match. This correspondence of identifying biometric signatures is the signal for recognition of an authorized user. The one-to-many matching process can cause delays in the identification of an authorized user and is the primary cause of errors in access control. The false acceptance rate (FAR) is a measure of unauthorized access; hence the imposer factor. While the false rejection rate (FRR) is a measure of rejection of authorized persons; hence the insult factor (Hendrey, 1997).

The biometric feature to be used as an identifier must be easily measured without undue inconvenience to the person seeking access (Hendrey, 1997). That is, detection at a distance is preferable where non-intrusive measurement of the biometric feature is performed. The measurement of the biometric feature must be immutable, with no change in the measured feature according to the perspective of the image.

Some technologies that have been developed and gained market acceptability include voice patterns, retina scans, signature dynamics, iris recognition, key-stroke dynamics, and signature recognition. Other physical characteristics that have been investigated as potential biometric identifiers include hand palm (Diaz *et al.*, 2004), hand topograghy (Vuori and Smith, 1997), facial recognition (Pretzel, 2004; Espinosa-Duro *et al.*, 2004), 3-D facial recognition (Russ *et al.*, 2004), and handwriting (Deng *et al.*, 2003).

The one-to-one match of biometric signature on a smart card or the one-to-many match of a biometric signature to a library of ID signatures has still to be resolved, but the trend seems to indicate that biometrics and smart cards still have some distance to travel.

For higher security applications, the trend towards multiple identifiers is increasing with two biometric signatures, or a biometric signature and a pass-word, or a biometric signature and a PIN being required for access to a facility or computer. Multiple identifiers considerably reduce the FAR for the access control system, and assist to ensure that only authorized persons are granted access to the facility.

Conclusion

This chapter has presented the case for the application of security technology within the domain of the security management plan and the asset protection strategy. The security benefits from technology are not endorsed outside a thor-oughly planned security strategy. As a consequence, the application of security technology to protect the assets of an organization must be supported by security theories and principles in order to justify this approach. The security theories of *defence in depth* and *crime prevention through environmental design* both support the application of security technology within the contexts of the principles of the protection of assets.

An understanding of the schematic structure of security technology is needed in order to comprehend the trends in developments of security systems. Quantum advances in components of security systems can provide a marked advance in the capacity of a system to detect, recognize and identify objects in restricted areas. The concepts associated with intelligent security systems continue to be advanced with important *breakthroughs* at regular intervals.

The trends in security technology can be considered across the spectrum of security devices using a wide range of physical principles at the detecting compo-nent in the sensors. This chapter has considered trends in the CCTV and intelli-gent imaging technologies as these represent a major component of the current and future security industry. Also, considerable advances in perimeter protection has recently occurred with further improvements expected in the future. The impact of terrorism on the protection of people, information, and property has necessitated the protection of perimeter boundaries of local and national infrastructure facilities. Smarter perimeter protection will reduce the risk associated with the threat of terrorism. Finally, access control through biometric identification being associated with smart cards has the potential to both enhance and simplify access for authorized persons to facilities and computing systems. The trends for comprehensive access control with reliable and valid protocols have captured the imagination of the security community.

Key readings

A definitive discussion of CPTED and its applications is presented in the landmark reference by Crowe, T.D. (2000) *Crime Prevention Through Environmental Design 2nd edn*, Boston: Butterworth-Heinemann. A generalist view of security and its technology is introduced in the standard reference Fischer, R.J. and Green, G. (2004) *Introduction to Security 7th edn*, Elsevier Boston: Butterworth-Heinemann. However, a most comprehensive review of security technologies and applications is presented in a theoretical model to justify inclusion by Garcia, M.L. (2001) *The Design and Evaluation of Physical Protection Systems*, Boston: Butterworth-Heinemann. An excellent reference edited by Van Renesse, R.L. (1998) *Optical Document Security 2nd edn*, Delft, The Netherlands: Artech House, pp. 451–79 addresses the technical issues associated with biometric identification. The remainder of the reference provides comprehensive discussions on optical and photometric applications of document security. Finally, Walsh, T.J. and Healy, R.J. (2004) *Protection of Assets: Vols. 1–5*, Santa Monica, CA: Merritt Publishing is recognized as the *bible* for applications of security in physical security. Its currency is maintained through the insertion and removal of materials into the five volumes of the reference to reflect current security philosophies and approaches.

References

Ashby, R. and Pritchard, D.A. (2004) Seeing Beyond the Perimeter: The Advanced Exterior Sensor (AES), proceedings of the IEEE 38th Annual 2004 International Carnahan Conference on Security Technology, pp. 182–8.

Backx, A.J. and Harman, R.K. (2002) Intrepid Micropoint System – European Fence Experience, proceedings of the IEEE 36th Annual 2002 International Carnahan Conference on Security Technology, pp. 80–6.

Berger, D. (1999) *Industrial Security 2nd edn*, Stoneham, MA: Butterworth-Heinemann.

Brooks, D.J. and Smith, C.L. (2002) 'Public Street Surveillance: A Psychometric Study on the Perceived Social Risk', in W. Hutchinson (ed.) 3rd Australian Information Warfare and Security Conference 2002 Proceedings, pp. 29–42.

Campbell, K. (2003) Security Concepts for Gated Communities and Residential Towers, Paper presented at the INTERSEC 2003 Conference, World Trade Centre, Dubai, January, 2003.

Cano, L.A. (2004) Smart Sensor Integration into Security Networks, proceedings of the IEEE 38th Annual 2004 International Carnahan Conference on Security Technology, pp. 82–4.

Cieszynski, J. (2001) *Closed Circuit Television*, London: Newnes.

Coretta, P. (1999) 'A Review of CCTV Evaluations: Crime Reduction Effects and Attitudes Towards Its Use', in K. Painter and N. Tilley (eds), Surveillance of Public Space: CCTV, Street Lighting and Crime Prevention, *Crime prevention Studies*, Vol. 10, pp. 157–78.

Crowe, T.D. (2000) *Crime Prevention Through Environmental Design 2nd edn*, Boston: Butterworth-Heinemann.

Cumming, N. (1992) *Security: A Guide to Security System Design, Equipment Selection, and Installation*, Newton, MA: Butterworth-Heinemann.

Damjanovski, V. (2000) *CCTV 3rd edn*, Boston: Butterworth-Heinemann.

Deng, P.S., Jaw, L.J., Wang, J.H. and Tung, C.T. (2003) Trace Copy Forgery for Handwritten Signature Verification, proceedings of the IEEE 37th Annual 2003 International Carnahan Conference on Security Technology, pp. 450–5.

Diaz, M.R, Travieso, C.M., Alonso, J.B. and Ferrer, M.A. (2004) Biometric System Based on the Feature of Human Hand, proceedings of the IEEE 38th Annual 2004 International Carnahan Conference on Security Technology, pp. 136–9.

Dreifus, H. and Monk, J.T. (1998) *Smart Cards a Guide to Building and Managing Smart Card Applications*, Boston: Butterworth-Heinemann.

Ellis, T. (2002) Multi-Camera Video Surveillance, proceedings of the IEEE 36th Annual 2002 International Carnahan Conference on Security Technology, pp. 228–33.

Espinosa-Duro, V., Faundez-Zanuy, M. and Ortega, J.A. (2004) Face Detection from a Video Camera Image Sequence, proceedings of the IEEE 38th Annual 2004 International Carnahan Conference on Security Technology, pp. 318–20.

Fay, J.J. (2002) *Contemporary Security Management*, Boston: Butterworth-Heinemann.

Fennelly, L.J. (1977) (ed.) *Effective Physical Security 2nd edn*, Newton: Butterworth-Heinemann.

Fischer, R.J. and Green, G. (2004) *Introduction to Security 7th edn*, Elsevier Boston: Butterworth-Heinemann.

Garcia, M.L. (2001) *The Design and Evaluation of Physical Protection Systems*, Boston: Butterworth-Heinemann.

Hendrey, M. (1997) *Smart Card Security and Applications*, Norwood: Artech House.

Honey, G. (2000) *Electronic Access Control*, Boston: Butterworth-Heinemann.

Horner, M., Leach, G. and O'Dwyer, T. (2000) AMETHYST: Automatic Alarm Assessment Operational Experience, proceedings of the IEEE 34th Annual 2000 International Carnahan Conference on Security Technology, pp. 107–12.

Konicek, J. and Little, K. (1997) *Security, ID Systems and Locks: The Book on Access Control*, Boston: Butterworth-Heinemann.

Kreugle, H. (1995) *CCTV Surveillance*, Boston: Butterworth-Heinemann.

Lipton, A.L. and Heartwell, C.H. (2002) Critical Asset Protection, Perimeter Monitoring, and Threat Detection using Automated Video Surveillance, proceedings of the IEEE 36th Annual 2002 International Carnahan Conference on Security Technology, p. 87.

Macalindin, I. (2001) Advantages of a Low Impedance Linear Magnetic Microphonic Sensor Cable, proceedings of the IEEE 35th Annual 2001 International Carnahan Conference on Security Technology, pp. 307–11.

Maki, M., Nieh, R. and Dickie, M. (2002) Field Testing of Outdoor Intrusion Detection Sensors, proceedings of the 36th Annual 2002 International Carnahan Conference on Security Technology, pp. 171–8.

Matchett, A.R. (2003) *CCTV for Security Professionals*, Boston: Butterworth-Heinemann.

McCrie, R.D. (2001) *Security Operations Management*, Boston: Butterworth-Heinemann.

Meyer, M., Hotter, M. and Ohmacht, T. (1998) New Options in Video Surveillance Applications using Multiple Views of a Scene, proceedings of the IEEE 32nd Annual 1998 International Carnahan Conference on Security Technology, pp. 216–19.

Most, M. (2002) 'Smart Cards and Biometrics: Technology Integration', DigitalIDWorld, www.digitalidworld.com

Murphy, T. (1999) 'The Admissibility of CCTV Evidence in Criminal Proceedings', *International Review of Law, Computers & Technology*, Vol. 13, No. 3.

Norris, C. and Armstrong, G. (1999a) *The Maximum Surveillance Society: The Rise of CCTV*, Berg: Oxford.

Norris, C. and Armstrong, G. (1999b) 'CCTV and the Social Structuring of Surveillance', in K. Painter and N. Tilley (eds) Surveillance of Public Space: CCTV, Street Lighting and Crime Prevention, *Crime prevention studies*, Vol. 10, pp. 157–78, New York: Criminal Justice Press.

Norton, M., Kindsfather, R. and Dixon, R. (1997) 'Short-wave Imagery Applications for Fun and Profit', *SPIE*, Vol. 2933, pp. 9–31.

Pierce, C. (2002) *The Professional's Guide to CCTV*, Boston: Butterworth-Heinemann.

Pretzel, A. (2004) Using Biometric Facial Recognition for Verification and Identification, proceedings of the IEEE 38th Annual 2004 International Carnahan Conference on Security Technology, pp. 309–17.

Purpura, P. (2002) *Security and Loss Prevention 4th edn*, Boston: Butterworth-Heinemann.

Rolf, M. and Cullity, J. (1997) in L.J. Fennelly (ed.) *Effective Physical Security*, Newton, MA: Butterworth-Heinemann.

Russ, T.D., Koch, M.W. and Little, C.Q. (2004) 3D Facial Recognition: A Quantitative Analysis, proceedings of the IEEE 38th Annual 2004 International Carnahan Conference on Security Technology, pp. 338–44.

Sanchez-Reillo, R. (2000) Securing Information and Operations in a Smart Card through Biometrics, proceedings of the IEEE 34th Annual 2000 International Carnahan Conference on Security Technology, pp. 52–5.

Smith, C.L. (2003) Understanding Concepts in the *Defence in Depth* Strategy, proceedings of the IEEE 37th Annual 2003 International Carnahan Conference on Security Technology, pp. 8–16.

Smith, C.L. (2004) The Development of a Security Systems Research and Test Laboratory at a University, proceedings of the IEEE 38th Annual 2004 International Carnahan Conference on Security Technology, pp. 111–15.

Smith, C.L., Cross, J.M. and Mehnert, A.J. (1993) Thermographic Imaging: Infrared Sensors for Positive Identification, proceedings of *Sensors: Theory, Development and Applications* Conference, Arab School of Science and Technology, Damascus, Syria, November.

Smith, C.L. and Robinson, M. (1999) The Understanding of Security Technology and its Applications, proceedings of the IEEE 33rd Annual 1999 International Carnahan Conference on Security Technology, pp. 26–37.

Smith, J.A. and Ballard, J.R. Jr (1999) 'Effect of Spatial Resolution on the Thermal and Near-infrared Sensing of Canopies', *Optical Engineering*, Vol. 38, No. 8, pp. 1413–23.

STAN Insight (2000) The Complete CCTV Program on CD-ROM, produced by STAN Insight, Inc.

Thiel, G. (1999) Automatic CCTV Surveillance – Towards the Virtual Guard, proceedings of the IEEE 33rd Annual 1999 International Carnahan Conference on Security Technology, pp. 42–8.

Toriumi, A., Herrmann, J.M. and Kawata, S. (1997) 'Nondestructive Readout of a Three-dimensional Photochromatic Optical Memory with a Near-infrared Differential Phase-contrast Microscope', *Optics letters*, Vol. 22, No. 8, pp. 555–7.

Van Renesse, R.L. (1998) *Optical Document Security 2nd edn*, Delft, The Netherlands: Artech House.

Vuori, T.A. and Smith, C.L. (1997) 'Three Dimensional Imaging System with Structured Lighting and Practical Constraints', *Journal of Electronic Imaging*, Vol. 6, No. 1, pp. 140–4.

Walsh, T.J. and Healy, R.J. (2004) *Protection of Assets: Vols. 1–5*, Santa Monica, CA: Merritt Publishing.

27
Theorizing About Security

Giovanni Manunta and Roberto Manunta

Were he still alive, the inarguable Chevalier de La Palice[1] would probably recommend that the first and essential step for addressing a security problem is deciding whether the problem at hand is indeed one of security.

The point is not as trite as it might seem, as it highlights the fundamental truth that problems of different nature have different premises and goals, different criteria of choice among options, which require consistent methods of analysis. Having decided we have a problem, the initial question of any problem-solving exercise should always be: what kind of problem are we *really* in?

Answering the question postulates the existence of a criterion for distinguishing *security* problems from others, i.e. an agreed definition of security. However, political, academic, public debates, and operations, are daily proof that security, as risk, means 'different things to different people and different things in different contexts' (The Royal Society, 1992: 7). Alas, many confuse means with ends, and equate security with deterrence, threat of mutual destruction, retaliation, war-readiness and restriction (Clutterbuck, 1993; Dougherty and Pfaltzgraff, 1980; Kitson, 1971; Mc Inness, 1992; Der Derian, 1992; Buzan *et al.*, 1998). Others argue that such a vision of security is a source of insecurity, hence the need for 'securing security' (Dillon, 1996).

What emerges is a confusion of concepts between safety and security, and a difference between approaches based on the physical sciences and those based on the social sciences. This cultural dispute has repercussions both on methodology and the basic definitions as, for example, those of hazard, threat and risk. This disagreement is longstanding. In 1983 the Royal Society, discussing safety, recognized that:

> One problem which the Study Group was faced with concerned the difference between technical or scientific use of terms such as risk, hazard, risk assessment and risk management and the colloquial use of these terms. The Study Group found difficulty in agreeing a common set of definitions to be used by each sub-group. (The Royal Society, 1983: 22)

In 1992, the Royal Society was still forced to acknowledge that:

> In the course of the study, it has become clear that these [terms] have limitations, but serve the purposes of the group of scientists and engineers concerned with putting numbers on risk (The Royal Society, 1992: 2)

Providing a decision has been made that the problem at hand is indeed one of 'security', then it becomes essential to decide upon its treatment. In security, analysis is often done by borrowing methods from other contexts (as, for example, military studies, insurance, engineering, criminal justice and management), without having first structured the problem and appreciated where, when and how should these tools be applied. Explanation involves unambiguous definitions and clarification of the methodology of analysis used for justifying decisions and actions. In order to address a security problem with a fair degree of confidence, and be able to explain our conclusions, we need to assess *where* we are and *what* we want to achieve, and appreciate *why*. Then we need to decide upon *how* to achieve the desired goal via a well defined set of intermediate objectives. *Having done this*, we need to understand which methods are best for our purposes, and make a reasoned decision about their utilization (SME, 1987). These fundamental steps of clarification are unavoidable in organizations, or in a court of justice, where the attribution of responsibilities, blame and liability is essential (Manunta, 2000a).

Justification is bound to be difficult. The condition of security is a dynamic equilibrium of opposing wills, desires, fears and actions. It follows a pattern of evolution and, by relying heavily on perception (of dangers, risks, threats, intentions ...), it is open to destabilization. Imaginative and reactive antagonists learning from errors, studying their targets and looking for gaps and opportunities to be created and exploited render even successful security decisions and operations rapidly obsolete (Manunta, 1997).

Difficult does not mean impossible. This contribution aims to assist students and professionals by offering a theoretical and methodological frame of reference, upon which reliable analysis can be based. It offers a formal definition of security, which identifies the components of a security context and describes its basic processes, and a framework of methodology, by which the formal definition is best applied to the verification, analysis, and explanation of possible security contexts.

The theory

The Socratic problem 'What is security?' is underestimated and under-researched. Different answers are given, which are often of value at the tactical and specific level. There is general agreement and a surfeit of information on the physical and formal aspects of security. Standards, technical details and codes of practice are easily available. Systems, procedures, planning, training and methodologies are covered in great detail by many sources. None of them appears to address and formalize the general concept of security.

This is not easy. The quest for security, as a condition, is both a need and a philosophical idea. As a need, the concept is linked to the daily struggle for life, and consequently depends on mental factors, such as awareness, will, determination and morale. As a philosophical idea, security is a desire for peace and tranquillity, the ideal condition for the achievement and preservation of freedom, wealth, peace of mind, and self-improvement. In contrast with the quantitative approaches derived by insurance and statistics, all seems to suggest that security is a complex, not fully quantifiable topic, but one dependent upon the integration of both its physical and psychological aspects. Maslow's hierarchy of needs comes immediately to mind.

The physical aspects are easily understood and learned; there is abundant reference to them in both literature and practice. These involve physical defences, such as fences, doors and safes, electronic alarms, access controls and closed circuit television (CCTV). By contrast, the psychological aspects appear to be relatively neglected in security literature. Most authors tend to surrender unconditionally to existing studies of risk perception, psychological insecurity, offender's motivation and victim's behaviour, and to avoid interpretation and systematization into an organic security-focused body of knowledge. Yet, all physical measures are conceived, planned, implemented and managed by humans, whose reasoning and behaviour is influenced by emotional, cultural and cognitive factors. Evidence proves that security decisions and actions are not exclusively rational, but are affected by human choices, beliefs, desires, fears, and constraints.

Physical and psychological aspects cannot be seen separately. Suppose we apply the prescribed standards, procedures and methods to the best technology in accord to our best practice. Can we *ipso facto* consider ourselves secure? The bitter evidence is that the mere implementation of the physical and formal aspects of security does not guarantee security. It might even increase insecurity (for example by attracting unwanted attention, infringing civil rights, suggesting treachery or bribery, increasing the level of conflict). Of these malign effects, we have many examples. In the absence of a clear definition of what 'security' is, and what it is for, we cannot explain the reasons of what we are doing, we are unsure of the causes of what we are achieving, and we cannot say that what we have done has achieved its goal (Manunta, 1996).

A definition of security

The current concept of security is so wide-ranging to be impracticable. It ranges from *philosophical* security as an ultimate goal (absence and freedom of worry and danger) to *operational* security, a precarious condition characterized by different approaches, different scopes, and different goals (e.g. logical security, physical security, personal security, industrial security, national security). A discussion on philosophical security would only divert this contribution from its practical objectives to the unsolved issues of certainty, free-will and determinism. Instead, the focus is here on finding criteria for the attribution of responsibility, liability, blame, and preparing a conceptual framework for the measurement of performance.

To reach the goal, the definition of security must be unambiguous. Defining a concept involves the identification of its essence, i.e. the consistent set of its defining properties, judged to be a necessary and sufficient condition to understand its meaning and to separate it from other similar concepts (A Dictionary of Philosophy, 1983: 86). To do this, let us start from its most general description. Dictionaries define security as *'freedom or protection from danger or worry'* and attribute the origin of the term to the Latin *'sine cura'*, that is: 'absence of care and worry' (Andrews, 1875: 1380).

The concept of security based on the clear-cut definition of 'absence of danger and worry' (a desirable, but exceptional condition in nature) is graphically represented in the following Figure 27.1: taking the whole of the Universe (U) and the whole of Security (S), then the Universe can be divided into two fields: security (S) and non-security (No-S):

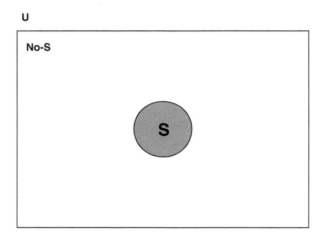

Figure 27.1   The ideal states of nature

In the diagram, the definition of security is represented by the boundary separating the two *ideal* states of affairs: the *perfect* state of security and the *perfect* state of non-security. Such definition is clearly insufficient for real life investigation. No 'perfect state of affairs' exists in nature, and security activities are not concerned with these, since in perfect security (S) there is no reason for 'freedom or protection', and in perfect non-security (N-S) there is no utility in trying to achieve this impossible result.

In real life, the concepts of security and that of non-security are not neatly separated, but coexist in a 'grey' area, which is the normal state of nature (Adams, 1995; Beck, 1992; Bueno, 2004).

This concept is explained in Figure 27.2 by adding to Figure 27.1 a second set (?S), here defined as 'insecurity', which has a lower limit, including what is certainly 'security' (S) and an upper limit, excluding what is certainly 'non-security' (N-S). In (?S), the characteristics of (S) and (No-S) coexist, in proportion dependent on nature, chance, and on the efficacy of the security activities. The grey area of instability, or 'indeterminacy', is, we submit, the domain of *operational* security. Here the activities aimed at transforming, and maintaining, the largest possible area of insecurity (?S) into a state of *practical* (vs. *philosophical*) security (P-S) have both sense and utility.

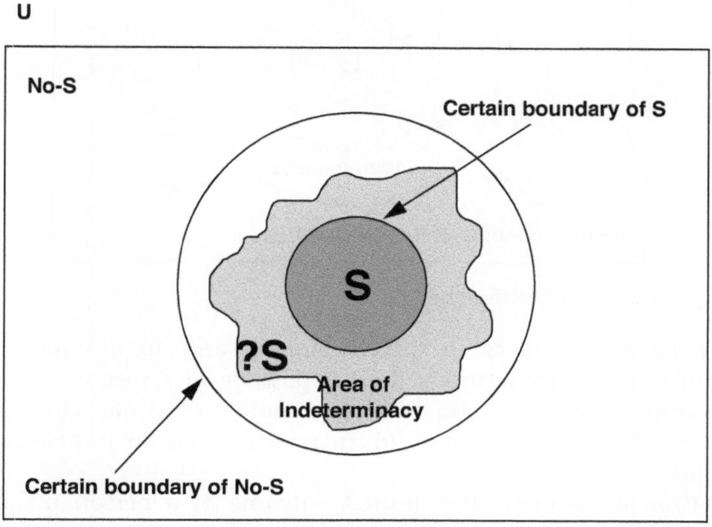

Figure 27.2   The existing states of affairs

Life is evolutionary and changing. The varying limit of the grey area of 'indeterminacy' cannot be exactly defined, with the processes going on with life. However, by the principle of approximation, the area can be arbitrarily subdivided into two sets, one (?S) where insecurity is dominant; the other (P-S) where nature, chance and specific activities (when they occur) maintain a prevalent state of security. This concept is represented in Figure 27.3.

The set (?S) has been subdivided into two areas, whose limit represents the momentary balance of the opposing forces. We are interested in the area of practical security, or (P-S), which includes the activities aimed to ensure '*freedom or protection from worry and danger*'. The extent of this area depends partly on nature and chance and mostly on a range of 'protective' measures aimed to oppose causes, or sources, of non-security.

Security as an activity welcomes the natural condition, or the accidental product of chance, but is a product of human rationality. Judicial, managerial and operational necessities relating to justification, performance and responsibility, require the limit of (P-S) to be identified, defined, and assessed.

The limit can be drawn in a number of ways. For instance, by studying and assessing the relative capabilities of the defensive and offensive forces aiming at achieving S or N-S, and implementing a security programme based upon a given

U

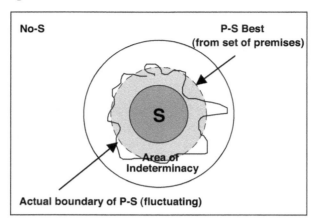

Figure 27.3   The area of indeterminacy

ratio of opposite capabilities, in a given moment and circumstance. Successful programmes show that setting a limit is possible in a specific case (e.g. in a bank's strong room), but also that this limit is dynamic. Obsolescence of defences, change of threats, time and circumstances dictate its assessment to be continuous.

This vision of security, the desired outcome of a person made process, assumes the existence of a conscious will capable of achieving it according to a rationale. Both will and rationale have limits. Operational security is a forced, and costly, response to someone else's initiative, related to a given set of assets and threats, perceived or assumed as real. Its rationale is biased by a significant degree of uncertainty, since decisions are based on incomplete information and subject to often unknown, nor controllable, adversary reactions. The achievement of security is within the limits of opposite human perceptions, wills, needs, interests, capabilities and intentions. Their balance, being the product of dynamic antagonism, is unstable (Clausewitz, 1832; Szafransky, 1997).

The identification of the basic actors of a security process comes as a consequence of previous reasoning. They are: the originator of the process, who fears an undesired event and acts to avoid it (Protector), and the entity that is considered capable of causing it (Threat).[2] Their existence and opposition is explained in security terms by the presence of an object of dispute (Asset). All three components are essential. The mere existence of an asset does not constitute a security situation. Neither protector nor threat can exist without an asset. The existence of a protector without the perception of a threat has no sense, and its activities cannot be defined as 'security'. The mere presence of a threat will not start a security process unless it is perceived by, and dealt with, a protector, with relation to an asset.

We can therefore say that the fundamental components of any security process are a Protector, an Asset, and a Threat to that Asset. These three basic components are to be understood as *functional* components, i.e. they may not be *physically* distinguishable. For example, the Asset and Protector may be one and the same. In this case, typical of personal security, the motivation to protect is, or should be, maximized. Similarly, *per absurdum*, Threat and Asset may coincide, as in the case of a suicide, who is a threat to himself. It may also be that the Threat and the Protector coincide.[3] It is therefore essential to distinguish the concept and function of each component from its physical manifestation.[4]

Intention, rationality and action are a *sine qua non* to operational security. A fully intentional security process does not arise until the proprietor of an asset has both *perceived* a source of damage to a given asset, and *acted* upon her perception after *weighing* some pro and contra, thus becoming a *rational* and *active* protector. The need, the will and the decision to proceed into a security context is presumably commensurate to the amount of 'perceived unacceptable damage', and to the credibility of the threat, to an asset considered worthy of the protection efforts.

The process leading an individual to move from the state of 'insecurity' and initiate security activities is seen here as being made of three separate stages. These stages are: the perception of the evidence of the possible existence of a threat (a noise, a shadow, …), the cognition that this evidence may indeed represent a threat, and the decision of acting upon this cognition. This decision marks the moment of entering the security context. It is submitted that only an *active* protector can provide security. In this vision, the *sine qua non* of protective action draws the demarcation line that separates security from risk management concepts, where the concept of risk-taking is accepted. Accordingly, one cannot deliberately accept an assessed risk to an asset without renouncing, at the same time, to his function of Protector. In the absence of protective decision and action, the context is the rich pageantry of life, not security.

Verifying the security context

It has been submitted that the presence of three basic elements (A, P, T) is the necessary and sufficient condition for a security context to be identified as such. Their presence identifies the 'essence' of security and provides a workable criterion of demarcation from other activities. A security context is the state of affairs to which this condition applies.

The verification of this state of affairs is considered the '*sine qua non*' of any security analysis. Consequently, the process of explanation derives from the analysis, within the security context, of the constituent actors (A, P, T), their interaction, the resultant processes, and relative output. Indeed, the existence of the three components in isolation is not a sufficient condition to establish a security context. This requires that they be interrelated.

Presence and interaction are the 'necessary and sufficient' condition for a full security context to exist. All three elements are present and interlinked, as required by the formal definition of security. This state of affairs is therefore used as the criterion of demarcation of 'security' from 'non-security'.

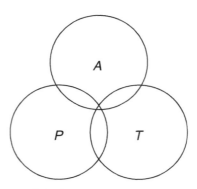

Figure 27.4   A, P and T are interlinked

It is important to note that security contexts are dynamic. Consequently, Figure 27.4 can be seen as a momentary representation of a security context in action. The Protector and the Threat are readjusting continuously to each other, centred on the Asset. It is now possible, using the diagram, to discuss different possibilities of interaction between the three components.

The basic model at work

The mere presence of interaction among all three actors (A, P, T) only means that a security context is present, as some ongoing processes amongst actors. Further analysis shows that Figure 27.4 represents a security problem, which has still to be solved.

In Figure 27.5 A, P and T are interacting with each other, but there is no area common to all three elements. Each of these areas offers a general representation of the intervening dynamics, which may be defined according to the focus of analysis (i.e. centred on A, or P, or T). For example, an interpretation may be the following. The area common to P and A can be taken to represent the **protection of A by P**. This area is *p* (protection). The area common to T and A represents the **extent to which A is vulnerable to T**. Vulnerable does not necessarily mean damaged. It only means that T is in a position to damage A, to an extent represented by the area of vulnerability, *v*. The area common to P and T represents all the activities of **P to prevent T** from attacking the asset, and **the responses of P** against attack or action by T. It includes all direct or indirect actions of P with regards to T. This area is *p/r*. (prevention/response). Similarly, if the analysis is focused on A, the area *v* may be interpreted as the area of damage, and (if the focus is on T) the area *p/r* may be considered to represent the activities of T against P.

The analysis follows keeping the original focus on P. A first observation indicates that the three areas do not overlap. This means that the Protector has perceived a Threat to his/her Asset, and is taking action (*p/r*). Yet, P has not understood T completely, as the lack of interaction between *p* and *v* clearly shows. In fact, P has made a wrong vulnerability analysis, and is protecting A in

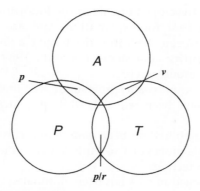

Figure 27.5   Preliminary analysis of the model

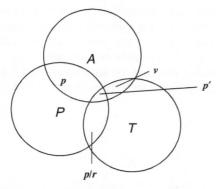

Figure 27.6   An adjustment of the security programme

those aspects (*p*) that are not, actually, under real threat (*v*). Moreover, P has not responded to the real vulnerability where T is/may attack A (*v*). It follows that the diagram represents an impending, unresolved, security problem.

Thus, this diagram helps to understand how the three elements interact, and assists identification of the problem. From this preliminary analysis, it is possible to formulate (or readdress) an appropriate correct security programme, designed to eliminate **v** and to increase **p/r** (p/r is at a maximum when T is neutralized via a counterattack). Analysis of this diagram clarifies understanding of the strategy behind the security programme. This will depend upon the aims of the Protector. These should derive from clear and definite choices in matters of security policy and management. This reasoning will be further analysed. Continuing the analysis, a number of cases might apply.

In Figure 27.6, P is more aware of the vulnerabilities of A with regards to T, and has adjusted its programme. The area **p'** represents the protection intended to reduce the perceived vulnerability. Yet, the way the diagram is drawn, implies that P still has to improve, because at this point, much of its efforts are nugatory. More, the protection has not been able to fully eliminate the vulnerabilities.

The concept can be developed further as the following examples show. They only aim to offer a tool for explanation, and are therefore incomplete. Different shapes have been used, in order to give a graphical explanation of different possible security approaches (Orlandi, 1989) and strategies (more focused assessments, resources, etc ...).

P has now definitely improved its programme. The ineffective protection measures and activities have been reduced, while *p'* and *p/r* have increased. See Figure 27.7.

In Figure 27.8 vulnerability has been eliminated. The Protector has been able to cover all the possible moves of T towards A, while minimizing the redundant and the ineffectual protection.

All unnecessary protection of A has been eliminated in Figure 27.9. All of P's actions are aimed at T or A. In this example, the area of P outside the process is intended. It represents a reserve, or additional P related to other A or T. This case illustrates a thoughtful and successful security programme, in which the resources are used to eliminate the vulnerabilities through full protection, while dedicating a part of the efforts to preventive and responsive activities, and to respond to foreseeable possible threats, not yet perceived.

Figure 27.10 illustrates the case in which security has priority over costs. The Protector values the Asset so highly that it decides to cover all possible

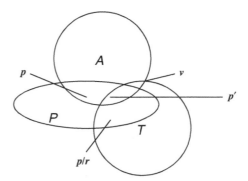

Figure 27.7   Ineffective protection has been reduced

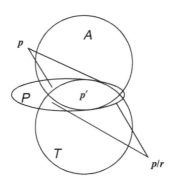

Figure 27.8   Vulnerability has been eliminated

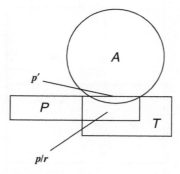

Figure 27.9   Maximum protection efficiency

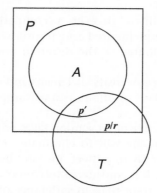

Figure 27.10   A probabilistic – competitive approach

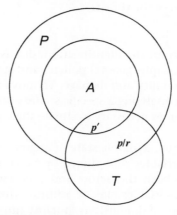

Figure 27.11   The organizational approach

vulnerabilities against all possible Threats. At the same time, efforts of prevention and response are directed against those Threats already identified and
considered more dangerous. The distribution of protection goes all around the
Asset, but in different strengths in different directions of Threat. This may be

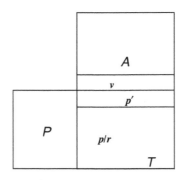

Figure 27.12   Deciding for prevention

an example of a 'probabilistic' or even a 'competitive' approach; different levels of protection are implemented and accord with the different probabilities (or capabilities) attributed to the different perceived Threats (Orlandi, 1989).

In Figure 27.11, the Protector treats all Threats and vulnerability as indifferent (equally possible). This state of affairs is an example of the 'organizational' approach (Orlandi, 1989).

In Figure 27.12, the objective of prevention takes priority over protection. Such decision might stem from the will to eliminate or to deter the Threat. The Protector has decided not only to protect the Asset but also, and particularly, to neutralize the Threat, which is considered too important to remain active. This goal is considered so important that, in sufferance of resources, the decision is made to leave the Asset unprotected at **(v)** and dedicate maximum resources to the certain neutralization of the threat.

From theory to practice

The A, P, T model allows for the identification, discussion, and explanation of basic concepts as, for example, general policies and strategies, prevention, protection, reaction, vulnerability and damage. To move from the conceptual to a practical level (e.g. when analysing a specific security process, or planning a security programme), it becomes necessary to situate the concepts in their particular circumstance.

Each context is a unique, dynamic state of affairs, characterized by a specific set of parameters and variables, and altered by a change in any of its variables. These factors influence both the actors and processes within *that* particular context. The number of variables may be infinite, with them deriving from the combination of a number of dimensions, notably time, psychological, political and administrative (Manunta, 1997). Only an assessment of the 'here and now' condition provides the cardinal parameters (identification, analysis and assessment of a specific case) to specify the operational reasoning. These are, for example: nature and setting of the asset, resources, defences around that asset, technology and *modi operandi*, but also local and global environment, laws, habits, culture, political, social, psychological, organizational, managerial and economic conditions.

At the operational level, the analysis of these situational factors should be as much detailed as necessary, since a minimum change of any of them can make the difference between protection and loss. At the general level of reasoning, a systemic rather than an analytic approach is more appropriate, as not the single value of each variable is relevant, but their total effect on the basic model. Hence, their influence on the actors and their relationships is here considered under the general term 'Situation', and discussed as the resulting balance of all of its factors.

It is on these premises that the following formal definition of security is based, and from the definition both the theory and the methodology follow.

$$S = f (A, P, T) \ Si$$

Operational security (from now on, Security) is a function of the presence and interaction of (at least) an Asset (A), a Protector (P) and a Threat (T) within their particular Situation (Si). This framework of reference provides a logical structure in which existing theories and analytical methodologies can easily be accommodated.

The way the formal definition is expressed indicates that (Si) is viewed as a 'factor of efficiency', not as a primary cause of a security process. It affects the actors' perception, cognition, decisions, and operations within the security process without producing it. (Si) is not an actor within the process, but a characterizing factor of influence on the basic actors.

Considerations

As the above diagrams and formal definition show, in order to understand the complexity of the context and its processes, the analysis should identify and evaluate all components (i.e. A, P, T), all relations between them, and relate each finding to the Situation, in order to understand possible influence.

Previous reasoning suggests that all relationships and dynamics are centred on the *perceived value* of the Asset, and characterized by a degree of antagonism between Protector and Threat with regards to that Asset. This view allows us to make the following considerations.

The driving forces behind security initiatives are the perception of a danger and/or the fear of damage, loss and/or injury. The condition of security is the result of rational activity aiming to avoid damages, losses and injuries. Daily evidence shows that the level of activities relates to the level of perception and fear. Two common assumptions at the basis of the concept and activities of security have been identified. The first is a need, which has been loosely described as: *'there is someone or something to be taken care of, because someone has the intention of, or is acting to, stealing, spying, damaging, or destroying it'*. The second is the pragmatic appreciation of the impossibility of eluding the task: *'I must personally perform this activity, because I will suffer the loss or damage, and nobody else (not even the State) will undertake it'*. Both assumptions link the decision of protecting to the will to protect and to a rationale.

The state or condition of security is a product of antagonism. Choice of the word 'antagonism' is deliberate. The more general term 'conflict' would include conflict with nature and chance. Such conflicts do not fall into the same framework of rationality as conflicts between opposite wills, thus are not considered in this research. Hence the use of the more specific term 'antagonism' for explaining a conflict between (at least) two human wills, the first seeking *'freedom or protection from worry or danger'*, the second being the cause of *'worry and danger'*.

These premises highlight three criteria, or limits, which contribute to a qualitative definition of the essential features of security processes, notably focus, self-interest and antagonism.

The criterion of <u>focus</u> is clear (i.e. avoiding, or protecting from, damage, loss, injury), and helps to understand the limits of security activities. Security conflicts are not intended to conquer or destroy, but to preserve. They are risk-adverse and thus a decision may be changed, or an activity interrupted, if a greatest risk arises from the conflict. However, this criterion alone does not assist a better definition of that area of fuzziness, which includes damages originating in accidental and intentional events. Their distinction is important to the attribution of responsibility and measurement of performance, and is offered via the criteria of self-interest and antagonism.

Self-interest. Security-related activities are aimed at protecting one's own interests, as long as these interests exists and are thought, or perceived, to be threatened. This criterion, which derives from basic survival instincts, leads to considerations of self-preservation, self-interest and risk-aversion, and has a number of consequences.

First, *security practitioners dedicate a large part of their efforts to avoidance and deterrence*. As long as possible, flight is preferred to fight. This preference separates security from risk-prone approaches (e.g. financial, entrepreneurial, and military). Accepting a significant risk (in the sense of possible damage deriving from a foreseen adverse event) is deemed to be a last resort and a danger to be avoided or diverted.

Second, *the owner of the asset only considers his/her own interests*. Security is egoistic in that it seeks to safeguard the holder's assets by using protective measures which may (and are often intended to) encourage the antagonist to direct his attention elsewhere. In the choice of security measures, deterrence intentionally exploits displacement.

Third, *security measures are conceived not on a 'defend to the last', but on a 'defend as long as justified' principle*. The principle of justification, which derives from the assumption of rationality, is largely influenced by the principle of self-utility, and contrasts with the 'crusader's approach' of security in modern international relations theories (e.g. peace-making and peace-keeping) and opens problems of ethics, scope and measurement.

Finally, *security considerations of self-interest, needs and expectations are affected by fear and worry and may be imposed from outside*. Apart from reducing losses, security measures can be taken to reduce fear, to ensure peace of mind, to comply with laws and regulations, to respond to a threat, to address political and social pressures, to detect, delay, deter, stop a potential antagonist, to appease the media, to improve control, to assert power or a status symbol. All of these reasons may conflict, and overwhelm, pure financial considerations, and challenge the application of the current 'risk management' paradigm to a number of security problems.

The criterion of <u>antagonism</u> (within the limits imposed by focus and self-interest) draws a clear demarcation between accidental and intentional events, thus brings a decisive contribution to the distinction between Safety and Security. A 'conflict' that originates from, and is conducted by, an antagonist is different, both in terms of processes and predictability, from a 'conflict' that originates in accident, or chance. When the antagonist is thoughtful, motivated by a purpose and reactive (or pro-active), the conflict originates in a choice, is driven by a will, motivated by fear and gain and supported by a rationale. The antagonist learns from the adversary's conduct, and adapts his course of actions to suit his interests according to the circumstances, and creates new opportunities and vulnerabilities when he cannot exploit the existing ones. Chess (a very simple game with a limited number of variables and rules, compared with security), with its almost infinite variety of contingency moves, depending on the activities of only one antagonist within limited dimensions in space and time, underlines the difference. The criterion of antagonism helps distinction and focuses analytical methodology on intelligence and strategy rather than statistics and determinism. Security analytical methodology <u>must</u> be different from that used in safety.

Besides these general considerations, there are some down to earth considerations to be done. Evidence and professional experience suggest that worry, interest, and antagonism play a major part in the processes, but also responsibility, degree of autonomy, initiative, liability, availability of resources (including information and access to key decision makers) and quality of management, to name a few. Relations are influenced by the value, visibility, accessibility, and vulnerabilities of the Asset, and depend on the comparison between each set of typical properties of each actor, as, for example, motivation, intention, capability, and determination, all of them influenced by their specific situational factors.

Apart from these situational, cultural and cognitive factors, actors are affected in their motivation, intention, capability and determination by the temporal phases (before, during, and after the given event), and the pressure caused by the event itself (Balloni and Viano, 1989; Holmes, 1985). An extreme example is the difference in intensity and impact of the relationship between Protector and Threat before, during, and after a physical confrontation, which might involve life and limb (Cooper, 1972). There is also evidence that these relations are affected by the actors' personal 'mood', mental and physical fitness, political and social attitudes (Dixon, 1976; Szafransky, 1997). At a tactical level, their resulting effects derive from the comparison between levels of motivation and the sum of factors constituting 'capability' both at a technical and a tactical level (SME, 1987; Speciale, 2002).

At this stage, which is only one of finding general concepts and attempting a theorization, it would be impossible to analyse how relationships will develop, and what effect they will produce. Security problems are hard to categorize, ranging from international to individual, from life-threatening situations to theft, fraud and slander (Barefoot and Maxwell, 1987; Buzan *et al.*, 1998; Der Derian, 1992). There are, however, a number of common issues that need to be addressed in dealing with any security problem, independently on its type. These have been categorized into the following questions:

- Is there a security problem?
- If yes, to what extent?
- Should we deal with this problem?
- What should we do to solve it?
- How can we be sure that the problem has been solved?
- Can we prove it?

The first question is essential. Clearly, a problem whose main decision criteria are consensus or budget over security is one of politics or accountancy, not security. The formal definition of security offers a workable criterion for distinguishing true from false security contexts.

Answering the second question (to what extent it is a problem) depends on the level of fear of its negative consequences. This is quite a subjective issue, with strong influence upon the decision-maker and his level of commitment. Assessing the gravity of the problem calls for a rationale and raises the issue of the reliability of its supporting arguments, which calls in the consistency of the methodology used. With security being often a pretext for increasing budgets and taking illiberal initiatives (Dillon, 1996), we need to know whether the methods we refer to are reliable and consistent, and whether we are using them properly. A degree of scepticism ensures that methods for solution are chosen <u>after</u> the identification of the problem, and applied only where their use is consistent with their axioms, potential and limits (Manunta, 2000b).

The third question (whether we should deal or not with the problem) depends on the acceptability of the expected harm/damage. Answering such question opens two areas of discussion about (a) the threshold which should trigger the decision of accepting or not a given risk (in the sense of expected damage), and (b) making a choice amongst risks of different nature. Such decisions are intrinsically subjective, with them being linked to at least three different issues: the different perception different people have about the same risk, the propensity to take risks, and the ratio between risks and expected advantages (The Royal Society, 1992). Within organizations, the interaction of different decision-makers, with their different mindsets, visions, ideologies, interests and goals, adds to complexity. Not only the setting of thresholds becomes inevitably political, but also it changes with time, knowledge, power and circumstances (Manunta, 2000c).

The fourth question (what should we do to solve the problem) is also matter for debate. Confusion between means and ends does not help. Many authors seem to equate protection with adherence to standards and think of solutions as a sort of shopping list, including fences, barriers, alarms, safes, CCTV, guards, weapons and guard dogs to name a few (Gigliotti and Jason, 1984; Biasiotti, 1991). Clearly, an 'automatic' set of prescriptions can hardly address a problem that is, by its very nature, dynamic and partially unknown. In order to know what to do, why, and for what purpose, we need first to identify actors, relations, processes and output, then build an informed and adequate security system.

This calls in the final question, about proof, explanation and justification. Security decisions and actions may have serious consequences. Calling for an act of faith on one's own claimed experience is hardly acceptable. Hence, the need for theorization. The complexity of the concept defies easy reductionism, which makes things difficult for those who confound numbers with knowledge. All considered, the main issue is epistemic. We need to reach a 'justified true belief' that the problem at hand has, indeed, been well addressed. The reasons supporting this belief must be robust enough to be acceptable by those in charge of its approval and funding, and in a court of justice (Manunta, 2000a).

Due to its conflictive nature, 'justified true beliefs' are attainable in security, but not for long. Threats, technologies, tactics and circumstances do change. The framework of analysis must be precise enough for attaining a 'justified true belief' in the validity of the reasoning, yet flexible enough to adapt to change.

In order to proceed, and demonstrate the applicability of this theoretical framework of understanding, we need to shift the discussion from the conceptual to the methodological level.

The methodology: an overview

Description is limited to general guidelines and comments, and is inevitably vague regarding the nature of the problem.[5] It aims to facilitate the understanding of this effort of theorization and to illustrate its relations with current risk management approaches.

An overview

The identification, evaluation and assessment of A, P, T, their relation and effects within their Si is the necessary premise to judgement. It allows for understanding, decision and action, which may vary according to the different phases of reasoning. Literary evidence and more than 20 years of professional security analysis based on Figure 27.13 suggests that a methodology for conducting such analysis should consider the following four main stages:

Context Analysis is concerned both with the verification of the existence of a security context, or, indeed of the different existing security contexts, and with the analysis of each specific security context in turn.

System Analysis aims at putting the different contexts within an organization in relationship, so as to identify general underlying patterns and behaviours. By

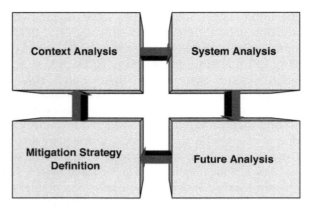

Figure 27.13   The general methodology

comparing the identified security contexts, it will also be possible to identify vulnerabilities, opportunities, motivations, capabilities and intentions.

Future Analysis is concerned with the formulation of scenarios and the identification and assessment of possible evolutionary dynamics. It is at this stage that risks and uncertainties are identified and analysed.

Only once Context, System and Future are analysed it is possible to enter the final stage of Mitigation Strategy Definition. This step is concerned with defining needs and means, and formulate the operational requirements for the resources that need to be deployed (people, intelligence, structures, systems, procedures and controls), according to the functions they must fulfil (prevention, detection, protection, reaction ...).

Although ideally these stages should be pursued in sequence, and then repeated cyclically, there is no *a priori* reason why they may not be pursued in parallel, as long as they are linked by a cyclical way of reasoning. There is often a trade-off to consider between time and available resources, which dictate the starting point of the analytical process and subsequent project planning.[6]

Context analysis

Context Analysis is the backbone of this methodology.[7] Whether in the private or public sectors, there is a widespread tendency to skip the assessment of Assets and Protectors, in order to dive directly into Threat Assessment, Security Surveys and Risk Management (sometimes informed by a general assessment of the Situation). However, this approach often leads to a poor definition of the Threat, with, consequently, an even poorer risk evaluation and mitigation strategies definition. A Threat can only be identified and assessed with respect to a specific Asset, and evaluated with respect to the Asset's Protector, within their specific Situation.

A single security process should be analysed as a combination/interaction of various distinct contexts.[8] By context the authors mean 'specific' context, i.e. the one resulting by combining a clearly defined set of specific/functional

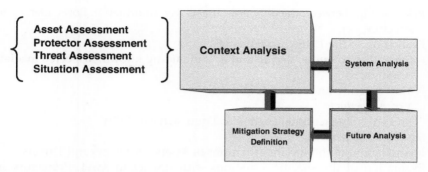

Figure 27.14   Context analysis

Asset, Protector, Threat and Situation. An Asset can also be a Protector and a Threat, within the same security process but functions vary in different contexts and according to different levels of analysis. For instance, a military genius is depending on the perspective, an Asset (to be protected), a Protector (to the nation), and a Threat (to the same nation if his genius exceeds political or operational capabilities/possibilities). Each aspect should be accounted for throughout specifically-focused analysis.

With regards to the Context Analysis see Figure 27.14, the issues that will have to be addressed are:

- Asset Assessment
    Identification of the Proprietor's general Assets (e.g. Personnel, Processes, Operations, Technology, Reputation, Financial Value, ...), locally and globally
    Relationships between Assets (e.g. information flows, hierarchical dependencies, ...)
    Identification of the Stakeholders (and the relationships between them)
    Identification of eventual Insurance and Lenders' Assets related to the Context
- Protector Assessment
    Identification of the Protector for each Asset (not all have formal Security responsibilities)
    Relationships between the different Protectors (e.g. information flows, hierarchical structure, ...)
    Evaluation of the Protectors in terms of
        Authority to know, decide and act
        Capability to know, decide and act (including available resources)
        Motivation to know, decide and act
        Accountability & Reporting
- Threat Assessment
    Identification of the actual and potential Threats for each Asset (not all Terrorists/Criminal)

Relationships between the different Threats (e.g. information flows, hierarchical structure, ...)

Evaluation of the Threats in terms of

Capability to know, decide and act (including known/suspected available resources)

Motivation to know, decide and act

Modus Operandi

Areas of influence and geographical outreach capability

- Situation Assessment

Identification of the specific Situations of Assets, Protectors and Threats

Evaluation of the specific Situations with respect to Asset, Protectors and Threats

System analysis

Once the Context has been adequately analysed, it is possible to relate the findings on Assets, Protectors and Threats, in their specific Situations, in order to identify possible relationships, interactions and dynamics, so to define all actual, foreseen and potential Security Contexts.[9] Each context will then be evaluated according to four broad dimensions see Figure 27.15: Vulnerability, Opportunity, Capability and Intention.

An apparently vulnerable Asset is not necessarily at risk if the Threat has no opportunity to attack. Similarly, the existence of an opportunity does not mean an attack will indeed take place if the Threat does not have the necessary capability and/or the intention. In the worst case scenario the intention of the Threat may be so strong as to lead to a rise in capability and the creation of opportunity and vulnerability. Only through a System Analysis it may be possible to interrelate all available information and deliver a truly multi-dimensional analysis, based on the following partial assessments:

- Vulnerability Assessment

Assessment of the vulnerability of the defined Assets to the defined Threats

Assessment of the vulnerability of the defined Protectors to the defined Threats

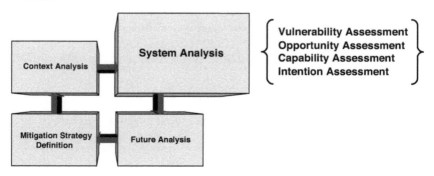

Figure 27.15   System analysis

Assessment of the vulnerability of the defined Threats to the defined Protectors

- Opportunity Assessment
Assessment of opportunities to the defined Assets (e.g. possibilities to improve value or resilience to potential damage, ...)
Assessment of opportunities to the defined Protectors (e.g. possibilities of proactive strategies or capability improvement/creation, ...)
Assessment of opportunities to the defined Threats (e.g. possibilities of exploiting environmental dynamics, or of creating temporary vulnerabilities to Assets or Protectors, ...)
- Capability Assessment
Of the Assets (e.g. to withstand a potential attack, ...)
Of the Protectors (e.g. reaction times and effectiveness to attack, including management of internal and external communication, ...)
Of the Threats (e.g. to bypass security, to find innovative tactical solutions, or to exploit secondary or tertiary damages, ...)
Of the Situation (e.g. to resist 'bad news', or to respond quickly to emergency situations, ...)
- Intention Assessment
Of Assets (e.g. to allow the implementation of protective measures, ...)
Of Protectors (e.g. to maintain adequate levels of alert and training, ...)
Of Threats (e.g. to invest in operational/tactical/strategic capabilities, ...)
Of Owners (e.g. to invest in strategic/tactical/operational defensive capabilities, ...)

Future analysis

Surprise is the single most effective principle of strategy, and a constant feature in security contexts. Security is a condition of dynamic equilibrium resulting from the decisions, actions and behaviours of Assets, Protectors and Threats in their specific Situation. Whilst the dynamics between Assets, Protectors and Threats may be considered, relative to one another, generally stable, their relationship (reactive, preventive, or proactive) with Situational factors may vary considerably and considerably quickly.[10] It is therefore necessary to extend the Analysis of the System to an analysis of plausible futures and evolutionary dynamics.

Based on the information gathered and analysed in the first two stages, and complying with the objective of interacting effectively at strategic level with the Proprietor and Stakeholders, the analysis should proceed with the following activities (see Figure 27.16):

- Scenario Planning
Prioritization of Security Contexts
Scenario Development
Description of Start conditions
Identification of stakeholders (favoured or damaged by the Scenario)

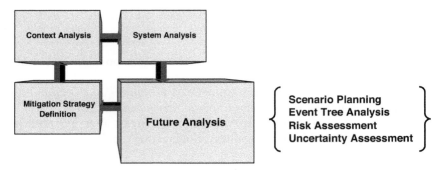

Figure 27.16   Future analysis

Identification of power holders (who can start, alter or inhibit the Scenario)
Description of Scenario
Description of End conditions
Development of general System Models for selected Scenarios
- Event Tree Analysis
Identification of relationships between Scenarios
Definition of chains of events leading to Scenarios
Development of specific System Models for selected Scenarios and Loop Analysis
- Risk Assessment (based on Scenarios and Event Trees)
Identification of quantifiable negative events (in terms of probabilities of occurrence and expected damage)
Development of Risk Matrices for quantifiable events
Loop Analysis (based on System Models) and identification of relevant Pressure Points
- Uncertainty Assessment
Identification of non-quantifiable events (where irrational to assign probabilities or impossible to adequately assess expected damages)
Loop Analysis (based on System Models) and identification of relevant Pressure Points

Mitigation strategy definition

According to the characteristics of the identified Scenarios, and the results of the Risk and Uncertainty Assessments, it will become possible to formulate strategies for mitigation. Strategy formulation, according to our methodology, consists in the design of appropriate sets of resources (people, intelligence, systems, structures, procedures and controls) to meet specific activities of the Threat, with respect to specific Assets in specific Situations.

The formulation of Mitigation Strategies, in order to be actionable, cannot stop at the definition of resource mixes, but must go to enough detail as to identify the operational requirements for the selected resources. These have been catego-

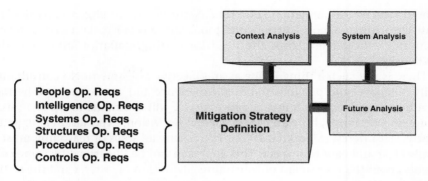

Figure 27.17   Mitigation strategy definition

rized into intelligence, people, structures, technological systems, procedures and controls, see Figure 27.17 (Manunta, 1997). The process consists therefore of:

- Definition of Operational Requirements for People
  Including: profiles, selection, necessary training, equipment, C^2 structure and information flows, etc.
- Definition of Operational Requirements for Intelligence
  Including: interaction between Security and Strategic Intelligence, identification of indicators, counter-intelligence needs and activities, internal investigation, etc.
- Definition of Operational Requirements for Technological Systems
  Including: location, definition of functions and conditions of operations, required performances, identification of potential providers, etc.
- Definition of Operational Requirements for Structures
  Including: location, definition of functions and conditions of operations, required performances, identification of potential providers, etc.
- Definition of Operational Requirements for Procedures
  Including: interface between Security, Safety, Crisis and Emergency procedures, procedures implementation and management system, training requirements, etc.
- Definition of Operational Requirements for Controls
  Including: definition of performance indicators, evaluation strategies, quality control strategies, maintenance strategies, etc.

Comments

The full implementation of the analytical methodology for a large corporate client or for a large public administration, with its complexity, importance and potential repercussions, requires a substantial effort in time and resources, comparable, perhaps, to a full quality assessment exercise. The need to validate intelligence amplifies the effort. Indeed, there is evidence enough that all the sources, particularly those with a vested interest in it, tend to present a biased view whose validation takes time. Security and intelligence, particularly anti-terrorism, are most instrumental tools, and specialists tend to disinformation and concealment, thus the need for vetting, collation and validation (Wilensky, 1967).

There is not such a thing in life as an objective assessment. No consultant is fully objective, and previous training, experience and education are a heritage that heavily influences his mental processes. He will contribute to the analysis, at times unconsciously, his own beliefs, mental set, vision, expectation and, particularly, self-interest (Manunta, 2002). This is why all steps of reasoning must be made clear and easy to inspect. This approach can be illustrated by some comments about the assessment of constraints, definition of criteria and the setting of decisional priorities.

Assessment of the constraints

Not all of the possible options can be pursued. Constraints are of a various nature, depending upon the class of context, the type of organization and the level of decision. Their correct identification helps avoiding errors, ensures feasibility, reduces the costs of implementation, and improves the effectiveness of the proposed measures.

A typical set of questions to be answered is the following: Upon which factors depends the actual level of security? How much the desired level of security depends upon factors that are external to the security system? What these factors are (e.g. Environmental, Political, Sociological, Legal, Normative, Economic, Cultural, Behavioural ...), and what is their weight in the specific Situation? What are the components of the security system to be considered relevant? What are their pro and contra? Will the proposed security system guarantee the desired level of security S1? Will its implementation create problems, and why?

The analysis allows for the identification not only of weaknesses (interference and constraints), but also of strengths (opportunities) and trends. The main characteristics to be considered are legal, physical, social, economic, political, human and technical. PESTEL and SWOT analysis techniques are generally useful. Each problem is unique, and referred to an open system (the organization and its environment). Operational answers can only be given for each specific case, with the caveat that they vary with level of decision, time, location and circumstance.

Definition of the criteria

Decisional criteria depend on context, organization, level of decision, location and circumstance. The process for their definition follows the same methodology of that of constraints, but choices are basically political. Each function within the organization contributes its own criteria, but the final decision (setting of standards and rules for measuring performances) is generally taken by one solver (the person in charge) after negotiations and compromise with other participants.

In the view of gaining weight in the negotiation, both the charisma and the professional credibility of the security responsible (and/or consultant, analyst) are essential. These qualities are certainly improved by his capability of communicating through media and languages (including techniques) understandable from the counterparts. If a credible, charismatic and easy-to-understand person presents a well-defined and structured security problem, where all steps of reasoning are clear, it seems reasonable to assume that the security criteria (timeliness, efficacy, utility ...) will not be overweighed by mere accounting considerations.

Setting of the subsequent priorities

This phase is very important, because (a) different weights attributed to each function lead to different profiles and to different costs (including interference) of the security system, and (b) different measures need different time to become effectual in the desired function.

The priorities of Assets, Threats, Events, Potential Damages, Criteria of Choice and Constraints have already been defined. Operational priorities are now essential. The Security Strategy defines (on the basis of the received Mission, within the guidelines of Policy and Strategy and with the aim of addressing assessed deficiencies) how to distribute efforts and resources amongst different functions of security (Prevention, Detection, Deterrence, Protection, Reaction ...), and according to which priority and timeline. This informs the choice of the components of the security system: People, Intelligence, Structure, Systems, Procedures and Controls, which should be summarized in a Security Programme, which describes and structures the desired state of affairs (S1), according to a definition of classes and categories, and under the supervision of a workable project planning.

It has been said that, besides reasoning and planning, operational security requires action and control, and all attempts to theorization should give careful thought to these phases. Before closing the argument, some considerations about the implementation and control phase may be useful.

Implementation

Even the perfect solution is only as good as its implementation. A number of factors may jeopardize the best programme. Good project management is essential, but not sufficient. Besides the quality of its installation, it is how the system is accepted, managed and maintained that becomes essential. This is linked to human factors, as awareness, determination, attention, care, in addition to recruitment, vetting, briefing and training. Sabotage and 'smart' installation and maintenance due to the action of an antagonist should not easily be discounted in this phase.

Control and feedback

Controls must be established, after deciding a set of rules (who, where, when, how, for what purpose, referring to whom, in which form and through which channels). These rules should be strictly related to those for measuring performance. Talking of control of the decision making process, this is only possible if the process has been well structured since its premises. By identifying which part of the process was wrong or incomplete, feedback allow for the immediate amendments and restart of the process at level where the fault has been identified. It is important to realize that, once implemented and active, the security system modifies the context and its environment, and teaches the Threat. This is accounted for by rerunning the assessment after time, and by remembering that the security process continues until Threat is present and interacting, and Proprietor maintains his will to protect.

Conclusions

This discussion has tried to demonstrate that there is both a need and the possibility for a theoretical approach to operational security.

The application of the formal definition of security, and the offered frame of methodology, may facilitate the study, by providing a criterion for demarcating security from other contexts, identifying the actors at the different levels, and focusing the attention upon their resulting dynamics and effects from a systemic-functional perspective.

Security, linked to the daily struggle for life, is both part of the complex process of an open system (the organization, the family, the individual ...), and a system on its own. The implementation of security measures interferes with, and is interfered by, individuals, community, environment and organizations (particularly the state) at all levels of life. It has ethical, social and political implications, which need to be evaluated when structuring the specific problem. To be accepted by and effective within, a larger system, a security system must be driven by a set of ethical, political and economic considerations proper to its specific context, level of analysis and situation. To be effective and useful as a system, security needs a clear definition of scope, relations and goals, thus of inputs, processes and outputs.

Security, like athletics, is a dynamic, antagonistic process that can best be explained by taking a series of photos, not just one. Good methodology should allow for repeated cycles of analysis, with assessments moving from qualitative to quantitative, allow for reasoned updating, control, feedback, and modification. This is deemed necessary to ensure, creativity, and wide open-minded approach, and to avoid possible malicious uses of methodology, where a too structured framework is offered prematurely to the decision-maker, so as to deceive, misdirect, or force his choice. Qualitative analysis at the less definable levels (mission, policy, and strategy) allows following and more definable levels of analysis to start from clear premises and with a clear, unmistakable focus. Quantitative analysis should only be considered after the problem has been structured and when relevant, possible, and consistent with the relative inputs/outputs.

To conclude, a word to the wise. There are no shortcuts to knowledge, and no panacea to security. Theorization is a necessary evil, and no profession can be considered mature without it. Methodology is just a set of tools, which are only as good as their user. To be useful and not damaging, methodology must be directed by a theory and a strategy of understanding which cannot be improvised, but results of study, thinking, discussion, criticism and rethinking. In security and risk matters, analysts, professional and decision-makers must always take the necessary time to think, validate, rethink and draw reliable conclusions. 'Fast-food' solutions are dangerous when dealing with a malevolent and creative opponent, and when life, limb, freedom and reputation are at stake.

Notes

1 Ecuyer to Francois I of France, and author of a book on horse dressage, where he stated: 'if you want your horse to turn right, you must first impede him to go to the left'. Killed in the battle of Pavia (1525), the inscription on his grave gave the passers-by a last taste of his wisdom: 'Here lies the Chevalier de La Palice, who, five minutes before being killed, was well alive'.
2 From now on, the antagonist of the protector is defined Threat. Capital letters are used for defining the basic elements of a security process, so to distinguish their use as such from the colloquial.
3 An example are the Sikhs bodyguards who were 'protecting' the late Indian Prime Minister Indira Gandhi.
4 More on this in the second part of this contribution (see 'Context analysis')
5 This methodology is heavily based on System Theory and System Thinking, For references on the philosophical and epistemological implications, see Bertalanffi (1951); Feyerabend (1993); Flood and Romm (1996); Geyer (1995); Johansen (1998); Johansen (1999); Mellor (1995); Yolles (1998).
6 A caveat. The aim is to offer the reader a path of reasoning, not an exhaustive discussion of the whole process. In full, the methodology based on this theory is quite detailed and supported by sophisticated techniques of Operational Research. According to our experience, its full delivery requires a two-week course of 120 hours, plus at least six weeks of directed studies.
7 Context Analysis follows directly from Manunta (1998).
8 The combination of the different contexts will be carried out in the following stage: System Analysis.
9 See Checkland (1993); Checkland and Scholes (1990); Coyle (1996).
10 See Hargreaves and Varoufakis (1995) for a critical account of the principles and methods of Game Theory, which is of particular relevance at this stage.

Key readings

Two references are directly concerned with security. One is Buzan, B., Weaver, O. and de Wilde, J. (1998) *Security: A New Framework for Analysis*, London: Lynne Rienner Publishers, which, by redefining the spectrum of security, redefines its scope and breadth of application. The second, for a more political approach to security, is Dillon, M. (1996) *Politics of Security*, London: Routledge. A redefinition of security leads to a review of the concept of risk. Two classic works are included here which will help the reader appreciate the full complexity and multi-dimensionality of the concept of 'risk': The Royal Society (1992) *Risk Analysis, Perception, Management*, London: The Royal Society and Adams, J. (1995) *Risk*, London: UCL Press Limited. For a discussion on the characteristics, problems and needs within the decision making process (whether directly or indirectly related to security), the authors make reference to two further classic works: from an intelligence perspective, Wilensky, H.L. (1967) *Organizational Intelligence*, London: Basic Books, Inc., and, for a more systemic approach, Easton, D. (1965) *A System Analysis of Political Life*, New York: Wiley.

References

A Dictionary of Philosophy 2ⁿᵈ edn rev. (1983) London: PAN Books.

Adams, J. (1995) *Risk*, London: UCL Press Limited.

Andrews, E.A. (1875) *Latin-English Lexicon 2ⁿᵈ edn*, London: Sampson, Low, Marston, Low Searle.

Balloni, A. and Viano, E. (1989) *IV Congresso Mondiale di Vittimologia*, Bologna: CLUEB.

Barefoot, J.K. and Maxwell, D.A. (1987) *Corporate Security Administration and Management*, Boston: Butterworths.

Beck, U. (1992) *Risk Society*, London: SAGE Publication.

Bertalanffi, L. (1951) 'An Outline of General System Theory', *British Journal of the Philosophy of Science*, Vol. 1, pp. 134–65.

Biasiotti, A. (1991) *I Sistemi di Sicurezza in Azienda*, Milano: Pirola.

Bovens, M. and Hart, P. (1995) 'Frame Multiplicity and Policy Fiascoes: Limits to Explanation', *Knowledge & Policy*, Vol. 8, Winter, pp. 61–83.

Bueno, G. (2004) *La vuelta a la caverna*, Barcelona: Ediciones B.S.A.

Buzan, B., Weaver, O. and de Wilde, J. (1998) *Security: A New Framework for Analysis*, London: Lynne Rienner Publishers.

Checkland, P. (1993) *System Thinking, System Practice*, Chichester: John Wiley & Sons.

Checkland, P. and Scholes, J. (1990) *Soft Systems Methodology in Action*, Chichester: John Wiley & Sons.

Clausewitz, C. von (1832) *Vom Kriege*, published in Penguin Classics (1982) On War, London: Penguin Books Limited.

Clutterbuck, R. (1993) *International Crisis and Conflict*, London: The Macmillan Press Ltd.

Cooper, J. (1972) *The Principles of Personal Defense*, Boulder, CO: Paladin Press.

Coyle, R.G. (1996) *System Dynamics Modelling*, London: Chapman & Hall.

Der Derian, J. (1992) *Antidiplomacy, Spies, Terror, Speed and War*, Oxford: Blackwell.

Dillon, M. (1996) *The Politics of Security*, London: Routledge.

Dixon, N. (1976) *On the Psychology of Military Incompetence*, London: Pimlico.

Dougherty, J.E. and Pfaltzgraff, R.L. Jr (1980) *Contending Theories of International Relations 3ʳᵈ edn*, New York: HarperCollins Publishers.

Dunbar, R. *et al.* (1996) 'A Frame for Deframing in Strategic Analysis', *Journal of Management Inquiry*, Vol. 5, March, pp. 23–35.

Feyerabend, P. (1993) *Against the Method 3ʳᵈ edn*, London: Verso.

Flood, R.L. and Romm, N.R.A. (1996) 'Contours of Diversity Management and Triple Loop Learning', *Kybernetes*, Vol. 25, No. 7/8.

Geyer, F. (1995) 'The Challenge of Sociocybernetics', *Kybernetes*, Vol. 24, No. 4.

Gigliotti, R. and Jason, R. (1984) *Security Design for Maximum Protection*, Stoneham, MA: Butterworths.

Hargreaves, S.P. and Varoufakis, Y. (1995) *Game Theory. A Critical Introduction*, London: Routledge.

Holmes, R. (1985) *Firing Line*, London: Pimlico.

Johansen, J.A. (1998) 'Organisations as Social Systems: The Search for a Systemic Theory of Organisational Innovation Processes', *Kybernetes*, Vol. 27, No. 4.

Johansen, J.A. (1999) 'Systemic Thinking as the Philosophical Foundation for Knowledge Management and Organisational Learning', *Kybernetes*, Vol. 28, No. 1.

Kitson, F. (1971) *Low Intensity Operations*, London: Faber and Faber Ltd.

Manunta, G. (1996) 'The Case Against: Private Security is not a Profession', *International Journal of Risk, Security and Crime Prevention*, Vol. 1, No. 3, pp. 233–9.

Manunta, G. (1997) *Towards a Security Science through a Theory and a Methodology*. PhD Thesis: University of Leicester.

Manunta, G. (1998). *Security: An Introduction*, Cranfield: Cranfield University Press.

Manunta, G. (2000a) 'The Management of Security: How Robust is the Justification Process?', *Security Journal*, Vol. 13, No. 1.

Manunta, G. (2000b) *Security and Methodology*, Diogenes Paper No. 2, RMCS Shrivenham: Cranfield Security Centre.

Manunta, G. (2000c) *Security and Decision Making*, Diogenes Paper No. 3, RMCS Shrivenham: Cranfield Security Centre.

Manunta, R. (2002) *Brief Notes on Modelling in Security*, SRSI Study Paper No. 1, Rome, SRSI.

Mc Inness, C. (ed.) (1992) *Security and Strategy in the New Europe*, London: Routledge.

Mellor, D.H. (1995) *The Facts of Causation*, London: Routledge.

Nicholau, E.V. (1995) 'Cybernetics: The Bridge Between Divided Knowledge and Transdisciplinarity', *Kybernetes*, Vol. 24, No. 7.

Orlandi, E. (1989) *Ingegneria del Rischio*, Milano: Franco Angeli.

SME (1987) *Il Metodo per la Risoluzione dei Problemi Operativi*, Civitavecchia: Scuola di Guerra.

Speciale, G. (2002) *Problem Solving in Security at the Conceptual, Organizational and Operational Level*, Rome: SRSI Study Paper 3.

Szafransky, R. (1997) 'Neocortical Warfare? The Acme of Skill', in J. Arquilla and D. Ronfeldt (eds) (1997) *In Athena´s Camp: Preparing for Conflict in the Information Age*, Santa Monica: RAND Corporation.

The Royal Society (1983) *Risk Assessment. A Study Group Report*, London: The Royal Society.

The Royal Society (1992) *Risk: Analysis Perception Management*, London: The Royal Society.

Yolles, M. (1998) 'A Cybernetic Exploration of Methodological Complementarism', *Kybernetes*, Vol. 27, No. 5.

Wilensky, H.L. (1967) *Organizational Intelligence*, London: Basic Books, Inc.

Index

National Association of Convenience
    Stores, 129
National Association of Security
    Companies, 130
National Center for the Analysis of Violent
    Crime (NCAVC), 250
National Center for Injury Prevention and
    Control (NCIPC), 249
National Center for Victims of Crime in
    Washington DC, 138
    quarterly magazine, *Victim Advocate*, 138
National Council of Investigation and
    Security Services (1975), 37
National Counterintelligence Officer for
    Economics, 55
National Crime Prevention Council (2005),
    41
National Crime Victim Bar Association, 138
National Crime Victimization Survey, 229
National Fire Protection Association, 139
    'Guide for Premises Security' (NFPA 730),
    139
National Geospatial-Intelligence Agency,
    171
National Institute for Occupational Safety
    and Health (NIOSH), 249
National Labor Relations Act of 1935, 163
National Occupational Health and Safety
    Commission (NOHSC), 230, 249
National Parking Association, 130
National Police Library, Bramshill, England,
    42
National Security Agency (NSA), 151
National Security Council (NSC), 147, 151,
    169
national security, 45, 54–5
    academics and corporations, diversity of
        approach, 55–6
    agencies, 58
    intelligence services, 12, 57, 147
    scholars, 53
national security studies, academic journals
    Contemporary Security Policy, 52
    Defense and Peace Economics, 52
    Defense and Security Analysis, 52
    Defense Studies, 52
    Intelligence and National Security, 52
    Journal of Security Studies, 52
    Security and Defense Review, 52
    Security Studies, 52
national versus corporate security, 45–6, 53
National Violence Against Women, 229
National Vocational Qualifications (NVQ),
    401

natural surveillance *see under* surveillance
Naylor, R., 278
network operations, 365
    Hypertext Transfer Protocol (HTTP), 365
    Internet Protocol (IP), 365
    Transport Control Protocol (TCP), 365
network security
    confidentiality, 365
    countermeasures, 368
    DoS attack detection devices, 369
        Intrusion Prevention Systems (IPS), 371
        Honeypots, 371
        Vulnerability scanning, 371
    entity authentication/firewalls, 368
    security mechanisms
        secure channels, 368–9
        three popular approaches, 369
    worms, severe threat posed by, 367
Nevada Supreme Court, The, 126
New York City's Port Authority Bus Station,
    183
New York State Tenement House
    Commission, 95
Newburn, T., 387, 392–3, 403, 454, 581
Newman, J.H., 243
Newman, O., 97, 101, 106
Nordby, 119
Norris, C., 449, 451
Northern Alliance, 334
Nuisance Alarm Rate (NAR), 83

offence, types of, 12
    commercial burglary, 12
    household burglary, 12
    shop theft, 12
    white-collar crimes, 12
Olson, J.N., 294
Oppal, W.T., 578
Osterburg, J., 137
Outcalt, 303
Oxnard Police Department, 250

Painter, K., 99, 443
Parfomak, P.W., 399, 401
Paternoster, R., 209–10
Paterson, Kenneth G., xxi, 13, 358
Pauchant, T.C., 537
Paulsen, D., 138
Pearl Harbor, 1941, 163
    attack, 146
    tragedy, 153
Pearson, N., 156
Pease, Ken, xxii, 12, 179
Peek-Asa, C., 251

Printed and bound by CPI Group (UK) Ltd, Croydon, CR0 4YY